The Prime Ministers

By the author

The Young Inheritors: A Portrait of Israel's Children
(Photographs by Gemma Levine)

Yehuda Avner

THE PRIME MINISTERS

AN INTIMATE NARRATIVE OF ISRAELI LEADERSHIP

The Toby Press

The Prime Ministers: An Intimate Narrative of Israeli Leadership

First Edition 2010

The Toby Press LLC
POB 8531, New Milford, CT 06676-8531, USA
& POB 2455, London W1A 5WY, England
& POB 4044, Jerusalem 91040, Israel
www.tobypress.com

© Yehuda Avner 2010

ISBN 978 159264 308 0, *paperback*

A CIP catalogue record for this title is available from the British Library

Printed in Israel

To my wife, Mimi,
our children,
our grandchildren,
and our great-grandchildren

Contents

Author's note

This is not a conventional biography or memoir, nor is it a work of fiction. It deals with factual events and real people, most notably Prime Ministers Levi Eshkol, Golda Meir, Yitzhak Rabin and Menachem Begin, all of whom I served in one capacity or another, junior and senior, over many years, and all of whom I have tried in these pages to bring back to life as I recall them. Having worked in their proximity in all manner of situations, good and bad – sometimes so bad as to call into question Israel's very survival – I have sought here to resurrect episodes which illustrate their responses in times of stress, recreate some unforgettable intimate moments, and reenact their intertwining relationships and their dealings with presidents, prime ministers and other dignitaries – all ratified, so to speak, by the viewpoint of the proverbial fly on the wall.

In so doing I have taken certain story-telling liberties by resorting to time-honored literary devices of narrative, dialogue, scene-setting, speech editing, impressionistic description, characterization, and reasonable constructs of conversations, without impinging too much, I trust, on historical truth.

Inevitably, an autobiographical footprint tiptoes – often stomps – through this personal narrative, firstly to illustrate the times into which I was born, secondly to introduce some extraordinary characters whose paths I crossed along the way, and thirdly and most significantly, to recapture how I came to be in the company of such amazing individuals, these early leaders of Israel, who were thrust into my life with such collision force that their hold on my imagination is intensely alive and personal still. I am everlastingly grateful for having had the opportunity to work for and alongside such prime ministers, and for having had my eyes opened to the fact that occasionally such larger-than-life champions of the Jewish people exist on earth.

For reasons which the reader will discover as the story unfolds, the most exceptional among them, in my eyes, was Menachem Begin.

Yehuda Avner
Jerusalem, 2010

Acknowledgements

Very many of the following pages are based on primary sources, not least my own copious records and notes. They exist because one of my tasks as a staff member for four prime ministers was to serve as their note-taker. Hence, in the preparation of this work I have been able to dip profusely into my own treasure trove of transcripts and personal diary notes. Additionally, I have had access to official correspondence and documentation, have perused biographies, have referenced autobiographies, and owe much to the testimony of people who feature prominently in this work and who gave generously of their time. I refer in the first instance to Yechiel Kadishai, Menachem Begin's closest aide and confidant, who was forever willing to share with me particulars of events to which he was witness, and answer my many questions concerning the prime minister's attitudes and inner thinking, though unwilling, rightly, to share responsibility with what I did with them. My profound gratitude to The Rt. Hon. Sir Martin Gilbert, who, with his learned historian's eye, perused the typescript, offered important suggestions, and graciously composed the foreword. Equally, to the Honorable Samuel Lewis, former United States ambassador to Israel, who not only shared with me his exhaustive oral history covering his tour of duty in Israel, but also rendered meticulous and invaluable help in my attempt to recreate certain of his crucial encounters with Prime Minister Begin. David Horovitz, editor-in-chief of the *Jerusalem Post*, kindly read the draft manuscript, and with his wise and critical attention to detail, offered invaluable suggestions.

It is with longing that I recall the late Harry Hurwitz, founder and first president of the Menachem Begin Heritage Center, Jerusalem, who vetted many of the Begin pages as they were initially composed. I venerate, too, the late Eric Silver, an assiduous journalist and a personal colleague, who himself authored an important biography on Menachem Begin, and who subsequently deposited with me his extensive archive, which includes exclusive interviews with a number of the foremost actors gathered in these pages.

My thanks to all at the Begin Heritage Center, and most particularly to its director of information resources, Yisrael Medad, who reviewed the chapters relating to Begin's command of the Irgun. Equally, I wish to thank the directors and staff of the various repositories in which I worked, or with which I corresponded, including the Israel Government Archives, the Jimmy Carter Library, and the Ronald Reagan Library.

My gratitude to all at *The* Toby Press for their judicious and expert attention to the book at every stage of publication, and most particularly to Matthew Miller, the man behind it all, for his patience and good fellowship. I am forever grateful to Deborah Meghnagi for her scrupulous and discerning editing in the highest professional fashion. Finally I am indebted to my literary agent, Joan Raines, of Raines and Raines, New York, without whose infinite persistence, encouragement, and indispensable advice I doubt I would ever have reached the last chapter.

Principal Characters

Menachem Begin: Israel's most extraordinary prime minister, infused with an overwhelming sense of Jewish history, a man of acute integrity, vision and compassion, who led a brutal fight against the British in Palestine, negotiated the historic peace treaty with Egypt, and launched a controversial war in Lebanon which was followed by his retirement into mysterious seclusion.

David Ben-Gurion: Legendary founding prime minister of the State of Israel, first minister of defense, intrepid pioneer and overseer of the country's initial development, who pugnaciously fought Begin every step along the way until, mellowed by age, sought a reconciliation.

Zbigniew Brzezinski: Polish-born national security adviser to President Jimmy Carter, who protested his admiration for Israel but never showed it.

Yosef Burg: Israel's longest-serving minister, brilliant scholar in both religious and classical studies, witty, sharp, and head of the negotiating team in the failed talks dealing with Palestinian self-rule in the late 1970s, early 1980s.

Esther Cailingold: Young teacher from England who died heroically in the hopeless battle to save Jerusalem's Old City from Arab conquest in the War of Independence and whose younger sister, Mimi, the author eventually married.

Jimmy Carter: American president with whom Prime Minister Yitzhak Rabin exchanged sharp words, as did Prime Minister Menachem Begin, but who, nevertheless, took a political gamble of historic dimensions in successfully navigating the Israel-Egyptian peace treaty, and then spent much of the rest of his life badmouthing Israel.

Moshe Dayan: Illustrious one-eyed warrior, architect of the Israel Defense Forces, darling of the nation, hero of the Six-Day War, and a wretched casualty of the Yom Kippur War.

Princess Diana: Enchanting first wife of future king of England, Charles, Prince of Wales, who thought Israel a "plucky little country."

Abba Eban: South African-born and Cambridge-educated, Israel's foreign minister (1966–1974), who was lauded in capitals the world over for his intellectual sophistication and Churchillian eloquence, but was derided at home as lacking strategic acumen.

Queen Elizabeth II: Long-serving British monarch who was mystified at the author's British origins when he presented his credentials as Israel's ambassador to the Court of St. James's.

Levi Eshkol: Seemingly lackluster prime minister who knew every inch of every water pipeline in Israel, and who displayed piercing diplomatic shrewdness in his efforts to avert the Six-Day War, yet readied the IDF for the fight of its life to win it.

Max Fisher: Detroit philanthropist, chairman of the board of the Jewish Agency, and trusted adviser on Israel and Jewish affairs to every Republican U.S. president since Eisenhower.

Gerald Ford: Foreign affairs neophyte who assumed the presidency of the United States following Nixon's resignation, and who triggered a grave crisis in the Israel-U.S. relationship when Prime Minister Rabin refused to relinquish strategic Sinai assets in Egypt's favor.

Yaakov Herzog: Brilliant Talmudist, philosopher and statesman, diplomatic adviser to Premier Eshkol, who was at one and the same time offered the posts of chief of the prime minister's office and chief rabbi of Great Britain.

Lyndon Baines Johnson: Beefy Texan rancher who, having failed to confound Egypt's hostile designs which culminated in the Six-Day War, was the first U.S. president to throw in America's strategic lot with Israel by becoming the Jewish State's major source of sophisticated weaponry.

Yechiel Kadishai: Menachem Begin's amiable long-time aide, chief factotum, and intimate confidant.

Henry Kissinger: A German-Jewish refugee who became secretary of state of the United States. In seeking to contain the Cold War reverberations of the Yom Kippur War, he sometimes aroused the ire of Prime Minister Golda Meir. Under President Ford, became virtually sovereign in setting the course of American foreign policy, thereby sometimes arousing the ire of Prime Minister Yitzhak Rabin.

Yossel Kolowitz: Yeshiva kid who survived the Holocaust by performing in the "Auschwitz Cabaret," whom the author met en route to Palestine. He attempted to jump ship, was arrested by the British, enlisted in the Irgun, and, decades later, met the author again under unexpected circumstances.

Samuel Lewis: American ambassador who earned Prime Minister Begin's confidence for much of the time, and whose appealing personality, diplomatic drive, and shrewd intuition won him access to numerous friends in high places.

The Lubavitcher Rebbe: World-renowned luminary who not only ignited Jewish souls the world over but also the reverence of a number of Israel's leaders, most notably Menachem Begin.

Golda Meir: Foreign minister who felt abandoned by fellow socialists and by African leaders to whose nations she had extended aid, but who, as prime minister, while totally ignorant of things military, emerged as one of Israel's greatest war leaders.

Richard Nixon: American president whose reputation as an anti-Semite did not preclude his appointment of a German Jewish refugee as his secretary of state, nor his resolve to massively aid the Jewish State when its survival was at stake and when he himself was enmeshed in the Watergate scandal, fighting for his own survival.

Shimon Peres: Forever suave and urbane with a propensity for hyperbole and tautology, popular worldwide as a peacemaker, and Yitzhak Rabin's nemesis for many years. Despite an illustrious career, he could never shed his reputation as an inveterate election loser, but he ultimately became one of the country's most esteemed presidents.

General Ephraim Poran: Commonly known as Freuka, served as military secretary first to Prime Minister Yitzhak Rabin and then to Prime Minister Menachem Begin.

Yitzhak Rabin: A conceptualizer with a highly structured and analytical mind, IDF chief of staff during the Six-Day War, ambassador to Washington, prime minister between 1974 and 1977 and again between 1992 and 1995 when, pursuing a controversial peace policy, was assassinated by a nationalist zealot.

Ronald Reagan: American president who led through instinct, and whose apparent reliance on cue cards belied his keen grasp of the Cold War power play and his resolve to stand by Israel despite frequent misunderstandings.

William Rogers: U.S. secretary of state whom Nixon and Kissinger let stew in his own juice when it suited their purposes.

Sam Rothberg: Plain-talking businessman from Peoria, Illinois, veteran leader of the Israel Bonds organization and Chairman of the Board of Governors of the Hebrew University, whom Begin sometimes treated as an ex-officio cabinet officer.

Anwar Sadat: President of Egypt, a man of grand gestures, convinced his peace mission was a sacred calling, irritated at Begin's insistence on precise agreements, yet forging with him a bond of mutual trust and friendship so deep as to leave Begin distraught when his peace partner was assassinated.

Margaret Thatcher: British prime minister dubbed the "Iron Lady" who, by reputation, surrounded herself with people she could trust to follow orders, not to give them, but who greatly admired Jews, and, though opposing Begin's settlement policies, had high regard for his principles and convictions.

Harry Truman: Retired U.S. president who invited the author to join him on a walk in which he related how his old Jewish pal from World War I, and later his partner in a haberdashery business, helped persuade him to recognize the Jewish State against the advice of cabinet colleagues.

Adi Yaffe: Prime Minister Levi Eshkol's chef de bureau, who initially paved the author's way into the foreign service and then the prime minister's office.

Foreword

By the Rt. Hon. Sir Martin Gilbert

Anyone who is interested in the first fifty years of the history of the State of Israel will be both enlightened and entranced by this book. From the moment that Yehuda Avner made his way from Manchester to Mandatory Palestine in 1947, to his years as Israel's Ambassador to Britain in the 1980s, he was a witness to, and increasingly a participant in, the events that shaped and molded the Jewish State.

Yehuda Avner's Zionism was born in Manchester, the British city where Israel's first president, Chaim Weizmann, had begun his extraordinary efforts to convince the British Government that a Jewish National Home in Palestine was in the British interest. Avner reached Palestine when the British commitment – given with such enthusiasm in the Balfour Declaration in 1917 – had waned and withered; when the bitterness between the British soldiers and officials in Palestine and the Jewish fighters for independence had reached a fever pitch of misunderstanding, recrimination, and violence.

The young Yehuda's diary, a precious contemporary document, sets out the strife and fears of the year before statehood was achieved, and the euphoria following that day in November 1947 when the United Nations voted for the establishment of both a Jewish and an Arab State in a partitioned Palestine. The Jews grasped the opportunity. The Arabs rejected it, and in May 1948 turned five armies in fury against the newly proclaimed Israel.

Throughout the formative years of the fledgling nation, Yehuda Avner was there. His diary, his memory, and his many notes made at the time, take us on a remarkable journey, full of insight, drama and humor, as he served four successive Israeli prime ministers, the giants of their day: Levy Eshkol, Golda Meir, Yitzhak Rabin and Menachem Begin. It was Begin who, from the outset, most attracted the young Yehuda, and who grew in stature in his mind as the two men worked increasingly closely together. Yet the others three leaders are not diminished in any way by Avner's preference; indeed, Levy Eshkol grows strongly in stature in these pages as he grasps the awful nettle of Israel's isolation and danger in 1967. Golda Meir emerges as a human being whose weaknesses were many and whose strength was formidable, and Yitzhak Rabin as a patriot who struggled with his inner demons as Israel began the long, hard, still uncompleted path toward Palestinian-Arab reconciliation.

Yehuda Avner draws the portraits of these four leaders with affection, yet he is never starry eyed. A wealth of sharply noted detail and contemporary documentation given from the standpoint of an independent-minded civil servant and diplomat – some of it never before seen in print – gives this book its theme, its charm and its importance. The book is, however, much more than a collection of individual portraits, vivid though these are. It is also the story of the life struggle of a new nation, small in territory, poor in natural resources, surrounded by enemies, absorbing vast numbers of immigrants from the Holocaust in Europe and from Arab and Muslim lands, forced to devote enormous resources to the usually penniless newcomers, and at the same time to sustain an army capable of defending – in war after war – its vulnerable citizens.

Israel's struggles, challenges and achievements are described in this book with all the enthusiasm of a lifelong Zionist for whom Zionism is not a rigid ideology or a clever theory, but a living expression of Jewish national aspirations, determination, culture, and a worldview that Jewish genius, Jewish hard work and Jewish idealism need a country of their own. As Winston Churchill told a delegation of Palestinian Arab leaders in 1921, when they urged him – even then – to halt Jewish immigration: "It is manifestly right that the Jews, who are scattered all over the world, should have a national center and a National Home, where some of them may be reunited. And where else could that be but in this land of Palestine, with which for more than three thousand years they have been intimately and profoundly associated?"

Yehuda Avner's book, with its cast of fascinating characters, its insights, its vigor, and its zeal, show how right Churchill was. A State was formed, whose leaders guarded it and moved it forward. Their most recent chronicler, himself so often at the center of the events he describes, has done them proud.

Martin Gilbert
26 May 2009

Part one

1939–1952

Beginites and Anti-Beginites

1939–1952

Key Events

1943 – Menachem Begin assumes command of the Irgun.

1944 – The 'Hunting Season': Irgun fighters are handed over by Hagana fighters to the British.

1945 – End of World War II.

1946 – The King David Hotel, Jerusalem, is blown up by the Irgun, in collaboration with the United Resistance Command.

1947 – Begin orders reprisals against British, measure for measure, hanging for hanging. U.N. Resolution on 29th November approved Partition Plan.

1948 – Jerusalem besieged; Israel declares independence; with the arrival of the Irgun arms ship, the *Altalena*, Israel finds itself on the brink of civil war.

Menachem Begin in Polish army uniform, with his wife Aliza, Tel Aviv, 12 December 1942. Courtesy of the Israel Government Press Office & the Jabotinsky Institute.

Chapter one

In the Beginning

T he first time the name Begin struck a massively resounding chord in my mind was on a sultry August afternoon in 1947, while walking down a street in the heart of Jewish Manchester. There, daubed in blood-red paint on a synagogue wall, was a splash of raw and angry graffiti: "HANG THE JEW TERRORIST BEGIN."

Though a mere school lad at the time, albeit close to graduation, I knew enough to know that Menachem Begin was the arch fiend of the British in Palestine. There was a price on his head, and they wanted him, dead or alive. For almost three years he had pitted his ragtag secret army – the *Irgun Zvai Leumi* – the National Army Organization, commonly called the Etzel or the Irgun – against British might, in a ferocious rebellion the aim of which was to drive them out of the country. It was a deadly underground combat which Begin called a fight for freedom and which the British called terrorism.

Ever since the early 1920s, Britain had held a mandate from the League of Nations to govern Palestine, with the aim of initiating a Jewish National Home there, as promised in the famous Balfour Declaration of 1917. But to all intents and purposes Palestine had been turned into a possession of the British Empire, and almost from the start, Arab enmity had swelled and grown in proportion to the influx of Jewish immigrants. As the seeds of strife became ever more bitter, London engaged in ever more convoluted exercises to appease the conflicting parties and interests.

It was in a neighborhood called Strangeways – the place into which I was born – that I came face to face with that alarming anti-Begin graffiti on the synagogue wall. Strangeways at that time was a seemingly irredeemable squalid slum, where for much of the year the air was so thick with smog that even the weeds wilted with grime. Chimneys of every sort billowed geysers of soot-saturated smoke from the textile mills, factories and foundries whose furnaces were fed by the coal pits of Lancashire. In the drab, rain-splashed, cobbled streets where the dwellings stood cheek-by-jowl – row upon Victorian row of bedroom to bedroom, kitchen to kitchen, outside lavatory to outside lavatory – the masonry was eternally black. When I joined the family in 1928, as the youngest of seven, my mother and father – she from Romania, he from Galicia – were eking out a living from behind a counter in a little drapery store whose kitchen in the rear and whose poky rooms upstairs housed us all.

My first childhood memories are of Friday nights. They were magical. When our mother covered her head with a silken white shawl, lit the Sabbath candles, and placed her fingers over her eyes in an attitude of hushed prayer, our humble kitchen was miraculously transformed. Gone were the shabby furnishings, with their suggestions of decay. Instead, in the glow of the candles everything looked palatial. The room was filled with hallowed aromas. And when we came home from shul and our father recited Kiddush standing at the head of the table in his Sabbath best, he looked grand. I sensed bliss on those Friday nights when our family cuddled up into a Shabbat peace that surpassed my comprehension.

Our Strangeways days came to a longed-for end in 1939, when my parents procured a small factory in which they manufactured pinafores and nightwear, enabling us to move into a leafier neighborhood and a finer house, with a garden. Soon thereafter humanity went into the sudden shock of World War II, but as a lad of eleven the war inflicted no particular trauma on me initially. Under barrage balloons as big as galleons that hung high in the sky I went out on shrapnel hunts, played around in bomb shelters, and engaged in all sorts of gas mask pranks. And at night, after the sirens sounded, I and my two brothers, Yitzhak and Moshe, would often sneak out of the cellar which our dad had reinforced as a shelter to watch the searchlight beams bouncing about the clouds trying to pick out enemy aircraft, until the shooting and the bombing began in earnest and we would be hauled back inside, with a smack on the behind or a pull of the ear.

But then the war intensified, and the boy became a teenager and the teenager a young man. The scenes of the heaps of Jewish corpses and the piles of bones of the cremated, and the dead-eyed death camp survivors too frail to survive, inflicted my soul with a piercing sense of helplessness. The horror, the frustration, and the bewilderment of the Holocaust clawed at my innards, and hardly had the flames of the crematoria of Hitler's "Final Solution" been doused before newsreels were showing the British Navy intercepting leaking boats of Jewish survivors off the shores of Palestine, and turning them back or interning them. Some of the pitiful vessels, searching in vain for a safe harbor, went down with their wretched cargo.

Was it any wonder, then, that a deep-buried fury burned within the Zionist circles of Manchester? And was it any wonder that a man of the stuff of Menachem Begin, driven by an inexpressible anguish, burst forth, and with more audacity than armory, led his small but well-entrenched Irgun underground army in a perilous revolt against the British in Palestine?

The first I learned of the Begin ideology was when I escorted my mother, who was a serious sympathizer, to a meeting of his supporters. World War II had just ended and many in the jam-packed hall were Holocaust survivors. The speaker was a man called Ivan Greenberg, longtime editor of Anglo-Jewry's most influential weekly, the *Jewish Chronicle*. Under his editorship the *Jewish Chronicle* had become so provocatively critical of British policy and so increasingly sympathetic toward Begin and his Irgun that some parliamentarians demanded the paper be prosecuted for seditious libel; eventually the *Jewish Chronicle*'s directors asked Greenberg to leave.

The recollection I have of him is that of a middle-sized, brisk intellectual with a mesmerizing command of florid Victorian English which he intoned in a manner that would put no actor to shame. This is what a now faded pro-Begin stenciled propaganda sheet quoted him as saying that evening:

> Freedom does not descend like manna from Heaven. It has to be won by trampling enemies, and advancing through the wilderness of past bondage into the blessings of future liberty. Menachem Begin is leading his people on that arduous and treacherous trek, away from the wastelands of exile. He is guiding the nation through the tempests of time. Stern and threatening though the storm clouds might be, by dint of infinite resolve, steel courage and boundless sacrifice he is ascending to the sunlit highlands of Jewish honor, of Jewish freedom, and of Jewish justice, in the land where Jewish history began.

This oratory evoked thunderous applause even from those who, like me, barely understood a word of it. And, as reported, Greenberg then went on to talk about the man whom Begin would forever describe as his "master and teacher" – Ze'ev Jabotinsky, the brilliant linguist, author, essayist, poet and philosopher who had established his own independent movement of Revisionist Zionism.

"Jabotinsky's Revisionist Zionism," said Greenberg, "is simple, direct, and candid, yet sophisticated in practice. It calls for the immediate establishment of a Jewish State. Its ideology emerges out of exasperation and disillusionment with the established Socialist-dominated Zionist leadership's fainthearted policies of abandonment, compromise, and indecisiveness, not to speak of excessive reliance on the British. Dr. Chaim Weizmann and Mr. David Ben-Gurion practiced this in the 1920s and 1930s, and they practice it now in the 1940s."[1]

Here, I understood, as I learned more, and grew more involved in following the struggle in Palestine, lay the key to Menachem Begin's unreserved defiance of David Ben-Gurion, titular head of the Jewish government-in-waiting in Palestine, and chief strategist of its mainstream underground fighting force, the Hagana. And while in the turbulent landscape of Palestinian Jewish politics Begin and Ben-Gurion – two breathtakingly courageous leaders – were intense ideological rivals, one left wing, the other right, at this juncture in time there was a lot more dividing them than dueling political philosophies. They wrangled bitterly over the contentious issue of when best to launch the final show-down against the British to drive them out of the country and declare Jewish independence.

Ben-Gurion was intensely pragmatic. He did not waste his energies on what he deemed to be quixotic crusades. As long as the Second World War lasted he clung to the belief that long-term Zionist interest necessitated a full and final Allied victory over the Nazis before battle could be joined with the British. This policy of self-restraint was, to Begin, fatally flawed. In his view, by 1944 the tide of war had irreversibly turned against Germany. Allied victory was in sight, and the closer it came into view the more European Jews in their hundreds of thousands were being driven, cattle-like, into the gas chambers of Auschwitz. So, in brazen opposition to Ben-Gurion, Menachem Begin proclaimed his manifesto of revolt, which read:

> We are at the last stage of the war. We stand before a historical decision and the fate of generations…There is no longer any armistice between the Jewish people and the British administration in Eretz

Yisrael, which hands our brothers over to Hitler. Our people are at war with this [British] regime – war to the end…Our fighting youth will not be deterred by sacrifice, torment, blood, and suffering. They will never surrender, nor shall they rest until our days of old are restored, and until our homeland, freedom, sustenance, and justice have been secured…This then is our demand: immediate transfer of power to a provisional Jewish government. We shall fight; every Jew in the homeland shall fight. The God of Israel, the Lord of Hosts, is with us. There shall be no retreat. FREEDOM OR DEATH!²

Decades later I would look at Menachem Begin, prime minister of Israel, searching for a likeness to the fugitive with a price on his head, but could find none. Nor could I discern any similarity between the hardened and unyielding Irgun underground commander and the statesman I would come to know. And as for his old Irgun comrades-in-arms, I quickly discovered that they were, by and large, an amiable lot, full of good cheer and public spirit, nothing like the terrorist gang their antagonists had portrayed them to be. Always a grand raconteur, in later years I heard Menachem Begin relate to his veterans how much time he spent conjuring up ways to outwit the British. As an example he reminded them of how Irgun youngsters had defied the British ban against blowing the shofar at the Western Wall on Yom Kippur.

The story really began on the Yom Kippur of 1928, when a *mechitza*, an improvised, collapsible screen to separate male and female worshippers, was set up in front of the Western Wall for prayers. This, to the Arabs, was an act of provocation, and they went wild.

"Jihad! Jihad!" flashed through the bazaars. "The Jews are trying to rebuild their Temple and destroy our al-Aksa Mosque."

Eyewitness accounts told of a white-bearded Chasid in a black caftan running for his life, chased by a mob through an alleyway leading to the Western Wall. The pursuers brandished clubs, sabers, and daggers, and howled: "Save our holy places from the Jews!" and, "Death to the Jewish dogs!" and, "*Allahu Akhbar!* God is great!" The fleeing Chasid, his bony face chalk white, stumbling through the narrow tunnel passages, was losing ground. He fell, sprang up again, and then inexplicably turned and, head-first, drove straight into the phalanx of the chasing mob, hollering hysterically, "*Shema Yisrael,*" as they cut him down.

Hundreds more were killed in the months that followed, culminating in the 1929 pogrom in Hebron, which snuffed out an entire ancient Jewish community – and all because of that flimsy screen at the Wall.

As the riots escalated the British set up an inquiry commission and, stirred by Muslim sensitivities, decreed that the Arabs were the sole owners of the Western Wall and that, henceforth, Jews would be forbidden to even blow the shofar in its precinct. Members of the Jewish community sat up and gasped. What are we, a myth? Do you claim that there never was a holy Temple on the Temple Mount? Our sacred texts are legends? Is it all a fairytale?

Some bravehearts defied the ban. Each year, as Yom Kippur approached its climax with the *Ne'ilah* service, a member of Betar, the youth movement of Ze'ev Jabotinsky's Revisionists, would surreptitiously sound the shofar; whereupon the British police would move in and hit out in all directions.

Menachem Begin was witness to one such *Ne'ilah* service, on the Yom Kippur of 1943. What he saw was a battalion of British policemen, armed with rifles and batons, trying to pick out who might turn out to be the shofar blower. And when the sun went down and the shadows lengthened, they squeezed in among the pious, elbowing their way towards the Wall, weapons angled and primed.

And then they heard it, and it drove them into a frenzy.

A ruddy-faced sergeant, livid at the insolence, dashed toward a short figure clutching a shofar to his lips and, slapping the lad hard across the face, bellowed, "Stop blowing that thing." Other policemen set upon worshippers trying to defend him, clobbering them with their batons. The young blower kicked the sergeant away and burrowed through the crush, spurting his way up the stairs, trying to reach the murky warrens adjacent to the Wall.

"Kill him, Stop him! Kill him! Stop him," cried the Arabs.

"Keep going! Run! Run! Run!" cried the Jews.

The boy dodged and leaped through the alleyways, until an officer felled him and pinned him to the ground.

Seeing the outrage for himself, Menachem Begin decided that the Irgun had to respond, to confound the low tricks of his people's enemies, who defiled this most sacred of sites. Thus it was that on the following Rosh Hashanah, in 1944 – ten days before Yom Kippur – he instructed his Irgun pamphleteers and poster-stickers to let it be known that any British policeman disturbing the service at the Western Wall "will be regarded as a criminal and be punished accordingly."

As the Day of Atonement drew nearer his warnings grew increasingly more strident, generating ever more grisly rumors as to what punishment Begin's Irgun men would mete out to the British policemen.

"Criminal lunacy!" cried the left-wing Hebrew press, fearful of innocent casualties at the Wall. "The blowing of the ram's horn at the close of the fast is a mere custom, not an obligatory act," declared a tremulous rabbinate. And British Intelligence speculated as to what casualties their police at the Wall might sustain if fired upon from unseen directions.

Came the culmination of Yom Kippur and the end of the *Ne'ilah* service, and in the deepening twilight the white-clad cantor, facing the gigantic shadowy blocks of ancient stones, chanted in a voice that swelled and soared, "*Shema Yisrael*... Hear, O Israel, the Lord is our God, the Lord is One." And the whole congregation affirmed this declaration with single-minded intensity.

And then, thrice, he trilled: "*Baruch shem kavod*... Blessed be the name of His Glorious Majesty for ever and ever," and thrice the assembly responded in passionate confirmation.

Seven times, the cantor intoned with trembling fervor, "The Lord is God. The Lord is God" and seven times the congregants avowed this invocation.

And as the cantor concluded the service with the final words of the Kaddish – "*Oseh shalom bimromav*... He who creates peace in His celestial heights, may He create peace for us and for all Israel; and say, Amen," – the British policemen looked on, tense, edgy, crouched in confrontation, waiting for the order to pounce at the sound of the shofar.

And the shofar sounded.

Rising on tiptoe, arms stiffened, eyes closed, hands trembling in excitement, the boy who had blown the shofar blew again; a sustained, robust, soaring, exalted, single blast, reaching the heights of pure perfection – and not a policeman stirred.

"Fall out," barked the ruddy-faced sergeant to his men. "Return to barracks. At the double – one, two, one, two, one two..."

"*L'shanah haba'ah b'Yerushalayim habenuyah*," hollered the crowd. "Next year in rebuilt Jerusalem!" And they danced their way triumphantly to their homes in the Jewish Quarter.

The following day Begin wrote in his Irgun underground paper:

Our ancient stones are not silent. They speak of the House that once stood here, of kings who once knelt here in prayer, of prophets and seers who declaimed their message here, of heroes who fell here, dying; and of how the great flame, at once destructive and illuminating, was kindled here. This House and this Land, with its prophets and kings and fighters, were ours long before the British were ever a nation.

When recalling that episode in later years, Menachem Begin could not contain a smile when he said, "It was never our intention to start a clash at the Wall, for fear of inflicting casualties. Our attacks were directed elsewhere – against British police fortresses in different parts of the country – and those we carried out as planned."[3]

Admirers were enthralled by these Scarlet Pimpernel tales, not least the narrow escapes from British manhunts when Begin sometimes had to creep from one hiding place to another as a dragnet closed in. With a flicker of a smile he would recount how he had first commanded his Irgun fighters from a little rented room in a small sea-front Tel Aviv hotel called the Savoy, adopting the pseudonym Ben Ze'ev after his father. He banked on the assumption that the least likely place the British would expect to find him was under their very noses, room seventeen of a public hotel.

For a while he was right, but eventually they caught his scent, and so he moved on to a small, run-down, isolated house in Machaneh Yehuda, on the fringes of the Yemenite quarter of Petach Tikva. And when that hovel came under scrutiny, he moved on again with his wife Aliza and little boy Benny, to yet another hovel in the Hassidoff Quarter, also near Petach Tikva. There, he took the alias Yisrael Halperin, and assumed the guise of a refugee law student heavily laden with books preparing for his bar exam.

"How well I remember the people at that *shteibel* – the homey, intimate little neighborhood synagogue where I used to pray on Shabbat and festivals," I once heard him say. "On the first Shabbat they honored me, as befits a newcomer, by calling me up to the reading of the Torah. The good *gabbai* – warden – asked me my full Hebrew name, as is customary. But believe it or not" – he said this with a chuckle and a cheeky smile – "I stumbled over it. The man gave me a suspicious stare. 'What's your name?' he asked again, and I had to remember not to give him my real name, but my Irgun name: not *Menachem*, but *Yisrael* ben Ze'ev Dov. After that I was always called to the Torah by that assumed name, and to this day I crave the Almighty's forgiveness for this deliberate misrepresentation in a holy place. But under the circumstances I'm sure He understood."

It was in the Hassidoff Quarter, in September 1944, that Begin experienced the closest of close shaves, when British patrols sealed off the whole of Petach Tikva, imposed a curfew, and began conducting house-to-house searches. By some unexplained stroke of good fortune – some would say Providence – the search parties passed over his off-the-beaten-track hovel. Tragedy struck, nevertheless. Dr. Arnold, his wife's brother and his own very close friend, died upon hearing of the search operation.

"He was in Tel Aviv at the time," Begin related sadly. "He knew where we were hiding, and it seems that the very thought of our being arrested shocked him so, distressed him so, that he collapsed and died.

"We, my wife and I, could not even attend his funeral. The British had their spying eyes at the cemetery waiting for us to show up. Those were terribly heartbreaking days for us both. My wife was inconsolable. I had lost a friend, but she had lost a brother: he was the last surviving member of her whole family. All I could do was to go to our little shul and recite Kaddish in his memory."

A time came when prying neighbors with left-wing views began to actively collaborate with the British to "liquidate the dissidents," as they put it. So the Begins left the Hassidoff Quarter and moved on again. This time they found what they considered an ideal hiding place – a tiny, dilapidated house in a nondescript, refuse-strewn, fly-infested and smelly Tel Aviv side street called Yehoshua Bin Nun. The reason for the flies and the smells was that the Begin's neighbors were the municipal abattoir on one side, and the municipal dogs' home on the other.

There, at Yehoshua Bin Nun Street, he changed his identity once more, posing this time as Reb Yisrael Sassover.

A photograph of him as Reb Yisrael Sassover shows nothing in his appearance to attract particular attention. Reb Yisrael looks at you through large, deep-set, and weary eyes in a lean, bearded face, a clever face which shows the sensitivity of a humble religious scholar more than the ruthlessness of a militia leader.

Truth to tell, people who knew him well at the time said it was not all that difficult for him to avoid the authorities' detection, since there was nothing in his appearance to stamp him as an underground fighter, let alone a commander-in-chief. In fact, a British dossier of the day titled *The Jewish Terrorist Index* profiled him as having "a long, hooked nose, bad teeth, and horn-rimmed spectacles." Time and again, British police on the lookout would pass him by without a second glance, seeing him as just another out-of-pocket law student, or a run-of-the-mill rabbinic scholar.

While living on Yehoshua Bin Nun Street, the Irgun chief again became a regular congregant at the local *shtiebel*.

Photograph credit: Israel Government Press Office

*Begin as Reb Yisrael Sassover, with his
wife and son Benny, 12 December 1946.*

"What a great little shul that was," I heard him reminisce. "There I found solace when life in the underground was at its harshest. That little *shtiebel* became a part of my daily life. The *balei batim* – congregants – were wonderful: a cross-section of hard-working Tel Aviv craftsmen, small shop-keepers, laborers, and artisans. They were true *amcha*, solid, down-to-earth, patriotic citizens. I regularly attended their evening Talmud classes, both because I enjoyed them and because they reinforced my cover."

Begin related this through a long sigh which mutated into a chortle when he added, "These wonderful people must have thought their Reb Yisrael Sassover was nothing but a *luftmensch*, a good-for-nothing loafer incapable of holding down a job who had to be kept by his wife, from whom he must have somehow managed to wring a substantial dowry."

He explained this reasoning by citing, part in jest, part in earnest, and much in mime, the excruciating quandary he once faced when the beadle, Reb Simcha, a short, red-bearded fellow full of good cheer, came calling on him to ask him to perform a simple *mitzvah*. Late one afternoon, just as he was about to enter his ramshackle home, Reb Simcha called out from the other side of the street, "Reb Yisrael, we need you for the *mincha minyan*" – the afternoon prayer quorum. He had to shout because of the cacophony of chained dogs barking from the municipal dogs' home, and the doomed cattle mooing and snorting in the municipal abattoir.

Reb Yisrael Sassover shouted back, "I shall join you presently. I just have to tell my wife I'm home."

When he entered, the chief of operations of the Irgun sighed in relief: "Menachem, thank God you're back. We were getting worried. We have an action in two hours."

"They're expecting me in shul for *mincha*," Menachem Begin told him. "I must go. I won't be long."

After the service, on the way out from the *shteibel*, Reb Simcha took Begin aside, and said to him, "I have a *mitzvah* for you to perform, Reb Yisrael."

"And what is that?"

"Our butcher, Reb Dovid, needs a favor."

"What kind of a favor?"

"In order for him to get his kashrus license renewed he needs two witnesses that he is totally *shomer Shabbos* – observant in every way. Since all the other congregants are hard at work all day and you seem to have lots of time on your hands I want you to come with me to the Chief Rabbinate's office to testify on Reb Dovid's behalf. It's a mere formality; won't take long. The *dayanim* – rabbinical judges – will ask you a few questions, that's all."

Begin shifted uneasily, not sure what he should answer. To be cross-examined by such sharp-eyed rabbis could unmask him totally.

"You have a problem with this, Reb Yisrael?" asked Reb Simcha.

"Of course not," replied Begin, trying to pull himself together, knowing that his chief operations officer was urgently awaiting his return to approve an action against a British police station that was to take place almost immediately. So he said, "I know Reb Dovid is a truly honest man with impeccable kosher credentials, but – "

"But what? All you have to do is to tell that to the *dayanim*. They'll believe you."

"I'm sure they will. It's just that – "

"Just that, what?"

"It's just that you'll have to ask somebody else."

"Somebody else? What's wrong with you, Reb Yisrael – you're so busy all of a sudden?"

"Yes, I am."

"With what?"

"Urgent things – things I have to attend to myself."

"What kind of urgent things?"

"Important things."

"Bah!" huffed the beadle, and he swung on his heels in disgust.

Years later at a political rally, an exalted Reb Simcha approached Mr. Begin and told him how, on the Saturday night following the declaration of independence, he was sitting at home with two of his shul-goers, one a stone mason, the other a plumber, drinking a *l'chayim* to the new state, and as they were sipping their schnapps they had their ears glued to the radio listening to a voice which they instantly recognized, a voice that declared, "Citizens of the Jewish homeland, the rule of oppression has been expelled. The State of Israel has arisen…"

"We couldn't believe that you, our Reb Yisrael Sassover, were Menachem Begin, our commander of the Irgun," said Reb Simcha jubilantly. And then, shoulders squared, "You knew, of course, I was a secret member of the Irgun."

"Of course I knew," said Begin. "So were almost half the *shtiebel*. But you all abided by the oath not to tell, and not to reveal to each other to which secret cell you belonged."

In truth, by the time I got to know Menachem Begin he did not talk all that often about those secretive days except when in the company of his old and trusted colleagues, and when he did his tone was more often wistful than gleeful and witty. For lurking behind his underground anecdotes was the anxiety and insecurity of living a fugitive existence, forever weighed down by the devastating responsibility of issuing life-and-death commands in response to the repressive actions of the British. Hunted ceaselessly, he could socialize with no one but his immediate family, select members of his Irgun High Command, and a few trusted couriers. Nevertheless, his military, moral, and ideological authority over the Irgun was uncontested. His followers admired him to the point of adulation. And by dint of his cunning and revolutionary strategies calculated to humiliate the British by hitting time and again at their symbols of power, compelling the authorities to choose between repression and withdrawal, he made his little Irgun army appear to British eyes much larger than it actually was.

It is estimated that at the height of the revolt leading toward Israel's independence in 1948 there were less than a thousand members who had taken the Irgun oath, and only a few hundred of them were capable of mounting operations at any one time. Hardly anybody served full-time, and only very few received any kind of pay. Almost all continued in their regular civilian jobs, which provided ideal cover for their activities, some of which were extraordinarily spectacular, others spectacularly controversial. One such was the blowing up, in July 1946, of Jerusalem's famed King David Hotel, a splendid imperial establishment of the day, on par with the Shepheard's in Cairo and Raffles in Singapore. In its early days the King David hosted such royalty as the Dowager Empress of Persia, the Queen Mother of the Egyptian royal house, and King Abdullah I of Jordan, who arrived with a retinue on horses and camels. The hotel also afforded asylum to three royal heads of state who had to flee their countries into exile: King Alfonso VIII of Spain, Emperor Haile Selassie of Ethiopia, and King George II of Greece.

During the Arab riots of 1936–1939, the British Army leased the hotel's top floor as emergency headquarters. In 1938, the authorities requisitioned two-thirds of the hotel's two hundred rooms to accommodate their military headquarters and government secretariat, taking over the whole of the southern wing, thus making the King David the nerve center of the British Government of Palestine. The hotel grounds were surrounded with a cordon of heavy barbed wire, butterfly nets to prevent grenades, and barricades manned by Bren-gun carriers and Argyll and Sutherland sentries. It was a fortress. But by the time I saw the King David Hotel, in the winter of 1947, it had been a ruin for over a year; a year in which the situation in Palestine had become more and more tense and explosive. The entire southern wing was a pile of rubble, dynamited to smithereens by an Irgun squad disguised as milkmen, delivering explosive-packed churns to the kitchens. Ninety-one people died in the blast: twenty-eight British, forty-one Arabs, seventeen Jews, two Armenians, one Russian, one Greek, and one Egyptian. Also killed was one of the operatives engaged in planting the explosives.

The action had been carried out with the approval of the United Resistance Command – an ad-hoc alliance embracing another underground splinter group called the Israel Freedom Fighters (Lechi), and headed by the mainstream Hagana. The bombing was a direct response to a British action named "Operation Agatha" taken some weeks before, when seventeen thousand British troops swept down upon Jewish settlements and confiscated vast quantities of hidden arms, arrested over two thousand activists, and took into custody prominent leaders of the Jewish community.

Among the spoils of Operation Agatha were believed to be

operational plans of the Hagana and the Irgun, implicating much of the Jewish leadership of Palestine in conspiracies to carry out anti-British acts. These Intelligence files were said to be housed in the southern wing of the King David Hotel. They could possibly have provided enough evidence to bring down death sentences on many a Jewish head. Hence, the approval given to the Irgun operation by the United Resistance Command.

Not only was the British press up in arms about the hotel bombing, so too was the Hebrew press. *Hamishmar* described the action as "Treason and Murder." *Haaretz* called it "A frightful blow to all the hopes of the Jewish people." The *Davar* headline read, "Without Cause, Without Atonement." And David Ben-Gurion, head of the Hagana, sought to distance himself from the whole thing by telling a French newspaper, "The Irgun is the enemy of the Jewish people."

For the rest of his days Menachem Begin would defend his King David action as a legitimate military target, and asserted that ample warning had been given to evacuate the hotel. The hotel switchboard had been told to vacate the building at least a half hour before the explosives were detonated, and calls also went out to the *Palestine Post* – forerunner of the *Jerusalem Post* – as well as a warning to the operator of the nearby French Consulate, to open all windows so as to avoid injury from flying glass. Even a string of firecrackers was set off in front of the hotel driveway to frighten pedestrians away.

"Oh yes, we did all we could," insisted Begin, talking to me, a new member of his prime ministerial staff, in 1977. "The warnings were given and received in time by the British authorities; they had time enough to evacuate the hotel twice over. Somebody, for some dark purpose, or because he lost his head, or to protect a spurious prestige, ordered that the hotel not be evacuated."

British retribution was harsh. Lt. General Sir Evelyn Barker, the General Officer in Command of Palestine, laid into the whole Jewish community, issuing a notoriously anti-Semitic order commanding his troops to cease all fraternization with all Jews of whatever sort:

> I am determined that they should be punished and made aware of our feelings of contempt and disgust at their behavior. I am certain that if my reasons are explained to the troops they will understand their duty and will punish the Jews in the manner this race dislikes the most: by hitting them in the pockets, which will demonstrate our disgust for them.[4]

The ruins of the King David Hotel, 22 July 1946.

After vehement protests, this order was rescinded; still, stringent curfews became routine, accompanied by mass round-ups and search operations. Every Jewish house was suspect. When British troops encamped in the grounds behind Begin's Tel Aviv hideaway on Yehoshua Bin Nun Street, he squeezed into a tiny cubbyhole prepared in advance for just such a contingency. There, he sat cramped, with hardly any food or water and little air, for three days, with no way of knowing how long the soldiers would bivouac. By the end of the third day he was faint with dehydration and lack of oxygen. Finally, on the morning of the fourth day, the soldiers moved on and Begin clambered out into the fresh air, gasping for breath, to plunge his head into a basinful of cold water.

There were some prudent voices in Whitehall who, hearing the death knell of Britain's thirty-year presence in Palestine, urged their Government to give up and get out. Most objected however; they remained either deaf or blind. Some even asserted that British imperial authority over the Holy Land was the will of the Almighty and, therefore, eternal.

As the Irgun revolt hardened so did the response to it. The authorities began sentencing captured Irgun fighters to the most savage forms of capital punishment: flogging for relatively minor offences and hanging for relatively major ones. Instantly, Menachem Begin responded by posting the following warning:

> "A Jewish soldier taken prisoner by the enemy was sentenced by an illegal British military court to the humiliating punishment of flogging. We warn the government of occupation not to carry out this punishment which is contrary to the laws of a soldier's honor. If it is put into effect, every officer of the British occupation army in Eretz Yisrael will be liable to the same punishment: eighteen lashes."[5]

When Begin's warning went unheeded he dared to defy the colossus of the British Empire and made good on his promise. He ordered the abduction of two British servicemen to be flogged, lash for lash. And as the tempo of the revolt quickened the searches and round-ups intensified. Jails were jammed. Hangings followed hangings, some contrary to normal procedure, without fair warning to the families, and in virtual secrecy. Begin gave no quarter. In the dead of night his underground press distributed the following leaflet in English for the British to see:

"We recognize no one-sided laws of war. If the British are determined that their way out of the country should be lined with an avenue of gallows and of weeping fathers, mothers, wives, and sweethearts, we shall see to it that, in this, there shall be no racial discrimination. The gallows will not be all of one color…The price will be paid in full."

He issued orders to kidnap a number of British servicemen and hold them hostage: hanging for hanging.

The first to be abducted insisted he was a victim of mistaken identity. He claimed not to be a military man at all, but a London businessman just arrived in Palestine from Cairo, called Collins. His executioners did not believe him. Nor did they believe his assertion that he was Jewish: what kind of a Jewish name is Collins? So, in the seclusion of an orange grove the execution party readied themselves to place the noose around the dazed man's neck, when he began to mumble incoherently *"Adon olam asher malach"* – the opening line of a Hebrew chant of divine praise. Then, with an equally terrible whimper, he muttered the lament for the dead – *"Yisgadal v'yiskadash sh'mei rabba."* Horrified at having almost murdered a fellow Jew, the executioners whisked him back to Tel Aviv, from whence he beat a quick retreat back to London.

So, two British sergeants, Cliff Martin and Mervyn Paice, were nabbed in his place. "Whatever is done to our people will be done to you," warned Begin's grim notices in the night.

The British executions were mostly carried out in the fortress of Acre, an imposing Crusader bastion that had been restored by the Turks, and was considered impregnable. In May 1947, in what was probably the Irgun's most daring exploit, a wall of this great citadel was breached, allowing for a mass escape. However, three of the attacking party – Avshalom Haviv, Yaakov Weiss, and Meir Nakar – were captured and condemned to death.

On the day of the execution, 29 July 1947, the District Commissioner of Galilee, a man with the unusual name of Thorne Thorne, visited the Acre prison accompanied by the Commissioner of Prisons, a Mr. Hackett, to ensure the gallows were readied and all other necessary arrangements in place.

It would be wrong to think of these men as in any way vindictive or malevolent. They were bureaucrats doing their job; their writ did not extend to pondering the iniquity of destroying healthy, conscious men. Their task was to see to the formalities of the hangings. So imagine their astonishment when, upon calling on the Acre prison superintendent in his quarters, he told them in no uncertain terms that he would not carry out the execution orders.

What these three officials said and did on that day was documented in an official report drawn up by the District Commissioner, Thorne Thorne, and classified "Top Secret & Confidential." Here is a construct of their exchange redacted from Thorne's meticulous testimony:

> *Charlton* [Acre Prison Superintendent]: I suppose you know that I
>   am not going to carry out these executions.
> *Hackett* [Commissioner of Prisons]: You are the officer detailed to
>   carry them out. I have here the warrants.
> *Charlton:* I do not agree with the policy of Government regarding
>   these hangings. The whole thing stinks. Why can't Govern-
>   ment carry out the executions in a normal manner, giving

the prisoners and relatives proper warning as usual? I want no part of it. I am unhappy about the whole affair. Please send me home. I've had enough of this.

Hackett: Do you absolutely refuse to carry out the death sentences?

Charlton: Yes. I have carried out forty-four executions during my service in this country and I have not raised any objections before. But now I'm adamant. I had a definite promise from Mr. Bromfield when he was acting Commissioner of Prisons that secret executions such as that carried out in the hanging of Dov Gruner [a young Irgun commander] will under no circumstances occur again. I will not preside under the circumstances you have outlined. I am ready to execute the men on Friday of this week [August 1] or next Tuesday [August 5] provided the proper open procedures are followed, meaning that the date is announced in advance and that the relatives are given the opportunity to visit the condemned men prior to the event.

Hackett: But the lawyer of the accused and their relatives will be informed prior to the event.

Charlton: I am not satisfied. Why can't Government carry out the executions in a normal manner, giving the prisoners and their relatives proper advance warning, as is usual procedure? The whole prison will be upset. It will be impossible for me to keep order or discipline if the executions are performed in a secretive manner. I am not going to carry out these executions, not because I am afraid but solely because it is against my conscience. If the executions are postponed as I suggest, and done later in a proper and regular manner I will certainly do as ordered.

Thorne [District Commissioner of Galilee] *to Hackett:* "The time now is 4.15 P.M. The intention to execute the three men will be made public in an hour-and-three-quarters, at 6.00 P.M. By that time the relatives will have been informed in Jerusalem. [*To Charlton*]: Unless you have someone else to carry out the executions, someone whom you can rely upon, we have to inform Government what is happening. I need hardly point out the political and other consequences if the executions are postponed because an Officer of the Crown refused to carry them out.

Charlton: I'm expecting Mr. Clow [superintendent of the Nablus jail] at five o'clock, and I'll ask him if he will carry out the executions. I cannot guarantee that he will.

Thorne: Under the circumstances, and in view of the fact that Clow may not get here in time, and given the importance of the time factor, I'm going to Haifa immediately and inform Government of the situation. [Haifa was the nearest place with a secure telephone line.]

Later, Thorne phoned Hackett from Haifa:

Thorne: Government confirms the executions must go forward as arranged. If Charlton still refuses to carry them out, either you or Clow must do so under all circumstances. Even if Charlton has a change of heart he has become so excited he won't be in a fit state to carry them out, so there is no use in pressing the matter further.

At 5.30 P.M. Clow, the superintendent of the Nablus prison, arrived at Acre.

Hackett by phone to Thorne: Clow is here. He will carry out the executions if that is Government's final instruction. He is pressing for a postponement though.

Thorne: A postponement is out of the question. The executions must be carried out as ordered. You have confirmed that the warrant is made out to "the superintendent of Acre prison" [and not to Charlton by name]. So I have relieved Mr. Charlton of that post and have appointed Mr. Clow as superintendent in his stead.

Hackett to Thorne [at midnight]: The tensions have relaxed. There will be no hitch in the executions.

And, indeed, there was none: Avshalom Haviv was hanged at four in the morning, Meir Nakar at 4:25, and Yaakov Weiss at 5:00.

No one in the Acre jail slept that night. One prisoner, whose Irgun name was Natan but whose real name was Chaim Wasserman, was in a nearby cell, and he smuggled out a letter to Menachem Begin describing what he saw and heard. He wrote:

Early this morning our three comrades went heroically to the gallows. We were already aware what was going to happen between four and five in the morning, and pressed against the bars with bated breath watching haplessly what was going on around the cell. The prison superintendent, Major Charlton, had left the place yesterday afternoon and was not seen again. Toward evening a party of hangmen arrived.

The officers went in and informed the condemned men they were to be executed between four and five in the morning. Their reply was to sing Hatikva and other songs in powerful voices. They then shouted to us that the hangings would begin at four o'clock, in this order: Avshalom Haviv, Meir Nakar, Yaakov Weiss. They added: "Avenge our blood! Avenge our blood!"

We shouted back, "Be strong! We are with you, and thousands of Jewish youth are with you in spirit." They replied, "Thanks," and went on singing.

At two a Sephardic rabbi whom we could not recognize from afar [Rabbi Nissim Ohana] was brought and stayed in the cell fifteen minutes.

At four in the morning Avshalom began singing Hatikva, and we joined in loudly, pressing against the bars. At once armed police came up to the visitors' fence near our cell. At 4.03 Avshalom was hanged. At 4.25 we were shaken by the powerful singing of Meir. Hardly able to breathe we nevertheless joined in. He was hanged at 4.28. At five o'clock the voice of Yaakov, this time alone, penetrated our cell, singing Hatikva. Again we joined in. Two minutes later he was hanged. Each of the bodies was left hanging twenty minutes before being carried off, one by one.

The chief hangmen were Hackett, Inspector of Prisons, and Clow, superintendent of the Nablus jail.

At dawn we informed the prison officers through an Arab warder that we would not be responsible for the life of any Englishman who dared enter the jail yard. We declared a fast and prayed. Later in the morning we found the following inscription on the wall of the cell of the condemned: "*They will not frighten the Hebrew youth in the Homeland with their hangings. Thousands will follow in our footsteps.*" Next to it was the Irgun insignia and their three names in the order they were executed.

News of the execution quickly seeped out, the whole country was put under curfew, and Menachem Begin made good on his threat – gallows for gallows. Sergeants Martin and Paice were summarily tried and duly hung, and it was the following day, that I, a Manchester school lad, had shivered at the sight of the blood-red graffiti on the synagogue wall, "HANG THE JEW TERRORIST BEGIN."

The grisly images of their bodies swinging from eucalyptus trees in a Netanya grove filled the front pages of British newspapers, and the public outcry was huge. But Begin remained undaunted. "Flogging for flogging, hanging for hanging, until all capital punishment ceases," he raged on a poster plastered on the walls of every Jewish quarter in Palestine in the dead of night. This measure for measure reprisal ultimately worked. Whitehall, humiliated into submission, quietly ordered a stop to capital punishment, a surrender which only served to deepen the frustration of an already demoralized Britain which, by 1947, was no longer great.

Exhausted and bankrupted by World War II, its influence on world affairs was essentially ended. Unemployment was high, austerity was everywhere, and everything was rationed. Pubs closed early for lack of beer. And on that particular oppressive August day in 1947 after the sergeants had been hung, the pub regulars, with nothing else to do, sat around feeding each other's rage at the gruesome news. It didn't take much for someone here and for someone there to spread the thought that it was time to show the Jews what real Englishmen thought of them. By late afternoon a mob had formed up and moved on Cheetham Hill Road, the heart of the Manchester Jewish ghetto.

Yelling "Yids go back to Palestine," "Beat up the Jews," "Down with the Sheenies," "Kick the kikes," and all sorts of other jingoistic slogans, the rioters flung stones and bricks at Jewish shop windows, homes, synagogues, and social halls. In one, a Jewish wedding was being celebrated, and like the men of Sodom at the door of Lot, the rabble pounded savagely on the hall's doors, which the terrified celebrants inside were trying to block. Saved in the nick of time by the arrival of the police, the horde was broken up temporarily but quickly regrouped to surround the place, howling and hurling threats and abuse and muck through its open windows.

Later that evening, the mob massed again, but this time they were met by a phalanx of vigilante Jewish ex-servicemen. The police, under orders to act firmly, broke up the scuffles, and by the end of the melee Cheetham Hill Road looked as it had a few years before, when it had borne the blast of German bombs. As far as the eye could see, broken glass littered the sidewalks, and shiftless thugs hung about nursing bruises amid wreckage of their own doing.

The next day, in school, I was accosted in class by a bully of a fellow whose father was serving with the British Police Force in Palestine. He had me pinned to the floor and was about to punch me in the nose when in walked our geography teacher, a fellow called Hogden, who bellowed, "Haffner" – that was my original family name – "what's going on?"

Pudgy, with a florid face and side-whiskers, and with a tendency to doze off after setting us an exam, Hogden automatically picked on me not only because I was a Jew but, equally, because I was not of the Church of England. Hogden had an aversion to anybody who was not of the Church of England. To him, there was only one path that led to the Almighty, and he was sure it did not pass through the synagogue or through Rome.

"Nothing, sir," I stammered, straightening myself up. "Nothing's going on."

"Oh yes there is, sir," blurted the bully. "Haffner's terrorist boss, Begin, strung up our two sergeants and he'll be hanging my dad next."

"Is that so, Haffner?" said Hogden in a voice brimming with scorn. "Would your Mr. Begin do a thing like that?"

"No, sir."

Hogden carried a long cane which he would frequently use on his wall map to point out the vast extent of the British Empire's dominions and colonies that stretched over an immense proportion of the globe. He handed me the cane, and smirked: "I want you to show the class on the map exactly where your Mr. Begin is carrying out his atrocities against our lads who are risking their lives to serve our country." Turning toward the class, he asked, "Who's risking their lives to serve our country, boys?"

"Our lads, sir,"

"Exactly! So, come on" – he had me by the collar and was frog-marching me to the map – "show us where your Palestine is."

Classmates sniggered and made faces.

"Here, sir," I stuttered, indicating the slender strip of territory on the eastern seaboard of the Mediterranean Sea.

"Quite right! Are you a Zionist, Haffner? Does Haffner look like a Zionist, boys?"

"Yes sir."

"What does he look like, boys?

"A Zionist, sir."

"And your mother's from Romania, is she not? Her English could do with a bit of a polish, I would think. What could Haffner's mother's English do with, boys?"

"A bit of a polish, sir."

"So, tell us, are there lots of Zionists in Romania – terrorists, too, perhaps?"

Like a zoologist bringing a real-live orangutan to his class, Mr. Hogden had me, the son of a native Zionist Romanian, as his exhibit. He knew of my mother's origins because, to my everlasting mortification, she had once introduced herself to him in her heavily-accented English at a parents' evening.

"Now show us on the map exactly where your mother comes from," he sneered.

I had no idea where my mum came from, exactly. I knew about *der heim* – the old homestead, in a place called Negresht – but I didn't have a clue where Negresht was.

"Stop idling," snapped Hogden. "You're keeping the class waiting." And to drive the point home he swished his cane this way and that over my head.

To this day I cannot fully explain what happened next. All I know is that my humiliation and despair yielded unexpectedly to an irresistible surge of courage. "*Geh in drerd,* sir," I blurted out.

"Gay in what?" hissed Hogden.

"*Geh in drerd,* sir," I repeated intrepidly.

"And what's that supposed to mean?"

"It's the name of my mother's village, sir."

"Is it? And where exactly is it? Show us on the map."

"Here, sir," said I, pointing to the Carpathian Mountains.

He peered over my shoulder: "I can't see any Gay-in-something."

"No sir. It's a small village, too small for this map."

Hogden gazed intently at the Carpathian Mountains. "What did you say the name was again?"

"*Geh in drerd,* sir."

The bigot stroked his chin and mused out loud, "Ah yes, of course. The name has a distinctive Latin ring to it, which is most characteristic of the Romanian language whose origins are largely Latin. What are the origins of the Romanian language, boys?"

"Largely Latin, sir."

At which point the bell rang, causing Hogden to gather up his belongings and make his exit, causing me to feel a huge rush of jubilation. For I had just given this anti-Semite his comeuppance. *"Geh in drerd"* is Yiddish for "Go to hell," and as far as I was concerned, I had feathered and tarred him good and proper.

Perhaps it was because I had by this time discovered a religious Zionist youth movement called Bnei Akiva – Akiva's children, named after the ancient scholar-warrior hero of the Jewish war of freedom against the Romans – that I dared be so impudent and bold. Today, when every value is contested and contestable, some readers might find it difficult to understand how, after the Holocaust, one such as me could become besotted to the point of almost mystical worship, with the idea that a new sort of religious Jew was called for, a scholar-peasant-fighter dedicated to building Utopia in the Promised Land through the establishment of religious kibbutz settlements to redeem the barren wastes and hasten the day of national freedom.

The romance of it so seized my imagination that a week or so later, when I graduated high school, I joined a training farm in the English countryside to ready myself for a life of pioneering and toil on the soil of Eretz Yisrael. And being such an exemplary devotee of this Bnei Akiva ideal, I was selected to travel to Jerusalem to attend a year-long course for cadres of Zionist activists at The Institute for Overseas Youth Leaders, commonly known as the *Machon*. It was a time when visas to Palestine were so hard to come by that, in obtaining one, I decided in my own mind I would not come back.

Came the day of departure, Monday the third of November, 1947, and I found myself waving farewell to an adoring family while listening to the most beautiful melody a young man heading for adventure can possibly hear: the steamy puff and jerk of the train pulling out of the railway station. I was eighteen, and I was on my way to Marseille to board a ship called the *Aegean Star* bound for Palestine.

As the train gently gathered pace and the waving hands of my brothers and sisters vanished from view, my excitement was suddenly moderated by melancholy – a stab of emotion that left me unstrung. It was a strange and nervous unease. I was leaving home, possibly for good. God knows when I would see my family again, not least my mother, who was bedridden with cancer. I opened the notebook which I had bought as a diary, and spontaneously scribbled on its first page:

> I went in to say good bye to Mammy. She is so sick. Dear God, I pray You fervently to return Mammy to normal health speedily. I

saw this morning when I said good bye her true and noble character. She cried a little but in spite of her bad health she held me tight and blessed me with a courage that is only common to my mother. I got a lump in my throat but quelled it down. I then took my leave of Daddy. I owe him more than I can pay to him. He has provided for me handsomely, more than another father would have done. Please God, bless my dear mother and father, for they deserve to be blessed.

And so I take my leave. It is a beautiful November morning. While I sit here I am overcome with a feeling of love and gratitude for my whole family. Please God, keep them safe. At the pit of my stomach there exists some inexplicable feeling. It is not excitement; it is a deep appreciation for your loved ones.

On arrival in London I purchased for myself a watch with the money given to me as a present from my brothers and sisters.

The author at the Machon, Jerusalem, November 1947

Chapter two

Desperate Hopes and Savage Defiance

The *Aegean Star* was a rusting steamship captained by a Greek mariner who strutted about in immaculate starched whites emblazoned with gold-braided cuffs, collar, and shoulders. From his bridge, he looked down his nose upon a cobbled, messy wharf bustling with pre-departure activity – winches, cranes, stevedores, crates, barrels, sacks, and teams of blue-smocked porters, rank with garlic, heaving passenger trunks up the gangway. A convoy of dilapidated yellow and green motor buses chugged into view, disgorging a procession of gray, matchstick women, men, and children, ill-clad and disheveled.

Without any spoken command, they arranged themselves in line in front of trestle tables manned by uniformed French officials, huddling one behind the other with the myopic, soup-kitchen stare of the downcast, long conditioned to obeying roll calls. Most of them, having no passports, clutched an International Red Cross document attesting to their stateless, refugee status as Holocaust survivors. Thick-muscled stewards herded them toward steerage, while the captain scrutinized them from above with a mean eye; resentful, perhaps, at having to make a living off Jewish charity money by transporting these Holocaust survivors from a place they were not welcome to a place they were not wanted.

"Hear this," he shouted at them in guttural English through a megaphone. "All passengers without valid entry certificates for Palestine travel on my ship at their own risk and responsibility. If, on arrival at Haifa, any one of you is arrested by the British authorities, you will obey their orders and disembark from my ship without resistance." And then, with extra bite, "There will be no disorder on my ship."

The refugees looked up at the captain passively, apparently accustomed to metallic voices barking at them through loudspeakers in languages they did not understand. I, wanting to get a closer look, descended to the lower deck and stumbled into a Yiddish babble of befuddled survivors trying to make sense of what the captain had just said.

"*Vos zugt der admiral?*" – What's the admiral talking about? – asked a young ultra-Orthodox boy of a neighbor.

"*Zol her ge'in brechen a fus,*" – Let him break a leg – snickered the neighbor in reply.

The *Aegean Star* was an old tub. She throbbed, quivered, and rolled as she moved across the Mediterranean, so that only the most intrepid risked the shipboard games. By far the most bracing of these was a ping-pong tournament on the lower stern deck, where the steerage refugees had set up a warped table. Here, between rusting anchor chains, lines of gray laundry, and cast-off deckchairs, two undersized teenagers who looked like invalids but played like combatants bashed the ball this way and that, their faces harsh, their stances tense, their strokes deadly.

One was the ultra-Orthodox lad. He was a yeshiva boy who looked about my age, and was dressed traditionally. Whenever he thrust forward in an offensive burst, his *bekeshe** flung open to reveal wildly swinging ritual fringes tucked into his black pantaloons. And when he laid out his strokes passionately, his long, tightly-curled *peyot*** flew over his shoulders like a horse's reins. Planted on his head was a black velvet pie hat, from the back of which protruded a white crocheted yarmulke. Deep scars parted both his eyebrows, and his beard was as flimsy as candy floss. His grimy garb hung loosely on his body and made him look like an emaciated scarecrow.

Yiddish-jabbering admirers crowded around him when he won the game hands down, but he burrowed straight through them to plant himself in front of me as if sporting for a fight. He did a long, slow slide with his eyes,

---

*   A long black coat.
** Sidelocks.

fanned his sweat with his bat, and insolently asked, "Where are you from, *macher* [hotshot]? You're not one of us. You're not steerage. Who are you?"

I gave him my name, and told him I was from Manchester, England, en route to a study course in Jerusalem. He gave me his name, Yossel Kolowitz, and told me he was from Auschwitz, Poland, en route to volunteer for Menachem Begin's army, the Irgun. "The Irgun is going to drive the British out of Palestine," he bragged. And then, with a cocky smirk, as if to say, I can make mincemeat out of you any time, he goaded, "I bet you can't play chess."

"I bet you I can."

"Then I'll take you on. And I'll bet I can smash you in less than ten moves. Want to try?" He spoke with the phony confidence of an unsure youth pretending to be sure of himself.

Half an hour later, as I was setting up the chessmen in my cabin, he walked in without a knock. "I've brought us some nosh," he said, retrieving a golden melon from under his *bekeshe*. "I got it from your first class kitchen."

"You stole it?" I was appalled.

Dismissing my censure, he chuckled, "Deception is my secret weapon, hotshot. It's how I survived Auschwitz." He rolled up his sleeves to reveal a turquoise death camp number tattooed into the chalky skin of his arm, and from a sheaf tucked inside his belt he produced a stiletto. As he sliced the lean blade into the thick melon flesh I caught sight of an SS emblem embedded in the knife's bone handle.

"I'm black," he announced. "I'm always black. You go first."

We played three games in almost total silence, and each time he finished me off in quick moves.

"It's my Talmudic training," he boasted. "Keeps my mind razor sharp. In Auschwitz I studied Talmud in my head. Played chess in my head, too. Played in the cabaret as well."

"Cabaret?"

"Sure, the Auschwitz cabaret."

Like a wily showman, he presented a gruesome tale about how his father had been a *badchan* – a traditional Yiddish wedding entertainer – and how he had picked up sufficient tricks of the trade to amuse the suffering Jews in the rat-filled Auschwitz blocs with jokes, mimicry, and stunts. One day, just before Christmas, he was hustled away by some guards. Expecting to be shot, or hanged, or maybe just tortured to death, he found himself instead being escorted to the office of the camp commandant, where he was told that his one-man performances had been noticed and that, henceforth, he would be given kitchen duties to fatten him up in time for the commandant's Christmas party.

"What a party that was!" cooed Yossel, grinning in a crooked sort of way. "What a show I put on!"

He was, he said, by turns, mimic, ventriloquist, magician, and comic. He did so well he was ordered to expand his repertoire for the further entertainment of the executioners.

"You keep us laughing and you keep on living," was the deal.

"But trust my luck," he went on lamely, "I came down with dysentery and was kicked out of the kitchen. A few days later I became so hunger-crazed that I sneaked back in and stole some scraps. An SS guard caught me, and bashed me across the brow with his rifle butt. And that's how I got these." He was pointing to his scarred eyebrows. "And then, on the day I was liberated, a Russian soldier shot that guard dead and that's how I got this."

Brandishing the Nazi knife in one hand, he ran the other through his shiny *peyot*, stroking and curling them with an automatic motion, and while he was doing this his features collapsed into a terrible sadness, and he whimpered, "You want to know what happened to my family in Auschwitz? They gassed my father, and my mother, and my brother, and my two sisters. There's no one left in my whole family but me."

The hush that followed was all the louder for Yossel's muffled sobs mingling with the thump and throb of the ship's engines and the sounds of the sea. I shivered. He had lived a nightmare beyond anything I could comprehend.

When our glances finally met he smiled in a cold, mirthless way and, all posturing gone, said he wanted to share a deep confidence. He was hell-bent on joining the Irgun because back in Poland his father had been a staunch supporter of Ze'ev Jabotinsky and Menachem Begin. From his father he had learned that only the Irgun's militant methods would succeed in driving the British out of Palestine. However, he had two uncles he must first meet. Both had offered him a home. The trouble was he didn't know which one to choose.

"Read these," he said, extracting two well-thumbed letters from his pocket.

The first was from his father's brother, a yeshiva scholar in Meah Shearim, Jerusalem's ultra-Orthodox neighborhood. It was written in a Hebrew script as impeccable as that of a Torah scroll, every word delicately realized.

"Your murdered parents," wrote his uncle, "lived for one thing – to rear you and your brother and your sisters as honorable, knowledgeable, and God-fearing Jews. Now you, Yossel, as the sole surviving member of your family, will surely wish to perpetuate their memory by building in Jerusalem a home of your own that will be a bastion of Torah and Yiddishkeit. In their name, Yossel, I stretch out my hand to you, I embrace you as my own son, and I ask you to come to where you belong. Please join us in Jerusalem."

The second letter was from his mother's brother, a member of a secular kibbutz called Mishmar HaEmek in the Jezreel Valley. It said: "Yossel, it's time to rid yourself of that old ghetto mentality, with its mumbo-jumbo texts and Talmud-obsessed rabbis whose anti-Zionist fanaticism ensnared thousands and thousands of Jews in the death trap of Nazi Europe. Start afresh, Yossel. Transform yourself into a new Jew. Forget the past with its religious superstitions. Be free. Get rid of that yeshiva garb. Join us. We are a kibbutz of socialist ideals. You belong here."

"*Nu* – what do you think?" Yossel asked, his fretful eyes holding mine.

What was I supposed to say? I stared blankly up at him and he stared darkly down at me, stroking, curling, and recurling his *peyot*. Finally, I babbled, "I'm not the person for this."

Yossel Kolowitz hurriedly rose and made for the cabin door, furious at himself at having wasted his time confiding in someone as lacking as me. There, at the door, he swung around and, in that put-on swagger of his, snarled, "I'm going to do something that will shock you, hotshot. I've no papers, no passport. I'm an illegal. And I'm not going to let the British catch me and put me behind barbed wire. I've spent too much of my life in concentration camps already. So when we get to Haifa I'm jumping ship."

I tried to hide a thick swallow. "And where will you go? To which uncle?"

"Who knows? All I do know is I'm going to learn how to use a gun and join the Irgun." With that, he slammed the cabin door, causing me to shudder inwardly, wondering what might become of an orphan so haunted as he.

At the end of its five-day journey, the *Aegean Star* approached the Palestine shore and we all crowded the rails, soaking up the view of Haifa. The faces of the steerage passengers were particularly radiant. One began to sing, hesitantly at first until, bit by bit, his song swelled and multiplied until virtually the whole vessel was alive with the stirring stanzas of the Zionist anthem of hope, "*Hatikva*":

As long as within the heart
A Jewish soul yearns,
And forward, toward the east,
An eye turns to Zion,

Our hope is not yet lost,
Our hope of two thousand years
To be a free people in our land,
The land of Zion and Jerusalem.

Survivors who thought they had no tears left, sobbed.

When the *Aegean Star* heaved to the dock, a battalion of British soldiers dressed in safari-like uniforms, red berets on their heads, trotted to their positions alongside the ship. They looked invincible. Behind them stood clusters of British policemen in starched uniforms, brassy parade-ground belts, navy-blue peaked caps, and burnished boots. With the cool confidence of jailers taking the measure of a convict transport, they scanned the Holocaust survivors crowding the ship's lower railing, picking out the illegals by the looks on their faces.

A gangplank was heaved out from a metal door in the belly of the ship, and a British officer barked an order that sent a contingent of the red-bereted paratroopers running up it with short springy steps, rifles at the ready. Then a clipped upper-class English voice, authoritative yet reasonable, declared over the captain's megaphone:

"Attention all passengers! Ladies and gentlemen, may I have your attention, please! Regular ticketed passengers will be so kind as to assemble in the main dining hall for passport inspection. Steerage passengers who have valid papers of entry into Palestine will be so kind as to remain in the stern section until escorted to the main deck for document inspection. Other passengers who do not have valid certificates of entry into Palestine will be so kind as to wait in the steerage section until all other passengers have disembarked. Your fullest cooperation will be appreciated. Thank you."

I rushed to my cabin to pack my remaining possessions, and made for the dining hall, dragging my trunk with me. There was only confusion and commotion. Everybody tried to keep an eye on their belongings while keeping their place in queues that snaked toward tables where assiduous British immigration officials, watched over by officers, checked passport photos against those presenting them.

Meanwhile, sinewy Arab porters in filthy balloon knickers and heavy-set Jewish porters in dirty brown shorts scrambled aboard the ship, carrying long straps and thick ropes about their bodies, the better to haul the huge trunks on their backs. They shouted unintelligible curses at each other as they grabbed hold of people's baggage to carry it off to the customs shed.

Survivors lucky enough to have some form of legal entry document gathered at the foot of the steep iron stairway leading from steerage up to the promenade deck, watched by paratroopers. Everybody was pressing forward against each other. Mothers held babies in tightly-wrapped bundles and fathers clutched children by the hand or high on their shoulders, promising them all manner of punishment if they dared misbehave. Faces strained upward bearing looks of anxious excitement, waiting to be told they could move to the upper deck to be processed and cleared for landing.

Hanging around in poses of anxiety in the rear of the stern were the illegals, those with no useful valid documents at all, waiting to be arrested.

"Jesus, how they stink," spat a beefy sergeant, his features twisting as if he had bitten into a lemon. Then, a cry of alarm went up.

A short, skeletal, black-clad yeshiva boy with wild eyes and deathly-white skin burst out of a covered lifeboat, jumped headlong into the steerage crowd, and darted to the rail, readying to jump.

The sergeant dashed after him, his face angry, his rifle cocked.

"'Ere, none of that," he bellowed. "Nobody's jumping this ship. Get back down 'ere." He grabbed Yossel's foot and broke his balance. Other soldiers ran forward, and Yossel kicked the sergeant away. He spurted back toward the crowd of shouting refugees who were now scattering in panic, abandoning their belongings. Fellow illegals took strength from Yossel's escape attempt, burrowing their way through the luggage, and shoving bags and sacks in the way of the pursuing soldiers. "Keep going, Yossel!" some cried. "Jump for it!"

Yossel dodged and leaped over the strewn baggage and between groups of startled passengers who parted to let him through. Not knowing which way to turn as his pursuers closed in, Yossel zigzagged around the deck. Two paratroopers crouched, ready to jump him in a rugby tackle, but he was too quick for them. Deftly, with unsuspected athleticism, he leaped around them and careened this way and that, desperately looking for an avenue of escape. Finding none, he fled up the stairway and up to the bridge house, straight into the grip of the outraged Greek captain who kicked him hard in the ribs and felled him.

Yossel made no further move to escape. His chest heaved and his nose bled. Three soldiers, expressionless, aimed their rifles directly at him while another shackled him with handcuffs.

"Hey, hotshot," Yossel Kolowitz yelled out to me through swollen lips, as he was hustled toward the gangway, "Begin will soon be kicking out these British bastards, and then – "

A single blow to the head from the beefy sergeant cut him short, and off he was dragged to a police van, to be driven to some barbed wire detention camp, God only knows where. Once the van disappeared off the dock, Yossel Kolowitz quickly became a vanishing memory, as a British official stamped my passport and, full of excitement, I disembarked from the *Aegean Star* and caught a bus to Jerusalem. The date was Friday, 14 November 1947.

Jerusalem! Its individuality is unique.

Something deep stirred within me when I entered it. I did not know what to call it then; I do not know what to call it now. It has the depth of an old masterpiece whose simplicity veils an immense sophistication. And like great music, its composition – the ancient and the modern, the religious and the secular, the Jews, the Muslims, the Christians, and their multiple tones and variations, all somehow synchronize into an incongruous harmony.

Yet, it is said that Jerusalem is the most disputed city in history; that more blood has been shed for Jerusalem than for any other spot on earth. Century after century, armies have fought to conquer and subjugate it: the Assyrians, the Babylonians, the Greeks, the Persians, the Syrians, the Romans, the Saracens, the Franks, the Arabs, the Turks, the Europeans, and again the Arabs. Nonetheless, throughout its three-thousand-year-long history Jerusalem has been capital to no one but the Jews.

I first set eyes on Jerusalem from afar, toward the end of the day, as the bus carrying me from Haifa snaked its way up the tortuous, twisting gorges of the Judean Hills. The lowering sun cast vivid rays across a sky aflame with scarlet and crimson. My Manchester eyes, attuned to cloud and rain, had never seen such a sky. As we arrived near the city center, Jerusalem's masonry seemed to suck up the hues, giving the walls a translucent, golden appearance. The bus slowed as it approached the bustling intersection of Jaffa Road and King George Street, where a sinewy Arab constable, perched on a pedestal and dressed in short pants and a lambswool fez, directed the traffic with a truncheon. When suddenly two sharp retorts rang out in quick succession, he began blowing a whistle and swinging his arms around like a windmill, doing his bungling best to halt the pre-Sabbath traffic so as to allow two English policemen to dart across the road, revolvers at the ready. Our driver agitatedly jumped up in his seat, and cried, "Look – the police! They're chasing a man. The man's throwing leaflets. He must be an Irgunist."

Leaflets fluttered around the intersection like so many laundered kerchiefs blowing in the breeze. One adhered briefly to my window. It displayed a roughly-printed Begin broadside: "JEWS ARISE! FREE THE HOMELAND OF THE BRITISH OPPRESSOR!" The flyer was crowned by an emblem in the form of a rifle thrust aloft by a clenched fist and ringed by the motto, "ONLY THUS!" It was the insignia of the Irgun.

All keyed up, our driver stuck his head out of the window to get a clearer view. "Oh my God," he gasped, "they've got him cornered. The poor fellow, he's down. They're beating him up. Oh, my God, he's bleeding."

People in the street were gazing in fright upon a young man – just a boy, really – lying prone on the opposite curb, his arms twisted behind his back, manacled. Blood oozed from a gash at the nape of his neck, staining the collar of his gray windbreaker. As he lay there, face down on his belly amid his scattered leaflets, his dark-blue beret askew on his curly ginger head, he kicked futilely at the British soldier who had him pinioned to the ground like a maimed steer.

The two English policemen with the revolvers came panting back and, gesticulating at the jammed traffic, barked orders to sort it out and open up a lane to let a police van through. They flung the handcuffed lad into this mobile dungeon, and soon the intersection returned to normal.

It had all been so public, so anonymous, so unbargained for, so fast, that I was transfixed, more stupefied than mortified. Here I was, less than twenty-four hours in the country, and already I had been witness to two clashes involving British police and soldiers accosting, battling, beating, and arresting two young, desperate, and reckless Begin boys. What seemed most alarming to me was their ruthless efficiency. Soldiers and policemen seemed to be on the prowl everywhere, primed for action, pouncing without quarter.

When the bus rolled on across the intersection down Jaffa Road, and passed what looked like a police station, I caught sight of a wall poster that sent a shiver down my spine:

WANTED: MENACHEM BEGIN DEAD OR ALIVE
TEN THOUSAND POUNDS REWARD
FOR INFORMATION
LEADING TO HIS CAPTURE

Staring grimly at me from the heart of the poster was a grimy, unshaven, coffin-like face with piercing black eyes framed in spectacles, wearing the desperate look of a man on the run.

That evening, after swiftly unpacking into cramped lodgings in the leafy suburb of Beit Hakerem where the *Machon* was housed, I rushed over to the nearby synagogue for Shabbat-evening prayers. Upon my return, I met my fellow students as we sat down around a table laden with Shabbat fare. There were twenty-four of us, all from English-speaking countries, and all keenly braced for a year-long intensive encounter with the Hebrew language, Hebrew culture, Jewish history, Zionist ideology, and all manner of other disciplines indispensable to a first-rate youth leader with aspirations to become a first-rate fighting pioneer.

Inevitably, by dinner's end the conversation had turned to the growing turbulence in the country, and since we represented virtually every shade of Zionist politics, the exchange quickly escalated into an argument. Two of the participants, one from Liverpool and one from Cleveland, almost came to blows over the animosity between the Hagana and the Irgun. The row was only defused when someone struck up a lively melody which soon swelled into a sing-along of patriotic songs which we all bellowed in unison at the tops of our voices.

Going to bed that night I could not erase the haunting image of Menachem Begin's face which I had seen on the "Wanted: Dead or Alive" poster. It was a ghastly introduction to Jerusalem. But it was representative of the desperate situation in Palestine in those final months of the Mandate. Like a Greek chorus frenetically chanting the finale of the final act of the final showdown, the gory Palestine opus climbed to a clamorous crescendo. The violent and ugly tit-for-tat rocketed sky-high – the shots in the night, the road mines, the sabotage, the threats, the kidnappings, the truck bombs, the killings. Increasingly, British forces imposed severe self-protective limits upon themselves. Personnel were ordered to move about in groups of no less than four. Cinemas, cafés, indeed whole districts, were placed out of bounds. Scores of Jewish families were forcibly ejected from their homes to make way for British military personnel dependents, women and children, in newly designated security enclosures surrounded by soaring fences. Bit by bit, the authorities were locking themselves up into barbed wire ghettoes. This was the Palestine which I had reached, just in time for one of the most significant events of Jewish history: A despairing Britain threw in the towel and placed the whole frightful Palestine mess in the lap of the United

Nations General Assembly, which, on 29 November 1947, voted to partition the bleeding and tattered country into a Jewish State and an Arab State.

November 29 was a Shabbat, so it was only in the early hours of the Sunday morning that we students at the *Machon* seminar heard the news. My diary entry of 30 November, headed in bold block letters "THE GREAT DAY," reads:

> Was woken up at 1:30 A.M. and told to get dressed. Got JEWISH STATE! Danced and woke up the whole district. Danced like hell till 5 in the morning. Got free drinks. Got drunk. Went to sleep. Woken up at 8 with a headache. Got dressed. Went into town. Terrific rejoicing. Went to the Jewish Agency. Everybody laughing and singing and dancing. Returned home 1:30 and went to bed till 5. After supper went with *chevra* – the pals – to Café Riva. Many British policemen there. Did not like it. Returned home at 9:30 and went to bed.

Two days later, on Tuesday, 2 December, at 11:30 in the morning, while in the middle of a Hebrew class, I was handed a telegram. It was from home. Unobtrusively, I opened it. It was a single ribbon of text. It said, "Mammy passed away peacefully in the night."

I felt a sudden tightness in my throat and a shortage of breath. Numbly, I walked out and made my way to my room. It was all so unreal, like sleepwalking. I locked the door and sat on the bed, deadened. I tried to cry but couldn't. I was too shocked and shaken to cry. I don't suppose there is a right and a wrong way to grieve, but what was infinitely painful was sitting there alone, away from the family, and feeling the guilt of having left my mother hardly three weeks beforehand knowing she was desperately ill, and being absent now from her funeral. So I sat out the long seven days of mourning – the *shiva* – alone. Fellow students at the *Machon* assembled each day to form a *minyan* – the prayer quorum – enabling me to recite Kaddish, but otherwise I sat solitary in my room sharing my feelings with no one, just mourning my mother.

The sole, admittedly powerful distraction, was the news that Arabs everywhere were up in arms over the UN partition resolution. They were vowing to destroy the Jewish State at birth. Bugles sounded the call to arms. Bit by bit, skirmishes mutated into operations, operations into battles, battles into campaigns, and campaigns into full-scale warfare. By the end

THE GREAT DAY.

Sunday Nov 30th

Was woken up by Elik____ at
1.30am & told to get dressed.
Got "JEWISH STATE". Danced &
woke up whole district. Collected
Sabras from neighbouring
Pension & got all students from
the Semin___. Danced like hell.
Went to קפה ריב׳. Got free drinks.
Got drunk. Danced afoul of
pub till 5. Went to sleep.
Woken up at 8 with a headache.
Got dressed. Went to town.
Terrific rejoicing went to
קולנוע. Took many photographs.
Everybody laughing & singing.
Returned home. 1.30 & went to
bed till 5pm. After supper went
with chevrah to קפה ריב׳. Many
British policemen there. Did
not like it. Returned home At 9.30

From author's diary, describing the festivities following UN partition resolution affirming the establishment of a Jewish State, 30 November 1947

Celebrations outside the Jewish Agency, Jerusalem, 30 November 1947, following the UN's partition resolution favoring the establishment of a Jewish State

of the year, just a couple of months after I'd arrived in Jerusalem, the city was under an intensifying siege.

My own scribbled teenage diary entries of those days mirror the pace of events and my reactions to them:

Sunday December 28: Much gunfire the whole day close at hand. Position more serious. Romema, [general area of today's Jerusalem Convention Center] populated by Arabs, was attacked by the Irgun. Bit risky getting into town through Romema. Arabs take potshots at the buses. Increasingly, buses under convoy.

Monday December 29: Gunfire so heavy was not allowed to go to shul in town to say Kaddish.

Wednesday December 31: Last day of year presents a picture full of death. Do not feel scared. Only wish I could have some training in order to help put a stop to this tragic killing. Cannot see an end to the troubles, but have faith in God. No post from home. They must be worried about me especially due to recent news of events here in the papers.

One hour later: Reporting for [training] duty January 3. Hurrah!

Thursday January 1: At 4 P.M. Much shooting from direction of Romema. In evening barrage started up from all directions. Shooting from the wadi at back of house. Strong explosions. Flares went up. All traffic into town stopped. Told big attack yet to come when British leave. Must keep faith in my God. Feel more worried that the family is not receiving mail. Trying to keep up with my ideals as a *chalutz* [pioneer] and will act accordingly. Every day presents a danger to life but yet I fear not, for God is with me. Like David I say "Thy rod and Thy staff comfort me."

Friday January 2: In evening expected lecture from Golda Meirson [Prime Minister Golda Meir to be]. Did not arrive. Went to bed early.

Monday January 5: Still unable to go to shul. Mobilized for trench digging and other fortifications.

Tuesday January 6: Went to daven at Zichron Moshe [near city center]. On the way into town while passing through Romema saw what a thorough job the Hagana has made of the place, not in its destruction but in clearing out the Arabs who had lived there. I did not see an Arab around. All the shops were closed. Many have been let to Jews. Whilst in town I saw a Tel Aviv convoy arrive. The convoy consisted of two armored buses and a few armored trucks. Following in the rear were the Jewish settlement police in open vans (poor fellows!)

Friday January 9: This morning, against advice, I went to shul. I did this because I realize the futility of a Kaddish said here [at the *Machon*] where everybody talks and eats and do not respect the prayer of putting on a hat. They know no better. I have been hearing more reports recently about the British activities. Ray, a reporter of the United Press, told me how the Irgun saved their compatriot who was wounded at Jaffa Gate on January 7. He was guarded over by a British policeman and outside Jaffa Gate was an armored car. The Irgun defied all and in the guise of doctors four of them came and carried the wounded fellow out to safety right under the noses of the British policeman and the armored car. I must give the Irgun credit.

No attempt is being made to feed the 1,500 Jews left in the Old City by the British, and they refuse to allow any help to be given by other Jews.

As I sum up everything in my own mind I see so clearly the mess the British are making here. Through them 1) The capital of the country is virtually cut off. 2) There is no access to the main hospital [Hadassa]. 3) There is no road to the [Hebrew] University. 4) Over 100 bodies are lying in Jerusalem hospitals because they cannot get to the cemetery on Har Hazeitim – Mount of Olives. 5) The courts are not functioning properly. 6) British show a definite bias in favor of the Arabs. The quicker they leave the better.

Shabbat January 10: Nothing spectacular to report.

Sunday January 11: Trench digging.

[...]

Wednesday February 4: After tea I went to shul for *mincha* [the afternoon service] to recite Kaddish since I could not get a *minyan* at the *Machon.* I was just about to board the bus when I heard a girl's voice calling my name. I turned and saw Esther Cailingold standing by the kiosk. It has been quite a few months since I last saw her. In the evening I met her at the corner of Ben Yehuda Street and we went to the Atara café and talked.

Sunday February 22: I delayed putting down this entry because my mood was too numbed. At 6:30 A.M. I was awoken by the sound of a terrific explosion. I got dressed and went to daven at Zichron Moshe. I noticed a few windows broken in shul but did not ask questions until I got back to Machaneh Yehuda. I asked the old fellow with the pot and pan shop near the bus stop what had happened and he told me about Ben Yehuda Street. I rushed down Jaffa Road and the nearer I got to the scene the more pronounced was the damage. Finally, I arrived at King George Avenue and saw what looked like the blast of a blitz. Up I walked to Ben Yehuda Street. My God! What a sight! Sheer and utter destruction. 55 killed and over 100 wounded. As I walked past the Bikur Cholim Hospital I saw and heard the screams and moans of the families of the victims. I could concentrate on nothing for the rest of the day. I knew the British had done it. [Actually, it was the work of British deserters in the pay of the Arabs.] Feelings are running high. The Irgun has put up posters that they will shoot every Britisher in Jerusalem. I listened to the Hagana underground broadcast in English. It was the voice of Esther Cailingold.

The author helps prepare a vegetable garden during the siege of Jerusalem, March 1948

Esther Cailingold, 22 years of age, February 1948

Chapter three

Esther

A few weeks later, through half-closed eyes, I peeped at the clock on my bedside table. It was eleven in the morning, and I winced at the sound of the phone jerking me out of a deep slumber after a sodden night of guard duty and a chilly dawn of trench digging.

"Who is this?" I croaked.

"Wake up! There are people I want you to meet."

It was Esther Cailingold. Older than me by a few years, I knew Esther from Bnei Akiva in England. She had come to settle in Jerusalem in 1946, to teach English at the then prestigious Evelina de Rothschild School for girls. However, since the advent of the siege she had become a full-time volunteer with the Hagana, but was not at all happy with the duties she was being asked to perform. In the space of a few months she had served as an underground broadcaster, messenger, arms courier, field cook, welfare officer, vetter of volunteers; in short, a general dogsbody.

"Where are you?" I shouted through the static.

"Schneller."

Schneller was a disused German Templar orphanage which the Hagana had taken over and converted into its main Jerusalem base.

"You'll like them," she teased. "They're characters."

"Who?"

"The people I want you to meet."

"Who are they?" I was in no mood for larks.

"Meet me at Café Atara in an hour, and you'll see."

"Café Atara? They've nothing to serve. I've hardly eaten in two days. I'm famished."

"Don't fret. I'll scrape together some leftovers from the Schneller mess. See you in an hour."

It was April 1948. The one narrow road that linked Jerusalem with Tel Aviv was by this point totally sealed off. It meandered down hairpin bends and through steep gorges. Arab irregulars were laying ambush to Jewish traffic at every twist and turn. As the British prepared to pull out of Palestine, the bloody battle for control of the strategically important road was escalating by the day. If that road could not be cleared of Arab fire, Jewish Jerusalem's hundred thousand inhabitants were doomed.

Britain's deadline for its final pullout was midnight, May 14. Until that hour, avowed British policy remained one of non-involvement and strict neutrality, standing aside while Jews and Arabs slogged it out.

Doomsayers claimed it was all a plot hatched in Whitehall. The British had no intention of evacuating Palestine, they said. Palestine was too strategically precious for the defense of the Suez Canal. Whitehall was actually conspiring to keep the Palestine pot boiling by pitting Arab against Jew, letting them kill each other off, until midnight May 14 when the surrounding Arab armies would invade Palestine to drive the outnumbered and outgunned Jews into the sea. And then, at that twelfth hour, the United Nations would adopt a British-instigated emergency resolution calling upon Britain to stay put in Palestine and restore the peace. Thus would England – perfidious Albion, as Napoleon had called the British – continue to rule Palestine with international consent, and scotch any prospect of a Jewish State.

So the doomsayers predicted.

In a city frequently pounded by shells, constantly hungry, and totally isolated, rumors like these fed feverish imaginations. Fewer and fewer food convoys were getting through. Meat, fish, milk, and eggs had disappeared. Streets, shops, classrooms and cinemas were empty. Fuel was in desperately short supply. Buses scarcely ran, all taxis had vanished, and private vehicles had been commandeered. There was no electricity, and the Arabs had cut the city's water pipeline. Whatever water there was was largely drawn from underground cisterns, some centuries old; in downtown Jerusalem a reservoir dug by the Romans was repaired and the winter rains stored.

The Hagana, much larger than the Irgun, had long since joined the offensive to fight the fight for independence, but there were pitifully few weapons to go round. And as the battle spread from neighborhood to neighborhood, the Old City's Jewish Quarter was cut off from the rest of Jewish Jerusalem, its inhabitants beleaguered in a siege within a siege. And all the while the British stood by, neutral, aloof, waiting.

Esther's call on that cheerless, dank April morning, with her promise of leftovers from the Schneller mess, was a bit of a tonic to the abiding Jerusalem misery. To get to Café Atara I had to pick my way around a tortured tangle of wires, steel shreds, stone blocks and concrete hulks that had once been a six-story residential and commercial building on Ben-Yehuda Street. Shattered armchairs, desks, filing cabinets, beds, china, clothing, and potted plants lay scattered amid the rubble. Cars that had flipped and burst into flames lay blackened and crumbled. This had been the third truck-bombing in downtown Jerusalem in a month – the first target was the *Palestine Post* building, then the Jewish Agency building, and now this – it seemed the Holy City was blowing itself to Kingdom Come.

Outside the Atara café three bone-skin lads were feeding a bonfire of twigs, trying to heat up a blackened pan of something called *khubeiza*, a plentiful weed which, when boiled, tasted like stringy spinach.

Atara's blasted windows were sealed with corrugated iron sheets on which a defiant "Business as Usual" sign was splashed in fresh white paint. Inside, candles and hurricane lamps cast a yellow glow that pushed back the dimness, diffusing the shapes and shades of the café's art deco charm.

"Over here. We're in the corner," Esther's voice came ringing out from the shadows.

She was dressed for war in a man's battledress two sizes too big for her, her slim figure seeming ridiculously vulnerable in the heavy khaki cloth. Under the tunic, she wore an enormous British Army sweater, and on her feet were clunky regulation three-quarter boots. Her neck was wrapped in a short khaki woolen scarf that could be rolled up into a forage cap. The only whisper of the old Esther was in her smart white gloves and black leather shoulder bag, gifts from her younger sister, Mimi, in London, about whom she often spoke.

The faint light of the café could not totally conceal the fatigue under Esther's eyes which, when turned on you, held a gleam no makeup could improve. Her quiet, heart-shaped face was as serene and unaffected as ever, and her petite physique and softness of voice offered no suggestion of the grit and guts she was soon to display in staggering measure in the hopeless battle for the Old City.

So preoccupied was I with the sight of her that I paid scant attention to the man at her side, his features backlit by the dim light. When he rose to introduce himself I saw he was in his mid-thirties, thick-set, in a kilt, and a Harris Tweed jacket. He had a wind-beaten face and a mop of curly hair that was the color of corn.

"Bonnie laddie!" he boomed, pumping my hand. "The name's Jock McAdam, from the Highlands. It's thanks to this here lassie that the divine whirlwind has swept us together. Pleased to meet you."

Next to him sat another man, as glum as the other was jolly. Esther introduced him as Leopold Mahler, a violinist, a member of the Berlin Philharmonic Orchestra before the war, and grand-nephew of the famous composer Gustav Mahler. He was cuddling a gray knapsack from which the neck of a violin case protruded.

Mahler half rose and offered me a limp hand. He was tall, with a scholarly stoop and thinning blond hair. He could have been anywhere between forty and fifty; it was hard to tell because his face was craggy and lean, and it had a haunted look, as did his shabby brown coat, fastened in front with a wooden toggle. Nothing about him fitted, yet everything about him spoke of refinement.

Esther explained that Mr. McAdam was a sheep farmer from the Scottish Highlands on a pilgrimage to Jerusalem, and was stranded because of the siege. Both he and Mahler were lodging at the YMCA opposite the bomb-damaged King David Hotel.

McAdam trumpeted in his rich Gaelic timbre, "You should know laddie, I've been trying my level best to get into Mr. Begin's army, the Irgun." He pronounced it *Eer-goon*, like some remote Highland loch. "But it seems they don't take Goyim like me. So I went to Schneller to try my luck with the Hagana – anything for the war effort – and this here lassie interviewed me. She put me through the meat grinder, I can tell you, and said you might have some useful job for me. Is that right?"

Esther interrupted to suggest I take him along to join our volunteer brigade of diggers and hackers, working on trenches and other fortifications on the city's western edge.

For some reason the Highlander was tickled pink at this idea, and he doubled over with laughter, rubbing his palms in delight, and slamming me hard on the shoulder. Mr. Mahler, on the other hand, looked at me with somber eyes and muttered morosely, "Since I'm stuck in Jerusalem, I might as well pitch in too." Then, with a wan smile, he explained how and why he had come to be stuck.

He told us that when the Nazis came to power in 1933 he had been heading the second violin section of the Berlin Philharmonic Orchestra. Ousted because he was a Jew, he was recruited by the newly formed Palestine Symphony Orchestra. However, one year of violence – this was at the start of the Arab 1936 riots – convinced him that Palestine was not for him, so he left to join the Paris Opera Orchestra. His next stop was the Drancy concentration camp, and after that Auschwitz. He arrived back in Palestine illegally in 1946, and now planned to go on to Australia where an opening with the Sydney Symphony Orchestra was reserved for him. However, by the time he had gotten his papers together and approved, the road out of Jerusalem was blocked. In desperation, he managed to get a place on an armored convoy intending to blast its way through to Tel Aviv. The convoy successfully crashed three roadblocks and was almost out of the mountains and into the safety of the coastal plain when it fell headlong into an ambush. The midsection of the convoy was smashed, blocking the road. So the front vehicles pressed on to Tel Aviv, while vehicles in the rear limped back to Jerusalem. He was in the rear. And that's why he was stuck in Jerusalem.

A waitress in a red cardigan waddled through the gloom with a menu. The fare was truly foul. Café Atara, known for its savory broths, egg medleys, sumptuous salads, sugar-encrusted chocolate cakes, and honeyed tortes, offered that day a menu of a slice of gray bread smeared with a yellowish paste, a half-omelet of powdered eggs, and the *khubeiza* weed.

Esther suggested the *khubeiza*, and then bent down to open a brown leather suitcase standing at her feet. From it she eased a shoe box and tipped its contents onto the table.

"With the compliments of the Schneller mess," she bubbled.

Out tumbled a chunk of black bread, a slab of margarine, triangles of cheese, olives, and sprigs of green onion. Greedily, I pounced.

As she was shutting her case I glimpsed at what else it contained, and saw it was crammed with her personal belongings. So, I asked her where on earth she hoped to be traveling to in the middle of the siege, to which she gave me a sharp nudge and told me not to be a nosy parker. But then, in Hebrew, she added that she had just been given a new posting for which she had volunteered, but could not talk about it in front of the others.

I didn't press her because the waitress came back with the boiled *khubeiza*, which we all tucked into, with the exception of Leopold Mahler. He speared one morsel of the gluey and stringy stuff on his fork, looked at it suspiciously, gave it a sniff and, after one chew, spat it out.

Jock McAdam was shocked. "Now, now, Mahler," he rebuked,

"there's no better greenery than God's vegetables, however humble. Moses led the Children of Israel through the wilderness for forty years, away from the fleshpots of Egypt. Note, the '*flesh*-pots' of Egypt! And what did they eat in the wilderness? – Manna from heaven. Now, you can't get more vegetarian than that. And what did Our Lord say? He said, 'Bread be my body.' *Bread*, not flesh."

With no trace of humor, Mahler cautioned, "You're digesting time-bombs, the lot of you. Swallow this now and you'll blow up at midnight."

McAdam exploded into laughter, but just as quickly his face darkened. He gave a short discreet cough, the kind that servants make when wishing to attract the attention of their masters, and his eyes flashed a "be careful" signal.

Standing in the doorway, silhouetted against the fading daylight, were two British soldiers, a corporal and a private. They peered into the dim interior of the café, hands in their pockets, Sten guns slung over their shoulders. Their eyes wandered toward Esther, but they walked past us to a nearby table. The waitress padded over to them with the menu which they didn't bother to look at. They just wanted raspberry water. When she returned with the glasses, the corporal dropped a few coins on the table and rummaged in his haversack, bringing out a black leather flask. Rotating his chair so that his back was toward us, he unscrewed the flask and knocked back a swig of liquor. He wiped his chin with the flat of his hand, lit a cigarette from the butt of his mate's, and curtly called the waitress to turn on the radio. A tinny baritone crooned *Brother, can you spare a dime?* The corporal reached once more into his haversack for the flask, and drank.

I whispered that the radio must be battery-powered, since electricity had long ago been cut off. But Esther barely listened. She was looking at the soldiers, her expression a combination of defiance and wariness. Scathingly, she hissed, "Their discipline has gone to rack and ruin. Thank God, we'll be rid of them soon, and then we'll declare independence."

Mahler, his tone acid, said she was talking rubbish. Did she not realize that at midnight on May 14, Arab armies would invade and make mincemeat of us all? And besides, how on earth could a few miserably-trained Jewish patriots like her, armed with popguns and peashooters, hope to sway the rulers of the mightiest empire on earth, Great Britain?

"Because it is preordained," intoned McAdam. "If God be for us who can be against us? The good Lord has given Begin the fortitude to drive them out of Palestine."

"Begin my foot!" raged the musician. "Even if the British do leave,

Begin will just plunge the Jews into civil war. Ben-Gurion is right to fear he'll try to mount an armed putsch and establish a dictatorship."

McAdam looked at the violinist benignly, and said, "Fiddlesticks! Begin is God's anointed. And as Scripture notes, 'He that bless Israel, I will bless.' The day you understand that, Mahler, you'll be a wiser and happier man."

"Will I? You are completely insane. Keeping company with a messianic saint like you is even worse than being one."

Esther and I exchanged glances. Clearly this was not their first duel on matters of theology and politics, sharing lodgings as they did at the YMCA.

McAdam, blazing with sincerity and injured rectitude, responded by saying that, true, he may well be insane; he would not deny that. After all, insanity was a relative thing and, in his case, it was madness put to good use. But by that same logic Mahler, too, was insane. For were they not both zealots, each in pursuit of perfection, on a quest for transcendence? And was there ever zealotry free from madness? Did not he, Mahler, worship his violin, just as he, McAdam, worshipped his God? When Mahler played did not his strings respond, just as when he, McAdam, prayed, did not God answer?

Never in my life had I heard such vainglory. No one could accuse Jock McAdam of lacking in self-belief. Or spirit. Or certitude. Or pontification. And as if to illustrate this disposition, the Scotsman sat back and drove a clenched fist into his palm, his eyes like fire, and added, "And I pray to God, Mahler, that you will never go to Australia, that you will never leave this Holy Land."

The musician, at a loss for words, sat there, a picture of tired, haggard dignity, looking into empty space. Finally, he asked, "Why do you pray I shall never leave this place? What's it to you?"

"To speed his coming," replied McAdam, calm as a rock.

"Who's coming?"

"Christ's."

Mahler shook his head in the deepest exasperation. "I don't understand a word you're saying."

"Then let me spell it out. You are a Jew. Your place is here. This is where you belong. This is where all Jews belong. All Jews should live in Palestine. There can be no Second Coming until all Jews leave Gentile lands and return to Jerusalem."

"Utter rot!"

"Shut your trap, Yid!" snapped the British corporal, swinging about to face us. "Can't you see we're trying to listen to the radio?"

Nelson Eddie was singing, *There's a song in the air.* The corporal's speech was warped with whisky.

Leopold Mahler cringed.

Jock McAdam rose, flicked a crumb of *khubeiza* from his jacket sleeve, smoothed his kilt, and walked over to the servicemen. Reaching their table, he stood and gazed pensively at them. Then he smiled at the corporal. "I'm Jock McAdam from the Scottish Highlands. You didn't mean what you just said, did you? It was a slip of the tongue."

The soldier took a swig of his courage, shook a cigarette from the pack, lit it and, rosetting his lips, blew a smoke-ring into McAdam's face.

McAdam closed his eyes for a flutter of a moment, coughed, and said: "I turn the other cheek. Just tell me you didn't mean it."

"Sorry Mister," said the corporal, taking another puff. "Too late. Already said it."

"Yes, but you can take it back."

"Can't take it back."

"Why is that?"

"Because Jews should shut their traps. They talk too much. Mouthy lot."

"Are they now?"

"And they're murderers, terrorists, like Begin."

"Are they now?"

"And they're double-crossers, too. Judases. Jesus killers."

"Are they now?"

"And they do other things, too."

"Like what?"

"Like hanky-panky."

"What kind of hanky-panky?"

"You know – *their* kind."

Jock McAdam smiled down benignly on the slouching corporal and, with the back of his hand, swiped him hard across the cheek. The corporal, utterly shaken, shot upright, holding his face. There were tears in his eyes.

The waitress, leaning against the wall, emitted a little shriek.

Still with the same smile, the Highlander eased the whisky flask from the soldier's grip and calmly poured its contents over his head. At this, the other lad, the private, jumped to his feet and began circling the table like a nervous boxer. The drunk, sniffing at himself and examining his stained uniform, mouthed a profanity.

"Now, now, none of that bad language," said McAdam amiably. "Perhaps you'd like to get up and leave now."

The corporal grumbled to his feet. His mate hurriedly shouldered his Sten gun and, slipping his hand though the crook of his arm, led him to the door. There he paused, turned, and called out to us in a contrite voice, "We're not all like him, you know. You can't judge us all by the likes of him."

"SKEDADDLE! SCRAM!" roared McAdam, making as if to rush the door.

We sat frozen, gazing at the Highlander, our mouths open. He dusted his hands in satisfaction and was moving to rejoin us when he was stopped mid-stride by an announcement coming over the radio which grabbed the attention of us all. Speaking as imperturbably as if he was reading cricket scores, the English announcer read a bulletin to the effect that initial steps for the British withdrawal from Palestine were under way, and to expedite the evacuation of materiel, sections of downtown Jerusalem would be sealed off at six the following morning until twelve midday. He detailed the streets to be closed, and by what authority.

Esther, rising to leave, said she had a ride back to Schneller from the nearby Zion Square, and handed Mahler and McAdam chits attaching them to my motley band of fortification diggers. She wished them the best of luck, and asked me to accompany her with the suitcase. As we entered Zion Square, housewives with bottles, tea kettles, pots and pans, were silently lining up in front of a donkey-towed water tank for their water ration. A couple of tin-helmeted British soldiers guarding the adjacent government compound dubiously eyed Esther's suitcase and uniform, but then went on tramping their beat. From the direction of the Old City came the sudden clatter of machine-gun fire, setting off a return stutter, followed by a dull explosive thud. Then everything went mute again.

Esther, checking her watch, breathed an exasperated sigh, and said, "My ride should have been here by now."

"So, tell me, where are you off to? Why the suitcase?" I was avidly curious.

She looked at me for what seemed a long time, her hands deep inside her battledress pockets. "I've got my new posting," she said finally, in a matter of fact way. "I'm going into the Jewish Quarter of the Old City."

I was dumbfounded. The Jewish Quarter of the Old City was the most imperiled place in the whole of imperiled Jerusalem. It was a place from which people fled, not one they entered. So I told her to be sensible

Esther Cailingold learning to fire a rifle, December 1947

and normal, stay out of trouble, stay at Schneller. But there was no point. She had made up her mind, and I felt totally inadequate.

Uncharacteristically, she gave me an affectionate squeeze of the hand, grinned – whether nervously or genuinely I could not tell – and said, "I wangled a police permit from the British to go in as a teacher. All I need now is a place on one of their supply convoys. There aren't that many, so every day I go to their assembly point in the hope of being taken. They select people at random, without rhyme or reason. It's all a matter of pot luck. That's why I carry my suitcase around with me every day, on the off chance I'll strike it lucky." And then, matter-of-factly, as if to make light of it, she added, "The Old City's Jewish Quarter defenders are in desperate need of reinforcements."

I knew that. I knew there were about two thousand Jews left in that ancient walled-in world, most of them old and pious. Arab irregulars had been hammering at them incessantly for months, and a bare three hundred poorly armed Jewish fighters – less than two hundred Hagana and less than one hundred Irgun – stood between them and certain massacre. British soldiers and police manned the Old City gates, effectively blocking reinforcements, ostensibly on the grounds of strict neutrality.

A lone car, smeared with crudely applied camouflage paint, its engine in full throttle, swung into Zion Square and screeched to a halt. Esther climbed in, and I dumped her suitcase in the back. The driver, a dusty fellow, revved the engine, released the break, hugged the wheel, and roared off.

There was not even time for a decent goodbye.

Esther finally got a seat on a convoy into the Old City on 7 May 1948, and went straight into battle with the Hagana.

Historians of the battle for the Old City attest that there was much mutual mistrust between the Hagana and the Irgun at first, but as their common lot sank in they began to collaborate closely. By 14 May, all contact between the Jewish Quarter of the Old City and the rest of Jewish Jerusalem was severed, and the final hopeless combat began.

Survivors would later testify how Esther Cailingold fought this last battle with grim and undaunted courage as the enemy closed in. They told of how she scrambled through the rubble from outpost to outpost, trying to maintain communication between the exhausted defenders, bringing them whatever little food was left, and delivering the dwindling ammunition. They also told of how, though injured, she tried to keep people's spirits up amid the dead and the wounded, the stench, the flies, and the crashing debris.

By 28 May there was nothing left to fight with. Most of the defenders were dead or injured. Esther Cailingold lay mortally wounded, and on the day the white flag was raised she died.

One of her last acts was to scribble a letter to her family in London, never knowing if it would reach its destination. Eventually, it did. This is what she wrote:

Dear Mummy and Daddy, and Everybody,

If you get this at all, it will be, I suppose, typical of all my hurried, messy letters. I am writing it to beg of you that whatever may have happened to me, you will make the effort to take it in the spirit that I want and to understand that for myself I have no regrets. We have had a bitter fight: I have tasted of Gehenom – but it has been worthwhile because I am quite convinced that the end will see a Jewish state and the realization of our longings.

I shall be only one of many who fell in sacrifice, and I was urged to write this because one in particular was killed today who meant a great deal to me. Because of the sorrow I felt, I want you to take it otherwise – to remember that we were soldiers and had the greatest and noblest cause to fight for. God is with us, I know, in His Holy City, and I am proud and ready to pay the price it may cost us to reprieve it.

Don't think I have taken 'unnecessary risks.' That does not pay when manpower is short. I hope you may have a chance of meeting any of my co-fighters who survive if I do not, and that you will be pleased and not sad of how they talk of me. Please, please, do not be sadder than you can help. I have lived my life fully if briefly, and I think this is the best way – 'short and sweet.' Very sweet it has been here in our own land. I hope you shall enjoy from Mimi and Asher the satisfaction you missed in me. Let it be without regrets, and then I too shall be happy. I am thinking of you all, every single one of you in the family, and am full of pleasure at the thought that you will, one day, very soon I hope, come and enjoy the fruits of that for which we are fighting.

Much, much love, be happy and remember me in happiness.
Shalom and Lehitraot,
Your loving Esther*

Esther Cailingold is buried in the military cemetery on Mount Herzl, Jerusalem. She was twenty-two. Her sister Mimi later became my wife, and her brother, Asher, one of my dearest friends.

---

* Esther's last letter is in the possession of her family.

Chapter four

Independence Day

The fourteenth of May 1948 was a Friday, and unbearably hot. A desert wind blew from the east, fanning the countryside like a blow dryer. For three consecutive sun-grilled days and restless nights we had been taking turns hacking trenches out of a chalky Jerusalem mountainside on the city's western edge, overlooking the Arab village of Ein Karem. There were about twenty-five of us, armed with pickaxes, shovels, and a dozen World War I Lee Enfield rifles – an untrained, inglorious bucket brigade of diggers and hackers fortifying a narrow sector of Jerusalem's western front.

In truth, there was no real frontline where we were, and, other than sporadic sniper fire and an occasional mortar shell, it was quiet. But rumor had it that an offensive would be launched from Ein Karem that night, against besieged Western Jerusalem. We'd heard that Iraqi irregulars were infiltrating Ein Karem to join up with a Jordanian brigade coming up from Jericho. We were supposed to stop them, but nobody knew how, least of all the man in charge, a fellow called Elisha Linder. With twelve obsolete rifles and a motley crew like ours, what was he supposed to do?

One insuperable problem was that he had no means of communication with the outside world – no field phone, no Intelligence, not even a radio. So in the absence of solid facts, rumor piled upon rumor: David Ben-Gurion had capitulated to Washington and would not declare independence; Menachem Begin was planning an uprising; Arab armies were invading; the United Nations was in emergency session to pass a resolution asking the British to stay.

In truth it was not the Arabs, but thirst, that was our principal foe that day. I was on the water-carrying detail with Leopold Mahler (Jock McAdam had gone off to the Red Cross as an ambulance driver).With the mountainside cisterns contaminated, the nearest water was in an abandoned orchard a mile away. To get to it we had to run a sniper's gauntlet – sprint up a steep zigzag path to the crest of the mountain, and then down to the orchard on the other side. There, in the shade of the trees, was a well, its water grubby but cool. We hauled it back in jerry cans, two to a man. The only way to drink it was through a handkerchief, so as not to swallow the bugs.

Under the noon sun the detail was punishing. Each jerry can seemed to weigh a ton and, dragging them, we stumbled over rocks and tripped through thickets of dry thistles, our half-naked bodies tormented by flies and mosquitoes. Try as he might, Leopold Mahler found it difficult to maintain the pace. He stopped frequently to catch his breath, drink, and put a wet cloth on his blistered hands as he painfully lugged his load, his violin case strapped into the knapsack on his back. Early in the afternoon, as we still were making our way back, a sniper's bullet whistled past Mahler's face and sliced clean through a tree branch just above his head. With a brittle crack, the branch struck his violin case so sharply it forced him to his knees. He looked up at me, dazed. "My violin," he gulped. "It's shattered. I'm finished."

I grabbed him by the shoulders and exhorted him to pull himself together. But he brushed me off, raised himself awkwardly onto a rock, unstrapped the knapsack, and very gently pulled out his wooden violin case. It was cracked. Cautiously, he opened the lid and lifted out the instrument, turning it this way and that, sliding his eyes very slowly over every inch of it. It looked to me as exquisite and delicate as a butterfly. He cradled the violin under his chin and, with closed eyes, meticulously tuned each string. Delicately, he replaced the instrument, returned the case to his knapsack and strapped it onto his back. While so doing he said in an exhausted voice, "My violin is perfect. If I don't survive, give it to the Philharmonic. And do me another favor, too. Tell God in your daily prayers, if there is a God, to save my soul, if we have souls," and he laughed, a thin and bitter laugh.

"That's daft talk," I said, helping him to pick up his load and, together, we stumbled back to the diggers on the mountainside. There, the medic, a retired x-ray technician, checked Mahler over and diagnosed dehydration and fatigue. Elisha Linder filled us in on the latest batch of rumors to come his way from a nearby emplacement: the Arabs were plundering downtown Jerusalem; a coordinated Arab offensive was under way; the British were siding with the Arabs; Ben-Gurion had put off the declaration of independence; Begin was rallying for a showdown against him.

As proof of the Irgun leader's intentions, Linder showed us an editorial in Begin's underground news-sheet, *Herut*, passed on to him by one of the diggers. It read:

> If, on Shabbat, the message goes out: "The Jewish State is hereby established," the whole people, the youth, will rally and fight shoulder to shoulder for our country and people. But if on that day a declaration of shameful surrender is issued, if the leadership succumbs to the tactics of the enemy and Jewish independence is destroyed before it comes to life – we shall rebel.

Groused Linder, "We have to find out what Begin's up to. We're totally blind up here," and he instructed Mahler to rest up and then hitch a ride into town any way he could, and find out what was actually going on. "Come back with hard news," he commanded.

Daylight was fading fast. Far to the west, the sun's last rays were receding behind the hilltops of Judea, heralding the Sabbath. Grimy, exhausted diggers assembled in the glow of a hurricane lamp hanging on the door of a stone ruin, hidden from enemy view, to recite the Sabbath prayers – *Kabbalat Shabbat*. It was a heavenly pause; Shabbat stillness suddenly seemed to reign over everything. But then, a series of dry, sluggish shots echoed across the hills and, seconds later, an angry rumble growled from Ein Karem and a shell shrieked and blasted the lower reaches of our mountainside, convulsing it into dust. A headlight briefly cut through the cypress trees at the approaches to the village, illuminating a group of Arabs with miscellaneous rifles, dressed in kaffiyehs and khakis. Elisha Linder screamed, "That's an armored car. To the trenches! Fire!"

We rolled, crawled, and scrambled wildly through the thistles, searching for cover, and everyone with a gun fired blindly into the night. I have no idea how long this went on for. Eventually, a command was passed from trench to trench to hold fire, and we all wondered what had happened. Was it just another skirmish, another probe, or an ignoble retreat? Nobody had an answer.

The Sabbath silence resumed, broken only by the crunch of rushing feet, panting breath, and the winded cry of Leopold Mahler running out of the blackness into the light of the hurricane lamp, shouting, "I have news! I have news!"

To a man, we raced back toward the flickering glow. Elisha Linder grabbed Mahler and snapped, "Well – talk. What did you find out? Is Begin rebelling? Has Ben-Gurion declared statehood? Are Arabs plundering downtown Jerusalem – what?"

Mahler wheezed that he had heard nothing about Begin. And as for the Arabs taking over downtown Jerusalem, the opposite was the case. The Jews were in control of the whole area. And to substantiate his claim he opened his shabby coat wide and displayed a Union Jack tied around his waist. He then began pulling from his bulging pockets forgotten luxuries; triangles of Kraft cheese, Mars Bars, and Cadbury chocolate. Then he unstrapped his knapsack, and from its side pockets spilled out cans of peaches, jars of Ovaltine, and a bottle of Carmel wine.

We watched, eyes popping, as Mahler told how he had come by his booty: it was from the abandoned officer's mess of the British police headquarters near Zion Square. The English had evacuated the area that morning, and the Jews had simply walked in without firing a shot. Moreover, he had heard with his own ears on the radio at Café Atara that all Union Jacks across the country had been hauled down at ten that morning when the British High Commissioner, Sir Alan Cunningham, reviewed a farewell guard of honor outside the King David Hotel. Cunningham had then been flown from Atarot airport, north of Jerusalem, to Haifa, where he boarded a cruiser that was due to cross the three-mile limit into international waters at midnight, formally ending the British rule of Palestine.

"Has Ben-Gurion declared independence, yes or no?" asked Elisha Linder, beside himself.

Mahler took a deep breath and solemnly said, "David Ben-Gurion declared independence this afternoon in Tel Aviv. The Jewish State comes into being at midnight."

There was a dead silence. Even the air seemed to be holding its breath. Midnight was minutes away.

"Oh, my God, what have we done?" cried one of the women diggers, fitfully rubbing her chin with the tips of her fingers. "What have we done? Oh, my God, what have we done?" and she burst into tears, whether in ecstasy or dismay I will never know. And then the air exploded in joyful tears and laughter. Every breast filled with exultation as we pumped hands and embraced, and roared the national anthem at the tops of our voices.

"Hey, Mahler!" shouted Elisha cutting through the hullabaloo. "Our state – what's its name?"

The violinist stared back blankly. "I don't know. I didn't think to ask."

"You don't know?"

Mahler shook his head.

"How about Yehuda?" suggested someone. "After all, King David's kingdom was called Yehuda – Judea."

"Zion," cried another. "It's an obvious choice."

"Israel!" called a third. "What's wrong with Israel?"

"Let's drink to that," said Elisha with delight, breaking open the bottle of wine and filling a tin mug to the brim. "A *l'chayim* to our new State, whatever its name!"

"Wait!" shouted a Chasid whom everybody knew as Nussen der chazzan – a cantor by calling, and a most diligent volunteer digger from Meah Shearim, the ultra-Orthodox area of Jerusalem. "It's Shabbos. Kiddush first."

Our crowd gathered around him in a hush, as Nussen der chazzan clasped the mug and, in a sweet cantorial tone began to chant *"Yom hashishi"* – the blessing for the sanctification of the Sabbath day.

As Nussen's sacred verses floated off to a higher place of Sabbath bliss his voice swelled, ululated, and trilled into the night, octave upon octave, his eyes closed, his cup stretched out and up. And as he concluded the final consecration – *"Blessed art thou O Lord who has hallowed the Sabbath"* – he rose on tiptoe, his arm stiffened, and rocking back and forth, voice trembling with emotion, he added the triumphantly exulted festival blessing to commemorate this first day of independence – *"shehecheyanu, vekiyemanu vehegiyanu lazman hazeh"* – Blessed are You, Lord our God, King of the Universe, who has given us life, sustained us, and brought us to this time.

"Amen!"

Not a squeak came out of Ein Karem throughout the rest of that night, and by morning we were replaced by a batch of trained fighters, relieved for a twenty-four-hour rest. We returned to a town that was bursting with excitement. As Sabbath noon became afternoon, and afternoon became evening, the mood grew from excitement to tumult. Despite the threat of shells, clusters of people roamed the streets, rejoicing. In the giant crater that had been blasted into the top of Ben Yehuda Street by a bomb a few weeks before, a bonfire was ablaze, and youngsters were leaping around it in a feisty folk dance – the *horah*. One young man, alight with the joy of the day, cartwheeled over to Mahler and me and slapped our backs. In

Zion Square, an old man with a trombone and a girl with a guitar were playing a spirited rendition of *hava nagilla*. Spying Leopold Mahler's violin, the musicians persuaded him to join in. Picking up the beat, Mahler began reworking it into wildly spiraling variations, his notes fluttering this way and that, improvisation upon improvisation, as if man and instrument were rediscovering each other in shared pleasure after a long separation.

Café Atara, still lit only by candles and hurricane lamps, was offering a free glass of wine to all comers. Four dusty-looking fellows with pistols at their belts – whom I learned were Irgun fighters, out and about openly for the first time – were fiddling with the battery-powered radio on the counter until they finally found the station they had been searching for.

"Keep the noise down everybody," one of them yelled. "Begin's about to speak."

"Where from?" somebody asked.

"The Irgun's secret radio station in Tel Aviv."

"What's he going to offer us – civil war?" shouted Mahler provocatively.

"Shut your trap and listen,"

A husky voice, rising and falling through the crackling airwaves, solemnly began addressing the nation:

"Citizens of the Jewish homeland, soldiers of Israel, Hebrew youth, sisters and brothers in Zion! After many years of underground warfare, years of persecution and moral and physical suffering, the rebels against the oppressor stand before you with a blessing of thanks on their lips and a prayer in their hearts. The blessing is the age-old benediction with which our fathers and forefathers have always greeted the Holy Days. Today is a true holiday, a Holy Day, and a new fruit is visible before our eyes. The Jewish revolt of nineteen forty-four to nineteen forty-eight has been blessed with success."

"Hurray," people yelped, but Leopold Mahler snorted for all to hear, "What's there to cheer about? Begin is about to launch his second revolt, this time against his own people."

"Shut up or you'll get this in your face," threatened an Irgunist, fist clenched, his features distorted with anger.

Mahler retreated, as Begin spoke on.

"The rule of oppression in our country has been defeated, uprooted; it has crumbled and been scattered. The State of Israel has arisen in bloody battle. The highway for the mass return to Zion has been opened. The foundation has been laid – but only the foundation – for true independence.

One phase of the battle for freedom, for the return of the whole people of Israel to its homeland, for the restoration of the whole Land of Israel to its God-covenanted owners, has ended. But only one phase.

"The State of Israel has arisen through blood, through fire, with an outstretched hand and a mighty arm, with suffering and with sacrifice. It could not have been otherwise. And yet, even before our State is able to establish its normal governing institutions, it is compelled to fight satanic enemies and bloodthirsty mercenaries on land, in the air, and at sea."

Here, Begin paused, and when he continued his voice was grim. "It is difficult to set up a State; it is even more difficult to keep it alive. Scores of generations and millions of wanderers, from one land of massacre to another, were needed, it seems; there had to be exile, it seems; burnings at the stake and torture in dungeons. We had to suffer agonizing disillusionments. We needed the warnings – though they often went unheeded – of prophets and seers. We needed the sweat and toil of generations of pioneers and builders. We had to have an uprising to crush the enemy. We had to face the gallows, the banishments across the seas, the prisons and the cages in the deserts. All this, evidently, was necessary so that we might reach the present stage where six hundred thousand Jews now dwell in our Homeland, where the rule of oppression has been driven out and Jewish independence declared in a part of the country, the whole of which is ours."

And then, forcefully, "We are surrounded by enemies who long for our destruction. And that same oppressor who has been defeated by us directly, is now trying indirectly to force us to surrender with the aid of mercenaries from the south, the north, and the east. Our one-day-old State has been established in the midst of the flames of battle. And the very first pillar of our State must, therefore, be victory, total victory, in the war which is raging all over the country. For this victory, without which we shall have neither freedom nor life, we need arms, weapons of all sorts, in order to strike our enemies, disperse the invaders, and free the entire length and breadth of the country from its would-be destroyers.

"But in addition to arms, each and every one of us has need of another weapon, a spiritual weapon, the weapon of unflinching endurance in the face of attacks, in the face of grievous casualties, in the face of disasters and temporary defeats – unflinching resistance to threats and cajolery. If, in the coming days and weeks, we can clad ourselves in this armor of an undying nation resurrected, we shall yet receive the blessed arms with which to drive off the enemy and bring freedom and peace to our nation and country.

"But even after emerging victorious from this campaign – and victorious we shall be – we shall still have to exert superhuman efforts in order to sustain our independence and liberty. First, it will be necessary to increase and strengthen the fighting arm of Israel without which there can be no freedom and no survival. Our Jewish army should and must be one of the best trained and equipped in the world. In modern warfare, it is not quantity that counts; the determining factors are brainpower and spirit. All our youth have proved that they possess this spirit ..."

Begin's voice suddenly broke up and was drowned in a storm of radio static, causing those crowding the receiver to groan in frustration. One fellow angrily banged the thing without effect, while another fiddled with the knob until, out of the quivering airwaves, the voice reemerged. "... Another primary pillar of our domestic policy is *Shivat Zion* – the Return to Zion. Ships! For Heaven's sake, let us have ships. Let us not mouth empty words questioning our capacity to absorb immigrants. Let us not impose restrictions on immigration for the sake of so-called 'efficiency.' Quickly! Quickly! Our nation has no time! Bring in hundreds of thousands of Jews now! If there won't be enough houses for them let us put up tents, or even let the skies, the blue skies of our land, be their roof, if necessary. We are in the midst of a war of survival, and our tomorrow – and theirs – depends upon the quickest ingathering of our nation's exiles."

And then, in a more level tone, "And within our homeland, justice shall be the supreme ruler, the ruler over all our rulers. There must be no tyranny. Ministers and officials of government must be the servants of the nation, not their masters. There must be no exploitation. There must be no man – be he citizen or foreigner – who will go hungry. 'Remember that you were strangers in the land of Egypt,' says our Book of Books. This supreme axiom must continually illuminate our path in our relations with the stranger within our gates. 'Righteousness, righteousness shall you pursue' says our Bible, and this must be the guiding principle in our relationships with each other."

Here, again, Begin seemed to take a deep breath, and when he next spoke his voice was fired with passionate conviction. "The Irgun is now leaving the underground. We, the Jews, now rule over a part of our homeland ourselves, and in that part, the law of a Jewish government prevails. This law is the law of the land; it is the only law. Hence, there is no longer a need for an armed underground. From now on we are all soldiers and builders of the State of Israel. And we shall all respect the government of the day, for it is *our* government ..."[6]

Leopold Mahler jumped up and made for the door, antagonism

written all over his face, "I've heard enough of this," he spat. "Do you really believe he's going to disarm his Irgun and knuckle under to a Ben-Gurion Government? Not a chance! I don't believe a word he says, and neither will Ben-Gurion. Watch out, you'll see."

Leopold Mahler was right. David Ben-Gurion who, with independence, became the provisional prime minister of the fledgling State, did not believe a word Menachem Begin said. He distrusted him almost to the point of obsession, considering him capable of the most fiendish of deeds. All politics are riddled with frictions, but Ben-Gurion's long feud with Menachem Begin seemed more ferocious than that of the Montagues and Capulets.

One reason had to do with the fighting units in Jerusalem. Despite the protestations of the Zionist leadership, the United Nations partition resolution of 1947 had determined that Jerusalem was to be internationalized as the city holy to the three monotheistic faiths. Neither Jew nor Arab would have suzerainty over it. Hence, while throughout the newly proclaimed Israel the Jewish underground organizations had voluntarily disbanded to form the Israel Defense Forces, in Jerusalem the Hagana and the Irgun still functioned under separate commands.

It was into this muddle, in mid-June, that a refitted Irgun arms ship called the *Altalena* arrived, carrying hundreds of volunteers and packed with desperately needed arms. Ben-Gurion demanded the weapons be handed over forthwith to the IDF, but Begin insisted that some be earmarked for his poorly equipped Irgun units in Jerusalem. From the outset Ben-Gurion credited Begin with fomenting a putsch, and no amount of mediation, explanation, and negotiation could persuade him otherwise. Besides, he charged that the *Altalena* was in violation of a UN-sponsored truce which he had brokered, and which banned the introduction of new arms and personnel into the country, be they for Arab or Jew. Hence, the *Altalena* was in violation of the truce. Due to bureaucratic bungling, the ship had been held up in a French port, and by the time it reached Tel Aviv it was long overdue. So Ben-Gurion ordered IDF units under his command to shell the ship. It caught fire, and in the blaze a score of innocent lives were lost, along with the invaluable cargo.

Embattled on every side by invading Arab armies, the fledgling Jewish State, hardly a month old, now stood at the brink of civil war – Jew against Jew. And it was on the very day – 22 June – when the *Altalena* reached Tel Aviv, and was beached, crippled and in flames, within spitting distance from the central promenade, that I, along with other *Machon* students, finally managed to get out of the still-blockaded Jerusalem. Our departure from Jerusalem had been engineered by our youth director, Abe Harman (a future Ambassador to Washington and a longtime president of the Hebrew University), who, fibbing on our behalf, persuaded the Red Cross that we were overseas students, plain and simple, caught in the siege, and now homeward bound. (None of us were.) This was sufficient for the Red Cross to accommodate us on one of their convoys that made its way through the Arab Legion lines.

The usual hour-and-a-half bus journey took us a debilitating five hours, but who cared? After months of deprivation and hazard we were about to enjoy a taste of the high life in the boisterous metropolis by the sea, which had remained untouched by the war. So as we approached the heart of Tel Aviv, and the boarding house where we were to be lodged, it was weird, indeed sinister, to hear the all too familiar sounds of gunshots and mortar fire issuing, so it seemed, from the end of the road leading to the sea front.

What went through my mind as the Red Cross bus pulled out of Jerusalem, and how I reacted to the shooting and the news about the *Altalena* are recorded in my diary entry of that Wednesday, 22 June, 1948:

> I write this on the bus going to Tel Aviv – the town of electricity, baths, showers, lavatories, cigarettes, crowded streets, and ice cream, if the Arab Legion will let us through. We have all been inspected and I am an innocent English student. It is 9:30 A.M. and we are off. Good bye Yerushalayim. I'll be back. We have just passed the Romema roadblock and the guard has shouted to us "Good luck." (We'll need it.) And so I travel along the road where all the blood of our boys was spilt. On both sides are the burned-out remains of trucks and armored cars…To my right is the height of Nebi Samuel from where we were bombarded more than once. We are now approaching Bab el Wad [Sha'ar Hagai] and I can see the dust of the lorries traveling over the Burma Road [a makeshift track carved out of the rocky terrain] bringing food to Jerusalem. It is a good feeling.
>
> We have stopped and a military policeman has just got on the bus and informed us we are approaching Arab lines. One fool of a fellow has a revolver and bullets. He hides the revolver in his sleeping bag and we each take a few of the bullets and put them in matchboxes.
>
> We are going on again and there before me by the battered police station of Latrun is a UN tent and Arab Legion guards. My fingers are crossed. Two of the Legion soldiers along with a UN

observer have just got on our bus and I feel like using the bullets in my pocket. They look like sturdy swine. Their search is not too intensive TG. They seem to be satisfied and we are allowed to go on. We are passing through their lines now. Now we are out on the road to Hulda. We made it!

We have been travelling for 5 hours (journey should take one-and-a-half) and there I can see Tel Aviv. I feel crazy with excitement. A wash, a change, a clean room, people in the streets – it seems too heavenly to believe after so long. It is just like a dream. By the side of the road is a kiosk stacked with chocolate and cigarettes. Everybody is looking at us and giving us a cheery smile. These people did try to help us in Jerusalem during the hard days.

Abe Harman took us to a deluxe hotel. I have switched on every light, pulled every lavatory chain, turned on every tap, and said Shalom to everybody in the most beautifully crowded streets. What a sight it is to see so many people. We lined up for a shower of showers. The dust just flaked itself off my body. I'm going to send off a telegram to the folks back home telling them I'm still alive and kicking.

From the window I could see a massive pillar of smoke coming from the harbor. That seems to be the ship everyone is talking about.

The shelling and burning of the Altalena, *22 June 1948*

Photograph credit: Hans Pinn & Israel Government Press Office

Abe took us to a deluxe restaurant and ordered the choicest of foods. I guess I need a bit of fattening up. I ate a few mouths full and then went back to the hotel and felt sick. I guess the stomach just can't take it. The rest of the group are in the same mess, so the doctor put us on a diet.

Outside the window there has been shooting over that ship and I feel like going back to Jerusalem. In spite of it all, I slept soundly through it between spotlessly clean sheets.

Nine months later I heard Menachem Begin talk about the *Altalena* at a public meeting. It was the first time I set eyes on the man and he had tears in his eyes. The meeting was being held in Tiberias, and I hitched a ride there together with a few other members of our Bnei Akiva pioneer contingent who had meanwhile arrived in the country from England. There were about forty of us, and we were initially housed in Yavne, a veteran kibbutz, to acclimatize ourselves to the tough conditions of working the land. A few months after that we moved to a primitive base camp called Sejera (now Ilaniya) in Galilee, to put together the paraphernalia needed to lay the foundations of our kibbutz. What followed was the most draining experience of my life – the backbreaking chore of clearing rocks and stones, which was why I was so anxious to travel to Tiberias to hear Menachem Begin speak: I desperately needed a break.

The pioneers of Kibbutz Lavi on the day of its founding, February 1949

Chapter five

The Rock Harvesters of Galilee

T he area we were settling was a waterless expanse of hard-hearted acreage, ten kilometers west of Tiberias. We called our kibbutz Lavi – Lioness – after an ancient inn of that name, and it was to a predesignated stony clearing that our convoy (if it can be called such: a truck, a tractor, and a trailer) groaned its way up the rock-strewn hillside. A nippy wind was blowing and there was a mutter of thunder in the air as we pitched our tents under slate-gray clouds that tumbled across the Galilean countryside.

By midday, the tents were up and the tureens on the kerosene burners in the makeshift kitchen were emitting tantalizing aromas that seduced people to down tools and tuck in. I, however, had one urgent chore I couldn't leave: dig the bog – the communal latrine.

It was a dreadful job. I had to burrow through the wet soil, shifting monstrous quantities of rock, and the deeper I dug, the more the water collected, until the area was as slimy as a mud pit. At one point, as I slid feebly into the mud with the sickening sensation of life plunging downward, I asked myself what on earth I was doing in this slimy mess. But then somebody came to relieve me, and after downing a plate of hot food, my spirits rose.

In the afternoon, a few minor political bureaucrats showed up to deliver animated speeches, be photographed, and be gone. By then, the sun had broken through the clouds and we could take in the surrounding countryside. It was spectacular. Looking to the right or to the left gave us radically different scenery to enjoy. On the right stretched the distant belt of the fertile Yavniel Valley plateau, a checkerboard of orchards and fields. To the left, northwards, towered a craggy hill with shoulders that resembled horns – hence its name, the Horns of Hittin – where Saladin once trounced the Crusaders. And beyond that loomed the slopes of Lower Galilee, ascending in swells and undulations to their upper ranges, on the crest of which sat the ancient town of kabalistic lore, Safed. A short walk to the east, meanwhile, brought into view the waters of the Kinneret, the Sea of Galilee, gently lapping the walls of old Tiberias on one shoreline and the purple foothills of the Golan Heights on the other.

Despite the temptation to do so, there was no time to stand and stare. Stones had to be cleared. The only harvest that nature provided in this infertile place, which had not seen a plow for a millennium and a half, were stones – stones in such abundance there seemed to be more of them than there was soil. And buzzing and creeping above and beneath the stones were mosquitoes, flies, scorpions, and the occasional snake.

Rock clearing became our singular preoccupation. The rocks had to be picked up one by one and carried away in baskets, then tossed onto a low trailer that carted them off to some distant tip. And that was what one did from daybreak till dusk – rock harvesting – with blistering hands, and backs that felt at times as if they were stretched on the rack. Even when we picked up the rhythm, and the technique of economizing energy, this was toil without end. And it would go on at Lavi for months; every member of our kibbutz, regardless of occupation, had to take a turn at this labor of rock reaping.

The toil mirrored the primitiveness of Kibbutz Lavi in the virgin terrain of those early days – there was no electricity, no sanitation, hardly a single solid roof; just army surplus tents and a simple basic diet consisting of semolina porridge, raw vegetables, a chunk of bread with margarine, and tea for breakfast; soup, raw vegetables, and half an egg with rice for lunch; and more soup, white cheese, olives and bread with diluted jam for supper. The weekly Shabbat treat was three slices of salami, which was enhanced a few months after our arrival with a piece of chicken.

My weekly letters home to my family in Manchester were full of elaborate lies about Lavi's dazzling progress. If anyone had happened upon the wooden barrack that served as our communal dining hall in those days, they would have seen a bunch of people in muddy work clothes, heavy boots and dunce-style sloppy hats sitting on benches at tables made of rough deal planks lit by spluttering Tilley lamps, reminiscent of Van Gogh's *The Potato Eaters*. Most would be slumped over their tin plates, elbows on table, spooning their soup in silence, too weary to talk.

Nevertheless, there was a poignant fellowship around those tables, and an indefinable quality of lighthearted camaraderie. People cared for each other in an almost mystical measure. We were as close to one another as family. Ours was a volunteer existence of heroic self-deprivation, dictated partly by poverty and partly by our collectivist ideology of mutual support. Above all, we were bonded by an awareness of being engaged in a wildly romantic religious pioneering adventure.

Of course, in a society so small, closely knit and isolated, where everybody inevitably lived under scrutiny and no secret could be hidden, petty quarrels were inevitable. And one such erupted one day over Menachem Begin. Somebody casually remarked that Begin was due to speak that evening in Tiberias and that he would like to go and hear him.

"You can't do that," cried another. "He's a terrorist."

"He's no such thing," retorted the first angrily. "He's a hero."

This was the thing about Begin: the mere mention of his name could arouse mighty and conflicting passions. Admirers adored him irrationally, and detractors loathed him irrationally. To some he was a great orator, to others a dangerous demagogue.

The fracas occurred shortly after Israel's first national election, in which Begin, having disbanded the Irgun, was now leader of his newly-founded political party, Herut – the Freedom Party.

With tempers at flash point it was left to a fellow called Wolfe to calm things down. "Anyone who wants to hear him should go and hear him," he arbitrated. "We could all do with a bit of a break anyway."

Wolfe was a sort of village counselor, a short, frail-looking man with thick-lensed glasses on a furrowed face which expressed strength, intelligence, and mildness. Everybody trusted Wolfe.

The public meeting took place in a ramshackle cinema, occupied mainly by Sephardic-looking Jews and weary pioneers like ourselves, from the newly established kibbutzim and moshavim round about. Some of us dozed off when Begin began to talk, until a sudden downpour of rain pelted the corrugated iron roof, drowning out the speaker and snapping us all to attention. Above the rat-a-tat of the downpour, Begin, unfazed, raised his hands heavenward and recited at the top of his voice a blessing for the abundance of rain in its season, at which he had the Sephardic crowd on its feet, stomping and applauding with delight.

This prompted me to focus more intently on the man, and to pay closer heed to what he was saying. He was a gifted orator, driving home his points with devastating clarity, at once moving and witty, inspiring and intimate. In appearance he looked to be in his mid-thirties, middle-sized, lean, and dressed in a baggy gray suit that looked as though it might smell of camphor balls. His clever, bright eyes – and it was my destiny, in time, to get to know them well – were framed by wire-rimmed spectacles. He had a tall brow capped by straight black hair that tended to fall backwards, and a round, pale face ornamented by a thick mustache. He did not look at all like the fearful man his enemies portrayed him to be.

He devoted the first part of his address to his claim that the Irgun, more than any of the other Jewish underground militias, had been the force that had compelled the British to evacuate the country, thus enabling Ben-Gurion to declare independence.

"Ben-Gurion had the privilege of declaring independence," he said, "but he did not set up the State. The nation set up the State. And without the Irgun in the lead we would still be living under the British yoke."

This issue was a source of agitated national debate between leaders of the Hagana and the Irgun, who constantly vied for the credit of having expelled the British. Indeed, the debate goes on to this day. In those days, all parties invested considerable energy in the argument, enlisting historians, educators, journalists, and other shapers of memory and myth, for in that first election of 1949 the political stakes were particularly high, the assumption being that whoever had expelled the British had, thereby, won the moral high ground, and the national right to lead the country.

Menachem Begin sought to mount an even higher plateau of moral certitude by invoking his personal intervention in saving the country from certain civil war. With the zeal of a prophet he told how twice he had pulled his irascible people back from the brink.

"We were almost at each other's throats," he declared, "not only in the matter of the *Altalena* arms ship, but even before that, in nineteen forty-four, when the Irgun rose up in revolt against the British, in defiance of Ben-Gurion's command."

Lowering his voice almost to a whisper, he led us deep into the beleaguered world of his Irgun underground, to shine a light on that black hole of 1944: "It was a year of unspeakable torment," he said forlornly. "Our sisters and brothers in Europe were being slaughtered in the millions.

But Ben-Gurion insisted we join the Allies in defeating the Nazis before rebelling to expel the British from our land. My colleagues and I thought otherwise. Ben-Gurion was so hostile to our revolt he tried to squash it by unleashing his Hagana men to round up our fighters and hand them over to the British. It was madness. It was tearing Jews apart. I could smell the stench of civil war."

Here he paused, his voice quivering slightly as he caressed his next words:

"So I told our men to go quietly, not to resist. It was extremely hard to order our men to restrain their natural instinct for revenge, but I had to do it. I had to do it, *Ki Yehudim anachnu!*" [Because we are Jews]

A tremendous applause shook the rafters of the tumbledown cinema, but Menachem Begin seemed not to hear. He wiped the corners of his eyes with the back of his hand, his pallid face fixed in an expression of gloomy recollection: "Oh yes, it was very hard. Yet our fighters understood my command and humbled their natural instinct for reprisal. They surrendered quietly, many of them to be transported to British detention camps in Eritrea. This roundup was given a name. It was given the name of a hunt. They called it 'open season,' and we were the fair game."

The speaker removed his spectacles and rubbed them vigorously with a handkerchief in an effort to subdue his emotions: "Many of you might remember that 'hunting season.' Our men were dismissed from their jobs. Their children were expelled from schools. Hagana men kidnapped our Irgun men. They were often treated grimly before being turned over to the British police. Lists of our members, officers and rank-and-file, were handed in by Jewish informers. There were daily roundups. Our arms caches and safe houses were exposed."

His voice caught again, but he turned it into a slight cough, a throat clearing, and in velvet words he went on: "All the love of which the human heart is capable wells up within me as I recall our underground fighters, unflinching, fearless, moved by a supreme fighting spirit, and who, nevertheless, allowed themselves to be flung into detention camps, thrown into dark cellars, starved, beaten, and maligned. And not one of them" – he rose to his full height, his eyes fierce with pain – "NOT ONE OF THEM broke his solemn oath not to retaliate! From the depths of Jewish history came the order not to fight back, and it was obeyed to the very last man."

He trumpeted this with a stab of the finger, his face as granite as his eyes, and the audience responded with another mighty wave of applause. But then a sudden rigidity came over him, and his shoulders lifted in the manner of a soldier at a march: "Now hear this each and every one of you, and hear it well. I live by an iron rule: a Jew must never lift a finger against a fellow Jew, NEVER. A Jew must never shed the blood of another Jew, NEVER. Twenty centuries ago we faced the bitter experience of the destruction of our Second Temple, the destruction of our capital Jerusalem. And why? Because of our senseless hatred of each other, a hatred that led to civil war and to our utter ruin: *bechiya ladorot* – generations of tears. And, therefore, I long ago took a solemn oath that no matter the provocation, no matter the circumstances, I would never ever be a party to a civil war, NEVER!"

He was standing ramrod straight, his face fearless, his hands balled, his voice choking with sincerity: "Do we not know from history what civil war does to a nation? Do we not know that generations pass before a nation at war with itself can ever heal? Therefore, I say to you tonight, a curse on him who preaches civil war. Let his hand be cut off before he raises it against another Jew. There will never be a civil war in Israel – NEVER!"

People jumped to their feet in excitement, I among them. I felt something I had never felt before. I could neither describe it nor name it. Only years later did I understand it. That night, in that run-down Tiberias movie house, I was listening to a leader possessed of a unique, all-encompassing sense of Jewish history. Menachem Begin's Jewish memory went back thousands of years, and his vision forward, thousands of years. The Jewish past nurtured his deepest convictions and instincts. It fed his fierce Jewish self-respect. It empowered him as a future premier to declare to kings and princes, to rulers of the world, "A Jew bows to no one but God." And something of that rousing feeling communicated itself to me that evening in Tiberias.

When the ovation subsided he struck a lighter pose, and in the easy tone of one whose authority on the matter was not to be disputed, said, "You know, ladies and gentlemen, I have to tell you in all honesty, there's a bright side to life in the underground. For living in the underground enforces seclusion, and that can be a good thing, because seclusion makes for clarity of mind and for deep thinking. Living in the underground can do wonders in turning a dark cellar into a high watch tower."

We, the audience, gazed up at him puzzled, and he smiled back at us, an intriguing little smile that narrowed his deep-set eyes and lit up his shrewd Jewish Polish face.

"Oh yes, we could see very far from the top of our watchtower in our cellar," he went on beguilingly, a bittersweet edge to his voice. "The visibility was excellent. From our watchtower in our cellar we could see that morning cometh after the night. But first we had to get through the night. And what did we see in that night?"

Grimly, he pounded out each of the next sentences with a thump of the podium. "In that night we saw our people in Europe in an endless procession of death. We saw the ghettoes going up in flames. We saw our enemies plotting against us all – the Hagana and the Irgun alike. And from down the corridors of time we heard the hideous echoes of that catastrophic civil war of almost two thousand years ago, which was Jerusalem's downfall. So seeing all that, we were seized by a profound Jewish instinct – an instinct that is as old as our nation. And that instinct cried out to us – nay, commanded us: Do not retaliate! Be abducted, be imprisoned, be tortured, but do not raise a finger against your tormentors, your fellow Jews."

He took a breather, had a sip of water, and, eyes still watery, began to speak of the arms ship, the *Altalena*.

"History teaches us," he intoned, "that on the heels of most wars of liberation, bloody civil strife almost inevitably breaks out. The fall of a regime resembles an earthquake, and an earthquake, even after it has spent itself, is often succeeded by a chain of subterranean aftershocks.

"Our Irgun revolt did, indeed, create aftershocks, at least in the minds of our detractors. So much so the British predicted that on their departure there would, indeed, be a Jewish civil war. It did not happen for the reasons I have already given. And because of those reasons we never indoctrinated our Irgun fighters to hate our political opponents. On the contrary, we impressed upon them that a day would come when they would be standing shoulder to shoulder in the battle for the Jewish State's defense, soldiers of a single Jewish army."

Again he paused, patted his forehead with a handkerchief, drank, and went on: "Remember, the singular goal of the Irgun was to achieve Jewish statehood, not political power. We broke away from the Hagana to revolt against the British because our national subjugation left us no alternative. We dissented in order to fight for our people, not to rule them. But Ben-Gurion never believed us. For years he and his colleagues maligned us. He and his colleagues insisted our struggle was nothing but a struggle for power. He spread libel throughout the Jewish world when he stated that we were planning a putsch. That's why he ordered the shelling of the *Altalena*. He spread the word I was launching a coup when, in fact, we were bringing in desperately needed arms and volunteers to assist in the general war effort."

He illustrated this by enumerating the particulars of the *Altalena's* cargo: 5,500 rifles, 300 Bren-guns, 50 Spandau machine guns, 4 million bullets, 10,000 aerial bombs, 50 anti-tank guns, 1,004 armored track vehicles, all this in addition to 900 volunteers.

Back and forth he swayed as he rolled off this manifest.

In his speech that night he made no mention of what befell him personally on board the burning *Altalena*. Eyewitnesses told me about that much later on. They told me how a loudspeaker was rigged on the ship to enable Begin to address the many people lining the Tel Aviv beach, some watching the crippled ship, others firing at it.

"People of Tel Aviv," Begin roared, "we of the Irgun have brought you arms to fight the enemy, but the Government is denying them to you." And then, to the soldiers firing at him from the beach: "For God's sake, help us unload these arms which are for our common defense. If there are differences among us, let us reason together."

One of the people who heard him say this was Yitzhak Rabin, then deputy commander of the Palmach – the Hagana's crack striking force. Thanks to the UN truce, he had taken a few days leave, and he happened to be at his Tel Aviv headquarters on some minor errand when, suddenly, he found himself in full view of the grounded *Altalena*, wedged on the rocks, helpless and immobile, some seven hundred yards from dry land.

"I honestly believed what Ben-Gurion was saying, that Begin was mounting a coup," he would tell me years later. "So when ordered to take command of a Palmach unit and open fire, I did. There was a gun battery nearby, a very old cannon, unequipped with sights and with a very slim chance of a direct hit. But clearly, this was no mere shelling to frighten off the people on board; it was meant to strike home. And strike home it did. The gun progressively zoned in on its target and the third shell hit it, setting the ship ablaze. And what a hit that was!"

Eye witnesses described Menachem Begin standing on the burning deck like some figure in a parable, black from the acrid smoke, flinging up his arms and yelling frantically to his men, "Don't shoot back! Don't open fire. No civil war!"

Fearful that the munitions packed below would explode in the spreading flames, the white flag was raised and the captain gave orders to flood the holds and abandon ship. Begin insisted on being the last man off, but his colleagues hurled him overboard. He was picked up in the water and carried ashore, a pitiful sight to behold, by all accounts.

That night, eyes dark-circled with anxiety and fatigue, he broadcast over the Irgun's secret transmitter, and spoke in tears about the *Altalena*, its arms, and its dead. He described the vessel's destruction as "a crime, an act of folly and of sheer blindness." He charged that a deliberate attempt had been made to kill him, snipers having aimed directly at him. "But you do not kill an idea by killing one of its loyal adherents," he cried, and he ended his address with an appeal for *ahavat Yisrael* – for mutual Jewish love. "Long live the people of Israel," he declared in a rasping voice. "Long live the Jewish homeland. Long live the soldiers of Israel, the heroes of Israel – for ever and ever."

And months later, to us, sitting there in the dilapidated Tiberias cinema, he lamented, "We had not yet buried our dead when Ben-Gurion claimed that the cannon he had commanded to fire at the *Altalena* was a holy weapon, worthy of a place in our future Temple. Oh, the shame of it! No wonder people of high moral stature and impeccable repute chastised him for mouthing such sacrilege, reminding him that no holy Temple can ever arise so long as there are Jews with the blood of other Jews on their hands."

And then: "To this day there are enemies who mock me because of the tears I shed in public that night in my radio address. Let them jeer! I feel no shame. There are tears of which no man need be ashamed. On the contrary, there are tears of which a man can be proud. Tears do not come only from the eyes; sometimes they well up, like blood, from the heart.

"Whoever has followed my story knows that fate has not pampered me. From my earliest youth I have known hunger and have been acquainted with sorrow. Death, too, has often brooded over me. But for such things I never ever wept. I did weep that night, however, for the *Altalena*. Why? I wept because there are fateful times when a choice has to be made between blood and tears. During our revolt against the British, blood had to take the place of tears. But at the time of the *Altalena* – Jew against Jew – tears had to take the place of blood. Far better for one Jew to shed tears from his heart than to cause many Jews to weep over graves."

And then, head high, chest out, pitching toward his finale, he ended:

"I say to you tonight, God forbid that a decision of a democratically elected government of Israel shall ever be defied by force. Whatever our differences, however strongly held are our differing convictions, however raucous the debate – these shall be expressed only through the legal avenues of legitimate dissent, as befits our parliamentary democracy. It is thanks to this democracy, set in a sea of despotism, that we shall weather every storm, overcome every hurdle, and withstand every test, as we shall grow, with God's help, from strength to strength."

The applause those words evoked went on and on and on.[7]

The election of 1949 was to be the first of many that Menachem Begin would lose. David Ben-Gurion demonstratively excluded him from every coalition government he headed, and he headed many. He stuck to the belief that Begin's party, Herut, and the communist party, Maki, were both a threat to democracy: the first wanting a right-wing, the second a left-wing dictatorship.

"He never understood," Begin was to say, "that the very essence of Ze'ev Jabotinsky's teachings was the establishment of a liberal parliamentary democracy."

Only in 1967 did Ben-Gurion's successor, Prime Minister Levi Eshkol, end the boycott, when he invited Menachem Begin to join his national unity government on the eve of the Six-Day War.

But that was sixteen years into the future. In that dismal winter of 1949, we weary pioneers of Kibbutz Lavi continued to endure our rock-clearing amid the piercing winds, the bone-numbing chills, the ubiquitous mud, and the relentless downpours. But finally the spring came, and it was a solace of Nature. The sun warmed the hillsides which were golden-green with pristine grasses, and the valleys, which were carpeted with wildflowers. Clusters of sunflowers bloomed here and there, hanging their heads as if in awe of the new village growing in their midst. The few acres freshly cleared of rocks and stones changed color from gray to green as shoots sprang up. And when the days lengthened, folk strolled around the patches, inspecting the ripening grain in anticipation of the first humble harvest.

One early evening, Wolfe tapped me on the shoulder in the dining hut and suggested we go for a walk, to see how the crop was doing. As it turned out, what he really wanted was a heart-to-heart. He told me that the kibbutz had received a letter from the executive of Bnei Akiva in Britain urging that I return to become the movement's general secretary. It would be my task to oversee the workings of the youth groups, coordinate educational programs such as summer camps and winter seminars, and edit the organization's magazine.

Wolfe contended I was morally obliged to take up the role because I had originally arrived in Israel on a Bnei Akiva scholarship to study at the *Machon* youth leadership training program, and was thus committed to three or four years service to the movement. Besides, he said, Lavi needed fresh recruits and it would be my job to help enlist them.

I gave Wolfe a shrug of submission, and said I would do whatever the kibbutz thought best. In truth, I was seized with a mixture of huge regret and tremendous relief – regret because I was under the powerful lure of Lavi, and relief because I was silently falling apart under the strain of the grueling rock clearing. So it was with mixed feelings that I bid farewell to Lavi in the summer of 1949 and plunged into the affairs of Bnei Akiva in Britain.

Chapter six

The Oxford Union

Returning to England, I was not the same person who had left. I felt like I had a new identity – a full-bodied Israeli identity. I continued to live the fantasy of Lavi by joining a small Bnei Akiva commune in a north London suburb, wore Kibbutz Lavi clothes – open-neck shirt, khaki cotton pants, windbreaker – wherever I went, spoke a stumbling Hebrew to whoever would listen, and reunited once more with my adoring family, made plain my intent to return to Lavi after a few years' work for Bnei Akiva.

I enjoyed arranging the educational programs most of all, and one afternoon in October 1952, I found myself in Oxford checking out premises for a Bnei Akiva winter seminar. With time to kill, I sauntered into one of Oxford's celebrated, well-stocked secondhand bookshops to browse around, and while inhaling the musty air I caught sight of a handbill announcing a debate that was to take place that evening at the Oxford Union. The announcement read:

MOTION: This House Condemns Zionism as Imperialism.
FOR THE MOTION: Dr. Ali el-Husseini, adviser to the secretary general of the Arab League, Abdul-Khalek Hassouna.
AGAINST THE MOTION: Dr. Gershon Levy, adviser to Israeli prime minister David Ben-Gurion.

Gershon Levy I knew. He had lectured at the *Machon*. So it was with high anticipation that I went to hear the debate.

The Oxford Union is celebrated as being the most prestigious debating society in the world, with a reputation for airing the most controversial issues. It is the battleground of British crossfire. One of its most outrageous motions was famously debated in 1933, just as Hitler rose to power. It read, *This House will under no circumstances fight for King and Country.* The motion was passed by a large majority, sparking off a national outcry. Winston Churchill denounced it as "this ever shameless motion," and editorialists suggested it contributed to Hitler's delusion that Britain would not fight, thus encouraging him to invade Poland without fear of a British declaration of war, which followed, in fact, six years later, igniting World War II.

Arriving well in time for the main debate, I sat crammed into the spectator's gallery, looking down on a chamber packed with students many of whom were attired in a dress code peculiar to the Oxford Union – eccentric hats, fancy waistcoats, brilliant neckties, and every kind of mustache.

A sanctuary for future statesmen, the Oxford Union had the appearance more of a cathedral than a students' debating society. Its oak benches were old and heavily pew-like, and its Tudor-style windows reached up to an oak-carved, arcaded ceiling from which hung wrought-iron chandeliers. Portraits of illustrious ex-Union presidents hung around the walls, interspersed with marble busts of former prime ministers who had once held Union office.

When I took my seat a satiric debate was in progress, a warm-up to the main contest. The motion was: *This House Considers Non-Perforated Postage Stamps a Menace to Society.* It was a scintillating exhibition of brilliant wit, clever quip, cutting irony, and hilarious anecdotes that reached an uproarious finale when the last speaker perorated: "And so, my Right Honorable Friends, after the Great War of 1914–18 – the war to end all wars – the victors carved up Europe into small pieces and called that making the world safe for democracy. All it really did was to create a glut of new, worthless, non-perforated postage stamps that made life damned complicated for collectors like me."

This set off a shower of guffaws. And when the union president on his mounted throne, dressed in traditional white tie and tails, called on the tellers to count the show of hands, he was greeted with light-hearted cheers. As the cheers died down, Gershon Levy and Ali el-Husseini took their places adjacent to the Dispatch Box from which they were to make their addresses, reminiscent of the House of Commons.

The el-Husseini name was well known to anybody who had lived in Palestine before 1948. They were one of the richest and most powerful of all the rival clans in the country. The most famous – or infamous – of them was Haj Amin el-Husseini, who had been the Grand Mufti of Jerusalem, leader of the Palestinian national movement, a perpetrator of early terrorism, and a collaborator of Hitler.

His younger kinsman, Ali, had a resonant voice, an appealing appearance, and the confident eloquence of one raised in a household whose daily fare was the politics of Palestine. Galvanizing his audience with grandiloquent verbal thrusts which he punctuated with disarming digressions, he triggered loud applause at the end of his presentation.

Next it was Gershon Levy's turn. He spoke as he looked: reserved, pensive, erudite, and thought-provoking. He spoke with an intellectual power that was without guile, laying out his facts with precision. And when he laced these with satiric irony, they cut like a scalpel, so that when he sat down people clapped hard for him too.

A short floor debate followed, students making brief points for and against, after which the two adversaries were invited to wind up their respective cases. Tempers were higher now, reaching a crescendo of an all-out war of words as both sought to clinch their arguments with every verbal trick they could muster in an effort to vanquish the other. The final cataclysmic salvo concerned a place called Deir Yassin.

Deir Yassin – now Har Nof – was a small Arab village on the western outskirts of Jerusalem, located across the valley from the suburb of Beit Hakerem, where I had lodged during the 1948 seige of Jerusalem. In the early spring of that year, Deir Yassin gunmen began taking pot shots at Beit Hakerem. Then, on 9 April, at five in the morning, an explosion from the direction of Deir Yassin roared across the valley with such force it practically knocked me out of bed. Two hours later another blast shook the building. I was told that Irgun fighters, with members of Lechi – the much smaller, radical breakaway underground group – were attacking the village.

"What happened at Deir Yassin," whipped Ali el-Husseini at the Oxford Union, in a voice that lashed like steel, "was emblematic of the notorious and horrific totality of Zionist massacres and imperialist crimes committed against my people. Menachem Begin stands indicted for the deliberate brutal massacre of two hundred and fifty-four innocent men, women and children at Deir Yassin. He ordered his thugs to descend upon this quiet village, savage its women, throw scores of mutilated bodies down the village wells, and burn the rest. Those who survived the massacre were, at Begin's command, loaded onto trucks and paraded throughout Jewish Jerusalem, to be stoned and spat upon, before being taken to a nearby quarry to be shot."

Then, climactically, bitterly, in a tear-smothered voice: "The Deir Yassin massacre and the resultant terror that seized the Palestinian people in its wake marked the beginning of the depopulation of Arab Palestine. For millions upon millions of Arabs this tiny village has become a symbol of Zionist imperialistic perfidy, brutality, aggression, and expansionism."

With that, he sat down and Gershon Levy jumped up. In an incensed voice that lifted to a shout, stopping all applause dead, he fumed, "What this House has just heard is an elaborate exercise in Arab myth-making and propaganda. On trial here is not what happened at Deir Yassin but what has been invented *about* Deir Yassin."

Then, tersely, vigorously, powerfully, as an attorney might address a jury, he made his points – that Deir Yassin, high on a ridge, was a village of strategic importance; that its inhabitants had been forewarned of the impending assault and given the opportunity to flee, thereby surrendering the element of surprise; that there was no deliberate massacre; that the fighting was house-to-house and, therefore, murderous, causing heavy civilian casualties; and that the number of dead was less than half of what Arab propaganda portrayed.

Turning to face Ali el-Husseini he said in a voice as cold as his eyes:

"I would advise you, sir, not to don the cloak of hypocrisy here, before an audience as perceptive as this Oxford Union. You cannot pull wool over their eyes. For they know it to be true that we Jews, unlike you Arabs, are not a martial people. And unlike the Arab nation" – he was talking to the pews again – "the legendary heroes of the Jewish nation were never warriors and conquerors but prophets and scribes. Warfare is not a part of our culture. It is not in our blood. There never was, never could be, a Begin policy of deliberately attacking civilians, as there has been a consistent Arab policy of doing just that. I speak of the policy of massacre and mutilation of Jews in the riots of nineteen twenty, in the riots of nineteen twenty-one, in the riots of nineteen twenty-nine, in the riots of nineteen thirty-six to nineteen thirty-nine, and in the recent war in which the Arabs set out to massacre and mutilate the Jewish State at birth; a war, during the course of which – to mention but a few instances – a convoy of seventy-seven doctors and nurses, in clearly marked ambulances en route to the Hadassah Hospital in Jerusalem met with massacre and mutilation, when all thirty-five members of a convoy en route to the Etzion Bloc met with ambush, massacre and mutilation, when all but four survivors of Kibbutz Kfar Etzion met with massacre and mutilation, or when – "

Cries of revulsion and nausea suddenly cut him short as a foul stench pervaded the hall. Outrageously, an unseen blackguard had hurled a handfull of stink bombs in the direction of the president's chair. They fell at his feet, and the reek was so pungent it reached up to the spectator's gallery. We all held our noses, our faces screwed up. People flailed their arms in an effort to waft the stink away. The president, handkerchief over his nose, began yelling, "Order! Order!" but his audience was fleeing in such droves he declared the debate null and void.

In the entrance hallway a dozen furious students were bawling epithets at each other, and thrusting fists into each others faces. There I caught sight of Gershon Levy in the company of a union officer, and he insisted I join him at the post-debate reception.

The reception was in an adjacent room, where some thirty-odd people stood about in high moods, drinking and laughing, and referring to the most famous Englishmen by their first names. The union president, glass in hand, called out that he would like to propose a toast.

"A toast, not a speech," teased a tower of a man with the posture of a Grenadier Guard and a Kaiser-style mustache, causing people to chuckle. He sounded tipsy.

The president responded with a polite smile, and said, "First, I'm sure everybody will agree that both our debaters tonight presented their cases and causes admirably."

"Hear hear," people grunted approvingly.

"Second, I wish to extend my deepest apologies for the inexcusable and insufferable incident that brought the debate to an abrupt close. It is my resolve to uncover the perpetrator, be it a prankster or a troublemaker. It seems this sort of behavior reflects the spirit of the times we live in."

Somebody piped up, "Was it not Goethe who said that what people call the spirit of the times is mostly their own spirit, in which the times mirror themselves? Ha, ha!"

The witty man looked hardly more than forty, yet he had a pronounced scholarly stoop and a prematurely balding scalp. He was, I learned, Isaiah Berlin, a brilliant philosopher and an ardent Zionist who, in later life, would be revered as Britain's most celebrated intellectual, philosopher, historian of ideas, and recipient of the highest award a British monarch can bestow – the Order of Merit.

Across the room someone began playing a popular chorus on a

grand piano and people gathered round to sing. Berlin sauntered over to congratulate Gershon Levy on his presentation, and surmised that the stink bomber was a student up to mischief, not politics.

Introduced to the philosopher, he asked me about my pedigree, and in an extraordinarily rapid manner of speech, proceeded to volunteer his own. He told me he was an agnostic Jew born in Riga to a devout family. His maternal grandfather had been a Chasidic rabbi of the Lubavitch tradition, and a direct descendant of the renowned eighteenth-century Lubavitch luminary, the Tzemach Tzedek, who had been himself, the grandson of the first Lubavitcher Rebbe. And in those circles there could be no higher pedigree than that.

"I say, old chaps, mind if we butt in?"

It was the Grenadier Guard type with the Kaiser mustache, accompanied by a skinny, long-necked lady with cobweb-like hair

"Please do," said Gershon Levy.

"Well the thing is this – nothing personal, you understand, I mean to say, well…" His voice was warped with whisky, and he dropped it to a conspiratorial whisper when he continued, "My wife and I were just talking: what we'd like to know is… well, you in the debate were talking about Israel being a Jewish State. What we'd like to know is, what exactly is a Jew? I mean, are you a religion, or a nation, or what? I mean to say, you seem to be so many things all at once, if you know what I mean."

"Both," answered Levy, amusement lurking in his eyes. "We are both a religion and a people – a nation-faith, so to speak."

To this, Berlin added enigmatically, "Remember memory! Don't forget memory. Jews are steeped in memory. We have longer memories than anybody else. Hence, we are aware of our continuity and heritage more than any other surviving community in the world."

"Oh dear," sighed the woman vacantly. "Now I understand why you Jews are such a clannish lot."

Her husband laughed with gusto and remarked in the breathy good-old-boy voice of the high-class alcoholic, "Well said, Ethel." Then, to us, "You chaps have to admit – calling yourselves Jews, well, I mean, it *is* a bit thick. Can you imagine me going around calling myself Gentile? It would sound funny, don't you think? What are you? – I'm a Gentile. Bloody alien it sounds to me."

Isaiah Berlin demonstratively turned his back on the awful pair, and said grumpily to us, "I can tell you as a researcher of the history of ideas that anti-Semitism is the most resilient prejudice in all of history. It is one of the strongest forces in world affairs. Amazing how many people are anti-Semites and don't even know it."

To that, Gershon Levy said, "That reminds me of a story. When the Germans conquered Paris they confiscated the grand houses of the French nobility. One such grand house was that of Philippe de Rothschild, and its new occupier was an SS general, a General Halle. Rothschild spent much of the war years in England with the Free French Forces, and when he returned to Paris at the war's end his mansion was restored to him. 'Felix,' said Rothschild to his old butler, who had remained in domestic service in the mansion throughout the war – 'Felix,' he said, 'the house must have been very quiet during my absence. What did you do?' 'Oh no, sir,' answered Felix, 'it wasn't quiet at all.' 'Not quiet?' asked Philippe de Rothschild. 'No sir,' said Felix respectfully. 'The SS general hosted receptions every night.' 'Every night?' asked Rothschild, baffled. 'But who came?' 'The same people who used to come to your receptions before you fled, sir,' answered Felix. 'The very same people.'"

Isaiah Berlin laughed, checked his watch, and said he had to be off. We escorted him to the exit, where he asked the doorman to hail him a taxi and, waiting, again complimented Levy on his debating skills. He did, however, rumble one stark reservation: "You were far too forgiving of Menachem Begin over Deir Yassin. Remember how your boss, Ben-Gurion, sent a letter of apology to King Abdullah of Jordan over the massacre?"

"True," countered Levy, "but from all the available evidence I have seen, a deliberate massacre was never proven, and that's the point I was trying to make. Besides" – this with a wry smile – "tonight was a no-holds-barred contest over the Jewish State's right to exist, and I was out to win it with every weapon I had."

"And win it you did," said Isaiah Berlin, crouching to enter his taxi. "But Deir Yassin remains a stain on Menachem Begin, nevertheless."

Decades later, in 1977, Begin was to astonish me by saying he knew nothing of the Deir Yassin operation until it was over. He explained that under the conditions of Jerusalem under siege, when he was in hiding and communications with Tel Aviv were at best erratic, he had given the local Irgun commander wide discretion in mounting operations. Nonetheless, as the Irgun's commander-in-chief, he never shirked in taking full responsibility for the action.

A few years after that revelation, in 1980, I found myself working alongside the man who had actually commanded the attack on Deir Yassin.

His name was Yehuda Lapidot, a soft-spoken professor of biological chemistry at the Hebrew University. At the time he had taken a leave of absence at the prime minister's bidding, in order to head up something called *Lishkat Hakesher*, a semi-covert operation that maintained contact with Jews locked behind the Iron Curtain during the Cold War.

One day, over coffee, I shared with him the diary I'd kept during the Jerusalem siege, and pointed to my entry of Friday, 9 April 1948 – the day of Deir Yassin. He mulled over the pages trying to decipher my boyish handwriting, which read:

> Practically knocked out of bed by explosion at 5 A.M. and then another at 7 A.M. They were explosions from Deir Yassin, a village just across the valley. Told that I.Z.L [Irgun] and Lechi attacked the village. Has always been very quiet and quite friendly. Told that Arab gangs had pushed themselves in. Went at 10 P.M. to investigate. Crawled down valley [and took cover] behind rock. Could see Jews maneuvering to positions. Crashed Jewish lorry [truck] on hill. Hagana asked for reinforcements for wounded etc. The village was captured by 2 P.M. Jewish flag raised over the destroyed mukhtar's house.

The diary went on:

> Prisoners taken around town by terrorists in lorry [truck] with their hands up. The idea is to bolster morale. Rumoured they were to be shot … [Later on] Walking home we saw the captured women and children sitting in a truck. They just stared. Many Jews around. I felt ashamed the way they cheered. Told that Haganah were going to hand them over to the British.

Lapidot sat quietly for a while, no doubt assembling his thoughts and dusting off his grim reminisces. When he spoke there was a tinge of sadness in his voice: No, there had been no deliberate massacre, he said. Things had not gone the way they had planned. They were being repeatedly hit, and the casualties were heavy. He had taken over command when the officer in charge, a fellow by the name of Ben-Zion Cohen, went down early in the fighting.

He then elaborated: "Our men were ordered to avoid bloodshed

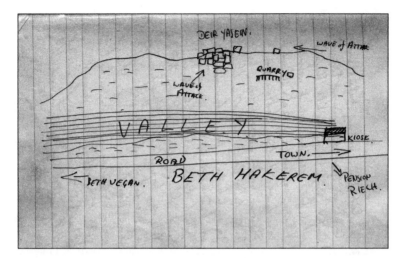

From the author's diary, sketching what he saw and heard of Deir Yassin, 9 April 1948

as much as possible. We had a loudspeaker mounted on an armored truck which was to drive ahead to warn the villagers, to give them a chance either to flee or surrender. The plan was to smash right into the center of the village with the truck and to blare a warning, but the vehicle plunged into a newly dug ditch at the very first row of houses, and that's when the calamity began. The overturned vehicle you'd seen on the crest of the hill was that loudspeaker truck. Though it had crashed we switched on the loudspeaker and made the announcement which said: 'You are being attacked by superior forces. The exit of Deir Yassin leading to Ein Karem is open! Run immediately! Don't hesitate! Our forces are advancing! Run to Ein Karem. Run!' Heavy fire was directed at the truck and injuries were reported. When the other units mounted their assault they were met with the most fierce resistance. Every house was a fortress. We had many wounded."

And then Lapidot said almost abashedly:

"We thought the Arabs would surrender. But having been alerted by our truck announcement they opened up with everything they had. Our hard luck was compounded further when one of the Arab sentries, spotting suspicious movements, shouted out: 'Mahmoud.' One of our men thought he'd said our password, '*Achdut*,' so he shouted back the second half of the password: '*Lohemet*.' That set off an even bigger barrage. We were pinned down. They were better armed than we were. We were about eighty men, and between us we had about twenty rifles, three Bren guns, thirty to forty

Sten-guns – most of which were defective – and grenades. They fought from house to house. We had no experience in house-to-house fighting; we'd never been in such a battle before."

Each house, Lapidot said, had to be taken individually. There was nothing to do but to toss grenades and spray gunfire. Some of the buildings were dynamited, and those were probably the explosions I'd heard in Beit Hakerem. So instead of smashing right through to the heart of the village as planned, it took two hours of horrific fighting to capture the mukhtar's house and raise the flag.

"So I say to you again, no, ABSOLUTELY NO: there was no deliberate massacre at Deir Yassin," swore Yehuda Lapidot. "The dazed and shaken Arabs you saw being driven through Jerusalem on trucks that Friday afternoon were not being taken away to be shot. That was a pernicious lie spread by the anti-Irgunists. They were taken to the Arab side of town and released."

The more I worked with Yehuda Lapidot the more I admired his decency and integrity. And so, yes, I readily accepted his version of events. Nevertheless, the misrepresentation of Deir Yassin lives on. Like Scheherazade narrating one of her never-ending tales of the *Arabian Nights*, Arab storytellers continue to weave their grisly fiction, resurrecting the ghosts of Deir Yassin from generation to generation.

Interregnum

Seven years are a goodly chunk of a person's life. The seven years between the Oxford Union debate and my joining the Israel Ministry of Foreign Affairs in 1959 were energetic, high-strung, edgy, crowded, and rich. These were the Truman and Stalin years, the Eisenhower and Khrushchev years, the King Hussein and Gamal Abdul Nasser years; the time of the global nuclear arms race, the 1956 Suez War, the advent of the PLO's Yasser Arafat; and in my own personal life, the time when I met and was smitten by Esther Cailingold's younger sister, Mimi, whom I married in grand style in London in 1953. A year or so later I introduced her to life in a one-room cabin in the still fledgling Kibbutz Lavi (with the latrine I had dug on its first day still in general use) and gathered from her reaction that we would soon be building our future elsewhere. Hardly a year went by and we did – living with a growing family on a shoestring in a rented, cramped Jerusalem apartment amid a regime of diapers, kindergartens, food rationing, kerosene stoves, and ultimately, by a stroke of good fortune for me, a career in the Foreign Service which was to bring me into the orbits of Prime Ministers Levi Eshkol, Golda Meir, Yitzhak Rabin, Shimon Peres, and Menachem Begin.

Part two

1959–1977

Coalitions and Oppositions

Prime Minister Levi Eshkol

1963–1969

1895 – Born of Chasidic stock in the Ukrainian village of Oratova.
1920 – An early pioneer of Kibbutz Deganya.
1937 – A founder of *Mekorot*, Israel's water utility.
1951 – Minister of Agriculture.
1952 – Minister of Finance.
1963 – Prime Minister and Minister of Defense.

Key Events of Prime Ministership

1964 – National Water Carrier is inaugurated.
1964 – Syria seeks to thwart National Water Carrier by diverting the headwaters of the River Jordan.
May 23–June 5, 1967 – Egyptian president Gamal Abdul Nasser mobilizes forces, blockades Eilat, assumes command of combined Arab armies, and declares intent to destroy Israel.
June 2, 1967 – Menachem Begin joins emergency national unity government.
June 5, 1967 – The Six-Day War begins.
September 1967 – Arab summit at Khartoum rejects Israeli peace overtures.
November 22, 1967 – UN Security Council Resolution 242 calls for Israeli withdrawal and establishment of defensible boundaries.
January 1968 – As the Soviet Union rearms Egypt and Syria, Eshkol pleads with President Johnson to help rearm Israel.
February 26, 1969 – Prime Minister Levi Eshkol dies at the age of 74; is succeeded by Golda Meir.

Chapter one

A Novice in the Foreign Ministry

I got into the Foreign Service by a fluke. Every major public estab-lishment in those days was a padlocked fiefdom of Mapai – the Hebrew acronym for the Workers' Party of Eretz Yisrael, Ben-Gurion's all-domi-nant Labor Party. Mapai was no mere political entity. It had but one idea of government – to preserve intact its absolute grip on the political power bequeathed to it by its historic dominance over the entire Zionist move-ment. It constituted the natural ruling class of Israel, and the body and soul of its socialist governorship. Mapainiks married into each other's families, supported each other, appointed each other, and kept outsiders outside. Climbing a career ladder was largely a matter of party allegiance, and the right connections – *protekzia*, in the vernacular. Mapai members filled the ranks of the civil service, the city halls, the local councils, the university senates, the officer corps, the industrial plants, and every other significant job on offer.

A branch of Mapai even operated within the Foreign Ministry itself, and the more senior you were, the more advantageous it was to be an active comrade. This Mapai branch not only determined the staff committee's annual elections but, by extension, all diplomatic appointments as well.

Menachem Begin was branded the drum major of everything

reactionary in the still-new country, and any mention of his name in a positive context could land you on the other side of the door, or on the other side of the world in some dead-end posting. So, to get on in the fledgling Israeli diplomatic service you had to be resourceful, a master of a couple of languages, and a good Mapainik – or you were a bit of a freak, as I was. For not only was I not a Mapainik, I was a supporter of a left-leaning religious Zionist party called Hapoel Mizrachi, loosely translated as the "Religious Zionist Workers' Party."

I got in thanks to a man called Adi Yaffe, who was head of the Ministry's Political Information Department. I was earning my bread at the time in an underpaid job editing an obscure Jewish Agency magazine. However, as luck would have it, I had a connection with a friend who had a connection with Adi Yaffe, and was able to supplement my income by moonlighting for his department, creating propaganda material calculated to woo the newly independent states of Africa.

One day, Adi, a bright, brisk and jolly sort of fellow, who exuded an irrepressible optimism, called to say that his boss, Golda Meir, the foreign minister, had launched an ambitious new initiative in Africa, putting such strain on his department that he had been authorized to recruit extra staff. "Are you interested?" he wanted to know.

"Very," said I, thrilled at the prospect.

"Then I shall recommend you to the Foreign Service appointments committee."

"But I'm not a Mapainik," I blurted out.

Adi laughed. "True, but you're an ex-kibbutznik, and that should be socialist enough for Golda Meir."

My kibbutz credentials, command of English, and a superficial familiarity with African affairs enabled me to pass muster with the appointments committee, and soon thereafter I became a probationer in the Jerusalem compound of the Ministry of Foreign Affairs. Commensurate with the austerity of the beleaguered little country it spoke for, the Ministry consisted of an assortment of huts as drab as a barracks.

On that very first day in 1959, I was one of fifteen greenhorns sitting stiffly upright in straight-backed chairs listening to Foreign Minister Golda Meir, Israel's most celebrated model of straight-laced probity, confessing to us that she was in the throes of a love affair with Africa.

In a tone full of conviction and in a Hebrew filled with Milwaukee-sounding pronunciations, she told us there were two things she wanted to drum into our heads. "One is, coming to the aid of African States now winning independence after decades of colonial rule is an emotional thing for me," she said. "It is the drive toward universal self-determination and international justice which lies at the heart of my socialist Zionist values. Indeed, my newly initiated African policy is a logical extension of the socialist principles in which I have always believed. And the second thing is, we Jews share with the African peoples a memory of centuries-long suffering. For both Jews and Africans alike, such expressions as discrimination, oppression, slavery – these are not mere catchwords. They don't refer to experiences of hundreds of years ago. They refer to the torment and degradation we suffered yesterday and today. Let me read to you something to illustrate my point."

She picked up a book and opened it at a marked page. "What I have here is a novel called *Altneuland – Old-new Land* – written, as you should know, in nineteen hundred and two, by the founder of the Zionist movement, Dr. Theodor Herzl. In it…" She paused to rummage inside her copious black leather handbag, from whose depths she extracted a pair of thick-rimmed spectacles which she perched on her nose. "In it, Dr. Herzl describes the Jewish State of the future, as he imagined it might be. I shall read you what he said about Africa. And remember, this was in nineteen hundred and two. 'There is still one question arising out of the disaster of the nations which remains unsolved to this day, and whose profound tragedy only a Jew can comprehend. This is the African question. Just call to mind all those terrible episodes of the slave trade, of human beings who merely because they were black, were stolen like cattle, taken prisoner, captured and sold. Their children grew up in strange lands, the objects of contempt and hostility because their complexions were different. I am not ashamed to say, though I may expose myself to ridicule in saying so, that once I have witnessed the redemption of the Jews, my own people, I wish also to assist in the redemption of the Africans.'"[8]

Golda Meir's matriarchal features wore an earnest and dedicated expression, and her voice went husky as she avowed, "It has fallen to me to carry out Dr. Theodor Herzl's vision. Each year, more and more African States are gaining national independence. Like us, their freedom was won only after years of struggle. Like us, they had to fight for their statehood. And like us, nobody handed them their sovereignty on a silver platter. In a world divided between 'the haves' and the 'have-nots,' Israel's nation-building experience is uniquely placed to lend a helping hand to the new African States. We have a vast amount of expertise to offer. For this purpose I have set up a new division for international cooperation – note what I say: international cooperation, not international aid – and you people are going to help staff it. We are going to send out to the new African states scores, even hundreds, thousands of Israeli experts of every sort – technologists, scientists, doctors, engineers, teachers, agronomists, irrigation experts. They will all have but one task – to unselfishly share their know-how with the African people."

She leaned into her chair, combed back her crinkly bobbed hair with the fingers of both hands, lit up a cigarette, and eyeing us through the flame of the match, said, "So now you understand why Africa is such an emotional issue for me. Does anybody have any questions?"

A hand went up. "Are you not afraid the Africans will view us as the new colonialists?"

"No, I'm not. Unlike the Europeans, Israel is totally free of the taint of colonial exploitation. And unlike wealthy America, we can't offer money to buy influence. What we have to offer is our nation-building experience, nothing else, no strings attached. Few developing countries in the world have accomplished what we have accomplished. As a new country, we built ourselves up from scratch. Now they, as new countries, are starting from scratch. We have the know-how, a vast reservoir of practical experience to share with them. We shall work with them side by side, in their fields, and in their workshops. All we ask from Africa in return is friendship."

"No political quid pro quo – nothing at all?" somebody else had the temerity to ask.

Golda Meir took a puff of her cigarette, inhaled deeply, pursed her lips, and gazed over our heads at the coils of smoke spiraling in expanding wreaths from her mouth to the ceiling. Then, in a small voice, she said, "At the end of the day, what we give to Africa we give without conditions."

"But why not something political in return – UN votes, for example?" asked the first questioner, persistent.

The foreign minister settled her elbows on the table, threw the doubter an expression of disapproval, and with exasperation, said, "Of course I am hoping for something in return, but I won't say so in public. Now that independent African States are beginning to emerge, I want to leapfrog over our hostile Arab neighbors and build bridges of fellowship to them."

She stubbed out her cigarette and brooded over an amethyst brooch pinned to the lapel of her plain black jacket, clearly pondering her next thought. When it came her voice was gritty: "But have I not got through to you? This is, first and foremost, a matter of principle, of ideology, of my socialist beliefs, of my Labor Zionist faith!"

Labor Zionist faith!

This crusading woman, then in her early sixties, was born in 1898 in Russia, and raised in Milwaukee, USA. She had studied to be a teacher, but in 1921 changed her calling to that of kibbutz pioneering in a malaria-ridden swamp in Palestine. The man she married, Morris Myerson, a reserved sort of fellow who earned a living as a sign painter, and who loved music and poetry, gave up on her ten years after their marriage, unable to keep up with her overwrought notions, whimsies, and grandiose Labor Zionist passions.

As plucky as Deborah, at times as witty as Wilde, she became as jovial as Jeremiah when pontificating about Labor Zionism. This was manifest when she held forth to us that day, speaking as though there was such a thing as an all-encompassing, all-conquering Labor Zionist ideology that need never bow to overwhelming odds. Her élan, her will to pit her Labor Zionist creed against the rest of the world, would, by her lights, enable the Jewish State to transcend the regional isolation imposed by the Arab States and extend its vision far beyond its frontiers, to Africa. This was to be Israel's equalizing factor in international affairs, and it was in this spirit that we were put to work, propagandizing Golda's Israel in Golda's Africa.

Golda Meir's bold African initiative did achieve impressive results. Leapfrogging over the Arab barricade, a vast structure of Israeli assistance programs gradually spread across the African continent, and the Foreign Ministry's Department of International Cooperation evolved into an enterprise of worldwide repute. Israel, a young state of only two-and-a-half million people, scarce in resources and short on manpower, was promoting the development of dozens of countries far and wide. Soon, hundreds of Israeli experts were rendering aid and sharing their know-how of one sort or another with some sixty-five countries, the vast majority of them in Africa.

Chapter two

A Greenhorn in the Prime Minister's Bureau

I n 1963, a small miracle fell into my lap when Adi Yaffe was promoted to become director of the prime minister's bureau, and arranged that I be seconded as the prime minister's English speech writer, note-taker, and responder to letters from the general public, most of which came from people with madcap ideas on how to wage war and make peace.

The prime minister of the day was Levi Eshkol, successor to Israel's founding father, the legendary David Ben-Gurion who, in 1963, amid a storm of rhetoric, abruptly renounced the premiership, quit his Labor Party in a war of principle, and went off in a huff to live in a hut on a remote desert kibbutz. There, surrounded by books, he relentlessly harangued his long-time trusted lieutenant, Eshkol, pouncing on him at every turn. Curiously, in 1965 he even set up his own rival rump party – Rafi – the Israel Workers' List – supported by his two young Turks, Moshe Dayan and Shimon Peres. They, in turn, lost no time in besmirching Levi Eshkol's competence, charging that his intellect was not as finely honed as that of his predecessor, that he did not enjoy Ben-Gurion's international reputation, that he was a military lightweight, and, to top it all, that he was an utter neophyte in matters of cabinet command.

This last was partially true.

I was present at a musical evening in London in 1986 when Abba Eban, exemplar par excellence of Israeli diplomacy, past master at witty stories, and droll purveyor of salacious gossip, regaled a circle of admiring guests with a tale about Levi Eshkol in his first days as prime minister. He related how Eshkol had summoned him to the prime minister's office to ask him what exactly the job of the prime-ministership entailed.

The former foreign minister was in terrific form that night as, with dry wit and subtle animation, he mimicked Eshkol beckoning him into his room, making sure the door was properly shut and the telephone off, and then asking Abba Eban to tell him as clearly as he possibly could, what exactly was involved in being prime minister of Israel. In his previous capacities as Minister of Agriculture and of Finance, Eshkol explained, he had dealt with concrete matters for which his responsibilities were clearly defined. But now, he had been sitting at his desk for a couple of days as prime minister, and he was not quite sure what he ought to be doing. He was so unused to his new position, he said, that at a public event the evening before, when the prime minister was announced, he had looked around to see who was entering.

Eban described how he had told Eshkol that, first and foremost, the job of a prime minister was very much like that of a conductor of a symphony orchestra. The conductor did not play an instrument, but his

The author with Abba Eban, London, 1986

will, personality, and interpretation decisively determined the sounds that emerged from the collective whole.

"And you, Mr. Eshkol, are our conductor," trumpeted Eban, impersonating a maestro waving a baton. "Your task is to persuade us, your cabinet ministers, to perform together in a single, harmonious whole in accordance with your program, your vision, and your interpretation."

This simile was particularly apt on that night in 1986, for as Israel's then ambassador to Britain, my wife and I were hosting a musical soiree at our residence in support of the Friends of the Israel Philharmonic Orchestra, whose chairman was Abba Eban. A goodly sprinkling of socialites and commercial big hitters were gathered in our spacious lounge to hear Daniel Barenboim's rendition of Beethoven piano sonatas, and it was in the glow of the post-recital drinks that Eban told his tale. He ended it off on a solemn note, saying bleakly, "I also advised Mr. Eshkol that if Israeli history was anything to go by, he would very soon find himself occupied with tasks bearing directly upon the Jewish State's very survival."

And indeed he was. Hardly a year went by before Eshkol found himself confronting a Syrian stratagem to divert the headwaters of the River Jordan in an effort to dry up Israel's main source of water. It was at this juncture of affairs that I started my new job as a junior member of the prime minister's staff.

The prime minister's office was located in the heart of the newly built government compound in Jerusalem, and Eshkol's office was a tastefully appointed wood-paneled chamber whose magisterial authority so overwhelmed me that when the man himself extended his hand and asked me my name, my throat clamped up and I stood there frozen, speechless. He beckoned me to take a seat, which I did with the ramrod posture of a new recruit.

"*Nu, yunger man,* tell me again, what is your name?" he grunted.

I cleared my throat and managed to squeak it out.

"And where are you from?"

"Manchester."

"Manchester?" His eyebrows rose a trifle and his eyes squinted in amusement when he teased. "Our first president, Dr. Chaim Weizmann, once told me that Manchester was a rainy place – a place to come from, not to go to. Ha! Ha! Actually, I hear it's a fine community. Been here long?"

"Twenty years, almost."

"Married?"

"Yes."

"*Oy vey.* That's not good. Children?"

"Four – a boy, three girls."

"*Oy vey!* That's not good at all." And then, lightheartedly, "This means you won't be able to be at my beck and call day and night. Never mind, I'll make do with what I can get."

I was quick to learn that this utterly likeable man was an accessible and easygoing chief, with no airs or graces. So devoid was he of personal vanity that one day, after instructing me about a letter he wanted drafted to former President Harry S. Truman, he turned to the doorman, who was holding open the door of his car preparatory to departure, and wryly asked him in Yiddish, "*Nu*, Yankele, how am I doing as your prime minister today? *Ere bist tzufreiden?*" – Are you satisfied?

Yankele, a dour, lean, stooping figure, closed one eye as if to take aim, and in a no-nonsense fashion, shot, "No, I'm not. My taxes are far too high. You have to bring them down. I'm being robbed."

The prime minister, one leg in, one leg out of the car, cupped a palm to his ear the better to hear the man out, and then spent the next few minutes explaining why taxation was still high and what was being done with the money.

"We have to buy weapons for our army to deter our enemies," he explained, "and that costs a lot of money – twenty percent of our budget. And we have to build homes for our refugee immigrants, schools for our children, hospitals for the sick, and factories for employment. The more we develop our economy, the quicker I'll be able to bring taxation down. So be patient, Yankele. Be patient."

"I hope you're right," grumbled Yankele, unconvinced. There was skepticism evident in his eyes as he whirled a salute, closed the door, and let the premier go. And I, mouth agape, watched the limousine move off, wondering how many other prime ministers ask a doorman for an opinion, listen, and then try to explain what they are endeavoring to do.

Eshkol was sixty-eight at the time, a bit on the paunchy side, with a high forehead and a solid square face. He wore half-framed spectacles that gave him a perpetually bemused expression and a wise, family-friend countenance. His thickset body, hefty shoulders, gnarled fingers and the waddle of his walk still suggested the period in his life when he had dug irrigation canals, swung a scythe, pushed a plow, heaved a sack, and sweated in the dust and heat of the Jordan Valley. The old pioneer was a man of the fields who had, at various times, been a kibbutznik, a labor leader, a planner of rural reclamation, a builder of new towns and factories, and finally, as Minister of Agriculture and then of Finance, the paramount overseer of Israel's economic development.

By nature a ponderer, Levi Eshkol's leadership style was that of a quiet persuader. He would spend hours talking problems through, collecting opinions, weighing their substance, and invariably easing tensions with droll Yiddishisms spoken in a lilting, singsong vernacular, charged with overtones and undertones and peppered with sentimentality, cupidity, and hilarity. His mixture of irreverence, affability, and authenticity was rooted in the soil of Oratova, the Ukrainian Chasidic *shtetl* near Kiev from whence his folksy banter and Yiddish witticisms sprang. Born into a family that traded in lumber, cattle, and fish, he spent his youth in *cheder*, then in *yeshiva*, and then in a Jewish high school in Vilna where he ran with the Zionist socialists who spawned a generation of pioneer nation builders.

As a politician he cut a bland figure, caring little for either material possessions or appearances. And as a public figure he suffered from one gross handicap: he had no rhetoric, no eloquence, no charisma. Yet, in some enigmatic way, his unassuming demeanor, nimble mind and keen instincts endowed him with an unaffected affability and an artless honesty that invited a confessional trust. People instinctively sensed he was not the sort of politician who would try to sell coals to Newcastle or ice to Eskimos.

Chapter three

A Walk with Harry Truman

The letter which Mr. Eshkol had asked me to draft to Harry Truman expressed appreciation to the former American president for having lent his name to a peace research institute at the Hebrew University in Jerusalem. Eshkol extolled the choice of name as emblematic of Israel's gratitude to the president for his moral and courageous decision to assert the power and prestige of the United States in his historic support of Israel's founding in 1948, against the advice of cabinet colleagues.

On the morning I placed the letter on the prime minister's desk for his signature he was receiving a delegation of fifteen or so of the top-ranking leaders of the Council of Jewish Federations – now the Jewish Federations of North America – who greeted him with zeal and pumped his palm with zest. Eshkol responded in kind, for he knew these American Jewish leaders were the genuinely dedicated ones, the ones who traveled tirelessly across the United States, elbowing their way into disinterested Jewish communities to fire them up for Israel, pounding on tables to demand a bigger slice of their funds, tearing up in disgust pledge cards they deemed inadequate, and sometimes even locking doors at fund-raising events so that no one could leave until more money had been raised for Israel – much more money.

If asked why they expended so much time, means, and prestige in doing what they did, most of these philanthropists would probably have said that the fate of the Jewish State was every Jew's responsibility. Some might have confided that their fund-raising for Israel was their last identifiable attachment to Jewish devotion of any sort. And some might have confessed a sense of guilt at the appalling record of their elders – the American Jewish leadership of the Holocaust years – who, paralyzed by inertia, ignorance, apathy, and indifference, had done too little too late to save Europe's Jews. Now, they were resolved that the Jewish State would not go the same way.

There was a predictable animated note to Eshkol's welcoming remarks as he informed his guests that the National Water Carrier, for which some of the people present had raised considerable funding through the sale of Israel Bonds, was finally up and running. They congratulated him heartily, knowing that this immense project was his personal brainchild, vision, and passion.

The National Water Carrier was Israel's largest development project to date, and to this day remains the hub of Israel's entire water system. Fed by winter rains and melting snows that swell the upper reaches of the River Jordan before cascading into the Sea of Galilee, the National Water Carrier is a mammoth network of canals, tunnels and pipelines – some as wide as jeeps – that funnels surplus waters from the north to the arid south, integrating local water systems along its route into a single national grid. With understandable pride, the premier illustrated this enterprise with photographs and maps.

When he had finished his presentation, one of the delegates announced, with much emotion, that he would like to make a personal announcement in the presence of the prime minister. Everyone straightened up. The man, a Los Angeles magnate whom everyone knew as Ruby, spoke with a heavy European accent.

Ruby was elderly and short, with a skinny neck, a big head, and white tusks of hair that stuck out on the sides of his head, reminiscent of Einstein. He closed his eyes when he rose to speak, pulling his mouth in at the corners. He twiddled the lobe of one ear, blew his nose to blink back tears, and rolled up a sleeve to reveal a tattooed death camp number. Sitting down again, he chokingly announced that, as a survivor who had lived to see this day, he was doubling his pledge to a million dollars.

All applauded, and the prime minister leaned across to shake the man by the hand and wish him *"a groise yishar koach"* – a hearty congratulation.

"Now, there you have it," piped up the leader of the group. He was a slim, trim elder with a shock of silvery hair, a patrician authority, and piercing blue eyes that never left Eshkol's face.

For the briefest moment the prime minister stared back at him perplexed. "Now there you have what, Henry?"

"There you have Ruby here doubling his pledge because he's moved by your remarkable water project, and there you have the rest of us working with him night and day for the love of Israel."

"And we certainly appreciate that," said Eshkol.

"I'm sure you do, and we ask for no reward in return. However, with all due respect, how many other Israelis appreciate what we are doing? How many other Israelis know how hard we voluntarily work for Israel? We Americans are expected to know about every new kibbutz and every new moshav going up here, yet how many Israelis have the slightest idea about what's going on inside our American Jewish community? What do they know of the problems we face trying to raise the funds you need? What do they know of our local needs? What do they know of our political lobbying for you, and of our other fund-raising commitments to aid the Jews suffering behind the Iron Curtain?

"Tell me, young fella, when was the last time you were in America?"

Henry – I don't remember his second name – was talking to me.

"Me? Never."

"Aha!" bayoneted Henry. "So there you have it. Here you have one of your own staff sitting here not knowing a thing about us, with no idea of the communities we come from, no idea how we organize ourselves, no idea how we volunteer our precious time, no idea what American Jewry – "

"So why don't you give him an idea," interrupted the prime minister, laughter in his voice. "Invite him. You have my permission."

"Okay, we will. We'll invite him on one condition."

"What's that?"

"That he keeps his mouth shut and doesn't make a single speech. We'll host him for a month or so and show him what the American Jewish community looks like. And you" – he was talking to me again – "you will observe, listen, ask as many questions as you like, and come back knowing a bit more about us than you do today. Is that a deal?"

"It's a deal," chuckled Eshkol on my behalf. "Will Independence, Missouri, be on his itinerary?"

"If need be. It's close to Kansas City. There's a generous Jewish community in Kansas City."

"In that case," said Eshkol, with a smile of satisfaction, handing me the Truman letter, "you'll be my courier and deliver this in person to the president as a token of my respect."

Head bubbling with anticipation, I thanked Henry profusely for his invitation – an invitation that took me across the continent to communities large and small, and which brought me, ultimately, to the front door of the former president of the United States, Harry S. Truman.

Two hundred and nineteen North Delaware Street, Independence, Missouri, was a spacious, rustic, white Victorian residence, with steep gables, corniced eaves, squared bay windows, and an elongated porch extravagantly decorated with elaborate ironwork.

The taxi driver who took me there was proud of its birthright, telling me in his flat-as-Kansas drawl that Bess Truman's maternal grandfather had built the house in 1860. Mr. and Mrs. Harry Truman had been living in it for the best part of fifty years, he said, and between 1945 and 1953, when Truman was president, it was known as the Summer White House.

A trimly attired middle-aged black maid answered the door and, informed of my purpose, said I was expected and bade me enter. She led me into the front parlor, took charge of the prime minister's letter, and told me to wait.

The parlor was a venerable repository of heirlooms. On the mantelpiece of the marble fireplace were all sorts of White House memorabilia, most notably a bronze miniature of Andrew Jackson on horseback. In one corner stood a piano, displaying the musical score of a piece called *The Missouri Waltz*, whose notes I tried to fathom.

"I don't give a damn about that waltz, young man, but I can't say that out loud in public because it's the state song of Missouri."

Harry S. Truman was standing in the doorway, his celebrated vim and vigor belying his eighty-odd years – though he did look his age. He was leaning on a cane, his famous face drawn and bony, his eyes disproportionately large behind thick steel-rimmed glasses. Buttoned up and scarved, he wore a dapper fedora on his head.

"I'm about to take my daily walk, young man," he said sprightly, "and I'd be pleased if you would care to join me."

A Secret Service agent maintained a discreet distance as Mr. Truman stepped out into the street and began walking with stiff, short steps. As I adjusted to his pace, he chuckled, "Old lady Anno Domini has been chasing me recently, so I have to take it a bit slowly." Then, genially, "Very kind of Prime Minister Eshkol to send you personally to deliver his letter, and kinder still to give me such credit for your nation's independence. But the man he really ought to be thanking is Eddie Jacobson, not me."

"How so?" I asked.

"Because when I wavered – and I wavered a lot – it was Eddie who made sure I kept America's weight behind Israeli statehood when it was most needed."

He paused at the memory of the man, and muttered, "Dear old Eddie. Best friend a man could ever have – honest to a fault. May he rest in peace."

Truman's voice mellowed when he spoke thus of his World War I buddy and long-time business partner. It mellowed even more when he confided, "Except for one time when he wanted me to see a Zionist leader I was not anxious to see, in all our thirty years of friendship there was never a sharp word between Eddie and me – and we had been through some tough times together, believe me. There was the Great War, and then our haberdashery venture, which was no howling success."

Edward Jacobson was the son of impoverished Lithuanian Jewish immigrants who moved from New York's Lower East Side to Kansas City. His biographers describe him as short, cheerful, and conscientious, with glasses and rapidly thinning hair. The haberdashery store, "Truman and Jacobson," specialized in "gents' furnishings" – shirts, socks, ties, belts, underwear, and hats. Harry kept the books, Eddie did the buying, and both took turns with the customers. The store opened for business in November 1919 and went under in 1934, crushed by the Great Depression.

"Good morning, Mr. Truman. Nice day, wouldn't you say?"

The ex-president looked up at the clouds scudding across the pale sky, sniffed the air and, tipping his hat to the elderly lady passing us by, amiably replied, "It sure is a nice day, Betsy. My best to Jim."

"Betsy's an old neighbor," he explained affectionately. And then, "So when Eddie came barging in to see me unannounced one day at the Oval Office – it must have been sometime in March forty-eight – I was surprised. In all my years in Washington he had never ever done that – never had he asked me for a thing. But on that day in the White House he was visibly upset. He said he wanted to talk to me about Palestine."

We were walking down a tree-lined street flanked by homes built with traditional Victorian-era elegance, much like his own. Suddenly, he halted, appalled. "Just look at that!" he snapped.

In the gutter lay two empty beer cans. President Harry S. Truman crouched down, scooped them up, tossed them into a wastebasket, dusted his hands, and groused, "Most mornings I have to do that nowadays, pick up litter. It's the Kansas City folk swallowing up Independence."

The rueful acceptance of this unhappy circumstance seemed

to trigger a sensitive nerve, for he suddenly turned on me and crisply exclaimed, "Let's cut out the crap. I'll tell you exactly why I was upset with Eddie when he came barging into my Oval Office – because his Zionist friends had been badgering me no end. Some were so disrespectful and mean to me I didn't want any more truck with them. Many chose to believe that their Zionist program was the same as my U.S. Palestine policy. It was not. They wanted me to engage America to stop Arab attacks on the Jews in Palestine, keep the British from supporting the Arabs, deploy American soldiers to do this, that, and the other. And all the while the British were putting it about that my interest in helping the Jews enter Palestine was because I didn't want them in America."

He pressed his lips together, showing his pique and, throwing me a piercing glance, went on, "I'll teach you an important lesson young man: never kick a turd on a hot day. And those were hot days. My patience was being drawn so tight I issued instructions that I didn't want to see any more Zionist spokesmen. That's why I had put off seeing Dr. Weizmann. He had come to the States especially to meet me. But Eddie was insistent I see him right away. I told him that if I saw Dr. Weizmann it would only result in more wrong interpretations of my Palestine policy. I'd had enough of that."

We had reached a bench at the end of the street, under a large and spectacular tree. "This is where I usually catch my breath," he said, sitting down.

I had the distinct impression he was trying to contain his cross feelings about those American Zionist activists who had come banging on his White House door, but his fixed eye and contracted brow showed that the sting of his recollection was too sharp to suppress.

"Because of them I had words with Eddie," he said vehemently. "He knew that the fate of the Jewish victims of Hitlerism was a matter of deep personal concern to me. The extermination of the Jews was one of the most shocking crimes of all times. Hitler's war against the Jews was not just a Jewish problem, it was an American problem. I had been seized of the issue from the day I became president. And now things had reached a point when I wanted to let the whole Palestine partition matter run its course in the United Nations. That's where it belonged."

He was sitting hunched on the edge of the bench, his chin resting on the handle of his cane, the picture of small-town genuineness. This man from the rural Midwest who had never been to a college, nor made a pretense of erudition, was giving me a taste of his celebrated reputation for relentless talking in a language that was plain, straightforward, decisive and honest.

"Let's go," he said, stiffly getting to his feet. He leaned hard on his cane, looked up at the lofty branches that canopied the bench, and clucked, "What a fine tree this is. It's a gingko." Whereupon, he gave the trunk a little pat, and said to it affably, "You're doing a good job."

For the next ten minutes we walked in total silence, interrupted only by two schoolgirls who asked for his autograph. A clutch of tourists was waiting for him outside his house and they clapped as he approached. With enormous good grace he posed with them for snapshot after snapshot.

I thought this a propitious moment to take my leave, but Harry Truman insisted I remain. So I followed him into his front parlor where the maid, whom he called Vietta, told him his wife had just left for her church rummage sale. Vietta helped him take off his double-breasted jacket, bringing bright red suspenders into full view, and eased him into an armchair. Then she left, and came straight back with bourbon, coffee, and two thick volumes which President Truman explained were his memoirs, intended for me as a memento.

Taking a sip of his bourbon and pointing to the mantelpiece above the marble fireplace, he exclaimed, "You see that statue of Andrew Jackson?"

He was marking the miniature bronze of the seventh president of the United States, on horseback.

"I had that in my Oval Office. Jackson is my lifelong hero. So when Eddie confronted me that day in the White House, insisting I see Chaim Weizmann, he waved to that statue and reminded me that when we had the haberdashery store together I was forever reading books about Andrew Jackson. He also reminded me that I had put up a Jackson statue in a Kansas City square. Then, Eddie said, and I remember his exact words – he said, 'Your hero is Andrew Jackson. I have a hero, too. He's the greatest Jew alive. I'm talking about Chaim Weizmann. He's an old man and very sick, and he has traveled thousands of miles to see you. And now you're putting him off. This isn't like you, Harry.' That's what he said. And I remember looking hard out of the window, and looking hard back at Eddie standing there, and my saying to him, "You baldheaded son-of-a-bitch. You win. I'll see him."

Wistfully, Truman went on, "Dr. Weizmann and I talked for almost an hour. He was a man of remarkable achievements and personality, who had known many disappointments and had grown patient and wise in them. He put it to me that the choice for his people was between statehood and extermination. It was then that I assured him that I would support Jewish statehood."

Leaning back then, right foot on left knee, Harry Truman began to speak about his own State Department as if it was the enemy.

"I knew then what I had to do," he said. "I had to handle those stripe-pants boys, the boys with the Harvard [he pronounced it 'Ha-vud'] accents. Those State Department fellows were always trying to put it over on me about Palestine, telling me that I really didn't understand what was going on there, and that I ought to leave it to the experts. Some were anti-Semitic, I'm sorry to say. Dealing with them was as rough as a cob. The last thing they wanted was instant American recognition of Jewish statehood. I had my own second thoughts and doubts, too. But I'd made my commitment to Dr. Weizmann. And my attitude was that as long as I was president, I'd see to it that I was the one who made policy, not the second or third echelons at the State Department. So, on the day the Jewish State was declared, I gave those officials about thirty minutes notice what I intended to do, no more, so that they couldn't throw a spanner into the works. And then, exactly eleven minutes after the proclamation of independence, I had my Press Secretary, Charlie Ross, issue the announcement that the United States recognized Israel de facto. And that was that."

A grin of self-satisfaction crept across his bony face as he took out his pen and dashed off an inscription to me on the title page of his memoirs. When I told him my son Danny was about to celebrate his bar mitzvah, he gladly inscribed the second volume to him.

Handing me the books, Harry Truman said, "Now, remind me, how did old Eddie use to say 'congratulations' in Hebrew – *mozol* something?"

"*Tov*," I proffered.

"Yeah, '*tov*,' that's right. *Mozol tov*." And he shook me warmly by the hand, with the command that I tender his personal best wishes to Prime Minister Eshkol, and thank him warmly for his letter.

Prime Minister Levy Eshkol with British Prime Minister Harold Wilson at 10 Downing Street

Chapter four

A Perfidious Syrian Design

Shortly after my return from the States, Eshkol summoned me to his office, listened to my brief report, and then, in a businesslike fashion, handed me a memo detailing a trip he was planning to London to confer with his fellow socialist, British prime minister Harold Wilson. He wanted Wilson to understand firsthand the implications of the perfidious Syrian design to divert the headwaters of the River Jordan, and to initiate negotiations for the acquisition of British weaponry in an effort to deter future escalation. Most particularly, he wanted the new British tank, the Chieftain.

Nurturing Israel's sparse water resources had always been Eshkol's abiding passion, and it was common knowledge that he was familiar with every stretch of every irrigation pipeline in the country. Hence the Syrian stratagem, backed by other Arab states led by Egypt, was to him not only an abominable act of belligerency, but an outrageous personal affront as well.

"Prepare me an airport arrival statement," he instructed. "Just a few lines. Try and say something without saying anything. And draft me a major speech for a dinner with the Joint Israel Appeal [now the United Jewish Israel Appeal]. It's a black-tie affair. Every *macher* in Anglo-Jewry will be there."

Panic-stricken at this sudden responsibility of drafting my first full-length speech, I croaked, "But what do you want to say?"

"Something inspirational. I'll talk about our refugee immigrants, the ingathering of the exiles, their human needs, and our longing for peace. But for God's sake, I don't want to talk about Israel being a light unto the nations. I've heard enough about that. Let's be a light unto ourselves first. And, oh yes, say a sentence or two about our National Water Carrier and Syria, but nothing too threatening. I don't want to declare war in London."

Came the day and Eshkol flew to Britain attired in a perfectly fitting dark suit and somber homburg, looking very much like a seasoned statesman. This being my first diplomatic trip I, too, tried to look the part when we disembarked from the El Al plane at Heathrow Airport, where the prime minister was greeted by children on the tarmac waving tiny blue and white flags and excitedly singing at the tops of their voices "*Heveinu shalom Aleichem*" [We welcome you in peace]. They cheered wildly when he approached them, grinning and waving his hat like a pennant, and when he posed among them, tenderly stroking their heads and muttering over and over again, "*Sheina Yiddisher kinderlach*" [beautiful Jewish children] their faces were radiant while cameras rolled, clicked, and flashed.

Inside the VIP lounge we were all greeted with gusto. A tall, handsome gentleman of elegant grooming, whose resolute air was enhanced by a bristling ginger mustache, a tightly rolled umbrella and a bowler hat, introduced himself as Colonel So-and-So from the Protocol Office, and officially welcomed Prime Minister Eshkol in the name of Prime Minister Harold Wilson. Lots of Israeli officials, in addition to leaders of the Anglo-Jewish community, squeezed, hugged, and lauded Eshkol endlessly. And when these welcoming rites were done, the prime minister, surrounded by guards of different sorts – Scotland Yard, Metropolitan Police, Diplomatic Protection Squad, and the Israeli Security Service – strode outside to the bouquet of microphones at the edge of the press pen. With immense gravitas, he read his arrival statement which, mercifully, he had found the time to check and correct before landing. In his characteristic gravelly voice he said:

> Israel and Great Britain have a long association. We share a history that was at times conflicted in the shadow of the greatest of tragedies that befell our people in World War Two. However, it is not the strife of the past that shapes our relationship, but the friendship of the present. This friendship binds our two democracies in an unbreakable alliance at a time when communist Russia is encouraging Syria and other regional dictatorships to engage in belligerent acts that demand our constant vigilance. I look forward to fruitful discussions with Prime Minister Wilson on this and on other topics of mutual interest, and am delighted at the opportunity to meet my fellow Jews, good citizens of this great land. Thank you."[9]

Reporters barked a few predictable questions which the prime minister answered good-naturedly and unsubstantially, whereupon he clambered into a glistening Rolls Royce that was adorned with the Israeli flag, and set off along the highway to London followed by a fleet of limousines bearing his entourage, escorted by police cars and outriders in cavalry formation. Entering the West End, he was driven along prestigious streets, through beautiful parks, and around elegant squares into the heart of London's classiest acre – Mayfair – and to its most exclusive hotel – Claridge's.

It was there, as the evening drew nigh, that the prime minister called me to his suite to rehearse his speech for the Joint Israel Appeal dinner, soon to begin in the banqueting hall downstairs. Given his partiality for lengthy consultations back home, he had found little time to go over my copy, so he was seeing much of it now for the first time.

I had, in its preparation, torn up a dozen or more drafts, leaving tooth marks on my pen as I wrote and rewrote page after page, scribbling deranged doodles while mentally struggling for concise, rhythmic and alliterative descriptions in my amateur effort to give the prime minister a defining oratory. Thus, in describing Israel's heterogeneous immigrant society I had written:

> Those of you who know our Jewish State know that there is much about Israeli life that is at once grotesque and heroic. We have a penchant for hyperbole and wild passions – visionary firebrands, biblical diehards, Tel Aviv high jinks, secular zealots and, of course, party dogmatists. It is hard to find a footing in the soft moss of composure in our land.

"*Stam narishkeiten*" – utter nonsense – growled the prime minister as he struck out the paragraph with his heavy fountain pen. "Can't you write plain English?"

Untutored as I still was in the craft and in his style, I realized I had blundered badly. Nevertheless, even as I acknowledged the extravagance of my language, I urged him to stick with the theme – that as a democracy of migrants we were a noisy and fractious lot, every citizen a prime minister unto himself. To reinforce my point I argued that the Zionist founding fathers had pledged that national freedom would rid us of the "ghetto mentality," exorcise the ghost of the "Wandering Jew," cure us of the "eternal victim" syndrome, and transform us into normal citizens of a normal country. Yet here we were, still strapped with a natural tendency to approach even minor matters with an air of suspicion and embattlement.

Levi Eshkol peered at me over the top of his spectacles, his face a severe frown. "*Boychik*," he said, "what's got into you? Don't you understand we are still at war? We are still beleaguered. We still face terrorism. We still live with menace. We are still absorbing hundreds of thousands of refugee immigrants. So how on earth can you expect us to be normal? We are a motley bunch of tribes trekking home, each with its own *pekelech* [packages] of neuroses."

He fell silent after that, presumably mulling over the enormity of it all, until, with a deep sigh, he stretched his shoulders as if to ease the burden, laid himself down on the couch, and, seeking sanctuary in his famed Yiddish wit, added, "*Mein teirer yunger man*, can't you understand disputation is in our blood? We're a stiff-necked people. Shouting at each other keeps us together. Argument is our nationality."

He then went back to the text, reading it out loud and scribbling numerous corrections as he went, while I naively tried to persuade him to liven up his delivery and put more pep into it. But he fobbed me off, admonishing, "At my age I'm not about to pretend to be what I am not – a performer."

Clearly exhausted, he leaned his head heavily against the back of the couch, and legs outstretched, closed his eyes and dozed off. After a few minutes his mouth fell open and he began to snore so loudly he woke himself up with a start. He looked uncertainly around the hotel suite, blinking, and then focused on the pages still in his hand.

"I dozed off," he said superfluously, rising from the couch. He peered at himself in the mirror, combed his fingers through his hair, centered his bow tie, pulled the sleeves of his jacket to restore its fit, and said, "Let's finish going over the speech."

"There's no time for that. All the guests are seated and waiting for you downstairs." It was Adi Yaffe in the doorway, come to collect his charge.

The prime minister handed me the pages: "Give me these when I go to the podium. I hope for your sake the rest of it makes sense."

People rose and applauded elatedly as Levi Eshkol entered the banqueting hall. Every seat was taken. So many black-ties and extravagant dresses! So many excited and grinning faces! So many cries of euphoria!

I took my seat at a reserved table up front while the prime minister was escorted to a dais, flanked left and right by big donors. After a long and flowery introduction by the banquet chairman, and upon the cue of a tailcoated master of ceremonies bearing a golden chain of office, I quickly handed over the speech and, gnawed by hang-wringing anxiety, watched the prime minister peer at it as if examining some piece of mumbo-jumbo.

In his rumbling accent, he began reading the text in fits and starts, his tongue twisting around wily consonants and tricky vowels in a hapless bid to anglicize his Yiddish diction, pausing frequently to double-check what he was saying. Soon enough he came to the paragraphs he had not yet had time to review, which spoke of the heavy drain on Israel's national economy caused by the mass inflow of penniless and skill-less refugee immigrants.

After all, this was a fund-raising occasion.

Incredulity crept into the prime minister's eyes and his voice trailed off in disbelief. Leaning across the podium, his eyes boring into mine, he called out in Hebrew, "What's this supposed to mean?"

I cringed in mortification as audible rustlings, murmurings, titters, nods, and nudges spread from table to table.

"What I just said is not true," declared Levi Eshkol to his baffled audience, without a trace of awkwardness. "The very opposite is the case." And then, syntax be damned, he proceeded to elaborate how each new immigrant was not a burden but an indispensable asset to the future growth of Israel's economy.

When he sat down he was greeted with a sprinkling of clapping that swelled incrementally into a crescendo. They gave him a standing ovation. They loved him. They loved his honesty, his authenticity, and his refreshing spontaneity. Face aglow, Levi Eshkol watched as they extracted their checkbooks, unscrewed their fountain pens, and upped their generosity abundantly.

The adoration done, Mr. Eshkol beckoned me over, and in a thin whisper, his nose almost touching mine, rasped, "*Boychik*, if you don't stop writing your fancy-schmancy nonsense and start writing what I want to say in the way I want to say it, I'll find somebody else who will."

"Yes, Prime Minister," I mumbled, eating a piece of humble pie I would spend a lifetime digesting.

During the days that followed, Eshkol made appearances on television, spoke to parliamentarians, visited a Jewish day school, briefed editors, academics, business barons, and Jewish leaders, and, at the very hub of it all, spent close to an hour and a half closeted with Prime Minister Harold Wilson behind the classic facade of the world's most famous black door, in Whitehall's most renowned cul-de-sac, Number 10 Downing Street.

Number 10 appears deceptively small from the outside, but behind its famous door there are more than sixty rooms – offices mainly – above which the prime minister and his family live in a self-contained apartment converted out of the attics by Mrs. Neville Chamberlain. And it was there, outside Number 10, that I once again got egg on my face.

Nowadays, for reasons of security, iron gates at the entrance to Downing Street obstruct public access, but not then. In those days, demonstrators were allowed to assemble on the sidewalk at the corner of Downing Street and Whitehall, and some twenty such demonstrators, Arabs carrying crude placards, were assembled when Eshkol's limousine swept into the street. The car in which I was traveling was the last in the motorcade, and by the time we turned to enter the street, the demonstration had become unruly, interfering with the traffic flow. So, inexperienced as I was in the logistics of prime ministerial motorcades, I decided to proceed on foot. It requires tremendous agility to sprint from a rear car to catch up with the one up front, which meant that by the time I reached Number 10, the door was closed.

"Move on," said the sergeant in charge.

"I'm with the Israeli party," I explained.

"Are you now?" He looked me up and down, peered at my lapel, and asked sanctimoniously, "So where's your security pin?"

Damn! Stupidly, I had left it attached to the dinner jacket I had worn the evening before.

"Shove off," he spat, and then, arms akimbo, planted himself in front of the Arab demonstrators who had meanwhile surged forward, shouting profanities.

"No you don't. Back you go," he hollered at them. "Nobody's going to demonstrate in this 'ere bloody street. You there, you in the black 'at" – he was looking at me – "move away from that door NOW, or I'll 'ave you arrested." He approached me menacingly, loosening the truncheon at his belt.

As I fell back into the crowd of Arabs, the policeman faced us squarely, fanning the air with his truncheon like a pendulum. One of the demonstrators tilted his placard as though to charge, and the sergeant instantly whacked his shoulder, causing him to yelp and his placard to clatter to the ground.

"Right! That's it," he bawled at us. "Off you go the lot of you, or I'll have you all in the clink. SCRAM!" He watched in contempt as the protestors slinked away, mumbling curses in a language neither he nor I understood.

"You too!" he hollered at me.

In desperation, I fumbled for my diplomatic passport. He glanced at it, consulted another constable, leafed through its pages and, satisfied I was who I claimed to be, said, "Sorry for the misunderstanding, sir. Please follow me."

Mustering my last shreds of dignity, I followed him to the door of the official residence, where he snapped to attention and gave me a whirling salute as I walked inside.

I was ushered into a red-carpeted parlor upstairs, where the two prime ministers were sitting by a grand marble fireplace under a portrait of a man attired in the uniform of an eighteenth-century admiral. Surrounded by their aides, they were exchanging small talk while a maid in a black dress and a lace collar poured tea with fastidious care from a silver teapot. To the raised eyebrows of Adi Yaffe, I planted myself as inconspicuously as I could on a chair by the door, and flipped open my pad to take notes.

"In my view, the main essentials of a successful prime minister are lots of sleep and a sense of history," Harold Wilson was saying genially to Levi Eshkol, in his rich northern accent. "Take this old house, for example. It's not the quietest of places to sleep in. It originally goes back to the sixteen-eighties. In seventeen thirty-two, I believe it was, King George the Second offered it to our first prime minister, Robert Walpole, but Walpole didn't like it. It was an uncomfortable place, poorly constructed on boggy soil, just like my Labor Party is today – shaky, unstable, and noisy."

"Not as noisy as mine," laughed Eshkol. "Put three Israelis in a room and you'll have four political parties."

The two men were jousting like the old socialist comrades they were, Harold Wilson looking very dapper in a powder blue shirt, pin-striped suit and bright red tie – nothing like your typical British prime minister. I had learned from a briefing paper that he was not yet fifty, came from a humble background, and had risen through scholarships to become one of the youngest Oxford dons of the century.

"Now, for our getting down to business," he went on with an impish smile, "I have to warn you, I'm a thoroughbred Yorkshireman, and we Yorkshiremen are a blunt lot. We're straight-talking, open, honest, and careful with our money. So, you and I will talk to each other as good friends must, candidly and honestly, and say exactly what's on our minds. And I know what's on *your* mind, Mr. Eshkol – this Syrian mischief over the River Jordan. Tell me about it."

Wilson's expression stilled and became somber as, for the next hour, while one sipped English and the other Russian tea, the two men earnestly mulled over the dangerous implications of the Syrian River Jordan diversion scheme.

"We've just completed what we call our National Water Carrier," Eshkol summed up grimly. "And now that it's up and running, the Syrians are doing their level best to dry us out. No country in the world would tolerate such premeditated aggression. If they go too far, things could easily escalate into full-scale war."

"A hot potato if ever there was one," remarked Wilson, puffing on his pipe. And then, "Tell me again, where exactly are the Syrians digging?"

Adi Yaffe jumped up and unfurled a map on the coffee table between the two men. Bending low over it, Eshkol pointed out two River Jordan tributaries tucked just inside the Syrian border, on the Golan Heights – the Banias and the Hazbani.

"If they succeed in diverting these," said Eshkol, "they will deprive the Jordan of about half of its annual flow. And that, as far as we are concerned, would be an act of war."

"My, my!" said the British prime minister, familiar enough with Middle East complexities to display genuine concern. "Is there nothing you can do to stop this, short of war?"

A parade of emotions raced across Levi Eshkol's face. "We are trying our best – our very best. We are using our guns to zone in on their earth-moving equipment – tractors and dredgers – without inflicting casualties. We want to hit their equipment to bring them to their senses. But who knows? They are retaliating, shelling our villages in the Hula Valley from their Golan Heights above. The engagements are sometimes fierce. They could easily escalate."

What he was really saying was that in the Middle East, butterfly wings can become typhoons, but Mr. Wilson was clearly not inclined to see it that way. He eyed a memo lying in front of him – composed, presumably, by his Foreign Office – on which he had made margin notes. With great solemnity, he sermonized, "I've no doubt you will display a responsible attitude and show maximum restraint to prevent this situation from getting out of hand. The last thing we need now is another fireball in the Middle East." And then, with a gust of goodwill, "I shall inform Parliament about this. I shall send a warning shot across the Syrian bow, to make plain our dissatisfaction with Damascus's behavior."

But when the Israeli prime minister raised the possibility of acquiring British Chieftain tanks so as to deter the enemy before it became too late, pointing out that Britain was already supplying such heavy armor to Arab countries on a considerable scale, the British prime minister suddenly looked visibly uncomfortable. Raising his hands in a dramatic gesture of reassurance, he began to speak elliptically about "silver linings" and "military balances," and "Israeli pluck," and "never letting an old socialist comrade down." And then, having exhausted his reassurances, he escorted his guest to the front door, where he bid him a fond farewell, waving a boisterous goodbye for the cameras to catch. Responding, Mr. Eshkol returned the wave with a forced smile and, entering his car, muttered to us in Yiddish under his breath, in a voice full of foreboding, *"Mir ret, mir ret und keiner hert nisht zu!"* [One talks and one talks, and nobody listens].[10]

Chapter five

The Gathering Storm

The Syrian water diversion stratagem continued to menace Israel like a floating mine, and by the late spring of 1967, the situation had deteriorated so drastically that war correspondents began descending on Israel in droves. With mounting audacity, provocation followed provocation as Egyptian president Gamal Abdul Nasser made common cause with Syria, moving his vast army and air force into the Sinai, ousting the United Nations peacekeeping forces, blockading Israel's Red Sea port Eilat by closing the narrow Straits of Tiran, and signing a war pact with King Hussein that put the Jordanian Army under Egyptian command. Other Arab states quickly adhered to the alliance, which Nasser told cheering Egyptians was designed to "totally annihilate the State of Israel once and for all."

Even before this dire peril, Israel's mood had been low. The nation was suffering from an unprecedented economic slump that put tens of thousands out of work. Record numbers had left the country, and the macabre joke of the day told of a sign at Lod – now Ben-Gurion – Airport, reading, "Will the last one to leave please switch off the lights."

As enemy forces mobilized in the north, the south, and the east, and mobs in Cairo, Baghdad and Damascus howled "Death to the Jews!" and "Throw the Jews into the sea!" people spoke with chilling seriousness of the possibility of total physical annihilation.

The Government Press Office, straining under the weight of processing accreditations to the seemingly endless flow of arriving war correspondents, asked me to pitch in, translating official communiqués and giving pro forma briefings in my spare time. This was what brought me to the King David Hotel's coffee shop on the afternoon of 27 May, to keep an appointment with two correspondents, one from the *Houston Chronicle*, and the other from the London *Guardian*. They were interested in an overall review and a quick tour of the shattered frontier zone that had sundered Jerusalem's heart in the battles of the 1948 War of Independence, and which, ever since, had been a looming front line, with East Jerusalem occupied by Jordan.

The coffee shop was packed with journalists sitting around like vultures, munching on peanuts, pretzels and potato chips, waiting for the war to begin. They ranged in age from their twenties to their sixties, and traded gossip at the tops of their voices in German, French, Spanish and English. By the looks of them, a good many might well have been plucked straight from an Ivy League yearbook. Most were casually dressed in sport shirts and jeans, or safari suits, and their easy chitchat made it plain they had met before, in other war zones. The hum of the place gave it the air of a theater bar crammed with critics waiting for the curtain to rise.

And rise it did.

The IDF reserves were fully mobilized, bringing normal life to a standstill and transforming usually bustling thoroughfares into eerie war zones. As we exited the King David Hotel, into St. Julian's Way – now King David Street – an air raid siren went off. It was only a test, but it prompted the few pedestrians in sight to scurry into the nearest sandbagged doorways. Posters on the shutters of the closed shops advertised advice about civil defense, bomb shelters and first aid. As we reached the street corner, a military policeman on a motorcycle gruffly stopped us to allow a number of armored vehicles to turn the bend leading to the border area where Israeli west Jerusalem and Jordanian-controlled east Jerusalem met.

There, rough concrete walls and high wooden barriers had been raised to protect pedestrians and traffic from the eyes of Arab sniper nests, observation posts, and gun positions perched on the Old City's ramparts and on its adjacent rooftops, some of which were only yards away. One such anti-sniper wall blocked Mamilla Road which, until the 1948 war, had been a graceless yet boisterous thoroughfare leading to the Old City's Jaffa Gate. It had once been lined with a hodgepodge of small shops, and teemed with pushcarts, loaded donkeys, and Arab and Jewish vendors and shoppers. Now it was a derelict border street, strewn with rubble, trash, and the strange dark weeds that always seem to sprout in the cracks of destroyed places. IDF soldiers in webbed helmets and battle harness, some scanning the scene with binoculars, stood in the shadow of the towering concrete wall, and as we approached they waved us back, one of them yelling, "Snipers! You might be spotted."

So we retraced our steps along St. Julian's Way to Yemin Moshe, also a stone's throw from the King David Hotel.

Yemin Moshe was a hillside quarter of red-roofed, chunky stone dwellings incongruously topped by a windmill, facing the Israeli-held Mount Zion and the Arab-held south-west corner of the Old City. This neighborhood had been virtually abandoned since the 1948 war, and it gave off the distinctive odor of dilapidation and decay. Its lower reaches were strung with thick entanglements of barbed wire festooned with the irretrievable refuse of no-man's land – spiked newspapers, rags and other filthy debris. Beyond the barbed wire was a no-man's land prowled by jackals and cats.

Adjoining the lane overlooking Yemin Moshe was an olive grove [now the Inbal Hotel and Liberty Bell Park] where an open jeep was parked. Two dusty soldiers in the wrinkled uniforms of reservists were sitting in the vehicle, and two more were leaning on it, rifles slung over their shoulders, talking to a civilian. He was a man in his fifties and was immaculately dressed.

"Who's that?" asked the *Houston Chronicle* fellow who, in contrast to his drably attired English colleague, was fitted out in full western regalia – cowboy boots, blue jeans, western shirt, a string tie, and a Camel cigarette dangling from his lips.

"Menachem Begin," I said, "Leader of the Opposition."

"Well kiss my rusty dusty, so it is. Hi there, Mr. Begin, mind if we ask you a few questions?"

"Presently, presently," Begin called back. He continued his conversation with the soldiers for a few more minutes and then, shaking the hand of each in turn, stood stiffly as if to attention, while the driver revved the engine, released the brake, and roared off.

"Inspecting the troops, Mr. Begin?" asked the *Guardian's* journalist, with an air of professional impudence.

Begin squeezed his face into something resembling a smile, and said, "Let me say, simply, I'm familiarizing myself with the lay of the land."

"And how is your land today?" asked the Englishman darkly.

"Beautiful as always," sparred Begin.

"Beautiful, but critically imperiled, wouldn't you say?" said the

Texan, aiming straight for the solar plexus. "Your tiny land is outmanned, outgunned, out-planed, out-tanked, and outflanked. How on earth are you going to survive the combined Arab onslaught Nasser is preparing?" He was staring intently at Begin as if awaiting some exciting spectacle.

"People all over the world are demonstrating their passionate support for you," added the English journalist. "Nobel laureates are lining up to sign petitions in sympathy for your plight. There is a fear this could be a second Holocaust. Could it be, Mr. Begin?"

Begin was already shaking his head, but the Texan plowed on: "Washington is asking Eshkol to hold back, to sweat it out until President Johnson rallies international support to break the blockade of Eilat and remove the *causus belli* for war. What say you to that?"

Defiance and melancholy harmonized strangely in Menachem Begin's voice when he said, "Gentlemen, what you call international support is, I fear, illusory. It has the ring more of compassion than support – compassion for a nation assumed to be on its deathbed. Well, let me assure you" – this with quiet emphasis – "Israel is not on its deathbed. We do not want war. We hate war. Premier Eshkol is doing his best to avoid war. But if war is thrust upon us, the Arabs will be hurt more than we will."

The journalists were scribbling, flipping page after page as the Opposition leader drove on. "The other day I told the Knesset that Israel must speak with one voice and with total clarity, warning our enemies of the dire consequences for them of their intended aggression. That, in itself, might bring them to their senses."

The Englishman looked up and asked, "Isn't it a bit late for words?"

"It is never too late. You may recall the famous story about your fellow countryman, Sir Edward Grey. He was the British Foreign Secretary on the eve of World War One. It was from his room that, as he put it, he observed 'the lamps going out all over Europe.' Well, at the war's end, analysts queried whether Edward Grey had been sufficiently outspoken in forewarning Germany of the consequences of its aggressive designs. Had he spoken up with greater clarity, more explicitly on England's behalf, that terrible war might never have happened. I told this to our Knesset. I told my colleagues that in order to prevent the situation from deteriorating into all-out war we, Israel, must speak up loud and clear so that our enemies will be under no illusion as to our resolve and capacity to protect our women and children, come what may." Then, peering at his watch, "Oh dear, forgive me gentlemen, I must go. I have to return the car."

He pointed with his chin to a dilapidated Peugeot half-hidden in the shade of an olive tree and, with a twinkle in his eye, said, "I've no car of my own, you see, and this one belongs to our Knesset faction. One of my colleagues is waiting to use it – so forgive me."

Walking to the vehicle, his gaze rested momentarily on the decaying masonry of Yemin Moshe, now tinted gold by the long shadows of the late afternoon sun. Pensively he said, "Gentlemen, what a beautiful city this could be without all that ugly barbed wire dividing it," and he folded himself into the seat next to the driver and was off.

Early the following morning I traveled by bus to Tel Aviv to keep an appointment with another clutch of journalists lodging at a beachfront hotel. The bus disgorged its passengers – many of them reservists – at the central bus station, from which I continued by foot. As I drew near the hotel, I caught sight of a hearse pulling up at the gateway of a small park overlooking the beach. Out of it tumbled half a dozen black-caftaned, pie-hatted, bearded members of the *chevra kadisha* – the burial society – one of whom, the driver, I recognized. He had been a member of the Jerusalem *chevra kadisha* team for as long as I could remember. He stood out because he was older than the rest, was a head taller, had a physique like an ox, and skin so weathered it looked like leather.

Immediately, two of the undertakers began pacing the park's grassy area, calling out distances to a third, who wrote down the measurements in a notebook. The other three began striding around the park's periphery crying out incantations in a whining howl, and while they were thus engaged the brawny driver stood leaning against the bonnet of his hearse, twirling his sidelocks and humming a Chasidic melody, as if this sort of thing was everyday fare.

A sudden shock of black premonition shot through me. Anxiously, I asked him what it was they were doing, and he coolly replied that his Jerusalem *chevra kadisha* had been instructed to help the Tel Aviv *chevra kadisha* consecrate city parks for cemeteries. Rabbis all over the country were consecrating parks for cemeteries. He himself had seen a warehouse stockpiled with tons of nylon rolls for wrapping bodies. Timber yards had been instructed to ready coffin boards.

"We're preparing for ten, twenty thousand dead," he remarked in an expressionless voice. "Some say forty thousand – who knows?"

I remonstrated with him not to spread such pernicious rumors, but as I continued on my way to the hotel, my every nerve leaped and shuddered.

The journalists smelled a rat immediately. There were half a dozen of them sitting around a lobby table, bored stiff. One of them, a woman with an Irish accent, shot me a look that could freeze water, and said, "You're nervous. You *really are* nervous. Why?"

"Performance anxiety," I blustered. "I'm new to the job."

"So, what do you have that's new to tell us?" asked a paunchy fellow in a linen suit. "Anything happening we don't know about?"

I extracted the official briefing paper that had been handed to me that morning, and read it out verbatim: "President Johnson has phoned Prime Minister Eshkol and has promised international action to lift the blockade of Eilat. Foreign Minister Abba Eban is to meet the president in Washington this afternoon when it is expected he will be given details of the plan to send an international flotilla through the Tiran Straits that lead to Eilat, thus breaking the Egyptian blockade."

"That's old news," snapped an upper echelon type, contempt in his eyes. "Our own sources have given us that already."

"There's not a chance in hell Johnson will be able to put together an international convoy," piped up a small thin man with a flashy bow tie. "He's asked eighteen nations to sign on and only four – Iceland, New Zealand, Australia, and the Netherlands – are on board. It's a non-starter. Johnson is just one big hulking Texan wishing he could help you out but can't. He's too bogged down in Vietnam. The whole thing is pie in the sky."

Squiggling in my seat I managed one more sentence: "I'm instructed also to say that Israel has received assurances from the president that on no account will he compromise Israel's national security."

"Bullshit!" spat one.

"You've come all the way from Jerusalem just to tell us that?" said another. "I don't believe a word you say. I think your people are hiding something. I think you guys are going to jump the gun, fire the first shot, and go to war."

"I'm not authorized to say anything more," I stammered, and made a hurried, graceless exit, leaving my briefing paper behind.

Three hours later, back at my desk in Jerusalem, still shaken and dismayed, I was sitting slumped, staring out of the window at the summer flowers, when the intercom rang like an alarm bell. It was the prime minister's secretary, telling me Eshkol wanted to see me. Assuming a calm exterior, I walked down the corridor into the elegantly carpeted hallway leading to the outer office of the prime minister's suite.

"He wants you to handle his letters of support," said the secretary, immersed in her typing. "They're coming in by the sack-load."

Two cartons the size of tea chests stood at the side of her desk, filled with envelopes.

When I walked into the premier's room, his head was bent low over a document, but it was easy to see that he looked more wan and sallow than I had ever seen him before.

"We're getting lots of letters and telegrams from some very important people," he grunted, hardly looking up. "Go through them and, where necessary, draft individual replies for my signature. Consult Yaakov if you're not sure what to say."

Dr. Yaakov Herzog was one of Israel's commanding intellects, possessed of a subtle and powerful mind, who was as equally at home with Bach as he was with the Bible. An impeccably dressed man, he had about him a quiet yet compelling charm, and his shrewd face showed the sensitivity of a scholar and the charisma of a cosmopolitan. A devout Jew, he was the son of a former Chief Rabbi of Israel and the younger brother of a future president. Described by Ben-Gurion as a genius in foreign affairs, and acknowledged by his peers as a prodigy in Talmud, philosophy, and theology, Levi Eshkol had recruited him early on as his most trusted foreign policy adviser. It is hard to overstate Yaakov Herzog's influence on my own worldview. To me he was a tutor, a guide, a counselor, and a mentor. Often he took me into his confidence in explaining his opinions and what shaped them, and his subtle and powerful mind left an indelible imprint on my thinking as a religious Zionist and public servant.

As I was about to leave the prime minister's room, Herzog strode in, followed by Colonel Yisrael Lior, Eshkol's military secretary. Herzog had obtained his early schooling in Dublin, where his father had once been Chief Rabbi, so his Hebrew was brushed with an Irish brogue, and this was greatly amplified when he told Eshkol that President Johnson had just sent a message through our Washington Embassy warning Israel not to fire the first shot. If Israel did spark a war, the Jewish State would have to go it alone. The United States needed more time to assemble an international flotilla to break the Egyptian blockade of Eilat and remove, thereby, the causes for war, said the message.

Eshkol listened glumly but did not say a word.

"There's more," continued Herzog, holding up another cable. "It's from the Soviets. The operative paragraph reads: 'If the Israeli Government insists on taking upon itself the responsibility for the outbreak of armed confrontation it will pay the full price of such action.'"

The prime minister still did not say a word. He just faced Herzog without looking directly at him.

"And there is still one thing more," his chief adviser went on, a chilling tone creeping into his voice. "Field Intelligence reports that poison gas equipment has been spotted in Sinai. There is a possibility the Egyptians intend to use it. Nasser has used poison gas before, in his recent war with the Yemen."

"And we have no stockpiles of gas masks," added a very pale Colonel Yisrael Lior.

"No gas masks?" asked the prime minister, his eyes locking onto Herzog's.

"Nothing to speak of," confirmed Herzog, his usually urbane manner distorted into extreme anxiety.

The prime minister turned his head, bit his lips, and sat there perfectly still for a moment. *"Blit vet zikh giessen vee vosser,"* [Blood will spill like water] he whispered to himself. And I, full of foreboding, moved to the door and closed it on them as the three leaned their heads together, speaking privately. The only words I caught were those of Eshkol saying to Herzog, *"Ikh darf reden mit'n der gelernter na'ar"* [I must speak to the learned fool]. He meant Foreign Minister Abba Eban.

That's how things now were between Eshkol and Eban, the South African-born and Cambridge-educated Foreign Minister. He was adored by Jewish communities the world over for his Churchillian eloquence, applauded at the United Nations for his brilliant and insightful oratory, highly sought after by high society for his erudition and sophistication, and lauded in virtually all capitals as a world-class statesman. Yet at home he existed on the leanest of power bases and, however unfairly, was seen by his own down-to-earth cabinet compatriots as an incongruous and pretentious outsider. These people gave little credence to Abba Eban's decision-making acumen. To them he was more a mouthpiece than a mind. No one questioned his exceptional diplomatic gifts and dazzling powers of communication, but few trusted his strategic thinking. Levi Eshkol didn't, Golda Meir didn't, Yitzhak Rabin didn't, and had Menachem Begin been asked he probably would have said he didn't either. Sardonically, Levi Eshkol once said of him: "Eban never gives the right solution, only the right speech."

"The prime minister must speak to Eban," called Yaakov Herzog to the secretary, sticking his head around the door. "He's due to meet President Johnson soon. Track him down in Washington."

As the secretary fussed with a phone directory, I lifted the first of the two cartons of letters to carry them to my room. When I returned for the second one I could distinctly hear Levi Eshkol's voice through the half-open door, yelling into the telephone: "You hear me, Eban? That's right – poison gas. Write down what I'm saying. I'm telling you to remind the president what he promised me. He promised me that the United States would stand by us if we were threatened. Yes, yes, in all circumstances – that's what he said. And remind him what he said to me when I asked him what would happen if one day Egypt attacked us and the United States had other problems on its head – what would be then? Write down that he said the same thing. And tell him this is what is about to happen, and with poison gas, too. Tell him the question is no longer freedom of shipping to Eilat. The question is Israel's existence." Then, totally beside himself with anger and frustration, he shrieked in Yiddish, *"Zug dem goy as mir haben tzu ton mot chayes. Ir hert – chayes!"* [Tell the goy we're dealing with animals. You hear – animals!]

I all but dropped the carton in fright as the prime minister slammed the phone down in anger.

*Eshkol with Chief of Staff Gen. Yitzhak Rabin, accompanied by General Tal,
during the crisis that culminated in the Six Day War, 25 May 1967*

Chapter six

An Uncommon Proposal and a Disastrous Broadcast

T he official prime minister's residence, a two-story box of a house, stood in an inconspicuous street in the fashionable Jerusalem neighborhood of Rehavia. The policeman at the garden gate, illuminated by the spill of light from a lamppost, stood stiffly to attention as Menachem Begin wished him a pleasant evening and made his way to the front door.

Levi Eshkol, his nose stuffed with a sudden cold and his eyes grave with anxiety, received Begin in his study. It was a room as unpretentious as himself – nondescript furniture, plain rugs, and dull paintings. There he briefed the leader of the Opposition on the latest menacing developments, and felt him out on the idea of establishing an emergency coalition of all the mainstream parties to unite the nation in this time of crisis. As Menachem Begin listened, Levi Eshkol thought he could detect sympathy in his eyes, for, like himself, Begin was a Jew from the old *shtetl* background, and despite their conflicting politics they got along well and understood each other.

But there was something else in Begin's eyes that Eshkol did not divine that night: relentless resolution. Unbeknownst to him, Menachem Begin had come not only to be briefed, but more importantly, to persuade the prime minister to resign. He wanted him to step aside in favor of David

Ben-Gurion, and demote himself to become Ben-Gurion's deputy, in charge of domestic affairs. He was not alone in this view.

"We are going to war," contended Begin, his voice soft yet firm. "When an enemy of our people says he intends to destroy us, the first thing we have to do is to believe him. People did not believe Hitler. The Arabs say they want to destroy us, and so we must believe them. We must seize the initiative and destroy their armies first."

"But how can you, of all people, ask me to step aside in favor of the man who has abused you at every turn, tried to bring you down at every turn?" asked an astonished Eshkol. And then, obdurately, "Besides, all our moves must be coordinated with the United States. It would be the wildest folly to act precipitately without exhausting the prospect of an American initiative to break the blockade. We, a country of two and a half million, cannot afford to thumb our noses at the United States and the rest of the world. We have no choice but to take world opinion into account."

"I do not believe the Americans are serious about marshalling an international flotilla to break the blockade," Begin replied. "And as for world public opinion, I agree it is important, but we must not allow ourselves to be intimidated by what the goyim think. Besides, we've called up all our reserves, and think what this mobilization is costing our economy!"

"So what are you proposing?"

Begin looked evenly at Eshkol: "I'm proposing we go on the offensive immediately. Time is of the essence. And I'm proposing you hand over the reins of government to Ben-Gurion and become his deputy in a national unity government. I have the highest regard for you personally, but I think the situation is so grave and your responsibilities so heavy, you cannot carry the burden on your shoulders. I am firmly of the belief that Ben-Gurion has to lead the nation in this hour of peril. He is a war leader."

Eshkol shot him a sharp look, and there followed a brittle silence which was broken when he snapped, "Impossible! Ben-Gurion is eighty-one."

"True, but I say again, he's a tried and tested war leader."

The prime minister, hurt to the core, stared upwards, studying the ceiling, trying to take it all in. Finally, he shot back, "You are asking me to do this after all Ben-Gurion has done and said about you over all these years? He's even compared you to Hitler."

"The enmity is his, not mine. I live by the maxim that a Jew should never hate another Jew."

Levi Eshkol let off a mighty sneeze, blew his nose, took a deep breath, rose, walked to the window, and gazed sullenly into the night, where he saw picketers encamped across the street holding up signs calling upon him to step aside. After what seemed a long time, he turned, gazed morosely upon Begin, and shook his head from side to side.

"If that's your feeling, "said Begin, "I shall go."

"No, no, stay," hastened Eshkol, resuming his seat. "Let's talk this through. The country is in such danger that every option must be thoroughly explored."

For the next hour almost, in an intimacy they had never shared before, they sat together mulling over the matter, weighing its pros and cons from every possible angle. Finally, a tired Eshkol rose, stretched his arms, yawned, looked at his visitor wearily, shook his head, and said, *"Dee tzvei fert kennen nisht shlepen de vagon tsuzamen"* [These two horses cannot pull the same wagon together].

"I understand," said the leader of the opposition. He got to his feet, made for the door, and was about to open it when the prime minister gripped him by the arm, and with a sad smile, said, "Thank you for coming, anyway. I know you think this is the best course for the nation. The immediate thing is to broaden the coalition, with you in it."

"But only if Ben-Gurion and Moshe Dayan are in it, too."

Levi Eshkol raised his palms, indicating that Begin had no need to belabor the point, and said, "Let's see what the next few days shall bring, and then we'll decide what course to take."[11]

Over the course of the next few days a good many people in Israel were anxiously sticking strips of adhesive tape onto their windows to reinforce them against the blasts of shells and bombs. It was a laborious chore, on the eve of a war of survival which everybody expected to begin at any moment. The prime minister and his most senior aides were ensconced in the war room, to which I had no access, so my wife and I were busily engaged in sticking tape to our windows when an announcement came over the radio that Eshkol was about to address the nation. Along with hundreds of thousands of others across the land, we were hoping for an encouraging word, so we stopped what we were doing and glued our ears to the set.

What we heard was a shuffling of papers, followed by a cough, a clearing of the throat, and then the distinctive gravelly voice. Eshkol talked bluntly of the anxiety the Arab troop concentrations were causing the nation, not least because of the Eilat blockade, and then he rattled on about how the Government had laid down principles for the continuation of its policy designed to promote an American-led international initiative calculated to avert war.

There then came the sound of more paper being rustled, accompanied this time by repeated grunts of "Err, err," as if Eshkol had lost his place, or was struggling to decipher scribbled alterations about "responsible decision-making" and "unity of purpose" – exactly as had happened at the Joint Israel Appeal dinner in London a few years before. Like then, he stumbled along, speaking in fits and starts, stuttering "Err, err" over and over again. But this was no fund-raising dinner. His audience was a frightened nation, and the more he stumbled over his reading, the more indecisive and panic-stricken he sounded, even when he rounded off with an assurance that Israel would know how to defend itself if attacked.

The broadcast shook everybody's nerves. Suddenly, the country seemed powerless and leaderless. Subsequent news reports told how Israel's enemies rejoiced while Israeli soldiers in the trenches smashed their transistors and broke down in tears.

Menachem Begin listened to the broadcast at his Tel Aviv home and recoiled in shock. He fiddled with the knobs of his radio to catch the BBC World Service to hear its commentary on the speech. What he got instead was the genteel voice of the BBC's Cairo correspondent describing the relentless Egyptian military buildup in Sinai, illustrated with a quote from the order of the day to the Egyptian forces:

> The eyes of the world are upon you in your most glorious war against Israeli imperialist aggression on the soil of our fatherland. Your holy war is for the recapture of the rights of the Arab nation and to reconquer the robbed land of Palestine by the power of your weapons and the will of your faith…

Begin switched off the radio in disgust and said to his wife Aliza, "I know Eshkol is suffering from a cold, but he sounded as if he's having a heart attack." And then, adamantly, "There's no doubt he must resign in favor of Ben-Gurion, and hand over the Defense Ministry to Moshe Dayan."

Next morning Israel's leading daily, *Haaretz*, said much the same thing:

> If we could truly believe that Eshkol was really capable of navigating the ship of state in these crucial days, we would willingly follow him. But we have no such belief after his radio address last night.

The proposal that Ben-Gurion be entrusted with the premiership and Moshe Dayan with the Ministry of Defense, while Eshkol takes charge of domestic affairs, seems to us a wise one.

When I walked into the prime minister's office that same day, I entered an atmosphere of gloom. Adi Yaffe took me aside to tell me what exactly had fouled up the radio broadcast. It had been a calamitous day from the start, he said – nerve-racking cabinet consultations, endless phone calls, party politicking, and the IDF General Staff straining at the leash like dogs penned up in kennels, wanting to strike the enemy before their buildup became impenetrable. In the eyes of the IDF, the delay was not due to military insufficiency but to political indecisiveness. Certain generals were even slinging accusations of cowardice at Eshkol. But he was shutting his ears to such epithets from men he saw as impetuous commanders who would lead him into war before he had exhausted every possibility of avoiding one. He insisted that if the American commitment to break the blockade came to naught then Washington's only moral choice would be to support Israel in a war thrust upon it.

Adi explained that, originally, Eshkol was to have prerecorded his address in the haven of his own room. However, because of his grueling schedule he did not get around to it until very late in the day. Going over the text drafted by Herzog and others, he quickly scribbled changes and, since his secretary had already gone home, Adi had sat down to retype the speech with one finger. He had hardly begun when the studio called to say it was too late to make a recording, and that if the prime minister wanted prime time he had to come to Broadcasting House immediately.

Exhausted from stress and croaky with his incipient cold, Eshkol entered the broadcasting booth and began reading a text he had not fully checked and which was crisscrossed with corrections he could not fully decipher. "At one point," said Adi dejectedly, "he signaled us, Herzog and me, that he wanted to cut the broadcast short, but we signaled back that he had no choice but to finish. And that's what happened."

On the following evening, David Ben-Gurion's wife, Paula, a short, stout, robust woman with a bulldog sort of a face, padded to the front door in a dressing gown to answer a gentle knock. "Ah, it's you," she said amiably, ushering in Menachem Begin and a couple of his party colleagues. "David is waiting for you."

Though the evening was hot and humid the leader of the Opposition wore, as was his custom, a formal suit and tie. He greeted Mrs. Ben-Gurion with genuine warmth. Paula liked Begin, and he liked her. In fact her husband was later to acknowledge this in an extraordinary letter he wrote to him in February 1969:

> For whatever reason, my Paula was always an admirer of yours. I opposed your path both before and after the establishment of the State, sometimes aggressively.... I remained an adamant opponent of certain of your positions and actions even after the State's inception and I have no regrets about that because I believe I was in the right (anyone can make a mistake without knowing it). But on the personal level I never felt ill-will toward you, and the more I got to know you in these past years the more have I come to respect you, and my Paula is happy about that.

This reconciliatory note suggested that the Old Man's ferocious animosity toward his longtime political adversary was finally cooling off, but this was hardly discernible that night when Begin and his colleagues walked into his Tel Aviv apartment.

Squat and stocky, and dressed in his signature open-necked khaki shirt and baggy cotton pants, David Ben-Gurion received them in his armchair, his silvery mane as untamed as ever and his face as pugnacious as ever. A man of issues, not of niceties, he snapped, "*Nu* – so what is it you've come to see me about?"

Begin, in a tone that suggested he and his colleagues had given considerable thought to the matter in hand, explained their proposal that he assume the leadership of an emergency national unity government, replacing Levi Eshkol. The Old Man's brows knitted into a frown and his bottom lip protruded in hard-pinched contemplation. Finally, he barked, "Me, Prime Minister again? Never!"

He then proceeded to make short shrift of their strategic concepts, chastising them for imperiling the nation by advocating a preemptive strike, insisting that the IDF could not win a war without the backing of a great power such as the United States, advising that any military action be restricted to reopening the passage to Eilat, no more, and generally accusing them of endangering the very existence of the Jewish State in a war it could not possibly win alone.

When Begin and his colleagues repaired to a nearby coffee shop to chew over Ben-Gurion's tirade they concluded that the man was completely uninformed, abysmally out of date, had no concept of the IDF's genuine strength, and had talked himself into believing that Israel did not have the grit to save itself by itself. In short, he had grown old and was politically extinct, and that disappointed Menachem Begin very much.

Steeling themselves for the battle of their lives, the people clamored for Dayan. Mass rallies chorused the same cry in city after city: "WE WANT DAYAN!" Wives of reserve officers – dubbed by one wit "the Merry Wives of Windsor" – marched in Tel Aviv chanting "DAYAN! DAYAN!" – Dayan, the legendary one-eyed warrior with the trademark black eye patch; Dayan, the internationally known Israeli hero; Dayan, the symbol of the Jewish State's fortitude; Dayan, the one-time Hagana commander and dashing Chief of Staff who had shaped the Israel Defense Forces and led the Jewish State from victory to victory. Only he could rally the nation in defending itself against yet another looming Holocaust. As for the unable-to-make-up-his-mind Levi Eshkol, most commentators were quick to assume he would carry on as prime minister in name only.

When Eshkol, pallid and grim, again approached Begin about joining an expanded emergency cabinet, he responded, "Only with Dayan as defense minister." This greatly aroused the ire of Golda Meir, then secretary-general of the Labor party, who ferociously opposed Dayan's appointment, never having forgiven him for quitting Labor when Ben-Gurion established his rival rump faction, Rafi. However, as the noose of war tightened ever more chokingly around the nation's neck, she acquiesced.

Thus it was, that on Thursday, 1 June, listeners to the evening news cheered with relief – and many with tears – upon learning that a national unity government, the first in the country's history, had at last been formed. That same night, Defense Minister designate Moshe Dayan and Minister without Portfolio designate Menachem Begin took their seats at the cabinet table and cast their votes in favor of a preemptive strike.

Also, that same evening, Chaim Herzog, Yaakov's elder brother, a former chief of military intelligence, a general in the reserves, and future president of Israel, told listeners in his highly rated daily morale-boosting broadcasts, "I must say in all sincerity that if I had to choose between flying an Egyptian bomber bound for Tel Aviv, or being in Tel Aviv, I would, out of a purely selfish desire for self-preservation, opt to be in Tel Aviv." For people digging slit trenches in their backyards in preparation for an Egyptian air bombardment, these were soothing words indeed.

On Sunday, 4 June 1967, the war cabinet passed the following resolution:

> After hearing reports on the military and diplomatic situation...the Government has determined that the armies of Egypt, Syria and Jordan are deployed for a multi-front attack that threatens Israel's existence. It is therefore decided to launch a military strike aimed at liberating Israel from encirclement and preventing the impending assault by the United Arab Command.[12]

With that, what had come to be known as the *hamtana* – the waiting period – was over. The Jewish State's 264,000 soldiers were now poised to pit their prowess and grit against the Arab States' 350,000, its 800 tanks against the Arab's 2,000, and its 300 combat aircraft against the Arab's 700. Such were the odds.

Chapter seven

A Prayer at the Wall

At 7:45 the following morning, 5 June, soldiers in the southern trenches looked upwards in response to a distant drone in the sky that expanded into roaring waves of combat aircraft flying in tight formations at such low altitudes they could easily discern the Stars of David on the fuselages. A few hours later Menachem Begin, accompanied by his closest aide, Yechiel Kadishai, climbed the stairs of the prime minister's Tel Aviv bureau where they found an exuberant Levi Eshkol in animated conversation with half-a-dozen equally elated ministers.

"*Mir dafen machen shecheyanu* – we have to recite a thanksgiving blessing," called Eshkol to Begin, and he made him privy to the single most spectacular piece of news he had ever heard in his life. In a surprise attack that morning, the Israeli Air Force had virtually wiped out the Egyptian Air Force. The blackened skeletons of more than three hundred Egyptian planes lay smoldering on the bombed runways of their bases. The Syrians, the Jordanians, and the Iraqis had all opened fire and, consequently, their air forces were also being demolished.

"*Baruch Hashem!*" [Thank God] exclaimed Begin, his eyes alive with excitement. And then, "Tell me, the Jordanian attack – how serious is it?"

Eshkol's face fell into its familiar worry lines: "So far just artillery exchanges, mainly in Jerusalem, with a few skirmishes around Mount Scopus. I have sent word to King Hussein through the UN and the Americans that if Jordan stays out of the war we won't touch them. The fighting in Sinai is much fiercer. Our tanks are just now penetrating the Egyptian fortifications, but we have total command of the skies. Up north, the Syrians are shelling townships and settlements from the Golan Heights. We are returning fire."

Hardly had Eshkol said these words when his military secretary, Colonel Yisrael Lior, walked in from the anteroom and handed him a note. The prime minister adjusted his spectacles and studied it.

"Aha! The Jordanians are intensifying their shelling. I presume this is King Hussein's reply to my message. He wants war!" There was a sharp and defiant bite to his words.

A deeply pensive look entered Begin's eyes, as if he was considering some staggering implications. He was! He was thinking that if the Jordanians persisted in their attack, the holy and historic national treasures the Jewish people had lost in the 1948 War of Independence might soon be liberated – the Old City, the Western Wall of the ancient Temple, Jerusalem reunited as the capital of Israel!

He shared this reverie with one man – the Minister of Labor, Yigal Allon. An old soldier, a veteran kibbutznik, a Labor leader, and an agnostic, Allon was, nevertheless, an ardent advocate of Jewish national rights in Eretz Yisrael. Begin suggested they go into the anteroom to talk things over. There they discussed their hopes, and Eshkol, sighting them through the open door of his office, pulled up his glasses and called out to them, "*Nu*, tell me what you two are hatching?"

"Jerusalem," said Allon. "Begin and I want the Old City of Jerusalem."

The prime minister rubbed his chin in the manner of a rabbi stroking his beard, and with twinkling eyes, replied, "*Dos iss a'gadank* – that is an interesting idea."

Amid the jeeps, half tracks, personnel carriers, fuel trucks, tank carriers, maintenance vehicles, ammunition trucks, and other assorted means of military transportation that congested the Tel Aviv-Jerusalem highway that afternoon was the car in which Menachem Begin was traveling. It was crawling along at a snail's pace. With him were Yechiel Kadishai and a couple of other intimate loyalists who had stood by him unflinchingly throughout the perilous underground days and during the long backwater years of the Opposition. And now, here they were, escorting him to Jerusalem to witness his formal swearing-in as a minister of the cabinet, a Knesset ceremony which, for them – indeed for all veteran Irgun comrades-in-arms – was a momentous moment of vindication. For here, at last, was a signal, albeit a slight one, that after almost two decades of virtual ostracism by the Labor-dominated establishment, the tectonic plates of Israeli politics were finally beginning to shift.

Begin's volunteer driver was so fed up with the congested highway that he threw caution to the wind and stepped on the gas, spurting along the road's narrow shoulder, overtaking a tank transporter groaning under a Centurion tank, and an open ammunition truck loaded with shells, avoiding collision by a hair's breadth.

"*Meshugenner!*" scolded Kadishai, with a wince. "Are you crazy? Get off the road at the next junction and take the roundabout route. At least there's a chance we'll get to Jerusalem in one piece!"

Yechiel Kadishai was a gregarious, quick-witted, irreverent, and self-assured man, in his mid-forties. He had just been released from the army, where he had spent the last few days and nights as a lackluster auxiliary guardsman, in order to attend upon the new ministerial needs of his boss, Begin. The side road, a rather dubious one in parts, led them along valley edges and through terraced hills, climbing and snaking along contours which steadily rose toward Jerusalem.

"Stop!" commanded Begin as they turned a hairpin bend. "We've just overtaken Golda. I must speak to her."

Yechiel Kadishai jumped out, with Begin hard on his heels, and flagged down Golda Meir's car.

"What's going on? What's so urgent?" she asked, head out of the window, a cigarette stuck on one side of her mouth, its smoke drifting across her face.

"Wonderful news! Wonderful news!" called Begin, his lips and eyes all smiles and his excitement inflated with the novelty of being a cabinet insider about to impart extraordinary information to a cabinet outsider. Breathlessly, he told her of the destruction of the enemy air forces. For the briefest moment Golda Meir hid her face in her hands, then glanced upward at the cloudless sky and gasped, "I don't believe it! After all these weeks of the terrible fear of air raids – thank God that threat is over."

Cars slowed at the sight of these two old political foes leaning toward each other through the open window, exchanging smiles and handshakes, wondering, no doubt, what it was they had to smile and congratulate each other about. For the nation had not yet been told of this remarkable early triumph.

Entering Jerusalem, Begin and his party sped through streets which had been emptied by almost nine hours of shelling. The thud of cannon could still be heard, and most of the city's residents were battened down in shelters. After a brief ceremonial visit to the graveside of their mentor Ze'ev Jabotinsky they drove to the Knesset, a flat-topped colonnaded parliament building of a style much favored by modern legislative assemblies. It was presently jammed with journalists anxious for news of the war, and some tried to waylay Begin, but he waved them off, and made his way to the second floor to shmooze – and no doubt to gloat – with David Ben-Gurion.

Volleys of cannon fire were still clearly audible and at one point everybody was shepherded into the basement shelter. Down there people applauded at the sight of Begin and Ben-Gurion elbowing their way to each other through the crush, like old friends. And there all sat on benches – ministers, Knesset members, officials, clerks, cleaning workers, religious, secular, left, right – all engaged in convivial conversation, and some gustily chorusing a robust sing-a-long. Never had Israel known such a sense of unity and common purpose as at that hour.

At one point a shell flew overhead and then whoo – oo – ooo – oooOOO – boom – bang, crashed into the nearby Israel Museum. When the shelling tapered off, Begin went back upstairs to the Knesset restaurant. The thought of capturing the Old City would not leave him. It appeared to be an ever more tantalizing prospect with each passing hour, so he instructed Kadishai to wait at the Knesset's driveway for the arrival of the prime minister from Tel Aviv.

"When you see him coming, let me know. I must talk to him," he said. "I'm going to ask him to convene an emergency session of the cabinet, even before the Knesset swearing-in ceremony. I'm going to try to persuade him to make a decision here and now about Jerusalem."

An hour later – it was 7:30 in the evening – Yechiel Kadishai came rushing back into the restaurant. "He's coming," he cried. "His car is drawing up."

Begin hastily made his way to the entrance where he accosted Eshkol as he was about to walk in. No man in Israel was better primed to perform the task in hand than was Menachem Begin at that moment. His ardor, his candor, his logic, all were brought to bear in convincing the prime minister to summon his ministers forthwith to the Knesset Cabinet Room.

The Knesset Cabinet Room is an elegant, wood-paneled and spherical chamber, with a ring-shaped mahogany conference table so large it takes up virtually the entire wall-to-wall red carpet. A floodlit floor-to-ceiling painting of a Galilean landscape, the work of a favored Israeli artist, Reuven

Rubin, dominates the room and, with this as his backdrop, Prime Minister Eshkol banged his gavel and gave Menachem Begin the floor.

"Mr. Prime Minister," he solemnly began, "The question before us is of unprecedented historic consequence – "

"Out, out. Shells are falling again. Out, out," cried the sergeant-at arms with terrible suddenness as he flung open the door. To the sound of a mortar bomb falling on the Knesset lawn and shattering the restaurant windows, two ushers pushed the ministers down to a lower level floor where the only private shelter space available was a long, narrow storeroom cluttered with brooms, buckets and mops, and stacked with old furniture, including about a dozen dusty chairs on which the prime minister and his colleagues planted themselves.

The sounds of the bombardment were filling this makeshift cabinet room as Prime Minister Eshkol again gave Begin the floor. Stuffy and tense though the room was, Eshkol showed no sign of stress. He was clearly in command. One could see it in his calm bulk, and in his candid, tranquil gaze as, cupping an ear, he listened to Begin solemnly saying, "Mr. Prime Minister, the question before us is of unprecedented historic consequence. This is the hour of our political test. We must occupy the Old City, in response both to the unheeded warnings we sent to King Hussein, and to the persistent Jordanian shelling since. The United Nations Security Council is currently in session debating a ceasefire. If we do not act promptly we are liable to again find ourselves outside the walls of Jerusalem, exactly as happened in nineteen forty-eight when we lost the Jewish Quarter and all our holy sites, and the city was left divided – all because of a UN ceasefire. I therefore propose we take immediate military action to liberate the Old City."

In an almost phlegmatic tone Eshkol explained that Defense Minister Moshe Dayan, who was not present at the meeting, had serious reservations. "His view," he said, "is that entering into the Old City will entail house-to-house fighting, and that will be costly. Moreover, there is a chance it will cause damage to the holy places of the other faiths, and that will bring the whole world crashing down on our heads. Presently, we still command a great deal of worldwide sympathy."

"There is much sense in that," said one of the ministers present.

"Moreover," continued Eshkol, "Dayan is of the view that it would be sufficient simply to surround the Old City. It would then fall to us like a ripe fruit."

Yigal Allon sharply disagreed. He insisted with martial authority that the Jordanian lines were fast crumbling and that given the order, the IDF could quickly surround the Old City in a pincer movement. "However," he went on, "unless and until Jewish feet are deep inside the Old City and on the Temple Mount, Jerusalem will remain forever divided. We have to occupy it physically."

Another minister mused that the Vatican would never countenance Jewish sovereignty over the Christian holy places, whereupon Eshkol revealed that the Vatican had already proposed declaring Jerusalem an open city, meaning it should be immune from attack by all sides. Washington was sympathetic to the idea, he said.

"Gentlemen," Begin said vehemently, "the Jordanian army is all but smashed, and our own army is at the city's gates. Our soldiers are almost in sight of the Western Wall. How can we tell them not to reach it? We have in our hands a gift of history. Future generations will never forgive us if we do not seize it."

Even as these emotions flared, the enemy's heavy guns opened up with renewed ferocity from the direction of the Old City, the thuds clearly heard by everyone in that cluttered, narrow shelter. Eshkol would not be distracted, however. Prudently, he continued to listen to the fiery debate, hearkening with sympathy to the pleas of Begin and Allon that it was now or never, and then pondering again the military and diplomatic merits of the Dayan argument, that a frontal attack was unnecessary. Those of this view exchanged pessimistic predictions, reinforcing each others' belief that the Christian and Muslim worlds would not tolerate damage to, let alone occupation of, their holy places, and that if it did occupy the Old City, Israel would surely be forced to withdraw. Behind all that, there was always the looming threat of Soviet intervention to think about.

In the end the prime minister called for order and proposed that in view of the situation created in Jerusalem by the Jordanian bombardment, and after the Israeli warnings to King Hussein had gone unheeded, "an opportunity has perhaps been created to capture the Old City."

"If it comes to it, I'll overrule Dayan," mumbled Eshkol to Begin as the meeting broke up.

That night, the Speaker of the Knesset banged his gavel, and the newly appointed ministers of the national unity government formally took their oaths of office. Also that night, as the Israel Defense Forces were smashing the Egyptians in Sinai, routing the Jordanians on the West Bank, and occupying the key strategic positions surrounding the Old City,

Menachem Begin's brain was so crammed with thoughts that he could not sleep. Tossing and turning, he was gripped by Jewish memories as old as time. His all-encompassing grasp of Jewish history stirred his deepest convictions, causing him to ponder how much longer Israel could wait before restoring to the bosom of its people Jewry's most sanctified treasures locked behind the Old City's walls. Who among his cabinet colleagues, besides Allon, would be brave enough to fight for a motion calling for the immediate storming of the Old City's walls?

At four in the morning he switched on the radio and heard the BBC announcer say that a UN Security Council ceasefire resolution was about to be voted upon with a clear majority. This was the last straw! Instantly, he phoned Eshkol.

"What is it?" the prime minister yawned.

"Forgive me for disturbing your sleep," said Begin, "but I've just heard the BBC. The Security Council is about to pass a ceasefire resolution. We have no time left. I propose the army be ordered to enter the Old City forthwith, before it is too late."

"Speak to Dayan," said Eshkol, his voice suddenly wide awake. "See what he thinks and get back to me."

Begin got hold of Dayan and urged him to agree to a quick cabinet meeting to decide on the storming of the Old City. He did. Again Begin spoke to Eshkol and it was decided the cabinet would convene at seven that morning. It was a quick meeting. By unanimous decision the order was given to immediately penetrate the Old City's walls, the troops to be spearheaded by a parachute brigade.

Some three hours later, after intense combat, the brigade crashed through the Lion Gate, and shortly thereafter came the commander's message over the wire: "The Temple Mount is in our hands! The Temple Mount is in our hands!"

Soldiers in their hundreds rushed to the *Kotel*, the Western Wall, and there broke into choruses of *"Yerushalayim Shel Zahav"* – Jerusalem of Gold – Israel's new, if unofficial, anthem of the day.

"Baruch Hashem!" cried a jubilant Begin, and he proposed there and then that work begin on the reconstruction of the ancient Jewish Quarter which had been razed to the ground in the 1948 War of Independence, and whose inhabitants had either been killed, or taken prisoner, or expelled.[13]

On the following day, a contingent of battle-weary and sweat-stained paratroopers peered over each other's shoulders at Menachem Begin and two of his compatriots as they made their way through the Lion's Gate toward the maze of shuttered, narrow passages that led to the Western Wall. A few cheered, and a few trailed along, guns slung on their shoulders, forming a sort of unofficial escort. A lingering smell of burning was everywhere, reminiscent of the battle they had just fought.

In those days, the Western Wall was one side of a filthy, narrow alleyway flanked by a profusion of ramshackle Arab slum dwellings that extended all the way westward to the edge of the sharp rise where the ruined Jewish Quarter began. As they moved through this grimy slum, called the Mugrahbi, they could still hear sporadic gunfire in the distance, and the sound of walkie-talkies and orders being shouted in nearby shadowy alleyways.

Step-by-step, Begin walked down the passageway leading to the Wall which he had not seen since 1948, his bespectacled, patrician features alive with a look of eagerness mixed with the reverence of one repossessing a long-lost, much cherished thing. It was that hour of the day when the sun's rays hit the ancient Wall's immense stone blocks, some of which were weathered while others appeared freshly hewn from the quarry. The sun's rays enhanced the Wall's cinnamon hue and brightened the bouquets of caper bushes that sprouted between the cracks of the higher crevices.

More soldiers showed up and soon a group of them formed a chanting circle around Mr. Begin, dancing and singing at the tops of their voices the song of Psalms, *"Zeh hayom asah Hashem"* [This is the day the Lord has wrought, let us rejoice and be glad in it].

As Begin touched the Wall, they ceased their song, and utter silence reigned when he laid his head upon one of its weathered stones. He spread out his arms in embrace, and then solemnly drew from his pocket a sheet of paper on which he had written a prayer. He had composed it himself for this very moment – a supplication suffused with scriptural and liturgical allusions to the Jewish people's rendezvous with their most sanctified of places – places from which they had been exiled for centuries; places which were what they were because of what had happened in them once upon a time; places which made Jerusalem and Israel what they were; places that made the Jewish people Jewish.

"O God of our fathers, Abraham, Isaac and Jacob," he recited, "Lord of Hosts, be Thou our help. Our enemies encompassed us – they encompassed us and arose to destroy us as a people. Yet their counsel came to naught and their evil was not accomplished. For there has arisen in our Homeland a new generation, a generation of liberators, a generation of warriors and heroes. And when they went forth to engage the enemy there burst forth from their hearts the call which echoes down the generations, the call from the father of the Prophets, the redeemer of Israel from the bondage of Egypt: 'Arise up O Lord and let Your enemies be scattered and let those that hate You be put to flight.'

"And we scattered and defeated them, and flee they did.

"The routed enemy has not yet laid down his arms. The Army of Israel continues to pursue and smite him. Lord, God of Israel, watch over our forces who, with their arms, are forging the Covenant You made with Your chosen people. May they return in peace – children to their parents, fathers to their children, and husbands to their wives. For we are but the surviving remnant of a people harried and persecuted, whose blood has been shed like water from generation to generation.

"Today we stand before the Western Wall, relic of the House of our Glory, in Jerusalem the redeemed, the city that is now all united together, and from the depths of our hearts there arises the prayer that the Temple may be rebuilt speedily in our days.

"And we shall yet come to Hebron – Kiryat Arba – and there we shall prostrate ourselves at the graves of the Patriarchs of our people. We shall yet reach Ephrat at the approaches to Bethlehem in Judea. There we shall pray at the tomb of Rachel and we shall recall the prayer of the prophet: 'A voice is heard in Ramah, wailing and bitter lamentation, Rachel weeping for her children, for they are not. Refrain your voice from weeping and your eyes from tears, for there is a reward for your labor says the Lord, and they shall return from the land of the enemy. And there is hope for your latter end, and your children shall return to their borders.'"[14]

"Amen!" bellowed the soldiers, and they sang and danced, shoulder to shoulder, in an ecstatic circle.

That evening a journalist, an old Begin acquaintance, called and asked him what had gone through his mind when he had touched the Wall.

"When I touched the Wall today I cried," he answered simply. "I suppose everyone had tears in their eyes. Nobody need be ashamed. They are men's tears. For the momentous truth is that on this day we Jews, for the first time since the Roman conquest of 70 C.E., have regained ownership of the last remaining remnant of our Temple site, and have won for ourselves free and unfettered access to pray there."

Three days later the Israel Defense Forces completed the capture of East Jerusalem and the entire West Bank from the Jordanians, the entire Sinai Peninsula and the Gaza Strip from the Egyptians, and the entire Golan

Heights from the Syrians. Israel then accepted the UN ceasefire, and felt the jubilation of David with Goliath prostate at his feet.

When the guns finally fell silent, bulldozers leveled the Mugrahbi slum quarter, opening up a vast plaza so that the Western Wall could finally breathe, and Jews could pray there in their multitudes. They prayed for peace, but the Arabs prayed for revenge. Gathering at a summit in Khartoum, Arab presidents and kings surveyed the debris of their shattered armies, shared the rage of their intolerable humiliation, and defiantly swore: "No peace with Israel, no recognition of Israel, and no negotiation with Israel." Whatever measures were necessary to drive the Jews back into their indefensible coastal strip – only ten miles wide at one point – were to be relentlessly pursued, beginning with the dispatch of procurement officers to the Soviet Union to fashion these threats into guns. Soviet Russia swiftly began replenishing Goliath's arsenals, and David's sling seemed to begin to lose something of its propellant thrust.

In Washington, President Lyndon Baines Johnson reviewed the inflammable situation in the Middle East which, by a quirk of geology, sits astride the largest reservoir of combustible energy in the world. Realizing what a precious commodity it was and understanding how easily it could reignite, he decided it was time to have a personal word with Prime Minister Levi Eshkol. Coincidentally, Levi Eshkol wanted a quiet word with him, too.

*Eshkol with Menachem Begin and O.C. Southern Command
General Gavish, visiting troops in Sinai, 13 June 1967*

*Eshkol & O.C. Israel Navy, Admiral Shlomo Harel, on a patrol vessel in the Straits
of Tiran, the blockade of which triggered the Six Day War, 20 June 1967*

Eshkol with President Johnson at the Texas ranch, 6 January 1968

Chapter eight
Deep in the Heart of Texas

On 6 January 1968, the White House issued the following matter-of-fact statement:

> The prime minister of Israel, Mr. Levi Eshkol, has accepted President Johnson's invitation to visit him at his Texas ranch…The president and the prime minister will discuss subjects of mutual interest in the bilateral relations between their two countries, as well as the situation in the Middle East in general.

An accompanying confidential directive to press officers, which later came my way, noted:

> In the absence of supplementary guidance, there should be no comment on specific details. However, if pressed on such questions as whether arms will be discussed, it may be said on background that since that subject is part of the overall picture, it is reasonable to assume it will be discussed along with all other subjects of the situation.[15]

This, above all, was what Eshkol wanted to talk to the president about – arms. France, Israel's longtime backer, had suddenly imposed an arms embargo on the very eve of the Six-Day War. Only the United States could redress the balance in face of the massive Soviet replenishment of the Arab arsenals. Eshkol was out to persuade Johnson to open up his armories and supply Israel, in the first instance, with America's newest state-of-the-art jet fighter-bomber – the F-4 Phantom.

I was at this time serving in the consulate general of Israel in New York, to which I had been precipitously posted toward the end of the war, to take charge of the political information section, and to assist Foreign Minister Abba Eban who, with dazzling diplomacy and oratory, was successfully fending off the Arab offensive at the UN Security Council, calculated to have Israel condemned and crippled with sanctions unless it withdrew back to the June 1967 pre-Six-Day War lines. Day after day Eban would dictate to me scintillating speeches with such perfection and accuracy that nary a comma was missing.

Before the summer's end I was joined by my family, and we quickly set up home in Riverdale thanks, largely, to the welcoming reputation of its Jewish community, and the excellence of its day school.

The first news I had of Prime Minister Eshkol's impending visit was the phone call I received from Adi Yaffe in Jerusalem, telling me – to my utter delight – that I was to put myself at the prime minister's disposal for the duration of his stay, doing what I always did: speech writing, note taking, and document drafting.

I joined the entourage immediately upon its arrival, and for the first couple of days we were lodged at the palatial New York Plaza Hotel on Fifth Avenue. I was so preoccupied with pressing assignments, however, that I had little time to indulge in its luxuries. I was only vaguely aware of the comings and goings of a host of Jewish leaders paying their respects to the prime minister, sandwiched between high-powered politicians like former vice president and presidential candidate Richard Nixon, governor of New York, Nelson Rockefeller, presidential candidate Senator Robert Kennedy, veteran New York senator Jacob Javits, and a galaxy of other household names all wishing – this being an election year – to be photographed with the leader of the Jewish State. Likewise, a goodly sprinkling of would-be senators and congressmen, state and federal, joined the prime minister for Sabbath morning services at the Fifth Avenue Synagogue, only to be left high and dry, and some ashen gray, upon discovering that no television or press photographers would be allowed into the sanctuary due to the sanctity of the day and place.

Meanwhile, Mrs. Miriam Eshkol, a prepossessing middle-aged lady, was being lavishly entertained by New York hostesses. Between a cocktail party and a fashion show she confided to me her fear that the gift she had commissioned for the Johnsons' new grandchild – a highly crafted, carpentered Noah's Ark – was perhaps a little too parsimonious for the occasion. So she asked me to try to find out what other gifts the grandchild had received from other visiting dignitaries. This was a delicate task requiring discreet enquiries at the White House Protocol Office from whom I learned, much to Mrs. Eshkol's satisfaction, that her gift was the most extravagant and elaborate the infant had yet received.

The presidential executive jet that eventually flew us to the LBJ ranch drew to a halt on an airstrip that reached almost up to President Johnson's front door, where a brawny fellow in a ten-gallon Stetson stood waiting by a station wagon, its engine running.

"Okay, Dale, I'll take over," said the president. "I want to show the prime minister my acres." And then, to us all, "This, folks, is Dale Malechek, my ranch foreman."

After an exchange of "Howdees" the president squeezed his bulk into the driver's seat, with Mr. Eshkol at his side, while Yaakov Herzog, Adi Yaffe and I squashed ourselves into the back.

The president drove at high speed across white-fenced fields and gunned his vehicle down rutted dirt tracks, causing us all to bounce crazily about. As we approached one particular pasture, a cluster of cows bolted in alarm at the sight of us, leaving just one cow that stubbornly refused to budge. The president honked his horn and nudged it with his vehicle's fender until it, too, skedaddled.

"That's Daisy," Johnson roared with laughter. "She's as pigheaded as a Texan senator with colic."

Holding firmly onto his homburg for fear it might fly off, Eshkol looked inquiringly at Dr. Herzog, and above the growl of the engine, asked, "*Vus rett der goy?*" – Yiddish for "What's the goy talking about?"

"This is my old homestead, Mr. Prime Minister," hollered Johnson in his pronounced southern drawl, oblivious to Herzog's effort to answer. "This hill country along the banks of the Pedernales River is where my mammy and my daddy brought me up. Most of my neighbors are my old playmates. I've known them all my life."

"Very nice," muttered Eshkol. "Very nice."

We came to a rambling barn where a cowman, wearing a soiled rubber apron and wiping his bloodstained hands on a cloth, moseyed over, stuck his head though the window, and said, "Howdee, Mr. President. Nellie's just calved."

Johnson's big face broke into a sunny grin. "This is Tim Chalker, folks, my chief stockman. Let's take a look at Nellie," and out he sprang, a towering Texan rancher followed by a paunchy Jerusalemite ex-kibbutznik, and together they walked toward a stall in the barn where they crouched to examine the cow and her wet and wobbly calf. No two men could appear more absolutely unalike in appearance and temperament. One was hardly more than five foot tall, stooped, bespectacled, stoical, with age spots on his balding scalp, the other, over a foot taller, vigorous, groomed, abrasive, commanding, and Brylcreemed. Yet, seeing them there together, squatting in the straw and exchanging deep farm talk, the impending Phantom aircraft request seemed suddenly that much more attainable.

Chummier now than ever before, the president showed refreshed delight speeding across his bumpy pastures back to his house, particularly when Eshkol remarked that the hills, dales, and trees of his ranch reminded him of parts of Galilee. This set off an eager technical exchange about rainfall and aquifers and irrigation techniques, both men hailing from areas of sparse water, and both having spent years searching for remedies. The president told the prime minister about the dams he had built in Texas and the prime minister told the president about the National Water Carrier he had built in Israel. Thus it was that by the time we drew up to the house, the president's eyes were crinkling in companionable warmth, with one heavily mottled, beefy hand on the wheel and the other resting amiably on Eshkol's shoulder.

"Time to freshen up," he said as he took long, lunging strides to his front door. "See you at dinner. Had a fine shoot early this morning. Pheasant! Excellent bird!"

We dined that night at two heavily laden round tables off the living room, with its frontier-size fireplace, antiques, sofas, and old oil paintings of the Texas Hill Country. The president's initials – "LBJ" – appeared on everything: on the rugs in the living room, the pillows on the sofas, the china on the tables, the flag in the garden, and on the two stone pillars flanking the front door.

Butlers served a mammoth meal of game bird, and butlers brandished vintage champagne and bottles of fine wine. Dr. Herzog, who was partnered with the secretary of state, Dean Rusk, beckoned over a butler to unobtrusively ask for two green salads, one for him, one for me. Rusk puckered his brow and muttered an apology: "Oh dear, I see our protocol people have slipped up. They should have known you both observe the dietary laws. Forgive us."

Herzog made light of it. "When I was ambassador in Ottawa," he chuckled, "I challenged the philosopher Arnold Toynbee to a public debate. He asserted that we Jews were a fossilized relic of an obsolete civilization – inert, petrified, dead. I argued we were a vitally alive people, so alive that History could not do without us. Presumably, were he here tonight he would say that keeping kosher is a fossil-like anachronism. And I would say to him it's a distinction of our eternal identity."

Even as he was humoring the secretary of state, I noted Herzog giving a sidelong glance at the next table where the president, in a light brown double-breasted suit, cut very full, was shoveling huge portions into his mouth and washing them down with Scotch, all the while keeping up a robust conversation with the prime minister.

Herzog, amusement lurking in his eyes, leaned over to whisper very softly into my ear, "You see why he chooses to host foreign dignitaries at his ranch, far from the Washington press and the bureaucrats? He can be himself here. He wants Eshkol to see *his* America as it really is; meet *his* people as they really are – just plain folk. That's why he showed him around the ranch. The media call it 'barbecue diplomacy.' It enables him to get a measure of people. This could never happen in Washington or Manhattan." At which point the president tinkled a glass, lifted his six-foot-four frame, announced he wanted to propose a toast, perched his spectacles on his bulbous nose, and, extracting a piece of paper from his inside pocket, read:

"Mr. Prime Minister, Mrs. Eshkol – welcome to our family table. We are honored and happy to have you here in our home. Here we ask only that you enjoy the warm ties of friendship and partnership that mean so much to each of us, and to both our peoples. Our peoples, Mr. Prime Minister, share many qualities of mind and heart. We both rise to challenge and the resourcefulness of the citizen-soldier. We each draw strength and purpose for today from the heroes of yesterday. We both know the thrill of bringing life from a hard yet rewarding land. But all Americans and all Israelis also know that prosperity is not enough – that none of our restless generation can ever live by bread alone. For we are, equally, nations in search of a dream. We share a vision and purpose far brighter than our abilities to make deserts bloom. We have been born and raised to seek and find peace. In that common spirit of our hopes, I respect our hope that a just and lasting peace shall prevail between Israel and her neighbors."

"Amen!" said Eshkol, prompting the president to elaborate in some detail on America's efforts for peace around the world – in Vietnam, in Cyprus, and in the Middle East – then adding: "God once made a promise to the children of Israel: 'I will make a covenant of peace with them. It shall be an everlasting covenant.'"

Having piously said these words, he raised his glass high, and trumpeted:

"Let that be our toast to each other – our governments and our peoples – as this New Year begins. Its days are brighter, Mr. Prime Minister, because you lighten them with your presence here, and the spirit you will leave behind. I drink to you *shalom!*"

"*Shalom!*" everybody called out, glasses high, imparting a blush of pleasure to Levi Eshkol's cheeks.

"Note what he said about the biblical covenant," whispered Yaakov to me. "It's significant. He had a deeply religious upbringing. Word has it that his grandfather exhorted him to take care of the Jews, and an old aunt supposedly told him if Israel is destroyed the world will end. That's the special feeling he has for us."

When Eshkol rose to reply I sat back, relaxed, having long ago learned to match my speech-writing to his style and intentions.

"Mr. President, Mrs. Johnson – for Mrs. Eshkol and myself this has been a wonderful experience to be here as your guests at your home in Texas. On our way we saw again the vastness and variety of America, and here in your home we feel the warmth of your friendship and the depth of your view that all peoples are equal, and that all have an equal right to be themselves and to live in peace. As I said to you earlier in the day, Mr. President, your great land of Texas reminds me very much of parts of my own country, though there is, of course, no comparison in size. But like at home, I can see here, too, the results of your pioneering and dedication, and the beauty that man can create when he is free."

After extolling Israel's desire for peace and praising the president's peacemaking efforts worldwide, Eshkol was about to wrap up the toast with a raise of his glass when Mrs. Eshkol tapped his sleeve to offer a corrective whisper. This prompted him to improvise. "Oh yes, of course. Mr. President and Mrs. Johnson – in the nearly four years which have passed since we last had the pleasure of meeting you, threefold congratulations have been in order. Twice you have played the role of father and mother to the bride, and now Mrs. Johnson and you have the joy of your first grandson. Please give the baby this modest gift from Mrs. Eshkol and myself." (He was pointing to the Noah's ark perched on a nearby side table). "And in drinking your health we wish Mrs. Johnson and yourself all personal joy in the years ahead, and for your country, in the realization of your dream for peace. *L'chayim.*"

"*L'chayim,*" everybody responded, glasses raised, the Johnsons grinning hugely while everybody ooh'ed and ah'ed over the Noah's Ark. And when the general chatter resumed, the first lady, known all her life as Lady Bird, began circling the tables, smiling and radiant in a lemon-colored dress. Moving from guest to guest, her gaze soon rested on the almost untouched green salads of Yaakov Herzog and myself, causing her to frown and say, "Gentlemen, oh dear! I see you did not eat the bird. Lyndon arranged for a special shoot this morning so that it would be fresh."

"Our friends observe kosher," remarked the secretary of state good-naturedly. "Evidently, protocol forgot to tell you."

"No, no, they did, they did," said the troubled First Lady. "But they told me it was only meat they weren't allowed to eat, but fowl they may. How stupid of me. Forgive me, please." She was genuinely upset.

"There is nothing to forgive," said Yaakov Herzog tactfully, and in hushed tones explained to her the rudiments of the kosher dietary laws.

"But I see your prime minister has no problem eating the bird," said Lady Bird, her chin pointing in the direction of her guest of honor.

Dr. Herzog assumed an innocent expression, and said artlessly, "May I share with you a confidence, Mrs. Johnson?"

"Of course, of course."

"The prime minister has one secret vice. He cannot resist fine gourmet. So you may take his lapse as a great compliment to your chef."

"Oh, I shall, I shall," said a charmed Mrs. Johnson, and off she went to greet her other guests. And thus ended my first tutorial as a novice diplomat on the niceties of kosher savoir faire in high places.

The next morning the talks began in the president's den – a mixture of warm leathers, rust couches, and a low oak table. The president sat the prime minister down on a couch with plush cushions that sank him deep into the upholstery, while he perched himself on a wooden rocking chair towering high above him. This seemed a deliberate stratagem.

After an exchange of "good morning" pleasantries Mr. Eshkol adjusted his spectacles, cleared his throat, and bent his mind to the hub of his argument: "The heart of my mission," he said, "is how to create peace in the Middle East at a time when the Syrian and Egyptian armies are being rebuilt at a menacing rate under Soviet guidance, so fast that the Arab leaders are contemplating renewed war."

"How fast?" asked Johnson. He was sitting at the very edge of his chair, his demeanor intense, the munificence of yesterday tempered by the hardheaded negotiation of today. A white dog at his feet barked and sniffed the prime minister's shoes, and the president snapped, "Quiet Yuki! Down!"

General Motti Hod, commander of the Israeli Air Force, who was present for his expertise, handed the prime minister a page from which he read:

"Egypt, Syria, and Iraq have already replenished their air forces to a combined strength of four hundred and sixty fighters and forty-seven bombers. Egypt is now almost back to its prewar air strength. From now on all further Russian supply will represent a net increase in their air power. Moreover, the quality of their aircraft is vastly improved."

"And their ground forces, what of them?" asked the president.

"In tanks," replied the prime minister, referring to another typed page, "the Egyptians are almost back to their prewar strength. The Egyptian Navy is stronger than before, with rocket-equipped vessels. The number of ground troops is rapidly rising beyond their June strength. We have evidence that Russia has provided Egypt with ground-to-ground missiles."

"Do you see signs of an actual Russian physical presence there?" asked the president.

"Certainly. Our assessment is that there are at least two thousand five hundred Soviet military experts in Egypt today."

"Okay, that's the Arab side. Now what about your side? What do you have?" The president was eyeing the prime minister unblinkingly, as if trying to track what lay behind his thoughts. Eshkol's response, when it came, was slow, soft, and disturbing:

"We have no more than one hundred and fifty aircraft, all French, sixty-six of them virtually obsolete. The French are contracted to send us fifty more, but we presume that because of their boycott we won't get them. In a word, Mr. President" – their eyes met and caught – "we presently do not have the minimum means to defend ourselves."

A flicker crossed Johnson's brow and he exchanged glances with his advisers. "So what are you asking for exactly? Spell it out." His voice was terse and tight.

Eshkol's whole body tensed and he pondered for a second, knowing this was the decisive moment. He adjusted his spectacles, cleared his throat, and in a measured tone, said, "What I am asking, Mr. President, is for the one aircraft which has the necessary range and versatility to enable us to face down our enemies. I'm asking for your F-4 Phantom jets."

Johnson's eyes seemed strangely veiled. He said nothing.

"Mr. President," continued Eshkol, a sudden edge of desperation in his voice, "please understand, my country is extremely vulnerable. One defeat in the field can be fatal to our survival. What I ask of you is the minimum for our self-defense. Without those Phantoms we will be deprived of our minimum security. We need fifty Phantoms as rapidly as possible."

"Fifty!"

Johnson gave Eshkol an unreceptive look, and there was a momentary pall over the conversation until the prime minister, really charged up now, fired off yet another cannonade:

"Mr. President, last June our enemies tried to destroy us and we defeated them all. Had we waited one more day, even one more hour, before forestalling them, the outcome might have been very different. Yet I come here with no sense of boastful triumph, nor have I entered the struggle for peace in the role of victor. The only feeling I have is one of relief that we were saved from national disaster, and I thank God for that. All my thoughts now are turned toward winning the peace – peace with honor between equals."

"That is a noble thought, Mr. Prime Minister," said Johnson amenably. "It is important that you have your thoughts turned to peace with honor."

"Thank you, but we need the tools to help bring that peace about. I regret that the United States is the only source we have for those tools. Within two years our Arab neighbors will have nine hundred to one thousand aircraft. So, it's an either-or situation." A sudden bitter irony crept into his voice. "Either the United States provides us with the arms we need, or you leave us to our fate. It's as simple as that. If I leave here empty handed, the Arabs will know that it was not only the French who said 'No' to us, but the Americans, too. Mr. President, Israel is pleading for your help."

Lyndon Baines Johnson put the back of one beefy hand against his mouth, chewed on his knuckles contemplatively, made a tent of his hairy fingers, and said, "I am impressed by your statement, Mr. Prime Minister. The United States is intensely concerned with conditions in the Middle East. However, as you know, we are facing a difficult situation in Vietnam, which is calling on our resources. At the same time we have made it clear to the world that we do not believe might makes right, nor that big nations be allowed to swallow up little nations. As for the weapons you seek, we suggest you look elsewhere to find them, and not only here in the United States."

Levi Eshkol threw him a cynical smile. "Please tell me where, Mr. President. I would be delighted to look elsewhere if you can give me an address."

"That's as may be, but I regret that your visit here is so closely tied to this matter of the Phantoms. Planes won't radically change your realities. The big problem is how two-and-a-half million Jews [Israel's population at the time] can live in a sea of Arabs."

Eshkol returned him a stony expression, as if to say, "You've not understood a word I've said," and he, Johnson, noting it, instantly raised a hand in a gesture of reassurance: "Look, don't get me wrong. I know what you're after. And what I'm saying doesn't mean I am unsympathetic to your military requirements. I follow your defense situation carefully and I certainly won't sit idly by and watch Israel suffer."

At which point, Secretary of State Dean Rusk, a solid sort of a fellow, with a fine intellect and a benevolent disposition, chimed in to say in a most reasonable and persuasive fashion, "Mr. Prime Minister, in all honesty, whatever efforts Israel makes in the field of military buildup, the Arabs are going to outdo you every time. If the Arabs see an Israel they cannot live with, one that is intolerable to them, they won't back away from an arms race. On the contrary, they will turn increasingly to the Soviets, to the detriment of the American interest. So what we would like to hear from you today is, what kind of an Israel do you want the Arabs to live with? What kind of an Israel do you want the American people to support? Surely, the answer to those questions is not to be found in military hardware."

The president leaned back, staring approvingly at the ceiling, and the prime minister sat forward, gazing squarely at Mr. Rusk.

"These are difficult remarks you are making, Mr. Secretary," he said coldly. "All I can say to you now is that our victory in the Six-Day War blocked the Soviet Union from taking over the Middle East, and that, surely, is an American interest. As for the kind of Israel the Arabs can live with and which the American people can support, the only answer I can presently give you is an Israel whose map will be different from the one of the eve of the Six-Day War."

"How different?" quizzed Rusk cagily.

The president hastily scribbled a note to his secretary of state: "Dean – go slow on this thing."

Eshkol, his voice brimming with sincerity, replied, "Please understand, we did not want that June war. We could have lived indefinitely within the old armistice lines. But now that there has been a war we cannot return to those old, vulnerable armistice frontiers that virtually invited hostilities. We won that war at a terrible cost. It is inconceivable that we cannot win the peace. We want actual treaties of peace. After three wars – 1948, 1956,

Hastily scribbled note from Pres. Johnson to Sec. of State Dean Rusk telling him to "go slow" on a sensitive issue during talks with Eshkol at the Texas ranch, 9 January 1968

1967 – Israel deserves peace. I will fight tooth and nail for peace. And in peace negotiations we will try to be as forthcoming as possible – but we must have the tools to deter another war."

Clearly not wanting this high-stress exchange to escalate into an all-out dispute, the president intervened and suggested a break. All rose as the two principals departed, leaving their aides behind to mull things over. I repaired to the bathroom, only to find it locked. As I was about to turn away, the door swung open and out strode the towering figure of the president of the United States.

"It's all yours, son," he boomed. "Be my guest."

"Thank you, Mr. President," I squeaked.

The seat was still warm.

When the talks resumed an hour later, the president said, "I have absolutely no argument with you, Mr. Prime Minister, as to your peace aims and the need to keep Israel secure. But there might be a difference of judgment as to how best to go about it. And it seems to me that the most useful thing that can be done in the first instance is for America to reach an agreement with the Soviets to avoid an arms race, while at the same time trying to get some kind of peace process going."

"*Halaveye*" [Would that but be possible], muttered Eshkol to himself.

"What was that, Mr. Prime Minister?"

"Nothing! Just a sigh – if only we could get a peace process going."

"The chances might be slight," continued the president, "but time must be given to try before the United States embarks on an irrevocable course."

"Mr. President, how much time?" interjected Eshkol with uncharacteristic adamancy. "I would love for somebody in the world – here in this room – to tell me when and where and how I can get a peace process going with the Arabs. I wouldn't be here asking for Phantoms if somebody could tell me how to do that. But instead of peace we are faced with an unprecedented Arab rearmament that again threatens our very existence. The immediate issue is the means to defend ourselves against another attempted onslaught. Surely, you can understand that. Israel feels weaker now than before the Six-Day War. Why? Because, as you rightly said, Mr. President, we are a small country of two-and-a-half million Jews surrounded by a sea of Arabs. They outnumber us in every possible way. So what are we supposed to do – wait until Russia gives them so many planes that they can dictate their terms at will? People used to say that a one-to-three ratio in aircraft in favor of the Arabs was adequate for our defense. Granted, our pilots are good. But my God, there is a limit!"

His face had gone white. "Mr. President," he galloped on, "the State of Israel is the last chance for the Jewish people. We Jews are in our land to rebuild a sovereign State which will, we hope, grow in population. I pray with all my heart to avoid another war. But I know of only one address to acquire the tools we need to defend ourselves – and that address is you. In a couple of years' time the Arabs will have nine hundred to one thousand first-line aircraft. To deter them we have to have three hundred and fifty to four hundred. We'll try to manage with that ratio. If I have to return home without a commitment from you on the Phantoms, our citizens will be demoralized and our Arab neighbors will rejoice, knowing that we have been abandoned. That will mean war. And I know of no other prescription for deterring it other than by you supplying us with the means to do so – the Phantoms."

Robert McNamara, the Secretary of Defense, rigid and erect, raised a finger. He was a handsome man in his early fifties, with a square chin, a fine mop of hair parted down the middle, and rimless glasses that gave him a distinguished and intellectual look. There was nothing about him to suggest he was in the midst of a Vietnam War that would prove one of the bloodiest America had ever fought.

"Having studied the evidence," he began with cool dispassion, "it seems clear to me that two-and-a-half million Jews truly cannot withstand the whole of the Arab world, particularly if the Arabs are assisted by the Russians. Therefore, action along the lines requested, namely the supply of a substantial number of the most sophisticated aircraft, could only increase Russian support for the Arabs. At the same time, there is no reason for Israel to say it has been abandoned. This will not occur while President Johnson is president. However, for the United States to supply you with planes might greatly increase the supply of Russian aircraft to the Arabs. So, given these unknowns, we have to proceed with great caution."

This obscure and contradictory comment aroused the ire of General Motti Hod who, with undisguised cynicism, countered, "The arms race, Mr. McNamara, has never been influenced by what we have in our hangers. Russian aircraft of all types are given to the Egyptians irrespective of the planes we fly. The only limiting factor is the Egyptian capacity to absorb them." And then, to the president, with all the chutzpa of a daredevil pilot: "Your Secretary of Defense says that as long as you, Mr. President, are president, Israel will never be abandoned. Might I suggest that the one way of guaranteeing that, and of assuring that United States forces will never have to come to our rescue, is by keeping Israel's Air Force strong."

The president took that well. He suggested another brief break for consultations, after which he said in summation:

"In the spirit of our talks I think we can agree on three objectives. First, there is the need to do what can be done to bring about a stable peace. Second, we are all anxious to deter, if possible, an arms race. Third, the United States has a hope and a purpose of assuring, if necessary, adequate equipment to the Israeli Air Force to defend itself. And in connection with this goal I suggest that the following sentence be written into our joint communiqué at the conclusion of this session." He picked up a paper and read: "The president agreed to keep Israel's defense capability under active and sympathetic review in light of all the relevant factors, including the shipment of military equipment by others into the area."

By way of explanation, he added, "This statement will be helpful in deterring the Arabs and might even push them toward restraint. It also says to the Soviets, 'Stop, look, and listen.' And it gives you something concrete to stand on."

In diplomatic-speak that translated into "Yes, you'll have your Phantoms," and a deeply relieved prime minister responded, "Thank you, Mr. President. I thank you from the heart."[16]

Chapter nine

An Unlikely Ambassador
and a Premier's Passing

Back in Jerusalem, Eshkol informed Chief of Staff Yitzhak Rabin of his Texas talks, and observed that if Lyndon Johnson remained true to his word – as he would – this could lead to a profound change in the future relationship between Jerusalem and Washington. "It might even be the makings one day of a de facto strategic alliance," he said.

"This is why," said Rabin, "that when I quit the army, my ambition is to be appointed Israel's ambassador to Washington."

Eshkol stifled a laugh. Genuinely astonished, he gasped, "You'd better grab a hold of me before I fall off my chair. You – ambassador? That's the last thing I would have expected."

"Why?"

"Are you telling me you're ready to stand around at tedious cocktail parties, sit though boring banquets, and play all those dreary diplomatic games diplomats have to play? Believe me, Yitzhak, you're no diplomat."

On the surface, Eshkol was right. This handsome, middle-aged, about-to-be-retired general appeared to possess few of the attributes commonly associated with diplomatic niceties. He was a no-nonsense and sometimes gruff sort of a fellow, shy to a fault, and bereft of any charismatic pretensions. Not one to suffer fools gladly, he was so uncomfortable with small talk that a stranger's innocuous "How are you?" could make him cringe as if his privacy had somehow been inexcusably invaded.

"Let me think about it," said Eshkol without bias. "And, of course, I'll have to talk to Abba Eban. After all, he is our Foreign Minister."

"Oh, I'm sure he'll have reservations," said Rabin brusquely. "He's not one of my greatest fans, and the feeling is mutual." But then, with the utmost earnestness, he went on to say, "The reason I want Washington is because strengthening our links with the United States is going to be our greatest political challenge in the years ahead, not to mention a vital condition for maintaining the power of the IDF. Here is a sphere in which I can make a contribution, and I would appreciate your support."

Eshkol ultimately gave it to him. He gave it to Rabin because, having worked closely with him since his appointment as chief of staff three years before, he knew the potency of the man's incisive mind and his diagnostic brain. Even Abba Eban, after a long interview, gave his approval. Of that interview Rabin would later scathingly write, "As is well known, dialogues with Eban have a way of turning into soliloquies, and it was very difficult for me to sound him out on ideas of my own."[17]

Yitzhak Rabin arrived in Washington on 17 February, 1969. Less than ten days later, on 26 February, 1969, he ordered that the Israeli flag that flew above the embassy's front door be lowered to half-mast, and a condolence book be opened for dignitaries to sign. Propped up in front of the condolence book stood an official portrait of Prime Minister Levi Eshkol draped with a black ribbon, flickeringly illuminated by a *yahrzeit* (memorial) candle. After a year of periodic ill health he had succumbed that day to a heart attack, at the age of seventy-four.

Very many mourned Levi Eshkol with the deepest of reverence; for all of his apparent prevarication, equivocation and convoluted diplomacy on the eve of the Six-Day War, it was beginning to dawn on more and more people that his gritty patience, nimble instincts and piercing shrewdness had ultimately convinced the world that Israel's very survival had been at stake, and that the Jewish State had done all it could to avoid that war. Hence the widespread moral backing Israel enjoyed, not least from the president of the United States. Moreover, there was widening appreciation that it had been his prudent prewar vision as prime minister and Defense Minister that had prepared the IDF for the fight of its life, just as it was his undaunted will that helped see the nation through. So yes, verily, the Six-Day War was Levi Eshkol's triumph.

Menachem Begin put it best at the cabinet meeting of 4 August, 1970, the day he resigned from the national unity government, chaired by Golda Meir who had replaced Eshkol as prime minister:

At the end of May 1967, I came to Prime Minister Levi Eshkol with what was surely for him a painful proposition – that he invite David Ben-Gurion to serve as prime minister of a national unity government, and that he, Eshkol, step aside and serve as his deputy. After I explained to him my considerations I said that if the proposal was objectionable to him he should stop me there and then, and I would have no recriminations. Not only did he not stop me, he suggested we talk the matter through, and we spoke for almost an hour. Indeed, I can verily say that from that day forth we not only established a relationship of understanding, but one of intimacy, too.

Nothing came of my proposal, and a few days later a national unity government came into being under Prime Minister Eshkol. All of us here recall those days leading up to the Six-Day War. We recall the anxiety, the alarm, and the decisive and historic decisions that were taken.

Prime Minister Levi Eshkol proved the spuriousness of the epithets hurled at him at the time – that he was irresolute and indecisive. The very opposite was the case: He took upon himself vital decisions, initiated measures and lent support to fateful judgments of historic consequence. It was Levi Eshkol who stood at the helm of the nation during the Six-Day War. Without his leadership, whatever was accomplished could never have come about. Thus it was that on the evening of Monday the fifth of June, nineteen sixty-seven, in a small Knesset air-raid shelter, we took the decision to liberate Jerusalem. Without Levi Eshkol, that decision would not have been taken. We decided in the final phase of the Six-Day War to ascend and occupy the Golan Heights. Without Levi Eshkol, that decision would not have been made. At the conclusion of the Six-Day War, the government, under Levi Eshkol, authorized the legislation to extend Israel's jurisdiction and administration over all of Jerusalem. Without him that law would not have come into being. It was on the basis of that law that we united Jerusalem, and I can verily say that without Levi Eshkol's backing, Jerusalem's reunification would not have been possible. And there is more, much more, that I can say of the accomplishments of the national unity government under the premiership of the late Levi Eshkol. Indeed, I believe his government was a unique phenomenon in Israel's history.

I was subsequently to learn from Abba Eban that when he had interviewed Rabin for the Washington posting he had expressed concern about his imperfect command of English. Rabin asked Eban if he could recommend somebody of experience who knew the language to work closely with him, and my name was mentioned. This resulted in my receiving a telephone call from the new Ambassador requesting I consider a transfer from the New York Consulate to his Washington Embassy, with the rank of Counselor. I grabbed at the opportunity, and spent the next four intense and highly rewarding years working at his side, in the course of which he was so parsimonious in his distribution of praise that the most gushing compliment he ever paid me was *"B'seder"* – That's okay.

At our first meeting he told me what he expected me to do, and I asked him what he expected of himself as ambassador. He stood up, thrust his hands into his pockets, walked to the window, stared out of it, features growing progressively more pensive, and then turned, and said, "My objectives in Washington are: One – to ensure that Israel is provided with her defense requirements. Two – coordinate the policies of the United States and of Israel in preparation for possible peace moves, or, alternatively, talks on a political settlement, or, at the very least, preventing a wide discrepancy in the policies between our two countries. Three – securing American financial support to cover our arms purchases and buttress our economy. And four – ensuring that America employs its deterrent strength to prevent direct Soviet military intervention against Israel in the event of war."

This, I soon learned, was classic Rabin: a conceptualizer with a highly structured and analytical mind. Whenever he had to grapple with an intricate issue he habitually did what I observed him doing on that first day: thrust his hands into his pockets, stare out of the window, mentally analyze the matter in hand, neaten it into an abstract model, and then typically say, "The whole thing boils down to four salient points. They are..." and he would tick them off one by one with unmistakable clarity.

On that particular afternoon, he was preparing himself for a meeting on the morrow with Dr. Henry Kissinger, then President Richard Nixon's National Security Adviser. Kissinger wanted Rabin's ideas on how to advance the implementation of the famous post–Six-Day War Security Council Resolution 242, which Abba Eban had so meticulously worked on. Most particularly he wanted Rabin's interpretation of the clause which spoke of withdrawal: "Withdrawal of Israeli armed forces from territories occupied in the recent conflict," and the establishment of "secure and recognized boundaries."

While Rabin gazed long and hard out of the window, hands deep in his pockets, I sat there waiting for what seemed an eternity until, finally, he said, "I'm going to deal with the matter in principle, not in detail," and on he went to dictate in a staccato Hebrew what I was expected to render into plain English. It said:

"On the meaning of withdrawal to secure and recognized boundaries: One – the Jewish people have an inalienable historic right to the whole of its biblical homeland. Two – since our objective is a Jewish and democratic state and not a binational state, the boundaries we seek are those which will give Israel a maximum area of the biblical homeland with a maximum number of Jews whom we can maximally defend. Israel, in peace, aspires to be a state that is Jewish by demography, society, and values, not just borders." And then: "On the measures to achieve such boundaries, peace cannot be accomplished through a single act such as a peace conference. Progress toward peace is a gradual, step-by-step process that will require much time to accomplish. It is dependent on four major steps: One – disengagement between the parties. This will eventually lead to Two – diffusion of the conflict between the parties. This will eventually lead to Three – trust between the parties. And this will eventually lead to Four – negotiation between the parties."

And that was that – no frills, no superfluities, no flourishes.

Measure these sentences against Yitzhak Rabin's strategic record and you will find that he held to these guiding principles with absolute consistency for the rest of his life. They informed his doctrine of peace diplomacy as a step-by-step process, evinced in his 1975 Sinai interim agreement with Egypt, his peace treaty with Jordan, his formula for a future peace with Syria, and his vision of peace with the Palestinians in his highly controversial 1993 Oslo Accords. All were based on the notion that Israel's integrity as a Jewish and democratic state could be assured only by dividing the land between its two peoples – Jew and Arab – embodying as they did two separate faiths, two separate languages, two separate nationalities, two separate narratives, and two separate destinies.

Long and hard did I work on that first talking paper on that first day. It was tricky precisely because Rabin's mind was so diagnostic and his Hebrew so laconic. By the time I had it polished and typed he had gone home for dinner, leaving instructions that I was to deliver it to his residence for a going-over preparatory to his meeting with Kissinger.

The maid who answered the door escorted me into a spacious L-shaped lounge where I caught sight of the Rabins supping with a couple of guests in shirt sleeves, one a short and lively man with leathery skin like a well polished boot, and the other tall and powerful with a fluff of silvery hair and a scar on his left cheek. I could see them clearly in an angled wall mirror which reflected the dining area where Leah Rabin, a striking, dark-eyed woman, was dishing out fruit salad while telling some tale that had them all rollicking with laughter.

Soon they sauntered into the lounge, where Yitzhak Rabin introduced me to his wife and guests – old army pals it transpired – and invited me to join them for coffee before going over the talking paper.

With his tie loosened, jacket off, drinking and chain smoking, Yitzhak – that's what everybody called him – listened rapturously to the army gossip his old mates were telling him in colorful detail. These were men on whom he had staked his life since the days of his youth as a fighter in the Palmach. The short man – I didn't catch their names – was drinking uninhibitedly, and began to hum an old Palmach ditty with dewy-eyed sentimentality. The rest hummed along, and all picked up the refrain, chanting in throaty harmony – all but Rabin, that is, who, incapable of holding a tune, sang along off beat in a grating, earnest bass.

As they chanted, the thought occurred to me that I was in the presence of a special breed: the Palmach generation – patriotic, agnostic, deeply anchored in the turf of their Hebrew culture, and consecrated wholly to the defense of their country. Whatever their diverse backgrounds they all seemed to share the same sort of crusty personality, speaking an often-ungrammatical Hebrew, expressing themselves in the most inexplicable slang, and sharing a strong aversion to suits and ties.

When Leah Rabin rose to leave them to get on with their masculine tittle-tattle, the warmth of her husband's smile echoed in his voice when he lovingly said to her, "Thanks for feeding us at such short notice. You know how the *chevra* – the pals – are, popping in at the drop of a hat." Everybody laughed, and I sat wondering at the warm and affectionate resonance of his words which were at such odds with the gruff and reserved individual I had encountered earlier in the day behind his desk at the embassy.

For this I was to learn about Yitzhak Rabin: put him in the bosom of his family, or among his old army buddies, and his warm passions instinctively flowed. He was relaxed, spontaneous, loving, even doting. But put him elsewhere and he invariably clammed up, and became introverted and shy. Such was his nature, and there was nothing he could do about it. He was not one to kindle a flame in public. His delivery of the English speeches I drafted for him was wooden. His words failed to resonate. Emotional language was foreign to his terse style. When he tried to put on a pose he looked ridiculous. He could be no one but himself, and because he spoke his mind with unembroidered frankness and didn't much care what anyone else thought, he could often infuriate his ideological detractors, while his supporters showered him with an innate trust. Certainly, neither side had any doubts as to who he was. At rock bottom Yitzhak Rabin had that most elusive yet indispensable attribute of leadership – authenticity. He never wore a mask.

Chapter ten

Envoy of the Year

Before moving to its new and smarter premises at 3514 International Drive in the late 1970s, the Israeli Embassy in Washington DC was located in a rather decrepit building on a ramshackle street of terraced houses at 22nd and R Street. There, in December 1969, Menachem Begin called on Ambassador Rabin to pay his respects and be briefed on the latest goings on in the American capital. Begin was visiting the United States on behalf of one of his pet causes: the Israel Bonds Organization, an operation headquartered in New York that was – and still is – dedicated to the sale of securities issued by the Israeli Government for the development of national infrastructure projects. It remains a hugely successful venture, boasting a multi-billion dollar portfolio of nationwide development programs.

Menachem Begin was still serving as a minister without portfolio in the national unity government, now headed by Golda Meir, and his visit to Washington coincided with media reports of a growing rift between the White House and the State Department. Indeed, the *Washington Post* asserted that very morning that President Nixon was worried that the squabbling between his National Security Adviser, Henry Kissinger, and his secretary of state, William Rogers, was so impeding United States diplomacy that its consequences had serious repercussions for America's relations with the Soviet Union, the still-raging war in Vietnam, and the deadlocked conflict in the Middle East. Begin wanted to learn what the Ambassador thought about it.

"Extraordinary times," said Rabin. "Yesterday, Bill Safire [who was then a presidential speechwriter before later rising to prominence as a *New York Times* columnist] told me off the record that Nixon had told him that he regretted the two men were not getting along. He quoted Nixon as saying, 'Their quarrel is really deep-seated. Henry thinks William isn't very deep and William thinks Henry is power-crazy.' That's what the president said."

"And what did Safire have to say about that?" asked Begin lightly.

Rabin, in a communicative mood that afternoon, smiled. "Safire said they are both egomaniacs!"

Begin laughed, and said a tad teasingly, "It sounds a bit like what's going on between you and the Foreign Ministry back home."

Rabin's face went amber. "Meaning?"

"Meaning, it is said in Jerusalem that you and Foreign Minister Abba Eban are hardly on speaking terms these days. Please don't take offense. I simply report what I hear."

"And I'm glad you have," said Rabin earnestly. "As a cabinet minister you have to know the facts. The fact is that Nixon prefers that national leaders maintain maximum direct contact with one another without going through their Foreign Ministers – in other words a back channel. So, when Golda was here a short while back, he proposed to her that she pass her messages directly to him through Kissinger via me, and vice versa. Golda approved. So, if that suggests a lack of confidence in Rogers by Nixon and in Eban by Golda that's hardly my fault, is it? The trouble is, I'm caught in the middle, and have to take the brunt of Eban's umbrage."

Begin was not surprised. Foreign Minister Eban had aired his complaints about Rabin to various cabinet members, Begin among them. He'd asserted that Rabin's wayward diplomatic behavior showed that he had no real comprehension of his ambassadorial tasks. Rabin was under the misapprehension, so Eban carped, that the hierarchy which applied to the IDF did not apply to the relations between his embassy and his ministry. This was evident in Rabin's cables. Some were thoughtful and moderate, others intemperate and aggressive. They invariably targeted members of the Foreign Ministry staff, or Eban himself, or other Ambassadors and, on occasion, even the Israel Government as a whole, not to speak of the Army Command which Rabin had so recently led. In short, he was acting more like a minister of Government than an official of the Foreign Ministry.

But Begin had no intention of getting involved in that spat. He wanted to get to the core of things, so he asked about Rabin's relations with President Nixon. "Rumor has it his door is open to you," he said.

"That's an exaggeration," answered Rabin dryly. "The truth is that in the presidential elections last year I did indicate my preference for him, and he seems to have appreciated that."

"Really? You, our Ambassador, spoke out in support of Richard Nixon against [Democratic candidate] Hubert Humphrey?"

By the manner Begin posed the question it was clear he was being more inquisitive than disparaging, and the way Rabin answered suggested he was being more bold than discreet, for he replied scathingly: "Our sensitive souls at our Foreign Ministry may find distasteful the notion of an Israeli Ambassador trying to set one presidential candidate against another on matters of vital importance to us. If that is what they think they understand nothing of the ways and means of American politics. It is not enough for an Israeli ambassador here to simply say 'I'm pursuing my country's best interests according to the book.' It doesn't work that way here in Washington. To promote our interests an Israeli Ambassador has to take advantage of the rivalries between the Democrats and the Republicans. If he doesn't do that he's not doing his job. An Israeli Ambassador who is either unwilling or unable to maneuver his way through the complex American political landscape to promote Israel's strategic interests would do well to pack his bags and go home."[18]

Begin let Rabin's forceful remarks sink in, but made no comment. He respected Rabin, first and foremost because he was a veteran general, and the old Irgun commander had high esteem and a soft spot for veteran Israeli generals, whatever their politics. Indeed, there was no resentment in Begin's mind when speaking to this old Palmachnik, who had once taken aim at the *Altalena*, with him on board. In fact, he greatly admired Rabin for being the soldier that he was, possessed of unbending intellectual honesty and forthrightness, so that when he spoke he conveyed authority and incisiveness. This was why Begin had no compunction now in saying to him rather cheekily, "People tell me Nixon's an anti-Semite. Is that true?"

Rabin smiled, but the smile didn't reach the eyes. "Confidentially," he said, "I reckon he is. He doesn't like the way Jews overwhelmingly vote Democrat, and he certainly doesn't like the way liberal Jews are leading the anti-Vietnam War campaign against him. Moreover, he probably believes Jews control the press, and he suspects many of them are more loyal to Israel than to America. However, this hasn't stopped him from appointing individual Jews to high places, like Henry Kissinger, based on their exceptional competence. I think he has high regard for our leaders, and admires our guts in defense of our national interests. Like now, for instance" – a grin was spreading across Rabin's usually acerbic features – "he seems to have no objection to my clipping the wings of Secretary of State William Rogers."

"And I hope you make a thorough job of it," agreed Begin, his face showing his contempt for Rogers, whom he did not like one bit.

Prime Minister Golda Meir also had a huge bone to pick with Bill Rogers, as did the whole of the Israeli cabinet. Without a by-your-leave the man had announced a comprehensive peace initiative of his own which, at rock bottom, required Israel to withdraw to its pre-1967 boundaries, with no binding Arab peace and security commitments in return. Instead, the Four Powers – the United States, Russia, Britain, and France – were to guarantee what Rogers called the establishment of a 'state of peace.' Note: not 'peace' plain and simple, but a nebulous something called a 'state of peace.'

"Preposterous!" Golda had fumed upon learning of the idea. "A disaster for Israel," she bristled. "Any Israeli government that would adopt such a plan would be betraying its country." And Yitzhak Rabin in Washington and Menachem Begin in Jerusalem had, at Golda's request, helped craft the cabinet statement of sharp protest, making plain Israel's utter rejection of the Rogers Plan. It smacked of an imposed settlement – an American-Soviet connivance to be forced on Israel. In those days Jerusalem lived in constant fear of precisely that – that Israel would be the victim of a Big Power policy that would lead to an imposed settlement favorable to the Arabs.

Sitting now with Ambassador Rabin mulling over this matter, Begin said, "Did not Mrs. Meir send a sharp personal letter to President Nixon for you to deliver?"

"She certainly did."

"And were you not authorized to launch an intensive public relations campaign against the Rogers Plan here in America?"

Leaning back in his chair, thumbs hitched in his belt, Yitzhak Rabin drew his lips into a tight smile, and said foxily. "Yes, I was. That's what I'm talking about. And Yehuda here" – he meant me – "can show you the kind of material we're distributing to a very select list of newsmen, congressmen, Jewish leaders, and other major opinion makers. We call it the Pink Sheet."

I handed a pack of pink stenciled pages to Mr. Begin.

"Why pink?" asked Begin, flipping through the sheets.

"Because when we hit on the idea it was very late at night – no secretaries," I explained. "And since I had to get it out very quickly, hand delivered, and since the only paper I could find in the stenciling room was pink, I used that."

"And we've used it ever since," added Rabin. "It gives it a distinctive look. A Pink Sheet is, in essence" – he was pointing to the pack in Begin's hands – "an expanded version of my talking papers with senior administration officials. We've made sure the media and the other people who get it know that. They know these are my actual arguments, often my actual words – from the horse's mouth, so to speak."

Begin loved to read memos and reports, loved getting briefed, speed-reading voluminous paper work, so he glanced at the Pink Sheets with the air of a man who requires only to look at a paper to grasp its contents, and said, "Forthright language indeed!" He was particularly struck by a paragraph which, by coincidence, had been quoted word for word the day before in a *New York Times* editorial:

> U.S. policy as it is now unfolding comes close to the advocacy and development of an imposed settlement. While this may not be deliberate, the mechanics and dynamics are moving in that direction. Israel will resist this. By addressing itself in detail to matters of substance, the U.S. proposals do more than undermine the principle of negotiation; they preempt its very prospect. If the United States has already determined what the "secure and recognized boundaries" are there is no point in Israel taking part in any negotiations with anybody at all. Why should the Arabs consent to give Israel more than what America is recommending publicly?

"That's saying it exactly as it is," commented Begin with approval. "But how is the State Department taking it, attacking them on their own turf?"

Rabin answered sardonically, "Oh, it's touched off a firestorm of controversy all right. Rogers is raging. He says such public attacks in the host capital are unacceptable. Abba Eban has complained to Golda about my embassy issuing such high-powered stuff without his approval. And Joe Sisco, the assistant secretary of state for Near Eastern affairs, has whispered in my ear that Yehuda here might have to be declared persona non grata for writing such stuff."

While there was more tease than truth in Rabin's tone, I hardly found it amusing.

"And yet, with it all, you seem to be so relaxed about the furor," said Begin. "Why so?"

The Ambassador's reply was pre-empted by a gentle knock on the door, and a secretary quietly entered with a tray of two steaming cups of coffee and a glass of lemon tea. The tea she handed to Begin, who took it with a grateful "Thank you." He placed a cube of sugar under his tongue, and repeated his question, "Why so?"

Rabin lit a cigarette and said, "Because Rogers presides over a State Department which Nixon and Kissinger have come to thoroughly distrust. You are a member of the cabinet, Mr. Begin, and you have a reputation of trustworthiness and discretion."

"I try. I try," said Begin demurely.

"Then I shall share with you in confidence how thorough the breakdown is." He unlocked a desk drawer and, rifling through some papers, extracted a brown envelope from which he took out a single sheet.

"This is a snippet of an exchange between Kissinger and Rogers a few days ago," he said. "It took place the day after a meeting I had with Kissinger. It speaks for itself. Please don't ask me how I got hold of it."

Peering over Begin's shoulder I read what he was reading:

> *Rogers:* The meeting you had last night with Rabin screwed it up badly.
> *Kissinger:* Don't be ridiculous.
> *Rogers:* I'm not being ridiculous.
> *Kissinger (shouting):* You are being absurd. If you have any complaint, talk to the president. I'm sick and tired of this.
> *Rogers:* You and I don't see eye-to-eye on these things. The Israelis have the impression that they have two channels to the president, and they exploit them differently.
> *Kissinger:* There is no separate channel.
> *Rogers:* Why do you think they go to you?
> *Kissinger:* To try to end-run you and to get the president to overrule you.
> *Rogers:* That's right!
> *Kissinger:* But that has never happened.
> *Rogers:* But why give them the impression that it might? I don't think you should see those people.[19]

Begin handed back the page, and with a twinkle in the eye, said, "How enlightening! I take it that Dr. Kissinger is here telling a – how did Churchill define a lie in Parliament? – a 'terminological inexactitude.' Tell me, how big a terminological inexactitude is Kissinger's assertion that there is no separate channel to the president?"

"This big," answered Rabin with a smile as wide as his outstretched arms. And then, "If I seem relaxed about our public relations campaign against Rogers it's because I have the blessings of the highest echelons."

"And how high are the highest echelons?"

"Nixon and Kissinger in person!"

Begin seemed dumbfounded.

Uncharacteristically animated, unable to resist his own extraordinary account of what was going on in the back channels of his diplomatic life, Yitzhak Rabin told how when he had gone to Kissinger with Golda Meir's letter to be transmitted to the president he decided to put his cards firmly on the table. "I said to Kissinger outright," he told Begin, "that we were embarking on a full-scale public relations campaign against the Rogers Plan and that I, personally, would do everything in my power, within the bounds of the American law, to arouse American public opinion against the Administration because of it."

"Strong words!" said Begin.

"Strong enough to crack Kissinger's sangfroid."

Rabin reopened the locked drawer and took out a yellow legal pad whose top page was filled with his own scribble. "This," he explained, waving the pad, "is a verbatim record of how Kissinger answered me. I wrote it down straight after the meeting. He said 'What is done is done, but under no circumstances, I beg you, under no circumstances, should you attack the president. It would mean a confrontation with the United States, and that's the last thing Israel can afford. The president has not spoken about the Rogers Plan, so his name is not associated with it. He has given Rogers a free hand. But as long as he, himself, is not publicly committed to it, you have a chance to take action. How you act is your affair. What you say to Rogers or against him are for you to decide. But I advise you again, don't attack the president!'"[20]

Rabin, more spirited than ever, added pepper to his tale by saying, "And then Kissinger sprang a huge surprise on me. As I was about to leave, he said, 'The president would like to shake your hand.' 'You're joking,' said I. 'No I'm not,' said he. 'Shall we go in and see him now?' I was totally bowled over. For an Ambassador of a tiny country to see the president of the United States at a moment's notice – unheard of!"

"And then what?"

"We crossed the street to the Executive Office Building to a room where Nixon closets himself when he wants peace and quiet. When we entered he was on his feet talking to Melvin Laird, the Defense Secretary.

The president welcomed me, and said" – again he referred to the scribbled page – "'I understand this is a difficult time for us all. I believe that the Israeli Government is perfectly entitled to express its feelings and views, and I regard that with complete understanding.' Then, to Kissinger, he said, 'Where do matters stand on Israel's requests for arms and equipment?' Kissinger replied in his usual evasive manner, 'We are in the midst of examining Israel's needs now.' The president, who was in a most genial mood, said, 'I promised that we would not only provide for Israel's defense needs, but for her economic needs as well.' To which Kissinger responded, 'The examination covers both.' Then Nixon turned back to me and said, 'I can well understand your concern. I know the difficulties you face in your campaign against terrorist operations, and I am particularly aware of your defense needs. In all matters connected with arms supplies, don't hesitate to approach Laird or Kissinger. Actually it would be better if you approached Kissinger.' Those were his exact words."

"How long did this go on for?"

"Seven or eight minutes. Back in the car I scribbled everything down, and could only wonder at the meaning of it all. Were Nixon and Kissinger trying to prove to me – and through me to our Government – that the president's attitude toward Israel differed from that of his State Department? Was he inviting me to drive a public wedge between them, or merely trying to ensure that we keep our fire far away from the White House? Whatever it was, it was as good a go-ahead as I could possibly get. Check those Pink Sheets. You won't find a single word against Nixon or against Kissinger, or against the Administration as such, only against Rogers and his State Department. And I can tell you, the man is already in retreat. A columnist quoted Kissinger the other day as saying to Nixon, 'Rogers is like a gambler on a losing streak. He wants to increase his stakes all the time. The whole thing is doomed to futility.'"

And, indeed, it was. The Rogers Plan died a slow but certain death, and Ambassador Rabin could pat himself on the back for having helped make it wither. As a result people in Washington began to take a closer look at this fellow – the envoy who consorted constantly with Kissinger and who occasionally met with the president himself.

Given his vast experience in military affairs, Rabin was a frequent guest at the Pentagon, too. Senior officials and generals sought his strategic assessments. On one occasion, in March 1972, Kissinger invited him for a private chat to solicit his views on the possible direction of an anticipated North Vietnamese offensive. Mulling over maps, Rabin pointed to a spot where the United States forces appeared particularly vulnerable, and said, "Your forces are not strong enough on this side, and my guess is the North Vietnamese will go for a flanking movement and try to encircle you through there."

"You're the only general who seems to think that way," said Kissinger skeptically. And then, when the offensive Rabin had predicted began, he confronted his top brass and snidely ribbed, "The only general who forecasted precisely the direction of the enemy's thrust was the Israeli Ambassador to Washington."

In truth, no other envoy succeeded in cultivating so much trust and respect in so short a time among the highest levels of the Administration, the all-powerful media, the dominant string-pullers on Capitol Hill, and the influential Jewish organizations. In the course of Rabin's five-year tenure he succeeded in turning a modest embassy into a prestigious address, so much so that in December 1972, as he wound down his tour of duty, *Newsweek* magazine crowned him "Ambassador of the Year."

I, by now back in Jerusalem, sent him a short congratulatory note, to which he replied on 19 December 1972 in his typical candid and blunt fashion:

> I confess it is a nice feeling to wind up one's tour of duty with 'flying colors,' particularly in view of the vilification campaign which was, and still is, being conducted against me by the Foreign Minister [Abba Eban] and his associates in the Foreign Ministry. Over the last two years the Foreign Ministry has done things unheard of in any self-respecting, enlightened society, and this for the sole purpose of damaging me personally.
>
> I don't need a write-up in *Newsweek* to know I've done a good job here. The problem is that our world is something of a dumbbell. Jews are still stricken with an excessive exile complex [a euphemism for a hang-up], and that goes for much of our Israeli public, too. They are forever in need of outside recognition to acknowledge that an Israeli, and even Israel itself, can actually succeed in accomplishing something worthwhile. And it is from that standpoint alone that the *Newsweek* write-up – which I did nothing to initiate – can be considered significant.
>
> Meanwhile, the situation here is unchanged. There has been a deterioration in the U.S. prospect of achieving an early settlement in Vietnam .... At the same time, I have no doubt that the fate of the

American involvement in Vietnam is a foregone conclusion and will be sealed in the course of 1973. Be that as it may, we have meanwhile gained precious time, which will bring us to the summer without any particular [imposed] initiative.

The next time I saw Yitzhak Rabin was over coffee in Jerusalem's Atara Café. It was shortly after his return from Washington, in March 1973, and he was grumpy. "Three times three different party big shots have promised me a cabinet position," he told me, "but nothing has come of any of them. It seems that if I want to go into politics I'll have to do it the hard way – doing my own campaigning – and not rely on Golda Meir's promises."

"Golda herself actually promised you something?" I asked.

"Once she did, but now she tells me there's nothing available. I'll have to wait until after the elections in October 1973. Then she hopes to find me a slot. That's as far as Golda was ready to go."

Opening page of letter from Yitzhak Rabin to author quoted in the text
pp. 195–196, bitterly complaining of the attitude of the foreign ministry under
Abba Eban while serving as ambassador to Washington, 9 December 1972

Prime Minister Golda Meir

1969–1974

1898 – Born in Kiev, Ukraine.

1906 – Migrates with family to Milwaukee, U.S.A.

1917 – Graduates teachers training college and marries Morris Myerson.

1921 – Emigrates to Palestine; joins Kibbutz Merhavya.

1924 – Leaves kibbutz and becomes leading figure in the Israel Labor Movement.

1938 – Separates from husband.

1948 – Israel's ambassador to the Soviet Union.

1949 – Appointed minister of labor.

1956 – Appointed minister of foreign affairs.

1966 – Appointed secretary-general of the Labor Party.

1969 – Appointed prime minister.

Key Events of Prime Ministership

April 1969 – War of Attrition along the Suez Canal.

1970 – American initiative for ceasefire; Menachem Begin resigns from her national unity government.

October 1973 – Confronts Austrian Chancellor Bruno Kreisky over Soviet Jewish emigration to Israel.

October 1973 – The Yom Kippur war.

1974 – Resigns the premiership; is succeeded by Yitzhak Rabin.

1978 – Dies at the age of 80.

Prime Minister Golda Meir addressing the Knesset, 10 March 1974

Chapter eleven

Changing of the Guard

When, on 7 March 1969, the Labor Party Central Committee elected Golda Meir as Levi Eshkol's successor – and Israel's first woman prime minister – she sobbed uncontrollably, and she made a point of saying so in her memoirs written six years later:

> I have often been asked how I felt at that moment, and I wish I had a poetic answer to the question. I know that tears rolled down my cheeks and that I had my head in my hands when the voting was over, but all that I could recall about my feelings is that I was dazed. I had never planned to be prime minister; I had never planned any position, in fact ... I only knew that now I would have to make decisions every day that would affect the lives of millions of people, and I think that is why perhaps I cried.[21]

I, a junior member of her staff, never saw her cry, though there were enough excruciating moments ahead when she had reason to do so. But Golda was made of sterner stuff. She was, as Abba Eban put it, a "tough lady with a domineering streak." Her "talent lay in the simplification of issues. She went straight to the crux and center of each problem .... When officials analyzed the contradictory waves of influence that flowed into decision-making, she tended to interrupt them with an abrupt request for the bottom line. The quest for the simple truth is not easy when the truth is not simple."[22]

For her, the bottom-line practical answers were rooted, first and foremost, in the creed of her Labor Zionist faith – a faith that never wavered even when it was rebuffed time and again by her fellow socialist delegates at the United Nations – the very same comrades with whom she happily hobnobbed in the committee rooms of the Socialist International, the worldwide association of social democrat, socialist, and labor parties, in which she played an active part. So she would oftentimes brood and be bitter, prowling the length of the carpet, arms rigid, head down, talking non stop in whole paragraphs about Israel's isolation in the international community because representatives of socialist countries behaved no differently toward the Jewish State than their reactionary counterparts, allowing anti-Israel resolutions to pass wholesale.

"I look around me at the United Nations," I once heard her say, "and I think to myself, we have no family here. Israel is entirely alone here, less than popular, and certainly misunderstood. All we have to fall back on is our own Zionist faith. But why should that be? Why? Why?"

Strangely, Golda Meir made no attempt to answer her own earth-shattering question: why, indeed, was the Jewish State the perennial odd state out in the family of nations?

I, having returned from Washington in the fall of 1972 to head up the prime minister's Foreign Press Bureau, was quick to realize that what she said of foreign relations very much applied to the foreign media as well: Israel was constantly being singled out by the press. On an average day, the Jewish State played host – still does – to one of the largest foreign press corps in the world. This seemed to me to reflect not mere international interest, not mere international curiosity, not mere international preoccupation; but an outright international obsession.

Foreign correspondents to Israel habitually camp out at the American Colony Hotel which, by Jerusalem standards, stands in a class of its own. Once a nineteenth-century Pasha's palace, it is suffused with an aura of understated elegance and a patrician grace, coupled with an aroma of British imperial stateliness. One can imagine Lawrence of Arabia chatting with General Allenby in its leafy courtyard, or Agatha Christie sipping tea with Sir Ronald Storrs in its spacious, high-windowed Pasha's Room upstairs.

With the passage of the years, as the tears of the Jewish-Arab conflict fell ever more heavily over the land, the international press corps found this genteel and very Gentile relic of cozier times conducive to their purposes. The American Colony Hotel is well situated on the seam between Jerusalem's east and west and, by common consent, its well stocked and companionable bar has long been designated as a kind of neutral watering hole where Jews and Arabs can meet foreign correspondents – and each other – free of constraints.

The first time I visited the place was the day after I started my new job, to keep an appointment with an independent television newsman from Chicago. Finding no sign of him in the lobby I sauntered upstairs to the Pasha's Room, where an Arab wedding was getting into stride. Streamers and balloons festooned its ornamental domed interior. It was filled with dark-suited males and virtuously clad females, socializing separately. A trio consisting of an accordionist, a saxophonist, and a mandolinist were playing soft Oriental melodies. When they switched beat to pound on tabors the men stepped onto the dance floor to perform the dabke dance, each resting a hand on his neighbor's shoulder, stomping in unison to the staccato tempo of the little drums, chanting praises to Allah.

Two middle-aged fellows with drooping mustaches, in dazzling white tasselled keffiyehs – the fathers of the bride and groom presumably – were heaved onto hefty shoulders and, to the shrill ululations and the clapping hands of the women, gyrated in extreme excitement, yelping and flailing the air with finely wrought ornamental daggers. Faster and faster they twirled, and only when the music rose to a crescendo and sounded an authoritative final chord did the dervish-like swirling ease and the ovation fade.

Spotting me, the man whom I had come to meet signaled recognition and, dabbing a sweaty brow, swiftly made his way to the door where I was hovering. He apologized for not having met me in the lobby as arranged, and panted, "It's this dancing. I lost all sense of time. Forgive me."

He was conspicuous in a gaudy, awning-striped shirt and a polka-dot bow tie, and his name was as chummy and as ebullient as his face: Buddy Bailey.

Over a drink in the bar, Buddy told me he had been commissioned to produce a television feature on Golda Meir and the future of Jerusalem, and that his Palestinian cameraman was the father of the bride upstairs, hence his hop, skip and jump on the Pasha Room's dance floor. What he wanted from me was assistance in arranging a couple of interviews, one with Prime Minister Meir, if possible, and also some insights into present-day Jerusalem.

Buddy Bailey admitted to only the most cursory knowledge of his subject, confessing that he was far too much on the go to be able to do much homework. "I know it sounds crazy," he owned up, "but I've only the vaguest recollection of your Six-Day War, and how you came to be in Arab East Jerusalem in the first place."

"Can I recommend a book or two before you start production?" I asked.

He sounded shocked. "Me – a book? I don't have time for books. Guys like me have to rely on guys like you for information."

"So how do you hope to produce – ?"

"You see those guys over there?" He stopped me, pointing to a group of fellow journalists. "How many of those people do you think ever do real research? Go on, ask them! Ask them how many know anything about the history of Zionism, or how the conflict began, or how you came to be in the West Bank. Go on, ask them." He was growing insolent in defense of his ignorance. "Ask them how many know your language – even those posted here. I bet not a one. All we journalists are slaves to all-news-all-the-time deadlines. We live by them, from one to the next. Who's got the time to do research? Our bosses want human action, not complicated facts."

"So how on earth do you dig up your information?" I asked naively.

"By poking our noses where your television cameras and newsmen poke theirs, and by picking the brains of guys like you, and by getting tips and gossip from Arab locals, like my cameraman upstairs."

Suddenly, he swiveled around. A hand had descended on his shoulder from behind, and he called out in delight, "Talk of the devil! Fayez – it's you! I was just talking about you. Join us. Wedding going okay?"

Fayez threw us a dazzling smile, dabbed his brow with a corner of his keffiyeh, and heaved mischievously, "I've been dancing far too much with my daughter, the bride, so I sneaked out to cool off and indulge in a little forbidden stimulant while my guests upstairs are not watching."

"A Scotch here, please, barman," called Buddy Bailey, snapping his fingers. "Black Label. Make it a double."

Fayez downed half his drink in a single swig, checking the room to make sure no one of his faith was catching him in the act, and downed the rest. Relaxed now, he chuckled, "Forgive my agitation. It's the excitement of the wedding."

"Fayez," said Buddy Bailey cheekily, throwing him a wink. "I have a question. I've been telling Yehuda here how tough it is for a foreign correspondent like me to get a grip on the conflict between you two. What do you think the chances are of you and Yehuda making up and shaking hands, eh?"

The man sounded a hiccup, "What do you mean, making up, shaking hands?"

"Peace. Making peace. Letting bygones be bygones."

Fayez looked me up and down, lazy laughter in his eyes, and said in perfect Hebrew, "You and me – peace?"

He removed his keffiyeh, scrubbed his curly graying hair with his knuckles, pulled back his shoulders, lifted his jaw, and in a voice warped with whisky, said, "*Habibi* – My friend – it won't work. Our genes are too different. You Jews come from everywhere. You are mongrels. We Arabs come from the desert. We are thoroughbreds. You think in subtleties, we think in primary colors."

"What do you mean – primary colors?" I asked.

He placed a hand on my shoulder, whether in fellowship or to steady himself I could not tell, and rambled on, "Primary colors means that there is nothing subtle about the desert. Everything there is in the extremes – blazing hot days, icy cold nights, arid sands, luscious oases. That's why we Arabs are most at ease in the extremes. It's in our blood. We can be over-generous one minute, over-greedy the next, hospitable one minute, cut-throat the next, fatalistic one minute, straining at the leash the next. And at this minute" – he had me by the hand – "I'm in a highly hospitable mood, so please come upstairs and join my daughter's wedding. No? You have other things to do? Fine! Then I shall go alone," and off he went, walking with the over-disciplined stride of a man under the influence.

"What was that supposed to mean?" asked Buddy, mystified.

Bemused myself, I answered, "I'm not at all sure. I'm not sure how much was him doing the talking and how much was the drink. But what I do know is that when it comes to our conflict they do appear most at ease in the extremes."

Chapter twelve

Golda and Oriana:
A Romance

During my two-year stint at the Foreign Press Bureau I discovered that the journalist whom Prime Minister Golda Meir admired and liked the most – loved even – was Oriana Fallaci.

Oriana Fallaci was all the rage in her native Italy. She had a reputation for brilliant and often controversial writing, as well as for being a fearless war correspondent. Her firsthand account of the Vietnam War – *Nothing, and So Be It* – was an international bestseller. Fallaci's talent for powerful and hard-hitting political interviews was world renowned, and it was said that she was the one journalist to whom virtually no prominent leader could ever afford to say no.

Her interviewing technique was unique. Unlike Buddy Bailey and his ilk, she would spend weeks researching her subjects in obsessive detail. Any attempt to patronize her, or to humor her with false conviviality, or to seek to justify an injustice of any sort could put a match to her Roman fury – as when she ripped off her chador in the middle of an interview with Ayatollah Khomeini when he said Muslim women must never uncover their faces, or when Fidel Castro huddled up to her a trifle too close and she told him he stank of body odor, or when she threw the microphone of her tape recorder in the face of the boxer, Muhammad Ali, when he belched into hers.

A mistress of theatrics, Oriana Fallaci could display irreverence one moment, and charming sweetness the next. She could tease out deeper meanings from answers to seemingly superficial questions. Even the toughest interviewees could be disarmed by her feigned innocence, by the impression she gave that all she asked was merely for her own enlightenment. Henry Kissinger wrote in his memoirs that his 1972 interview with her "was the single most disastrous conversation I have ever had with any member of the press." In it, Kissinger was seduced into acknowledging that the Vietnam War was "a useless war" and to absurdly admitting that he often thought of himself as "the cowboy who leads the wagon train by riding alone ahead on his horse."

When I met Oriana Fallaci in the lobby of the American Colony Hotel preparatory to her interview with Prime Minister Golda Meir, I had to fight an impulse to stare. Fallaci was a sinewy lady, hardly more than five foot tall, forty-odd years old, with a very Italian face full of chutzpah and mettle that demanded attention: a wealth of auburn hair, high cheek bones, and stubborn eyes. The moment I told her that the prime minister wanted to know what she wanted to talk to her about I got a taste of her tongue:

"Mrs. Meir shall know what I shall talk to her about when I talk to her. And if she has a problem with that, I shall pack my bags and go home right now."

When I reported back to Mrs. Meir she smiled a mischievous sort of a smile, and then, tellingly, on the appointed day, welcomed Oriana Fallaci into the comfort of her lounge at home, rather than to her office. Golda chose to wear a stylish black dress as any hostess might, and the first thing she did was to thank her visitor for the beautiful bouquet of roses, just delivered. She excused herself to go into the kitchen to put on the kettle for tea, and pouring, she insisted her guest try her cheesecake, as any mother would, and remarked upon how youthful and chic the journalist looked despite the rigors of her job. Golda then delved into an appreciation of Fallaci's recently published Vietnam War book, comparing that war with her own against terrorism.

An hour and a quarter later, a captivated Ms. Fallaci found that instead of the fighting bout she had expected to conduct, she had been engaged in a genial female chat, and an equally charmed prime minister said she would love to continue it sometime soon, and instructed me to arrange a date.

At the door Oriana Fallaci embraced Golda Meir, and entering my car, effused, "What am I to do with a woman like that? How am I to be objective? She reminds me so much of my mother – that same gray curly hair, her tired and wrinkled face, that sweet and energetic look. I think I have fallen in love with her." Then, exhaling a Gloria Swanson sigh, she heaved, "I need a drink. Take me back to the hotel. I have to think!"

By the time the second meeting took place, three days later, the journalist had retrieved her warrior professionalism fully, and she pummeled the prime minister with hard-hitting political questions which Golda parried with the tough, singular passion of a Deborah facing down a Sisera. But then, halfway through, Fallaci switched from fortissimo to pianissimo, from Valkyrie to Princess Charming, and gently asked some very personal questions, beginning with "Are you religious, Mrs. Meir?"

The prime minister answered with a dismissive wave of the hand, and said in a manner that left no room for doubt, "Me, religious? Never!! My family was traditional, but not religious. Only my grandfather was religious, but those were the days when we lived in Russia. In America we observed the festivals, but went to temple very seldom. I only went for the High Holy Days to accompany my mother. You see, to me being Jewish means, and has always meant, being proud to be part of a people that has maintained its distinct identity for more than two thousand years, with all the pain and torment inflicted on it."

Abruptly, her voice trailed away and she leaned deeply into her armchair, looking past Fallaci with a remote stare as if recapturing a second thought, an image so vivid she could clearly see it in her mind's eye. Quietly, almost reverentially, she said, "The one time I've ever really prayed was in a synagogue in Moscow. It was shortly after the establishment of the State and I was Israel's ambassador there. If I'd stayed in Russia I might have become religious – maybe. Who knows?"

"Why?"

"Because in communist Russia, the synagogue was the one place Jews could meet Jews. On Rosh Hashanah and Yom Kippur they came in their thousands. I stayed in the synagogue from morning till night. And I, who am an emotional person, really prayed. In fact, I'm the most sensitive creature you'll ever meet. It is no accident many accuse me of conducting public affairs with my heart instead of my head. Well, what if I do? I don't see anything wrong in that. I've always felt sorry for people who are afraid of their feelings, and who hide their emotions and can't cry wholeheartedly. Those who don't know how to weep with their whole heart don't know how to laugh either."

"And what about peace – when will there be peace?"

The prime minister shrugged her shoulders. "I fear war with the Arabs will go on for years because of the indifference with which their leaders send their people off to die."

"And what about Jerusalem? Will you ever agree to the redivision of Jerusalem?"

"Israel will never give up Jerusalem. I won't even agree to discuss it."

"And the Golan Heights – will Israel ever agree to give up the Golan Heights?"

"No, Israel will never come down from the Golan Heights."

"And Sinai – will you be willing to withdraw from the Sinai in return for peace with Egypt?"

"Yes, Israel will be ready to withdraw from much of the Sinai Peninsula in exchange for peace. But we won't take the risk of waking up one morning with the Sinai full of Egyptian troops again, as happened on the eve of the Six-Day War."

"And Arafat's PLO – are they a partner for peace?"

"Never, never, never will I talk to that terrorist Yasser Arafat."

"And the Palestinian refugees – will you ever agree to their return?"

"No. What hope can the Arab refugees have so long as the Arab countries exploit them as a weapon against us by deliberately keeping them confined in squalid camps?"

And thus they went at it, the premier and the journalist, tit for tat until, again, Fallaci switched roles and sweet-talked Golda into letting down her guard so willingly that she began to reveal things about herself she had never revealed so fully to anybody before:

"Is this the Israel you dreamed of when you came here as a pioneer so long ago?" asked the interviewer.

Golda lit a cigarette, and blowing smoke through her nostrils, sighed, "No, this is not the Israel I dreamed of. I naively thought that in a Jewish State there would not be all the evils that afflict other societies – theft, murder, prostitution. It's something that breaks my heart. On the other hand" – her voice became resonant, even buoyant – "speaking as a Jewish socialist, Israel is more than I could ever have dreamed of, because the realization of Zionism is part of my socialism. Justice for the Jewish people has been the purpose of my life. Forty or fifty years ago I had no hopes that we Jews would ever have a sovereign state to call our own. Now that we have one, it doesn't seem to me right to worry too much about its defects. We have a soil on which to put our feet, and that's already a lot.

"And as for my socialism, to be honest there's a big difference between socialist ideology and socialism in practice. All socialist parties that have risen to power soon stoop to compromise. The dream I had, the dream of a just world united in socialism, has long gone to the devil. You can have all the dreams you like, but when you're dreaming you're not awake. And when you wake up you realize your dream has very little in common with reality."

The two women were now leaning closer to one another, speaking almost secretly, as if I was not there, and Golda, clearly under Fallaci's spell, began confessing such private feminine intimacies I felt my cheeks heat up:

"It was hard, hard, hard!" she lamented, recalling her motherly neglect of her children when they were very young and they most needed her. "When you're at your job you're thinking all the time of the children you've left at home, and when you're at home you're thinking of the work you should be doing at your job. It breaks one's heart to pieces. My children, Sarah and Menachem, suffered so much on my account. I left them alone so often. I was never with them when I should have been. And when I had to stay home because of a headache or something like that, they were so happy. They would jump up and down, and laugh and sing, 'Mamma's staying home. Mama's got a headache. Mama's staying home.'"

Meekly, she went on:

"If your husband is not a social animal like yourself, and feels uncomfortable with an active wife like myself, a wife for whom it's not enough to be a wife, there's bound to be friction. And the friction may even break up the marriage, as it did mine. So, yes" – she paused to extract a handkerchief from her handbag and blow her nose – "I've paid for being what I am. I've paid a lot."

Fallaci bent closer, and whispered. "That sense of guilt toward your children, did you also feel it toward your husband?"

Golda sat bolt upright, and with a wag of a finger, admonished, "Oriana, I never, ever talk about my husband. Change the subject."

"But did you?" The Italian's eyes were compelling, magnetic, her voice mesmeric.

The prime minister studied her fingernails in pensive silence, and said in a thawed tone, "Well, all right, for you I'll try."

Dabbing an eye with her handkerchief, she said morosely, "My husband, Morris, was an extraordinarily nice person – educated, kind, good. Everything about him was good. I met him when I was fifteen. We got married soon afterwards. From him I learned all the beautiful things, like music and poetry. But I was too different from him. He was only interested in his family, his home, his music, his books. For me, domestic bliss wasn't enough. I wasn't born to be satisfied with music and poetry. He wanted me to stay at home and forget politics. Instead, I was always out, always in politics. I had to be doing what I was doing. I couldn't help myself."

She took a breather to light another cigarette, and following the trail of the smoke with a dismal eye, flared, "Yes, of course I have a sense of guilt toward him. I made him suffer so much. He came to this country for me because I wanted to come. He came to kibbutz for me because I wanted the kibbutz. He took up a way of life that did not suit him because it was the kind of life I could not do without. It was a tragedy," – her mouth tightened – "a great tragedy. He was such a wonderful man. With a different sort of a woman he could have been so very happy."

"Did you not ever make an effort to adapt yourself to him, to please him?"

Golda's dark brown eyes were full of pain. "For him I made the biggest sacrifice of my life: I left the kibbutz. There was nothing I loved more than the kibbutz: the work, the camaraderie. In the beginning our kibbutz was nothing but swamp and sand, but soon it became a garden full of orange trees, full of fruits. Just to look at it gave me such joy that I could have spent my whole life there. But Morris couldn't stand it. He couldn't stand the hard work. He couldn't stand the hot climate. He couldn't stand the communal way of life. He was too individualistic, too introverted, too delicate. He got sick and we had to leave for Tel Aviv."

Restlessly, she began to stroke the arm of her chair, and between clenched teeth went on, "My feeling of anguish at leaving kibbutz still goes through me like a needle. It was really a tragedy for me. But I put up with it for his sake, thinking that in Tel Aviv our family life would be more tranquil, more harmonious, but it wasn't. In nineteen thirty-eight we separated. In nineteen fifty-one he died."

"Wasn't he proud of you, at least in the last years?" asked Fallaci compassionately.

Golda answered with a twisted smile: "I don't know. I don't think so. I don't know what he thought in his last years. He was so withdrawn that it was impossible to guess. Anyway, his tragedy did not come from the fact of not understanding me. His tragedy came from the fact that he understood me only too well, but could not change me. He understood I had no choice but to do what I was doing, and he did not approve of what I was doing. It was as simple as that. And who knows" – this with a shrug and in almost a whimper – "if he wasn't right?"

"But you never thought of getting a divorce, never thought of remarrying?"

Golda Meir answered with a vigorous shake of the head. "Never! Such an idea never entered my mind. You have to understand, I've always gone on thinking I'm married to Morris. Even though we were so different and incapable of living together, there was always love between us. Ours was a great love! It lasted from the day we met to the day he died. And a love like that can never be replaced, never."

The prime minister rose to her feet, and pumping cheer back into her voice said, "So now you know, Oriana, what I've never told anybody else. Come back soon, but without that thing, eh?" She was pointing to the tape recorder. "Come back just for a chat, over a cup of tea!"

"Oh, I shall, I shall," gushed Fallaci with a huge hug, and I drove her back to the American Colony Hotel where the concierge informed her that her flight to Rome, scheduled for the following day, had been duly confirmed. We parted, and I assumed that was the last I would see of her.

I was wrong. The following night, at an outrageous hour – two in the morning according to my bedside clock – I was jerked out of bed by the peal of the telephone and, fumbling for the receiver, yawned into it, "Who is this?"

"Oriana Fallaci. I'm in Rome." She sounded distraught.

"I know you're in Rome. What do you want?"

Sobbingly she said, "I've been robbed."

"Robbed – of what?"

"The tapes of my Golda interview. All my Golda Meir tapes have been stolen."

I sat up. "How? When? Who?"

She churned out the answer in an intense machine-gun ratter: "I checked into the hotel. I took the tapes out of my purse. I put them in an envelope on the desk. I left the room. I locked the door. I gave the key to the desk clerk. I was away for no more than fifteen minutes. When I got back the key was gone. The door of my room was open. None of my valuables were taken, just the tapes. The police are here now. They suspect it's a political theft, as if I don't know that already."

"But by whom?"

"An Arab looking for information, maybe; some personal enemy of Golda, maybe; even some journalist jealous of me, maybe. One thing for sure: I was followed. Somebody knew I was arriving in Rome today.

Somebody knew the hour of my arrival. And somebody knew the hotel I'm staying at."

"So what do you want of me?"

There was a pause, and I could hear her catching her breath. "I want you to arrange a repeat interview with Mrs. Meir."

"That's asking a hell of a lot." I was wide awake now.

"Please try, please." She was sobbing again.

"Okay, I'll try. But I can't promise anything. Send me a telegram explaining what happened and I'll show it to Golda. It might help."

Next morning the telegram came. It read:

MRS. MEIR EVERYTHING STOLEN STOP REPEAT EVERY-
THING STOLEN STOP TRY SEEING ME AGAIN PLEASE

When I explained the circumstances, Golda's face turned grim. "The poor, poor thing," she said in motherly pity. But then her eyes went steely and her voice obstinate: "Obviously, someone doesn't want this interview to be published, so we'll just have to do it again. Tell her, yes, and find me a couple of hours soon."

It was with much joy that the two women embraced one another once again when, a couple of weeks later, the interview was repeated – even better than before. Again, Golda Meir gave Oriana Fallaci all the time she needed.

Recalling the episode, Fallaci was to write:

Naturally, the police never got to the core of the mystery surround-ing the theft of the tapes. But a clue did offer itself. At about the same time as my interview with Golda Meir, I had asked for one with Muammar el-Kaddafi [president of Libya]. And he, through a high official of the Libyan Ministry of Information, had let me know he would grant it. But all of a sudden, a few days after the theft of the tapes, he granted an interview to a rival Italian weekly. By some coincidence, Kaddafi regaled the correspondent with sentences that sounded like answers Mrs. Meir had told me ... How was it possible for Mr. Kaddafi to answer something that had never been published and that no one, other than myself, knew? Had Mr. Kaddafi listened to my tapes? Had he actually received them from someone who had stolen them from me?[23]

Shortly thereafter, Oriana Fallaci sent me a copy of her Vietnam War book, *Nothing, and So Be It*, with a dedication that read:

To my friend Yehuda Avner who shared a drama of mine and, thank God, did not share this Vietnam one. With love and thanks – Oriana Fallaci.

This bold chronicler of people and of wars was the only journalist I knew who had talked four times and for over six hours with Prime Minister Golda Meir. Well do I recall her last question at her last session which she put in a seemingly off-the-cuff manner:

"Mrs. Meir, do you really intend to retire soon?"

Golda's response was a resolute earful:

"Oriana, I give you my word. In May next year, nineteen seventy-three, I'll be seventy-five. I'm old. I'm exhausted. Old age is like a plane flying through a storm. Once you're aboard there's nothing you can do. You can't stop the plane, you can't stop the storm, you can't stop time, so one might as well accept it calmly, wisely. So no, I can't go on with this madness forever. If you only knew how many times I say to myself: To hell with everything, to hell with everybody. I've done my share, now let the others do theirs. Enough! Enough! Enough!"

She said this jabbing the air as if pointing to those who should be making her life easier. But then, she leaned back, and with one corner of her mouth pulled in a slight smile, she chuckled: "What people don't know about me, Oriana, is that I'm really bone lazy by nature. I'm not one of those who *has* to keep busy all day. In fact, I like nothing better than to sit in an armchair doing nothing. Mind you, I do enjoy cleaning the house, ironing, cooking, and things like that. In fact, I'm an excellent cook. And, oh, something else – I like to sleep. Oh, how I love to sleep! And I also like being with people. To hell with serious political talk – I just like to chat about trivial, everyday things. And I love going to the theater and to the movies – but without bodyguards underfoot. Whenever I want to see a film they send out the army reserves. You call this a life? There are days when I would just love to pack it all in and walk away without telling a soul. If I've stayed so long in the job it's only out of a sense of duty, nothing else. Yes, yes, I know, people don't believe me. Well, they'd better believe me now! I'll even give you the date when I'll step down: October nineteen seventy-three. In October seventy-three there'll be elections. Once they're over, I'm gone. It's goodbye!"

Skeptics across the political spectrum tended to take her protestations with a pinch of salt. After all, Golda Meir could never resist a challenge, and she was becoming increasingly embroiled in one right now – a fight against the spreading scourge of Arab terrorism. And when confronted with that kind of warfare she was no Venus; she was Mars.

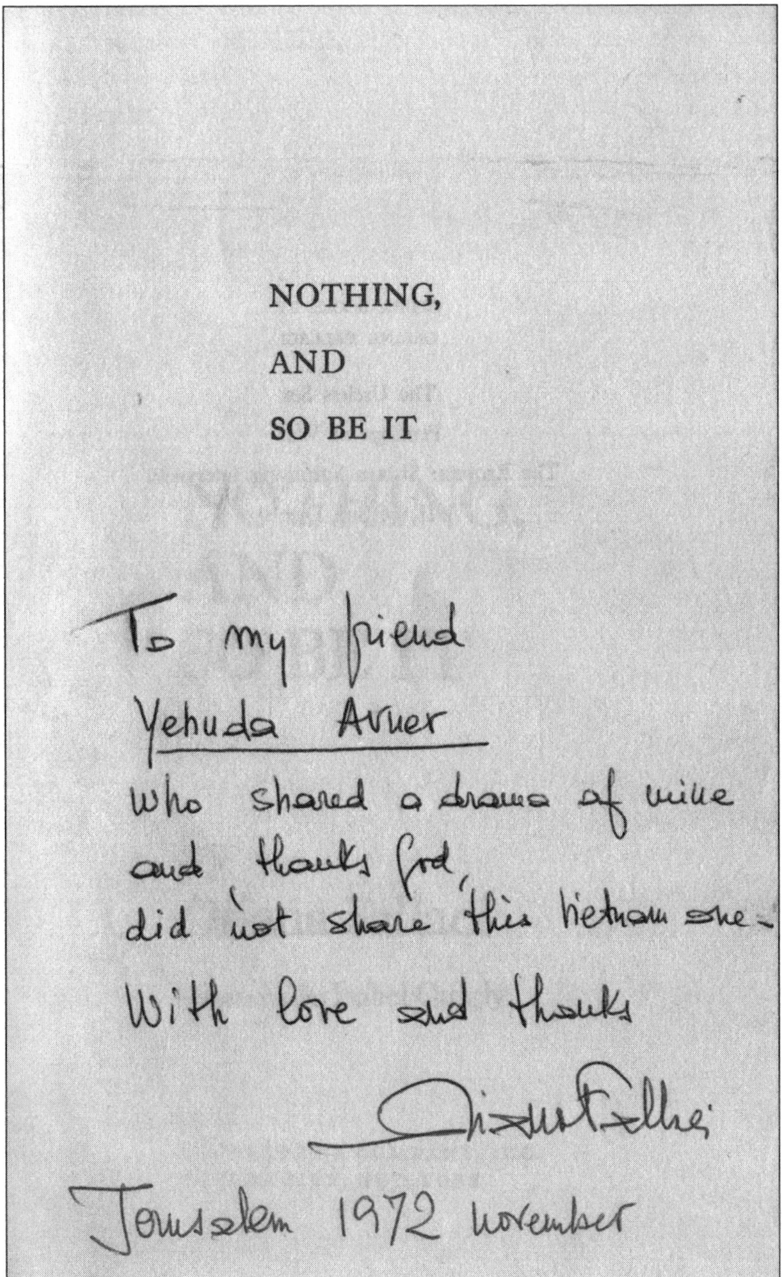

NOTHING,

AND

SO BE IT

To my friend
Yehuda Avner
who shared a drama of mine
and thanks God,
did not share this vietnam one.
With love and thanks

Oriana Fallaci

Jerusalem 1972 November

Photograph credit: Chanania Herman & Israel Government Press Office

Prime Minister Golda Meir consulting with her defense minister Moshe Dayan, 10 April 1973

Chapter thirteen

The Shame of Schoenau

How does one treat with terrorists? Deal with them and you're done for; don't, and innocents die.

During 1972 and 1973, Arab terrorism against Israeli and Jewish targets was spreading like an epidemic across the whole of Western Europe: a Belgian plane hijacked en route to Israel; a Lebanese woman carrying weapons apprehended at Rome airport; eleven Israeli athletes mowed down at the Munich Olympics; a courier carrying weapons arrested at Amsterdam airport as he was about to board a plane for Israel; a Palestinian arrested at London airport charged with planning attacks on Israeli embassies in Scandinavia; an attack planned on the Israeli Embassy in Paris; an attempted attack on El Al passengers at Rome airport; an attempted attack on the Israeli Embassy and on an Israeli aircraft at Nicosia; an attack on the El Al office in Rome; letter bombs to Jewish and Israeli addresses in Britain and Holland; an attack on the El Al office in Athens.

And then came the shame of Schoenau – a tale of infamy that seized the assemblage of the Council of Europe in September 1973.

The Council of Europe in Strasbourg is that continent's approximation of a representative House. At the time in question its approximately four hundred delegates watched with varying degrees of curiosity as Prime Minister Golda Meir, stooped and stern, mounted the podium. She was there at the invitation of the Council of Europe to state the case for Israel.

Generally speaking, Golda preferred to speak extemporaneously, but since this was a formal occasion protocol required she deliver a pre-prepared address. I, her in-house speechwriter, drafted one. It thanked the Council and individual European parliaments for raising their voices in support of Soviet Jewry's right to freely emigrate to Israel [this was at the height of the worldwide "Let My People Go" campaign], delved into the intricacies of the Middle East conflict, pleaded for "the Council of Europe's help to enable the Middle East to emulate the model of peaceful coexistence that the Council itself has established," and concluded with a quote from the great European statesman, Jean Monnet, that "Peace depends not only on treaties and promises. It depends essentially upon the creation of conditions which, if they do not change the nature of men, at least guide their behavior towards each other in a peaceful direction."

To my consternation, Golda never enunciated a single one of these words. Instead, she scanned the assembly from end to end, jaw jutting, brandished the written speech, and in a caustic voice, said, "I have here my prepared address, a copy of which I believe you have before you. But I have decided at the last minute not to place between you and me the paper on which my speech is written. Instead, you will forgive me if I break with protocol and speak in an impromptu fashion. I say this in light of what has occurred in Austria during the last few days."

Clearly, the woman had decided it was idiotic to read her formal address after the devastating news which had reached her just before leaving Israel for Strasbourg.

A train carrying Jews from communist Russia to Israel via Vienna had been hijacked on 29 September by two Arab terrorists at a railway crossing on the Austrian frontier. Seven Jews were taken hostage, among them a seventy-three-year-old man, an ailing woman, and a three-year-old child. The terrorists issued an ultimatum that unless the Austrian government instantly closed down Schoenau, the Jewish Agency's transit facility near Vienna where émigrés were processed before being flown on to Israel, not only would the hostages be killed, but Austria itself would become the target of violent retaliation.

The Austrian cabinet hastily met and, led by Chancellor Bruno Kreisky, capitulated. Kreisky announced that Schoenau would be closed, and the terrorists were hustled to the airport for safe passage to Libya.

The entire Arab world could hardly contain its glee, and a fuming Golda Meir instructed her aides to arrange a flight to Vienna after her meeting in Strasbourg, where she intended to confront Chancellor Kreisky, a fellow socialist and fellow Jew.

To the Council of Europe she said, "Since the Arab terrorists have failed in their ghastly efforts to wreak havoc in Israel, they have increasingly taken their atrocities against Israeli and Jewish targets into Europe, aided and abetted by Arab governments."

This remark caused a fidgety buzz to drone around the chamber, and it seemed to deepen when she spoke in particular, and with great bitterness, about the eleven Israeli athletes kidnapped and murdered at the Munich Olympics the previous summer, an outrage compounded by the German Government's subsequent release of the captured killers in return for the freeing of a hijacked Lufthansa plane and its passengers.

"Oh yes, I fully understand your feelings," said Golda cynically, arms folded as tight as a drawbridge. "I fully understand the feelings of a European prime minister saying, 'For God's sake, leave us out of this! Fight your own wars on your own turf. What do your enmities have to do with us? Leave us be!' And I can even understand" – this in a voice that was grimmer than ever – "why some governments might even decide that the only way to rid themselves of this insidious threat is to declare their countries out of bounds, if not to Jews generally then certainly to Israeli Jews, or Jews en route to Israel. It seems to me this is the moral choice which every European government has to make these days."

And then, in a voice hardened ruthlessly, she thundered, "European governments have no alternative but to decide what they are going to do. To each one that upholds the rule of law I suggest there is but only one answer – no deals with terrorists; no truck with terrorism. Any government which strikes a deal with these killers does so at its own peril. What happened in Vienna is that a democratic government, a European government, came to an agreement with terrorists. In so doing it has brought shame upon itself. In so doing it has breached a basic principle of the rule of law, the basic principle of the freedom of the movement of peoples – or should I just say the basic freedom of the movement of Jews fleeing Russia? Oh, what a victory for terrorism this is!"

The ensuing applause told Golda that she had gotten her message across to a goodly portion of the Council of Europe, so off she flew to Vienna.

She was ushered into the presence of the Austrian chancellor; an affluently dressed, bespectacled, heavy-set man in his mid-sixties whom she knew to be the son of a Jewish clothing manufacturer from Vienna. She extended her hand, which he shook while rising with the merest sketch of a bow, not emerging from behind the solid protection of his desk. "Please take a seat, Prime Minister Meir," he said formally.

"Thank you, Chancellor Kreisky," said Golda, settling into the chair opposite him, placing her copious black leather handbag on the floor. "I presume you know why I am here."

"I believe I do," answered Kreisky, whose body language bore all the signs of one who was not relishing this appointment.

"You and I have known each other for a long time," said Golda softly.

"We have," said the Chancellor.

"And I know that, as a Jew, you have never displayed any interest in the Jewish State. Is that not correct?"

"That is correct. I have never made any secret of my belief that Zionism is not the solution to whatever problems the Jewish people might face."

"Which is all the more reason why we are grateful to your government for all that it has done to enable thousands of Jews to transit through Austria from the Soviet Union to Israel," said Golda diplomatically.

"But the Schoenau transit camp has been a problem to us for some time," said Kreisky stonily.

"What sort of a problem?"

"For a start, it has always been an obvious terrorist target – "

Golda cut him off, and with a strong suggestion of reproach, said, "Herr Kreisky, if you close down Schoenau it will never end. Wherever Jews gather in Europe for transit to Israel they will be held to ransom by the terrorists."

"But why should Austria have to carry this burden alone?" countered Kreisky with bite. "Why not others?"

"Such as whom?"

"Such as the Dutch. Fly the immigrants to Holland. After all, the Dutch represent you in Russia."

It was true. Ever since the Russians had broken off diplomatic relations with Israel during the 1967 Six-Day War the Dutch Embassy in Moscow had represented Israel's interests there.

"Oh, I'm sure the Dutch would be prepared to share the burden if they could," responded Golda, trying to sound even-tempered. "But they can't. It doesn't depend on them. It depends entirely on the Russians. And the Russians have made it clear that they will not allow the Jews to fly out of Moscow. If they could we would fly them directly to Israel. The only way they can leave is by train, and the only country they will allow Jews to transit through is yours."

"So let them be picked up by your own people immediately upon arrival in Vienna, and flown straight to Israel," argued the Chancellor, holding his own.

"That's not practicable. You know and I know that it takes guts for a Jew to even apply for an exit permit to leave Russia to come to us. They lose their jobs, they lose their citizenship, and they are kept waiting for years. And once a permit is granted most are given hardly more than a week's notice to pack up, say their goodbyes, and leave. They come out to freedom in dribs and drabs, and we never know how many there are on any given train arriving in Vienna. So we need a collecting point, a transit camp. We need Schoenau."

The Chancellor settled his elbows on the desk, steepled his fingers, looked Golda Meir directly in the eye, and said sanctimoniously, "Mrs. Meir, it is Austria's humanitarian duty to aid refugees from whatever country they come, but not when it puts Austria at risk. I shall never be responsible for any bloodshed on the soil of Austria."

"And is it also not a humanitarian duty not to succumb to terrorist blackmail, Herr Chancellor?"

What had begun as conflicting views between opponents was now becoming a nasty cut and thrust duel between antagonists.

Kreisky shot back: "Austria is a small country, and unlike major powers, small countries have few options in dealing with the blackmail of terrorists."

"I disagree," seethed Golda. "There can be no deals with terrorism whatever the circumstances. What you have done is certain to encourage more hostage-taking. You have betrayed the Jewish émigrés."

The man's brows drew together in an affronted frown. "I cannot accept such language, Mrs. Meir. I cannot – "

"You have opened the door to terrorism, Herr Chancellor," the prime minister spat, undeterred. "You have brought renewed shame on Austria. I've just come from the Council of Europe. They condemn your act almost to a man. Only the Arab world proclaims you their hero."

"Well, there is nothing I can do about that," said the Austrian in an expressionless voice, looking uncomfortably still. And then, with a hint of a shrug, "You and I belong to two different worlds."

"Indeed we do, Herr Kreisky," said Golda Meir, in a voice cracked with derisive Jewish weariness. "You and I belong to two *very very* different worlds," and she rose, picked up her handbag, and made for the door. As she did so, an aide to the Chancellor entered to say the press were gathered in an adjacent room, awaiting a joint press conference.

Golda shook her head. She asked herself, what was the point? Nothing she could say to the media could make any difference. Kreisky wanted to stay in the good books of the Arabs – it was as simple as that. So, she turned and hissed in Hebrew to her aides, "I have no intention of sharing a platform with that man. He can tell them what he wants. I'm going to the airport." To him she said contemptuously, "I shall forego the pleasure of a press conference. I have nothing to say to them. I'm going home," and she exited through a back stairway.

Five hours later she told the waiting Israeli press at Ben-Gurion Airport, "I think the best way of summing up the nature of my meeting with Chancellor Kreisky is to say this: he didn't even offer me a glass of water."

As feared, Schoenau was shut down, and for days the Kreisky crisis made international headlines, focusing interest on the question of how the rights of Russian Jewish émigrés could be protected against the outrages of Arab terrorists. Golda Meir's remonstrations had triggered such an international whirl of protest, however, that the Austrian Chancellor had no choice but to offer alternative arrangements. These were more discreetly administered than the previous ones, and the intermittent exodus of Jews from communist Russia via Austria continued. But the prime minister of Israel was quickly distracted by another and far more urgent crisis on returning home. Intelligence reports indicated large scale Egyptian and Syrian troop movements which her military experts explained away as mere maneuvers – a calamitous misinterpretation that swiftly exploded into a war of Vesuvian proportions – the Yom Kippur War.[24]

Chapter fourteen

The SAMS of Suez

The overture to the Yom Kippur War of October 1973 came in the form of a now all-but-forgotten conflagration called the War of Attrition. It was orchestrated by the thousands of Soviet instructors in Egypt who were rapidly retraining and re-equipping that country's battered army after the debacle of the 1967 Six-Day War.

The Six-Day War ended with the IDF controlling the east bank of the Suez Canal, and in the autumn of 1968 Egyptian artillery bombardments across the Canal started up again, one of them killing ten Israeli soldiers. In retaliation, Israeli aircraft bombed bridges over the Nile, and the construction of fortifications along the whole of the Canal's length began. It was dubbed the Bar-Lev line, after the then Chief of Staff, Chaim Bar-Lev. From that day forth bursting shells rained ever more relentlessly and lethally upon the IDF's forward Canal positions, and as casualties mounted, Israel hit back with ever-escalating and deeper-penetrating ferocity. Yet the Egyptians pounded on, intent on compelling the IDF to abandon the Bar-Lev line while pushing forward with their sophisticated Soviet surface-to-air missiles – the SAMS – to neutralize Israel's overwhelming air superiority. The one hope the Egyptians had of regaining the Sinai Peninsula by force was by first knocking out Israel's aircraft from the skies over the Canal so as to enable their amphibious forces to cross it. The Soviet-manned SAM missile umbrella was designed to do just that. By the mid-1970s not only were some two hundred Soviet pilots flying Egyptian aircraft, but another fifteen thousand Soviet officers and men were manning eighty SAM missile sites.

The War of Attrition went on for more than two years until, in August 1970, the Americans, under President Richard Nixon, and through his Secretary of State William Rogers, brokered a ceasefire. The Rogers initiative, as it was called – as opposed to the earlier Rogers plan which Golda Meir had categorically rejected – was a political-military package in which both sides agreed to stop shooting and start talking under UN auspices. The envisaged talks were to be essentially based on the famous Security Council Resolution 242 which called, inter alia, for Israeli "Withdrawal from territories occupied in the recent [1967] conflict."

To Menachem Begin, still serving in the national unity government, this language was anathema, but after much wrangling, Prime Minister Golda Meir accepted the initiative, prompting Begin and his Party colleagues to resign. As Begin saw it, Israel was being asked to commit itself to a withdrawal before a concrete peace proposal was even in sight. This, to him, was irresponsible – a squandering of precious territorial assets whose loss could be justified only within the framework of a fully fledged peace treaty.

However, worse was to follow when, hours after the ceasefire came into effect in August 1970, Egypt brazenly violated it by rushing its SAM missile umbrella into what was designated as the "standstill zone" adjacent to the Canal, thereby achieving by stealth what it had failed to accomplish by attrition. Cairo finally had the means to clear the skies of Israeli aircraft whenever it felt strong enough to strike across the Canal.

Golda fumed. She demanded the missiles be removed forthwith. But President Nixon, embroiled in the war he was losing in Vietnam, and fearful of a direct confrontation with the Soviets, procrastinated. He showered the prime minister with hopeful reassurances until she ultimately succumbed for the sake of Israel's critical strategic relationship with Washington. This ignited Begin's fury even more, particularly when Washington refused to even officially acknowledge that a violation had taken place at all. His indignation launched him into a barrage of dire Jeremiah-like prophecy as he told a packed Knesset:

> The Egyptians, with the aid of their Russian advisers, have violated the ceasefire in a manner so gross it threatens our security and future. They have already deployed nine batteries of their enhanced SAM missiles, and are presently installing a further nine, all penetrating to a depth of ten to fifteen kilometers over our side of the Canal.

Hence, the conclusion has to be drawn, and the Knesset and the people have to be aware of the implications of this conclusion, that when President Nasser of Egypt decides to reopen fire – and knowing the realities as we do we have to assume such a day shall surely come – he will have a decisive advantage over us…. Given his expanded missile umbrella it will be very difficult for our Air Force to hit back without sustaining substantial losses in pilots and aircraft. This is the reality, and the Americans know it to be so.

In other words, the United States had misled Israel and had placed its security in jeopardy.

After ending his speech in a crescendo of righteous indignation, Begin stepped down from the podium into a crowd of admirers who showered him with praise, to which he responded with grace. He then made his way to the Knesset dining room where Prime Minister Golda Meir was conversing with Yitzhak Rabin, then still Israel's Ambassador to Washington.

"That was some fire and brimstone," hissed Golda derisively as the Opposition leader walked by. She had heard his address over the loudspeaker in her office.

"And I hope you took note of my every word, Madame Prime Minister," said Begin with an air of impudence and gravitas in delicate balance.

"What you don't seem to understand," scolded Golda, "is that there would be no ceasefire unless we accepted all the conditions of the Rogers initiative. We couldn't choose half the package without the other."

"But they hardly consulted us, Mrs. Meir," countered Begin, his voice gentle in order not to make his reproof too offensive. "Rogers gave us a document to sign. We initially rejected it. We had reservations and you rightly sought to insert changes, but in the end, it was all but dictated to us."

"Nonsense!"

"Is it? Remember the earlier Rogers plan when he wanted to impose upon us a withdrawal from virtually all the territories we legitimately occupied in the Six-Day War, and you instructed Ambassador Rabin" – this with an approving glance at him – "to launch what was a highly successful public campaign against it? Why not launch such a campaign now?"

"Because the situation is entirely different now, that's why."

"In my view there is the stench of an imposed U.S.-Soviet settlement brewing in the air," huffed Begin. "Nixon is going to sell us out!"

This irked Golda so much she raised her voice: "You know very well I've totally rejected any whiff of an attempt to impose a settlement on us. I will not go back to the nineteen sixty-seven lines, and I've made this plain both to Rogers and to the president. I told them both that Israel will neither be a victim to American appeasement of the Arabs nor of their big power politics with Russia."

"True, but you should have never given in to their appeasement over these latest ceasefire violations. We shall pay a heavy price for those violations one day. Moreover, I genuinely believe your acceptance of the language of Resolution 242 on 'withdrawal' is the beginning of a major unconditional retreat from all the ceasefire lines."

"Goodness gracious, Begin, how you get carried away by your own rhetoric!" scorned Golda, her eyebrows arching challengingly. "If only you stammered or hesitated occasionally."

Unperturbed, Begin countered, "This is an instance when *you* have gotten carried away by your own wishful thinking. Nixon, I fear, is playing chess with the fate of Israel. This could be a Middle East Munich. America seems to be more interested in Arab oil than in Israel's future."

"With all due respect, Mr. Begin, President Nixon recently told me the very opposite of what you've just said." It was Ambassador Yitzhak Rabin speaking, his voice respectful but firm.

Begin sat down uninvited. "So how does that square with Rogers' ceasefire initiative, which is tantamount to appeasing the Arabs?" he asked.

"It squares," said Rabin in his deep baritone, "because all along Nixon and Kissinger have known that in the War of Attrition the Soviets and the Egyptians were putting us both to a test – not only us, but America as well. The Americans know the Soviets are feeding and manipulating the entire Egyptian war effort. That's why I strongly advocated the use of our Air Force to strike hard deep inside Egyptian territory, to prove to the Americans that we have the mettle to stand up to them. Just about the most encouraging breath of fresh air the Nixon Administration has been enjoying recently has been our military operations against Egypt and the Soviet advisers and weaponry there. Our actions have undermined both Nasser's and the Russians' credibility and standing in the whole of the Middle East. I will go further: the American willingness to supply us with arms is dependent upon our giving the Egyptians and the Soviets a bloody nose. Our deep penetration raids into Egyptian airspace during the War of Attrition not only changed the balance of power along the fighting front, but also tipped the scales of the superpower confrontation in America's favor. But with all that, Nixon still has to strike a balance so as not to lose the Arab world entirely to the Russians because of us."

Rabin extracted a sheet of paper. "You will recall Eban recently met with Nixon in my presence. He asked us, I quote, 'In view of the Soviet involvement, is Israel's position still – as I once heard Ambassador Rabin say – "Give us the tools and we'll do the job?"' Much to Eban's chagrin, I gave the answer. 'Yes, it is,' I said. Listen to how the president replied." Rabin read:

> Good! That was all I wanted to know. If it were just a question of you and the Egyptians and the Syrians, I'd say, "Let 'em have it! Let 'em have it! Hit 'em as hard as you can." Every time I hear about you penetrating into their territory and hitting them hard I get a feeling of satisfaction. But it's not just a problem of Egypt and Syria. The other Arab states are watching also. I don't have the slightest doubt about that. We don't have any choice. We have to play it so that we don't lose everything in the Middle East. We want to help you without harming ourselves.

And then:

> Damn the oil! We can get it from other sources. We have to stand by decent nations in the Middle East. We will back you militarily, but the military escalation can't go on endlessly. We must do something politically.[25]

Added Rabin with self-satisfaction, "I, personally, don't think any American president has ever uttered such a pro-Israel sentiment before."

"So, again I ask, how does that square with his Rogers ceasefire initiative which is tantamount to appeasing the Arabs?" pressed Begin.

"It squares because he has to play it in such a way that the Russians will not be allowed to better Israel, while at the same time ensuring that America will not lose all of the Middle East to the Russians. So yes, he's greatly expanded our military aid, which is excellent, while launching the Rogers initiative, not all of which is to our liking but which has placated the Arabs enough to bring about a ceasefire."

"Add to that," said the prime minister, brimming with gratification at her ambassador's first-class analysis, "in return for our accepting the Rogers package Nixon has promised us that we will not be expected to withdraw a single soldier from the ceasefire lines except in the context of a contractual peace agreement which we would regard as satisfactory to our security needs. Moreover, had we not accepted the Rogers initiative we wouldn't be getting any more American arms, as Rabin has just explained. So how can you argue with that?"

Begin dismissed this clincher with a perfunctory wave of the hand. "What do you mean we wouldn't be getting American arms? We would demand them."

"You know, Begin," said Golda sarcastically, "you sometimes make me think you're a mystic. You've convinced yourself that all we have to do is to go on telling the United States that we won't give in to pressure and that if we do this long and loud enough, then one day that pressure will vanish."

"My good lady," responded Begin in an equally patronizing vein, "you trivialize Israel's importance to the United States of America."

"Do I? I think that though the American commitment to Israel's survival is certainly great, I'm afraid we need Mr. Nixon and Mr. Rogers much more than they need us."

"I disagree!" said Begin. "The Americans don't give us arms out of the kindness of their hearts. Israel is doing more for America in keeping the Soviet Union at bay in the Middle East than what America is doing for Israel to defend itself. And I dare say Mr. Nixon is fully aware of that. Besides, you must never underestimate the voice of American Jewry."

"Oh, I don't. But I'm afraid our policies can't be based entirely on the assumption that American Jewry either would or could force Mr. Nixon to adopt a position against his will and better judgment, especially when he doesn't like liberal-minded Jews."

"We shall see," said Begin, rising, and turning to Rabin he said with a smile, "I beg of you, please, do not misconstrue this argument between the prime minister and myself as personal. Mrs. Meir and I differ on many issues, but I want to assure you that I view her with the highest regard as a proud and courageous Jewess."

"Stop being a shmoozer," sniffed Golda, with a grin that greatly softened her craggy and aging features.

"No, no, Madame, I say this not in flattery. I look back on my three years in the national unity government, first under Eshkol and then under you, as a very beautiful period in my life. I miss the camaraderie, and the deliberations we had together, sometimes on vital issues of life and death. To me you were always the first among equals. But now that I have returned to the Opposition I shall have to oppose you whenever I believe you are in error, just as I did in the Knesset today. But on a personal level my respect for you shall never waver."

With that, Mr. Begin shook Rabin's hand, and said, "I wish you continued success in Washington for all our sakes." And to Mrs. Meir, with a bow of the head, "Madame Prime Minister, I pray that all my predictions will prove to be unfounded. Yet I fear they will not." To which Golda returned him a reprimanding stare as he walked off to join a table of fellow oppositionists for a glass of lemon tea.

According to what Henry Kissinger subsequently wrote in his memoirs, Menachem Begin was perfectly correct in asserting that America's backing of Israel at that juncture was not a matter of mere benevolence, and that Israel's obstinate demands for U.S. support resonated among Washington's decision makers. In his memoirs he wrote:

> Israel is dependent on the U.S. as no other country is on a friendly power. Increasingly, Washington is the sole capital to stand by Israel in international forums. We are its exclusive military supplier, its only military ally (though no formal obligation exists)…It takes a special brand of heroism to turn total dependence into defiance, to insist on support as a matter of right rather than as a favor; to turn every American deviation from an Israeli cabinet consensus into a betrayal to be punished rather than a disagreement to be negotiated. And yet Israel's obstinacy, maddening as it can be, serves the purposes of both our countries best. A subservient client would soon face an accumulation of ever-growing pressures. It would tempt Israel's neighbors to escalate their demands. It would saddle us with opprobrium for every deadlock…. Our relationship with Israel is exhilarating and frustrating, ennobled by the devotion and faith that contain a lesson for an age of cynicism; exasperating because the interests of a superpower and of a regional ministate are not always easy to reconcile, and are on occasion unbridgeable. Israel affects our decisions through inspiration, persistence, and a judicious, not always subtle or discreet influence on our domestic policy.[26]

Chapter fifteen

Once Upon a *Sukka* Time

At one time or another we are most of us like Don Quixote, all more or less the dupes of our own illusions. Even the alleged infallibility of the Israeli intelligence community is not immune. Thus, when the headlines of 28 September 1970 blazed the news that President Nasser of Egypt had died of a heart attack, and that his successor was to be Vice President Anwar Sadat, the little that was known of this long-limbed, balding, joyless-looking, deeply religious model of anti-charisma suggested he was hiding spinelessness beneath his extravagant uniforms. It was thus widely assumed that Sadat would merely serve as a temporary stand-in until someone of more stellar rank would come along.

Imagine then the shock on the Yom Kippur day of October 1973, when Sadat dispatched his army in a massive surprise attack across the Suez Canal, in coordination with a Syrian invasion of the Golan Heights, sending the Israel Defense Forces scrambling on both fronts. Israel's highest echelons had seemingly taken a holiday from reality – less than a month earlier they had estimated that hostilities were not in the offing. They were still saying as much twenty-four hours before they began.

As head of the Foreign Press Bureau I had no reason to doubt their assurances. On the eve of that Yom Kippur I closed my office early – as does everybody on that day – and, making my way out, bumped into a British correspondent, Eric Silver, who represented the London *Observer* and the *Guardian*. He wanted to know what would happen in the event of a national emergency, all services being shut down on the Day of Atonement, including the radio.

Full of self-assurance, I answered, "But what could possibly happen? It's Yom Kippur."

"Yes, but what if something *does* happen?"

"Like what?"

"I don't know – a war, maybe."

"A war? There will be no war!"

"But what if there is one?"

"How can there be a war on Yom Kippur?"

The next day, on this holiest of holy days, war came, accompanied by an inexpressible astonishment as people heard in horror the wailing of air raid sirens filling the sky. Military vehicles violated the awesome silence of the sacred day as they sped along normally empty streets on errands of high emergency, and radios blared out code names for instant mobilization. The cantors' chanting of the brokenhearted liturgical, *U'netaneh tokef* – "Who shall live and who shall die" – was followed by rabbis telling their congregants, wrapped in prayer shawls, that they were to report forthwith to their reserve units, and that those mobilized may break this most stringent of fast days.

A postwar Blue Ribbon commission of inquiry – the Agranat Commission – would conclude that had Israel's leaders put their ears to the ground they would have heard the rumble of the approaching chariots of war long before the juggernaut came. Yet even those who *were* listening were so duped by their own preconceived notions that they misread what they were hearing. The very idea of an Arab onslaught was an affront to Israel's enshrined military doctrine which expressed certainty that neither Egypt nor Syria was capable of waging renewed all-out warfare at this time. And much as actors at dress rehearsals reassure their anxious producers, "Don't worry, it'll be all right on the night," so did Israel's military reassure Prime Minister Golda Meir, "Don't worry, the IDF will be ready on the day, if such a day should ever dawn."

Yet dawn it did, and the IDF was not ready. The thinly held lines in the north and in the south were sent bleeding and reeling under the hammer blows of the combined Egyptian-Syrian surprise attack, splintering and crushing the army's defenses. A combination of highly effective preparations and deceptions, astutely planned to appear to be training maneuvers, allowed the Egyptians and the Syrians vast opening-day victories.

Along the Suez Canal, four hundred and fifty Israeli soldiers with fifty artillery pieces tried in vain to stop one hundred thousand Egyptian troops crossing the waterway under the covering fire of two thousand artillery pieces, and under an umbrella of one of the most expansive SAM missile umbrellas in the world, just as Menachem Begin had predicted. The SAMs quickly knocked fifty Israeli aircraft out of the skies, and within a few days two whole Egyptian armies had occupied the entire Israeli-held east bank of the Suez Canal. Simultaneously, in the north, fourteen hundred Syrian tanks hurled themselves against Israel's one hundred and sixty. The defenders fought ferociously at point blank range, lurching and roaring and dying in an unequal entanglement of tanks and armored personnel carriers and howitzers and other lethal paraphernalia that culminated in a contest of wills which left Israel hemorrhaging.

The bloodiest and most desperate battle of those very first days was fought on the Golan Heights, in a place called the Kuneitra Valley, dubbed by those who fought there the Vale of Tears. Golda Meir wanted to see this frightful place with her own eyes, so on her insistence, a last-minute inspection tour was arranged on the seventh day of the war. It included a six-man foreign media press pool under my care. She wanted the world to know the odds Israel was up against.

"Mrs. Meir, may I put a question to you?" asked one of the pool members as the prime minister was about to board her helicopter.

"If it's about the war the answer is no," she replied impatiently.

"It's not about the war. It's about Africa."

"What about Africa?"

"Well, word has it that, because of the war, your whole assistance enterprise in Africa, which you initiated as Foreign Minister, has collapsed; that under Arab pressure African leaders are severing diplomatic ties with Israel, some even branding you a war criminal. Surely, you must be saddened, disillusioned, by this."

"Saddened, yes, disillusioned, no."

"But don't you feel it was a waste of time and effort?"

"Nothing is cheaper than that sort of blanket, after-the-fact ridicule."

"Yet you have to admit that you took your bighearted African policy too seriously. You were almost messianic about it."

"Utter nonsense! A setback is not a failure. A disappointment is not a ruin. A frustration is not a catastrophe. Not every enterprise can give immediate returns. Nothing ever goes to waste. Time will tell."

"But how can you be sure the Africans will want you back after giving you such a slap in the face?"

"Because what I did for Africa was not just a policy of enlightened self-interest. I did it for the benefit of the African peoples, and deep in their hearts they know this to be true. It was an expression of my deepest historic instincts as a Jew, and a demonstration of my most profound and cherished values as a Labor Zionist."

With that, she was assisted into the helicopter by her veteran minister of defense, Moshe Dayan, and her ruggedly handsome chief of staff, General David (Dado) Elazar. Less than an hour later these two warriors, faces gray for lack of sleep, watched with expert eyes as squads of dusty men, some staggering with fatigue, loaded tanks with shells, refueled their engines, and waved them off, clanking and snarling, back to the slaughter of the shifting front. Other metal brutes clawed and ripped at the rock-strewn path up the slope to the plateau designated as the tank replenishment depot, where the prime minister and her entourage were standing. Centurions, much the worse for wear, were parked higgledy-piggledy, taking on ammunition and fuel before returning to battle.

From this vantage point, Golda Meir, her face deeply scored, stared out across the Vale of Tears, and her eyes reddened. It was one of the intermediate days of the festival of Sukkot. The distant thud of heavy guns pounding the road to Damascus could be distinctly heard. The chief of staff propped up a map of the Golan Heights on the hull of a battered tank, and with sweeps of his pen, resurrected the lines of battle for the benefit of this knotted old woman whose ignorance of things military was absolute.

Moshe Dayan handed her his binoculars the better to view the distant valley floor strewn with the hideous debris of war: pulverized howitzers, blown-out trucks, banged up armored personnel carriers, burned-out tanks punched through with bull's eyes, some still smoldering – and the dead. The stench of death, cordite, diesel, and exhaust, was overwhelming.

As she scanned this cadaverous landscape through the binoculars the creases in her face sharpened, and she fumbled for a pack of cigarettes from her black leather handbag. Dado struck her a match and she inhaled deeply, sparking a blaze of photo flashes from the accompanying journalists who were in my charge.

Given the improvised and sensitive nature of the trip it had been agreed that there would be no press conference, but one journalist pugnaciously called out, "Share with us, if you will, prime minister, what's going through your mind as you look out upon this battlefield?"

Golda stared back at him, her features livid, and with a dismissive wave of the hand as though brushing away a fly from her plain gray suit,

*Golda Meir and Defense Minister Moshe Dayan speaking with
soldiers on Golan Heights during the Yom Kippur War*

Golda Meir with Israeli troops on Golan Heights during the Yom Kippur War

she turned to Dayan and Dado, and said, "Come, I want to talk to the men at the *sukka*. I want to hear what they have to say."

She moved off in the direction of an armored personnel carrier which, incongruously, was canopied by a *sukka* – a booth – in honor of the festival. The *sukka* was thatched with palm branches in imitation of the fragile huts the Israelites lived in during their wanderings in the desert after the Exodus from Egypt. And as she walked toward this mobile field *sukka*, pigheaded photographers walked backward, shooting pictures of her every stride.

Inside, about fifteen soldiers were chanting a prayer, their backs toward Golda and her companions. Each was draped in a prayer shawl, and each clutched a *lulav* and *etrog*, *hadassim* and *aravot* – the Four Species. They were shaking them gently, first forward to the east, then right to the south, over their right shoulder to the west, then left to the north, and then up, and then down, in replication of the ancient Temple's *Sukkot* ceremony, symbolizing that God is everywhere. Only when they had completed their ritual did they notice who was silently gazing at them.

"*Chag sameach!*" called Golda, and the soldiers returned the festive greeting with wide-eyed astonishment. They were reservists, plucked from their synagogues on Yom Kippur to reinforce the desperately stretched line that was holding back the Syrians along the crest of the Golan Heights, in a frenzied effort to stop them from capturing the highway below, which would have opened the road to Haifa. While their tanks were being hastily refueled, rearmed, and serviced, they had taken the time to pray and recite the blessings over the Four Species, the *Arba Minim*, in this makeshift *sukka*.

Straightening her skirt, Golda Meir asked the men about their families, her countenance that of a concerned grandmother, and learned by-the-by that she was talking to lawyers, bakers, teachers, falafel vendors, accountants, shopkeepers, and hi-tech executives. Other soldiers were drawn into the circle, and the prime minister asked them many questions. Then she wrapped the session up with, "Now, is there anyone who would like to ask me something?"

One tank crew member – he seemed to be in his mid-twenties – raised his hand. He was caked with black basalt dust from head to toe, and his only contrasting feature were the whites of his eyes. "I have a question," he said, in a voice throaty with exhaustion. "My father was killed in the war of forty-eight, and we won. My uncle was killed in the war of fifty-six, and we won. My brother lost an arm in the sixty-seven war, and we won. Last week I lost my best friend over there," – he was pointing to the Vale of

Tears – "and we're going to win. But is all our sacrifice worthwhile, Golda? What's the use of our sacrifice if we can't win the peace?"

An edgy murmur passed through the group of unshaven, weary, and unkempt soldiers.

The prime minister returned the young soldier a long and sad look, and there was a strange reserve in her eyes, a remote stare, as though she was looking way inside herself. For on that *Sukkot* day, this indefatigable and implacable old woman represented the very essence of Jewish self-defense; she was the fervent agent of the view that it was infinitely preferable to deal with power's confounding implications than to be powerless again.

So she answered, in a deeply compassionate tone, saying, "I weep for your loss, just as I grieve for all our dead. I lie awake at night thinking of them. And I must tell you in all honesty, were our sacrifices for ourselves alone, then perhaps you would be right; I'm not at all sure they would be worthwhile. But if our sacrifices are for the sake of the *whole* Jewish people, then I believe with all my heart that any price is worthwhile."

A faintly bemused smile tipped the corners of her mouth, and though her face was gnarled with age, a girl looked out of her eyes as she said, "Let me tell you a story. In nineteen forty-eight, in this season of the year, I arrived in Moscow as Israel's first ambassador to the Soviet Union. The State of Israel was brand new. Stalinism was at its height. Jews as Jews had no rights. They had been cut off from their fellow Jews for thirty years, since the communist Revolution of nineteen seventeen. Stalin had proclaimed war against Judaism. He declared Zionism a crime. Hebrew was banned. Torah study was banned. One was sent to the gulag or to Siberia for far less.

"The first Shabbat after I had presented my credentials, my embassy staff joined me for services at the Moscow Great Synagogue. It was practically empty. But the news of our arrival in Moscow spread quickly so that when we went a second time the street in front of the synagogue was jam-packed. Close to fifty thousand people were waiting for us – old people and teenagers, babies in parents' arms, even men in officer uniforms of the Red Army. Despite all the risks, despite all the official threats to stay away from us, these Jews had come to demonstrate their kinship with us.

"Inside the synagogue," she went on, "the demonstration was the same. Without speeches or parades, these Jews were showing their love for Israel and the Jewish people, and I was their symbol. I prayed together with them on that festival. Oh, how I prayed. I was caught up in a torrent of love so strong it literally took my breath away. People surged around me, stretching out their hands, and crying, *'Sholem aleychem Goldele'* [Yiddish for, 'Welcome Golda']. *'Goldele, lebn zolstu'* [Golda, a long life to you]. *'Gutt yontev Goldele'* [Happy Holiday, Golda]. And all I could say over and over again was, *'A dank eych vos ir zayt gebliben Yidn'* [I thank you for remaining Jews]. And some cried back to me, *'Mir danken Medinas Yisroel'* [We thank the State of Israel]. And that was when I knew for sure that our sacrifices are not in vain."[27]

A day later, a despondent Defense Minister Moshe Dayan walked into the prime minister's room, closed the door, stood in front of her, and asked outright, "Do you want me to resign? I am prepared to do so if you think I should. Unless I have your confidence, I can't go on."

Golda Meir shook her head from side to side. "No Moshe, under no circumstances do I want you to resign. If I wanted you to, I would have said so."

Clearly relieved, Dayan proceeded to share with her what to him was becoming increasingly obvious: that this war was not going to be a short one. Even while the enemy was being held at bay and in certain sectors was even being pushed back, Israel's casualties were mounting and its arsenals were rapidly being depleted.

"What we saw up north on the Golan Heights," said the Defense Minister, "confirms my fears that the hostilities are going to continue for an extended period, and the attrition is enormous."

"So what are you saying?"

"I'm saying that unless our stocks are speedily replenished we won't be left with sufficient arms to defend ourselves – there won't be enough tanks and planes; there won't be enough trained personnel."

Golda, shocked at this prospect of national annihilation coming from the man who heretofore had embodied the Jewish State's undaunted defiance, gasped, "Are you saying that we'll ultimately have to surrender to the Syrians and the Egyptians for lack of arms?"

It was as if David had aimed with his sling and missed.

"What I'm saying," said Dayan, "is that if our stocks are not replenished at a much faster rate we may well have to pull back to shorter, more defensible lines, particularly in Sinai."

"Pull back? Retreat?"

Golda Meir's face went ivory white. She looked despairingly at her defense minister, covered her face with trembling fingers, then rose to stare out of the window. The more she pondered, the more the color seeped back into her cheeks until, composure restored, she turned back to face Dayan and said, "Moshe, one way or another I'll get you your weapons. Your job is to bring us victory, mine is to give you the means to do so." Then, picking up the telephone, she instructed her secretary, "Get me Simcha."

Simcha Dinitz was then Israel's ambassador to Washington.

"But it's three in the morning there," said the secretary.

"Wake him up!" snapped the prime minister. And then, to Dayan: "Simcha is going to have to persuade Kissinger to persuade the president to speed up a massive airlift, otherwise I'll go to Washington myself. The Soviet Union is replenishing the Arabs around the clock. And so, yes, the whole of the Arab world is arraigned against us, but at the end of the day this war is not just between us and them, it's a duel in the Cold War between America and the Soviet Union, and that surely Washington can understand."

Her red telephone buzzed. "The ambassador is on the line," said the secretary.

"Simcha – Dayan is here with me. I want you to call Kissinger immediately – "

"I can't speak to anyone right now, Golda," said Dinitz, suddenly wide awake. "It's much too early. It's three in the morning here."

The prime minister refused to listen to reason. "I don't give a damn what time it is. We are in desperate need of a military airlift. Call him right now. We need the help today because tomorrow may be too late."

"So what do you want me to tell him exactly?"

"Tell him he must speak to the president. Tell him what he already knows – that huge military transports of Soviet aid are being supplied by sea and air to the Syrians and the Egyptians. Tell him that we're feverishly shopping around for foreign carriers to transport materiel to us, but they refuse. Tell him that European governments, notably the French and the British, have chosen to impose an arms embargo on us when we are fighting for our lives. Tell him that we are losing aircraft to the Soviet SAMs at an intolerable rate. Tell him I'm ready to fly to Washington incognito right now to talk directly to the president myself if I have to."[28]

But Golda did not have to. Washington understood only too well that the direction this war was taking could drag America into a perilous confrontation with the Soviet Union, with consequences too terrible to contemplate. For as much as it was primarily a gory conflict in the Middle East it was, indeed, becoming an increasingly menacing confrontation between the world's two superpowers. So, on 14 October, soon after Golda had spoken to Dinitz, and after she herself had spoken to Washington personally any number of times, President Richard Nixon telephoned Secretary of State Henry Kissinger from his retreat in Key Biscayne, Florida, where he was taking refuge from the ever-mounting legal and congressional pressures brought to bear on him because of the Watergate scandal.

Pundits claim that by this time the president was drinking heavily, was losing sleep, and was so distracted by the shadow of possible impeachment that he was not fully focused on the Middle East inferno. It was, in fact, rumored, that he was leaving it all to Secretary of State Kissinger to handle. And while this was mere speculation, the reader might be forgiven for concluding that he was indeed under the influence, given the slurred and rambling nature of some of his remarks. Whether this was so or not, once it came to the decision-making crunch he was absolutely categorical: he did not want Israel to lose this war, but neither did he want it to win outright.

This is how the transcript of that 14 October telephone conversation – on the ninth day of the war – reads:

Nixon: Hi, Henry, how are you?

Kissinger: Okay.

N: Anything new this morning?

K: Yes, the Egyptians have launched a big offensive and it's hard to know exactly what is really going on in an early stage of an offensive.

N: Of course.

K: The Israelis have claimed they have knocked out one hundred and fifty tanks and that they've lost about fifteen of their own. But that, in itself, would not prove anything – it depends where the Egyptians go to. The last information we have, that is not absolutely firm, is that they may have reached close to the Mitla Pass, which is about thirty kilometers beyond the Canal, and which would be the key Israeli defensive position. There are two possibilities: One – the Israelis are trying to draw the Egyptians beyond the SAM belt in order to knock out a lot of their forces, and in that case the battle could be fairly decisive [in Israel's favor]. Or two – the Israelis are really in trouble and we should know that by tonight in any event."

[…]

N: Look, we've got to face this… we've got to come off with something on the diplomatic front. If we go the ceasefire route, the Russians will figure that we get the ceasefire and then the Israelis will dig in and we'll back them as we always have. That's putting it quite bluntly, but it's quite true, Henry, isn't it?"

K: There's a lot in that."

N: They can't be in that position, so we have to be in a position to offer them [the Russians] something.

K: Well I …

N: Because we've got to squeeze the Israelis when this is over and the Russians have to know it. We've got to squeeze them goddamn hard. And that's the way it's going to be done. But I don't know how to get that across now [to the Russians]. We've told them before we'd squeeze them and we didn't.

K: Well, we are going to squeeze them; we are going to start diplomacy in November right after the Israeli … [elections].

N: I know we were, but …

K: And we have made all the preparations for that, but that's now water over the dam. I think what we need now – if we can find a [UN] resolution that doesn't flatly say the sixty-seven borders, but leaves it open – something that invokes the Security Council Resolution 242 that speaks of withdrawals, and that's something everybody has agreed to once. Plus a [peace] conference or something like that. Then perhaps by tomorrow we can move it to a vote in the Security Council.

N: Yeah, yeah. Certainly a conference would be fine.

[…]

K: By the end of the day this thing will be a lot clearer because the battle now in Sinai, whatever happens in Syria, the battles cannot be extremely protracted because supplies from both sides have to come a fairly long distance.

N: Desert battles are not protracted – we know that, that they move quickly. The other point I want to make, what are we doing on the supply side [to the Israelis]?

K: I could call you in an hour …

N: All right.

K: … when I can give you an accurate report. Basically what we are trying to do is to stop military planes and put commercial charters in.

N: Yes, yes. As I say though, it's got to be the works. What I mean is –

we are going to get blamed [by the Arabs] just as much for three planes as for three hundred – not going to let the Russians come in there for – with a free hand. On the other hand, this is a deadly course, I know, but what I mean is, Henry, I have no patience with the view that we send in a couple of planes, even though they carry sixty some... My point is, when we are going to make a move, it's going to cost us out there. I don't think it's going to cost us a damn bit more to send in more and – I have to emphasize to you that I think the way it's being handled in terms of our things – we are sending supplies, but only for the purpose of maintaining the balance [with the Russian resupply to the Arabs] so that we can create the conditions that will lead to an equitable settlement. The point is, if you don't say it that way, it looks as though we are sending in supplies to have the war go on indefinitely, and that is not a tenable position.

K: Right. Right. If it hasn't been said before, we'll say it certainly today.

N: The thought is basically: the purpose of supplies is not simply to fuel the war; the purpose is to maintain the balance, which is quite accurate incidentally, and then – because only with the balance in that area can there be an equitable settlement that doesn't do in one side or the other. That's really what we're talking about.

K: Right, Mr. President.

N: But now, on the Russians...

K: I expect formally to hear from the Russians. I didn't get through talking to the Russians till ten last night. And I gave them really a terrific...

N: We can't have this business of defending them all over the place... What ought to happen is that even though the Israelis will squeal like stuck pigs, we ought to tell the Russians that Brezhnev [the Soviet leader] and Nixon will settle this damn thing. That ought to be done. You know that....

K: That's exactly right.

N: If he [Brezhnev] gets that through, I think maybe he'd like it. I'll call you in an hour; you call me in an hour.

K: Right, Mr. President.

N: Bye. Right.

Two hours later Richard Nixon called Henry Kissinger. It has been suggested that given his even more incoherent flow of words he was, by now, truly inebriated.

N: Hi, Henry. I got a fill-in [on the airlift]. I'm glad to know we are going all out on this.

K: Oh, it's a massive airlift, Mr. President. The planes are going to land every fifteen minutes.

N: That's right. Get them there. The only addition – I want to check the European theater to see if there were some of those smaller planes [Skyhawks] that they need, and fly them down there so that they can replace the aircraft losses. And the other thing is that these big planes [cargo c-5 Galaxies] you can put some of those good tanks, those m-60 tanks on if necessary, if that would have some good effect, and put a few in there too.

K: Right, Mr. President.

N: So, in other words, don't – if we are going to do it – don't spare the horses. Just let…

K: Actually, the big planes, Mr. President, we have also flexibility. We can fly the Skyhawks in them.

N: Put them on the plane, you mean?

K: Yes. I don't think there is another way – no [European] country will let them overfly [nor grant refueling rights].

N: All right. How many can a big plane take?

K: It can take five or six.

N: All right – put some Skyhawks in; do that too. You understand what I mean – if we are going to take heat for this, well, let's go.

K: I think that is right. And I think, Mr. President, we can offer to stop the airlift if the Russians do after a ceasefire is signed.

N: Exactly. I think we should say – I think a personal message now should go. I mean you have been sending messages, but one should go from me to Brezhnev.

K: Everything I am sending is in your name.

N: Good. But I think he should know – now look here: the peace is not only for this area but the whole future relationship [with the Russians] is at stake here, and we are prepared to stop if you are, and we are prepared – you know what I mean. I don't know – have you got anything developed along those lines so that we just don't have…?

K: I have. I'm developing it now and I think I could call Dobrynin [the Soviet ambassador] and point it out to him.

N: Right. Right. Put it in a very conciliatory but very tough way that I do this [the airlift] with great regret – great reluctance – but that we cannot have a situation that has now developed and that we are prepared to give tit for tat. Nothing on the battle so far?

K: On this morning's battle, it is the Israelis – it has not been announced yet; *they* have knocked out one hundred and fifty tanks.

N: And lost fifteen. Yes, I heard that this morning.

K: Something like ten thirty this morning.

N: The Egyptians...

K: They seem to be heading more south than east and are not really trying to break into the Sinai at this point. So they are just keeping their defensive position down the coast. And they may be going for [garbled]. But, ah...

N: Nothing new on Syria?

K: In Syria the Israelis have told us this morning they have stopped their advance on Damascus. They stopped about twenty kilometers short. There are reports from some foreign correspondents that went up to the front from Damascus on the Syrian side and indicated the Syrian army now was getting to be demoralized and were abandoning equipment. But still, Mr. President, they are the reason why the Egyptians are able to hold on.... The estimate of our group is that it would take the Israelis three more days to knock out the Syrians and that they couldn't really turn to the Egyptians for another four to five days.

N: What do we plan then?

K: Well, we plan to try to get it wound up this week.

N: [garbled]

K: Yes.

N: ...Well at least I feel better. The airlift thing, if I contributed anything to the discussion it is the business that, don't fool around with three planes. By golly, no matter how big they are, just go gung ho.

K: One of the lessons I have learned from you, Mr. President, is that if you do something, you might as well do it completely.[29]

247

And do it completely he did. Over the course of the ensuing days and weeks U.S. resupply aircraft conducted 815 sorties delivering more than 27,900 tonnes of materiel, replenishing Israel's arsenals and enabling the IDF to decisively move over to the offensive.

When a bleary-eyed and weary prime minister addressed the Knesset a couple of days after this conversation she expressed Israel's fervent gratitude to the president and people of the United States for the airlift, and caused an optimistic stir when she revealed that even as she was speaking, a task force of the Israel Defense Forces had succeeded in crossing the Suez Canal and was engaging the enemy on its western bank.

But the principal reason Golda Meir chose to address the Knesset that day, when the war was still at its height and Israel still in peril, was because she wanted the world to know what the Jewish State's fate would have been had it ever bowed to the constant international pressure to withdraw to the pre–Six-Day War lines of 1967. She wanted the world to know why she and her predecessor, Levi Eshkol, had rebuffed that pressure so stubbornly. To the approving nods of Menachem Begin, who was listening to her with appreciation, she told the House in a voice that rang with sudden command:

> One need not have a fertile imagination to realize what the situation of the State of Israel would have been if we had been deployed on the June fourth sixty-seven lines. Anyone who finds it difficult to visualize this nightmarish picture should direct his mind and attention to what happened on the northern front – on the Golan Heights – during the first days of the war. Syria's aspirations are not limited to a piece of land, but to deploying their artillery batteries once again on the Golan Heights against the Galilee settlements, to setting up missile batteries against our aircraft, so as to provide cover for the breakthrough of their armies into the heart of Israel.
>
> Nor is a fertile imagination required to imagine the fate of the State of Israel had the Egyptian armies managed to overcome the Israel Defense Forces in the expanses of Sinai and to move in full force towards Israel's borders.... This is a war against our very existence as a state and a nation. The Arab rulers pretend that their objective is limited to reaching the lines of June fourth sixty-seven, but we know their true objective: the total subjugation of the State of Israel. It is our duty to realize this truth; it is our duty to make

it clear to all men of goodwill who tend to ignore this truth. We need to realize this truth in all its gravity, so that we may continue to mobilize from among ourselves and from the Jewish people all the resources necessary to overcome our enemies, to fight back until we have defeated the aggressors.

Toward the end of October, the Arabs sued for a ceasefire. What had begun three weeks earlier as an ignoble retreat of the Israelis ended in an almost total rout of the Egyptians and the Syrians, and the humiliation of their patron, the Soviet Union. Reenergized and reequipped, the IDF advanced to forty kilometers [not twenty as Kissinger had told Nixon] from the gates of Damascus, battled its way along the highway to Cairo, smashed two Egyptian armies, surrounded a third, and was poised to strike a knockout blow against that Third Army when Nixon and Kissinger put the squeeze on Israel, saying in effect, "Okay Golda! Good job! Enough! Stop, it's over!"

Exactly as the president and the secretary had envisaged in their jumbled and rambling telephone exchanges two weeks before, the squeeze rescued Egypt's remaining forces from total annihilation and Israel was robbed of a decisive military victory. Fretfully and fatalistically, Prime Minister Meir put it this way to her cabinet:

> Let's call things by their proper name. Black is black and white is white. There is only one country to which we can turn, and sometimes we have to give in to it – even when we know we shouldn't. But it is the only real friend we have, and a very powerful one at that. We don't have to say yes to everything, but let's call things by their proper name. There is nothing to be ashamed of when a small country like Israel, in this situation, has to give in sometimes to the United States. And when we do say yes, let's, for God's sake, not pretend that it is otherwise and that black is white.[30]

The fact that the last remnant of Egyptian military power – the Third Army – had not been routed and had not surrendered, enabled President Sadat to declare to his people that he had wiped clean the shame of 1967, and enabled Secretary of State Kissinger to fly into the Middle East to begin reaping the political harvest of Washington's diplomacy. Using the currency of Israeli concessions, he set out to convince President Sadat that Washington, not Moscow, was henceforth the arbiter of affairs in the Middle East, and that it paid to be a friend of the United States of America.

The first full Knesset debate on the Yom Kippur War took place on 13 November 1973, and Leader of the Opposition Menachem Begin, dressed in a dark gray double-breasted suit, walked into the parliament building spoiling for a fight. He had not uttered a word of criticism against the prime minister and her government so long as the war raged, but now that it was over, the political gloves were off. Golda Meir had to be made to account to the nation why she had allowed a war to break out in the first place – a war that had sent two thousand, six hundred and eighty-eight Israeli soldiers to their graves.

At four o'clock that afternoon a press secretary poked his head through the door of the Knesset restaurant and shouted, "Begin's speaking," causing a stampede of parliamentary correspondents to pile out of the eatery, up the stairway and into the press gallery, where they peered down on the Opposition leader standing at the podium beginning to address a House crammed to the rafters. Usually, Mr. Begin delighted in dropping a cool nugget of irony into the most heated of debates, and then watching with satisfaction the resultant effervescence bubble and pop, but not today. Today was not a time for rhetorical antics. It was a time to be grim, lucid, terse, accusatory and, above all, to state the opposition case so unanswerably as to vanquish the government and compel it to resign.

Up in the press gallery foreign correspondents crowded around me, some kneeling, some sitting on the floor, scribbling furiously while straining to hear my stage-whispered, amateurish simultaneous translation above the amplified voice of the speaker. Menachem Begin was pointing an accusatory finger at the prime minister, who was sitting at the government table in the well of the chamber, shoulders hunched, face pale, her hair somewhat disheveled, surrounded by her brooding ministers, and all knowing what was about to come. What came was a growling Begin with a contemptuous eye, scornfully reproving:

"Did we, Madame Prime Minister, at noontime on Yom Kippur, have armor and infantry mobilized along the two fronts, north and south, ready to inflict a preemptive blow on the enemy? No, Madame, we did not! What did we have along those fronts?" He surveyed the House as if expecting an answer. "We had the finest and bravest troops any nation could wish for, but they were so thinly stretched, any preemptive action on their part would have been suicidal. Perhaps our Air Force might have been brought into play, but given the advanced weaponry at the enemy's command, their deadly ground-to-air missiles – the sams – plus their four thousand tanks and their multiple divisions poised to strike, it is unreasonable to assume our pilots could have prevented such a coordinated assault that had been so meticulously planned."

As he spoke, the packed assembly kept on shifting its gaze from his face to that of the prime minister's, like a crowd watching a tennis match.

"The question every household in Israel is asking," battered Begin in full stride, "is, why was it that between Rosh Hashanah and Yom Kippur you did not mobilize the reserves and move our armor forward? What prevented you, Madame Prime Minister, from taking this most elementary of precautionary measures? You knew well in advance of the massive Egyptian and Syrian preparations for an imminent attack, and yet you did not even admit this to your own government, and you overruled your own chief of staff when he wanted to stage a preemptive strike."

He abruptly dropped his voice from a high octave to a low one when he continued reasonably:

"Oh yes, I agree that to decide to launch such an all-out preemptive strike in such circumstances would, indeed, have been a momentous decision. One would have had to ponder it a thousand times. But with an enemy concentrating his forces before your very eyes" – again, he was up on the high ground, strident and harsh – "and still to do virtually nothing? And all the while, between Rosh Hashanah and Yom Kippur you were receiving confirmatory reports about those troop and weapon concentrations, yet you still did not take the most elementary precautions. How is this possible?"

He tossed up his arms in bafflement and stared hard at the premier and her cabinet ministers, searching their faces. Golda Meir sat there immersed in papers, as though engaged in other affairs. There was the blank, impassive face of Defense Minister Moshe Dayan, the intellectual, paunchy face of Foreign Minister Abba Eban, the closed expression of Deputy Prime Minister Yigal Allon; there were the veiled eyes of Minister without Portfolio Yisrael Galilee, whom some called Golda's Svengali; the sharp and intelligent eyes of Interior Affairs Minister Dr. Yosef Burg, and the shrewd and clever gaze of Finance Minister Pinchas Sapir – among others.

"Just imagine," said Begin to the people at that table, "and I say this with restrained yet indescribable frustration, that we had called out the reserves, say, four days before Yom Kippur, and at the same time moved our heavy weaponry forward. I'm speaking here of five hundred tanks to the Golan Heights and seven hundred to the Suez Canal, which would have still left us with an ample strategic reserve; just imagine those twelve hundred tanks readied in the north and in the south, the difference it would have made. One of two things would then have happened: either there would have been no war at all. Soviet spy satellites would have spotted our presence and Cairo and Damascus would have been forewarned by Moscow: 'Don't attack – the Jews are ready and waiting;' or, yes, the enemy would have attacked, but the Egyptians would never have gotten across the Canal, certainly not with seventy thousand infantry, nine hundred tanks and hundreds of artillery pieces. The Israel Defense Forces would have fulfilled its vow: 'They shall not pass!' and we would not have had to pull back in the north, abandoning almost half of the Golan Heights, creating an intolerable threat to the villages in the valley below. We would have smashed the Syrian assault just as we would have routed the Egyptian aggressors, because we would have had the means to do so."

Then, really letting go, he unleashed a mighty barrage with unreserved passion:

"But where, Madame Prime Minister, were those forces at noontime on Yom Kippur when our sworn enemies set out to destroy us? Where were those twelve hundred tanks? Where were their crews? Where were their gunners? I shall tell you where they were, Madame Prime Minister: the weapons were in the depots and the crews were at home."

At this, several scores of voices exploded in a tumult of resentment: "All right, all right. We know about that. Sit down. Enough!" And there were some voices that were raised almost to a squeal: "Stop the demagoguery! You don't know what you're talking about! You don't have all the facts! You're imagining things!"

"Am I? I don't think so," snapped Begin, his inflection sarcastic. And then, every word plainly enunciated, "What I'm asserting is that our ability to have blocked the enemy at the very outset is not a figment of my imagination. It is an objective fact. And the proof is that, despite our not having mobilized the reserves in time, despite our not having moved our tanks to the front in time, despite the appalling chaos, and despite the resultant logistical breakdowns, despite all of these terrible things, when the actual crunch came – and this I say to the everlasting credit of the IDF – our forces managed on both fronts, with that same approximate number of tanks, to trounce our enemies, grind them underfoot, and send them reeling."

Assured even more than before, his finger jabbing the air like a prosecutor scolding a witness, he admonished: "Yet, Madame Prime Minister, you did not mobilize our forces in time. You did not move our weaponry forward in time. So I am compelled to ask you, from whence this irresponsible flippancy? Why don't you just come out and openly admit to the nation that you made a mistake?"

Golda Meir looked up sharply, and returned Menachem Begin's gaze with hard, fearless eyes, as if to say, You know very well the reason why. You know very well my hands were tied by the Americans who told me in no uncertain terms not to fire the first shot, whose Intelligence was as misguided as our own, and who, therefore, warned us against full-scale mobilization for fear it might transform what appeared to be enemy training maneuvers into an enemy offensive assault.

But whether Menachem Begin knew this or not, he was not to be assuaged. He had reached the very pinnacle of his speech and having climbed there, his eyes still riveted on this old woman whose face was obdurate, he said to her in an almost intimate fashion, without malice or spite:

"Mrs. Meir, you know full well that a government which fails in a matter so fateful to the life of a nation – and certainly to our nation, surrounded by enemies bent on our destruction – such a government inevitably loses the trust of the people. So I ask you, by what moral authority do you stay in office after being responsible for such a misfortune? How can you possibly think you can continue to conduct the affairs of our nation in light of the fateful decisions that still lie ahead? I am compelled to say to you, not as a politician, not as a party member, but as a father and a grandfather, that I can no longer depend on your Government to ensure the future of my children and grandchildren. So, with all the respect and the regard I hold for you, I have to say to you, please go now – right now. Go to the president and hand him your resignation. You are duty-bound to do so in the name of truth. Please go!"

Cries of "Yes, yes! Resign! Resign!" rose from the opposition benches, but Prime Minister Golda Meir paid no heed to them. And when Menachem Begin stepped down from the podium and returned to his seat, the whole House in an uproar, she stared at him with disgust in her eyes as he passed her bench.

She was disgusted too, nay furious, at her fellow socialist comrades, leaders of European governments, who had refused to allow the fighter aircraft to land and refuel in their territories as part of the airlift which America was rushing through to replenish the crippling IDF losses. So she phoned Willie Brandt, Chancellor of West Germany and a highly respected leader of the Socialist International, to ask for a meeting of that body.

"I have no demands to make of any one of them," she told him stiffly. "I just want to talk to my friends, my fellow socialists. For my own good I want to know what possible meaning socialism can have when not a single socialist country in all of Europe was prepared to come to the aid of the only democratic nation in the Middle East. Is it possible that democracy and fraternity do not apply in our case? Anyhow, I want to hear for myself, with my own ears, what it was that kept the heads of these socialist governments from helping us."

In a word, she wanted to look them straight in the eye.

The requested conference convened in London shortly thereafter, and was attended by all the heads of socialist parties, those in government as well as those in parliamentary opposition. Having been the one to ask for the meeting, Golda was the first to speak. Rising to do so, she had to impose an iron control on herself: lifelong Labor Zionist that she was, she understood that she was about to face a moment of quintessential truth. Was the Jewish State a rightful member of this socialist fraternity, or was it irredeemably the odd state out in the family of nations?

She began by reminding her fellow socialists how Israel had been taken by surprise, fooled into misinterpreting Arab intentions, and how it had been touch and go for days until the enemy was driven back and the Jewish State emerged staggering but victorious.

And then she laid it on thick: "I just want to understand, truly understand, in light of what I have told you, what socialism is really about today. Here you are, all of you. Not one inch of your territory was put at our disposal for refueling the planes that saved us from destruction. Now suppose Richard Nixon had said, 'I'm sorry, but since we have nowhere to refuel in Europe, we just can't do anything for you, after all.' What would all of you have done then? You know us and who we are. We are all old comrades, long-standing friends. What do you think? On what grounds did you make your decisions not to let those planes refuel? Believe me, I am the last person to belittle the fact that we are only one tiny Jewish State and that there are over twenty Arab States with vast territories, endless oil, and billions of dollars. Of course you have your interests. But what I want to know from you today is whether these things are decisive factors in socialist thinking too?"

"Would anybody like the floor?" asked the chairman when Golda Meir sat down. Nobody did. The silence was palpable. It was broken only by a man's voice behind her who said audibly, "Of course they won't talk. They can't talk. Their throats are choked with oil."

"I never found out whose voice that was," she told a colleague on her return home. "I couldn't bring myself to turn my head and look at him for fear I might embarrass him. But that man, whose face I never saw, said it all."[31]

To which Menachem Begin, had he been present, might well have said, "Golda, old friend, welcome to the Jewish people."

Meanwhile, for all her disappointments and setbacks, Golda Meir had absolutely no intention of resigning. In her mind she still had work to do. Secretary of State Henry Kissinger was shuttling back and forth between Jerusalem and Cairo, and then between Jerusalem and Damascus, painstakingly hammering out separation-of-forces agreements and prisoner of war exchanges. Not only that, but Egypt was in such dire straits that the prospect of a diplomatic breakthrough toward peace seemed possible for the first time – and she wanted to be around if and when it happened.

So she carried on, and surprisingly to some, her Labor Party won the postwar general election – the election Golda Meir had told Oriana Fallaci would be her last. Labor was returned to office again, albeit with a reduced number of Knesset seats. Still, public doubt and criticism were growing over the very questions which Menachem Begin had raised in his Knesset speech: the mistaken Intelligence assessments, the failure to implement a full-scale mobilization in time, and the misplaced confidence in the ability of the IDF regular forces to hold the line while the reserves were being mobilized. Who was responsible for these fatal errors? The government, surely! More than that, the Yom Kippur War seemed to debunk the popular delusion that the spectacular victory of the Six-Day War was proof positive that the IDF was invincible. In Golda's mind it was. Israel's performance in the Yom Kippur War, she contended, exceeded its military successes in the Six-Day War. Many an expert tended to agree.

But, inevitably, once the electoral dust settled the public protests began in earnest, and what started as a one-man vigil outside the prime minister's office quickly burgeoned into mass, countrywide demonstrations as more and more reservists were demobilized and came home angry. It was an anger fueled by that matchless fury which Israelis reserve for their fallen idols. They were so angry, in fact, that in April 1974, following the findings of the inescapable inquiry commission, the once-indomitable

Golda Meir, the woman who was an epic embodiment of true legends and legendary truths, became so discredited in the eyes of her exhausted and grieving nation that she and her fellow ministers, morally crippled, were compelled to resign. In stepping down, the path was paved for Yitzhak Rabin to step up to the plate.

Prime Minister Yitzhak Rabin

First Term: 1974–1977

March 1 1922 – Born in Jerusalem.

1941 – Joins Palmach, the Hagana commando force.

1948 – Leads the Palmach 'Harel' Brigade in helping to smash the siege of Jerusalem.

1964 – Appointed Chief of Staff of the IDF.

1967 – Chief of Staff of the Six-Day War.

1968–1973 – Ambassador to Washington.

1974–1977 – Prime Minister.

Key Events of Prime Ministership

1975 – Negotiates through Kissinger interim agreement with Egypt entailing deep withdrawal in Sinai.

1976 – The Entebbe, Uganda, rescue operation.

1977 – Resigns because of his wife's illegal bank account.

1992 – Re-elected prime minister.

1995 – Assassinated by a Jewish extremist.

Prime Minister Yitzhak Rabin and Sec. of State Henry Kissinger
at a joint press conference, 12 July 1975

Chapter sixteen

The Instant Premier

Yitzhak Rabin had long wanted to go into politics, and less than a year had passed since his return from his Washington posting in the spring of 1973 when greatness was suddenly thrust upon him. His meteoric rise to the premiership, for which he was thoroughly unprepared, was due to the Labor Party's disarray, still reeling as it was from the near-fatal surprise attack of the Yom Kippur War, its gruesome cost, and Golda Meir's resignation. So the Party bosses scrambled around for a fresh face, one unblemished by the war, and by a process of elimination their gaze settled on him. Though still a political novice he seemed a fitting candidate: he was both a former IDF Chief of Staff and had been a highly effective ambassador to the United States, qualifications that gave him an intimate and intuitive knowledge of the country's two most vital preoccupations: national defense and relations with Washington. Besides, he was a *sabra* – born of the land – and people liked the idea of a native Israeli ascending to the prime ministership for the first time.

The one person to oppose him was his fellow Laborite Shimon Peres, a man as single-minded as himself, whom he had disliked and distrusted ever since their personal and professional clashes in the early sixties, when Rabin was an aspiring IDF general and Peres an exceptionally young director-general of the ministry of defense. Both were enormously competent, but their personalities and dispositions were so different that whenever they confronted each other in the political arena their disagreements became gladiatorial combats for influence and power. This was what happened now in the Labor Party's Central Committee, when Rabin beat his arch rival by a narrow margin of 298:254. Given his fellow contender's powerful showing, the new and inexperienced prime minister had no choice but to offer him the second most influential spot in the cabinet: minister of defense. It was an appointment the chagrined Rabin would regret as "an error whose price I would pay in full for a long time to come."[32]

Yitzhak Rabin took his prime ministerial oath of office on 3 June 1974, and soon afterwards invited a few of his old Washington hands to join his personal staff. He appointed me his adviser on Diaspora affairs as well as his English-language wordsmith. Hardly had we settled into our jobs when we were notified that President Nixon himself was planning a tour of the Middle East, accompanied by Secretary of State Henry Kissinger. No president of the United States had ever visited the Jewish State before, and the advance work this entailed was backbreaking.

"Never mind," said Rabin, at his first planning session. "It is a good opportunity for me, so soon after taking office, to talk to Nixon and Kissinger face-to-face about continuing the disengagement negotiations begun by Golda after the war, and to firm up Nixon's military supply commitments for the future. But if Nixon thinks his trip is going to wash away Watergate he'd better think again. That scandal will be waiting for him when he gets back to Washington, without a doubt."

Comments of a similar nature echoed among the crush of correspondents and photographers in the main dining hall of the King David Hotel some two weeks later, as they waited for Secretary of State Kissinger to show up for a press conference. What brought me there was not only the press conference, but also an old Washington friend by the name of Willie Fort whom I had arranged to meet in the coffee shop. Not finding him there I sauntered into the dining hall, which was laid out theater-style for the press conference, and bumped into a Bonn correspondent whom I vaguely remembered from my days in the foreign press bureau. He was arguing earnestly with a gum-chewing American journalist that, as a German, he could read Kissinger's mind better than any American.

"You don't say?" said the American snidely. "And what's your take on him today?"

"My take is that though Nixon has many pressing foreign policy headaches to deal with, and certainly enough to have kept him in Washington, here he is in the Middle East. I put this down to Kissinger. Of course Nixon took to the idea of coming here, because it distracts people's attention from Watergate. Besides, he wants to take credit for Kissinger's success in bringing about the military disengagements after the Yom Kippur War. But behind it all is Kissinger's thinking – to do something big here, really big – something truly global."

"Buster, to these people *everything* is global," scoffed the American. "When they look at the Middle East they see the Soviet Union before they see Israelis and Arabs. That's how they read maps. It's the Cold War, my friend."

"For Kissinger it's Metternich, too," said the German smugly.

"Who?"

"Metternich."

This was not the first time I had heard a Kissinger connoisseur draw a parallel between Prince Klemens von Metternich of Austria and the American secretary of state. Von Metternich was a brilliant and cunning nineteenth-century statesman whose diplomacy resembled the intricacies of a game of chess, and had played a decisive role in the Congress of Vienna, which essentially redrew Europe's political map after the Napoleonic Wars. Supposedly, Kissinger so admired Metternich that he modeled himself on him.

"So, what Metternich wizardry is Kissinger conjuring up now, wise guy?" asked the American.

"Kissinger has persuaded Nixon it's time to push the Russians out of the Middle East entirely," said the German. "He can only do that if he convinces the Arabs that Washington, not Moscow, has the ability to deliver Israel. America alone has the influence and the wherewithal to pressure Israel into giving back the territories the Arabs lost in the Six-Day War. If Kissinger succeeds in doing that the Arab world will automatically align itself with Washington. Then you would have here a *pax Americana* – America's domination of the whole of the Middle East. And that's a pure Metternich maneuver."

"Bullshit!" said the American. "Kissinger's a Jew. He lost God knows how many of his relatives in the Holocaust. Sure, he'll twist Israel's arm, but do you really think he's going to jeopardize the country's very existence to get the Russians out, which is what would happen if you're right? And even if Kissinger tried, Rabin wouldn't play ball. We saw in America how he tore the Rogers Plan to pieces. Besides, Rabin's the general who captured those territories in sixty-seven, and those territories are the one card he holds which the Arabs desperately want back. He'll give it back to them but only in return for something approximating peace. His doctrine is a piece of territory for a piece of peace – step-by-step. I've heard him say so umpteen times."

"Hi, Yehuda! Sorry I'm late."

It was Willie Fort, the man I had come to meet, pushing his way through the crowd. We grabbed a couple of chairs, took ourselves off to a corner by the door, and plunged into family news and politics.

Willie was about my age, in his mid-forties, but you would not have thought so by his looks. Short and chubby, he had a boyish face topped by jet black hair that flowed from a center parting and glistened like shining glass, a bit like Bob Hope. There was mirth in his clever eyes, and his wardrobe – he habitually sported extravagantly patterned suits over flashy shirts and flamboyant ties – exuded an irrepressible bonhomie.

Given my new position as adviser on Diaspora affairs, Professor William Fort was a good man to know. He was on intimate terms with all sorts of Washington grandees, and was also a prominent leader of his community. He was active in the United Jewish Appeal, Israel Bonds, and was a generous contributor to Israeli cultural causes. He had a reputation as an exceptionally gifted psychiatrist, with a professorship at Johns Hopkins University and an affluent practice in Georgetown, favored, so it was whispered, by White House neurotics and fashionable hostesses with hyphenated names.

Our chitchat was interrupted by a newspaperman standing close by, who suddenly called out in a most rascally fashion, "Here he comes – it's King K. himself."

Television lights from the mezzanine balcony overlooking the marble lobby bathed the place in a luminescent glow as an armored limousine with a gold-tasseled American flag drew up. Out of it emerged Secretary of State Henry Kissinger, surrounded by a phalanx of security. He blew in like a cyclone, exuding immense authority, and the guests in the roped-off lobby applauded while cameramen and photographers filmed and clicked as he, half-smiling, waved back over the heads of his bodyguards.

Mounting the dais, he said in his famous Bavarian accent, "I have no opening statement, so let's get straight to the questions."

A dozen hands shot up and multiple voices barked questions. The most strident, clearly Californian, asked: "Mr. Secretary, would you not say that President Nixon is a damaged leader, seeking to trump Watergate by coming here to the Middle East and thereby escape his crisis back home by trying to project an image of a confident world statesman – and all in an effort to keep himself in office?"

Everybody began scribbling as the secretary of state shot back, "President's Nixon's visit to the Middle East is a political event of the highest magnitude. The president has proven beyond doubt that he is indispensable as a peacemaker in this region. His administration's accomplishments in helping to broker disengagement agreements, both on the Egyptian and the Syrian fronts after the Yom Kippur War, open up the long road to a permanent settlement. This is why – "

The Californian broke in: "But how can he focus on these momentous issues when he's facing possible impeachment back home? He's fighting for his presidential life."

Kissinger ignored the interruption and pointed to another questioner, but before he could open his mouth Kissinger swung back, aimed an accusing finger at the Californian, and snapped: "It seems to me that your question is more a media fixation than a presidential preoccupation. Wherever the president has traveled this last week and more" – he ticked off the names: Egypt, Saudi Arabia, Syria, Israel – "he has been received with enormous enthusiasm, as those of you who have been traveling with us can testify."

"There wasn't much evidence of that in Damascus," growled the Californian in a stage whisper.

"That's because you didn't see what happened at the Damascus airport when President Nixon said goodbye to President Assad," answered Kissinger, a sudden smile sneaking across his face. "The Syrian president kissed him on both cheeks, which is an extraordinarily important gesture in Arab culture, all the more so coming from one with a reputation of being the leading anti-American firebrand of the Arab world."[33]

Chuckles rippled across the hall.

"Mr. Secretary" – this from the German correspondent – "it is said a diplomatic tilt is taking place here in the Middle East."

"It depends on what you mean by tilt. What's your question?"

"Is the tilt in favor of the Arabs, and will it have a long-term impact on the outcome of the Israel-Arab conflict?"

It was clear that the secretary of state liked the question. He leaned leisurely against the podium, dusted his hands, pursed his lips as if to gather his thoughts, and in an authoritative fashion proclaimed, "Until six or seven months ago, the Middle East was polarized between the Arab world and Israel. Every tension in this region had the insoluble quality of a superpower confrontation. The Arab states were backed by the Soviet Union and Israel by the United States. This is no longer the case. Now, a diplomatic turn has taken place. Without giving up our traditional friendship and support for Israel, we, the United States, have moved into a position where we can be helpful to all parties in a negotiation process. And because of this shift – or what you call a tilt – the Arab countries are reconsidering their previous one-sided alliance with one country alone."

"Meaning the Soviet Union?"

"Exactly! The disengagement negotiations initiated by the United States after the Yom Kippur War, which have culminated in President Nixon's current visit, are an affirmation of a dramatic reversal in the historic evolution of this area. The United States has now begun a relationship with all the countries in the region, not based on the exigencies of a particular crisis but on the basis of a long-term strategy of peace, prosperity, and progress. President Nixon's visit has served to crystallize this direction. If we can stay this course by continuing the negotiation process, step by step – and we all know this is a very tricky and complicated part of the world – it could mark a historic turning point in the direction of a general peace, with America serving as honest broker."[34]

All the ensuing answers were amplifications of this premise, and when the secretary of state stepped down and made his way back toward the lobby, Willie Fort, standing amid the crush, pressed forward against the velvet rope barrier and called out to him as he passed, "Heinz! Heinz!"

Caught off guard, Kissinger halted mid-stride, and momentarily stared at Willie.

Singularly excited, Willie shouted with a beaming smile and an outstretched hand, "Heinz – recognize me? Wilhelm Furtwangler from Furth. Remember?"

The secretary of state flushed, threw Willie a contemptuous look, and strode on. His bodyguards, too, eyed Willie as if he was diseased, and shouldered him out of the way.

"What on earth was that about?" I asked Willie, flabbergasted.

White as a shroud, Willie seemed about to answer, but did not. Instead, he shook his head, smiled glumly to himself, and skulked off toward the coffee shop.

"What did you tell Kissinger your name was?" I asked, pulling up a chair.

Stoutly, as if testifying before a court of law, he replied, "My name is Wilhelm Furtwangler from Furth, Bavaria, the same place Heinz Kissinger comes from. We were at school together. My family escaped Germany and got to America in thirty-seven, his in thirty-eight. We were both fifteen. We settled in Washington Heights on Manhattan's Upper West Side, where there were so many German Jewish refugees they called it the Fourth Reich. We went to the same school, George Washington High, and prayed at the same shul, Rabbi Breuer's, very orthodox."

I swallowed. "But there's absolutely nothing German about you. You're as Yankee as baseball."

His mouth spread into a thin-lipped smile. "Me, a Yankee? I'm a German refugee kid in disguise, you jerk. I've been working at it all my life."

"Then how come Kissinger has such a heavy accent and you've got none?"

"Because as a kid Heinz was shy and a bit withdrawn, and any speech therapist will tell you that shyness inhibits the ability to mimic, and you have to be a mimic like me to acquire accent-free fluency. Our indefatigable English teacher at George Washington High, Miss Bachman, tried with endless patience to rid Heinz of his Bavarian accent. 'Henry, you have a chronic English-language speech disability,' mimicked Willie impersonating Miss Bachman's schoolmarm's wheedling voice. 'You must try harder to Americanize it.'"

"So when did Furtwangler become Fort?" I asked.

"The day I graduated medical school. It was an obvious choice."

To prove it he formed his mouth into an oval and, with a long, drawn-out breath, exhaled the name F-U-R-T-W-A-N-G-L-E-R, and then 'F-U-R-T-H,' each time exaggerating the guttural 'R' and the spiked umlaut.

"Get it? Wilhelm Furtwangler from Furth morphs into Willie Fort from Washington."

As he acted out this nomenclature I tried to rethink his life story, and he, as if reading my mind, said with amused contempt, "And now Heinz is the American secretary of state. When Nixon appointed him in seventy-three, I sent him a congratulatory note with an old photo of him holding up the football I'd given him for his bar mitzvah. He was crazy about football as a kid. But do you think he acknowledged it? Not a chance!"

"Were you that close as boys?"

A glint of fond reminiscence entered his eyes and he chuckled at the thought of it: "There was no one closer. Even though he was a bit of a bookworm and I wasn't, we had great times together. We sometimes even got our ears boxed for fooling around."

"And what happened when the Nazis came?"

Willie let the reminiscences flow like unstoppable water through the cracks of a dam: "When the Nazis came our neighbors told our parents not to worry: Hitler was just another anti-Semitic street brawler disseminating mad propaganda, best ignored. But gradually they changed their tune and said, look at the good things Hitler was doing for Germany. And soon after that we weren't allowed to play with their children anymore, and Heinz's father lost his prestigious job as a State school teacher, and we were expelled from the State-run high school and had to go to a special Jewish school, and we weren't allowed to go to football matches, so we set up our own soccer team, and we weren't allowed to go to the municipal swimming pool, and we weren't allowed to go anywhere where it said '*Juden Verboten!*' And the Gestapo came banging on our doors, and the Hitler Youth beat us up. And so we ran away until we reached America."

Gripped with such dark memories, Willie's usually bright demeanor slumped into melancholy. He rose and said, "I need fresh air. I'm going for a walk."

Outside, the ceaseless hum of traffic along King David Street was punctuated by the sharp tongue of an angry cab driver shouting at an Israeli security guard whose car was occupying his spot in the hotel's taxi rank. Two other taxi drivers, ignoring the row, were idly playing cards, while well-dressed, muscular American security agents with crewcuts lolled about the driveway, maintaining a watch.

"Let's walk," said Willie, as if hoping the breeze and the sun would wash away the brooding hurt. But since I had nothing worthy to say he had only his pain for company. He took a seat on a bench overlooking the Old City walls, and said contemplatively, "It's so complicated, so very complicated."

"What is?"

"Kissinger. He's trying so hard to repress his feelings, he's obsessed by them. The years of Nazi persecution are locked deep inside him."

There was an expression of sympathy in Willie Fort's voice intermingled with a sort of frustration, which explained itself when he added, "I'm speaking professionally, as a psychiatrist. I believe he needs help."

"What sort of help?"

"Psychiatric help. There are basic tensions in that man's psyche which influence how he perceives the world and, consequently, how he arrives at his decisions. There's no separating his personality from his policies."

This was an intriguing and unsettling thought, so I asked Willie to elaborate.

"By all means," he said. "I shall offer you an off-the-peg, extemporaneous psychoanalysis of Henry-Heinz Kissinger, based on reliable hearsay

and anecdotal observations, and shared by many of my professional colleagues. You might wish to write some of this down. It could be of interest
to your prime minister."

I took out my pen and prepared to write.

Henry Kissinger, he said, habitually insisted he had no lasting memories of his childhood persecutions in Germany. This was nonsense! In 1938,
when Jews were being beaten and murdered in the streets, and his family
had to flee for their lives, he was at the most impressionable age of fifteen.
At that age he would have remembered everything: his feelings of insecurity,
the trauma of being expelled, of not being accepted; what it meant to lose
control of one's life, to be powerless, to see one's beloved heroes suddenly
helpless, overtaken by brutal events, most notably his father, whom he
greatly admired and who was expelled from his prestigious teaching post,
leaving the family devastated. Those demons would never leave Henry
Kissinger, however hard he tried to drown them in self-delusion.

Outwardly, the secretary of state presented an image of self-assurance, strong will, and arrogance, Willie went on. Inwardly, however, because
of his suppressed emotions and state of denial, he was possessed of a deeply
depressive disposition, an apocalyptic view of life, a tendency to paranoia,
and an excessive sense of failure when things did not go his way. Typically,
such inner doubts triggered displays of petulance, tantrums, and temper.
Persons of such a nature were invariably overly solicitous of their superiors
and overly harsh toward their subordinates. They had an excessive need to
be loved and admired, and an extreme ambition to excel.

Henry Kissinger's Jewishness was equally a source of neurosis,
according to Willie Fort. Reared as a deeply observant Jew, Kissinger
slipped away from beneath the Orthodox shadow of his parental home
when he was drafted into the American army in 1943. His rebellion was
absolute and his assimilation total. Yet, try as he might, Henry Kissinger
would never be able to shed his thin Jewish refugee skin.

Willie emitted a sudden cynical laugh, and observed, "I've learned
through the White House grapevine that whenever Nixon feels Kissinger
is getting too big for his boots he is not averse to resorting to nasty anti-
Semitic barbs to cut him down to size. He has even been known to call him
'my Jew boy' to his face. And he takes a perverse satisfaction in humiliating
and taunting him with anti-Semitic slurs about how the Jews put Israel's
interests ahead of America's, and how cliquey they are, wielding far too
much power because of their wealth, and too much influence because of
their control of the media, things like that. It is said that Kissinger is careful

not to bring Jewish staff members to meetings with the President for fear of arousing his anti-Semitic streak. And when it *is* aroused he pretends to shrug it off, concealing his humiliation, but then, back in the privacy of his room, he invariably goes into a tantrum and takes it out on his subordinates."

"So how does this impact on his role as mediator between us and the Arabs?" I asked.

"People like him invariably over-compensate. They go to great lengths to subdue whatever emotional bias they might feel, and lean over backward in favor of the other side to prove they are being even-handed and objective." And having said that, Willie sprang suddenly to his feet, his old buoyant self again, and strolling back to the hotel rounded off his extemporaneous diagnosis thus: "What happened in the King David lobby suggests that our brilliant American secretary of state – forty-fourth in line since Thomas Jefferson – behaved in a neurotic fashion. One minute he was glorying in the world's spotlight at his press conference, and the next, when he saw me, he was hurtled back into Jewish memories he'd spent a lifetime trying to suppress. He certainly recognized me. You noted how he bridled at my mention of his name, Heinz. He utterly despised me for that. So yes, I have to conclude that the man is disturbed. Tell Yitzhak Rabin he should be most wary in dealing with our secretary of state. Tell him that deep inside him is an insecure and paranoid Jew."

A few hours later Air Force One lifted off from Ben-Gurion Airport carrying the president and his secretary of state back home to Washington – and to Watergate. After seeing them off with all due ceremony, Prime Minister Rabin traveled back to Jerusalem to hold a press conference of his own at the King David Hotel, where he assessed the positive significance of the visit and the boost it had given to the U.S.-Israeli relationship.

Asked by the German correspondent what, in his view, had brought about the Arab tilt toward Washington and away from Moscow, Rabin answered categorically: "The reason is President Nixon's policy of keeping Israel strong, by giving us the means to defend ourselves by ourselves. Ever since the airlift of the Yom Kippur War, the Arabs have come to understand that America will not allow Israel to be weakened. A defeat of Israel is a victory for the USSR. Paradoxically, this is what has raised America's prestige in the Arab world, and has given Washington leverage. Today in the Middle East, Moscow is a synonym for instability and war, Washington for stability and negotiation."

"But is there not a negative aspect to this change from your standpoint?" asked a reporter from the *New York Times*.

"What sort of negative aspect?"

"A few hours ago, in this very room, Dr. Kissinger told us that America no longer stands exclusively on the side of Israel. Does that not do something to diminish the U.S.-Israel relationship?"

"The opposite is true," contended Rabin. "Not only have the relations not been diminished, our friendship and cooperation have grown." But then he paused, and after a moment's reflection, added with his typical candor: "I must confess it is only natural that in certain aspects there is concern for the loss of the pre–Yom Kippur War exclusivity in the Israel-U.S. relationship. But we have to acknowledge that we are living in changed circumstances, and it is impossible to remain oblivious to those changes. So now we must seek the greatest possible benefit from them. This means our ability to utilize the closer Arab association with the United States in order to initiate new political movement toward a peace, with America serving as an honest broker. This can't be done by a single act such as a peace conference. It is a phased, patient, step-by-step process."[35]

It pleased Rabin shortly thereafter to hear from Kissinger that President Nixon had said much the same in a letter to President Sadat, penned on 25 June, shortly after his visit to Cairo, in which he wrote:

> …As a result of our talks each of us has a better understanding of the other's concerns, hopes and political realities. I particularly welcomed the opportunity to describe to you our concept of approaching a final settlement step-by-step, so that each succeeding step will build on the confidence and experience gained in the preceding one…. Mr. President, I am convinced that we have witnessed in recent months a turning point in the history of the Middle East – a turning toward an honorable, just, an endurable peace – and have ushered in a new era in U.S.-Arab relations. A direction has been set, and it is my firm intention to stay on the course we have charted.[36]

But the American people had other ideas for President Nixon's course for the future. Even as he was putting his signature to this diplomatic note in the privacy of his Oval office, the House Judiciary Committee was conducting public impeachment proceedings against him on Capitol Hill. And the deeper the committee probed, the deeper Mr. Nixon ensnared himself in his Watergate morass, so that by the end of August he threw in the towel and did what no other American President had ever done before: he resigned.

Vice President Gerald Ford entered the White House in Nixon's stead, and being a total neophyte in international affairs, he promptly picked up the phone to Dr. Kissinger, and said, "Henry, I need you. The country needs you. I want you to stay. I'll do everything I can to work with you."

"I thank you for the trust you place in me, Mr. President," answered an elated secretary of state, and when he replaced the receiver he felt more alive than he had ever felt before, knowing that he was now virtually sovereign in setting the course of American foreign policy.[37]

One of his first acts was to recommend to President Ford that he invite Prime Minister Rabin to Washington to discuss the next step.

Chapter seventeen

Yeduha

The prime minister and his advisers arrived in the American capital on 10 September 1974, and the talks generally went well. All agreed that a comprehensive settlement was too utopian to contemplate at this stage, and that the best way forward was to continue the step-by-step approach. Rabin, however, expressed one important reservation. He told Ford and Kissinger, "I'm facing considerable criticism back home regarding my step-by-step approach, not least from the leader of our opposition, Mr. Begin. Begin argues that withdrawals without peace ruin the very chances of peace. Peace, he contends, will be advanced only when we adopt a policy that leads to overall serious peace commitments, not mere disengagements or partial settlements. I take serious note of this. If we go ahead giving up a piece of land without getting a piece of peace in return, we'll end up squandering everything without gaining anything. Hence, it is imperative that any future step of withdrawal on our part be recompensed by a political step toward peace on the part of the Egyptians."

The president and the secretary of state had no argument with that, and it was decided that Kissinger would soon revisit the region to examine the feasibility of this course.

Rabin's Washington visit ended in the grandest of styles. President Ford – a tall, affable, athletic-looking fellow in his early sixties – hosted an official state banquet in his honor. It was a sumptuous and extravagant affair that took place in the State banqueting hall. From his gilded frame above the fireplace Abraham Lincoln looked down on more than two hundred black-tied and opulently gowned guests sitting at round tables in the historic room, as exalted as a museum gallery that emanated power, influence, and fortune. Elongated amber mirrors reflected the enormous, shimmering brass chandelier at the ceiling's center, casting a pleasing flaxen light over the entire setting. Two ushers opened double doors and heralded the entry of twenty violinists, all attired in the crimson dress uniform of the Marines Corps. Two by two, their bows rising and falling in perfect synchronization, they advanced down the center aisle playing an emotive medley of Israeli tunes. An embossed card present at each table explained that these musicians belonged to the strings section of the Marine Chamber Orchestra which, itself, was a part of the famed Marine Band, America's oldest musical organization, established by an Act of Congress in 1798, and traditionally called "The President's Own."

A tableau of animated faces watched President Ford rise to welcome his guests and to say to Rabin by way of introduction, "As I was sitting here chatting with you and Mrs. Rabin, I couldn't help but note that nineteen forty-eight was a somewhat significant year as far as your country is concerned. And it just so happens, it was quite a year for the Fords, too. It was the year we got married."

"So did we," called out Leah Rabin, to laughter and applause.

Toasts followed a predictable script, host and guest of honor lauding each other's enduring friendship, eternal alliance, and common values, after which, at an unseen signal, liveried butlers fanned out across the room, each bearing feasts of roasted pheasant, sizzling roast potatoes, and decorative garnished beans. Soon, everybody was chomping on their succulent fare except me. I had pre-ordered a vegetarian kosher dish which, for some reason, tarried. Perhaps it was because my place card had been misspelled: instead of "Yehuda" it was engraved "Yeduha Avner."

A couple of chairs away the Chairman of the Joint Chiefs of Staff, General George Brown, was chatting with Barbara Walters, the famous television celebrity, who was sitting on my right. Within minutes, the general caught sight of my still-empty place setting and, craning his neck to note my name card, boomed, "Yeduha, not eating with us tonight?" Whereupon, as if on cue, a butler stepped forward and placed before me a vegetarian extravaganza consisting of a base of lettuce as thick as a Bible, on top of which sat a mound of diced fruit, on top of that a glob of cottage cheese, and on top of that a swish of whipped cream, so that the whole thingamajig

White House dinner invitation

Table card for Yeduha

must have stood about a foot high. In contrast to everybody else's deep brown roasted pheasant, it glittered and sparkled like a firework.

Gasps of admiration greeted this fiesta of color, and Barbara Walters began to applaud. This attracted the attention of President Ford who, half rising to see what the commotion was about, whispered something into Yitzhak Rabin's ear, who whispered something back into his. Then, rising to his full height and grinning from ear to ear, the president raised his glass high and called out to me with an overflow of well-being, "Happy birthday young fella! Let's sing a toast to our birthday boy."

With that, the entire banqueting hall rose to its feet and, goblets aloft, chorused a hearty, "Happy birthday dear Yeduha." And as they sang I slouched sheepishly further into my chair, mortified.

In the ballroom after dinner I asked Rabin why on earth he had told the President it was my birthday, and he shot back, "What else should I have told him – the truth? If I did that, tomorrow there'd be a headline in the newspapers that you ate kosher and I didn't, and the religious parties will bolt the coalition, and I'll have a government crisis on my hands. *Ani meshuga?* Am I crazy?" And then, with a sudden startled gaze, "Oh my God, look at that! What am I supposed to do now? Save me somebody!"

He was watching as a beaming President Ford swept Leah Rabin onto the brightly lit ballroom floor and waltzed her around to general applause, while an expectant First Lady Barbara Ford flashed a smile at Rabin, awaiting his invitation to follow suit. With nowhere to run he grimly made his way toward Mrs. Ford as if walking the plank, bowed awkwardly, and croaked, "Please forgive me, I can't do it."

"Can't do what?"

"Can't dance."

"Can't dance?" The woman seemed astounded, as if she had never heard of such a thing.

"Not a step," blushed the prime minister. "I'll be treading on your toes all the while. I've tried it before. I'm no good at it."

"Have no fear, Mr. Prime Minister," chortled a buoyant Mrs. Ford, taking him by the hand and leading him onto the ballroom floor. "When I was younger I used to teach dance, and I protected my toes from men far less skillful than you. Now this is how you do it: put your hand here. That's right. And your other hand here. Very good! And now relax, and let's go: one-two-three; one-two-three; one-two-three. Excellent! You're doing fine, getting the hang of it!" and she rotated the crimson-faced premier around and around, he staring fixedly at the First Lady's toes until

Dr. Kissinger – himself no swinger – tapped him on the shoulder, and said in deadly seriousness, "Yitzhak, give up while you're ahead. Let me take over. Mrs. Ford, may I have this dance?"

"By all means," said she, letting go of Rabin, who tottered toward his chuckling staffers, muttering, "If Henry Kissinger does nothing else for Israel but save me from that embarrassment I shall be forever in his debt."

A few months later, in March 1975, Secretary of State Kissinger returned to the Middle East to test the political waters, embarking on a remarkable odyssey unheard of in international relations. It was dubbed shuttle diplomacy – a whirlwind, improvised to and fro between Egypt and Israel to badger Rabin and Sadat into negotiating the next step. In a marathon schedule that created convoluted complications of timing, Kissinger would arrive in Jerusalem at abnormal hours of the day and depart for Cairo at eccentric hours of the night. He flitted back and forth in an antiquated Boeing 707 which had been Lyndon Johnson's plane when he was Kennedy's vice president.

Since the talks were held at all hours of the day and the night, and frequently in haste, people's nerves easily frayed. Rabin soon felt he was being unduly pressured, sensing that Kissinger was cajoling him into accepting an IDF withdrawal in Sinai deeper than he was prepared to concede in return for an Egyptian step toward peace smaller than he was ready to accept. In short, he felt Henry Kissinger was seeking a deal at almost any price to demonstrate to the Egyptian president that America alone could deliver Israel.

The indefatigable secretary of state conjured up concessions and trade-offs, wheedling, rhapsodizing, hectoring, threatening, and sometimes going out of his way to charm his hosts with jokes against himself as a means of relaxing tensions. At one such session a furious row broke out over Rabin's incessant insistence that Sadat give him something politically substantial in return for a sizeable IDF withdrawal in Sinai, just as he had advocated in Washington. He wanted the Egyptian president to commit himself once and for all to a "termination of the state of belligerency" with the Jewish State.

"Sadat will never accept such language," flared Kissinger. "It would be tantamount to his acknowledging the end of the state of war while your army still occupies huge swathes of his territory. The furthest I might persuade him to go is a commitment to the 'non-use of force' in return for your IDF pull-back." But Rabin refused to budge, and his obduracy drove

Kissinger berserk. The ever-composed Joe Sisco, Kissinger's chief deputy, proposed a recess, and the legal advisers were brought in to try and come up with some ingenious linguistic compromise. While they were at it, Kissinger, poking fun at himself in an effort to reduce tensions, said, "Yitzhak, you have to understand that since English is my second language I may not always grasp its nuances. When I arrived in America it took me a while before I understood that maniac and fool were not terms of endearment. And, only recently, I offered to teach English to the Syrian President Hafez al-Assad. I told him, if you would allow me to teach you the language, you would be the first Arab leader to speak English with a German accent."

Such self-effacing wit – something Rabin himself did not possess – did succeed in bringing temperatures down, and the talks resumed in a less heated spirit.

In those shuttle days, the media could not get enough of Henry Kissinger. Headlines catapulted him to superstardom, crediting him with the ability to perform deeds unheard of in contemporary diplomacy. This man crafted the doctrine of detente with the USSR, nudged Moscow to the arms control negotiation table, paved the way for Nixon to China, brokered the first disengagement deal between Egypt and Israel, and then between Syria and Israel after the Yom Kippur War, and coerced Hanoi into the Paris peace talks, opening up the prospect of an honorable U.S. exit from Vietnam.

Wherever he traveled, the international press followed in droves. The most privileged were the "Kissinger 14" – so nicknamed because they were the senior Washington correspondents for whom the fourteen seats in the extreme rear section of the secretary's aging aircraft were reserved. And though having to put up with much discomfort in flight, they alone were privy to the secretary's midair, off-the-record, not-for-attribution deep briefings, given under the thin disguise of a "senior official." These fourteen were more familiar with Kissinger's inner thoughts than most of the Israeli officials who dealt directly with him. This I knew because I was acquainted with most of the "14" from my Washington and foreign press bureau days, and occasionally pumped them for information myself.

Late one night, seven of the "14" straggled into the King David Hotel's coffee shop, where I was passing the time with other correspondents. They had just arrived with Kissinger from Cairo for the umpteenth time (the shuttle had begun on 8 March and this was 21 March). They were NBC's Richard Valeriani, ABC's Ted Koppel, CBS's Bernard Kalb, the *Washington Post's* Marlyn Berger, the *New York Time's* Bernard Gwertzman, *Time's* Jerrold Schecter, and *Newsweek's* Bruce van Voorst. All had the jet-lagged, haggard look of long-distance flyers. As they shuffled in, bleary-eyed and weary, the jaded correspondents already slouching in the coffee shop, bored for lack of news, offered them their chairs in the hope of picking their brains. I, too, was intent on acquiring information, with the aim of passing on to Rabin whatever useful tidbits might come my way.

One lean Londoner from the *Daily Telegraph*, spotting a badge on Richard Valeriani's lapel, called out, "Hey Dick, what's that badge you're wearing?"

The tall, gangling NBC man responded by throwing him a mischievous grin, and turned to all corners of the room so that all present could clearly see his lapel, onto which a campaign-style button was pinned. All were in fits of laughter as they read: *"FREE THE KISSINGER 14."*

This show of camaraderie triggered colossal applause, and as it soared a fellow with a camera clicked and shouted, "Hey, you '14,' is it true that King K. has confided to you, not for attribution, that President Ford is alive and well after all, but he's just fast asleep?" Another wisecracked: "And is it true that Mr. Fix-it spills you '14' so many beans his plane is flying on natural gas?" And a third called out, simply, "Will there be an agreement, yes or no?"

A different pitch then took hold as the other journalists crowded around the seven, pressing them with specific questions: Was Rabin truly refusing to surrender the Mitla and Gidi passes in the Sinai desert? Was he still insisting on his "termination of belligerency" formula in return for a deep withdrawal? Was Kissinger truly threatening to fly back to Washington if Rabin refused to compromise, blaming Israel for the failure of his mission?

The overwrought tone of these questions faithfully reflected the mood pervading the smoke-filled conference room at the prime minister's office, with exhausted negotiators vainly seeking to break the impasse into which they had floundered. When I entered, Henry Kissinger was shoving a map across the table at the prime minister, and grumbling, "For God's sake, Yitzhak, draw me a final line to show how far you are prepared to pull back in Sinai. Whenever I go to Sadat, he's ready with his answers on the spot!"

Rabin, with deliberate emphasis, responded, "Henry, unlike Egypt, Israel is a democracy. I will not be dictated to. Those passes hold the key to an Egyptian invasion of Israel. You will get the final line only after I get final approval from the cabinet."

"And how long will that take?" asked Kissinger scornfully.

"The last cabinet session lasted ten hours," returned Rabin, provocatively.

Kissinger threw down his pen. "You know what? I no longer care. Do with the map whatever you want."

There was a sudden silence: no movement, not even the whisper of a sound, until the door gently opened and in walked an American security agent. He approached the secretary of state reverentially, and whispered, "You left these in the car, sir."

He was holding a pair of spectacles.

Kissinger glowered at him in contempt, as if to say, how dare you approach the secretary of state without permission?

Humiliated, the security agent froze, the spectacles in his hand, not knowing what to do with them. U.S. Ambassador Kenneth Keating came to his aid by relieving him of the glasses, leaning across the table to hand them to Joseph Sisco who, in turn, handed them to Dr. Kissinger. The hierarchy of protocol thus preserved, the secretary pocketed his spectacles, gathered up his papers, muttered, "I'm off" and moved toward the door, his features downcast, knowing his mission had failed.

"Henry!"

It was the charged, deep voice of Yitzhak Rabin.

Kissinger turned. The two men's eyes locked.

"You know very well we have offered a compromise at every step along the way," fumed Rabin. "You know we have agreed to adopt your language on the 'non-use of force,' which means much less than a 'termination of belligerency.' You know we have agreed to hand over the Sinai oil fields. You know we have agreed, in principle, to pull back as far as the eastern end of the passes. You know we have agreed to allow the Egyptian army to advance from its present positions and occupy the buffer zone. And you know we have agreed that they may set up two forward positions at the western entrances to the passes. After all this display of goodwill and flexibility for the sake of the success of your mission – and at great risk to ourselves – to then accuse us of causing the failure of your mission, instead of laying the blame on Sadat's intransigence, is a total distortion of the facts."

Kissinger listened, turned, and without another word walked out of the room. The Israeli negotiating team – which included Defense Minister Shimon Peres, Foreign Minister Yigal Allon, and Ambassador Simcha Dinitz – exchanged shocked looks. Instantly, Rabin picked up a phone and instructed his assistant to call the cabinet into emergency session. In the course of that session, a courier arrived with an urgent message from President Gerald Ford. Rabin read out the message to his ministers. It said:

Kissinger has notified me of the forthcoming suspension of his mission. I wish to express my profound disappointment over Israel's attitude during the course of the negotiations. From our conversations, you know the great importance I attached to the success of the United States' efforts to achieve an agreement. Kissinger's mission, encouraged by your Government, expresses vital United States interests in the region. Failure of the negotiations will have a far-reaching impact on the region and on our relations. I have given instructions for a reassessment of United States policy in the region, including our relations with Israel, with the aim of ensuring that our overall American interests are protected.[38]

This was about as brutal a message as diplomatic dispatches get, and the cabinet ministers listened to it in dry-throated silence, weighing each word with the same intensity that its author had put into its drafting. There was no doubt in Rabin's mind who that author was, just as his ministers had no doubt that it heralded the gravest of possible crises between the two countries. Gloomily they discussed consequences, and they were in the midst of their pessimistic assessments when an assistant entered to inform the prime minister that Kissinger was on the line asking if he could come over right away.

Rabin received him in his inner sanctum, where the secretary of state, breathing heavily, tried hard to retain his composure.

"Yitzhak, I want you to know I had nothing to do with the President's message," he said.

Rabin, lighting a cigarette, glared at him through the flame of his lighter, and said, "Henry, I don't believe you. You asked the President to send that message. You dictated it yourself."

Kissinger, shocked, began shouting, "How dare you suggest such a thing? Do you think the president of the United States is a puppet and I pull his strings?"

Rabin did not answer. He just stood there in stony silence.

Kissinger, beside himself with frustration and rage, yelled, "You don't understand, I'm trying to save you. The American public won't stand for this. You are making me, the secretary of state of the United States of America, wander around the Middle East like a Levantine rug merchant. And for what – to bargain over a few hundred meters of sand in the desert? Are you out of your mind? I represent America. You are losing the battle of American public opinion. Our step-by-step doctrine is being throttled. The

United States is losing control of events. There will be insurmountable pressure to convene a Geneva conference with Russia sharing the chair. A war might break out, the Russians are going to come back in, and you'll have to fight without an American military airlift because the American public won't support one." Then, tantrum full-blown: "I warn you, Yitzhak, you will yet be responsible for the destruction of the third Jewish commonwealth."

Rabin, red in the face, hurled back, "And I warn you, Henry, you will be judged not by American history but by Jewish history!"

The following morning the two men – longtime friends and longtime adversaries – closeted themselves in a room at Ben-Gurion airport and, according to what Rabin later told us, had an extremely emotional exchange. Rabin once again told Kissinger exactly what he felt – that though he fully realized the new situation could deteriorate into war, Israel could compromise no further. This was not just a matter of acute political consequence to him as prime minister, but, equally, of acute anxiety to him as a man, for he felt personally responsible for every IDF soldier, as though they were his sons. Indeed, at that very moment his own son was serving on Sinai's front line, in command of a tank platoon, as was his daughter's husband, who commanded a tank battalion, and he knew what their fate might be in the event of war.

"And how did Kissinger react to that?" we asked him.

"I've never seen him so moved," responded Rabin. "He may have wished to reply but his voice was so cracked with emotion he couldn't. It was time to go out to his plane where we both were to make brief farewell statements. When it came to his turn he was so full of emotion he could hardly speak. Besides being upset at the failure of his mission I could see his inner turmoil, as a Jew and as an American."[39]

Once airborne, the secretary of state made his way to the rear of his aircraft to brief the "14," as was his wont. He told them, 'not for attribution,' that Israel was to blame for the breakdown of the negotiations; that the failure of his mission would inevitably radicalize the Middle East; that war was now likely and, with it, an oil embargo; that the Egyptian and Syrian post–Yom Kippur War disengagement agreements would collapse; that the mandate of the United Nations forces deployed under those agreements would not be renewed; that Russia would replace America and again become the dominant force in the Middle East; that Europe would turn its back totally on Israel; that Russia and the Arabs would rush to convene an international conference at Geneva, leaving America without a policy and Israel without an ally; and that American public opinion would swing against Israel for having squandered the one chance of an interim agreement – a chance that had taken a year-and-a-half to germinate.

Hearing this from Rabin, who had heard the story from one of the journalists on the plane, I recalled Professor William Fort's conjectures about the convoluted psychological profile of Dr. Henry Kissinger – his tendency to overreact when things did not go his way, his penchant for petulance and tantrum when crossed, his Machiavellian manipulations, and his innate inclination to bend over backward in the name of a spurious objectivity.

Prime Minister Rabin with leader of the opposition Menachem Begin, 3 September 1975

Chapter eighteen

Collusion at Salzburg

L ike a concert audience come to hear a classical recital, the journalists in the press gallery of the Knesset chamber stirred with anticipation as Yitzhak Rabin stepped down from the podium having given a dry, matter-of-fact report on the crumbled negotiations with Egypt, and Menachem Begin stepped up to respond. This oratorical virtuoso, whose mastery of style and pace could grasp and command any gathering, got off to a flying start when he fixed Rabin in his determined gaze, and said to him in a schoolmasterly voice:

"Mr. Prime Minister, I would have wished that you and your colleagues had refrained from insisting on the use of the expression 'termination of belligerency.' It stems from the Latin *bellum gero*, and its practical meaning is so vague and obscure that nobody really understands what it legally implies."

Cries of offense and defense rose from the benches, stretching from wall to wall.

"The point I am making, Mr. Speaker," pressed Begin, cutting through the clamor and stabbing a finger at the government benches, "is this: why ask for something so nebulous as a 'termination of belligerency' when you should have been demanding an end to the state of war?"

Again, cries for and against swept the House floor, and Begin switched tone from stern hammering to thunder:

"Yes, that's right, you understand me well. I'm talking about a peace treaty. No withdrawal in Sinai without a peace treaty. And the first clause of any peace treaty speaks not about the termination of belligerency but about the cessation, the termination, of the state of war, plain and simple. It should, therefore, be made clear to all free nations, and most particularly to our American friends, what our enemy's intentions truly are – his refusal to end the state of war even in return for a deep IDF withdrawal and even after further and ever-deeper IDF withdrawals."

Rabin sat listening, the expression on his face difficult to parse. I knew he was deeply anxious. It was a stalemate, and pessimism filled the air around him. To get through it he needed a show of national unity; he needed to display to Gerald Ford and Henry Kissinger that the nation stood squarely behind him. Hence, his one concern during that moment was not Begin's remonstrations, but whether, at the end of the debate, he would support the government's actions or not.

Like a cavalry horse answering the bugle, Begin continued galloping headlong into the fray, flinging an arm in a sweeping arc as he denounced what he called "the prime minister's excessive concessions for the sake of a so-called interim agreement which, were it to be carried out, would fritter away the country's security in return for war and more war."

Rabin's angry supporters began bawling epithets so shrill that the Speaker, a gaunt, self-effacing, gentle man, banged his gavel over and over again, shouting all the while "Order! Order!" No one paid attention. So Begin stood there patiently, waiting for the din to run its course, where-upon, he again addressed Rabin, but this time with a degree of empathy.

"Mr. Prime Minister," he said reassuringly, to a now totally silent chamber, "even after the grave charges I've laid against you in your having vainly tried to exchange Sinai for something much less than peace, I say now, given the seriousness of the situation in our relations with America and, perhaps even the danger of war, I deem it a propitious hour for us all to display national unity."

Involuntarily, a flicker of a smile rose at the edges of Rabin's mouth, and a buzz of approval spread around much of the hall. The support of this complex, shrewd, iron-willed leader of the opposition would surely give pause to the American president and his secretary of state as they pondered their "reassessment" policy to punish Israel.

"Under no circumstances is your government to be blamed for the failure of these negotiations," continued Begin, his right hand held out as if he wanted to shake that of the prime minister's. "Responsibility for the failure of Dr. Kissinger's mission is Egypt's alone."

And then, with a thump of the podium, jaw jutting, he snarled, "The Egyptians have had the effrontery to treat us as though we were the defeated nation and they the victors, demanding we accept their dictates. The chutzpah of it! Thank God the government put a stop to it, and from the moment it did, our nation has straightened its back so that we stand tall once more, confident in the moral justice of our cause. American and world Jewry will surely stand by us in this hour of crisis, together with our many other American friends, be they in Congress or elsewhere. Indeed, good people of goodwill everywhere will stand by us and lend us support."

He paused once more as if gathering himself, and his next sentence resounded around the chamber like a clarion call:

"Mr. Speaker, ladies and gentlemen of the Knesset: we of the opposition shall stand united with the government in facing whatever challenges lie ahead so that, with the help of He who brought us out of the house of Egyptian bondage and led us here to Eretz Yisrael, we shall emerge victorious together."

As he stepped down from the dais and made his way through the crowded aisle, accepting congratulations on his speech from Knesset members who pressed forward to shake his hand, Yitzhak Rabin intercepted him by the cabinet bench. He extended his hand, and with a lopsided smile, said, "It takes true leadership to do what you just did, Begin. I thank you for that."

"It was my simple duty," responded the opposition leader with immense formality. But then, he smiled, and added teasingly, "And now it is your turn to perform an act of unusual national leadership. Go up to the podium and announce for all the world to hear that in this hour of national unity you, as prime minister, call upon the youth of Israel to volunteer to establish new settlements throughout the whole of our homeland – to settle all the waste places of Eretz Yisrael."

Rabin smirked. "I know exactly what you're after," he said, "you're after my job."

"Exactly," bantered Begin, "and as soon as possible." But then, in all seriousness, "The truth is, if we don't fill up the barren areas of Yehuda and Shomron with our settlements they will be occupied one day by that terrorist murderer Yasser Arafat and his so-called PLO. Then every Israeli town and village will be in range of their guns."

In his reply, irritation burst through Rabin's usually guarded tone: "You know very well where I stand," he said. "The West Bank is our one bargaining chip for a future peace with the Palestinians. Fill it up with settlements and you destroy the very hope of peace."

Resignedly, Begin responded, "Mr. Rabin, you go your way and I'll go mine, and may the Almighty spread his tent of peace over us all."[40]

Some two months into the battle for American public opinion, Yitzhak Rabin, full of spirit, and euphoric, strode into my office waving a piece of paper, and exclaimed, "Take a look at this – a gift of the gods from Congress! Our campaign is bearing fruit."

It was a cable from our Washington Embassy, citing an open letter addressed to President Ford and signed by seventy-six senators urging the president to support Israel in any future negotiation on an interim settlement with Egypt. It said:

> "We urge you to make it clear, as we do, that the United States, acting in its own national interests, stands firmly with Israel in the search for peace in future negotiations, and that this premise is the basis of the current reassessment of U.S. policy in the Middle East."[41]

"Ford and Kissinger won't like this one bit," gloated Rabin, in a rare show of glee. "We have to thank the American Jewish organizations for this, particularly AIPAC."*

Had Rabin been able to gaze into a crystal ball that day, and divine what the American president would say to the Egyptian president about that letter a week later, on the second of June, he would have been far less sanguine. "The importance of that letter," Ford told Sadat, "is being distorted out of all proportion. Half of the senators didn't read it, and a quarter didn't understand it. Only the additional quarter knew what they were doing. The impact of the letter is negligible."

The president said this when he and Kissinger met with Sadat and his foreign minister, Ismail Fahmi, at the Residenz, a baroque edifice in the heart of "Old Town" Salzburg, Austria. They were sitting in a high-ceilinged parlor whose walls were hung with majestic portraits of royal Hapsburgs and church eminences, relics of a time when Salzburg was an ecclesiastical state and when the Residenz was the archbishop's seat of governance. Now it was an official guest house.

What had brought the Americans to Europe was a NATO summit, and what led the Egyptians to rendezvous with them at this place with its

---

* The American-Israel Public Affairs Committee, the largest and most influential pro-Israel lobby in the United States.

spectacular Alpine view was a desire to revisit the possibility of an interim Sinai agreement.

In the course of the Egyptian-American deliberations a number of new ideas were put on the table to sweeten the terms so as to make an agreement more palatable to Israel. One such concerned the status of the early warning stations in Sinai. Rabin had insisted that in the event of a withdrawal these would remain under Israeli control. Sadat had strongly objected. Now, pondering the matter afresh, the Egyptian president suggested that perhaps they could be manned by American personnel. Kissinger immediately seized upon the idea and adroitly renovated it, as only he knew how, into a dazzling exercise in diplomatic flattery:

> *Kissinger:* Again, President Sadat, you reveal yourself as a statesman. I think we can sell this idea. If the Israelis think about it carefully, the idea of Americans manning the warning stations is an interesting one. It is very novel. From the Israeli point of view an American presence is better than an agreement of limited duration. The idea of Americans manning the warning stations engages the United States in a permanent way. It is a better assurance for Israel.
>
> *Ford:* I believe it is very saleable to the American public. Moreover, if Israel accepts the proposal, the Israeli supporters [in Congress] would help.
>
> *Kissinger (to Ford):* It is very important that this should not be told to Rabin next week [when he was due again in Washington]. *(To Sadat):* We will indicate to Rabin that you will be willing to look at the question of the early warning stations, without going into details. And then two weeks after Rabin goes home we will get back to him specifically with your creative idea.
>
> *Sadat (to Ford):* You have said that it is saleable in America?
>
> *Kissinger (to Sadat):* It is important that you not look too eager for an interim agreement. Say you are going back to Cairo to think about it. If we get tough with Rabin we have a chance of pulling this off. *(To Ford):* You will first have to shake up Rabin, and then you could send me out to the area again.
>
> *Sadat:* You mean to present it as an American proposal? You could then adopt the posture of putting pressure on me to accept it. You could say that you insist I modify my position.

Kissinger: This would enable us to say that President Ford was the one to have broken the impasse.

Sadat (to Egyptian Foreign Minister Fahmi): Work out the language with Henry.

Fahmi: This will bring about a major crisis between Egypt and the Soviets.

Sadat (to the Americans): You have nothing to fear from the Soviets. The Soviets are clumsy and suspicious. The United States will have the upper hand.

Kisisnger: They cannot do anything.

Ford: I believe President Sadat's ideas are saleable.

Kissinger: To sum up – I believe our approach here ought to be that you [Sadat] are going home to consider what each of us has said and weigh our conversation. You should not appear too anxious to get an interim agreement. Say that the prospects are fifty-fifty. We can tell the press that the atmosphere of our talks here was excellent and that both President Ford and President Sadat are going back home to think about the substance of our conversations.

Sadat: And at the appropriate time I will bear witness that it was President Ford who was responsible for finally breaking the impasse and achieving an interim agreement.[42]

Thus it was that after more comings and goings, triggering recriminations and vindications, initial tentative understandings began to emerge until, finally, the obstacles to a Sinai interim agreement, which came to be known as Sinai II, began to melt away, one by one. As scripted in Salzburg, President Sadat wobbled about the desirability of such a settlement at all, saying its prospects were at best "fifty-fifty." President Ford promptly "pressured" him into a rethink, and proposed an American presence in Sinai. Rabin agreed, as did the Egyptian leader, after much questioning and hesitation. Sadat then applauded the American president for having finally broken the impasse, and Secretary of State Kissinger flew out once more to the Middle East to wrap up the whole thing.

The Israeli line at the eastern end of the Sinai passes – the Gidi and the Mitla – was finally settled, an American presence in the early warning stations (the Sinai Support Mission) was put into place, the Sinai oilfields were transferred back to Egypt, and, with that, the agreement was ready for signing.

Needless to say, President Ford was delighted at the successful outcome of his and Kissinger's efforts and on the day of the signing, 1 September (1975), he telephoned Rabin in Jerusalem to express his congratulations. Tasked with transcribing the exchange, I hardly recorded a word of it because it turned out to be a four-minute swap of unexceptional platitudes. Not so in the case of the call the president made to Anwar Sadat in Alexandria on the same day.

There are times when heads of states stumble into the theater of the absurd, and when gestures intended to be acts of higher diplomacy turn into riotous burlesque worthy of the Marx Brothers. This was the case with that telephone call:

President Ford: Hello. President Sadat?

President Sadat: Hello. This is President Sadat.

President Ford: How are you this morning? I wanted to call you and congratulate you on the great role that you played in the negotiations that have culminated in this agreement.

President Sadat: Hello? [Inaudible]

President Ford: Unfortunately, I don't hear you too well, Mr. President. I hope that my conversation is coming through more clearly. Let me express most emphatically on behalf of my Government the appreciation for your statesmanship, despite adversity and some criticism, the spirit in which you have approached the need for an agreement. I am most grateful for the leadership that you have given, and look forward to continuing the work with you…

President Sadat: Hello?

President Ford: Hello. Can you hear me, Mr. President?

President Sadat: Hello?

President Ford: I am asking, can you hear me, Mr. President?

President Sadat: This is President Sadat.

President Ford: I am asking, can you hear me, Mr. President?

President Sadat: Not very well.

President Ford: I know that you and I recognize that stagnation and stalemate in the Middle East would have been potentially disastrous, and your leadership in working with Secretary Kissinger and with the Israelis – all of us are most grateful for. And as we continue to work together, personally, as well as government-to-government…

President Sadat: Hello? This is President Sadat speaking.

President Ford: Yes, I can hear you, Mr. President. I hope you can hear me, Mr. President.

President Sadat: President Ford? Hello.

President Ford: I don't hear you too well, Mr. President.

President Sadat: Is that President Ford speaking?

President Ford: Yes, this is President Ford.

President Sadat: Go ahead, please.

President Ford: The connection, unfortunately, is not too good for me to hear your comments, Mr. President. Let me say, if I might, despite the difficulties, that Mrs. Ford and I hope that Mrs. Sadat and you and your children will visit the United States sometime this fall. Secretary Kissinger has told me of the very warm hospitality that you have extended to him and Mrs. Kissinger, and we look forward to reciprocating when you come to the United States in the fall of 1975.

President Sadat: Hello?

President Ford: I regret that I can't hear you. The connection is very bad. I hope you can hear me and my comments from the United States. Mr. President, I understand that Secretary Kissinger is coming to Alexandria to personally deliver the documents for your initialing, and I have asked Henry to extend to you on that occasion the gratitude...

President Sadat: Hello?

President Ford: Hello, Mr. President.

President Sadat: Hello, Mr. President.

President Ford: I can hear you better now.

President Sadat: Mr. President, I hope you and your family are well.

President Ford: I am feeling very well, Mr. President, and I hope you are, too.

President Sadat: I want to thank you for your personal message [Inaudible].

President Ford: I, unfortunately, could not hear as well as I would like the last comments you made. The connection from here is not, apparently, as good as I hope you have there, but...

President Sadat: I hear you quite well.

President Ford: The efforts of Secretary Kissinger and myself, we feel, were completely worth what we have done, but our efforts could not have been successful without your leadership and statesmanship.

President Sadat: Thank you, Mr. President, very much.

President Ford: We will see you soon, I hope.

President Sadat: We are looking forward to coming, with pleasure, and convey my good wishes to your family.

President Ford: And my best to yours, sir.

President Sadat: Thank you very much.

President Ford: I would just wish to add…

President Sadat: Hello?

President Ford: Hello? [Inaudible].

President Sadat: Hello! Hello!

With that the line went dead.[43]

Chapter nineteen
A Presidential Letter

The prime minister's room in the Knesset had two seating areas, one around a large desk and the other around a couch, both of which were a rather drab brown but toned well, nevertheless, with the chestnut-colored curtains and carpet. As was his practice when wanting to engage a visitor in personal conversation, it was toward the couch that the prime minister guided the leader of the opposition in the early afternoon of 2 September 1975. Rabin wished to explain to Begin what had transpired between February and March of that year, when he had withstood American pressure to conclude an interim agreement with Egypt, and the previous day, when he had signed one.

In contrast to Begin's immaculate self, Rabin looked awful. Lighting a cigarette, he dragged on it as though sucking in oxygen, his whole body bearing the signs of the strain and the anxieties of the past months. His eyes were puffy and his shoulders stooped; he was exhausted from the late-night negotiation sessions that had culminated in his initialing the agreement in the presence of an elated Kissinger.

"I wanted this meeting so that I could explain to you, as leader of the opposition, the essence of what we've just signed," Rabin began.

"Mr. Prime Minister," responded Begin in formal fashion, "I fully appreciate your gesture. However, I have already been shown the contents of the document, so I don't think there is much to explain. What I do know is that in February you categorically told us that you would not hand over any of the Sinai assets – the oilfields, the passes, the early warning stations – let alone commit yourself to a deep withdrawal, unless the Egyptians responded with a commitment to end the state of war. In March you told us that an Egyptian commitment to 'the non-use of force' was meaningless verbiage. Now, here we are, a few months later, and you have turned the whole thing on its head, as if our public is mindless."

Wearily, Rabin said. "I have not turned the whole thing on its head. Events have moved on since March. We have now negotiated a new and improved situation, enabling us to reach an understanding."

"But with all respect, Mr. Prime Minister, you cannot expect our people to believe that what you signed yesterday changes the fabric of our relations with Egypt today. From March onward, when you refused to bow to the Egyptian dictates and to American pressure – and you won our total support for that…"

"Indeed I did."

"…Kissinger constantly stepped up the heat through his so-called 'reassessment' policy and his grim prophecies, not one of which material-ized, until you finally capitulated, and you signed."

Genuinely upset, Rabin sat up, and in a firm and tight voice, snapped, "Mr. Begin, that is preposterous. I did not capitulate. My government entered into this improved interim accord of its own volition because it holds out the promise of a new strategic situation in our relations with Egypt, and a new threshold of support from America. The alternative" – this with derision – "is the renewal of the Geneva peace conference."

The Geneva peace conference was the official negotiation frame-work established by the United Nations after the Yom Kippur War, headed jointly by the United States and the Soviet Union. It met only once in the immediate aftermath of the war, and had since become defunct.

"Let them convene Geneva," huffed Begin. "We have nothing to fear from Geneva. The Arab representatives will make their case and we shall make ours. It will be an excellent international platform to broadcast to the whole world the justice of our cause."

"On the contrary, we will be totally isolated," retorted Rabin. "The whole world will line up to pressure us to return to the old sixty-seven lines. This partial settlement with Egypt gives us a chance to tempt Sadat away from the military option and adopt a political one, backed by the United States. He will do so if he concludes it's worth his while."

Begin sneered, "That's an illusion."

"I don't think so," said Rabin, and he began to navigate his way into the underlying concept which he wanted to put across to his visitor:

"Egypt is the largest and most powerful of all the Arab states. In population it is almost half of the Arab world. It is the leader of the Arab world. No war has ever been launched against us which has not been initiated by Egypt, and then the other Arab states followed. And no war has ever ended without Egypt being the first to pull out and then the others followed. This Sinai interim arrangement is a first step in the effort toward taking Egypt out of the alliance of violence against us."

Begin threw Rabin a skeptical look: "Many of us don't see it that way, Mr. Prime Minister. We see it as an unacceptable gamble."

Continuing his conceptualization, Rabin postulated: "Security is not merely a matter of territory, as you know full well. Given our willingness to withdraw to a new defensive line deep inside Sinai, Sadat is now being given, for the first time, genuine motivation to reopen the Suez Canal [closed since the 1967 Six-Day War], and to rebuild his cities along its banks [destroyed in the 1969–1970 War of Attrition]. That, in itself, grants us substantial added security. Also, the return of the Sinai oilfields gives Sadat yet another good reason to maintain his side of the bargain. In other words, the agreement is largely self-policing. And on a broader strategic level it gives Egypt an added impetus to totally move out of the Soviet orbit and into the Western one. Moreover, it widens the rift between Egypt and Syria, putting an end to the most dangerous regional alliance against us – the Cairo-Damascus axis."

Begin, his face hard and somber, remained unconvinced. "Speak to the man in the street," he said brusquely. "He's no fool. He feels he's being led down the garden path. You promise him a step toward peace and all he sees are the fruits of victory being frittered away under his very nose. He senses an inherent contradiction between your orders to the IDF to carry out a most significant withdrawal in Sinai, and Sadat's orders to maintain the state of war. He feels that not an inch of territory should be returned to Egypt except in return for a full contractual peace."

Rabin took his time responding, as if weighing the merits of what his visitor had just said. Eventually, he demurred, "We have to put this agreement to the test of time. Time will tell, Mr. Begin."

Begin bridled: "Time to enable the Egyptians to repeat what they did after our last withdrawal in August nineteen seventy, when they brazenly violated the ceasefire by rushing their SAM missiles into the area we had just evacuated, and for which we soon paid a terrible price in the Yom Kippur War, just as I had predicted. And now here we are again making the same mistake. By your abandoning the Mitla and the Gidi Passes, in a total reversal of your original stance, you are practically inviting the Egyptians to duplicate their deceptions."

"We are not abandoning the passes," retorted Rabin, irked to the core.

"You decidedly are, Mr. Prime Minister. According to the map attached to the documents shown to me, you are certainly moving out of the passes."

"Yes, but we are retaining total control of them," countered Rabin, with unyielding earnestness. "We shall continue to encircle them and dominate them from the eastern ridges. Any Egyptian tank which tries to enter those passes from the western side will be a sitting duck. Besides, there will be American monitors in the passes. Study the map again, please."

Begin grunted a "bah," and shifted his line of argument:

"Few things are more important in diplomacy than credibility, and your government has lost its credibility. Your government has caved in on some of the most vital issues on which you initially refused to budge. So now everybody knows that when Israel says no to a specific demand, all one has to do is to exert pressure and we shall change our minds. In these last few months the Arabs have learned a lesson or two about how to negotiate with Israel."

Rabin knew Begin enough to know he was not simply playing party politics. He knew he was genuinely troubled. So he said to him in a placatory fashion, "Let me share with you my strategic philosophy. It might help you to understand why I see hope in this agreement. I see hope in this agreement because it contains the three fundamental elements essential for peacemaking. One: it deepens the disengagement between our opposing forces. Two: it strengthens the element of diffusion. And three: it holds out the prospect of fortifying trust. If we are ever going to move toward peace with any of our neighbors it will be by these three steps: disengagement, diffusion, and trust. Only when we have trust can we conduct a genuine face-to-face negotiation. This is what I believe. And I believe in one thing more besides."

He took a letter from his pocket, and said, "I believe, wherever possible, we have to synchronize our best interests with those of America. And I believe that to advance peace, America must keep us militarily strong. This new agreement cements our ties with Washington in both senses. It places the U.S.-Israel relationship on an entirely new footing. Please read this letter. It is from President Ford. It was delivered to me last night after the initialing."

Mr. Begin took the letter, adjusted his glasses, and read:

Dear Mr. Prime Minister – The Israeli-Egyptian Interim Agreement entailing withdrawal from vital areas in the Sinai constitutes an act of great significance on Israel's part in the pursuit of final peace and imposes additional heavy military and economic burdens on Israel.

It is my resolve to continue to maintain Israel's defensive strength through the supply of advanced types of equipment, such as the F-16 aircraft...enter into a joint study of high technology and sophisticated items, including the Pershing Ground-to-ground missiles with conventional warheads, with the view to giving a positive response...submit annually for approval by the U.S. Congress a request for military and economic assistance in order to help meet Israel's economic and military needs...Should the U.S. desire in the future to put forward proposals of its own, it will make every effort to coordinate with Israel its proposals with a view to refraining from putting forth proposals that Israel would consider unsatisfactory.

Asked for the precise meaning of these last words, Rabin explained that they were meant to remove once and for all the ever-hovering fear of a Great Power–imposed settlement on Israel.

And then Begin read the final paragraph:

The U.S. has not developed a final position on the borders. Should it do so it will give great weight to Israel's position that any peace agreement with Syria must be predicated on Israel remaining on the Golan Heights.[44]

"Well, that *is* interesting," he said. "It's hardly a binding commitment to support our retention of the Golan Heights, but it's important nevertheless. And what, pray, was Kissinger's role in the composition of this letter?"

"We negotiated every word through him. Without these new presidential commitments I would never have signed the agreement."

Menachem Begin sank deeper into the sofa, clasped his hands around one knee, and in a collegial fashion, asked, "I've never asked you this before, but what do you make of Kissinger? You've known him a long time. That last paragraph on final borders and the Golan Heights for example – has he ever spoken to you about what he thinks our final borders should be?"

Rabin could not contain a wry smile as he answered, "One day on my last visit to Washington I asked him about that point blank. I said, 'Henry, we've known each other for years and have had hundreds of conversations on every subject under the sun. Yet I have never heard you express your opinion on what Israel's final borders ought to be. Now that we're here alone, all by ourselves, tell me, what is your view?'"

"And his answer?"

"He raised both arms as if to say, 'Please don't shoot me,' and said, 'Yitzhak, you've never heard me talk about your final borders and you never will. Moreover, I pray that when the time comes to decide on those final borders I shall no longer be secretary of state.'"

"Very witty," said Begin, not at all amused. "What conclusions have you drawn about the man after all he's said and done over these past months?"

"Oh, he's a complicated Jew all right. He's full of contradictions when it comes to us. Need I tell you, he's a virtuoso at negotiations. Not only can he be tough, he can also be dangerous, as we saw when the negotiations collapsed."

"Is he duplicitous?"

"I would say he has a Metternich system of telling only half the truth when it suits him. He doesn't lie. He would lose all credibility if he lied. He simply emphasizes different shadings to different listeners. It's a negotiation technique."

"A chameleon, eh?"

"That's one way of putting it. Although I have to say I believe that underneath it all he cares deeply about us. And you should know" – this with a sudden bite that sharpened to anger – "he was devastated by the vicious attacks on his Jewishness at the demonstrations mounted against him by *Gush Emunim*."

Rabin was referring to a series of mass anti-Kissinger demonstrations organized by the religious nationalist settlement group called *Gush Emunim* – the Bloc of the Faithful – that had taken place in front of the King David Hotel and outside the Knesset when Kissinger was in Israel. Placards had read *JEW BOY GO HOME, JEW TRAITOR*, and *HITLER SPARED YOU SO YOU COULD FINISH OFF THE JOB*.

"I call that unadulterated Jewish anti-Semitism in the heart of the Jewish State," seethed Rabin. "These self-styled religious chauvinists are ruining the chances of peace. Countless times I have argued that we Jews should not assert our right to settle in the West Bank, with the exception of areas vital to our security."[45]

"The whole of what you call the West Bank and what I call by its original biblical names, Yehuda and Shomron," said Begin indignantly, "is vital to our security."

"I beg to differ," answered Rabin icily. "The planting of Jewish settlements in regions densely populated by Arabs is a prescription for violence. We Jews have to make a choice between remaining a Jewish and democratic state or retaining control of the whole of Eretz Yisrael. We can't have both. The two are a contradiction in terms."

"Not if we grant full autonomy to the Palestinian Arabs."

"They will never accept it."

"Why should they when you constantly advocate handing back to them whole chunks of our tiny homeland?"

"But don't you understand, precisely *because* the Arabs desperately want the West Bank and Gaza that these territories are the real key to peace with them? They are our most valuable bargaining chips. But now, those settler hooligans who masquerade as the champions of Eretz Yisrael – "

"Which they are," interrupted Begin firmly. "They would give their lives for Eretz Yisrael."

"They are a threat to our democracy," countered Rabin. "One of their leaders dared write that Kissinger deserves to meet the same fate as Count Bernadotte." [Count Bernadotte was a UN mediator assassinated in Israel in 1948.]

Begin, shocked, said, "I never heard of such a thing."

"Well I have. Those fanatics have been storming through Jerusalem's streets like common rabble. They even laid siege to the Knesset while Kissinger was there. We barely succeeded in getting him out through a rear exit, and safely back to the hotel. It was disgusting, totally outrageous. I felt thoroughly ashamed."

"You sound as if those demonstrations took you by surprise, Mr. Prime Minister," said Begin carefully.

"Their ferocious antagonism in the name of a divine authority certainly did take me by surprise," snapped Rabin. "I will not tolerate such demonstrations. I have ordered the chief of police to break them up, by force if necessary."

"Mr. Prime Minister," said Begin, in a voice full of rebuke. "I ask you, please, to rescind that order. These people are not as you say. They are the salt of the earth. They are the last vestige of our pioneering elite. Yes, I accept, their behavior is sometimes overzealous, but it is because of their passionate love of their country. And they are very angry these days, very angry indeed, and rightly so, because of what you have just committed our country to. For years every Israeli government has said no to withdrawal in the absence of peace. This has penetrated deep into the nation's psyche.

So, is it any wonder that people demonstrate? And where else to demonstrate if not in the streets?"

"Those demonstrations violate the rules of democracy," retorted Rabin, with equal fervor.

"Really?" countered Begin, his voice touched with sarcasm. "Your party has nothing to teach our national camp about the rules of democracy. We have proven our fidelity to democracy throughout the whole of our public lives, sometimes in the face of the greatest provocation. Moreover, to the best of my knowledge, in free countries demonstrations are not considered a threat to democracy, but rather a demonstration of it."

Then, rising to his feet, tone prim and official, he said, "You understand, Mr. Prime Minister, that I shall be voicing my opposition to your so-called interim agreement from the rostrum of the Knesset and from every other platform I can find."

"I expect nothing less, Mr. Begin," said Rabin, with a mirthless smile. "Are you not in the habit of saying that the job of the opposition is to oppose? Well, feel free – oppose, and I shall answer."

Yitzhak Rabin looked upon his 1975 interim agreement as a historic step on the road to peace with Egypt, and felt embittered that his contribution was never publicly recognized. He said as much in his 1979 memoir:

> When President Sadat made his historic visit to Jerusalem on 19 November 1977 I was no longer prime minister. Yet that visit – and the subsequent moves toward achieving a peace treaty – could never have come about were it not for the course my government adopted in signing the 1975 interim agreement. That our policy provoked the anger of Likud has not prevented Mr. Begin's government from reaping the fruits of our labors. Of course, that is how things should be, since the quest for peace is not a contest between political parties.... The 1975 agreement with Egypt was never meant to be an end in itself. As its title implies, it was designed to advance the momentum toward peace, and in that sense it achieved its objective.[46]

Chapter twenty

Entebbe – Flight 139

P rime Minister Yitzhak Rabin's military secretary, Brigadier-General Ephraim Poran – otherwise known as Freuka – was an unexcitable, soft-spoken soldier who had a reputation for keeping his head while others around him were losing theirs. So when Rabin saw him enter the Cabinet Room in the middle of a session and bear down on him with a note in his hand and a troubled look on his face he knew something seriously untoward was afoot. It was Sunday, 27 June 1976. Rabin's features paled when he read the note:

> An Air France plane, Flight 139 from Tel Aviv to Paris, has been hijacked after taking off from a stopover in Athens.

Rabin leaned forward to frown over the papers in front of him as if he was studying their contents, but he was, in fact, desperately trying to decide what to do. Not since the Six-Day War had he been smitten with such a sudden blow of anxiety. Finally, he turned the note over and scribbled on its back:

> Freuka – find out: 1) How many Israelis are on board. 2) How many hijackers are on board. 3) Where the plane is heading.

Rabin then banged his gavel to silence a minister who was working himself up over the price of bread, and informed his cabinet of the shocking news.

Adjourning the meeting, he asked Foreign Minister Yigal Allon, Defense Minister Shimon Peres, Transport Minister Gad Yaakobi, Justice Minister Chaim Zadok, and Minister without Portfolio Yisrael Galilee to meet him forthwith in the conference room downstairs, to consider a course of action.

On his way down he told Yaakobi to contact Ben-Gurion Airport to go on instant and full alert. "The hijackers might want to do another Sabena," he said.

He was referring to an incident in May of 1972 when a passenger aircraft of the Belgian-owned Sabena airline was hijacked during a flight from Vienna to Tel Aviv. It landed at Ben-Gurion airport and the hijackers demanded the release of hundreds of Palestinian terrorists, otherwise they would blow up the plane together with its passengers. The next day Israeli commandos successfully stormed the aircraft.

"The only thing we know for sure right now," said Rabin, opening the emergency ministerial meeting, "is that the hijacked plane is Air France. What exactly is the legal status of passengers on board that plane?"

He was addressing Minister of Justice Chaim Zadok, a corpulent, round-shouldered, middle-aged gentleman who possessed an encyclopedic legal mind.

"By law, the passengers are under French sovereign protection," he answered authoritatively. "The French government is responsible for the fate of them all."

"Yigal" – this to Foreign Minister Allon – "have your people inform the French Government, and tell them we're issuing a public statement to that effect. Ask Paris to keep us informed of their actions." To me, he said, "Prepare a draft of the statement."

As I began to scribble, Allon rose to leave the room, and was almost out of the door when Zadok called after him, "And tell them they must make no distinction between the Israeli passengers and the rest."

"That goes without saying," muttered Allon, slightly huffed.

Now Freuka came barging in with a fresh note, which Rabin read out loud:

There are 230 passengers on board, 83 of them Israeli, and 12 crew members. The Libyans have allowed the plane to land at Benghazi.

"So now at least we know where the passengers are," said the prime minister, lighting a cigarette, his face a frown. "But there are three crucial things we still don't know. We don't know whether Benghazi will be their final stop. We don't know who the hijackers are. And we don't know what their demands are."

For the next half hour the ministers mulled over these three unknowns, until a secretary entered and passed a note to Allon. "Aha, it's from the French Ambassador," he said, and he read:

> The government of France wishes to inform the government of Israel that the French government bears full responsibility for the safety of all the passengers without distinction on Air France flight 139, and shall keep the government of Israel apprised of its actions in this regard.

"That is satisfactory," said Zadok, and for lack of fresh information, and in the absence of anything useful more to say, the prime minister adjourned the meeting, asking everyone to stay close to a phone.

It rang in the late afternoon, and the committee reconvened early that evening. Rabin, now once again every bit the hard-nosed commander he used to be, ran his eyes up and down a dossier in front of him, and said, "Here is the new information. The plane was seven hours on the ground at Benghazi, for refueling. One passenger, a pregnant woman, was released. The plane took off and the terrorists requested permission to land at Khartoum. Permission was not granted, despite the fact that Sudan is a haven for Palestinian terrorists. We have no idea where the plane is heading now. Meanwhile, Ben-Gurion Airport is on the highest alert. As for the identity of the hijackers, it seems there are four – two Arabs from the Popular Front for the Liberation of Palestine, and two Germans from a terrorist splinter group calling itself the 'Revolutionary Cells.' That's as much as we know."

An anxious exchange followed which added nothing to the sum total of knowledge or ideas, so Rabin brought the meeting to a close. That night he fell into a woolly sleep until jerked blinking back into reality by the shrill ring of his bedside telephone:

"Who is this?"

"Freuka."

"What time is it?"

"Four in the morning. Sorry for waking you up. The plane has landed in Entebbe, Uganda."

Rabin, instantly alert, said, "Better there than an Arab country. We know the Ugandan President, Idi Amin."

"Didn't he do his parachute training here?"

"He did. And during the heyday of Golda Meir's African aid program quite a few of our specialists worked in Uganda. Some should know him personally so, hopefully, we can straighten this thing out soon. Try and find out who knows him. Any word yet of the hijackers' demands?"

"None."

"Convene a meeting first thing."

"Shall do. Try and get back to sleep."

"Shall do."

The next day was Tuesday 29 June, and at 8:30 in the morning a somewhat bleary-eyed and slouched Rabin reported the new facts to the committee. Hardly had the ministers absorbed what he was saying when Freuka's assistant came rushing in with a note. The general quickly ran his eyes over it and instantly passed it on to the prime minister who, after a single glance, said, "This is what we've been waiting for. The hijackers have broadcast their demands over Ugandan radio."

He paused to study the page and absorb its full meaning, and then shared its contents in a slow and deliberate manner with the men around him. They sat with a too-well-controlled steadiness as if to conceal their uneasiness.

"In return for the hostages," the prime minister said, "the hijackers want the release of terrorists – they call them freedom fighters – imprisoned in five countries: forty from us, six from West Germany, five from Kenya, one from Switzerland, and one from France. They've issued an ultimatum. Within forty-eight hours the released terrorists are to be flown to Entebbe. Those freed by us are to be transported by Air France; the other countries can decide on their own mode of transport."

"And if not?" asked Yisrael Galilee in his characteristic solid and phlegmatic way. "What happens if they are not freed?"

Yisrael Galilee had the white hair of an Einstein, the stocky build of a kibbutznik, the shrewdness of an entrepreneur, and the veiled eyes of a Svengali. The reason he was a minister without portfolio was because he did not need one. He was Rabin's closest political confidante, having also had the ear of virtually every prime minister before him.

"If the terrorists are not freed," answered Rabin, his voice grim, "they threaten to begin killing the hostages as of two o'clock Thursday afternoon, July the first. That is the day after tomorrow."

The group emitted a collective gasp. The first to break the silence was Defense Minister Shimon Peres, who delivered an impassioned address on the implications of capitulation to terrorist blackmail.

Rabin turned to look at Peres with contempt. In his memoirs he would revile Peres as an "inveterate schemer," one who would stop at nothing to advance his own ambitions. Now he stared back at Peres with a gaze that said, 'Say what you will, I'm in charge,' and cut him short with a sardonic, "Before the Defense Minister sermonizes any further I suggest we adjourn to think the matter through, with all its implications. We'll meet again at five thirty this afternoon and, hopefully, come up with some ideas."

Rabin promptly called a meeting of his personal staff and opened it by letting off steam about what he regarded as Peres' self-serving homilies. He then asked for a report on the attempts to persuade Idi Amin to intercede on behalf of the passengers, and what he learned caused him to snarl and to say with a bitter smile, "Nothing will surprise me about what that man Amin is capable of. He runs his country like a personal fiefdom. He probably has his own fish to fry in this mess, in cahoots with the terrorists."

To Freuka he said he wanted the IDF chief of staff, General Mordechai (Motta) Gur, to come to the 5:30 meeting, and to me he said he wanted another brief for the foreign media emphasizing, again, France's responsibility.

"Why do you need the chief of staff?" asked Freuka. "You have something in mind for him?"

He answered, "I want to know what the IDF thinks about this whole matter. I don't have the slightest doubt that Peres' pontifications about not surrendering to terrorist blackmail are for the record only, so that he'll be able to claim later that he was in favor of military action from the start. The problem is his rhetoric is so persuasive he believes it himself."

The prime minister opened the 5:30 meeting with a direct question to the chief of staff: "Motta, does the IDF have any possible way to rescue the hostages with a military operation?"

Peres, irate, intervened: "There has been no consideration of the matter in the defense establishment. I haven't discussed it yet with the chief of staff."

"What?" spluttered Rabin, the veins on his forehead seeming ready to pop. "Fifty-three hours after we learn of the hijacking you have not yet consulted the chief of staff on the possibility of using military means to rescue the hostages?" His fury was palpable. "Motta," he repeated, staring sharply at the general, his voice crisp and commanding, "do you have a military plan, yes or no? If you do have a military plan, that will be our top preference. But remember, any operation has to provide for a way of bringing the hostages back. It won't be good enough just to eliminate the terrorists. We have to be able to bring our people home."

Again, Peres was about to say something, but Rabin forestalled him, insisting that Motta Gur answer his question.

"When I received your message to attend this meeting," replied the general, a hefty parachutist who had led the assault to free the Old City in the Six-Day War, "I assumed it was to seek my advice on a military option. Consequently, before coming here I ordered the chief of operations to start a preliminary examination to see whether an operation is feasible, and if so, at what cost. A major problem is our lack of reliable information on the attitude of Idi Amin. If the Ugandans cooperate with us our chances for a successful operation would be that much greater."

"Obviously," said Rabin, and then, to the whole table, "but the reports we are receiving about Amin are not encouraging. The point is that, as of this moment, there is no concrete military solution, so we shall have to..." – he paused, as if hesitant to express his next thought – "...consider negotiating with the terrorist hijackers for the release of the hostages."

Peres promptly rose and left the room, followed by General Gur, presumably to speed back to the Ministry of Defense in Tel Aviv to see what military plan they could come up with, if at all. The rest of the committee engaged in a fretful discussion about the frightening thought of attempting to rescue so many hostages, thousands of miles away in the heart of Africa, and the unthinkable alternative of negotiating with the killers for the release of *their* killers in exchange for innocents.

Later that evening, over a drink in the privacy of his room – the prime minister was drinking and smoking more heavily now – Rabin confided his inner thoughts with these words: "When it comes to negotiating with terrorists, I long ago made a decision of principle, well before I became prime minister, that if a situation were ever to arise when terrorists would be holding our people hostage on foreign soil and we were faced with an ultimatum either to free killers in our custody or let our own people be killed, I would, in the absence of a military option, give in to the terrorists. I would free killers to save our people. So I say now, if the defense minister and the chief of staff cannot come up with a credible military plan, I intend to negotiate with the terrorists. I would never be able to look a mother in the eye if her hostage soldier or child, or whoever it was, was murdered because of a refusal to negotiate, or because of a botched operation."[47]

On the following day – Wednesday 30 June – Rabin opened the next ministerial committee meeting with this chilling news:

"The terrorists have carried out a selection. They have separated the Jews from the non-Jews. There are ninety-eight Jews. The non-Jews have been released. The Jewish hostages are threatened with execution. There is now absolutely no doubt that Idi Amin is eager to ingratiate himself with the Arabs and is fully collaborating with the terrorists. The ultimatum expires in less than twenty-four hours. So, again, I ask the chief of staff – Motta, do you have a military plan?"

"We are looking at three possible options," answered the general. "One is to launch a seaborne attack on the airport from Lake Victoria; the second is to induce the hijackers to transact an exchange here in Israel, and then jump them; and the third is to drop parachutists over Entebbe."

There was a silent pause. "Are any of these plans operational?" asked the prime minister, his face cold, hard-pinched. "Can you recommend any one of them to the government?"

"No."

"In that case," said Rabin with alacrity, "since the terrorist ultimatum is scheduled to run out at two P.M. tomorrow, I intend to propose to the full cabinet that we negotiate with the hijackers for the release of the hostages. We will negotiate through the French. If we are unable to rescue them by force we have no moral right to abandon them. We must exchange them for terrorists held here in our jails in Israel. Our negotiations will be in earnest, not a tactical ruse to gain time. And we will keep our side of any deal we strike."

"I object," countered Peres.

"I'm sure you do," muttered Rabin between his teeth, but this time Peres was not to be silenced.

"We have never agreed in the past to free prisoners who have murdered innocent civilians," he thundered. "If we give in to the hijackers' demands and release terrorists, everyone will understand us but no one will respect us. If, on the other hand, we conduct a military operation to free the hostages, it is possible that no one will understand us, but everyone will respect us, depending, of course" – this in a whisper – "on the outcome of the operation."

Rabin, glowering, decanted his unrestrained rage: "For God's sake, Shimon, our problem at this moment is not more of your heroic rhetoric. If you have a better proposal, let's hear it. What do you suggest? You know as well as I do that the relatives of the hostages are stalking us day and night. They are beside themselves with fear, clamoring for us to make an exchange, and for good reason. What do they say? They say that Israel freed terrorists after the Yom Kippur War in exchange for the bodies of dead soldiers, so how can we refuse to free terrorists in exchange for living people, our own people, their loved ones, when their lives are in imminent danger?"

Peres, features frozen, said nothing, and when it came to the vote he raised his hand together with the rest of his morose colleagues to negotiate for the release of the hostages though the auspices of the French government.[48]

The next morning, with hardly more than a few hours to spare before the executions were to begin, the prime minister reported the facts to the full cabinet which, likewise, voted unanimously to open negotiations through the French. Said Rabin as he brought the meeting to a close, "It has to be understood that the IDF will continue to seek a military option, but this in no way detracts from the earnestness of the decision we have just taken to negotiate."

Then, pale-faced, he strode into an adjacent room, where members of the prestigious Knesset Foreign Affairs and Security Committee (composed primarily of non-ministerial leaders of the major parties, among them Menachem Begin), were waiting to hear his report. "Gentlemen," he said tensely, "the cabinet has just made the decision to open negotiations with the terrorists to exchange killers in our hands for the Jewish hostages."

Glances were exchanged as uneasiness and trepidation pervaded the atmosphere. An agonizing argument broke out which Rabin cut short by saying, "We simply have no choice. We have no credible military option. The terrorists' ultimatum expires in a few hours time, at two o'clock, after which they will begin executing a Jew every half hour."

"Mr. Prime Minister, may I request a brief interval for consultations with my colleagues?" said Menachem Begin.

Rabin looked at his watch. "Yes, but please be quick. Time is running out. We have yet to relay our position to the French."

The leader of the opposition rose quickly and departed for an adjacent room, together with a number of his party members. There he said in a voice that rang with the command of one who had lived a life of hard choices, "Who knows better than me what it means to take a stand on a matter of principle? One of my principles is not to negotiate with terrorists. But when Jewish lives are at stake every principle must go by the board. We must rescue our brethren from execution. Therefore, I propose we inform the prime minister that we of the Likud opposition share in the public responsibility for the decision to open negotiations with the terrorists."

Nobody demurred, and within minutes they were back.

"Mr. Prime Minister," said Begin with enormous gravitas, "this is not a partisan matter for debate between the coalition and the opposition. It is a national issue of the highest order. We, the opposition, shall support any decision the government adopts to save the lives of Jews. And we shall make our decision known to the public."

"Thank you," said Rabin, clearly moved. When he reported what Begin had said to the ministerial committee, the defense minister looked taken aback. Rabin remarked sarcastically to his own staff people as he left the meeting, "It seems Mr. Begin's display of national responsibility descended on Mr. Peres like a cold shower, cooling off his demagoguery. And now I must quickly inform the French to proceed with the negotiations."

Within the hour, the news was blazoned around the world: *"ISRAEL SURRENDERS!"*

All of us working with the prime minister were gnawed by a supercharged tension while waiting for a response from Entebbe – all of us, that is, except Rabin himself. He summoned me to review the day's correspondence, and even as I sat there trying to suppress my flutters he seemed unnaturally composed, as if morally fortified by the principled decision he had taken. Once his mind was made up, his clarity of focus never wavered. So when his red emergency phone, which was linked directly to the intelligence people in Tel Aviv, suddenly buzzed, he answered it calmly with a tranquil "Hello." And then, nodding his head in comprehension, said, "Yes, I see. Good. Thank you. That gives us a little more time," and he replaced the receiver.

"Any news?" I blurted.

"Yes," he said, and he pressed the intercom button to speak to his military secretary, General Poran: "The French have just notified us that the terrorists have extended their ultimatum to Sunday July the fourth, to allow for the negotiations to proceed. Please inform the members of the ministerial committee. I'll speak directly to the defense minister and the chief of staff. Hopefully they will come up with a military plan before then."

A couple of hours later I was chatting with Freuka in his room when Rabin walked in, red in the face, accompanied by his press secretary, Dan Patir. "You won't believe it," growled Rabin. "Here I am, waiting for the defense minister and the chief of staff to come up with a military plan to beat the new deadline, and there they are backing the most outlandish proposal I've ever heard in my life. They want me to send Moshe Dayan – MOSHE DAYAN OF ALL PEOPLE – to Uganda to talk to Idi Amin! They have to be out of their minds, to suggest that we hand over one of our best-known public figures to that crazy tyrant so that he can hand him over to the terrorists as their prize hostage. It's outrageous!"

"But I hear a military plan is beginning to take shape," said General Poran, in an effort to calm him down.

"I've heard that too," said Rabin, skeptically. "But I'll believe it when I see it. Motta and Peres say they might have something to show me in the morning."

And indeed they did – a spectacularly daring plan to which Rabin gave his ultimate approval after much refining with his practiced and professional military eye. He then summoned the full cabinet into emergency session. Since the item on the agenda was a matter of life and death, despite the fact that it was Saturday 3 July and therefore the Sabbath, all the religious ministers attended the meeting, arriving at the venue by foot, since driving is not permissible.

The prime minister opened: "What I'm about to say is top secret. We have a military plan."

Some ministers sat back stunned, others gasped, still others immersed themselves in their paperwork as if to hide their thrill or their agitation, depending on their temperament, and yet others simply sat expressionless, waiting.

Flatly and factually, without a trace of emotion, Rabin explained, "As you know, so long as we had no military option I was in favor of conducting serious negotiations with the hijackers. But now the situation has changed."

"Can you give us an idea of anticipated casualties?" asked one of the ministers apprehensively.

Rabin looked the questioner squarely in the eye: "The rescue operation will entail casualties both among the hostages as well as their rescuers. I don't know how many. But even if we have fifteen or twenty dead – and we can all see what a heavy price that would be – I am in favor of the operation."

"And are you positive there is no other way out, besides negotiating with the terrorists?" asked another.

"Yes, I am. If we have a military option we have to take it, even if the price is heavy, rather than give in to the terrorists." He paused to scan the faces of his colleagues and gauge their moods. Most expressions were closed and dubious. So it was with uncharacteristic passion that he pressed them, declaring, "I have said all along that in the absence of a military plan we have to negotiate in earnest. Now that we have a military plan we have to implement it, even at a heavy cost."

Motta Gur presented the essentials of the plan, code-named Operation Thunderbolt. A substantial military force was to be landed at Entebbe by Hercules transport planes, rather than by parachute. He described the stealth, caution and subterfuge that lay at the heart of the plan, all designed to catch the terrorists and the Ugandans off guard. He wrapped up by saying, "Gentlemen, after having attended the rehearsal of Operation Thunderbolt last night I can recommend it to the cabinet."

A brief debate followed, after which the cabinet gave its approval. Rabin then stepped into an adjacent room to meet once more with the leading figures of the Knesset Foreign Affairs and Security Committee, who had gathered there at his behest. Hearing what the prime minister reported, Menachem Begin, again speaking in the name of the opposition, responded with solemn goodwill:

"Mr. Prime Minister, yesterday, when you had no military plan, I said that since the issue was a matter of saving Jewish lives we of the opposition would lend the government our fullest support. Today, now that you have a military rescue plan, I say again, we of the opposition shall lend the government our fullest support. And may the Almighty bring home all our people safe and sound."

The green light given, Rabin went to sit quietly, alone in his room, until he was interrupted by Freuka, who said, "I've just received the signal. Our forces are on their way." Rabin responded resignedly, "So be it. There is nothing more I can do." And he poured himself a drink.

As the Hercules planes roared through the night toward Entebbe, the prime minister departed for home to try and grab a nap. When he awoke, he drove to the defense ministry, where a loudspeaker link-up was installed to relay reports from the IDF force landing at Entebbe. They could see nothing, but heard everything, relayed through an Israeli 707 command aircraft trailing at a safe distance and overseeing the whole operation: how the Hercules planes landed before midnight, their cargo bays disgorging a burnished black Mercedes and Land Rovers together with elite troops, to create the impression that Idi Amin himself was being driven toward the terminal with a military escort; how the IDF commandos burst into the terminal yelling to the startled hostages in Hebrew, "Shalom, shalom. We are Israeli soldiers here to rescue you. Stay down, stay down"; how they had burst into room after room gunning down the terrorists; how more aircraft landed to reinforce the troops and take the hostages home.

It was the longest night of Yitzhak Rabin's life and, in many respects, his finest hour. Reflecting back on it, he would write this in his memoirs:

The military transmissions, laconic and dry, heralded the brilliant success of the operation, which was the furthest ever conducted from Israeli territory. It was carried out in an orderly fashion, exactly according to plan. The first plane took off from Entebbe within thirty minutes of landing and carried the hostages, the French crew, part of the assault force, and the casualties.... When the news came through that the last of our planes had left Entebbe, we drank a toast to the success of the venture. A few hours later people were literally dancing in the streets as a wave of elation swept over Israel.[49]

Uri Dan, a well-known Israeli journalist, full of vim and chutzpah, managed to get through to Idi Amin on the telephone. When he described to him what was going on in Israel – the singing, the dancing, the elation – the Ugandan dictator wailed, "What have you done to me? I am carrying the bodies of my soldiers in my arms. I treated the hostages so nicely. I gave them soup, soap, and toilet paper."[50]

Five Jews met their deaths at Entebbe, one of them Lieutenant Colonel Yonatan (Yoni) Netanyahu, brother of Binyamin (Bibi) Netanyahu. He fell commanding the first assault group which broke into the terminal. In homage to his valor the mission's code-name was changed from Operation Thunderbolt to Operation Yonatan.

On the very day the hostages were brought home, the fourth of July, Menachem Begin rose to address a special session of the Knesset. He said:

"Not since the Six-Day War has our nation known such a profound sense of unity. We shared a common anxiety and a sense of fraternal love for our people, emanating from the resolve to rescue our brothers and our sisters in peril. Perhaps it was because of this unity that we found within ourselves the capacity to mount such a momentous operation – a rescue mission unprecedented in gallantry and daring.

"There are no battles without sacrifices. We bow our heads before the grieving families who lost loved ones, among them a most valiant commander who charged at the head of his troops with the battle cry, 'Follow me.'

"In the name of the whole nation of Israel we pay tribute to our armed forces, to our chief of staff, and to his comrades-in-arms. These officers and men have proven that the generation of the Maccabees has risen anew."

Turning toward Yitzhak Rabin, who was sitting at the head of the cabinet bench in the well of the chamber, he said:

"Mr. Prime Minister, you and I belong to different political factions.

Photograph credit: Moshe Milner & Israel Government Press Office

*Rescued Entebbe hostages waving to the crowd upon
landing at Ben Gurion Airport, 4 July 1976*

Our outlooks differ, and in this parliament of free debate we shall assuredly continue to argue over matters of fundamental import, sometimes fiercely so. But not today. On this day I say to you with a full heart in the name of the opposition: Mr. Prime Minister, I salute you. I salute you for what you have done. I salute, too, the minister of defense, as indeed I do all members of the cabinet, and everyone else involved in the most difficult of decisions a nation's leaders can possibly make. But you, Mr. Prime Minister, you who are the leader of the team – and I have some knowledge of being a leader of a team – I say that while all your colleagues have a share in the decision-making responsibility, upon your shoulders rests an extra morsel of responsibility. And who can measure the weight of that extra morsel?"

Then, to the whole House:

"What did we see at Entebbe? We saw an extremist left-wing German Nazi point a finger at the hostages: who shall go to the left and who shall go to the right – non-Jews one way, Jews the other. And we asked ourselves, *Ribono shel olam* – God Almighty – hardly thirty years after the Auschwitz crematoria, that cemetery without end, with the image of Dr. Mengele still fresh in our minds, standing there among the rows of Jews – of the men and of the women, of the children and of the babies – pointing his finger, 'To the right: to death; to the left: to life.' And there was no one to save them.

"Well, now there is. Now we declare for all to hear: Never again!

Our generation has taken a solemn oath consecrated in the blood of our slain mothers, our butchered fathers, our asphyxiated babes, and our fallen brave – never again will the blood of the Jew be shed with impunity. Never again will Jewish honor be easy prey.

"We are no empire. We are but a small nation…but after all that has befallen our nation throughout all the generations – and not least the generation of the Holocaust – we declare that if there be anyone anywhere who is persecuted, or humiliated, or threatened, or abducted, or is in any way endangered simply because he or she is a Jew, then let the whole world know that we, Israel, the Jewish State, shall marshal all our strength to come to their aid and bring them to the safe haven of our homeland. This is the message of Entebbe."[51]

A week later, a shy and awkward Yitzhak Rabin hosted an exuberant American Jewish solidarity mission in the garden of his official Jerusalem residence. The one-hundred-odd guests, gripped still with a Fourth-of-July-like euphoria, stood in line to pump the prime minister's hand, slap him on the back, and announce uncommonly generous pledges for the cause of Israel.

A handsome rabbi, tall, trim, and tanned, strode up to the microphone in cowboy boots, planted a large multi-colored skull cap on his head, opened up a Bible, and delivered an invocation in a resonant baritone, telling the tale of an earlier rescue mission when Jew saved Jew. He was reading from Genesis, chapter fourteen, when Abraham came to the rescue of his nephew, Lot, who was in the hands of enemy kings. As the rabbi continued his description of the rescue, more and more men put their hands into their pockets to place skullcaps on their heads, out of respect for the biblical text. Rabin, seeing what was going on, stuck a handkerchief on his, but it was so starched it stuck up like an alabaster tripod. And when, in peroration, the rabbi stretched out his arms dramatically and began conferring the priestly blessing upon Rabin, he smiled and blushed bashfully, and deciding he'd had enough, quickly thanked everybody for coming and beat a quick retreat, leaving me behind to wind up the proceedings.

At the evening's end, many of the visitors were moved to register their feelings of solidarity and kinship in the prime minister's official guest book, located in the hallway. Leafing through it after they had gone I was struck by the warmth and spontaneity of their sentiments. Admittedly, not all were elegantly phrased. In fact, some were prize nuggets. I list them here below, names and addresses omitted for propriety's sake:

"Mr. Rabin, I think you're doing a swell job, but next time it would be nice if you'd put on a proper yarmulke."

"Yitzhak – because of what our boys did at Entebbe I upped my pledge to a couple of grand. I'll up it again if you rub out Arafat."

"You are proof, Mr. Prime Minister, that to be a great leader you have to have a great war. God bless you for it."

"Our President back in Washington has been fool enough to swallow all the Arab propaganda. We Jews rely on you for more Entebbes. Give 'em hell."

"Well done at Entebbe. I'm sorry I did not have an opportunity to have a quiet chat with you about the future of your country. I have some definite views on the matter. You might wish to phone me. My number is with your security man at the door."

"When Maria married me 35 years ago she went through the whole conversion spiel. We encouraged our boy, Milton, to make aliya, so as to be sure he'd meet a nice Jewish girl. He got a job in Beersheba and married a shikse from Russia. Where does that leave me? Anyway, congrats on Entebbe."

"Our President demands reform in the Arab world. My Temple demands Reform in the Jewish State. Do something about it, please."

"This is my first visit to the Holy Land and I, a Christian, support your just cause for the greater glory of Jesus Christ our Lord. Entebbe was an expression of His glory. This Land is your land. Stay the course."

"Dear Yitzhak. You won't mind me calling you Yitzhak. We must be about the same age, you and I. You're Number One in my eyes. *Congrat-u-laaaations!* My late husband, Phil, left me well provided for, so I've made out a check for $2,000 for you to spend as you please. (Your bodyguard knows where to find me.)"

"Mr. Prime Minister, I run a big business, so if you'd like some help on how to run your little country I'd be happy to oblige free, gratis, and for nothing."

"I congratulate you on your extraordinary rescue feat. But as a clinical psychologist I detect in you a bashful and timid reserve. Diagnostically, I would say you have a depressive personality. Its root cause is an inability to elicit love. You're in search of a hero. Henry Kissinger wrestles with the same problem."

"I had planned a private word in your ear but I can't push in a crowd because of a back problem. What I wanted to say is, you're doing a good job and I've donated a tidy sum. But isn't it time you stopped being a socialist and become a proper Yiddisher mensch?"

"I leave this extraordinary country after five days feeling enriched and strengthened. God bless you for saving our people. Sure, you still have problems. But don't worry – we Jews thrive on problems. If we didn't have problems we'd invent them, otherwise we'd die of boredom. Keep it up. Next year in Jerusalem!"

"Great country! Great visit! Great people! Question: Is it true that you and Peres don't hit it off? Terrific! I feel exactly the same way."

"Mr. Rabin, yashar koach. These are Moshiach times. Consult the Lubavicher Rebbe. He knows what's what. Am Yisrael Chai!"

"It was lovely. I just wish you would speak English a little better."

Chapter twenty-one

Enter Jimmy Carter

Mr. Begin – time for a question?"

The *Jerusalem Post* parliamentary correspondent, Asher Walfish, had chanced upon the opposition leader as he was exiting the Knesset chamber on his way to the cafeteria for his mid-afternoon refreshment.

"For you, always," said Begin, his smile widening in recognition. "Please join me for a glass of tea." He beckoned the journalist to a corner table, thanked the waitress profusely for serving them so promptly, took a sip of his tea, and asked, "Now, what is it you'd like to talk to me about?"

"Yesterday's American election," answered the correspondent, readying his pen and pad. "Now that Jimmy Carter has won, and has announced Kissinger is not his choice for secretary of state, do you have any comment on Prime Minister Rabin's statement that we shall yet look back on the Kissinger years with nostalgia?"

The date was 3 November 1976, and Jimmy Carter, former governor of Georgia, had just beaten the incumbent President Gerald Ford in the race for the White House.

"Ah, nostalgia!" chortled Begin, beaming like a boy. "What a word! I'm not even sure Mr. Rabin understands its full meaning. It is derived, as you know, from the Greek *nostos* – a connotation of longing for a former happy circumstance."

Begin took pleasure in showing off his penchant for classical languages, picked up as a law student at Warsaw University, and he assumed the man he was talking to, an Oxford graduate, would appreciate his little dip into etymology. But Walfish refused to accept such an answer, so he pressed, "Do you think it was an inappropriate thing for Rabin to say?"

Begin allowed his smile to cool off: "You tell me, Mr. Walfish – would *you* call Dr. Kissinger a former happy circumstance to be nostalgic about?"

"That's my question, sir."

Begin's brows furrowed and his eyes frowned: "For a prime minister of our country to say that Israel shall yet yearn for Secretary of State Dr. Henry Kissinger is tantamount to saying to the American people: what a pity you elected Mr. Jimmy Carter as your next president."

"Then you *are* concerned?"

"Concerned? Of course I'm concerned. Let me reveal to you something that has not yet been reported. During the height of the American election campaign I called on the prime minister in the company of a number of my colleagues to express dismay at certain of his public statements, which could only be construed as crass interference in their elections."

"You're talking about his complimentary remarks about President Ford and the enhanced military and economic aid we are now getting?"

"I am. We told him that his biased statements were undermining the bipartisan support Israel enjoys from democrats and republicans alike. Moreover, Mr. Rabin has done this before. When he was ambassador in Washington he brazenly came out in favor of Richard Nixon against Hubert Humphrey. Actually" – this with an impish smile – "it paid off at the time, since Nixon won by a huge margin, as you will recall."

Walfish's mouth lifted into a sarcastic smile, and he teased, "So now that Kissinger is about to leave office might *you*, Mr. Begin, have cause to miss him – as a Jew, I mean?"

Measure for measure, Begin bantered, "So, now that you've finished your glass of tea might *you*, Mr Walfish, like another – as a friend, I mean?"

The *Jerusalem Post* man chuckled and shook his head. Being a veteran, he had had experience with the good humor and easy rapport which made Begin such a favorite with the press.

"In that case, allow me to indulge on my own," said Begin, and he raised a finger to catch the waitress's eye. Then, "As to your question, I got to know Dr. Kissinger quite well over the course of time, and I would say, yes, as a Jew he has a certain feeling toward us. But how can I be expected to feel nostalgia at his departure after all the occasions he exerted such pressure on us that caused us incalculable harm?"

"Such as when?" The correspondent's eyes were focused firmly on Mr. Begin but his pen carried on writing as if of its own accord.

"Such as when Mr. Rabin initially said no to the so-called interim agreement with Egypt, and Kissinger imposed a so-called 'reassessment' policy on us between March and August last year. He claimed it was President Ford's doing, but we all know it was his, and his pressure became so relentless that he ultimately forced Rabin to pull back deep into Sinai, abandon the Mitla and the Gidi Passes, surrender the oil fields, and all for what – for peace? Fiddlesticks! Sadat did not even renounce his state of war, let alone lift his boycott and allow our ships through the Suez Canal." And then, without pause, "Please excuse me a moment, otherwise I'll be in trouble with my wife."

Begin put his hand in his pocket, extracted a pill, swilled it down with his tea, said with a twinkle, "Now you are a witness that I've followed my wife's orders," and then returned weightily to the subject in hand: "You didn't by any chance follow the second TV debate between Carter and Ford, did you?" he asked the journalist.

"No, I'm afraid not."

"Carter accused Ford of virtually bringing Israel to its knees – those were his words: *'to its knees'* – because of the 'reassessment' policy. And then there was the matter of the airlift during the Yom Kippur War, which was Nixon's doing much more than Kissinger's. And what about" – he was running on all cylinders now – "when he rescued the Egyptian Third Army from inevitable surrender in the Yom Kippur War, depriving us of the chance of reaching some sort of an accommodation with the Egyptians? We had a whole Egyptian army at our mercy, and there was he, Kissinger, banging on the table trying to panic Prime Minister Golda Meir into believing the Soviets were about to march against us if we didn't lift the siege. I've seen the transcripts. I've seen his actual words. He said, 'Mrs. Meir, you want the Third Army? Well, the United States has no intention of entering World War Three because you want the Egyptian Third Army.' That was his language."

Begin paused to take a long sip of his tea, and a sudden glint entered his eyes. It was a puckish shine, a shine of reminiscence, that said, "I have a good story to tell," and tell it he did:

"I once addressed Kissinger from the rostrum of the Knesset. I spoke to him as if he was standing right there in front of me. 'Dr. Kissinger,' I said, 'you are a Jew. You are not the first Jew to achieve high office in the country of your domicile. Do not forget those other Jews, who had such complexes about being accused of bias in favor of their own people that they did the very opposite. They bent over backward. Don't forget those Jews, Dr. Kissinger.'"

"I recall that," said Walfish. "And I recall you were taken to task for it by government people."

"I was," said Begin, the glint still in his eyes. "There were some who railed against me. But I don't regret a word I said, because I spoke the truth. And do you know what?" – the glint flowered into a grin – "I met Dr. Kissinger some time later and he, with that dry wit of his, said to me with mock sulkiness, as if I'd just berated him, 'Mr. Begin,' he said, 'I heard you gave me hell in the Knesset.' And I said, 'Dr. Kissinger, me – hell? Never! Paradise is where you belong. Do the right thing by Israel,' I said, 'and you'll earn your place in Paradise.'"

"And what did he say to that?"

"Oh, he just laughed, but we both knew it was *yenim's g'lechter*" [Yiddish for "no laughing matter"].

A couple of months after that conversation, in mid-January 1977, Rabin called me in to say he wanted me to draft a letter to Kissinger.

"He's stepping down in a few days," the prime minister said, "and I want to send him a farewell message."

"What kind, official or informal?" I asked.

Rabin pondered, and said, "A bit of both. We've had such a topsy-turvy relationship over the years – good times, bad times, friendship, fights. I have to think about it."

Hands in pockets, he strode over to the window, stared into the murkiness of the winter twilight, and when his thoughts had germinated, turned and told me what he wanted to say. It was this:

Dear Dr. Kissinger,

This letter, addressed to you now on the eve of your departure from the State Department, is no mere formal communication of appreciation. We have known each other too long and too well for that. I, therefore, ask you to read my letter in the personal spirit in which it is written.

I look forward to a time when we shall have the opportunity to meet and chat about your days in government over these past eight years. These have been fateful years for America and the world, and if their direction has led mankind a step or two closer to international sanity, I have no doubt that you have had something to do with it. The chapter entitled "The Kissinger Period" in future history books will tell of one of the most dramatic, incisive and imaginative periods in American foreign policy. As you clear your desk at the State Department you can take satisfaction in the knowledge that you leave the affairs of nations in a somewhat better condition than you found them.

Hopefully, this applies also to my own part of the globe. In the course of our many personal and formal discussions we have not always seen eye to eye on the affairs of the Middle East. But I believe we have always understood each other, just as I know that we have been impelled by the same common concerns and aspirations for peace.

Few men have brought to the negotiating exercise such knowledge of our region, such skill, such an understanding and, if I may add, such boundless energy, as yourself. It is my hope that the building blocks you helped so assiduously to create will prove to be a foundation for a structure more permanent and firm. Certainly, we are determined to try.

In some important respects the Israel you knew when you came into office is now a stronger place. And I know that, in this area too, you have had a share in making it possible. Which is why we owe you much gratitude for helping to translate words into deeds, sentiments into actions and, not least, goodwill into policy. I will add that you leave office having helped create a period of unprecedented understanding in the history of the American-Israel relationship…It is in the spirit of these sentiments that I extend to you now my very best wishes and all good fortune for the future.

After Rabin had approved and signed the letter, I asked him if he truly believed he would miss Kissinger that much, given all the fights and the ups and the downs over the years. He gave me a dour look, lit a cigarette, bent down to extract a tumbler from a bottom drawer, filled it with Scotch and water, and with absolute conviction, said, "Yes, I'll miss him."

"Why?"

"For three reasons: One – he's the only secretary of state who ever truly understood the Israel-Arab conflict. Two – the interim agreement is working out fine; not a single Israeli soldier has fallen on the Egyptian front since we signed it. And three – our relationship with Washington has never been better. What we now have is tantamount to a strategic alliance."

"And Jimmy Carter – what do you make of him?"

Rabin rolled his eyes. "God knows! From what I've heard he sounds like a pie-in-the-sky do-gooder, with visions of curing all the ills of the world, beginning with our own. My fear is he's going to embark on a misbegotten crusade to bring peace to the Holy Land and end up a misinformed meddler embroiling us all in an inferno."

Imagine, then, his pleasant surprise when President Jimmy Carter welcomed him to the White House – this was on 7 March 1977 – and emphasized in his public greeting America's "long-standing commitment and friendship to Israel," saying how "our two peoples are forever bound by our sharing of democratic principles and human liberty, and our constant search for peace." The Jewish State, he said, "must have defensible borders so that peace commitments would never be violated," and that, "in welcoming you and your delegation, I wish to reassure you at the outset, Mr. Prime Minister, that the United States is deeply committed to the security and welfare of Israel. There is no intention of our imposing upon your country any settlement that you feel might jeopardize your security. In fact, our commitment to Israel's security takes precedence over any other interest in the area."

What could possibly sound better than that? But behind closed doors the official talks that got under way took an ominous turn as President Carter began to press Rabin to reconvene the international Geneva peace conference in order to establish a comprehensive settlement with all of Israel's neighbors. Rabin abhorred the idea of an international peace conference. It would mean facing Russia as a co-chairman with the U.S. and a solid bloc of hostile Arab states, backed by Moscow and the non-aligned nations, all intent on enfeebling Israel – a sure prescription for failure, if not outright war.

There was more: President Carter wanted not only Geneva; he wanted to know how the Palestine Liberation Organization, led by Yasser Arafat, would fit into the whole negotiation process. This core question was picked up by the Speaker of the House, Thomas (Tip) O'Neill, at a stag working dinner given by Carter for some sixty political heavyweights.

Tip O'Neill was a big, shambling Irish-American, and when he rose to ask about the PLO he did so in a deceptively innocent fashion – deceptive in that Rabin suspected he was speaking not only for himself but for President Carter, too.

Photograph credit: Moshe Milner & Israel Government Press Office

Rabin meets with President Carter at the White House, 7 March 1977

Author in conversation with Prime Minister Rabin and wife Leah, en route to Washington on presidential flight, March 1977

"Mr. Prime Minister," he said, "why can't you bring yourself to nego-tiate with the PLO? Why can't we ask you to do what we did? We talked to the Vietcong, not just with the North Vietnamese. If that's what we did as representatives of a Great Power, why can't you do the same? Why could the French negotiate with the Algerian FLN and conclude an agreement with them? Why were the British able to negotiate with underground movements all over the world – yours included – while you are unable to negotiate with the PLO? Why?"

Rabin's answer was delivered with tremendous conviction.

"Mr. O'Neill," he said, "let me ask you in return: did the Vietcong refuse to recognize the existence of the United States? Was their basic program a 'Vietcong Covenant' denying America's right to exist? [an allu-sion to the PLO's National Covenant denying Israel's right to exist]. Did the FLN plan to annihilate France? Did the underground organizations in Israel and elsewhere challenge the existence of Great Britain? What basis is there for negotiations with the PLO, whose avowed raison d'être is to destroy the State of Israel and replace it with a Palestinian state?"

This logic did not move Jimmy Carter, and the visit, which had begun on such a hopeful note, ended with the two leaders locked on a collision course.

In his diary entry of 7 March 1977, President Jimmy Carter wrote this:

> Prime Minister Rabin came over from Israel. I've put in an awful lot of time studying the Middle East question and was hoping Rabin would give me some outline of what Israel ultimately hopes to see achieved in a permanent peace settlement. I found him very timid, very stubborn, and also somewhat ill at ease. At the working supper Speaker Tip O'Neill asked him, for instance, under what circum-stances he would permit the Palestinians to be represented at the Geneva talks, and he was adamantly opposed to any meeting if the PLO or other representatives of the Palestinians were there. When he went upstairs with me, just the two of us, I asked him to tell me what Israel wanted me to do when I met with the Arab leaders, and if there was something specific, for instance, that I could propose to Sadat. He didn't unbend at all, nor did he respond. It seems to me that the Israelis, at least Rabin, don't trust our government or any of their neighbors. I guess there is some justification for this distrust. I've never met any of the Arab leaders, but am looking forward to see if they are more flexible than Rabin."[52]

And of that same occasion Yitzhak Rabin wrote:

> [I was given] reassurances from the President that the contents of
> our conversations would under no circumstances be allowed to leak
> out or be publicized in any manner. I was therefore all the more sur-
> prised to hear of the President's far-reaching statements at a press
> conference the next day [which] succeeded in dashing my spirits...
> In explicating his views on peace, borders, and other issues related
> to Middle East peace negotiations, Carter practically committed the
> United States and the presidency to an explicit position – in com-
> plete contradiction to all that had been said to me during our meet-
> ings. His remark on Israel's withdrawal to the 4 June 1967 lines, with
> minor modifications, was the worst part of it. No President before
> him had ever committed the United States to such a position. Even
> so, it never occurred to me that only ten days later Carter would
> speak of the need for a 'Palestinian homeland,' a further dramatic
> change in traditional U.S. policy.[53]

No wonder Rabin was full of foreboding when he departed Washington. With his statement, Jimmy Carter had publicly all but unilaterally
sided with the Arabs in saying that Israel would have to withdraw back to
the pre–Six-Day War 1967 lines, which reduced the Jewish State to a vulnerable nine-mile waist along the densely populated coastal plain where
the bulk of the nation's population resided, and where the greater part of
its economic infrastructure was located, leaving the country with no defensive depth and rendering it vulnerable to attack after attack. Moreover, the
president was advocating the establishment of a Palestinian 'homeland'
which, in Rabin's eyes, was a euphemism for a Palestinian state – and all
this under the umbrella of an international conference in which the PLO
would be a partner. For all of the president's reassurances, here were the
seeds of an imposed settlement, and one which, in essence, was almost
indistinguishable from the reviled Rogers Plan of 1969.

Such acrimony, such a breakdown of trust between an Israeli prime
minister and an American president, had not occurred in decades. When I
discussed with Rabin the two major speeches he was still to deliver before
leaving America, one for a black-tie Israel Bonds affair at the Fontainebleau
in Miami Beach and the other at a United Jewish Appeal dinner at the New
York Waldorf Astoria – speeches which I had yet to draft – he told me to

put a brave face on things and totally downplay his differences with the president, just as he was doing with the Israeli press.

Our final day in America was a Shabbat, and we rested up before flying home that night. Generally, the prime minister enjoyed a chat over a nightcap after take-off, but on this occasion he was unusually uncommunicative, so we lounged about and tried to get some sleep as best we might. Seven hours later, nibbling on an El Al breakfast, Rabin told us that he had spent much of the night ruminating over Jimmy Carter's abysmal ignorance of our affairs, and thinking about how the situation would affect the forthcoming Israeli general election three months hence. The last thing he needed before polling day was a crisis with Washington, he said. What he did not tell us was that he was brooding on something else as well, the dirtiest trick fate could possibly have played on him. It had sneaked up on him from behind, and it would eventually catapult him headlong into his own political waterloo. This defeat did not come from his political opponent's electoral advantages, and not from his acrimonious dealings with the president of the United States; it was as a result of the accidental discovery of an illegal bank account belonging to his wife, at the National Bank in Washington DC.

Chapter twenty-two

Swansong

On the very day Yitzhak Rabin was locked in his vinegary
dispute with Jimmy Carter at the White House, Leah Rabin was spotted
making a withdrawal at the Dupont Circle branch of the National Bank
by a security officer at the Israeli Embassy. Her transaction was trivial
enough, and would have gone unnoticed but for the fact that at that time
it was an offense for an Israeli citizen to hold a bank account abroad. The
account was a leftover from the Rabins' ambassadorial days, and should
have been closed once their time in America was over. It contained some
twenty thousand dollars.

Tipped off, Dan Margolit, the Washington correspondent of the
influential Israeli daily *Haaretz*, dashed off to the branch in question, and
thinking quickly, told the teller he owed the Rabins money, and would like
to deposit a fifty-dollar check into their account. The unsuspecting teller
examined the customer file, confirmed the existence of the account, and
jotted down the account number on the back of Margolit's check prior
to depositing it. Margolit, quick as a Roadrunner, memorized the digits,
scribbled them down, and scurried off to ask the prime minister's press
secretary, Dan Patir, if Mr. Rabin had any comment to make. Rabin said
he had none, but asked that the story be held up for one day, to enable
him to fly home before it broke. It was this that was preying on the prime
minister's mind as he winged his way back to Ben-Gurion airport, not just
his row with Jimmy Carter.

Israel's attorney general at the time, Aharon Barak – later to become president of the Supreme Court – initially regarded the matter as a mere technical infringement, to be handled on an administrative level. But being something of a doctrinarian, ultimately he underwent a change of heart and insisted that the law be allowed to take its inexorable course, which meant that Leah Rabin would have to stand trial.

"Me, too," insisted an outraged Rabin when given the news. "I will not let Leah face this alone. Morally and formally we share responsibility. True, Leah was the one who actually used the account, because she always handled our finances. But the account was registered in both our names and I share full responsibility. If she is to blame, so am I. I will not allow a distinction to be drawn between me and my wife."

Three people were witness to this outburst – Freuka Poran, in the prime minister's office to report on some military matter, Dan Patir, Rabin's press secretary, who was there to report on the day's media, and myself. I was there to report on a document that required his attention. Embarrassed and dismayed, the three of us sat speechless as we watched this most private and decent of men, as honest a one as ever had crossed the threshold of Israel's political life, being thus besmirched and humiliated.

Came the day of the trial, and Yitzhak Rabin publicly escorted his wife to the courthouse, where she was found guilty and heavily fined. Even before the trial, Rabin had decided to resign from the prime ministership as a matter of principle. This was an act so exceptional in Israeli political life it came to be seen as a legendary deed of noble proportions. However, Israeli constitutional law forbids a prime minister to resign once a new election date has been set, and an election was already scheduled for three months hence. So Rabin announced his withdrawal from the electoral race as leader of the Labor Party, and his natural successor was, predictably, his longtime nemesis and arch-rival, Minister of Defense Shimon Peres. Unable by law to resign, Rabin did the next best thing: he took what was tantamount to a leave of absence. But, here, too, the law did not totally relieve him of his overall responsibilities, most notably on matters to do with public security, so he continued to come daily to the office, as did we, his personal staff. I, personally, had little to do other than to write an occasional speech, letter, or position paper for Shimon Peres, who conducted whatever affairs of government he was engaged in either from the Cabinet Room on the floor above, or from his ministry of defense office in Tel Aviv.

As election day approached, his secretary called to say he wanted to see me to talk about a job following the elections. I was totally taken aback;

the very thought of working for Shimon Peres, after having worked so long for Rabin, was abhorrent to me and I went in search of Rabin to tell him so.

There can be few things worse for a politician than to be an out-of-work prime minister: the Rabin I met that day looked forlorn and abandoned. His eyes were red and swollen. He stood grimly at his desk scanning newspapers, a bent shadow of his old self.

"Stop torturing yourself with that stuff," I said as I walked into his room. "The media is wallowing in your crucifixion."

"Swine!" he hissed. "They twist everything around." But, then, with a spark of spirit he pointed to a paragraph in *Davar* – the Labor Party daily, now defunct – and said, "Here I'm being called obstinate and inflexible, but honest to a fault. Is that a compliment or not?"

"A backhanded one, I suppose," I replied.

He obviously did not want to be alone, for he invited me to take a seat, and in a wry and unusually candid fashion, said, "You've known me long enough to know I can be pretty inflexible, and I do know that I am honest to a fault. This has sometimes got me into a lot of hot water, not least in the army."

"And in Washington, too," I reminded him. "How many times were you rapped over the knuckles by Abba Eban because you said exactly what you thought of him?"

Grumpily, he concurred, and added, "And now, this business of the bank: I brought myself down by insisting on resigning – the law does not require it – because I thought it was the only decent thing to do."

"So whose genes are these? Whom did you inherit it from?" I asked this flippantly in the hope of lightening things up a bit.

Rabin began toying with a statuette on his desk – one of those executive playthings built of multiple metal parts – and smiling his crooked smile, said, "My mother, mainly. My mother, Rosa, was as obstinate as a mule, and strict and straight as a die. She inherited her character from her father – the Cohen from Petrograd. She used to tell stories – to my sister Rachel and me – about what a man of strict principle our grandfather was. He was very religious, and was one of the few Jews allowed to live in Petrograd."

"How so? What did he do?"

"He was a timber merchant. He used to manage forests for some relative of the Tsar, which was why he was allowed to live in Petrograd. They even installed a telephone in his house – one of the first in Petrograd. Now, I ask you – how many people in those days in Russia had telephones? So, when it rang you knew somebody very important was on the other end of the line. But our mother told us that our grandfather had such strong religious principles, and was such a stalwart character, that he would never answer the telephone on Shabbat. The man could have lost everything – all his privileges – but he would never answer the telephone on Shabbat. Now, what do you make of that for a character?"

I had one sudden lucid thought: "It's a pity nothing of your grandfather's Shabbat observance ever rubbed off on you," I said.

He shrugged as if the very notion of it was beyond his realm of reasoning, and said simply, "My mother rebelled against religion and left home to come here. But enough of me. What about you?"

A sudden spikiness had gripped his voice which I knew meant his defenses were back in place and that the Rabin I knew had returned – the Rabin of no nonsense, no frills, no flourishes, just unembroidered frankness and privacy.

"What about you?" he asked again. "What are you going to be doing now that I'm going?"

"Peres wants to see me," I told him. "His secretary tells me he's going to offer me a job. But I'd prefer to go back to the foreign ministry, under the circumstances."

He looked at me sharply. "What do you mean – under what circumstances?"

"Under the circumstances of having worked with you for nearly a decade; under the circumstances of feeling a deep sense of personal loyalty toward you; and under the circumstances that I can't simply switch horses overnight, from you to Peres."

Without a word he walked over to the window, hands thrust in his trouser pockets. However dark his mood had been when I'd entered the room, it was even darker now as he turned, and in a flat, uninflected tone, the tone he used at press conferences, scolded, "*Shtuyot!* Rubbish! You were never involved in my differences with Shimon Peres, and I'm not going to let you get involved now."

"That's easier said than done," I muttered.

"Maybe. But by what moral right will you say to the next prime minister of Israel that you refuse to work with him because of me? If Shimon Peres has the same view of you as I do – and I think he has – that's all that matters. Must everything be a matter of personal allegiances? What about the country? What about the people? You have no right to refuse him. You're not a politician, you're a civil servant. Keep it that way."

Bruised by this moralistic tirade, I said in a mood of genuine truculence, "You know it's not that simple. You can't stand Peres' guts and he can't stand yours. Imagine a situation – he's sitting in that chair where you are now and he has a go at you, as he inevitably will, because of some speech you've made, or some stand you've taken. What am I supposed to do, get up and walk out?"

Blithely, Rabin replied, "Don't worry, Peres will be careful not to bad-mouth me in your presence. And besides, I'll give him no cause to do so."

"Meaning what?"

"Meaning I've decided to stay in the Knesset but lie low for a while – keep a low profile, out of the public eye. After that we'll see what happens."

"What do you think is going to happen?"

"Trouble."

"What kind of trouble – war?"

"Maybe, but not necessarily. The Arabs will certainly have to show Jimmy Carter they have the military muscle to make trouble, otherwise their diplomatic moves will be toothless. And we'll have to show Carter that we have even more military muscle, otherwise our diplomatic moves will be toothless. We have to be ready to put up a fight. The problem is that ever since my March meeting with Carter an impenetrable cloud has been hanging over Washington."

"Impenetrable – what does that mean?"

Rabin's voice dropped from a pebbly baritone to a gravelly bass, a sure sign he was about to say something confidential. "Simcha Dinitz can't get his hand on any hard information, but the indicators are that President Sadat has won Jimmy Carter's absolute trust, at our expense. They're cooking up something – something to do with a Geneva confer-ence. Kissinger even phoned Dinitz to warn him he's heard that a plan is in the offing, but even he doesn't know exactly what. And because of Carter's essential ignorance of Middle East affairs, Kissinger is truly wor-ried that we could find ourselves in a grave situation, so grave that he said that as a Jew he could not stand by without alerting us. I even sent over a special emissary to meet quietly with some of our friends over there, but the picture is still murky."

I blew a long whistle of surprise. "You think things are that serious?"

He strode toward the window again, stared out of it for a while, and said softly, more to himself than to me, "I think Kissinger is exaggerating. You know how paranoid he can get."

I asked him whether the cabinet was fully cognizant of the state of affairs he had just described.

"Certainly," he said. "I felt I had to be on record before leaving office that I've done all that I could to get hold of all the facts."

"And what's Peres' view?"

"Peres is anxious that nothing gets out before the elections, which I can well understand."

"And after the elections – will he have a problem putting together a coalition quickly to handle this?"

His feet now up on the desk, hands pillowed behind his head, he speculated, "My guess is that if Labor makes a decent showing, Peres should be able to form a coalition in a reasonable amount of time. But if Labor does badly he'll use the Carter crisis to cobble together an emergency coalition – a national unity government together with Menachem Begin. The nation will go along with that under the circumstances."

"And are you that convinced Peres is truly our next prime minister?"

"As things stand now, yes. Begin has suffered a severe heart attack at the worst possible moment for his party. The elections are imminent and he's virtually out of the picture. They have nobody else of Begin's stature – so who are they going to vote for? That is why I take it for granted Peres will form the new government, and that you, Yehuda, will be as loyal to him as you have been to me."

Then, purposefully, "I've got to write a farewell letter to Jimmy Carter, but I'll be damned if I know what to say. Let's think."

He began to pace the room slowly, immersed in thought, and when he next spoke there was fire in his eyes and grit in his voice: "I've got it! I'm going to say that any furthering of the American disengagement from Israel could lead to war, and that any strengthening of America's special relationship with Israel could lead to peace. Let's try it out – the thrust of it. Let's see what it looks like."

In its final version it looked like this:

Dear Mr. President – I depart from my duties as prime minister after three years of unremitting effort to advance the cause of peace in our region. This is a cause which was and remains the highest aspiration of every government of Israel. It is my conviction that if the building blocks for a negotiated peace with security are to be constructively exploited this will depend primarily on the continuation and intensification of the special relationship that has traditionally marked the ties between our two countries. I believe we are entering a crucial period in which the prospects for further movement toward peace will be determined, ultimately, by the credibility of the Israel-U.S. dialogue and the intimacy of understanding it invokes. Over and over again, experience has shown that the atmosphere of this dialogue influences and shapes the atmosphere of the peace climate in the area.

Extremely satisfied with this paragraph, which said exactly what he wanted it to say, he did something unheard of: this painfully shy man walked around the desk and with an overflowing of camaraderie gave me a hug so huge it left me speechless.

"*B'seder*," he said – "OK."

I kept my appointment with Shimon Peres that afternoon, and I confess that his propensity for hyperbole, poetry, and tautology – the very opposite of Yitzhak Rabin – got under my skin. He listened patiently when I told him that I felt too great a personal loyalty to Rabin to switch horses overnight, but being the canny and tested politician that he was, he disarmingly brushed off my protestations, and suavely responded that had I been less loyal to Rabin he would have thought less of me.

He then went on to regale me with lyrical and optimistic rhetoric about how he was going to beat Menachem Begin roundly, how Begin was virtually out of the race anyway because of his heart attack, and how all the polls were going his way. And then, taking me by the arm and guiding me toward the door, he said with enormous poignancy, "Yehuda, everything I know tells me I shall be the next prime minister of Israel. Psychologically, I'm living with that responsibility night and day, so it's only natural I should be thinking now about who I want to work with. And one of the people I want to work with is you. I have lots of new ideas, and you have an important role at my side." Whereupon, he gave my hand a final squeeze and, full of energy, said, "Get ready for hard work. Expect a call after the victory."[54]

Part three
The Last Patriarch

Prime Minister Menachem Begin

1977–1983

August 16, 1913 – Born Brisk [Brest-Litovsk], Russia.

1935 – Warsaw University Law School.

1939 – Head of Betar, Poland (the influential youth wing of the Zionist Revisionist movement founded by Ze'ev Jabotinsky).

1939 – Marries Aliza Arnold.

1940 – Sentenced to eight years in Siberian labor camps by Soviet secret police for Zionist activism.

1941 – Released to join Free Polish Forces following the Nazi invasion of the Soviet Union.

1942 – Arrives in Eretz Yisrael with the Free Polish Forces.

1943 – Assumes command of the underground *Irgun Zvai Leumi* (The National Fighting Organization).

1944 – Leads uprising against the British rule of Eretz Yisrael.

Key Events of Political Life

1948 – Begin disbands the Irgun following Israel's independence and establishes the Herut (later the Likud) Party.

1967 – Helps initiate the national unity government on the eve of the Six-Day War.

1970 – Resigns from the national unity government.

May 1977 – Elected prime minister.

November 1977 – Egyptian President Anwar Sadat visits Jerusalem.

1978 – The Camp David Accords are signed with Egypt, facilitated by President Jimmy Carter.

1978 – Awarded the Nobel Peace Prize.

1979 – Peace treaty with Egypt.

1980 – 'Operation Moses' – the initial covert mass rescue of the black Jews of Ethiopia.

January 1981 – Ronald Reagan assumes the U.S. presidency.

June 7 1981 – Israeli air force destroys Iraq's nuclear reactor.

June 30 1981 – Begin reelected prime minister.

October 1981 – Egyptian President Anwar Sadat is assassinated.

June 1982 – Operation Peace for Galilee.

September 1982 – The Sabra and Shatila massacre.

November 1982 – Aliza Begin dies.

February 1983 – The Kahan Commission report on the Sabra and Shatila massacre.

October 1983 – Begin resigns the prime ministership and retires from public life.

March 9 1992 – Begin dies at the age of 79.

Photograph credit: Ya'acov Sa'ar & Israel Government Press Office

Prime Minister Designate Menachem Begin praying at the Western Wall upon receiving the mandate to form the new government, 7 June 1977

Chapter one

Upheaval

At eleven o'clock in the evening of 17 May 1977, I was sitting cross-legged in front of the television in the company of my wife and four kids, listening to the station's chief anchorman, Chaim Yavin, repeating for the umpteenth time the word *"Mahapach!"* – Upheaval! – and breathlessly announcing that according to the television's sample poll Menachem Begin, leader of the opposition Likud Party, had roundly trounced Labor's Shimon Peres in the elections that day.

"I don't believe it," I cried out in disbelief. "Peres just offered me a job."

The phone rang. It was General Freuka Poran. In a supercharged voice, he snarled, "Are you watching the TV? Look at them – those Beginites. They're our new bosses. Ever since I was a youngster in the Hagana I've been allergic to that man and his minions. He's a" – his voice climbed – "he's a ghetto windbag, an ex-terrorist, a fanatic!"

"Cut it out," I shot back.

"I won't work for him," he shouted.

"But you're a soldier," I said angrily. "You can't opt out because of a political whim. Are you telling me you're not going to follow the orders of the next prime minister of Israel, which apply to me" – he knew about my last talk with Rabin – "and which apply to you even more so, General Poran?"

He shot back, feisty as hell. "Do they? Well let me tell you something. This is no whim. That man is going to lead us into war, and I want no part of it. I'm quitting the army. *Layla tov!*" [Good night!] And he hung up.

I went back to join my family, who remained transfixed by the political theater filling the screen. It showed the hall at Begin's party headquarters in Tel Aviv where hundreds of loyalists were applauding in incredulity and ecstasy, all bellowing in a single voice, "BE-GIN! BE-GIN! BE-GIN!" The din was so ear-battering that the jostled television reporter on the floor had given up trying to describe what the clamor was about. But then, as we watched, he cupped his hand around his microphone and yelled for all he was worth, "Here he comes! He's coming now," and the camera zoomed in on the prime minister–elect entering the hall, crowded in on every side. Despite the grainy picture on our black-and-white screen, the signs of his recent heart attack were distinct. His face was sallow, his cheekbones were pronounced, his semi-bald crown was thrown into prominence. Yet his ravaged features were animated by a dazzling smile as he moved with obvious joy into the shoe-stomping, raucous throng crushing in upon him on every side. And as he moved, the thrilled assembly chorused his name ever louder:

"BE-GIN! BE-GIN! BE-GIN!"

Anxious guards, stewards, aides, and policemen pushed and elbowed the adoring crowd, cutting a channel through the crush to let the victor enter. Inching his way toward the stage, Begin waved with both hands high, and when he finally mounted the platform, the entire jamboree exploded into the thumping patriotic chant, *Am Yisrael Chai* – The People of Israel Live.

His figure was all aglow in camera flashes as he led the throng, clapping his hands and bending his knees up and down to the rhythm of the beat, like a Chasidic rabbi.

Swiftly seizing the opportunity as the champion raised his palms to quell the applause, the television commentator explained that Menachem Begin was sixty-three, and had been in Israel for thirty-five years.

The singing and shouting gradually settled into a deep hush, and those pressing around the prime minister-elect peeled aside to give him center stage, leaving him standing alone beneath the giant portraits of his two ideological heroes, Theodor Herzl and Ze'ev Jabotinsky. And there he stood, isolated in the stillness, drinking in the crowd's adoration, a slender, frail-looking figure in a dark suit, his face pale yet his eyes bright.

With deep reverence, he drew from his pocket a black yarmulke and recited the *Shehecheyanu* blessing, thanking the Almighty for enabling him to reach and celebrate this day. A resounding "Amen!" roared around the hall with such energy it caused the microphone to shriek with feedback. Next Begin recited a psalm of gratitude, and, after that, his victory address, an oration of reconciliation, in which he appealed for a spirit of national unity, capping his address with the compelling phrases of Abraham Lincoln: "With malice toward none; with charity to all; with firmness in the right, as God gives us to see the right, let us strive to finish the work we are in."

As the applause swelled again, Menachem Begin turned toward his wife, Aliza, a petite woman with springy gray hair and thick glasses, wearing a simple gray suit, who all this while had been standing modestly behind him. One could see the embrace in his eyes as he told her, in a voice husky with emotion, of his eternal love and his everlasting debt toward her, for the way she had stood by him through thick and thin, in unbounded devotion and sacrifice, for forty years.

"I remember you, the kindness of your youth," he lauded, quoting the Prophet Jeremiah. "I remember you, the love of your betrothal, when you followed me into the wilderness, into a land that was not sown." And then, paraphrasing, "I remember you when you followed me into a land that was strewn on every side with deadly minefields, and yet you followed me."

These deeply passionate feelings spoken so openly stood in such sharp contrast to Yitzhak Rabin's famed emotional austerity that they triggered shouts of approval from the entire assembly. The clapping and the whistles went on for so long that many probably missed Begin's invocation of the memory of his "master and teacher," Ze'ev Jabotinsky, the charismatic nationalist ideologue, founder of the Revisionist Zionist Movement, in whose footsteps he devoutly walked.

"Prodigious and startling were Ze'ev Jabotinsky's gifts," he declared. "He was decades ahead of his time, a giant Zionist warrior-statesman, a true prophet of his people, the man who led the movement for the settlement of the whole of biblical Israel, who was the first to sound the alarm of the coming holocaust, and the war cry for a Jewish army to fight for freedom and a sovereign Jewish State."

Ending with a promise to fulfill Jabotinsky's legacy, he bowed low, and the whole hall rose to chant the anthem of national hope, "*Hatikva*." People pumped hands and hugged each other, not wanting the moment ever to end, even though it was three in the morning. But end it did, and Begin, shielded once more by a cordon of security personnel and officials, waved his way off the platform, beaming, shaking every palm he could reach and kissing the knuckles of every woman who thrust her hand at him, with all the gallantry of a Polish peer.[55]

Instantly, the camera shifted to the floodlit street outside, where loudspeakers blared patriotic music and devotees milled around singing and dancing under blue and white paper bunting. Men and women of every age were there, from youngsters to oldsters, most of them olive-skinned. They originated from places like Morocco, Tunisia, Yemen, Iraq, Libya, Kurdistan, Algeria, Egypt, Iran, and India. Commentators would later explain that it was they, these Oriental immigrants, who had catapulted Menachem Begin into power after almost thirty years in the political wilderness. They were the impoverished and the God-fearing, Sephardic Jews mainly, who, having felt left out and passed by, fed up of slum life and handouts, had finally flexed their muscles, put their energy behind Mr. Begin, and settled their score with the paternalistic and elitist European Labor old-timers of whom Shimon Peres was the epitome.

Scores gathered eagerly around a television commentator who had thrust his microphone into their faces.

"Why did you vote for Menachem Begin?" he asked. "What makes him so different from Shimon Peres? Peres' name was originally Perski. Both were born in Poland. Is not Begin as much an Ashkenazi as Peres?"

"Ashke-NAZI!" yelled somebody off-camera.

"Shut up!" bellowed a man with the sloped shoulders of a boxer, dressed in a waiter's jacket. "You want to know why we voted Begin? We voted Begin because he's not a godless socialist like Shimon Peres and his atheist lot. Begin never lined his pockets the way they have. He's humble and honest. Begin speaks like a Jew, the way a Jew should speak. He's not ashamed to say 'God.' He speaks with a Jewish heart. That's why Labor always ridiculed him, and treated him the way they always treated us – like scum."

"Are you saying that Peres and the entire secular Labor crowd are not really Jews?" asked the interviewer, provocatively.

The man spat. There was contempt in his eyes. "They may be Jews, but they behave like goyim. Have you ever seen one of them inside a *beit knesset* – a synagogue? What's a Jew without a synagogue sometimes? Where's their self-respect, their pride?"

"*Ya, habibi*," cut in someone else, sporting a thick crown of greased black hair, also wearing a waiter's jacket. "Thirty years ago those Labor bigwigs duped us. They brought us here telling us this was the *Geula*, the Redemption. Cheap labor, that's what they brought us here for. In Casablanca my father was an honored member of the community. He was the patriarch of our family. He had *kavod* – respect."

"*KAVOD!!*" the crowd chorused in corroboration.

"Everybody gave him *kavod* because he ran his own spice shop in the

Kasba. Now what does he do? He breaks his back on a building site. Who's going to give him *kavod* now? In Morocco only Arabs work on building sites. His *kavod* has been stolen."

Heads nodded vigorously.

"What's your name?" asked the interviewer.

"Marcel."

"So, tell us Marcel, what did you do in Casablanca?"

"I was a bookkeeper. That's an occupation of *kavod*. Now I'm a waiter. In Morocco, only Arabs are waiters. In Casablanca we lived in a big house with a courtyard. Now, I, my wife, my three children, my mother, my father – all of us live in four ramshackle rooms. Our *kavod* has been trampled upon. The Ashkenazi Labor bosses did that. And now Menachem Begin is giving us our *kavod* back."

He said this in such a triumphant tone that one man began jumping up and down in front of the camera, clapping his hands in excitement and shouting something in a Moroccan Hebrew I could not understand. Other people cheered and burst forth into a rousing singsong. Spontaneously, they formed a chain, hands on each other's shoulders, and ecstatically weaved around and about, singing at the tops of their voices, *"Begin, Melech Yisrael"* – Begin, King of Israel.

This, assuredly, was their field day. To them – half of Israel's population – the name Menachem Begin had an almost mystical appeal. Without sycophancy or pretense, he had won their hearts, knocking down the high walls of arrogance and sectarianism which had cut them off from mainstream Israel since their mass immigration two and three decades before. Ever since national independence, and long before that as well, the country had known only one ruling party – Mapai, the Labor Party – and it saw itself as an all big-guns political battleship designed to rule the political seas forever. But it went off course and was caught off guard by a vessel captained by Menachem Begin who, running silent, running deep, rose incrementally from election to election – from fifteen, to seventeen, to twenty-six, to thirty-nine – until he surfaced with a spectacular showing in the battle of 1977 with the largest number of Knesset seats of any single party, forty-three: enough to form a coalition.

The shocked Laborites drew up petitions, held meetings, organized protests, made speeches, wrote articles, and convened conferences. Many insisted that their downfall was really the fault of President Jimmy Carter. He had publicly tilted toward the Arabs. He had publicly challenged Yitzhak Rabin. He had publicly produced what was tantamount to a unilateral peace plan. He had stabbed Labor in the back by making nonsense of the accepted axiom that they, and they alone, with their vast experience in international affairs, could win and retain the trust of the White House and the American people. But at the end of the day, the truth was much simpler. Labor lost because it had defeated itself. It had been in office for far too long. Its blood was tired and its rank and file flabby.

This was why much of the nation was ready to give Menachem Begin his chance. His integrity shone through. Even his opponents acknowledged his modest, almost monastic lifestyle, and his strict personal uprightness. So, many a moderate gave him the vote as well, on the assumption – and in the hope – that the burdens and realities of office would mellow his passionate vow never to surrender a single inch of the beloved *moledet* – the biblical homeland: Eretz Yisrael. And so they, too, dumped Labor and with the untested Begin at the helm, slipped the national anchor from its familiar moorings, and pushed off on an untutored course into uncharted waters.

Cables from our Washington Embassy reported dismay at Menachem Begin's victory. Some of President Carter's aides suggested he snub the prime minister-elect by not inviting him to Washington. After watching a Begin interview on ABC's *Issues and Answers*, Jimmy Carter was so aghast at what he heard that he wrote in his diary on 23 May 1977:

> I had them replay the *Issues and Answers* interview with Menachem Begin, chairman of the Likud Party and the prospective prime minister of Israel. It was frightening to watch his adamant position on issues that must be resolved if a Middle Eastern peace settlement is going to be realized…. In his first answer he stated that the entire West Bank was an integral part of Israel's sovereignty, that it had been 'liberated' during the Six-Day War, and that a Jewish majority and an Arab minority would be established there. The statement was a radical departure from past Israeli policy, and seemed to throw United Nations Resolution 242, for which Israel had voted, out of the window. I could not believe what I was hearing.[56]

The international media pilloried Begin; *Time* magazine even headlined its election story with an anti-Semitic slur: "BEGIN (rhymes with Fagin) WINS," and the London *Times* led its comment on the election result with the Roman proverb: "Whom the gods want to destroy, they first drive them mad." Prominent Diaspora community leaders, unused to any Israeli leadership but the pragmatic Laborites, were startled at Begin's electoral success and urged him to moderate his public statements, particularly on settlement policy. The day after his victory, Begin had traveled to an IDF encampment called Kaddum, near Nablus, in the heart of the densely Arab populated hill country, and in the course of an impromptu press conference announced a settlement drive to embrace the whole of the West Bank, which he insisted on calling by its biblical name – Judea and Samaria.

"In that case, what is the future of the occupied territories?" asked a journalist.

Like a patient schoolteacher gently correcting an uninformed pupil, Begin replied, "These, my friend, are not occupied territories. You've used this expression for ten years, since sixty-seven. But now it is seventy-seven, and I hope that from now on you'll start using the term liberated territories. A Jew has every right to settle in these liberated territories of the Jewish homeland."

"And what about the Arabs living here?" somebody asked.

Begin answered, "We don't want to evict anyone from his land. In this beautiful country there is room for the Arabs who are working their lands, and for Jews who will come to make the homeland blossom."

"Do you actually plan to annex these territories?" queried another.

"We don't use the word annexation," chided Begin. "You annex foreign territory, not your own country."

"But what about international law – the Fourth Geneva Convention, which expressly forbids settling occupied land?" pressed the questioner.

Begin would not be provoked. Gently, patiently, he explained, "I advise you to look carefully into the legal status of the territories of which you speak, and you will then understand that the Fourth Geneva Convention does not apply. The UN 1947 partition resolution, which the Arabs refused to recognize, is null and void. The area which you call 'occupied' remains a part of what the League of Nations Supreme Council defined on the twenty-fourth of July nineteen twenty-two as the area to be reconstituted as the National Home of the Jewish people; and Jews have lived in, owned land, and tilled their soil here in these areas for hundreds of years prior to being evicted because of Arab wars of aggression."

"So will Israeli law be introduced into the West Bank?"

Begin benignly replied," My friend, what you call the West Bank is Judea and Samaria. Please use these terms in the future. They are, after all, their original biblical names. As for Israeli law, this is a matter for consideration. Once I have formed a government, we shall go to the Knesset and ask for a vote of confidence, and then we shall consider what steps to take. Thank you," and off he went to join a group of would-be settlers, who were singing and dancing as they celebrated installing a new Torah scroll in their makeshift synagogue, which event is what had brought Begin to Kaddum in the first place.

A few days later, Begin was rushed to hospital. It was rumored that he had suffered yet another heart attack. His doctors denied this. What he'd suffered was a cardiac complication brought on by overwork, they said, and what he needed was a rest. So he rested, and from his hospital bed he drew up his new cabinet which he duly presented to the Knesset on 29 June 1977.

It was an exquisite day, and he began it by going to the *Kotel* – the Western Wall – to pray. A crowd of onlookers included black-clad worshippers, Hawaiian-topped tourists, and a host of others, all gawking at a gray Plymouth saloon with three radio masts following an off-white Peugeot 504, out of which Begin emerged, ringed by a squad of bodyguards. Sephardic women ululated with excitement, yeshiva boys sang and danced, and the gleeful throng quickly surrounded the prime minister's group, already swelled by a clutch of newsmen and photographers, recording every stride the prime minister took.

Menachem Begin made his way toward the Wall, his bespectacled, patrician features alive with a glittering smile as he waved and nodded heartily to the assembly. There, at the Wall, he laid his head on a weathered stone, a spontaneous gesture so symbolic that it sparked a blaze of photo flashes. A flock of starlings startled, and went wheeling and screeching out of the crevices above, where bouquets of caper bushes sprouted.

From his pocket, Begin solemnly drew a book of psalms, and recited both lamentations and thanksgivings with reverence. He was deeply aware that within a matter of hours the Knesset would give him its vote of confidence, and the burden of leadership would rest upon his shoulders for the first time.

People watched in silence as he prayed. When he kissed the Wall, and turned to go back to his vehicle, many formed a chanting chain around him, singing *Begin, King of Israel* at the tops of their voices.

Above the din, a voice called out, "So, under your prime ministership, Mr. Begin, how do you visualize a solution to the Palestinian refugee problem?"

The question came from a big-boned man in a safari jacket on whose lapel hung a *New York Times* tab.

"I see a ready solution," answered Begin, unhesitatingly. "In nineteen forty-eight, on the day of our independence, five Arab armies invaded us. We defeated them at great human cost. As a result of that aggression, not one, but two refugee problems arose – Jewish as well as Arab. An almost equal number of Jews fled to Israel from Arab and Moslem lands, as did Arabs from here to Arab lands. Hence, a de facto exchange of populations has already taken place."

"And would you be willing to negotiate this and other matters directly with Mr. Yasser Arafat and his PLO?" asked a tall, gray-haired *Christian Science Monitor* journalist, in the precise tones of a Boston Brahmin.

Something flickered far back in Begin's eyes. The sun caught his glasses, sending a fierce flash across his face, and in a tone reserved for stubborn doctrines, replied, "No, sir – never! That man is the godfather of international terrorism. His organization, the so-called PLO, is a gang of murderers bent on destroying the State of Israel. His so-called Palestine Charter is an Arab *Mein Kampf.* We will never conduct talks with that archcriminal about our own destruction."

"And what if Mr. Arafat recognizes Israel's existence – would you negotiate with him then?"

"No, sir!"

"Why not?"

"Because I wouldn't believe him. It would be a trick, a subterfuge, a phase in his plan to destroy the Jewish State in stages."

"May I butt in at this point," insinuated a tall, debonair chap in a bow tie, with a deep, perfectly pitched BBC voice. "Mr. Arafat asserts that the Jewish State is an illegitimate entity with no right of existence in international law. Arab governments hold to that same view. What say you to that?" His rich English accent was provocative.

Begin, sniffing the foul odor of prejudice, but honed by years of legal training, restrained himself and, with the demeanor of a practiced lawyer, said, "Traditionally, there are four major criteria of statehood under international law. One: an effective and independent government. Two: an effective and independent control of the population. Three: a defined territory. And four: the capacity to freely engage in foreign relations. Israel is in possession of all four and, hence, is a fully fledged sovereign state and a fully accredited member of the United Nations."

The BBC man's acerbic comment on Israel's right to exist had so infuriated Begin that he wrote a last-minute addition to the address which he was shortly to deliver in the Knesset, presenting his government for a vote of parliamentary confidence. And when the time came, in a House already buzzing with excitement, every seat taken, the president in his chair of honor, senior officials cramming into their reserved sections, and all the galleries packed with ambassadors, senior officers and other dignitaries, Menachem Begin, a picture of robust self-assurance, mounted the podium to present his cabinet for approval.

Old-timers, noting that he held in his hand a sheaf of papers, called out to each other in surprise, "Look, he's going to read his speech!"

Menachem Begin had not read a speech since he addressed his compatriots over the Irgun underground radio on the day of Israel's birth twenty-nine years before. In deference to the magnitude of the moment, he, the undisputed master of the impromptu word, began reading his address.

Begin started dryly, by outlining the democratic processes that had led to the present changing of the guard from Labor to Likud, but when he came to the body of his remarks, a deepening passion crept into his voice. Recalling Israel's rebirth and its inherent right to exist in the family of nations, he wagged a finger, and asked in a trembling tone, "Would it enter the mind of any Briton or Frenchman, Belgian or Dutchman, Hungarian or Bulgarian, Russian or American, to request for its people the recognition of its right to exist? Their existence per se is their right to exist!"

As he said these words he rose up on his toes, and every chattering voice in the chamber stilled. He made an arch out of the tips of his fingers, glared at his text, and thundered, "We were granted our right to exist by the God of our fathers at the glimmer of the dawn of human civilization four thousand years ago! And so it is that the Jewish people have an historic, eternal and inalienable right to Eretz Yisrael, the land of our forefathers. And for that right, which has been sanctified in Jewish blood from generation to generation, we have paid a price unequalled in the annals of the nations."

Applause rose from the coalition benches. Many got to their feet. It was a stirring moment, but the man sitting on my left in the section reserved for senior aides did not seem to be particularly moved. Busying himself with a notepad, he was scribbling down names and numbers in a handwriting so bold I could not help but notice them. I threw him a glance and he grinned back with a wide and disarming smile.

"Yechiel Kadishai," he said above the ovation, introducing himself, and he gave my hand a friendly shake.

He was in his mid-fifties, of medium height, with silvering hair bordering a high forehead. Knesset old-timers gossiped fondly about Yechiel Kadishai, for he was a gregarious sort, quick-witted and irreverent. Yet for all his bonhomie and easy-going manner, he was reputed to be the most influential member of the Begin coterie, his most intimate confidant, his alter ego, his factotum, the man who saw him unshaven in pajamas in the morning.

As Begin resumed his extravagant oratory, Kadishai returned to his notepad, but soon enough he got up and left, presumably on some urgent errand. At this point his master's speech gradually cooled to a dry and factual outline of the policy aims of his new government, and the naming of the ministers who would carry them out, after which speakers from all parties spoke.

When Moshe Dayan rose to speak, a sudden restlessness seized the Labor benches. Eyes glared and hatred flashed at this one-time war hero and stalwart of the Labor movement who, forever the maverick, had jumped ship to join Menachem Begin's cabinet as his foreign minister. The moment he opened his mouth, the wrath of his former comrades was flung at him.

"Traitor!" one of them screamed

"Turncoat!" yelled another.

"Give back your seat!" bawled a third.

"Resign!" shouted a fourth.

"Shame on you!" bellowed somebody else.

Amid the jeers, hissing and name-calling, Moshe Dayan kept his temper, his face masklike. He delivered his address, mentioning Israel's intention to attend a Geneva peace conference on the basis of UN Security Council Resolution 242, and affirming that no step would be taken to annex Judea and Samaria while Israel conducted peace negotiations with its neighbors.

One Labor member, totally beside himself, jumped up and cried out, "You are unfit to represent Israel as our foreign minister. Get out of our sight!" This evoked such a squall that the Speaker of the House shouted that he was of a mind to close the meeting. Yet without missing a beat, Moshe Dayan pressed on, insisting that Israel was heading toward crucial decisions and that national unity was more urgent than ever. Few could hear him, because the barrage of abuse shattered virtually every second sentence he uttered.

As the heckling rose and fell, Freuka Poran, who was sitting behind me, leaned across to say, "That's exactly how Dayan behaves under fire, with that same expression on his face – blank! Shells can be bursting all around him but he carries on as if he's not hearing a thing. That's what he's doing now – he's cut himself off from reality. People can shout till kingdom come, he won't bat an eyelid."

Hours later, well past midnight, and after what had died down to a largely humdrum debate, the vote of confidence in the new government was carried, and Menachem Begin and his newly appointed ministers stepped up to the podium one by one, to take the oath of office. When the Speaker finally banged his gavel to declare the session closed, I caught sight of Yitzhak Rabin edging his way around the crowd to join the cluster of well-wishers surrounding the new prime minister.

"*Mazal tov!*" said Rabin with his shy, lopsided smile, extending his hand in congratulation.

Begin returned the handshake, bowed, and said, "If it is convenient may I call on you at the prime minister's office tomorrow morning at nine?"

Rabin's smile spread into a grin. "Convenient? I shall make it convenient. You're the prime minister now!"

At 8:45 on the following morning, Yitzhak Rabin, casually dressed in a long-sleeve white shirt and flannel slacks, walked into the outer office of the prime minister's bureau looking stress-free and even cheery, as if his cup of bitterness had miraculously emptied overnight.

"Time to call it a day," he said with mock relief to us, his handful of personal aides, gathered together to make our farewells. Rabin had ended his self-imposed leave of absence the day Begin won the election, and as the law prescribed, resumed the prime ministership until the prime minister-elect had wrapped up the haggling and horse-trading that always accompanies the formation of a new coalition. That day had finally dawned, and while Rabin waited for Begin's nine o'clock arrival we engaged in chitchat about the furor Dayan had caused in the Knesset the evening before. Not only were Labor people furious over his desertion and his appointment as foreign minister, but bereaved families from the Yom Kippur War were outraged, too. They had never forgiven him for the war's initial failures. Wherever he appeared in public they jeered and booed him, and sometimes threw rotten vegetables at him as well, so the fact that he had now been made foreign minister filled them with renewed anger.

Though never a Dayanist, Rabin thought the appointment a shrewd move on Begin's part. Begin needed Dayan, he said. The new prime minister was virtually unknown outside the Jewish world, whereas Dayan was an international figure. His appointment was proof to foreign governments that Begin's cabinet was serious, not a bunch of former terrorists.

"Believe me," said Rabin with a smirk, "when an ambassador calls on Foreign Minister Moshe Dayan he'll make sure his tie is straight when he walks into his room, and he'll watch his every word. Nobody else in Begin's cabinet comes close to Dayan's eminence."

While this chitchat was going on I opened the door leading into the prime minister's inner sanctum.

"Close that door!" said Rabin.

"Why – you're not going to receive Begin in your room?" I asked.

"That room's no longer mine. I'll walk into it when I'm invited." Then, to Dan Patir, his media adviser, "Are the press assembled next door?"

The adjacent conference room was where the formal handover ceremony was to take place. Patir assured him that the reporters and photographers were all present, together with senior staffers, and he showed him the running order of the ceremony. It was to be a straightforward, modest affair – a couple of speeches and toasts, no more.

Satisfied, Rabin, hands in pockets, walked over to the window to stare at the road along which Menachem Begin's car would shortly pass. He glanced at his watch – less than two minutes to go.

A silence settled on the room. It was an awkward moment. There was nothing more to say. Our desks were cleared, the drawers emptied, the last calls made, and the farewells done. Rabin, without turning, said he hoped we'd continue to see something of each other, and we said we would, but we knew we wouldn't. We were, for the most part, office colleagues, not personal friends. We had worked together as a team because Rabin had galvanized us to serve him loyally in that marvelously cosseted and privileged environment known as the prime minister's bureau. But now that he was going, so were we – off on our separate ways, driven by dissimilar interests and ambitions, and miscellaneous insecurities. As for myself, I would be moving back to the crabby bureaucracy of the foreign ministry, to be offered, no doubt, a posting in some far-off Third World capital that would leave me and my family unsettled and itinerant.

Ironically, the one man slated to remain with Begin was his biggest detractor – General Ephraim Poran. The novice prime minister had asked him to stay on as his military secretary and, predictably, Rabin had told him in the plainest of terms that it was his soldierly duty to accept. Rabin insisted that Freuka alone had the expertise to manage the sensitive liaison between the new prime minister and the chiefs of the IDF, the Intelligence services, and the defense ministry. Freuka was persuaded to put off his retirement for another year.

"Here he comes!" said Rabin, abruptly stepping back from the window. "He's making sure to arrive on the dot of nine. I'll go down to receive him."

The off-white Peugeot 504 curb-crawled along the road, followed by the gray Plymouth saloon filled with its bevy of security agents. Soon, the vehicles drew up under the portico of the prime minister's office, and a doorman saluted. Policemen encircled the car, cameras clicked, and bystanders applauded. The man inside reached out to clasp the welcoming hand of the man standing outside to welcome him.

In the brightness of that June morning, the formal and impeccably neat attire of Prime Minister Menachem Begin looked like a costume of high rank compared to Yitzhak Rabin's dressed-down shirt and pants. This, in Ze'ev Jabotinsky's parlance, signified *hadar*, Hebrew for 'splendor.' *Hadar* suggested not just style, but a frame of mind and attitude. It implied nobility of spirit, chivalry, self-esteem, majesty, honor, and stateliness. A Jew should conduct himself with *hadar*. And on this morning, Begin's *hadar* advertised a fresh kind of government, a nationalist creed with a social-liberal bent, in place of the discredited informal, bare-chested socialist habit of yesteryear.

Begin, smiling broadly, escorted by Rabin and trailed by an entourage of three, Yechiel Kadishai among them, mounted the stairs and entered the outer office, where he pumped our hands enthusiastically. Rabin then stepped forward to open the door to the inner sanctum and gestured to its new occupant to enter, but Begin held back. Putting on a mock frown, he insisted Rabin enter first.

"But it's your room now," said Rabin, partly tease, partly earnest.

"Indeed it is," replied Begin, in the highest of spirits. "Therefore I, not you, am the host. It is I who must open the door for you. I insist you go in first."

They crossed the threshold together, and commandeered a corner for a tête-à-tête while we aides engaged in stiff small talk. Eventually, Begin called Kadishai over to show Rabin a letter he had just received from the president of the United States, Mr. Jimmy Carter. Kadishai dipped into his jam-packed briefcase and, in a jiffy, extracted the document and gave it to Rabin, whose eyebrows rose as he read it. He whispered something into Begin's ear that caused him to throw me a quick, assessing look, and he then suggested they join the assembly awaiting them in the adjacent conference room. Entering together, they were greeted with applause amid the whirling and clicking and flashing of cameras.

Yitzhak Rabin, though no orator, handed over the reins of government with articulate grace. He spoke of the privilege of having devoted his life to the service of his people, and of his democratic responsibility to ensure the smooth changing of the guard from himself to Mr. Begin, and his prayer for the success of Begin's administration.

In turn, Begin thanked Rabin profusely for his "dedicated years." He was "immensely proud of the mature expression of democracy that made an election day in Israel a day of such beauty." Moreover, "words cannot adequately express the nation's gratitude for the manner whereby Knesset member Rabin has overseen the historic change of administrations."

Each speech ended with a toast, followed by round after round of handshaking, which trailed off only after the two men briefly embraced for the benefit of the cameramen. Then came a final wave of the hand and a thank-you, and the newly installed prime minister turned to enter his room. As he was about to do so, a bold *Jerusalem Post* reporter called out after him, "Mr. Begin, what does it feel like to walk into that room after so many years in opposition?"

Begin paused, pushed his bottom lip forward in thought, and with much gravity, said, "It is a compelling moment, my friend. It is a compelling moment of extraordinary opposites."

"Like what, Mr. Begin?"

"Like…" He held up his right palm and rotated it slightly to underscore the paradox of what he was about to say. "Like, on the one hand, it is a terrifying feeling, and on the other, it is an exhilarating one. It is a feeling of the highest privilege, and it is a feeling of the deepest humility. It is a feeling of grave responsibility, and it is a feeling of wonderful hopefulness. It is a feeling of sisterhood and of brotherhood, and it is a feeling of solitude. It is…" Again he paused, and for a lingering moment stared hard at the door as if trying to absorb the full consequences of his walking through it, and then, in a tone of absolute conviction, said, "I have the feeling of the *chazan* – the cantor – on the High Holy Days when he stands alone before the Holy Ark and he appeals to the Almighty in the name of the whole congregation, and he says to God, 'I have come to plead before you on behalf of your people, Israel, who have made me their messenger, even though I am unworthy of the task. Therefore, I beseech you, O Lord, make my mission successful.'"

"Amen!" exclaimed somebody from the back of the room.

"*Ken yehi ratzon*" [May it be so], echoed Begin, and with an air of consecration, hands clasped and eyes lowered, he walked into the office of the prime minister.

Photograph credit: Ya'acov Sa'ar & Israel Government Press Office

Rabin and Prime Minister Begin with top staff members at the official handing-over ceremony, Prime Minister's office, Jerusalem, 21 June 1977

Photograph credit: Ya'acov Sa'ar & Israel Government Press Office

Begin proposes a toast upon assuming the premiership, Jerusalem, 21 June 1977

Chapter two

A Jew of Many Parts

A half hour later, feet perched on my empty desk, I stared crankily out of the window, dismayed at the prospect of having to keep an appointment with the bureaucrat in the personnel department of the foreign ministry with whom I had just spoken. It was a glorious day of sun and shade and summer flowers, just the kind of day to take a nostalgic stroll down memory lane before saying goodbye to this room for good, which is what I was doing when the phone rang, jerking me out of my reverie.

"This is Yechiel Kadishai. The prime minister wants to see you."

"Me? When?"

"Now!"

I tried to assume a calm demeanor as I hurried down the corridor, through the security barrier and into the elegantly carpeted hallway which led to the outer office of the prime minister's suite. Kadishai told me to go straight in.

As I opened the door, Menachem Begin glanced up. He seemed dwarfed by the gigantic mahogany desk behind which he sat and, close-up, the signs of the heart attack were still upon him. His face was sallow and drawn, yet still he was imperious, like a patrician, a man to be addressed by title, not by name. I walked across the persian carpet and, clearing my throat, said, "Mr. Prime Minister, as a citizen I wish you every success for the sake of us all."

He rose halfway, shook my hand automatically, and nodded at the chair where I was to sit. I did so with the ramrod posture of a new recruit as he began searching through a pile of papers, declaring while doing so in a voice so formal it sounded like an official pronouncement: "I have this day received an important communication from the president of the United States of America, Mr. Jimmy Carter, and Knesset member Rabin suggests I show it to you with a view to preparing a reply. He tells me you have some experience in these matters."

Wholly taken aback at this unexpected turn of events, all I could do was to nod and look about me in controlled excitement while he hunted for the letter.

But for the removal of personal photos, trophies, awards, and decorations, the wood-paneled room was exactly as Yitzhak Rabin had left it. A row of high-backed chairs stood in front of the prime minister's desk like well-drilled guardsmen, and behind the desk were shelves filled with volumes of parliamentary legislation with deep blue covers, and timeless Jewish classics in gold-tooled, brown calf antiquarian bindings. Next to the shelves was a floor-to-ceiling relief map of Israel, with the national flag by its side. A second seating area, lounge style, occupied much of the rest of the room, where a visitor reclining in one of the sky blue armchairs could look up at the wall in front of him and take in a huge black-and-white aerial photograph of Jerusalem's Old City, the heart and soul of the nation's eternal and indivisible capital. On the third wall, facing three bullet-proof lace-curtained windows, was an imposing world map and, close to that, tucked in a corner well above eye-level, a discreet photo gallery of Menachem Begin's predecessors: David Ben-Gurion, Moshe Sharett, Levi Eshkol, and Golda Meir. There was ample room left for the framed likeness of Yitzhak Rabin.

"Please read this," said Mr. Begin, handing me the letter.

I asked his permission to retire to peruse its contents and draft a reply, as had been my wont with his predecessors, but he said in a tone that was just a shade supercilious that there was no need for that anymore. It was not his habit to put his signature to anything which he had not composed himself, including his speeches and English letters.

"I shall prepare my response to the president," he said, "and you" – this with a warm smile, and in English – "shall polish my Polish English. You will be my Shakespeare. You will shakespearize it."

I was quick to learn that Begin delighted in inventing neologisms – creating new words or new meanings for established words. He had just invented one now.

The telephone buzzed.

The prime minister had two telephones on his desk, one cream-colored – a regular line with press buttons – and the second a red point-to-point military set, linked directly to the defense people in Tel Aviv. He stared at the buzzing red mechanism as if he had an aversion to it. Tightening his lips, he delicately picked up the receiver and gravely said, "Hello. Begin speaking."

It was Ezer Weizman, his defense minister, and I gathered from what was being said that there had been two Katyusha rocket attacks by the PLO, from southern Lebanon into northern Israel, albeit with no casualties or damage. Also, overnight, Moslem militia had mounted an assault on a Christian Maronite village in northern Lebanon, slaughtering civilians.

While Begin interrogated Weizman, Freuka walked in, obviously aware of what was going on. Urgently, he scribbled a note which he placed in front of Begin who, upon reading it, said sharply into the phone, "General Poran suggests the PLO attack could be a deliberate provocation to test my will on my first day in office. I am going to assume he's right, so please consult the chief of staff about a firm response, and keep me informed." Then, in a tone that was even more dogged and authoritarian, "As for the Moslem attack on the Christian civilians, the policy of this government is clear: it is our moral duty as a Jewish State to come to the aid of the Lebanese Christian minority. We Jews know what it is to suffer as a minority. We shall come to the aid of any persecuted minority in the Middle East. The Christian world has abandoned the Lebanese Christians. We shall not abandon them. We shall discuss this in detail in the cabinet meeting."

When he put the receiver down, you could see the veins throbbing in his neck.

Freuka looked disturbed. He shifted uneasily from foot to foot. Menachem Begin had just turned Israel's Lebanon doctrine on its head. Yitzhak Rabin had never permitted Israeli forces to become directly entangled in the Lebanese bloodbath for fear of being sucked into its infernal civil war, which had been ravaging the country since 1975. He wanted clarification, but as he was about to ask for it, Yechiel Kadishai stuck his head around the door to say that Reb Raphael was on the line.

"Put him through," said Begin, his face lighting up. He slouched back in his chair, crossed his legs, and cuddled the cream receiver to his ear. "This won't take a minute," he said contritely to General Poran, and then, with fondness, into the receiver, "Ah, Reb Raphael, how good it is to hear from you."

General Poran stroked his mustache and waited.

"I have been thinking much of your dear father of blessed memory," the prime minister continued. "I know how he prayed and sacrificed for this day when we would form the government. We shall remain faithful to his legacy, I promise you."

Reb Raphael was a name I knew. His late father was the widely adored saintly Reb Aryeh Levine – "the Prisoners' Rabbi" – a legend in his lifetime. When Britain ruled Palestine and Menachem Begin commanded the Irgun, Reb Aryeh had toiled to render aid and comfort to captured Irgun fighters, many of whom were condemned to long terms of imprisonment, or sentenced to death by hanging. The last embrace they felt at the foot of the gallows was invariably Reb Aryeh's. Now, his son ran the small Jerusalem yeshiva which his father had founded.

The prime minister inquired about the yeshiva's welfare, and as he listened, his features became compassionate and troubled. "*Oy vey!*" he sighed, "I'm so sorry, Reb Raphael, to hear things are so difficult. I shall speak to one or two friends to help. Meanwhile, send the electricity, water, and telephone bills to Yechiel Kadishai. I shall see to them personally. It's a *mitzvah* I want to perform. So don't fret, Reb Raphael. Your task is to sit and learn and teach. We shall see to the rest."

It was clear from the look on his face that with Lebanon on the boil, General Poran found this benevolent tête-à-tête with an obscure yeshiva rabbi too much to swallow. He about-faced and made his way to the door, where Begin stopped him. "General Poran!" he said, in a low yet commanding voice.

Freuka spun around.

"You shall have an opportunity to express your views on my Lebanon policy at another time, not now. Now, I need you to keep me informed on our retaliation in response to the PLO attacks. Please wake me at night if necessary. And please tell Yechiel Kadishai to come in."

Begin spent the next few minutes briefing Yechiel about Reb Raphael's plight, and asked him to get hold of a certain Sir Isaac Wolfson in London. (The most important thing about Sir Isaac Wolfson was that he was a very rich Jew.) He then mused out loud how he should reply to President Carter, and asked me, businesslike, "Have you finished reading the president's letter?"

I nodded an affirmative.

"In that case tell me, other than the usual pleasantries and expressions of mutual values and interests, etcetera, do you find anything particularly exceptional in his invitation to Washington, as I do?"

The way he said it, I had the distinct impression he was putting me through my paces.

"I think so," I ventured.

"What, exactly?"

"The last paragraph." I read it out loud: "I would like, therefore, to invite you to visit the United States during the week of July 18 and join with you in a partnership of principle leading to a just and peaceful settlement of the dispute between Israel and its neighbors. We are both blessed with the historic opportunity to give substance to the religious meaning of our societies."

"So?" asked the prime minister, in a testing tone.

"There is something idiosyncratic in that last sentence, coming as it does from the president of a country where the separation of church and state is so sacrosanct," I hazarded.

"*Azoy?*" responded Begin, with a varnish of irony. "Yet, would you not agree there is often more content to religious life in America than there is here? What else do you find?"

Clearly, I was on trial.

"The first sentence – its innuendo," I said. "Carter is inviting you to Washington to join with him in what he calls 'a partnership of principle leading to a just and peaceful settlement.' What is 'a partnership of principle'? It's a new term. There is a set diplomatic vernacular in our dialogue with America, and I've never heard this expression before. So Carter seems to be saying he wants to meet you to see if he can establish a partnership of principle, meaning a common strategy. As of now, he's not sure there is a common strategy."

Begin's eyebrows arched a trifle. "I agree. That's my reading, too."

The cream phone buzzed again, and the prime minister's eyes brightened in pleasure when he recognized the voice at the other end of the line. "Sir Isaac!" he boomed. "How glad I am to have found you."

As he listened to Sir Isaac Wolfson, he settled back into his chair, and then in an English that was accented but perfect, responded by thanking him profusely for his expressions of congratulation and support. He promised, "*B'ezrat Hashem* – with God's help – our new government will do good things for Israel and for the Jewish people." Then, with a roguish glint in his eye and sarcasm in his voice, he asked, "So tell me, Sir Isaac, the British press, do they have a good word to say about me on my first day in office, or am I still their favorite fiend?"

Sir Isaac Wolfson's answer, whatever it was, wiped the impish look from the premier's face. He clucked his tongue and wagged his head, and in a tone huffy with disdain, said, "So The *Times* is at it again, preaching Middle East appeasement, just as it preached German appeasement in the thirties. That's the newspaper, remember, which dismissed the atrocities of Hitler's Brownshirts as mere 'revolutionary exuberance.' Bah! What do they want of me now – another Munich? They want me to give up the security of Judea and Samaria, like Neville Chamberlain forced Czechoslovakia to give up the security of the Sudetenland? What are we supposed to do – commit suicide like Czechoslovakia?"

Sir Isaac continued, obviously reporting other things that upset Begin, and as he listened, incredulity issued from him in the form of words like "Unbelievable!" "Amazing!" "Outrageous!" Finally, in a tone of resignation, he lamented, "So, there are still people out there who think of me only as the ex-terrorist, eh? After all these years they are still blinded by their prejudices. But I do not complain. It's *their* neurosis, not mine." He then breathed a long and audible sigh and, through it, muttered, "Sad! Very sad! Yet the truth will out. It always does."

This maxim seemed to have restored Begin's spirit, for he rose to his feet, squared his shoulders, stiffened his voice, and declared, "You know the truth, Sir Isaac. You know we in the Irgun were never terrorists. We were freedom fighters. We fought bravely, fair and square, man-to-man, soldier-to-soldier, against the British. Never did we deliberately hurt civilians. And yet you tell me there are still people out there who call me a terrorist and Yasser Arafat a freedom fighter? Well, let me say to you, sir, I have nothing but contempt for them."

Flushed now, he thundered on: "That so-called Palestine Liberation Organization…'liberation?' Bah!…that murderous Nazi organization led by that war criminal Yasser Arafat, they target civilians exclusively, children, women and men. So, yes, Sir Isaac, I say it again: THE TRUTH WILL OUT AND JUSTICE WILL WIN THE DAY!"

He trumpeted these words with such triumph, it sounded like the finale of a speech at a rally. Having thus let off steam, he lowered himself back into his chair, leaned in repose, and in an unruffled and winning fashion spent the next few minutes expanding on the actual purpose of his call. This he wrapped up with an appeal that came from the bottom of his heart: "Sir Isaac, I would not be troubling you now did I not sincerely believe that saving Reb Raphael's yeshiva is a *mitzvah* – a sacred and noble deed. And knowing of your charity, I thought you might want to have a share in it."

The philanthropist's response was so generous it brought a blush of pleasure to Menachem Begin's cheeks, and over and over again he responded with his thanks. As he did so, I felt a tingle running down the length of my spine. Had a passerby happened to overhear how Begin had opened his heart to Reb Raphael, and to Sir Isaac Wolfson, he might have gone away thinking an Israeli prime minister's job was to run some sort of yeshiva appeal, punctuated by affairs of state. Just to watch him handle, in one and the same breath, and with equal zeal, a presidential letter from the White House, a military flare-up in Lebanon, and a yeshiva solicitation in Jerusalem, was a spellbinding experience.

To me, an observant Jew, this was heady stuff indeed. I had served Levi Eshkol, Golda Meir and, until this morning, Yitzhak Rabin – all illustrious pioneers and idealistic Zionist diehards, but none of them possessed the depth of Menachem Begin's reverence for Jewish tradition, his cozy acknowledgement of God, his familiarity with ancient customs, and his innate sense of Jewish kinship. He came from the heart of Jewish Poland, and though not strictly observant, was an old-school traditionalist with an infectious common touch which made Jews everywhere feel they really mattered. Here, at last, was a prime minister after my own heart – the quintessential Jew.

Yet even as I drank in this intoxicating brew, there lingered in my mind the image of Begin the politician, the iron-cored patriarch who was neutral in nothing. He was the most ideological prime minister Israel had ever elected. So I was stunned when he put the phone down, and asked me with the fullest expectation of being obeyed, "I take it you will remain a member of my personal staff?" That he, the leader of a victorious, power-hungry party, many of whose stalwarts had fought under him in the underground and had stood by him through thick and thin during his decades in the political wilderness – that he should invite me, an unknown outsider, onto his personal staff, was flattering and staggering – so staggering that I blurted out impulsively, "But Mr. Begin, I'm not a member of your party."

"I never asked you if you were. Are you saying this to disqualify yourself?"

"No, but – "

"But what?"

I paused, hesitant to express my next thought, which was *I've always thought we should agree to territorial concessions; a piece of land for a piece of peace.* But those words never came out, because my throat went dry. My throat went dry because those words were not my own; they were Eshkol's, they were Golda's, they were Rabin's. They were the essence of the speeches and letters and memoranda galore I had written for almost twenty years in their names and upon their instruction. That had been my job. But now I needed to find my own voice, sort out my own thoughts, arrange them in my own way, and speak them in my own name. So, I said, "Mr. Prime Minister, may I take a little time to think this through?"

"As much as you need," he said forbearingly.

I rose, and was halfway to the door when he called me back. "What exactly was your status working with the previous prime ministers? Were you a political appointee or a civil servant?" he asked.

"A civil servant," I answered, "seconded from the foreign ministry at the request of each of the prime ministers."

"In that case," said Begin, emphatically, "I renew that request. This government has come to serve, not to reap. Do you understand that?"

I shrugged my shoulders.

"Then I shall elucidate. This is the first time there has been a change of political administration in Israel, and we have no intention of plundering power. There has to be continuity. This is a democratic transition. The world must see this; the nation must see this. I will allow no dismissals of the professional civil service except in exceptional cases which I consider reasonable." And then, wryly, "My model is the British system, where civil servants know to say the right thing in the right way at the right time to the right people in the name of the right government. And the right government is always the elected government of the day. Now do you understand?"

I said that I did, but he was no longer looking at me. He was looking past me, at the door, his eyes bright. "Nehamale!" he exclaimed. "What a surprise! How wonderful! Like the good old days!"

A tea lady in a red cardigan waddled across the carpet with her trolley and shook the prime minister's hand, her wrinkled face beaming. "*Mazal tov*, Mr. Begin!" She smiled. "Congratulations! Good to see you back."

They were obviously old acquaintances from the days when Begin had been minister without portfolio in Levi Eshkol and Golda Meir's national unity government.

"Same as usual?" asked Nehama archly.

"Same as usual," answered Begin heartily.

She poured him a plain glass of tea, with lemon and a sweetener.

To me, he said, "Whatever your response, please meet me at four o'clock this afternoon, when we'll go over my reply to President Carter, and you shall shakespearize it for me."

Back in my room I picked up the phone to Rabin. "Yitzhak," I blurted, "Begin has just offered me a job. Should I take it?"

"Of course you should take it. He is an honest man and a responsible man. I've known him for a very long time and I can tell you that he always puts the national interest above his own. Besides, he's your kind of Jew. You'll enjoy working with him."

Menachem Begin's draft reply to President Jimmy Carter covered three pages which had been ripped out of a shorthand notepad, apparently the only paper he had to hand. It was written in red ink, in a handwriting that was tight, taut and cramped. My pen was black, and as I painstakingly navigated my way through his congested scrawl, stylizing as I went, my black ink increasingly superimposed itself upon his red, so that in the end, the pages looked as if a spider had scrawled across it. His way with words was skillful; his syntax less so.

He sat silently as I worked my way down the page, occasionally leaning across the desk to scrutinize my 'shakespearization.' And when I handed him the finished product, he carefully studied the corrections and, allowing himself a hint of a smile, complimented me on my touches, but expressed reservations about certain word changes I had made. He didn't like my 'misting' his adjectives, as he put it. For instance, where he had written 'lofty,' I had written 'noble.' 'Fruitful' should be 'fruitful,' not 'constructive.' And, yes, he deliberately chose to open his letter with 'Your Excellency,' and not 'Dear Mr. President.' After all, he was addressing a head of state.

Try as I might to persuade him that 'Your Excellency' was simply not accurate in this situation, he simply shook his head in disbelief, saying that it was inconceivable not to address the president of the world's mightiest power other than by such an honorific. So he decided to call the chief of protocol at the foreign ministry to double check. And while he cross-examined the poor man I sat wondering how many times a man stranded for well nigh three decades in Israel's political wilderness might have had cause to write a letter to the president of the United States. Whatever Menachem Begin's grasp of international affairs might be – and I was to discover that it was vast – his familiarity with the trivialities of diplomatic etiquette on that first day on the job was inadequate.

He acknowledged as much when, replacing the receiver, he threw me an amiable shrug and owned up, "You're right!" and with a chuckle added, "but I'm in good company. When Theodore Roosevelt became president of the United States he received letters of congratulation from the kaiser of Germany and the king of England. Not caring about diplomatic protocol, and never having communicated with either of them before, he blithely addressed the kaiser as, 'My Dear Emperor William,' and the king as, 'My Dear King Edward,' instead of 'Your Royal Majesty,' which was appropriate for both. Eyebrows were raised in the royal courts and American ambassadors were sent in to apologize."

Menachem Begin related this nugget of gossip with absolute delight, and when I asked him whether history was his preferred reading, he concurred, saying, "History and political biographies are my favorite topics, and these I generally read in English." By way of illustration, he cited four different authors he had recently read, and by the offhand way he tossed out their names I realized that here was a man of many parts: not only meticulous, but erudite, an intellectual of the Polish mold but in the Jewish idiom.

Waiting for his letter to be typed up, he entertained me with the tale of how he had perfected his command of English. It was during his days in the Irgun, when he was hiding from the British – a time of sharp wits and subterfuge, when survival hung on knowing what the other side was thinking, saying, planning, writing, reading, and broadcasting. Words were weapons; he had to learn them. So day by day, night by night, he sat glued to the BBC World Service, frenetically mastering the news and the King's English. He loved the BBC's economy of style, its unexcitable precision, and its clarity of speech.

He developed a lush English vocabulary; one could sense his love of words for their own sakes. As in the underground, so too, throughout all his years in opposition, words were his sole arsenal. He was a man of passionate polemic and gripping oratory. He loved the Knesset. He loved to debate. He loved to write. He loved to read. He loved to preach. He loved journalism. He loved letters. Letter writing, he lamented, was a dying skill. Language was being robbed of precision and clarity. Politicians were the prime pirates of this despoilment. Parliamentary debate was on the wane everywhere. Congress and Westminster were still relatively decent chambers, and the Knesset, too, had its rare moments. Too rare! But, generally speaking, good talk for good talk's sake was gone. A man or woman gets up to speak, and says nothing. Nobody listens – and then everybody disagrees. Duels occur without real cause. Politicians had become hard-nosed, bottom-line pragmatists, bereft of humor. "Where is the parliamentarian today," he remarked cuttingly, "who can dispose of an opponent with the elegance of Benjamin Disraeli calling across the aisle to Gladstone, 'The Honorable Gentleman is a sophistical rhetorician inebriated with the exuberance of his own verbosity?'"

The exactitude with which he pronounced this quote was so stunning I asked him how on earth he remembered it. Smugly, he replied, "I learned it by heart from the BBC when I was in the underground. I used it as a vocabulary exercise. To this day, the first thing I do on rising at five in the morning is to switch on the BBC."

Indeed, in the fullness of time I would discover that there were occasions when Menachem Begin based his political decisions partly or wholly on what he'd heard on the BBC, aware that while its commentators did not spare the rod in criticizing Israeli policy, they were, for the most part, impartial, accurate, and bound by the ethic of fair play. Indeed, to Menachem Begin, the British Broadcasting Corporation was the gold standard of faithful reporting.[57]

In the late afternoon the prime minister asked if his letter of reply to President Jimmy Carter was ready for checking. It was not. Norma, my secretary, was understandably edgy, trying her best to make sense of Begin's red scribbles and my superimposed black ones. Her typing was taking much longer than usual, and by the time the letter was done, the prime minister had to leave for his next appointment. He and Mrs. Begin were hosting a tea at the King David Hotel in honor of close friends who had flown in from overseas. He suggested I accompany him to the hotel, and he would go over the letter en route.

Once we were sitting in his official limousine, he settled back and, head cocked in concentration, began reading. He disapproved of a word here and added a phrase there, and was still hastily scribbling some final corrections when the car drew up at the hotel's entrance. Switching on a smile, he bounced out to be met by well-wishers with outstretched hands, and such was the crush inside the lobby that I had to insinuate myself behind his phalanx of security men, trying to edge my way forward in a vain attempt to retrieve the letter. As he reached the elevator he recognized a familiar face among the crowd of applauding guests. His smile widened, and with an outstretched hand, he called, "Sir Isaiah, welcome to Jerusalem!"

Sir Isaiah Berlin, the celebrated British thinker, philosopher and Oxford professor, whom I had met briefly many years before at an Oxford

Union reception, flushed darkly, threw the prime minister a jaundiced look, and contemptuously turned his back on him. Begin stiffened, pressed his lips together, lifted his chin, and assuming all the dignity he could muster, stepped into the elevator, the letter crumpled in his hand. I watched, frozen, as the door glided shut in my face.

I suddenly felt the need for a drink.

The bar off the main lobby was jam-packed, and I had to elbow my way to the counter, where everybody was talking loudly, sipping drinks and munching peanuts, pretzels and potato chips. Suddenly, out of the crush, Sir Isaiah Berlin emerged, his jowled face cold and hard-pinched. In a dark-colored three-piece suit and a somber tie, he looked totally out of place among this high-spirited crowd with their shirts, cotton slacks, and blue jeans.

"Have I not seen you in the past?" he called out to me, above the hubbub.

I reminded him of the brief encounter at the Oxford Union, but he had no recollection of it.

"I have, however, seen you with Yitzhak Rabin when he was prime minister, have I not?" he pressed.

I confirmed that he had, in London and in Jerusalem.

"But did I not see you just now in the company of Menachem Begin?" he asked, a frown of disapproval on his face. With his large bespectacled eyes, scholar's stoop, thick whitening brows, graying hair, and balding scalp, he looked like an aggrieved proctor.

I verified that he had, and I could almost taste the distaste in his voice when he growled, "So what are you doing now with Begin?"

He listened, aloofly at first, as I explained how I had become a member of his staff, but then he suddenly began to contemplate me closely, as if I represented some sort of a philosophic conundrum. "I understand," he muttered. "You're a civil servant, eh? Tight spot! You have no choice. Proper thing to do." Whereupon he sternly downed a whisky and, after that, a long glass of soda, and then promptly dived into a monologue spoken so rapidly that it was partly incomprehensible. Whether this was his regular manner of speech or an emotional outburst, I could not tell. The gist of it was that, though he considered himself a well-tempered and composed Oxfordian, not given to vehement public stands, he could not, as a Jew, stand the sight of Menachem Begin as prime minister. He could not shake the man's hand. It was too much to ask of him. He feared what harm Begin would do to the country. He feared for Israel's Zionist dream. He feared for his own Zionist dream. He was terribly shaken and perplexed.

All his life, he said, he had been a two-state Zionist – a Jewish State alongside a Palestinian State. Moral life could entertain nothing less. The Arab-Israel quarrel was a conflict between two rights of self-determination of equal validity. Israel, therefore, had to concede territories. Partition! This was his profound philosophical view as a Jew.

And, as a Jew, he loathed violence. Terrorism of any kind, for whatever noble a goal, was abhorrent. In the 1960s he had condemned the French for their brutal war of counterinsurgency against the Algerians, and then had condemned the Algerian FLN for their counterterrorism against French civilians. So how could he shake the hand of Menachem Begin who, in 1946, had ordered this very hotel to be blown up, which resulted in the loss of ninety lives?

I cut in to insist that there were different versions of that old episode, but he kept on going at such a helter-skelter pace he could not have heard me. Only when I raised my voice to argue that, at the end of the day, we Israelis had democratically elected our own prime minister in a free and secret ballot, did he pause to concede: "Well, yes, that's true. Besides, who am I to offer you people advice? You would never want to accept it anyway. I'm no better understood in the Jewish State than I am in other places. As often as I come here, I don't know if I understand Israel at all. I don't know how many Jews in the Diaspora really understand Israel. I don't know how many Israelis understand the Diaspora, for that matter."

With this thought, he fumbled with a tiny magnifying glass that was dangling on the end of a chain from his vest pocket, placed it close to his eyes to check his watch in the dim light of the bar, and apologized that he had to run.

"So do I," I said.

I took the elevator up to the prime minister's suite on the sixth floor, knocked, and was greeted by a smiling Mrs. Begin, who beckoned me inside with a motherly invitation to have a cup of coffee.

"Ah, there you are," called the prime minister, detaching himself from his guests and extracting the letter to President Carter from his pocket. I began to apologize for my tardiness, but he apologized back, handing me the letter and saying, "I'm sorry it's so crumpled. There were so many hands to shake when I walked into the hotel lobby I inadvertently stuffed it into my pocket."

He drew me into the lounge to introduce me to his guests – a half dozen middle-aged, extremely well-dressed couples, talking to each other in an admixture of Yiddish, Polish, and English. They had the look of affluent Holocaust survivors, from America.

"I was just talking to my friends here about Sir Isaiah Berlin," said Begin, sardonically.

"Stop taking it to heart, Menachem," chided Mrs. Begin. "For more than thirty years you've had so many people turn their backs on you, and suddenly you're surprised that some still do. Sit down. Relax. Try one of these." She proffered a tray of rolls, pastries, and cookies, together with a glass of steaming tea.

"Sir Isaiah has, of course, an extraordinary mind," granted Begin, seating himself on a couch surrounded by his admirers. Between a sip of tea and a nibble of a cookie, he continued, "As a philosopher, he's a genuinely original theorist. But as a Zionist thinker he's a …" – a rascally look lurked in his eyes – "he's a J.W.T.K."

"A what?"

"A Jew with trembling knees."

The people around him laughed.

"Those utopian Zionists like Berlin wove a fantasy that bewitched the Zionist movement for decades," continued Begin, in a voice that had gone absolutely earnest. "Had we followed the Isaiah Berlin path we would never have had a Jewish State. Their flight of fancy led them to the delusion that the Arabs would eventually come to terms with us for the sake of their economic progress. What utter nonsense! Ze'ev Jabotinsky had too much respect for the Arabs to believe they would come to the peace table for the sake of a mess of pottage."

The mention of Jabotinsky's name prompted a number of these old Revisionists to begin reminiscing about their late leader with all the adoration of disciples. I, standing on the periphery, heard Menachem Begin muse about his "master and teacher," as though he were a prophet. He reminded his guests how Jabotinsky's Revisionist Zionism was the only unblinking realism in the crumbling Jewish world that ended in the Holocaust. He was the first to warn against the coming European catastrophe; the first to organize illegal rescue boats to Eretz Yisrael; the first to sound the warcry for a Jewish army; the first to maintain that we have to fight for a Jewish State; the first to advocate the building of an 'iron wall' of deterrence that would ultimately convince the Arabs that they had no alternative but to come to terms with a Jewish State.

"Ze'ev Jabotinsky foresaw this 'iron wall' doctrine already in the twenties," concluded Begin. "And ultimately, it was to become the strategic imperative of all of Israel's leaders. What are the Israel Defense Forces if not an iron wall? Surely, few men have been so vindicated by history."

I deemed this an appropriate moment to take my leave and ready the prime minister's letter for dispatch to the American president. And as I did so, the thought occurred to me that what I had just witnessed was high drama – Begin and Berlin: two extraordinary men, perfectly representing the warring sides of the Jewish character and the contradictory visions of the Jewish narrative and Jewish survival.

An echo of this was reflected in the contents of the letter to the president, which read:

Dear Mr. President,

Thank you for your warm letter of congratulations. My colleagues and I are deeply grateful for your wishes for the success of the new government of Israel. On May 17 our free people decided by the ballot upon a change of administration. Since then, three acts took place in accordance with our constitution. The president of the republic charged me with the task of forming a new government. The Knesset expressed its confidence by a majority vote in the government presented to our parliament. My colleagues and I took in the House the oath of allegiance to our country and to its constitution.

Proof has been given that liberty and democracy reign in our land. Transfer of power took place in a most orderly way. We have learned much from the dignified manner in which such transfer was carried out in the United States.

Mr. President, with all the differences in might between our country and the United States of America I share your view that both nations have much in common. Lofty ideas of humanity, democracy, individual liberty and deep faith in Divine Providence are the cherished heritage of the great American people and the renascent Israel. May I assure you, Mr. President, that the friendship between our countries is, and always will be, the foundation of our policy reflected in our special relationship and based also, as I believe, on the recognition of a community of interests.

The people of Israel seek peace, yearn and pray for peace. It is therefore natural that as Israel's elected spokesmen, my colleagues and I will do our utmost to achieve real peace with our neighbors. It is in this spirit that I gratefully accept your invitation to visit your great country during the week of July 18th and I look forward to meeting with you and to have a most fruitful exchange of views with the president of the United States who is also the leader of the free world. With my best wishes,

Sincerely

M. Begin

Prime Minister Begin scans the morning papers with Yechiel Kadishai, 21 June 1977

Chapter three

Yechiel and Begin

Compared to the efficiency of the bureaus of the previous prime ministers I had served, Menachem Begin's was a bit chaotic. Yechiel Kadishai, who ran it, was in a constant whirl of banter, ideas, deliberation, and good deeds. Forever amiable, Yechiel had no head for systematic planning and staff work. He delegated to a fault. Nevertheless, as hectic as the bureau could be, he ran it with a remarkable flair for improvisation and a gift for divining the location of any document the prime minister might require. People of every sort – down-and-outs, immigrants, fans, journalists, politicians, charlatans – were constantly in and out of his open door. On one occasion, a week or so after I had adjusted to his pulse, a bedraggled-looking fellow in a battered trilby and tattered raincoat walked out of Yechiel's office just as I was about to walk in. I recognized him; he was a peddler in downtown Jerusalem.

"What's that hawker doing here?" I asked. "Do you know him?"

"Sure. His name is Kreisky."

"Who?"

"Shaul Kreisky, brother of the chancellor of Austria, Bruno Kreisky."

Yechiel's face remained totally deadpan as he said this, and my mouth dropped open as I watched the visitor shuffling down the corridor toward the exit. Could he really be the brother of the Austrian chancellor whom Golda Meir had hauled over the coals because he had surrendered to Arab terrorist blackmail?

"You're pulling my leg!" I said.

"No, I'm not," answered Yechiel. "He's lived here for years. The prime minister occasionally helps him out. He's a great admirer of Begin. Run after him and ask him."

I did. It was absolutely true.

The trappings of rank interested Yechiel Kadishai not one bit. He refused a car and driver, which were his due, and opted instead to travel to Jerusalem from his Tel Aviv home on an early bus, often at sunrise. Predictably, he and his wife Bambi were now on everyone's invitation list, and he had the enviable ability to walk into a room filled with strangers, confident he would walk out of it having made a sourpuss smile and a cold fish laugh. At one diplomatic reception soon after he was installed in his new job I watched him turn his irrepressible bonhomie on a cluster of stiff ambassadors, diverting them with the tale of when he first set eyes on Menachem Begin. It had been in 1942, in a Tel Aviv basement, empty but for plain wooden benches on which everyone sat. A meeting of Betar and Irgun members was in progress, most of them volunteers in the special Palestine regiment of the British Army. They were gathered to hear a talk on the fate of the Jews of Europe. Rumors of their mass slaughter were already beginning to circulate.

"In walked a sallow-looking fellow dressed in an ill-fitting British army uniform and wearing John Lennon glasses," recounted Yechiel. "He wore army-issue short baggy pants down to his knees, and a forage cap with a Polish eagle stuck into it, symbol of the Free Polish Forces in Exile. When he asked for the floor, he said, plain and simple, that the only way to save European Jewry was to compel the British to quit Palestine as quickly as possible and then open the country's gates to free immigration. I asked people who this fellow was and they told me his name was Menachem Begin, and that back in Poland he'd been head of the Betar movement. I'd never heard of him before."

Yechiel then went on to relate how, over the course of the following two years, he had served in the Western Desert and in Europe, and it was while doing duty in the European displaced persons camps that he heard that Menachem Begin had been appointed commander of the Irgun underground.

"What exactly were your duties in the camps at that time?" asked one of the diplomats.

"Smuggling," answered Yechiel artlessly. "King George's uniform did

Photograph credit: Gemma Levine, London, UK

Yechiel Kadishai and author, November 1978

wonders for my tricks as a smuggler." He declared this with such irreverence that a couple of the ambassadors threw their heads back in great peals of laughter, while others cast him startled stares.

"What on earth were you smuggling? Or is that too delicate a question?" asked one.

"Death camp survivors, across frontiers to southern ports for so-called 'illegal immigration' to Eretz Yisrael," Yechiel shot back. He then went on to tell them how he himself had returned home in the summer of 1948 on the ill-fated Irgun ship, the *Altalena*, only to be fired upon on arrival by fellow Jews.

"And after that?" queried another.

"After that I began working on behalf of families of the Irgun fallen and the wounded. In those early days our ministry of defense discriminated against our people in favor of the former Hagana fighters. However, I discovered a number of fair-minded sorts working in the ministry and they helped me out. It was during the course of that work that I came to Mr. Begin's attention, and I began working for him in sixty-four. I haven't stopped since."

Later, among themselves, or so I was told, the ambassadors discussed Kadishai's natural exuberance. One of them, claiming private knowledge, said that loyalty meant more to Begin than ability. All concurred that the two men were inseparable, Kadishai having been unswervingly loyal during Begin's solitary years in the political wilderness of opposition, during which he suffered eight consecutive electoral defeats. Kadishai, they concluded, was the man to cultivate.

I learned quickly that Yechiel had an intuitive ability to anticipate Begin's every wish, as though they communicated telepathically. Yechiel was the one person outside the family with whom Begin could totally unwind. With him he could share both confidences and casual chitchat. Yet even Yechiel's natural gusto tended to subside into a restrained reverence whenever he entered Begin's presence, and this proved true of all of Begin's old-time underground fighters. He still expected absolute obedience. Daily, I noted how these veterans related to him with a fidelity that bordered on total submission. To them, he was a patriarch.

"Sure, he'll sometimes ask my opinion, but that's usually to convince me of the correctness of his own," Yechiel once confided to me. "Most of the time we understand each other without talking."

This made him invaluable as chief of the prime minister's bureau.

Yechiel knew who to recommend for positions of influence in the sure knowledge that Begin would approve them; he would soften up Knesset bigwigs and party ringmasters before they entered the prime minister's presence; while absenting himself from meetings he would know exactly who said what to whom; he arranged the prime minister's visitors' schedule without having to consult him; and he intercepted and deflected those he knew Begin would not want to see.

As for the prime minister himself, for one who had recently suffered a heart attack, his day was jam-packed. Up at dawn, he would start his day's work with a glass of lemon tea and a survey of the news. He would listen to the BBC on the radio, read all the major dailies with intense concentration, occasionally making notes, and committing the papers' contents to his photographic memory. Next was a perusal of the foreign press. Then he would look over any documents he was currently dealing with, eat a light breakfast, make a few calls to cabinet colleagues, and arrive at the office by eight. There, he studied the overnight cables, sat with his staff for briefings and issued instructions, and then he would move from his desk to the lounge corner of his office, where he received a steady flow of callers. He would go home for lunch with his wife at one without fail, which he followed with a nap, and a return to the office at three thirty. He stayed until six. The last hour was usually spent dictating and signing letters, after which he would review the forthcoming day's schedule, bid a personal goodnight to each of his secretaries, and exit the building in the company of Yechiel, who would hand Begin's briefcase to the head of his security squad. The briefcase contained two files, one relating to domestic affairs, the other to defense and foreign affairs.

Most evenings were taken up with public engagements, at the end of which the prime minister would ascend the stairs to his private quarters, study the two sets of files at the kitchen table over a final glass of lemon tea, retire to bed with a book, and be up four or five hours later to start the next day afresh.

Although Begin took pride in thinking of himself as first among equals, he ruled his cabinet with a rod of iron. His opening words at the inaugural meeting were "There shall be no smoking!" He then insisted his ministers pay due respect to the Knesset by attending whenever it was in session – most particularly on Mondays and Tuesdays, when much of the parliamentary work was done.

Photograph credit: Ya'acov Sa'ar & Israel Government Press Office

Begin chatting with his foreign minister Moshe Dayan, 20 June 1977

Grunts of objection rolled around the table. They were cut short when the prime minister asked for silence so that he could give them a piece of his mind.

"We have to restore the dignity of the Knesset to our national life by improving our attendance," he admonished. "It is shameful that the public see a virtually empty chamber every time they switch on their television sets. If we cabinet members set an example, the rest of the Knesset will follow."

Defense Minister Ezer Weizman whispered to Agricultural Minister Ariel Sharon, "It's a crazy idea! It won't work!" A look from the prime minister told Weizman he had been heard, and the former commander of the air force muttered a request for forgiveness. Moshe Dayan passed Begin a note that prompted the prime minister to pause and say, "The foreign minister thinks my request is not feasible, since it will leave you too little time to run your ministries. I therefore accept his recommendation, that you divide your Knesset attendance equally between you – half of the cabinet to attend on Mondays and half on Tuesdays."

The sigh of relief over the reprieve was palpable.

Compared to the temper of Rabin's cabinet ministers, Begin's were meek. Rabin had Peres to contend with; he had to watch his back. Not that this was unusual in Labor circles. Labor cabinets were invariably cacophonous, punctured with caustic leaks and acerbic blasts. Labor leaders were for the most part a single-minded, disputatious lot – trade unionists, kibbutzniks, party strongmen – united by an adherence to the socialist creed, but fractured by its multiple nuances. Internecine warfare was the norm, each leader creating his own camp followers, and each wheeling and dealing behind the others' backs. In contrast, the new Likud cabinet, with its one commanding, charismatic figure in the chair, was disciplined and leakproof, at least to start off with.

Lack of leaks drove the media to distraction, particularly when the prime minister was preparing himself for his first meeting with the American president, and every official mouth was tight-lipped. Menachem Begin knew that to Jimmy Carter and his chief advisers – National Security Adviser Zbigniew Brzezinski and Secretary of State Cyrus Vance – the paramount element of the Middle East dispute was not so much the enmity of the Arab states, threatening though that was, but the Palestinian question. Solve the Palestinian question, they contended, and you have the key to peace. This was Carter's ambition – a comprehensive settlement to be achieved through a Middle East peace conference at Geneva, with a Palestinian representation at the table. To this end he had already met most of the Arab heads of state, and we anticipated that this president would readily ignore the earlier Ford-Kissinger pledge to keep Arafat and his PLO out of the process as long as they did not recognize Israel's right to exist. Moreover, we assumed that if and when Begin launched his promised settlement drive in the West Bank and the Gaza Strip, the chances were that Israel would risk not merely U.S. reprimand, but perhaps U.S. economic and military sanctions, too. Indeed, by one official estimate, "The vastly differing approaches of Begin and Carter reveal a philosophical chasm that may prove impossible to bridge, and unless a mutually acceptable formula is found, the times ahead could be so abrasive as to bring the U.S.-Israeli relationship to its lowest ebb since the establishment of the state."

Meanwhile, a new American ambassador had come to town and was making the rounds. Houston born, and a Yale man, Samuel Lewis was a career diplomat with a great deal of experience, self-confidence, a sense of humor, and an open mind. Over our first cup of coffee he told me with absolute candor – clearly for Begin's ears – that the president was very impatient to get his Middle East diplomacy going, and that he would not shrink from being 'confrontational' if that was what it would take to make it happen. With equal candor, he confided, "I've informed Washington that Mr. Begin needs careful handling, and honey is going to get us a lot further than vinegar. I'm flying ahead to Washington in the hope of cooling things down a bit."

The prime minister made no comment when I reported this to him. He was devoting every spare waking hour to planning his own pitch with the president. Again and again he pored over the protocols of the March Rabin-Carter clash, and read and reread the entire file of the president's declarations on the Middle East. Almost daily, he sat with his senior ministers to finesse Israel's position on the convening of a Geneva peace conference. At one such meeting he summed up his feelings about the American president:

"I believe Jimmy Carter to be a decent man, and his impulse is entirely sincere. He is a truly religious Southern Baptist. I'm told that he prays privately several times a day and that each night, before retiring, he and his wife study the Bible together in Spanish, to lend scope to their learning. As a genuine born-again Christian he lives by the conviction that God has placed him on this earth to fulfill a destiny. He sees himself as a healer, and as a healer he wants to bring peace to the Holy Land. Yet much as I respect his religious convictions, I doubt, as did Rabin, his grasp of the complexities of the Middle East. Certainly, he shows little comprehension of the Jewish right to Eretz Yisrael, nor of our genuine security concerns. But since I believe him to be an honest man I have to believe he can detect the truth when he sees it, and is, therefore, open to persuasion."

With that he turned to General Poran, and said, "Freuka, please prepare for me three maps – the first showing PLO concentrations in southern Lebanon, the second showing Israel's minute size compared to our twenty-two Arab neighbors, and the third, the tiny distance between the old nineteen sixty-seven border and the Mediterranean Sea. And since Americans love to put initials to everything" – this with that cheeky look – "let's call that third map the INSM."

"Which stands for?" asked Freuka.

"Israel's National Security Map, of course," he replied. Then, to Kadishai, "Yechiel, prepare a list of American towns with biblical names, state by state. And finally, to me, "Please try and make yourself available this coming Shabbat afternoon? We're hosting an open house. You'll help us entertain."

Chapter four

The Open House

The weather in Jerusalem was warm and breezy that Shabbat afternoon, adding spice to the smell of poplar and pine that always fills the air of Rehavia in high summer. In this upscale neighborhood stands the spacious official residence of the prime minister, and on this particular Shabbat, under a blue sky streaked with tangerine wisps of cirrus that heralded the onset of sunset, tourists, soldiers, yeshiva boys, neighbors, and even casual passersby lined up at the gate waiting their turn to enter.

For as long as anyone could remember, the Begins had hosted a Shabbat afternoon open house in their modest Tel Aviv home. They were intent on continuing this practice in their official Jerusalem residence. The contrast between the two dwellings was staggering. In Tel Aviv they welcomed their guests into a cramped, two-room, ground-floor apartment at Number 1 Rosenbaum Street, where they had raised their son and two daughters. Friends, acquaintances – anyone – would drop by to say "*Shabbat shalom,*" shmooze over a glass of orange juice, and with the coming of the night, wish one another a *shavua tov* – a good week – and be on their way.

When Menachem Begin unexpectedly became leader of the country and word spread that he intended to continue the open house tradition, the anticipation of it became a source of matchless pleasure to the general public and an unmatched migraine to the security service. No prime minister had ever flung open his door to all and sundry before, and the people in charge of his security were at a loss as to how to handle it.

"*Shabbat shalom.* Come in. Have a cold drink," cried Mr. and Mrs. Begin welcomingly, extending a hand to all visitors as they walked through the door. Many were holding housewarming gifts of cake, flowers, chocolate, and wine. Some were so awestruck they instinctively bowed and tiptoed across the threshold.

Once inside, visitors hung about gawking at the expansive living room, with its blend of old-style European and contemporary Israeli furnishings set out on rich carpets. They silently admired the crystal chandelier in the dining room, the paintings on the walls by famous Israeli artists, the solid silver Shabbat candelabras still coated with wax, and the framed pictures of the grandchildren on the grand piano. And while they stood and stared, the two Begin daughters, Hassya and Leah, and an older grandchild, circulated among them, carrying trays of juice and soda and cookies, and urging everybody to feel at home.

One skinny old man dressed in his Shabbat best, with pockets of fatigue under his eyes, and jaws and jowls drooping with mourning, peered into Mr. Begin's face as though studying an object at a museum. He refused to let the prime minister go until he had examined a snapshot of his wife and four children, discolored and crumbling. He thrust it under Begin's nose, gesticulating and shouting in Yiddish, that in all his years at Auschwitz, where his family was gassed, he had never let go of this photograph, and that whenever the SS searched him he stuffed it into his mouth, which was why it was so cracked and creased and smeared.

Begin clasped the man to his breast and the survivor's voice gradually trailed away, and his eyes went misty. A silent thread of communication passed between them, calming the man immensely. He blinked back his tears and wordlessly walked away.

Next, a Yemenite with a wispy beard, tight side-curls and a white skullcap with a tassel on top stepped forward, and introduced himself as a grocer. Asked where his place of business was, he named a run-down neighborhood, prompting the prime minister to announce, "I want you to tell your customers and all your friends, in my name, that we are going to renew your neighborhood."

"Renew? What does that mean?" The grocer was totally perplexed.

"It means our new government is elaborating a plan called Project Renewal. With the help of our Diaspora brethren – the United Jewish Appeal and Keren Hayesod – we shall eliminate all the slums of Israel, including yours. We shall restore your homes and build new ones in consultation with you, the inhabitants. It will be a cooperative effort and, *b'ezrat*

Hashem [God willing], we shall make all our neighborhoods places where people will be proud to live."

The grocer listened intently, trust softening his sun-blasted face, and then he abruptly bent his knee to deferentially kiss the prime minister's hand. But Mr. Begin would have none of it. "A Jew bends his knee to no one but to God," he reprimanded gently.

By now the place was packed, so I stepped into the garden that led off from the living room to get some air. Here, too, people were gathered, among them a driver I recognized from the prime minister's office. His name was Rahamim, and he was in the company of a dozen or so muscular young men, all wearing T-shirts and expertly cracking roasted sunflower seeds between their teeth. Insisting I join them in their feast, they regaled me with tales of Menachem Begin's love fest with Sephardic Jews like themselves.

It was the twilight hour, and the prime minister himself stepped out of the crowded living room into the floodlit garden, his animated features lit by a dazzling smile. His entry was welcomed with whistles and applause. Among the eager faces which greeted him was one belonging to a frail figure in a baggy suit, with the pale skin of an underfed convict and teeth the color of khaki. Most of his hair was gone except for a crescent of iron-gray bristles. He looked at least fifty, and he bowed with a stiff, brittle dignity as he clasped Mr. Begin's hand.

Speaking in a fluent Hebrew, he said his name was Misha Lippu, an artist by profession, and that he had just been released from a Romanian penal colony after five years of imprisonment. He had arrived in Israel two days before, under the quota system which the Israeli government negotiated annually at a high price with the Romanian communist dictator, Nicolae Ceauşescu, enabling a trickle of Jews to emigrate.

All guests within earshot stood in rigid attentiveness as Begin gripped the man by the shoulders and in a tone of fervent compassion and respect, said, *"Shalom Aleichem! Baruch haba!"* [Welcome! Welcome!]

Lippu lowered his gaze and compressed his lips which began to tremble in emotion, causing Begin to grip him harder, saying softly, "It's all right Mr. Lippu. You're among your own now. You're home. You're safe. No one can harm you." And then, brightening up, "From whence your Hebrew? It's so fluent."

Energized by the question, Lippu wiped his eyes and explained that in his younger years he had studied at a yeshiva, and that in the penal colony there had been a Catholic priest, a Father Oradea, who knew classical

Hebrew well. So they spoke it and did exercises together. "Father Oradea was imprisoned as an *agent provocateur*," said Lippu, matter of factly.

"And you – what was your crime?" probed Begin.

"I was charged with being a Zionist conspirator."

Begin closed his eyes for a moment, and mumbled knowingly, "I am very familiar with the term. And what, specifically, were you found guilty of?"

A parade of intense emotions raced across Misha Lippu's face, and he chewed on his knuckles to get a grip on himself. "Jewish and Zionist art," he answered flatly.

Begin was nonplussed.

Compulsively, Lippu told Begin that after he'd left the yeshiva world he'd followed his artistic calling and enrolled in an art academy. When the Stalinists came to power they enforced a proletarian style of art for which he received many commissions over many years. He became well known, and was showered with honors. This won him disdain from connoisseurs and adulation from those he disdained – the fat cats and the apparatchiks. So, in the end he gave that up and began painting Jewish devotional and Zionist themes that expressed his innermost emotions. He was warned many times to stop, but he didn't. Under the Stalinist penal code this amounted to conspiracy against the state. And that's what landed him in the penal colony, where he was sent into the quarries to smash rocks.

The prime minister stared back at him with watery eyes, and said, "I, too, spent time in a gulag smashing rocks."

Dumbfounded, Misha Lippu gazed hard at Begin, and whispered, "You were a prisoner of the communists, too?"

Begin nodded, and related how, on one fine day in September 1940, three Russian security agents came knocking on his door in Vilna, and took him away. At the time he was head of Betar in Poland and, a Soviet court declared him guilty of 'deviationism,' and sentenced him to eight years hard labor in a Siberian gulag. His Soviet interrogator told him, "You will never see a Jewish State," and most fellow prisoners were equally disheartening, one telling him that the supposed date of his release – 20 September 1948 – was a fiction. Nobody ever left the camps alive. But then fate intervened. In the spring of 1941, Germany attacked Russia and the Soviets concluded an agreement with the Polish Government-in-Exile that led to his release. He joined the Free Polish Forces and reached Palestine with one of its units in 1942.

"Time for *Maariv*" [the evening service], somebody called out. Peo-

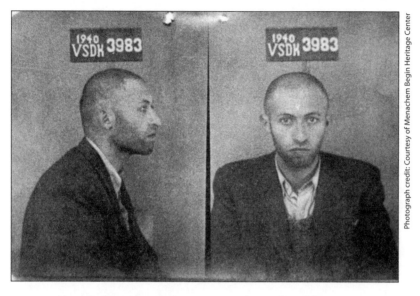

Mugshot of Menachem Begin, 1940, as a prisoner in a Soviet labor camp

ple gazed heavenward to check that three stars were visible in the sky, this being the sign that the Sabbath day was over. A group of men assembled in a corner of the garden to pray, and while they were doing so Mrs. Begin brought in from the kitchen a thick plaited candle, a silver spice box, and an overflowing goblet of wine. The brief service done, Mr. Begin lifted a granddaughter onto a chair, lit the candle, placed it in the child's hand, and as she held it aloft, raised the wine goblet and recited *havdalah*, the closing ceremony of the Sabbath day. Then the whole throng chanted in full-throated chorus, *"shavua tov"* – the words that expressed the hope for a good week to come.

As the guests were leaving, the prime minister called out after them, again and again, "We leave for Washington shortly. Please come back and visit us after we return." And the guests, bursting with delight, called back, "We will. We will."

"No, they won't," muttered the exhausted and agitated chief security officer to his subordinates. "Such a free-for-all will not happen again. To the prime minister he said, "Sir, if you want to maintain your open-house tradition, all visitors will have to register beforehand, and each will be thoroughly vetted."

"Pity," sighed Begin. "It's been such a beautiful way to keep in touch with the *amcha*" [the ordinary folk].

Chapter five

The Bible Circle

Though Mr. Begin had to forego his open house, he did open up his home to a Bible study circle which convened every Saturday evening. Approximately twenty people, among them Bible scholars of repute, would seat themselves around the couch on which the prime minister sat, and for an hour or more they would delve into some particularly attention-grabbing passage of the Book of Books. I would participate as a matter of course; being in attendance on the prime minister was part of my job.

On the first such Saturday night, held on the very eve of Begin's departure for Washington, the chosen passage was from the Book of Numbers, chapters twenty-two to twenty-four, in which the Bible records how, thirty-eight years after the children of Israel embarked on their Exodus from Egypt, and two years before entering the Promised Land, the heathen prophet Balaam was coaxed – bribed actually – by the Moabite King Balak, to curse the advancing Israelites and thereby devastate them before they could devastate him. However, Balaam, impelled by God's command, and much to Balak's displeasure, found himself involuntarily blessing them instead.

That evening's discussion centered primarily on the evocative verse nine of chapter twenty-three, in which Balaam foretells with remarkable prescience the future destiny of the Jewish people, predicting, "...this is a people that shall dwell alone and shall not be reckoned among the nations."

Reading the verse out loud, Prime Minister Begin gave a mild chuckle and said, "One does not have to be a mystic for the imagination to be stirred by such an improbable vision of a nation forever 'dwelling alone.' Is it not a startlingly accurate prophecy of our Jewish people's experience in all of history?"

Even as he was saying this, I vividly recalled the remark Prime Minister Golda Meir had once made about how lonely she invariably felt when attending a session at the United Nations. "We have no family there," she had said. "Israel is entirely alone there. But why should that be?"

Being a socialist, with no bent for theology, Golda Meir had made no attempt to answer her own momentous question. But now Menachem Begin was opening discussion on this indisputable reality.

"Why does the Jewish State so frequently face solitude in the family of nations?" he asked rhetorically. "Is it because we are the only country in the world that is Jewish? Is it because we are the one country in the world whose language is Hebrew? But why are there no other Jewish states? Why are there no other Hebrew-speaking states, just as there are multiple Christian states, Moslem states, Hindu states, Buddhist states, English-speaking, Arabic-speaking, French-speaking, Chinese-speaking states? In short, why have we no sovereign kith and kin anywhere in the world? In the United Nations, everybody is grouped into regional blocs, each bloc bound by a common geography, religion, history, culture, and language. They vote with one another in solidarity. But no other country in the world shares our unique narrative. Geographically, we are located in Asia, but the Asian bloc won't have us. Our Arab neighbors see to that. Indeed, they want to destroy us. So, geographically, we really belong nowhere. And since membership in the Security Council is in accordance with regional blocs, we have no realistic chance of being elected to it. The one blood tie, the one kindred bond we have with anybody at all in the world, is with our own fellow Jews in the Diaspora, and everywhere they are a minority and nowhere do they enjoy any form of national or cultural autonomy."

Professor Ephraim Auerbach, a rotund, semi-bald scholar of refinement, wit and brilliance, picked up the theme, citing classic commentators who suggested that the meaning of "dwelling alone," as cited by the heathen prophet Balaam, really meant voluntarily setting oneself apart. In other words, the Jewish nation distinguished itself from other peoples by virtue of its distinctive religious and moral laws, and by the fact that it had been chosen by God as the instrument of a divine purpose within the family of nations. "In that sense, the Jewish people dwells alone of its own volition," he said.

A woman in her fifties asked for permission to comment. She was tall and lean, her face equine, her dress and hat plain, and her eyes brilliantly intelligent. This was Nehama Leibowitz, a renowned Bible scholar famous for her immensely popular weekly Torah commentaries, composed in a highly comprehensible style. Deftly, she drew attention to the verse's grammatical structure, elaborating upon and reinforcing Professor Auerbach's comment, explaining that the word *yitchashav*, generally translated in English to mean 'reckoned' – "this is a people that shall not be *reckoned* among the nations" – was rendered in the reflexive form, which therefore gave the meaning, "this is a people that *does not reckon itself* among the nations." And as an aside, she pointed out that this form of that particular word occurs but once in the whole of Scripture.

Professor Yaakov Katz, a slight figure with dour features and a deeply analytical disposition, broke in to refer to the eminent Talmudist Marcus Jastrow. Citing Jastrow's Talmudic sources, Katz showed that the reflexive form of the root word *chashav* ['reckon'] signifies "to conspire," meaning that Israel "is a people that dwells alone and does not *conspire* against other nations."

Professor Harel Fisch, educator, literary scholar, and future laureate of the prestigious Israel Prize, raised a finger for attention. Stroking his goatee, he mused that in modern society the Jewish people were unique in personifying a seamless blend of peoplehood and religion, born out of the two seminal events that forged the Jewish national personality: the Exodus from Egypt, when Jews entered history as a people, and the giving of the Torah at Sinai, when Jews entered history as a nation-faith. A Jew, therefore, was a synergy of both – Exodus and Sinai. He could not be the one without the other, though many throughout the centuries had tried to keep them apart. Whether one was a believer or a skeptic, this subtle nation-faith individuality was indivisible. And since this was what distinguished the Jewish people from all other peoples, they would always, uniquely, "dwell alone."

Another participant, whom everybody knew simply as Srulik, a bushy-haired archaeologist and Bible prodigy wearing an emerald green yarmulke which he had picked up at the door, provocatively remarked that whichever way one interpreted Balaam's prophecy, it stamped the Jewish people as an eternally abnormal nation within the family of nations – and that this flew in the face of the classic Zionist creed, which expounded that Zionism's aim was to normalize the Jewish people so that it could become a *goy k'chol hagoyim* – a nation like all other nations. Indeed, the central thesis of the Zionist thinkers of the late nineteenth and early twentieth centuries, particularly the Labor Zionists, was that once Jews possessed what every other normal nation possesses – a land of their own – they would automatically become a normal nation within the family of nations. And the consequence of that, so the classic Zionist theory held, would be that anti-Semitism would wither and die. Well, it hadn't withered and died. On the contrary, the very existence of the Jewish State was often a cause for anti-Semitic prejudice, and this, surely, cast a shadow on a fundamental article of Zionist faith.

To which Dr. Chaim Gevaryahu, chairman of the Israel Bible Society, added that he wondered what led those brilliant secular Zionist founding fathers of yesteryear to predict so confidently that Jewish self-determination would, of itself, lead to national normalization and put an end to anti-Semitism. Indeed, once Jews became a normal people they would cease being Jews. But that could never happen, because nothing could ever put an end to anti-Semitism. In fact, one thing to be learned from the biblical portion under review was that the so-called prophet Balaam was the archetypical anti-Semite. His whole intent was to curse the Jews, not to bless them. The blessing was God's doing, not his.

Irresistibly, the prime minister plunged in once again, expanding on the uniqueness of the Jewish national identity, saying, "As Professor Harel Fisch has pointed out, other peoples are multi-religious; other religions are multinational. But we Jews are one and the same – religion and nationhood both. And as Professor Auerbach and Professor Leibowitz have indicated, we have forever maintained this distinctiveness by refusing to assimilate into other nations. It all began with the father of our nation, Abraham of Ur of the Chaldees, who, at the age of seventy-five, deduced the eternal truth of the One God, and bolted the idolatry of his parental home in order to worship Him. Hundreds of years later we see his descendents, by now an enslaved people, again embarking on a God-commanded journey – the Exodus from the idolatrous land of Egypt – again in order to worship the One God. In both instances their destination was Eretz Yisrael, there to fulfill their religious-national destiny. Never in Jewish history was this identity severed." Then the line of his mouth tightened a fraction showing he was about to draw a practical conclusion: "And since there can be no separation between nation and faith, this means there can be no total separation between religion and state in the Jewish State."

This triggered off a firestorm of controversy, because while some of the scholars present took the Bible as a paradigm of God's own writing, others related to it secularly, as a piece of extraordinary literature. Listening attentively, Mr. Begin lowered the temperature by saying in an earnest voice that whatever the differences of view, the eternal fact remained that, by any reading of the text, the Jewish people did, indeed, constitute an exceptional phenomenon in world history. To illustrate his point he picked up a volume of the utterances of Dr. Yaakov Herzog, whom readers might recall had been my mentor, counselor and inspiration when I took my first steps into the world of diplomacy. Yaakov died prematurely in 1972 at the age of fifty, and Menachem Begin appropriately described him that evening as "a master of the perplexities of international diplomacy and a prodigy in the field of Jewish erudition." He continued, "In fact, he is the only man I ever met who was given the choice at one and the same time of being asked by Levi Eshkol to be chief of the prime minister's office, and approached by Anglo-Jewry to be chief rabbi of Great Britain."

In closing the discussion that night, Menachem Begin read from Herzog's profound philosophical anthology, *A People That Dwells Alone*:

> The theory of classic Zionism was national normalization. What was wrong with the theory? It was the belief that the idea of a 'people that dwells alone' is an abnormal concept, when actually a 'people that dwells alone' is the natural concept of the Jewish people. That is why this one phrase still describes the totality of the extraordinary phenomenon of Israel's revival. If one asks how the ingathering of the exiles, which no one could have imagined in his wildest dreams, came about, or how the State of Israel could endure such severe security challenges, or how it has built up such a flourishing economy, or how the unity of the Jewish people throughout the Diaspora has been preserved, one must come back to the primary idea that this is 'a people that dwells alone.' More than that, one must invoke this phrase not only to understand how the Jews have existed for so long; one must invoke it as a testimony to the Jewish right to exist at all in the land of their rebirth.[58]

"So there you have it," concluded Begin snapping the book shut. "Cease dwelling alone and we cease to exist. What a conundrum!"

Chapter six

Washington

AT EASE!"
"ATTENTION!"
"PRESENT ARMS!"

Compelled by the roll of military drums, the honor guard saluted the prime minister as, head held high, shoulders back, chin out, he inspected the IDF parade, then bowed respectfully before the thicket of regimental banners which were dipped in ceremonial salute.

Dr. Yosef Burg, the always witty and highly erudite minister of the interior, leaned across to where I was standing in the receiving line and whispered naughtily into my ear, "There hasn't been a state departure ceremony like this since Golda Meir put a stop to it five years ago. Jabotinsky would love it. For Begin this is *hadar!*"

The pomp, the show, the *hadar*, were all entirely his. Begin wanted to underscore to the nation the momentous purpose he attributed to his journey. A 'Who's Who' of Israeli public life had turned out at Ben-Gurion Airport to see the prime minister off, although he was taking a regular commercial El Al flight. The entire cabinet was there, as was the diplomatic corps, the high command, religious dignitaries, Knesset members, and various other important officials. The VIPs lined the carpet that snaked toward the gleaming blue and white airplane whose passengers crowded the windows to gawk at the rare show unfolding on the tarmac below. Moving leisurely along the line, the prime minister shook hands and squeezed shoulders, the nature of his leave-taking dependent on how partial he was to each of the well-wishers.

Standing on a podium he declared he was leaving for the shores of America filled with hope, and that he was bringing to the president of the United States a far-reaching and concrete proposal for the advancement of peace. "Let the word go forth," he fervently declared, "that the people of Israel want peace, a lasting peace, a genuine peace, a just peace. Our people have too often been bereaved and orphaned. There is not a home in our land that has not lost someone – a father, a mother, a brother, a son – and the grief is forever with us, to our last breath. We detest war, we hate bloodshed, we threaten no one." And then, addressing his remarks at the Egyptian president, who had recently made a statement threatening Israel if it did not accede to his demands, the prime minister scornfully reprimanded, "Really, President Sadat! Might I suggest you cease threatening us? After all, Israel is not exactly famous for its lack of courage, is it?" And then, with a sweeping gesture, caught up on the wave of his own enthusiasm and righteousness, he proclaimed, "Yes, President Sadat, we want peace. But if we are attacked, we shall defend ourselves and fling back the aggressor with all our might – as it was avowed in the days of yore, in the Book of Books, where it is written, *'Kuma Hashem v'yafutzu oyvecha v'yanusu sonecha mipanecha'*: Rise up, O Lord, and let Thy enemies be scattered, and let them that despise Thee flee before Thee."

Softly, with deep feeling, he ended, "Citizens of Israel, I need your prayers for the success of the assignment I undertake in your name today. And even though I am unworthy of the task, I beseech the Almighty that He allows my mission to prosper, for the sake of the whole House of Israel."[59]

With that, the drums beat yet another lengthy roll and Menachem Begin, his face resolute and dedicated, stood ramrod straight as the military band played the national anthem.

Over Germany, the premier asked his spokesman, Dan Patir – a relic from the previous administration, like myself – to invite the Israeli press on board to come up to the first-class section for an informal, off-the-record chat. Soon, a dozen or so journalists were crowded around Begin, kneeling in seats and on the floor, straining to hear him above the engines and scribbling ferociously, trying to capture all the information coming their way.

Begin had known most of these correspondents for years, and so it was with relaxed familiarity, jacket and tie off, that he shared what he thought of Jimmy Carter. His intention, as always, was to tug these opinion makers into the orbit of his tough choices, hoping to win them over in the event of a fight with the president of the United States.

Then came the questions, which tumbled out one after the other in rapid succession:

"Is it true that Carter is preparing a chilly reception for you?"

"We'll have to wait and see," replied Begin cagily.

"The pomp and pageantry of your farewell ceremony at Ben-Gurion Airport – your critics say you're obsessed with red carpets. Are you?"

Begin sounded a deep and honest laugh: "Stuff and nonsense! I'm obsessed with *hadar* – national dignity and Jewish honor – yes. But those who suggest that I indulge in self-aggrandizement don't remember, or don't want to remember, that I lived in the underground for five years without a carpet of any sort. The only people that can talk such nonsense are those who never savored an underground struggle, and don't know what total anonymity is – an absolutely gray existence in which you cannot visit a friend and a friend cannot visit you."

"But Mr. Begin, now you can," said someone. "So why have you been avoiding us? Why are you suddenly so press-shy? Why have you been so tight-lipped? What do you have up your sleeve for Mr. Carter?"

"Aha! No leaks out of my cabinet, eh? My apologies!" He said this with a smug laugh and an air of victory.

"So tell us, what's really happening?"

Deadly serious now, the prime minister explained that he had been deeply immersed during the past week in preparing for this visit, and that he was carrying with him to Washington the results of his labors. It was a confidential document whose contents the cabinet had approved unanimously. The document was entitled, "The Framework for the Peacemaking Process," and it dealt with the whole matter of the proposed Geneva peace conference. Most significantly, it pre-empted the Arab demand that Yasser Arafat and his PLO participate in the intended conference.

"And if Carter insists?" asked one.

"Then I shall resist. They shall not participate under any circumstances!" His words were raw, but he instantly controlled himself and explained that out of respect for the president he could not share the contents of the document with the press now. "The president must be the first to hear about it, directly from me," he said. "Remember, this is my first visit as prime minister to Washington, and it will set the tone of my relationship with President Carter for a long time to come."

"So, if it's that important why isn't Foreign Minister Dayan with you?" asked one.

"Because at this first meeting it is important that President Carter and I have a chance to take a very close look at each other, man to man, with no intermediaries; just him and me."

Five hours later, well over the Atlantic, I awoke from a fitful doze to the startling sight of the prime minister, vigorous, freshly shaven, and properly attired, bending down on one knee, unsuccessfully trying to help his wife put on her shoe. From across the aisle where I sat, I handed Mrs. Begin a neat little shoehorn that was tucked into the cunningly designed toilet kit, compliments of the airline.

"Menachem," teased Mrs. Begin. "You can get up off your knees now. Yehuda has given me a shoehorn."

Begin rose and said with fake petulance, "Marriage is not a word. Marriage is a sentence."

Encouraged by this intimacy, I asked how long they had been married. Mrs. Begin answered that it was thirty-six years, since May 1939, three months before the German occupation. And he, with amusement in his eyes and loving laughter in his voice, revealed, "We met at the home of a mutual friend, a veteran Betar member in Poland. Sitting at the table were the Arnold girls, twin sisters. Seventeen! They looked identical, but I could tell they were different. On the spot I decided that this one" – he jerked his thumb – "would be my wife. The next day I wrote her a letter."

Mrs. Begin shook her head and in mock sarcasm, scoffed, "What a letter!"

The prime minister smiled with beautiful forthrightness, and said, "I wrote to her: 'My dear lady – I saw you for the first time but I feel I have known you all my life.' Then, later, I told her how hard life would be. There would be no money, there would be plenty of trouble, and there might even be jail. We have to fight for Eretz Yisrael, I told her."

"And what did you answer?" I dared ask Aliza Begin.

She gave me an easy smile, but he replied for her: "She said, 'I'm not afraid of trouble.' That's exactly what she said."

I told them that the American ambassador, Samuel Lewis, had told me that an internal state department brief drawn up preparatory to their visit described their marriage as "exemplary."

"Till now," cracked Aliza, whom Begin and their intimate friends called Alla. "I'm providing him with *this* world, he's providing me with the next."

He chuckled and said with appealing openness, "We toast each other every day. May it last forever," and his hand stole across the armrest and fondled hers in a possessive gesture.

On arrival at Kennedy Airport, Abraham Beame, New York's diminutive and effervescent mayor, stepped up to the microphone to pronounce words of welcome in the name of the Big Apple, and on behalf of the thirty or forty local politicians, Jewish leaders and Israeli officials who were crowding around. The prime minister responded in kind, after which reporters began barking questions, which he fielded with experienced deftness. The first one was asked by the *Jewish Press*:

"Mr. Prime Minister, both you and President Carter are known to be deeply religious men, well acquainted with religious quotations. I would like to know to what extent these feelings and your knowledge of the Bible will enter into your discussions?"

Answered Begin, "I know President Carter to be a man of faith, and I am not at all ashamed to state I believe in Divine Providence. I think it is a very positive quality to have in common for the promotion of a constructive dialogue."

The last question was posed by a woman representing the *Village Voice*, with pronounced bluntness. "Mr. Prime Minister, you say you are here to meet the president to talk about advancing the peace, but how can you advance the peace without agreeing to the establishment of a Palestinian state?"

"Madam, what you are suggesting is ceaseless warfare and bloodshed," rumbled Begin. "What you term a Palestinian state would mean a mortal danger to the Jewish State. Such a state can never come into being."

"But what if Yasser Arafat will recognize your right to a Jewish State?"

"The leader of the so-called PLO is the godfather of international terrorism. There are people, particularly in Europe and no doubt some here in America, too, who have a delusive impulse to read into his rhetoric messages of amiability, sobriety, and compromise. It's all lies. Thank you."

That night – it was a Friday – Menachem Begin slept the sleep of a Sabbath lover in his Waldorf Astoria bed. During most of the following day he had his feet up reading, and spent an hour or two entertaining old friends.

Sunday he had meetings with lay and religious leaders across the full spectrum of American Jewry. He spent a goodly hour with Rabbi Joseph B. Soloveitchik, whom he had known for years. Soloveitchik was the scion of an eminent rabbinic dynasty, a Talmudic mastermind and outstanding teacher who was the head of the Yeshiva University's rabbinical seminary. A religious leader par excellence, he was the seminal figure of Modern Orthodoxy, serving as guide, mentor and role model to hundreds of thousands of Jews across America and beyond.

With easy familiarity they chatted about developments within Jewry in general, and in Israel and the United States in particular. They then went on to converse about the relevance of the religious fast of Tisha b'Av [the ninth day of the Hebrew month of Av] to modern times. The fast, which commemorates the most tragic events in the Jewish calendar, was only days away, and the prime minister wanted the rabbi's thoughts concerning the appropriateness of integrating the Holocaust commemoration within this traditional saddest of saddest days (In Israel, the official Holocaust memorial day coincides with the anniversary of the Warsaw Ghetto Uprising). The Rav – that is how his disciples reverently referred to him – thought the idea merited serious consideration. Rabbinic tradition, he said, favored the merging of such commemorations. By combining the two anniversaries, the one ancient and the other all too modern, the themes of Jewish suffering, destiny, and eternity would be dramatically reinforced.

Rabbi Soloveitchik and Menachem Begin parted with enormous affability, and then the prime minister readied himself for his next appointment, which was a meeting with another old friend – Rabbi Menachem Mendel Schneerson, the Lubavitcher Rebbe.

Rabbi Schneerson stood at the entrance of the Lubavitch movement headquarters at 770 Eastern Parkway, in the Crown Heights section of Brooklyn, waiting to receive his guest. Amid a blaze of photoflashes the two men embraced. The Rebbe's face was beaming as they exchanged greetings. His was an angelic face, half-curtained by a square gray beard, and topped by the trademark black fedora of the Lubavitch Chasidim. On him, it seemed to have the effect of a bastion protecting the mind from iniquitous invasions.

One reporter called out, "Mr. Begin, why have you come to see the Rebbe? Surely, you being the newly elected prime minister of Israel, he should be coming to see you?"

"Why, indeed?" the prime minister responded with grace, showing

Begin and the Lubavitcher Rebbe, Brooklyn, New York, 17 July 1977

Photograph credit: Ya'acov Sa'ar & Israel Government Press Office

an easy rapport. "A good question." And then, with an air of deep reverence, "I have come to see the Rebbe because I am en route to Washington
to meet President Carter for the first time. So, it is most natural for me to
want to seek the blessings of this great sage of the Jewish people."

"How great is he?" asked another reporter.

"Rabbi Schneerson is one of the paramount Jewish personalities of
our time. His status is unique among our people. So I am certain his blessings will strengthen me as I embark on a mission of acute importance for
our future."

"Would the rabbi care to comment on that?" asked yet another.

"Only to reiterate my fullest blessings," said the Rebbe, in his heavily accented English. "And also to add that I accept the honor of the prime
minister's visit to me not on my own account, but in recognition of the
Lubavitch movement's dedicated work in spreading the love of God and
His Torah among our fellow Jews, wherever they may be."

The two men closeted themselves together for a good hour, at the
end of which Mr. Begin informed Rabbi Schneerson that when we returned
from Washington, I, his aide, would return to brief him on how the White
House talks had fared.

Chapter seven

The Presidential Encounter

T he prime minister's motorcade made its way to Blair House, the official guest residence across the street from the White House, escorted by police outriders through streets bedecked with Israeli flags. The next morning, at 10.30 prompt, to the martial salute of an army, navy and air force guard of honor, Prime Minister and Mrs. Begin were driven at a stately pace to the South Lawn of the White House, there to be greeted by the President and Mrs. Carter amid pageantry so grand as to make the send-off at Ben-Gurion airport appear provincial.

Under a cloudless sky, the Army Old Guard Fife and Drum Corps paraded across the flag-bedecked South Lawn, to the delight of over two hundred guests. Led by a standard-bearer carrying the troupe's tasseled colors, to the trill of tiny flutes and the staccato beat of the drummers, the white-liveried Corps drilled in flawless formation, drawing up before the presidential platform for review as a nineteen-gun salute thudded imperiously through the air, commanding everyone's silence.

The president delivered his welcoming remarks with perfectly chosen words, going out of his way to praise Menachem Begin:

"To me, having read the writings and the biography of our distinguished visitor, there is a great parallel between what Israel is and what it stands for, and what Prime Minister Begin is and what he stands for. He is a man who has demonstrated a willingness to suffer for principle, a man who has shown superlative personal courage in the face of trial, challenge, and disappointment, but who has ultimately prevailed because of the depth of his commitment and his own personal characteristics."

Then he singled out for acclaim Begin's "deep and unswerving religious commitment. This," he said with surprising familiarity, "has always been a guiding factor in his consciousness and in his pursuit of unswerving goals. There is a quietness about him, which goes with determination and a fiery spirit in his expressions of his beliefs to the public. And that is how it should be."[60]

Yechiel Kadishai, next to whom I was placed in the line-up, gave my arm a monstrous pinch of satisfaction, and Ambassador Sam Lewis, three or four paces away, threw me a huge wink and made a circle with his thumb and forefinger, as if to signal, 'Right on the ball!' Perhaps Lewis had had a hand in the composition of the speech. Certainly, the whole reception reflected his attitude; that honey will go a lot further than vinegar.

The prime minister stood on the platform in pleased surprise. Such praise! Such honor! So unexpected! So moved was Begin by the conviviality of the welcome that he declaimed the opening words of his response in an impromptu and lyrical Hebrew, saying, "Mr. President, I have come from the Land of Zion and Jerusalem as the spokesman of an ancient people and a young nation. God's blessings on America, the hope of the human race. Peace unto your great nation."

He then continued by extemporizing in English with equal zest about how "we, in Israel, see in you, Mr. President, not only the first citizen of your great and mighty country, but also the leader and defender of the whole free world." He dwelt much on Israel's struggle for peace, and how the free world was shrinking in the face of the Soviet threat. "Democracies can be likened in our time to an island battered by bitter winds, by stormy seas, by high waves," he surged. "Therefore, all free men and women should stand together to persevere in the struggle for human rights, to preserve human liberty, to make sure that government of the people, by the people, for the people shall not perish from the earth."

Eager applause was subsumed in the sustained beat of the drums, and not a person stirred as the marine band, their instruments, buckles, straps, and insignia glistening brilliantly in the sunshine, struck up *"Hatikva"* and then the "Star Spangled Banner." Whereupon, the president took Begin lightly by the elbow and said, "Come, let us start our talks." The rest of us fell into step, and followed them at a respectful distance into the White House.

An easy smile played at the corners of President Carter's mouth as he opened the talks by saying, "Mr. Prime Minister, we are all pleased and honored that you are with us. And, as you know, there is a great deal of excitement and anticipation to see how well you and I get along together. There are dire predictions."

The smile widened into a considerable grin.

"Oh yes, our newspapers back home are predicting big fireworks today," laughed Mr. Begin, humor glinting in his eyes.

"Fireworks? This is July the nineteenth, not the fourth. No firework displays today," said the president.

The laughter around the grand oak conference table was genuine. Coffee was served and the president and the prime minister sipped for a moment in silence. We were sitting in the Cabinet Room, an austere, colonial-style oblong chamber with off-white walls, one of which bore a life-size portrait of Harry S. Truman hanging over a mantelpiece. The only real splashes of color in the room were the golden drapes of the windows and the presidential banners standing in a corner, suspended from silver standards. The hush in the old room was magnified by the clinking of the china, the discreet chitchat of the officials and the muffled drone of a plane overhead.

Leaning forward in his chair and bringing his charm to bear, Carter resumed his words of welcome: "I am delighted that tonight we shall be having supper together. We have invited fifty-nine people. That's the largest dinner we've had since I took office. So many Americans want to meet you. And I have asked the prime minister" – this to his aides – "to give me some more of his time after supper, so that we can have a private chat, to get to know each other a little more."

"It will be my honor," said Begin, bowing his head to his host.

The president peered at his notes and speaking forcefully now, said, "So now I shall begin."

The Middle East, he explained, was a very high priority of his administration, and if a settlement could not be accomplished in 1977 it would be more difficult to attain after that. America wanted to be an intermediary who would win the trust of all parties, Israel and the Arabs alike. Therefore, whatever he was sharing with the prime minister today he had already conveyed in exactly the same terms and with exactly the same connotations to the Arab leaders whom he had met earlier – Sadat of Egypt, Hussein of Jordan, and Assad of Syria.

He emphasized that his administration was abandoning the strategy of his predecessor, President Gerald Ford, and his secretary of state, Henry

Kissinger, whose policy had been to try and achieve a slow, incremental, step-by-step process toward peace. Now the time was ripe for a comprehensive peace settlement, a complete solution of the Israel-Arab conflict. With this as the goal, a conference of all the parties should be convened as soon as possible at Geneva. And for this to take place there was a need for a general agreement by all the parties on a few basic principles. These, he had already aired with the Arab leaders.

First and foremost, he said, was the principle of the acceptance of the 1967 UN Security Council Resolution 242 as the legal basis of the conference. However, he, Carter, had decided to expand upon that Resolution and to take it a step further. In its original version it merely called for "an end of the state of belligerency" as the object of an Arab-Israel negotiation. This was insufficient. Now, he was widening its connotation to mean a full-blown peace settlement. In other words, the object of the Geneva talks would be a genuine and comprehensive peace.

"And how did the Arab leaders respond to that?" asked Begin.

"It is a difficult concept for them to accept," replied Carter candidly, "but they did not disavow it."

The prime minister could not resist an enigmatic smile, and he leaned back with excessive nonchalance. This was good news! No American president had ever defined 242 this way before; none had envisaged an Israel-Arab peace settlement as categorical as this. But Begin kept his counsel. He wanted to hear more. He wanted to know what the president had to say on the other two issues which preyed heavily on his mind – the land issue, meaning the territorial integrity of Eretz Yisrael, and the issue of the Palestinian representation at Geneva, meaning the exclusion of Arafat's PLO.

As if reading his mind, the president ran his eyes down his notes and said almost casually that on the territorial issue, Israel, clearly, would have to withdraw from occupied territories to new borders, which would be secure and mutually recognized. On the future of the Palestinians, the Arab leaders had told him they should be treated as a separate nation. His position, however, was that they should have a 'homeland' tied to Jordan, not an independent state. But there was no actual concrete plan. And as for the procedural question of the Palestinian representation at Geneva, the Arab leaders themselves were not of one mind. Egypt and Jordan thought the Palestinians could be part of the Jordanian delegation, while Syria preferred a single Arab delegation negotiating as a single body.

At this point President Carter leaned forward and examined the faces of his colleagues. "Anybody else have anything to add?" he asked.

"It seems not, Mr. President," said Secretary of State Cyrus Vance, speaking on behalf of them all. He squeezed his long, tired face into something resembling a smile of approval, and confirmed, "You've summarized it all very accurately."

The president turned back to Begin with eyes which seemed to express more challenge than curiosity, and said, "The floor is yours, Mr. Prime Minister. We are eager to hear your concepts. What role do you want us to play? What ideas do you have about Geneva? What's your thinking on the question of Arab good faith – and your good faith, for that matter? What can your government do to encourage the Arabs to place their trust in you?" And then, in a rarefied southern way, "And, oh yes, I have to add that not everybody really trusts America either, do they?" suggesting vaguely that Begin was one of them. "But I can promise you one thing, Mr. Prime Minister, with all my heart" – his eyebrows had risen with his avowal of sincerity – "we shall try, we shall honestly and truly try, to act as best we can for the sake of peace. Hence, we are keen to hear your feelings and your thinking."

With deference, Menachem Begin expressed his gratitude for the president's reception, and then, drawing his lips in thoughtfully, stated, "Before I address myself to the important issues you raise, I have something significant to say about Ethiopia."

All the Americans looked up sharply. Carter drew a breath. His mouth seemed suddenly thinner, his lips tighter. "Ethiopia?" he said. "What's your urgent interest in Ethiopia that requires you to bring it up at the very outset of our talks? We've had problems galore with that country."

With the Cold War at its height, the Soviet Union was engaged in a high-stakes battle for control of the Horn of Africa. The reality of African politics was that tribal allegiances were ephemeral and alliances shifted back and forth unpredictably; a situation the Soviet Union used to its own advantage. First they had sided with Somalia in a war against Ethiopia, and then they had switched sides to help Ethiopia push back the Somalis. At the time of this first meeting between Carter and Begin, they were supporting a Sudanese invasion deep into Ethiopia.

Menachem Begin gazed at President Carter with deceptively mild eyes. "Early this morning, Mr. President," he said, "I received a message from Mengistu, the ruler of Ethiopia. It was an appeal for help. Mengistu communicated it to me directly and personally. He says Soviet-backed invaders are on the point of dismembering his country. It is as serious as that. His appeal made a deep impression on me. He asked me to tell you that he has a proposition to make to improve your relations with his country. I feel duty-bound to bring his plea to your attention."

"Cy, Zbig, any such message come your way?" asked the president of his secretary of state and national security adviser.

Both men shook their heads, puzzled.

"Tell us again, who exactly sent the message?" asked Zbigniew Brzezinski, a cold-eyed intellectual of unmistakable Polish origin.

"The Ethiopian head of state, Colonel Mengistu Hailé Mariam, in the early hours of this morning," answered Begin.

The message had reached him at Blair House via a Mossad channel, and he had read it with mixed feelings. His relationship with the Ethiopian president was convoluted. Mengistu was a seedy despot with a moral claim on Israel. Over the years he had provided port and air facilities to Israeli ships and planes when they had been in desperate straits in the waters and skies of the Horn of Africa, which was surrounded by hostile Moslem territories. And now, Begin needed Mengistu's goodwill more than ever. In Ethiopia there were tens of thousands of Jews – black Jews, who were impoverished and threatened by famine and war. Begin wanted to bring them out. He wanted to bring this entire remote, archaic community, whose history traced back to the Middle Ages or earlier, to Israel. His emissaries were already in contact with them. But Ethiopia's Jews came at a price; there was a ransom. Mengistu wanted military and economic aid in return for their exodus. A plan was already being developed under conditions of utmost secrecy: Israel would fly military supplies into Ethiopia and fill the returning planes with Ethiopian Jews. That had been the deal – but as of this morning, a new twist had arisen. The Mengistu note to Begin carried with it the implication that the Ethiopian Jews were now hostage to Begin transmitting this message to Carter, and to Carter's favorable response. Of all this, Begin said nothing. Given Mengistu's record of corruption and cruelty, and his duplicity in his dealings with the Americans, he could not be sure how Jimmy Carter would react to a deal which was intended to liberate the Jews of Ethiopia. It might even backfire. So he chose to couch his case in the language of American interest, saying, "You will agree, Mr. President, that under the circumstances of the Cold War, given Ethiopia's location in the Horn of Africa, it is a country of great strategic importance. And given the fact that Mengistu has become disillusioned with the Soviets because they are now aiding his enemies, he wants you to know he has changed sides and he writes to me to intercede with you."

Carter listened intently, stroking his cheek with the back of his knuckles, while Vance and Brzezinski huddled with him, whispering words of advice. When they were through, Carter asked, a bite in his voice, "Would you mind giving me a copy of the text of that message?"

"Gladly!"

"Thank you. We had a fairly substantial amount of aid going into Ethiopia over a long period of time, but they turned their backs on us. So this is a difficult thing for us to swallow. Mengistu's human rights record is abysmal. All I can say is that we'll look into it. I can promise nothing."

He stared at the prime minister with an indecipherable expression in his eyes, and Begin could do no more than to thank him for taking the matter into consideration. Then he said, "Before I get to your specific questions concerning Geneva, I would like to turn to the matter of southern Lebanon. I have a map of the area which I would like you to see."

General Poran quickly unfurled a map on an easel. It displayed tiny clusters of Christian villages, colored in green, surrounded by an abundant sprinkling of Moslem villages, in red. As Begin began describing the threats which the isolated Christian villagers were facing, Freuka indicated with a pointer how the scattered green dots were dominated by the excessive profusion of the red. The Christians were not merely isolated, said Begin, but abandoned amidst five thousand well-armed PLO terrorists who had

Photograph credit: Ya'acov Sa'ar & Israel Government Press Office

After the meetings in Washington with President Carter, Begin visited the UN to discuss, again, the Lebanese border tensions, using the same map. Here, with UN Sec. Gen. Waldheim and author, 22 July 1977

taken over southern Lebanon and who were shelling them regularly every night. It was due to this situation that the Israeli government had reviewed its policy vis-à-vis Lebanon, and had reached conclusions somewhat different from those of its Labor predecessor.

"The points of our policy are these," declared Begin unequivocally:

"One – we don't want any part of Lebanon, not a single inch.

"Two – we don't want a war to result from the situation in Lebanon.

"Three – we will not let the Christian minority in Lebanon down.

"And four – whatever happens we shall never take you, Mr. President, by surprise. If contingencies arise that might require action, we shall always consult you."

And then, with a cautionary lift of the hand, "But I think, above all, we have to say to you that we cannot turn our backs on the Christians. We have a human duty as Jews – nay a sacred duty – never to allow the Christian minority to be destroyed."

Carter's voice rose in surprise. "Do you not feel the Lebanese central government is the best source of protection for the Christians? We are thinking of extending them assistance."

"The Lebanese President, Elias Sarkis is, of course, a Christian, but he is virtually helpless, as I'm sure your specialists will confirm," said Begin.

Brzezinski cupped his hand and hastily whispered something into Carter's ear. The president nodded and reiterated to the prime minister, "Nevertheless, it is our inclination to give him military assistance."

"Good!" said Begin, but then he continued, in an ominous tone, "But I have to tell you, Arafat is destroying Lebanon. Presently, he is engaged against the Christians. And the Christians must be given the means to protect themselves. But a day will come when he will surely turn against us, too."

Carter made no response. The issue was becoming too knotty. He did not want to be drawn in. So, jaw tight, gazing upon the prime minister with narrowed eyes, he said, "Might I suggest we move on to your next point."

"Certainly," said Begin, and he breezily turned to the man sitting on his left, whom he introduced as Dr. Shmuel Katz, his chief information adviser. "I'd like my friend and old comrade, Dr. Katz, to describe for you the way we look upon Judea, Samaria and the Gaza District in their broader historical context," he told the president.

A soft-spoken intellectual originally from South Africa, Shmuel Katz was a former member of the Irgun High Command, and its chief ideologue. Indeed, within the Begin camp, Katz was the keeper of the

Jabotinsky conscience, the guardian against corrupters of the Eretz Yisrael creed. Clearly, he was here as an ideological voice. At this first encounter with the American president, Menachem Begin wanted his interlocutors to know exactly what he stood for.

Shmuel Katz's usual melancholy demeanor deepened as he held up a map of the Middle East on which were displayed twenty-two Arab states surrounding one tiny Jewish State, prominent in its abject isolation.

"Every child in every one of these twenty-two Arab states," Katz began, "is taught from an early age that it is a patriotic duty and a moral imperative that this tiny state" – his fingertip was resting on Israel, blotting it out entirely – "be eliminated from the face of the earth, as a divisive and immoral element intruding into the Arab world."

The president listened, his face impassive.

"Indeed, in the Palestinian Covenant, which is the National Charter of the PLO, the expulsion of the so-called 'Zionist imperialists' from the Arab world takes precedence over the 'purging of the Zionist presence in Palestine.'"

Carter pressed his lips together. Clearly, he had no tolerance for national dogmas of this sort. His mind was empirical, that of an engineer, focused only on results. You could sense it in the way he fixed his steely, impatient, pale-blue eyes on Katz, as if to say, "What's your bottom line?" Recognizing this gaze, Carter's advisers began shifting about restlessly, shooting wary glances at each other. In contrast, Begin sat expressionless while Dr. Katz elaborated further:

"Logically, the PLO was recognized as the sole representative of the Palestinian people by all the Arab states, for the PLO is an instrument of all the Arab states, armed by them, financed by them, and trained by them. To bolster the scenario of a people driven from their homeland by a predatory Israel they have built up a mythological history which bears no relation to the facts. In 1974, Arafat addressed the United Nations, claiming that the Palestinians were engaged continuously for thousands of years in farming and cultural activity in Palestine. It is hard to imagine a description in harsher contrast to the facts."

"How is that?" asked Vance mildly.

"Because the land was virtually empty. As Americans, you will be interested in the firsthand testimony of one of your own – testimony that refutes the absurd Arab claim. I urge you to read, or reread, Mark Twain's *Innocents Abroad.*"

Katz hunched over his file and extracted from it a page photocopied from the book. He adjusted his spectacles, coughed a little cough, and said, "This is Mark Twain in eighteen sixty-seven, writing about the scene he saw in Upper Galilee: 'There is not a solitary village throughout its whole extent, not for thirty miles in either direction. There are two or three clusters of Bedouin tents, but not a single permanent habitation. One may ride ten miles hereabouts, and not see ten human beings.... Gray lizards, those heirs of ruin, of sepulchres and desolation, glided in and out among the rocks and lay still and sunned themselves. Where prosperity has reigned and fallen; where glory has flamed and gone out; where gladness was and sorrow is; where the pomp of life has been, and silence and death brood in its high places, there this reptile makes its home, and mocks at human vanity.'"[61]

"Oh, how Mark Twain could write!" gushed Menachem Begin, his smile pure sunlight. "Whoever would have thought that a day would come when his words would become testimony filled with such pertinent political significance?" He sat back and beamed contentedly at the old brass chandelier hanging above the table. "A beautiful piece," he observed.

Katz continued, "And Twain's is only one of a series of testimonies between the eighteenth and twentieth centuries that describe the utter desolation of the Land of Israel. Indeed, Palestine was never, never ever" – he tapped Twain for added weight – "a homeland of any other people; never, never ever, a national center to anybody else except to the Jewish people. *Their* links were forever continuous. It is part of western culture that Palestine was always a Jewish country."

The president wore a mask of politeness, but it was easy to see by his clenched teeth that anger lurked beneath. Apparently, not only did he resent the lengthy Katz litany; he found no joy in hearing America's foremost literary prodigy being quoted back at him in such a fashion.

"Yes, indeed, a Jewish country," echoed Begin, striking a defiant pose. "When the British Mandate was adopted at the San Remo Conference in 1920, the language used was, 'Recognition having been given to the historical connection between the Jewish people and Palestine.' Note, Mr. President, the *Jewish* people and Palestine. The name, Palestine," he crisply clarified, "was given to the area by the Roman emperor Hadrian when he crushed the Bar Kochba revolt in 133 C.E. He sought to erase every last trace of Jewish existence by calling the country *Syria et Palestina*, after the long-extinct Philistines. Yet throughout history, the historical connection was recognized by all civilized nations as between the Jewish people and Palestine, and not any other people."

Shmuel Katz picked up the theme. "The present-day Arabs in the country are, for the most part, fairly recent arrivals, beginning with the nineteenth century, and especially since the Zionist revival in the twentieth. That is probably why so many got up and ran in forty-eight. That is not how a rooted peasantry behaves. The really indigenous Arabs are the ones who stayed."

"Is that so? Tell us more!" Thus Brzezinski, his voice brimming with cynicism.

Carter looked at Katz with a cold, hard, pinched expression, his patience long gone. More than half the allotted time for the meeting had passed, yet not a word had been said by Begin about Geneva. Others around the table fidgeted, eyeing comrades with sideways squints. But Katz would not be stopped. He spoke of how the old Zionist organizations in America, and elsewhere, axiomatically used the name Palestine in their titles, since Palestine was axiomatically the Jewish land; he spoke of how the 1919 agreement between the Emir Faisal and Chaim Weizmann stated explicitly that here was a pact between 'the Arab state,' meaning the Arabs, and 'Palestine,' meaning the Jews; he spoke of how the Arabs themselves had once insisted that there was no such country as Palestine, and that it was really southern Syria; he spoke of how, by international law, Israel was entitled to the ownership of Judea and Samaria because their occupation by the Kingdom of Trans-Jordan in 1948 was an act of aggression and an illegal invasion, and Israel enjoyed a 'preferred right of ownership'; and he spoke of how the British, for imperial reasons, had given the Arabs three-quarters of the original Palestine – now the Kingdom of Jordan – and how the PLO insisted that the Palestinian homeland still stretched across both sides of the River Jordan. Therefore, they already had a homeland, on the other side of the Jordan. As he finished this sentence, the prime minister placed a gentle restraining hand on his arm and, in a voice low yet intense, interjected, "With your permission, Mr. President, I have something important to say."

"By all means," said Carter, his eyes still stirred to anger at the direction the meeting had taken.

Menachem Begin returned the stare with a look that was grave and commanding: "Mr. President, I wish to tell you something personal – not about me, but about my generation. What you have just heard may seem academic, theoretical, even moot to you, but not to my generation. To my generation of Jews, these are indisputable facts. They touch upon the very core of our national being. For we are a nation of returnees, back to our homeland, Eretz Yisrael. Ours is the generation of destruction and redemption. Ours is an almost biblical generation of suffering and courage. Ours is the generation that rose up from the bottomless pit of hell."

The voice was mesmeric, the room quiet. The speaker's passion had nudged all at the table out of their restlessness.

"We were a helpless people, Mr. President," continued Begin. "We were bled, not once, not twice, but century after century, over and over again. We lost a third of our people in one generation – mine. One-and-a-half million of them were children – ours. No one came to our rescue. We suffered and died alone. We could do nothing about it. But now we can. Now we can defend ourselves."

Suddenly, he was on his feet, his posture militant, his face iron, as he said intrepidly, "Permit me to show you a map. I call it the INSM – the Israel National Security Map. General Poran, the map, please."

Freuka jumped to unroll the chart on the table between the president and the prime minister, who set about explaining it. "Mr. President, there is nothing remarkable about this map. It's quite a standard one of our country, displaying the old forty-nine armistice line as it existed until the sixty-seven Six-Day War, the so-called Green Line."

He ran his finger along the defunct frontier which meandered down the center of the country.

"As you see, our military cartographers have delineated the tiny area we had for defense in that war. It was a war of survival in the most literal sense. Our backs were to the sea. We had absolutely no defensive depth. The distances were tiny. Permit me to show you how tiny they were. I shall begin with the north."

He leaned across the table and pointed to the mountainous area which covered the upper section of the map, the section closest to Carter.

"You see these mountains, Mr. President. The Syrians and the Lebanese sat on the top of them and we were at the bottom."

His finger marked the Golan Heights and the mountains of South Lebanon, and then rested on the green panhandle squeezed in between.

"This is the Hula Valley. It is hardly ten miles wide. They shelled our towns and villages in that valley from up on top of these mountains, day and night."

Carter nodded, his hands clamped under his chin.

The prime minister's finger now moved southward, to Haifa.

"Haifa, as you know, Mr. President, is our major port city. The armistice line was only twenty miles away."

The President nodded again.

The finger shifted still further south, halting at the resort city of Netanya.

"Here, at Netanya, the distance to the old indefensible line was nine miles. Our country was reduced to a narrow waist."

"I understand," said the President, pursing his lips in contemplation.

But the prime minister was not sure that he did. His finger trembled and his voice rumbled, "Nine miles, Mr. President! Inconceivable! Indefensible!"

Carter made no comment.

The finger now hovered over Tel Aviv, and it drummed the map.

"Here, in the Tel Aviv area, live a million Jews, twelve miles from that indefensible armistice line. And here, between Haifa in the north and Ashkelon in the south" – his finger was running up and down the coastal plain – "live two million Jews, two-thirds of our total population, together with virtually our entire national infrastructure. This coastal plain is so narrow in parts that a surprise thrust by a column of tanks could cut the country in two in a matter of minutes. For whosoever sits in these mountains" – his fingertip tapped Judea and Samaria, whose heights dominated the narrow coastal plain – "holds the jugular vein of Israel in his hands. The Soviet-supplied artillery possessed by our neighbors has a range of forty-three point eight kilometers. In other words, from any point along this so-called Green Line, their conventional artillery can hit every city and township in our country; every house, every man, woman and child. It would be a mortal danger. It would mean the beginning of the end of our statehood, independence, and liberty."

Begin's dark, watchful eyes swept the somber faces of the powerful men in front of him, and he declared tersely, "Gentlemen, I submit to you, no nation in our region can be rendered so vulnerable and hope to survive. There is no going back to those lines. Abba Eban called them the Auschwitz lines. No nation can live on borrowed time."

Carter bent his head forward, the better to inspect the map, but still said nothing, and his features remained unfathomable.

Begin fixed his eyes upon him more intently, and in a tone that was official, precise, every word weighed, he proclaimed, "To Israel, the term national security is not an excuse for self-aggrandizement. National security is not a cloak to mask an expansionist ambition. National security is precisely that – survival; it is the lives of every man, woman and child in our country."

As he spoke these words, something stirred deep inside him. There was a sudden detachment in his eyes, a distant gaze, as if he was looking at this dispassionate born-again Southern Baptist from way inside himself, from that most intimate of Jewish recesses – that private space of Jewish remembrance and of Jewish weeping and of Jewish hope. And, standing there in that place he declared in a voice that would not tolerate indifference, "Sir, the distinction between Jewish national security in the past and Jewish national security in the present is that in the present, our men can defend their women and children. In the past, in the Holocaust, they had to deliver them; they had to deliver them to their executioners. We were tertiated, Mr. President."

Jimmy Carter lifted his head. "What was that word, Mr. Prime Minister?"

"Tertiated, not decimated. The origin of the word decimation is one in ten. When a Roman legion was found guilty of insubordination one in ten was put to the sword. In the case of our people it was one in three – TERTIATED!"

And then, in a tone that was stubborn, defiant, obdurate, he rose to his full height, banged his fist on the table, and thundered, "MR. PRESIDENT, I TAKE AN OATH BEFORE YOU IN THE NAME OF THE JEWISH PEOPLE! THIS WILL NEVER, EVER, HAPPEN AGAIN."

And then he broke. His lips trembled. He clenched his fists and pressed them so tightly against the tabletop his knuckles went white. Unseeing, he stared at the map, struggling to blink back tears. Who could tell what ruined faces of kith and kin were staring back at him at that moment as he stood there, dignified, weeping within.

Silence settled on the chamber. The tick of the antique clock on the marble mantelpiece became audible. An eternity seemed to hang between each tick. All the president's men lowered their eyes until, by degrees, in slow motion, Menachem Begin straightened himself. Gradually the room came back to life.

"Would you like a recess, Mr. Prime Minister?" asked the president, seemingly moved.

"No, no," answered Begin, pain still flickering in his eyes. "I apologize for speaking at such length. You see, I have so many things to say about my people, about our land, about our history, about our suffering, and about our future. But above all, I have to say this to you – you, the leader of the free world: our fathers and mothers were killed because they were Jews. We don't want our grandchildren to suffer the same fate. I believe that were we to go back to those old lines, we would lose the very chance of peace."

Like a cold wind blowing in from the Arctic, Zbigniew Brzezinski asked if this was the prime minister's rationale for planting Jewish settlements in the West Bank and the Gaza Strip. Was he contending that the proposed settlements were a matter of national security. Begin answered that they assuredly were. This was what he had meant when he'd said that for Israel, national security was not just an excuse for self-aggrandizement or a cloak for expansionist ambition. The settlements were critical to security. Equally, they were an expression of the inherent right of the Jewish people to settle in any part of their historic homeland.

Cyrus Vance seemed unruffled as a rule, but now displayed a great deal of agitation, contending that the new settlements would prove an insurmountable obstacle to peace and would destroy any hope for a successful Geneva conference. Carter thought so, too. The Rabin administration had taken the attitude of discouraging such settlements, he contended.

But Begin pooh-poohed the pessimism. Jews and Arabs already lived side by side in places like Jaffa, Jerusalem, and Haifa, he argued. Besides, no new settlements would be built on Arab-owned land, only on untilled, rocky and uncultivable land, of which there was plenty.

The Americans exchanged guarded glances. This was the Begin they had heard of – the inflexible and obstinate nationalist. Their disquiet was articulated by the president who said, "I shall have more to say on this very thorny question in a minute. Meanwhile, I am waiting to hear what you have to say on a Geneva peace conference."

But Menachem Begin wasn't ready for that just yet. He wouldn't be rushed. He had one more thing to add, and add it he would.

"One last word, Mr. President," he said.

He took out a piece of paper from his inside pocket, adjusted his spectacles, peered at the page, absorbed its contents, and then said with sudden good humor, "Mr. President, here in the United States of America there are eleven places named Hebron, five places named Shiloh, four places named Bethel, and six places named Bethlehem."

Jimmy Carter's eyes grew faintly amused. "Indeed there are. Within twenty miles of my home there is a Bethel and a Shiloh."

"May I be permitted to visit them one day?"

"Of course. With pleasure! There are three good Baptist churches there."

"In that case, I shall bring along our chief rabbi to protect me."

Everybody laughed, but it was a hollow laugh.

"Allow me to put to you a hypothetical question. Imagine one day that the governors of the states in which these Hebrons and Shilohs and Bethels and Bethlehems were located were to issue a decree, declaring that any citizen of the United States was free to settle in any one of these places except for one category – the Jews. Jews are forbidden to build homes in the Shilohs and the Hebrons and the Bethels and the Bethlehems of America – so it would be decreed!"

Begin threw up his hands and let out an inflated sigh: "Oh dear! Everybody is welcome to settle in any of these places whose names derive from the Book of Books except for the People of the Book. Good women and men everywhere would cry from the rooftops – 'Scandalous!' 'Discrimination!' 'Bigotry!' Am I not right?"

Jimmy Carter heard the penny drop and did not like the sound of it. "Hypothetically," he said, not amused.

Whereupon Begin clinched his argument. "So how can you expect me, a Jewish prime minister of the Jewish State who heads a cabinet of fifteen Jews, free men all – how can you expect me to forbid my fellow Jews from acquiring a piece of land and building a home in the *original* Shiloh, in the *original* Bethel, in the *original* Bethlehem, and in the *original* Hebron, from whence our Jewish forefathers *originally* came? Would that not be scandalous?"

Impatiently, Jimmy Carter brought out the heavy artillery. "Not if building such a home would prove an obstacle to peace, and prevent a Geneva conference from being convened," he chided. "My impression is, it would be regarded as an indication of bad faith, a signal of your apparent intention to make the military occupation of the West Bank and the Gaza Strip permanent. It might very well close off all hope of negotiations. On the other hand, if you would refrain from creating new settlements while we prepare for Geneva, that would be a gracious and encouraging sign." And then, totally exasperated, "Mr. Begin, it would be incompatible with my responsibilities as president of the United States if I did not put this to you as bluntly and as candidly as I possibly could."

The prime minister leaned back and settled his gaze on the ceiling above the president's head. The two men were on vastly different trajectories, a no-exit confrontation on the settlements. But Begin was not going to wrangle. There was no point in a tug-of-war. He knew that on this issue of the settlements, the president was as determined as he was. Nevertheless, he somehow had to persuade this judgmental president who wanted to be a healer that he too honestly and truly wanted peace. So he shifted focus, and in an utterly composed and civil manner, said, "Mr. President, on behalf of the government of Israel I have the honor to present to you our official proposal on the convening of a Geneva peace conference. It is entitled, 'The Framework for the Peacemaking Process,'" and he laid the document on the table before the president.

As Carter leafed through the pages, Begin went on, "We fully concur with your view that the goal of Geneva has to be a full and normal peace. For too long, we Jews have been the exception of history. We now have our own country, and the normal rules of nations must apply. After wars come peace treaties, and the purpose of negotiations should be peace treaties. This is why we stand on the principle of direct negotiations – direct negotiations without any prior conditions."

"On everything? Are you saying everything is negotiable?" Thus Brzezinski, in an accent as Polish as Begin's own. "Borders, withdrawals, the West Bank, everything is on the table – is that what you're really saying?"

"Dr. Brzezinski, the word 'non-negotiable' is not a part of our vocabulary," retorted Begin smugly. "Everything is open to negotiation. Everybody is at liberty to put on the table any subject he deems fit. Take Sadat of Egypt for example. Sadat says we have to retreat to the old sixty-seven armistice lines and that a so-called Palestinian state must be established in Judea and Samaria, and linked – Heaven forbid! – by an extra-territorial corridor across our Negev to the Gaza Strip. We say to President Sadat, that's what you want? Fine! You are fully entitled to bring that position to Geneva, just as we are entitled to bring ours. Another example – Jerusalem. In Israel there is an almost total national consensus that the city shall forever remain the undivided and eternal capital of the Jewish people. Yet we are not asking the Arabs to accept this position in advance as our condition for going to Geneva. Not at all! This is what I mean when I say no prior conditions. Gentlemen, please understand, Israel has no conditions, only positions!"

"That's positive," responded the president, thawing. But then, sharply, "What about Security Council Resolution 242 – do you agree that it should serve as the legal basis for the negotiations? Do you accept that?"

"Absolutely! It is written into our proposal. Actually, our proposal refers to Resolution 338, which already embodies 242 but specifies the additional need for negotiations directly between the parties. And I will be happy to say so in public."

"That will help a lot," said the president.

The prime minister then went on to list the other features of his Geneva proposal: that Israel would be willing to participate in the conference as of 10 October 1977 – that is, after the Jewish Holy Days; that the other participants should be the accredited representatives of Syria, Egypt, Jordan, and Lebanon; that there should be an inaugural session at which the parties would make public opening statements; after that, separate bilateral committees should be established – Egypt-Israel, Syria-Israel, Jordan-Israel, Lebanon-Israel – and these should go to work to negotiate the respective peace treaties. Once done, the public session should be reconvened for the signing ceremonies.

"And if Egypt refuses to attend unless the PLO is invited, then what?" asked the president, his eyes sharp and assessing.

"Then Egypt makes Geneva impossible," retorted Begin, without batting an eye. "The Israeli position was, and remains, that the PLO cannot attend under any circumstances. They have their charter, their covenant, which calls for the destruction of the Jewish State. So if the PLO shows up, Israel walks out. The PLO is a terrorist organization. However" – this reassuringly – "we have no objection to Palestinians as such participating in the Jordanian delegation; we shall not investigate their personal credentials."

Everybody seemed happy with that, which prompted Begin to quip, "And by the by, we Jews, too, are Palestinians. Under the British mandate we all had Palestinian passports. There were Palestinian Arabs and there were Palestinian Jews."

Nobody seemed to appreciate this, and the president plowed on, "But if the PLO recognizes the right of Israel to exist, would you not then talk to them? We have notified the PLO that if they fully endorse Resolutions 242 and 338 and acknowledge Israel's right to exist we will begin to talk, and listen to their positions."

Begin met fire with fire: "I say to you, Mr. President, I don't need anybody to recognize my right to exist, and even if that terrorist Arafat were to make such a declaration, I wouldn't believe a word he says. It would be tantamount to somebody approaching me with a knife and saying, 'Take this knife and thrust it into your heart.' I would reply, 'but why should I agree to stick a knife into my own heart?' And he would say, 'For the sake of peace. Please commit suicide for the sake of peace.' You are asking me to consider talking to such a person? The PLO's vision of peace is our destruction. No! ABSOLUTELY NO!"

"But what happens if the bilateral committee idea which you have suggested flounders because of the boycott of the PLO?" asked Secretary of State Vance, trying to account for every possible pitfall.

"Then quiet American diplomacy should seek to establish other avenues of negotiation," answered Begin.

"Such as what?

"Such as, for example, proximity talks. Let an American mediator move back and forth between our delegations, meeting in close proximity under the same roof, until he comes up with something. And there are other ways. The important thing is to get going. I have given you, Mr. President, the essence of our 'Framework for the Peacemaking Process.' We consider them serious proposals, designed to start an initiative, to keep momentum alive, and to bring to realization our yearnings for peace. We have an open mind on all these propositions. And with God's help, and with the help of the United States, we shall surely make progress."[62]

At the end of the two-hour session the White House Press Office issued the following statement:

> The meeting this morning was devoted to a thorough and searching discussion of how to move forward toward an overall settlement of the Arab-Israeli conflict. The president and the prime minister each developed their ideas on the issues involved. They agreed that all the issues must be settled through negotiations between the parties based on Security Council Resolutions 242 and 338, which all the governments directly concerned have accepted. They also agreed that this goal would best be served by moving rapidly toward the convening of the Geneva Conference this year, keeping in mind at the same time the importance of careful preparation…. The president and the prime minister will meet again tonight at the working dinner, which the president is giving at the White House.

Photograph credit: Ya'acov Sa'ar & Israel Government Press Office

Following the White House dinner President Carter escorts Begin arm-in-arm to his private quarters for a nocturnal chat, 19 July 1977

Chapter eight

The Dinner

Jimmy Carter ran an austere White House, and, consonant with his innate Calvinism, cast himself in the role of citizen-President. He banned *Hail to the Chief,* slashed the entertainment budget, sold the presidential yacht, pruned the limousine fleet, and generally rid his mansion of foppery, artifice, and pretentiousness. He even carried his own bags. So the dinner that evening in the Executive Dining Room was, characteristically, a business suit affair. It was gracious, nevertheless, the president smiling as he opened the proceedings with an announcement:

"Ladies and gentlemen – history is being made here tonight. This is the first time ever that a wholly kosher menu under strict rabbinic supervision is being served in the White House. And this, in honor of, and out of respect for, our esteemed guest of honor, the prime minister of the State of Israel, Mr. Menachem Begin."

I joined in the applause wholeheartedly, recalling those occasions when I had dined in this place in the entourage of other prime ministers, picking at some vegetable dish while they enjoyed gourmet *treyf.* A couple of weeks before our trip Begin had charged me with the almost impossible task of recommending a high-class kosher caterer for the occasion, this at the request of the White House, and in consultation with our embassy. The task was next to impossible because of the ferocious competition between the potential candidates. I quickly surrendered the challenge to the Rabbinical Council of America, a central rabbinic organization which, together with the White House housekeeper, Mary Lou, vetted menus and cast the deciding vote. The result was a succulent banquet of roast lamb, sun-dried tomatoes, roasted potatoes and green beans with almonds, followed by fruit and assorted desserts, all washed down with fine Israeli wines.

The guests were of the Georgetown media elite and politicians, with a goodly sprinkling of Jewish establishment bigwigs, and all applauded and laughed when Mr. Begin, rising to toast his host said, tongue-in-cheek, "Mr. President, before I thank you for your warm hospitality, I have a personal statement to make. I owe you and some others in this historic room a profound apology. I know that my electoral victory came to you as a total surprise, so I crave your forgiveness. And by the by, my name does rhyme with Fagin."

"Oh my God, is *he* funny!" enthused the woman sitting opposite me, grabbing a pen and jotting down his comment. We were sitting at a long dining table, one of four that branched, candelabra-like, from the top table, where the president and prime minister sat. Hamilton Jordan, the president's youthful chief of staff, had introduced her to me earlier, giving a name that sounded like Merry Trash. The hand she had extended was cluttered with rings. She was wrapped in garb that looked like grain sacks. Her face was creased, and divided by a pair of horn-rimmed dark glasses. I had gathered that she was a high-flying Washington gossip columnist.

"Wow!" exploded Merry Trash, with a sharp intake of breath. She was reacting to an observation Mr. Begin had just made in his toast that "Israel is a tiny land which God, in His wisdom, endowed with virtually no natural resources. Why? Because when the Almighty took us out of Egypt He told Moses to turn left instead of right. So Ishmael got the oil and Israel got the stones – two tablets of stone with their ten 'shalts' and 'shalt nots.' And by them did we shape a moral civilization, and by them do we strive to live."

"Oh my God, he sounds so scriptural," gushed Merry Trash, in a Gloria Swanson surge of passion. "He carries his faith like a humble burden."

Ignoring this outburst, the man on my right, Senator Richard Stone of Florida, observed dryly, "I understand that things today with the president went somewhat better than expected."

I concurred.

"Perhaps not stratospherically better," the senator added, "but apparently you Israelis put a little more on the table than you were expected to, and found a little more than you expected in return."

"I think the prime minister and the president just liked one another a little more than they expected to," said Hamilton Jordan easily. He was in his mid-thirties, and looked like an athlete.

Ambassador Samuel Lewis leaned toward us and, lighting up a cigar, remarked. "As you probably know, Senator, the atmosphere of this visit just didn't happen of itself. A few of us had to work very hard to persuade some people around the president" – he was staring at Hamilton Jordan, who smiled back at him – "to reshape the preparations, to give the visit a different spirit, not to be too confrontational."

Merry Trash began to record what the ambassador was saying, so he threw her a peppery glance and made it clear he was talking off the record. She laid down her pen and, he, pointing with his cigar in the direction of the national security adviser, Zbigniew Brzezinski, added, "Zbig, I think, is still skeptical about the soft-touch approach. He would like the president to be tougher with Begin. But in my view the president has got it just right – co-opting the man, bringing him along, not engaging him too sharply. The object, after all, is to get him to Geneva."

Merry Trash (could that really be her name?) effused, "But Ambassador, *darling*, what has Mr. Begin actually conceded? What compromises has he *really* made? What's he giving that will make the Arabs *want* to go to Geneva?"

A butler distracted Lewis's attention by asking what he would like for dessert. Selecting the lemon meringue pie, Lewis tossed a smile at Merry Trash, and said, "My dear, that's what it's all about – making the right choices." Then, puffing on his cigar, he looked up at the ceiling, as if gazing into an inscrutable future. Obviously, he was not going to be drawn into a question and answer session with this gossip columnist.

"What do you make of Begin as a man?" Senator Stone asked Lewis. "Or is that an indiscreet question?"

"Not at all. I like him. I think we've hit it off. I get a different sense of him one-on-one than I'd gotten from the briefings I'd read. Contrary to his popular image, he is determined not to lead Israel into war. My belief is he wants to go down in history as a peacemaker, as a Moses, not a Samson."

"Good quote," crunched Merry Trash, her mouth full of apple pie. "Can I use it?"

"No!" said Lewis.

"So, are you saying," continued the senator, "there's a chance that ultimately he'll soften up, go along with Carter on things like the PLO and the settlements?"

"No, I'm not. He will be as stubborn as hell on those things, and will resist anything that can be characterized as pressure."

Dinner now over, people began to mingle, and suddenly I felt a gentle tap on my shoulder. I turned to see a distinguished-looking man with cropped silver hair and jovial, guileless eyes encased in thick spectacles, smiling down at me.

"Remember me?" he beamed.

"Justice Goldberg!"

Everyone within reach rose to shake the man's hand, for no Jew enjoyed more public esteem in American life than did Arthur Goldberg. Now seventy, this son of eastern European immigrants, a one-time labor leader, had been President Kennedy's secretary of labor and, after that, a supreme court justice. President Johnson made him ambassador to the United Nations and in that role he had been a principal draftsman of the celebrated United Nations Resolution 242. I knew him slightly, having been introduced to him by previous prime ministers.

"May I trouble you for a private word," he asked affably, and he slipped his hand through the crook of my arm to walk me through the socializing guests, half a dozen of whom were lining up under a Lincoln portrait to rub shoulders with the president and the prime minister, some asking for their autographs.

We crossed a marble hallway to a lounge whose walls were covered in a red silk fabric and where two naval orderlies, all starched in white and gold, saluted rigidly as we entered, and then left. Clearly, Arthur Goldberg was familiar with these corridors.

The elder statesman closed the door and, all his affability gone, said, "I've dragged you in here because you're the one person I recognize from the old days. There are some hard truths your new people in Jerusalem have to understand."

Flabbergasted, I opened my mouth to respond, but he held up his hand to silence me, saying he expected no comment, no response, no observation; that I was just to listen to what he had to say and pass it on to whomever I saw fit. The first part of the message was that Begin's visit was not what it appeared to be. Carter, he said, was trying very hard to put a positive gloss on things, to avoid a confrontation. Begin had to appreciate that all American presidents, secretaries of state, and pentagon officials knew only one kind of Israel – Labor Israel, the Israel of Ben-Gurion, Eshkol, Golda, Rabin – the Israel that was pragmatic, ready for territorial compromise for the sake of peace.

Then, even more passionately, "To most Americans, Begin's ideology is an enigma. To the president, the 'not an inch' posture on the Land of Israel is baffling. It is equally puzzling to most American Jews. Sure, American Jews will support the prime minister in public. It's the right thing to do. Begin, after all, is the head of a freely elected democratic government. But in private, many Jews are troubled and confused, myself included."

I tried to get a word in, to tell him he should say this to Begin to his face, not to me, but again he shut me up and went on relentlessly. "The president has sincere feelings toward Israel. But I fear one day, in frustration, he might decide that Begin's vision of retaining the whole of biblical Israel is so unreasonable – so unreasonable, so unrealistic, so liable to suck the United States into war, that he will decide it is his unbounded duty, nay his religious duty, to save Israel from itself. And if that were to happen, whatever the official disclaimers might be, it would mean only one thing – a settlement imposed on Israel by the Great Powers against its will."

"But we have a September first, nineteen seventy-five letter from President Ford assuring Rabin that America would never impose a settlement to Israel's disadvantage," I said hotly.

"Forget that letter; it's not a binding commitment. And just in case you're thinking somebody in the Oval Office has put me up to this, think again. This is me, Arthur Goldberg, talking from the bottom of my heart, Jew to Jew. That's all I have to say. Thanks for listening. And now I suggest you go back to the party. I'm going home." And off he went, leaving me with the feeling that a stiletto had just punctured my innards.

When I walked back into the dining room it was resounding with a standing ovation. The president and the prime minister were on the point of leaving, and were waving their farewells. Carter took a step back to allow Begin to fully enjoy the limelight before leading him upstairs to his private quarters for a candid, face-to-face chat. I was now in a position to make an intelligent guess as to what that chat would be about.

Joining the exiting guests who were proceeding from the dining room to the marble entrance hall, where a string trio was serenading us goodnight, I fell into step with Merry Trash, who was in conversation with a large, sharp-nosed lady in green.

"*Darling*, you look stunning," said the lady, adding conspiratorially, "You know what Aliza Begin is up to tonight, don't you?"

"Of course I know," answered the gossip columnist, as if her professionalism had been called into question. "She's been taken for dinner at La Grand Scene and then to the Kennedy Center to see *Porgy and Bess.*"

"Quite a woman, don't you think?" said the lady in green.

"Millicent darling," exclaimed Merry Trash, flipping a page of her notebook, "if you have a story to tell me about Aliza Begin – speak!"

"Well, you know that Grace Vance [wife of the secretary of state] gave Mrs. Begin a luncheon today."

"Of course I know," said Merry Trash archly. "What else is new?"

"Well, I swear you won't believe what I'm about to say."

"Try me."

"When Grace Vance got up and introduced Aliza Begin, we all sat there clapping and waiting – there must have been about seventy-five of us – waiting for her to stand up and make a speech. But she just sat there."

"Waddyanno?!"

"I swear! Frankly, it became a bit awkward. There we were applauding, and there was she just sitting there. Finally, Grace prevailed upon her to stand up. So this gray-haired little thing gets up, and she says, 'Forgive me everybody. I'm the Greta Garbo of the family. I'm the silent one. I don't make speeches.' Boy, did we laugh! But then, someone at the next table insisted on asking her what she thought of her husband's position about the settlements on the West Bank."

"And her answer?" Merry Trash was scrawling ferociously.

"Strike me dead if she didn't go straight up to that woman, put a hand on her shoulder, and say, 'You want to know what *I* think, Madame? Forgive me, but a question like that you have to ask my husband. He was elected prime minister, not me.' Well, wow! She had us all on our feet in fits of laughter. Talk about class! She's some smart cookie, that lady."

"Alla!" Menachem Begin called to his wife, in the highest of spirits, as he strode into the Blair House lounge, still outfitted as it had been a century-and-a-half ago, with immense, overstuffed, carved and inlaid furnishings. Yechiel Kadishai, General Poran, Dan Patir and I traipsed in after him. We had been killing time in an adjacent room, waiting for his return from his private chat with the president.

Clasping his wife's hands, he beamed, "It went very well, Alla, better than I expected. We reached an understanding on important matters. We parted on the most heartwarming of terms."

Aliza Begin, dressed in an unpretentious housecoat, laughed her mellifluous laugh, lit a cigarette, and while a fume of smoke coiled from her nose to the ceiling, said in her tobacco-roughened voice, "Excellent! Now sit down and relax, Menachem, and I'll make you a cup of tea."

A table had been set in front of the fireplace. It held a large china teapot surrounded by cups and saucers and, around them, rolls, pastries, cheeses, dips, and homemade bread and butter. A business card with the name of a kosher caterer from Baltimore also sat on the table.

I decided this was the moment to tell Begin about my encounter with Arthur Goldberg. He said nothing for a while, leaning forward and burying his face in his hands, deep in thought. Eventually he said, "*Azoy!* So that's Goldberg's reading, is it? Well, it's not mine. Despite our differences, I think my meeting with Carter went encouragingly well, and so I shall report."

He settled himself on the gold couch by the fireplace, took a hearty sip of the cup of lemon tea his wife had poured for him, and then said he wanted to compose a cable for Foreign Minister Moshe Dayan and Defense Minister Ezer Weizman immediately. They would be waiting to hear what had transpired.

It was close to midnight, but despite his long day, Begin was fully alive, energetic, aggressive. Leaning back into the couch he recounted by way of prologue how, after the dinner, the president had given him a tour of the Treaty Room where President Ulysses Grant's cabinet used to meet. Grant's table was still there. It had seven drawers in it, one for each member of the cabinet to stow his papers. "Now, that's what I call economical government," Carter had joked. And the prime minister, in retelling the tale, divulged with a chuckle that he had the strongest sense that the president, in taking him to see the treaty room, was out to flatter him, win him over, soften him up. Indeed, as they were walking up to the president's private apartment, Carter had put a friendly hand on his shoulder, and said, "I'm glad we have this opportunity to get to know each other a little better. You'll find me a straightforward man. I like to speak openly."

"For sure, Mr. President, but do you also like to listen openly?" Begin had responded. This seemed to have broken the ice between them, and got them off to a good start.

Still chuckling at the memory, Menachem Begin took a pastry, and eating with a slow circular motion, told us about how the president had asked him about his role in the War of Independence, of which he knew little. "I told him that our proclamation of revolt against the British in forty-four was to me no less an imperative than was the revolt of the American founding fathers against the British two hundred years before – perhaps even more so. Then, Carter asked me about my youth in Brisk and I told him about what it was like to live among anti-Semites, and how my father,

Ze'ev Dov, taught me never to stand by when a fellow Jew was being persecuted. I told Carter how, one day, my father was walking in the street with
a rabbi when a Polish police sergeant tried to cut off the rabbi's beard – a
popular sport among anti-Semitic bullies in those days. My father did not
hesitate. He hit the sergeant's hand with his cane which, in those times, was
tantamount to inviting a pogrom. The rabbi and my father were arrested,
I told the president. They were taken to the River Bug, threatened with
drowning, and then beaten until they bled. My father came home that day
in terrible shape, but he was happy. He was happy because he had defended
the honor of the Jewish people and the honor of the rabbi."

Concluding this account on a pugnacious note, he said, "I looked
Carter straight in the eye, and told him, 'Mr. President, from that day forth
I have forever remembered those two things about my youth: the persecution of our helpless Jews, and the courage of my father in defending their
honor.' And I made it plain to him that these were the bedrock of my thinking to this very day. I wanted him to know from whence I came and what
kind of a Jew he was dealing with."

He then got stiffly to his feet, braced himself, told Yechiel he was
ready to dictate his cable to his ministers, and began slowly to prowl the
room in thought. As he did so, his features became ever more firmly set.
Those who knew Begin well recognized that look: he was mentally orga-
nizing what he wanted to report, paragraph by paragraph. This was how
he prepared his speeches, how he created his amazing rhetorical flow as
an orator, his beautifully structured passages – all pre-assembled and composed in the alcoves of his mind.

The first thing he wanted his ministers to know – thus did he dictate
to Yechiel – was that, contrary to speculations, there had been no direct
confrontation with the president of the United States, no pressures. They
had reached understandings on important issues. And on those issues on
which understandings had not been reached, "we behaved as friends do –
we agreed to disagree." Thus, he could inform his ministers that, thanks to
Israel's new approach to Middle East peacemaking as formally embodied
in the document "The Framework for the Peacemaking Process," he had
succeeded in dispelling the lingering effect of the very serious confrontation that had marred the relations between Carter and Rabin in their
March meeting.

Here he paused, downed the remainder of his tea, and before
proceeding with the rest of his dictation, shared with us his thinking as
to why his meeting with the president that day had gone well, whereas

Rabin's March meeting had not. Wagging a finger like a rabbi reprimanding a student, he sighed, "Rabin invited pressure on himself in March. He should never have gone to that meeting. It was folly! He knew Carter was bent on a comprehensive settlement through a Geneva conference, but Rabin was still stuck with his step-by-step doctrine, as advocated by Kissinger. So what was the point of him even trying to reach an understanding with Carter on territorial matters ahead of Geneva when they were miles apart? The timing was all wrong. For all of Rabin's readiness for territorial compromise he, like me, refuses to withdraw back to the sixty-seven lines. That's precisely what Carter is asking for – our virtual total withdrawal. So what made Rabin think Carter would support his peace map more than he would support mine? To have asked him to do so ahead of Geneva was merely to invite pressure. And that's precisely what Rabin did. And that's precisely what I've avoided by elaborating a concrete Geneva proposal – 'The Framework for the Peacemaking Process.'"

Satisfied he'd been well understood, he went back to dictating to Yechiel. "I invited no pressure since I proposed no prior agreement of substance. On the contrary, I made it plain to the president that the negotiations in Geneva about peace would be between Israel and our Arab neighbors, not with our American friends. And the Geneva format will have to guarantee this. With respect to that, I emphasized that negotiations which are direct are not just a matter of form but constitute, of themselves, content and substance. President Carter accepted this approach. The important thing is that there is now an Israeli initiative on the table – 'The Framework for the Peacemaking Process' – to which our Arab neighbors will have to address themselves."

Further, "The president pledged to avoid statements [of the sort he made after his Rabin talks] that would preempt Israel's negotiation positions at Geneva, such as talking publicly of Israel having to withdraw back to the sixty-seven frontiers with minor rectifications, or using the term, 'the right of the Palestinians to a homeland.' In return, the president wanted a commitment from me that all settlement activity be halted until the Geneva Conference. I refused to make such a commitment."

With regard to Geneva itself, "The president expected the Arabs and the Israelis to come to the conference without prior conditions. I assured the president that this was exactly our view. Israel has no conditions, only positions. Moreover, the president thought "The Framework for the Peacemaking Process" was a solid proposal, and he undertook to bring it to the attention of the Arabs for their reaction. Most significantly, the president agreed that the goal of the Geneva negotiations would be full-fledged peace treaties, not mere short-term, interim accommodations as in the past. I also indicated to the president that, independently of Geneva, I would put out feelers for meetings with top Arab leaders, beginning with President Sadat of Egypt."

Menachem Begin then informed his ministers – for their eyes only – how he had disclosed, "with absolute discretion and in a highly confidential fashion, the Top Secret section of 'The Framework for the Peacemaking Process,' about which I had said nothing at the morning session, because so many aides were present. There, I had spoken about procedure. Now, alone with the president, I spoke about substance. Before reading to Carter this highly classified page composed of three short paragraphs, I said I thought it proper that he, the president, should know about them as a friend and as the leader of the free world. I told him that they deal with the substantive principles of how Israel visualizes conditions of peace with each of our neighbors, and I emphasized that brief though each paragraph be, each has a vital bearing upon our future. I then read him the principles:

"One – regarding Egypt: In view of the large area separating the two countries, Israel is prepared, within the framework of a peace treaty, to make a significant withdrawal of its forces in Sinai.

"Two – regarding Syria: Israel will remain on the Golan Heights. But within the framework of a peace treaty we shall be prepared to withdraw our forces from their present lines and redeploy them along a line to be established as the permanent boundary.

"Three – regarding the 'West Bank': Israel will not transfer Judea, Samaria and the Gaza District to any foreign sovereign authority. There is a dual basis for this position: the historic rights of our nation to this land, and the needs of our national security which demand a capacity for the defense of our state and the lives of our citizens.'

"This, in summary, is what I told President Carter."[63]

The judicious crafting of these three sensitive paragraphs were meant to create the trails up the tough mountain track toward Geneva, and Foreign Minister Moshe Dayan had been a tenacious scout in helping to blaze them. For days he had closeted himself with the prime minister prior to the Washington visit, hammering out the 'Framework' document. The hardest nut to crack was paragraph three, the one dealing with the hypersensitive issue of the West Bank. Begin had wanted to declare outright and without obfuscation Israel's manifest moral, legal and historic right and claim to the whole of Judea, Samaria and Gaza. To him this was the very kernel of the 'Framework.' Even while the mule in him reared up against any West Bank concessions, the statesman within him strained to rein in his own impulses as he rummaged for a formula that would make plain his claim to the whole of Eretz Yisrael without tipping over the president's Geneva apple cart. As he mulled over words and weighed up idioms, Moshe Dayan finally persuaded him to swallow a bitter pill, which he did reluctantly, in the knowledge that if he refused, there might be a far more unpalatable one to digest further along the trail. He acquiesced, therefore, to the use of Dayan's shrewd formula that stated, "Israel will not transfer Judea, Samaria and the Gaza District to any foreign sovereign authority." This formula was not an outright avowal of Israeli sovereignty, but nor was it a concession to anybody else's, and for the moment Menachem Begin could live with that.[64]

Breakfast with Brzezinski

Although President Carter had accepted Begin's proposed "Framework for the Peacemaking Process" as a reasonable passage to a negotiation, we knew that his national security adviser, Zbigniew Brzezinski, had advised against it. Carter, anxious to get to Geneva as speedily as possible, had over-ridden him. "We'll cross the sovereignty bridge when we get to it," he said.

All of us on the prime minister's staff were curious to know what sort of a man this national security adviser was – this Democrat version of Kissinger, with the almost unpronounceable name. We wondered if there might be some sort of cultural affinity, some natural rapport between him and Begin, both of them being of Polish origin. But other than their accents, we found none. How could there be? Theirs was not a shared Polish background; one was the son of a Catholic diplomat, the other of a downtrodden yet proud Jew.

"Poles apart!" cracked Yechiel.

And indeed, they were. Between them lay the ghosts of pogroms past, and the bleak, immeasurable distance of one thousand years of Polish Jewish civilization obliterated almost overnight. Yet despite this, Menachem Begin did find a powerful way to touch Brzezinski's emotions. He invited the national security adviser to breakfast at Blair House on the second morning of his stay, and on arrival, Brzezinski was surprised to find a crowd of TV cameras and photographers awaiting him – surprised because he had been given to understand that the breakfast was to be a tête-à-tête.

He was even more astonished when the prime minister greeted him with a smile so effusive it was obviously meant for the cameras.

Menachem Begin was holding in his hand a dossier. Raising it high for all to see, he announced to the media that the documents it contained had recently come to light in a Holocaust archive in Jerusalem. They testified to the fact that when Zbigniew Brzezinski's father, Tadeusz Brzezinski, had served as a Polish diplomat in Germany between 1931 and 1935, he had been witness to the rise of the Nazis and had been involved in efforts to rescue European Jews from Nazi concentration camps. Wishing now to bring this to world attention he, Begin, had invited the press to record his presentation of the dossier to Brzezinski the son. And doing so, the prime minister pronounced words of such high praise to the memory of the father, that the son was almost in tears.

Over breakfast, Brzezinski confided that the prime minister's gesture had touched him all the more because it came at a time when he was the subject of harsh personal attacks from certain sections of the Jewish community, and the media at large. A number of dailies, magazines and TV correspondents had been casting him as the anti-Israeli of the president's team.

"I am not," he said. "Some have even insinuated I'm an anti-Semite, making much of my Polish-Catholic ancestry. I am not." And, as if to emphasize he was not, he solemnly declared, "I cannot but express to you, Mr. Prime Minister, my admiration for the degree to which you live the suffering of your people and yet are, also, the personification of the triumph of Israel. May that triumph soon become permanent under your leadership through a peaceful accommodation with your neighbors."

A discussion then ensued about the wording of the joint U.S.-Israeli statement to be issued later in the day at the conclusion of the Washington talks. The national security adviser had brought with him a draft for the prime minister's approval, and after analyzing each phrase with his eagle eye, Begin said, "Totally acceptable but for two sentences."

"And what are they?"

"Please delete 'The United States affirms Israel's inherent right to exist.'"

"Why so?"

"Because the United States' affirmation of Israel's right to exist is not a favor, nor is it a negotiable concession. I shall not negotiate my existence with anybody, and I need nobody's affirmation of it."

Brzezinski's expression was one of surprise. "But to the best of my knowledge every Israeli prime minister has asked for such a pledge."

"I sincerely appreciate the president's sentiment," said Begin, "but our Hebrew Bible made that pledge and established our right over our land millennia ago. Never, throughout the centuries, did we ever abandon or forfeit that right. Therefore, it would be incompatible with my responsibilities as prime minister of Israel were I not to ask you to erase this sentence." And then, without pause, "Please delete, too, the language regarding the U.S. commitment to Israel's survival."

"And in what sense do you find that objectionable?"

"In the sense that we, the Jewish people alone, are responsible for our country's survival, no one else."

Wordlessly, and seemingly perplexed, the national security adviser deleted the offensive sentences, upon which the prime minister expressed himself totally satisfied.[65]

Brzezinski examines the portfolio of his father's rescue efforts of German Jews in the 1930s, presented to him by Begin, with Yechiel Kadishai looking on, 20 July 1977

Photograph credit: Ya'acov Sa'ar & Israel Government Press Office

Chapter nine

To Ignite the Soul

A s previously arranged, after the White House talks I returned to New York to call upon the Lubavitcher Rebbe and report to him on how we had fared. There, at 770 Eastern Parkway, I found myself settled with the sage in his unadorned wood-paneled chamber, where he greeted me with a beaming smile. Dog-eared Talmudic tomes and other heavy, well-thumbed volumes lined his bookshelves, representing centuries of scholarship and disputation.

We spoke in Hebrew; the Rebbe's classic, mine modern. What lured me most as we talked were the Rebbe's eyes. They were wide apart, sheltering under a heavy brow, but fine eyebrows. Their hue was the azure of the deep sea, intense and compelling, although I knew that when the Rebbe's soul turned turbulent, they could dim to an ominous grey, like a leaden sky. They exuded wisdom, awareness, kindness, and good fellowship; they were the eyes of one who could see mystery in the obvious, poetry in the mundane, and large issues in small things; eyes that captivated believers in gladness, and joy, and sacrifice.

As he dissected my account, his air of authority seemed to deepen. It came of something beyond knowledge. It was in his state of being, something he possessed in his soul which I cannot possibly begin to explain, something given to him under the chestnut and maple trees of Brooklyn rather than under the poplars and pines of Jerusalem to which, mysteriously, he had never journeyed.

I never asked him why, because I felt that he dwelt on an entirely different plane – a profoundly mystical plane, one to which I, a mere diplomat, could never aspire. The Lubavitcher Rebbe was a theologian, not a political Zionist. But if Zionism is an unconditional, passionate devotion to the Land of Israel and to its security and welfare, then Rabbi Menachem Mendel Schneerson was a fanatical Zionist.

My presentation, his interrogation, and his further clarification took close to three hours. By the time we finished it was nearly two in the morning. I was utterly exhausted, but not the Rebbe. He was full of vim and vigor when he said, "After listening to what you have told me I wish to communicate the following message to Mr. Begin," and he began dictating in a voice that was soft but touched with fire:

"By maintaining your firm stand on Eretz Yisroel in the White House you have given strength to the whole of the Jewish people. You have succeeded in safeguarding the integrity of Eretz Yisroel while avoiding a confrontation with the United States. That is true Jewish statesmanship: forthright, bold, without pretense or apology. Continue to be strong and of good courage."

Then to me:

"What do I mean when I say to Mr. Begin, 'Be strong and of good courage?' I mean that the Jewish people in Eretz Yisroel cannot live by physical power alone. For what is physical power? It is made up of four major components: One – weaponry: do you have the weaponry to assert your physical power? Two – will: do you have the will to employ your weaponry? Three – competence: do you have the competence to employ your weaponry effectively? And four – perception: does the enemy perceive that you have the weaponry, the will, and the competence to effectively employ your physical power so as to ensure your deterrent strength?"

And then, gently, "But even if you have all of these, Reb Yehuda, but you are bereft of the spirit of *'Mi hu ze Melech hakavod? Hashem izuz v'gibor, Hashem gibor milchama'* [Who is the King of glory? The Lord strong and mighty, the Lord mighty in battle] then all your physical power is doomed to fail, for it has no Jewish moral compass to sustain it."

At this his usually benign features became grim, and his eyes dimmed to an ominous gray when he added, "For in every generation an Amalek rises up against us, but the *Ribono shel Olam* [the Almighty] ensures that every tyrant in every age who seeks our destruction is himself destroyed. *Am Yisrael chai* [the people of Israel lives on] only by virtue of *hashgocho* [divine protection]. Time and again, our brethren in Eretz Yisroel have been threatened with destruction. Time and again they have floundered and stumbled and been bled. Yet time and again, *b'siyata d'Shamaya* [with the Almighty's help] they have weathered every storm, overcome every hurdle, withstood every test and, at the end of the day, emerged stronger than before. That is *hashgocho.*"

Relaxing, he fixed me with those eyes, and with a surprisingly sweet smile, said, "Now tell me, Reb Yehuda, you visit us so often yet you are not a Lubavitcher. Why?"

Still trying to absorb what he had said, I sat back, stunned at the directness of the question. It was true. This, probably, was my fifth or sixth meeting with the Rebbe. Over the years I had become a sort of unofficial liaison between the various prime ministers I served and the Lubavitch court.

Swallowing thickly, I muttered, "Maybe it is because I have met so many people who ascribe to the Rebbe, powers which the Rebbe does not ascribe to himself."

Even as I said this I realized I had presumed too much, and I could hear my voice trailing away as I spoke.

The Rebbe's brows knitted, and his deep blue eyes grayed again, into something between solemnity and sadness, and he said, "*Yesh k'nireh anashim hazekukim l'kobayim*" [There are evidently people who are in need of crutches]. The way he said it conveyed infinite compassion.

Then, as if tracking my thoughts, he raised his palm in a gesture of reassurance, and with an encouraging smile, said, "Reb Yehuda, let me tell you what I try to do. Imagine you're looking at a candle. What you are really seeing is a mere lump of wax with a thread down its middle. So when do the thread and wax become a candle? Or, in other words, when do they fulfill the purpose for which they were created? When you put a flame to the thread, then the wax and the thread become a candle."

Then his voice flowed into the rhythmic cadence of the Talmud scholar poring over his text, so that what he said next came out as a chant:

"The wax is the body and the wick is the soul. Bring the flame of Torah to the soul, then the body will fulfill the purpose for which it was created. And that, Reb Yehuda, is what I try to do – to ignite the soul of every Jew and Jewess with the fire of Torah, with the passion of our tradition, and with the sanctity of our heritage, so that each individual will fulfill the real purpose for which he or she was created."

A buzzer had been sounding periodically, indicating that others from around the world were awaiting their turns for an audience. When I rose to bid my farewells, the Rebbe escorted me to the door, and there I asked him, "Has the Rebbe lit my candle?"

"No," he said, clasping my hand. "I have given you the match. Only you can light your own candle."

I all but trembled as I left his presence.

Prime Minister Begin's own New York itinerary prior to his departure for home was intense. He called on the secretary-general of the United Nations, briefed editors and columnists, met with academics and business leaders, attended synagogue on Tisha b'Av eve, where he sat in bereavement on the floor and listened to Jeremiah's lamentations over the destruction of ancient Jerusalem, and on the day after appeared on NBC's *Meet the Press*, where Bill Monroe of NBC News kicked off by asking him, "Tell us, Mr. Prime Minister, how did your talks with President Carter go?"

"Before I respond to this very important question," answered Begin, "I would like to say a few words about this day on which we meet, because of its universal importance. Today, in accordance with our Jewish calendar, is the ninth day of the month of Av. It is the day when, one thousand, nine hundred and seven years ago, Roman legions – the Fifth and the Twelfth Legions – launched their ultimate onslaught on the Temple Mount, set the Temple ablaze, and destroyed Jerusalem, subjugating our people and conquering our land. Historically, this was the beginning of all the suffering of our people, who were dispersed, humiliated, and ultimately, a generation ago, almost physically wiped out. We forever remember this day, which we call Tisha b'Av, and now we have the responsibility to make sure that never again will our independence be destroyed, and never again will the Jew become homeless and defenseless. This, in truth, is the crux of the problem we face in the future – making sure it will never ever happen again. And that, in a nutshell, was the underlying theme of my talks with President Carter."[66]

Other than this extraordinary introduction, the essence of the prime minister's message was the same wherever he went: Israel's new peacemaking strategy, with its concrete goal of concluding peace treaties within the framework of a Geneva conference, has led to a newfound understanding between Israel and the president of the United States.

At a packed Jewish assembly in Manhattan, Begin delivered an inspirational address that had people who had thought him a warmonger rise to their feet, enraptured. "Proud Jews of America," he exhorted them, "lift up your voices high, so that all the world may hear you and be witness to our everlasting Jewish camaraderie, our unity, our eternal sisterhood and brotherhood, in solidarity with Zion, forever."

Finally, to the sound of summer thunder on the night of 24 July, the El Al jumbo jet carrying the premier and his party home growled off the Kennedy runway, racing across rooftops, trees and lakes, banking sharply over the broad sound of Long Island, until, finally, it settled into a steady drone homeward. The prime minister unfastened his safety belt, helped his wife take off her shoes, and beckoned me over. He wanted to dispatch a farewell message to the president from the plane. "Use this to write on. It won't be a long message," he said.

Begin helping his wife Aliza with her shoes, July 1977

He handed me the flight menu and I, down on one knee, leaned the menu on the prime minister's armrest, and with Yechiel, Freuka and Patir bending over me like spectators at a chess match, I scribbled Begin's message exactly as he dictated it. Clearly, his perfumed rhetoric was calculated to dispel whatever odors of Rabin's March meeting that still lingered in the Oval Office. And since he wanted the captain to dispatch his message right away, I had no time to 'shakespearize' it. So this is how it read:

Dear Mr. President,

On leaving the airspace of the United States en route home to Jerusalem may I, on behalf of my wife, my colleagues and myself, express our deepest gratitude to you and to Mrs. Carter, and to your close associates, for the wonderful hospitality you bestowed upon us during our stay in your country. Mr. President, great days in my time have been few. We've lived through horrible atrocities. We fought and suffered and mourned. May I tell you that the Washington days were some of the best of my life. They will never be forgotten, thanks to you and to your gracious attitude. I remember well our personal agreements, always to speak and write with candor, to strive for a complete understanding, and that even if there are differences of opinion they shall never cause a rift between us and between our nations. I go back home with the deep hope we are making progress toward peace in goodwill and good faith. Much depends on the other side. Let us hope they will not reject the hand we extend to them wholeheartedly.

Politics aside, Begin's relationship with opposition leader Shimon Peres
remained cordial, as seen here following a stormy Knesset debate

Chapter ten

A Duel in the Knesset

Begin's speaking!" cried Dan Patir, poking his head through the door of the Knesset restaurant.

Parliamentarians hurried to their seats, gossipers dispersed in a flash, and like hounds to the call of a horn, the parliamentary correspondents jumped up as a pack and piled up the stairway into the press gallery, where they peered down at the podium, waiting expectantly to hear Begin's flashes of wit and practiced prose.

It was September 1977, a couple of months after the prime minister's talks with the American president, and a day-long foreign affairs debate was drawing to a close. The prime minister had opened it by revealing that he was engaged in drafting a prototype peace treaty in readiness for a Geneva parley. Shimon Peres, the leader of the opposition, ridiculed the notion of a draft peace treaty, calling it "pie in the sky." Israel would never have peace with its neighbors, he contended, so long as the Begin government was unwilling to make painful and far-reaching territorial concessions on the West Bank and the Gaza Strip, not to speak of Sinai and the Golan Heights. "So stop lulling the nation into pipe dreams," he had mocked.

"Knesset Member Shimon Peres," responded Begin in his closing remarks, "I should like to read you some quotations." He held up a sheet of paper, brandishing it for all to see. "I'm quite sure they will sound familiar to you, Mr. Peres," he said.

The prime minister looked immensely pleased with himself, relishing the parliamentary challenge he was about to present. He moved the page closer to his eyes, adjusted his spectacles and, glancing toward the press gallery to make sure the pack was in place, exclaimed in a faintly theatrical tone: "It is a fallacy to believe that the solution to the Arab-Israeli conflict depends on our willingness to grant territorial concessions."

"Well?" snickered Begin in Peres' direction, flourishing the page. "Who do you think wrote that?"

Letting the question hang, he scanned the Chamber from end to end, jaw jutting, his expression derisive, his gaze finally settling back on the object of his scorn, who sat bristling in the number one seat of the opposition front bench, looking daggers back at him.

"Knesset Member Shimon Peres, you wrote that did you not? And who wrote" – again he peered at the page: "'I know that no territorial concession proposed by us will meet with a positive Arab response. To think otherwise is futile.' Who wrote that, Mr. Peres?"

A buzz began to drone around the packed chamber. Members sat grinning, grimacing or glowering, according to their allegiances.

"I ask again, who wrote that?" goaded Begin.

The buzz in the chamber rose. "Quiet!" bellowed the Speaker. "Order!"

"I'll tell you who wrote it," snarled Begin. "Knesset Member Shimon Peres wrote it! And who wrote: 'How can anybody believe that if we just settled East Shomron the Arabs would be more amenable to peace than were we to settle West Shomron?' Who wrote that?"

The glowerers and gloaters now began to heckle one another. Not a one heeded the frantic gaveling of the Speaker.

"Knesset Member Shimon Peres wrote that," teased Begin, above the tumult. "And who said, 'Everybody agrees we must hold on to the Golan Heights because they are the strategic high ground. But there is also strategic high ground in Judea and Samaria, at the foot of which lies Israel's most densely populated center, the coastal plain.' Who said that?"

The gavel of the Speaker of the House rose and fell as if it were some ineffectual, noiseless thing. Slowly, he got to his feet, his face distorted with frustration. In vast contrast, the prime minister seemed amused. He was leaning nonchalantly against the podium, fingers steepled, a smug smile hovering over his lips. Once the uproar began to subside, he rearranged his expression into a frown, straightened himself up, and pointing a grim finger at the leader of the opposition, nettled him like a faultfinding referee to an outmatched contestant: "Now listen well to what I'm about to add, Mr.

Peres. It is important that the nation hear the facts. It is important they know what kind of a leader advocates one policy one day and another the next."

Caustic and contemptuous, Peres shot back: "I always listen well to your Knesset routines, Mr. Prime Minister. But don't think you can mislead the nation today. Everybody here knows those statements you attribute to me were made at a different time under different circumstances."

Upon extracting this admission of authorship, the prime minister stroked his chin with great satisfaction. *"Really!"* he said, in feigned surprise. "I've heard you speak many times and you always stated your conviction that it was fallacious to think that territorial compromise would bring peace. Those quotations I just cited expressed your earnest and honest political beliefs – until recently, that is. So, what suddenly made you change your mind, Mr. Peres? What happened between the time you made those statements I've just quoted, and the dovish views you express these days? Tell us Mr. Peres."

You could sense by the sudden razor bite in his voice that he was readying for the kill, but Peres forestalled him. "Conditions change, positions change. Only fools don't change," he retorted. "Only fools cling to fantasies and to obsolete dreams."

Every syllable was annunciated sharply; clearly he had steeled himself for this duel. His devotees rallied around him with vigorous applause, while he leaned back with the confident ease of a swordsman who has just parried a tricky play.

Begin responded with a cheeky little grin. "Only fools, you say? Was it not Winston Churchill who said that the greatest lesson in life is to know that even fools are right sometimes? Well, Knesset Member Shimon Peres, tonight I am right!"

"And wasn't it Churchill who said 'I'd rather be right than consistent'?" shot back Peres, causing everyone present, government and opposition, to shout with laughter.

Begin cut in, "Well he might have, but I shall now tell the House exactly what turned you from a hawk to a dove, Mr. Peres – what brought about your change of mind. You decided you wanted to seize the leadership of your Labor Party from Yitzhak Rabin. You wanted to position yourself to become prime minister. But to remove Rabin, you first had to win the support of your party's left-wingers. And the only way you could do that was to trade in your ideological colors, to reinvent yourself from hawk to dove. And that's exactly what you did. Am I not right, Knesset Member Peres?"

Peres was on his feet, shaking his head violently, chopping the air with balled fists, shooting looks at his opponent that could freeze water. After all, Shimon Peres was no pushover. Whatever ill-will existed between himself and Rabin, he had an illustrious career to his credit. He had initiated Israel's nuclear Dimona project. He had essentially built the nation's aerospace industry. And now he had inherited a disillusioned party who lost the last elections, but was rebuilding it bit by bit with skill and patience. No wonder his usually rumbling, melancholy voice was strident with wrath as he shouted back at Begin that never in his life had he "sacrificed principle for expediency," or "sold his soul for a mess of political pottage." He had always been "a pragmatist and a realist, yet guided by moral imperatives." Israel was engaged in "a struggle for its very existence," and had to constantly "be alive to new circumstances." He, therefore, refused "to remain a prisoner of outmoded doctrines." Indeed, his "sheer integrity compelled him to reappraise and reassess the situation." Never once had he misled the people as the prime minister was doing now.

"Never did I promise the nation that I would bring them instant and total peace wrapped up in a peace treaty, without concessions," he raged. "That is not a policy; it is an irresponsible flight of the imagination!"

This hit home.

Motionless, arms folded, lips pressed, his face blanched and his eyes granite, Menachem Begin said quietly, stubbornly, grimly, "Never did I make such a promise in my life, Mr. Peres. You have plucked this spurious charge out of thin air. It is a fiction! I challenge you to prove otherwise."

But his opponent was not to be cowed. Knowing how his words had the power to wound, he hurled more: "Repeatedly, you insinuate that we stand at the threshold of peace as defined in a peace treaty. You said as much again today."

Anger hung in the air between them like an invisible knife, their eyes locked in open warfare.

"Knesset Member Shimon Peres," seethed Begin, "I have just quoted to this House words you spoke and wrote yourself. I quoted them word for word. Now, I challenge you to bring to this podium quotes from me, in my own words, asserting that we stand at the threshold of peace. I have never said it. The members of this House know I have never said it. They are well informed. You can't pull wool over their eyes."

"Indeed you can't," countered Peres. "That is why most people here see right through your whimsical flights of fancy. You're so enamored with your own words that you think they can move mountains. Well they can't. You think a good speech is all that it takes to get things done. Well it can't.

You think that you can run a government by oratory. Well you can't. You think that just because you've prepared a draft of a peace treaty it's as good as done. Well it isn't."

Begin responded in a tone that evoked high purpose and responsibility. "Let me assure you, and the whole House," he said solemnly, "I have no illusions about the obstacles awaiting us at a Geneva peace conference, if one will take place. I have left in the hands of the American president a proposal as to how we believe such a conference should be structured and who should participate, no more. Indeed, if anything, it is *your* party Mr. Peres, the Labor Party, that has been deceiving our nation for years, telling us tales about territorial compromises in exchange for peace. For years you have been proposing to our Arab neighbors enormous concessions, and their answer has always been universally the same: 'Totally unacceptable!'"

He stopped for a moment and straightened up, and with an expression both teasing and taunting, said, "So at least have the grace to be a good loser, Mr. Peres. You lost the elections, remember. Take it like a man. Stop sulking. Criticize us if you will. This is a free, democratic parliament. But why resort to such excessive rancor? Why the uncontrolled fury? Why the baseless allegations? What's gotten into you, Mr. Peres? Get a grip on yourself." And with that he stepped down from the podium into the well of the Chamber, his mouth curved into the impish smile of one satisfied that he had had the last word.[67]

What he did not know, could not possibly know, as he took his seat at the head of the horseshoe cabinet table amid a cacophony of boos and hurrahs, was that his model peace treaty would not gather dust for all that long. Seemingly out of the blue, an event occurred soon after of such mind-boggling proportions it would change the course of history and render Jimmy Carter's Geneva exertions obsolete.

Anwar Sadat, President of Egypt, decided to travel to Jerusalem to speak to Menachem Begin about peace.

The night that changed history: Egyptian president Anwar Sadat arrives, 19 November 1977

Chapter eleven

The Night Sadat Came

W hat time does Shabbat end?" asked Begin, in an impatient voice.

Yechiel Kadishai flipped through his pocket calendar, and said, "This coming Shabbat, November nineteenth, it ends at five twelve."

The prime minister's face became sunny. "So, that's fine, Sam. You can tell your Cairo Embassy to tell the Egyptians eight o'clock is perfectly in order. It will give us time enough to prepare everything for President Sadat's arrival without our desecrating the Sabbath."

This exchange took place on Wednesday afternoon, 16 November, 1977. The prime minister was addressing Ambassador Samuel Lewis, who had asked to see him urgently to deliver a message from the Egyptian president. He wanted to know what time on Saturday night he could land at Ben-Gurion Airport.

The drama behind this sudden and astonishing question had begun a week earlier when, in a rambling address to his parliament – the People's Assembly – Anwar Sadat had tucked in the following sentence: "Israel will be stunned to hear me tell you that I am ready to go to the ends of the earth, and even to their home, to the Knesset itself, to argue with them, in order to prevent one Egyptian soldier from being wounded."

"*Allahu Akbar!*" [God is great!] chanted the assembly in collective affirmation.

Upon hearing this on the BBC World Service at dawn the following morning, Begin mumbled to himself skeptically, "We'll see how serious he is about this!" On arrival at the office, he said to Yechiel, "We have to put Sadat to the test," and he summoned his adviser on Arab affairs to assist in drafting a welcoming response in Arabic, to be aired on television and radio. In it, the prime minister assured the Egyptian people of a reception worthy of their president's stature, and uttered words that have since entered history books: "Let us give a silent oath to one another: no more war, no more bloodshed, no more threats. Let us make peace. Let us start on the path of friendship."[68]

Sam Lewis – now dubbed the "happy postman" on account of his coming and going with messages between Jerusalem and Cairo – was soon back to say President Sadat had heard the prime minister's statement, but wanted an actual written invitation.

"By all means," said the prime minister, and on the spot he wrote: "On behalf of the Government of Israel I have the honor to extend to you our cordial invitation to come to Jerusalem and to visit our country. Your Excellency's readiness to undertake such a visit, as expressed to the People's Assembly of Egypt, has been noted here with deep and positive interest, as has been your statement that you would wish to address the members of our Parliament, the Knesset, and to meet with me.

"If, as I hope, you will accept our invitation, arrangements will be made for you to address the Knesset from its rostrum. You will also, should you so desire, be enabled to meet with our various parliamentary groups, those supporting the government as well as those in opposition…. May I assure you, Mr. President, that the parliament, the government and the people of Israel will receive you with respect and cordiality."

From that moment, Israel quivered with anticipation, while President Jimmy Carter fretted over how this direct contact between the belligerents squared with his statement issued with the Soviet Union the month before, announcing the intention to convene a Geneva Peace Conference under their joint chairmanship. Carter would later explain:

> Since the only forum the United States had to work on was the Geneva Conference under the aegis of the United Nations, we had to get the Soviet Union, as co-chairman, to agree to the format we were laboriously evolving. On September 23, during my meeting with [Soviet] Foreign Minister Gromyko, he told me, "If we can just establish a miniature state for the Palestinians as big as a pencil eraser, this will lead to a resolution of the PLO problem for the Geneva Conference." He smiled as I pointed out the difficulty of

such a tiny state being formed, and then agreed that peace would have to be more than the end of war in the Middle East. The ultimate goal, he acknowledged, was normal relationships between the Arab and Israeli governments and people.[69]

It is clear that Menachem Begin and Anwar Sadat had an instinctive sense of global geopolitics that told them that such a conference would place Soviet Russia squarely back into the heart of the Middle East equation. The Egyptian president had kicked the Russians out, and he was not about to slip under their thumb again. This led him to conclude that it was infinitely better to implement a bilateral peace move with Israel, rather than to again become a mere pawn in the superpower Middle East play. Begin wholeheartedly agreed. His own instincts had been greatly energized by reports from Foreign Minister Moshe Dayan, who had secretly met with a senior Sadat confidant in Morocco some months before, and from whom he had learned that "the Soviets would not play any positive or constructive role in future negotiations." At the same time, Begin himself had visited Bucharest, to impress upon the Romanian dictator, Nicolae Ceaușescu, his desire to come to terms with Egypt. When Ceaușescu subsequently met the Egyptian president, he told him, "Begin is a hard man to negotiate with, but once he agrees to something he will implement it to the last dot and comma. You can trust Begin." Similar advice was given by the Shah of Iran, whom Begin had discreetly met in Teheran, ahead of a Sadat visit there (in those days, Israel maintained a close relationship with the Shah of Iran, albeit discreetly and unofficially. There was even an Israeli Embassy in Teheran, but it was not labeled as such; it was merely called "The Diplomatic Representative." It bore no plaque, flew no flag, and did not appear in any embassy listing).[70]

Having put out these feelers, the Israeli premier was not taken entirely by surprise when the Egyptian president resolved in his almost theatrical fashion to circumvent Geneva by flying to Israel to talk peace. "The irony of it all," confided Begin to us, his staff, "is that after all the years of my being slandered and vilified as a warmonger and a terrorist, I am the one Sadat has chosen to visit."

Thus it was, that at 7:58 on Saturday night, 19 November, a seventy-two-man guard of honor drawn from officer cadets of every branch of the IDF dipped its flags and presented arms, while buglers sounded a fanfare, signaling the arrival of the president of Israel, Ephraim Katzir, and Prime Minister Menachem Begin, who had come to welcome the president of Egypt. The multitude of high-ranking dignitaries lining the unusually long red carpet was all-anticipation, watching the approaching white lights in the sky. The roar of the descending aircraft drowned out the scattered applause as the plane touched down, slowed, turned, and taxied toward the waiting throng.

The presidential Boeing arrived exactly as prescribed – eight o'clock. On its bright white fuselage, made all the brighter by the searchlights shining on it, were emblazoned the words ARAB REPUBLIC OF EGYPT. Even the dourest of cynics beamed with delight at the sight of it, like the Mona Lisa breaking into a grin.

A marshal's voice barked, "ATTENTION! PRESENT ARMS!" and the officer cadets moved with choreographed precision, their weapons clasped rigidly upright as the aircraft drew to a halt at the red carpet's floodlit edge.

Never had Ben-Gurion Airport been more festooned as on that Saturday night – it was awash with light and color, hung with hundreds of flapping flags, Israeli and Egyptian. Rows of parading troops, their regimental ensigns aloft, framed the tarmac, and at one end was arranged a military band, its brass instruments flashing in the floodlights (the conductor, Yitzhak Graziani, unable to find a copy of the Egyptian national anthem, had hastily transcribed its notes from an end-of-day Radio Cairo broadcast).

A ramp was quickly rolled into position, and an expectant hush settled on the assembly. Even the air seemed to be holding its breath. However, for reasons unknown, the aircraft's door did not open, and the anticipatory adrenalin gradually faded as people put their heads together, their faces faintly unsettled, murmuring softly to each other about the inordinate amount of time passing by.

Might something untoward be afoot?

A few cast speculative glances at the chief of staff, General Mordechai [Motta] Gur, who had suggested publicly that the Egyptian president's sudden impulse to visit Jerusalem might be a ruse, a subterfuge that would lend him an advantageous starting point for the next Israel-Arab war. Might Egyptian commandos be poised behind that door, readying themselves to mow down the entire Israeli cabinet?

Notwithstanding the tension, Prime Minister Begin stood stolidly at the foot of the ramp, looking up at the sealed door with no hint of restiveness in his demeanor, his face as impassive as a sphinx. He knew this was no ruse.

When the door finally swung ajar, an unruly horde of journalists burst through it, descended the ramp, and jostled each other for strategic positions at its base. This caused the mass of correspondents, television crews and photographers contained behind the barriers of the official press grandstand – an estimated four thousand – to shout their frustration, their line of vision of the impending first handshake between the leaders of Egypt and of Israel being entirely blocked by the just-landed Cairo crowd. So they surged forward through the police barrier, causing such a crush along the red carpet that numerous VIPs were pushed aside into the second and third rows of the receiving line.

Still, the plane's doorway remained empty and dark. The hubbub continued to swell, until, like a burst of dazzling fireworks, a thousand camera shutters sliced the night, engulfing the lone figure who had just stepped into the doorway in blazing lights.

Tall and immaculately groomed, President Anwar Sadat stood there blinking in the glare, basking in the fanfare of trumpets and the fervent applause which greeted him. In extreme slow motion he descended the steps, accompanied by the Israeli chief of protocol, who formally introduced the president of Egypt to the president and the prime minister of Israel at the foot of the ramp.

Stampeded by the crush of the pressmen, I ended up by the side of Golda Meir, who was remarking sarcastically to Yitzhak Rabin, "*Now* he comes! Couldn't he have come before the Yom Kippur War and saved all those dead, his and ours?"

Rabin's reply, whatever it was, was drowned out by the applause as Prime Minister Begin introduced his guest to his ministers who were lining the carpet. Reaching Ariel Sharon, the commander who led the Israeli counterattack across the Suez Canal in the Yom Kippur War, the Egyptian president paused, and said good-naturedly, "Aha, here you are! I tried to chase you in the desert. If you try to cross my canal again, I'll have to lock you up."

"No need for that," laughed Sharon. "I am glad to have you here. I'm minister of agriculture now," and they shook hands warmly.

To Foreign Minister Moshe Dayan I heard him say, "Don't worry Moshe, it will be alright." But someone in earshot claimed he also quipped, "You must let me know in advance when you are coming to Cairo, so that I can lock up my museums" – a dig at Dayan's penchant for helping himself to ancient relics when conducting private excavations in Israel.

To Chief of Staff General Motta Gur, he said, grinning, "See, General, it is no trick. I was not bluffing."

Israeli and Egyptian flags festoon Ben Gurion Airport, 19 November 1977

Prime Minister Begin welcomes President Sadat, with President Ephraim Katzir

*Sadat, Begin & Katzir stand at attention during the playing
of the Egyptian and Israeli national anthems*

*Sadat and Begin in discussion in the course of a working dinner
at the King David Hotel, Jerusalem, 19 November 1977*

The general's response was a formal salute.

And now he stood face to face with Golda Meir. They looked at each other solemnly, he half bowing as he took her hand.

"I have wanted to talk to you for a long time," he said.

"And I have been waiting for you for a long time," she answered.

"But now I am here," he said.

"Shalom. Welcome," she said.

He continued along the carpet, shaking the hands of the rest of the ministers and of the other notables, until, at a given signal, a young captain of the guard, head high, chest out, marched forward, and with a whirling salute informed the Egyptian president that the IDF guard of honor was ready for his inspection. Walking with measured steps, President Sadat inspected the ranks, semi-bowed to the blue-and-white flag, and then, standing side by side with President Katzir and Prime Minister Begin, heard the band play his national anthem, followed by "*Hatikva*," their contrasting harmonies punctuated by the thumps of a twenty-one-gun salute.

An armored limousine pulled up alongside the Egyptian president, but a pack of pugnacious newsmen mobbed the vehicle, overwhelming President Katzir, who was Sadat's intended traveling companion for the ride to Jerusalem. He, being an elderly, genteel man, slow of gait, was pushed aside and would have been left behind were it not for the quick-wittedness of a security agent trotting alongside the car who saw him safely inside.

Thus did the presidential motorcade set off for the drive up to Jerusalem, where houses were bedecked with Israeli and Egyptian flags, and cheering crowds filled the streets. Here was history in the making. Strangers embraced in unbounded optimism, and the sound of wave upon wave of hurrahs swept through the windows of the King David Hotel, where the president of Egypt was lodging. Common folk stood vigil all through the night outside, as if silently entreating the man inside to be the bearer of good tidings that the wars were ended for good.

Most of the thirty-six hours of the Egyptian president's stay were taken up with ceremonial and public events: a prayer service at the al-Aksa Mosque on the Temple Mount, a visit to the Yad Vashem Holocaust Memorial, meetings with representatives of the parliamentary parties, a working lunch with the prime minister and his senior colleagues, a festive dinner, and a joint press conference. At the center of it all, was his address to the Knesset.

That day, the crowded parliament chamber had an air of high, almost tear-jerking expectancy. All rose and applauded at length at the entrance of the president of Egypt accompanied by the president of Israel.

"I have come to the Knesset," the visitor began, "so that together we can build a new life, founded on peace."

The clapping rattled the rafters, and it continued during Sadat's lengthy ode-to-peace, given in a stilted English. It was only when he moved on to list the conditions with which Israel would have to agree if it ever wanted Arab acceptance, conditions untenable to the overwhelming majority, that the chamber stilled to an intensely grave attentiveness. No, the president of Egypt told his audience, he would not sign a separate peace agreement. No, he would not enter into any interim arrangements. No, he would not bargain over a single inch of Arab territory. No, he would not compromise over Jerusalem. And no, there could be no peace without a Palestinian state.

Begin's response was cordial but emphatic: His guest had known before embarking on his journey to Jerusalem exactly where Israel stood on each of these issues. He urged negotiations without prior conditions. With goodwill, he added, a redeeming formula could be found to resolve all the admittedly complex matters.

Perhaps in the course of their private conversations the two leaders had found ways to bridge this seemingly impassable chasm. Perhaps Sadat's declared conditions for peace were not so set in stone, because after his plane had left en route to Cairo, an exuberant Begin beckoned me over, across the tarmac, and said, "I want to send off a cable to President Carter straight away," and on the spot he began to dictate while walking to his car. As anyone who has tried it well knows, writing while walking is no easy feat, and my resultant scribble was so illegible I had tremendous difficulty deciphering it. Once I did, it came out like this:

> Dear Mr. President – Last night President Sadat and I sat till after midnight. We are going to avert another war in the Middle East, and we made practical arrangements to achieve that quest. I will give you the details in a written report. The exchanges were very confidential, very far-reaching from his point of view. I am very tired. I work twenty hours a day. There are differences of opinion. We are going to discuss them. I have a request. You will plan another trip to various parts of the world. Please visit both Egypt and Israel during that trip. Sadat was very moved by the reception of our people.

You will come to Israel and we will give you a wonderful time. So will Egypt. Give two days to Jerusalem and Cairo. Please take this into consideration.

Draft of the official written report sent to President Carter, reporting on Sadat's visit to Jerusalem, 23 November 1977

That same night, the prime minister, exhausted though he was, received a four-man delegation of United Jewish Appeal philanthropists who had flown in from the U.S. especially to witness the historic event.

Among them was an old acquaintance of mine from Columbus, Ohio – Gordon Zacks, commonly known as Gordie.

Gordie was a vigorous, enterprising, big-hearted and idealistic man who not only gave generously but also thought innovatively. In 1975, while then U.S. Secretary of State Henry Kissinger was shuttling back and forth between Cairo and Jerusalem in the arduous attempt to hammer out an interim Sinai agreement between Sadat and the then prime minister Rabin, he had embarked on a peacemaking mission of his own. He had flown to Egypt to identify a hundred projects in the fields of medicine, agriculture, irrigation, industry, and social welfare which he envisioned as possible joint Egyptian-Israeli enterprises. He saw these servinge as stepping-stones to peace, and carrying his proposal to Israel he asked me to arrange a meeting with Rabin.

As Rabin had flicked through the bulky project folder, Gordie leaned across and said to him with enormous zest, "Yitzhak, listen to me, this is a no-lose deal."

"Meaning what, exactly?" asked Rabin, slamming the folder shut without even pretending to examine a single one of its projects.

"Meaning, here is a way of testing Sadat's true intentions toward peace."

"Gordie, what world are you living in?" scoffed Rabin sarcastically, pushing the folder away as if its author was one of the proverbial babes in the wood.

"I'm telling you, this is a solid proposal," countered Gordie indignantly. "Israel could offer to become a part of any or of all these projects. It could lay the foundations for the beginnings of a true dialogue."

"And if the Egyptians say we don't want you, as I'm sure they will?"

"Then what you do is publicly offer them two projects a week for fifty weeks. You will come out smelling of roses as the peacemaker, while Sadat will be seen as the intransigent one."

"Crazy, naive American," said Rabin, rising and extending a hand of farewell. "Gordie, old friend, this is just another public relations gimmick. Go back home to America and do what you do best: raise money for the United Jewish Appeal."

And off Gordie went, dejected.

Two years later, when Menachem Begin assumed the premiership, he asked to see all materials concerning Israel's past peacemaking efforts with Egypt. Among the documents was Gordon Zacks' proposal. It aroused enough curiosity for the premier to ask me who the man was, and when

I told him of his UJA leadership role and his political activism on Israel's behalf, he said, "His ideas are a fantasy, but they show daring and imagination. I'd like to meet him one day."

I phoned this through to Gordie and within a week he was having lunch with the prime minister in the Olive Room at the King David Hotel.

"Mr. Zacks, have you ever been in jail?" asked Begin, while the first course was being served.

"No, Mr. Prime Minister," answered Gordie testily, wondering what Begin was getting at, "I've never been in jail."

"That's a pity," said Begin enigmatically, nibbling on his chicken. "You see, I have been in three different jails."

Gordie Zacks sat back, stunned. "Three? How come?"

"The first time the communists arrested me was in Vilna. I was in the middle of a game of chess. When the Soviet agents dragged me off, I remember calling out to my colleague, 'I concede the game. You win.' The Soviets locked me up in one of their prisons. I was held there for six weeks, and all I could think about was getting out and going back home. The second prison was a forced labor camp – a gulag – in Siberia. By the sixth week, I dreamt of being back in that first prison cell. The third time, the Soviets put me in solitary confinement, and I dreamt of being back in that Siberian labor camp. So, you see, Mr. Zacks, my job as prime minister of Israel is to make sure that Jewish children dream the dreams of a free people, and never about prisons, or labor camps, or solitary confinement. I want to bring them peace, but in our region peace can be won only through strength."

"So, how can I help?" asked Gordie, with his characteristic wholeheartedness.

"By telling me about your trip to Egypt, and the nature of the projects we might do together with the Egyptians once we have peace."

It was no wonder, with that history, that Gordie Zacks displayed such excitement that night at the conclusion of Sadat's visit, when Begin told him and his colleagues, "Friends, you will be pleased to hear that President Sadat and I have come to an understanding. We still have our differences, as you heard in his Knesset speech and in my response to him, but we agreed there will be no more war. I already wrote as much to President Carter. Yehuda" – this to me – "you sent off my cable?"

"Of course, as soon as I got back to Jerusalem from Ben-Gurion."

"Then let's call the president now – hear his reaction."

"Do you have his number?" I asked.

Begin shook his head with an air of innocent ignorance.

"Then I'd better rush over to the office. I have it in the classified telephone directory," I said.

"Why not call the international exchange, and ask for the White House switchboard," suggested Gordie helpfully. "I'm pretty sure they have a general number."

"I'll try," I said, and soon enough I got through to 001 202 456 1414. I was standing in the hallway, speaking to a woman at the White House switchboard, who thought I was a crank.

"I'm sorry, mister," she said in a steely voice, "but you can't speak to the president of the United States."

"It's not me, it's the prime minister of Israel, Mr. Menachem Begin," I said haughtily.

To which she responded dubiously, "Menakem who?"

"Begin."

"Hold the line."

"Hello, how can I help you?" This from a lady with a more gentle tone.

I explained the matter, and she said reasonably, "Please give me the prime minister's number and we'll get back to you."

I checked the phone to see the number. There was none. How could there be? This was the prime minister's residence, and his number was not on public display for prying eyes to see. So I called out to the prime minister, who was sitting in the lounge with his guests, "Mr. Begin, what's your number?"

"I've no idea. I never phone myself," he said. And then, moving into the hallway he shouted up the stairwell to his wife, "Alla, what's our phone number?"

"Six six four, seven six three," she shouted back.

I scribbled it down and repeated it to Washington.

"Thank you," said the voice, "we'll get back to you presently." And, sure enough, within minutes, the phone rang and the voice said, "Please put the prime minister on the line. I'm putting the president through now."

I handed over the receiver and stood aside to take notes. With no extension to hand, I could only record one side of the conversation, what Mr. Begin was saying.

"I hope you received my message, Mr. President," he said beamingly.

Long pause.

"Oh yes, of course. Tomorrow I shall send you a full account, through our ambassador," he said.

Another long pause.

"Certainly, indeed, Mr. President. Yes, there are immediate concrete results. President Sadat and I agreed to continue our dialogue on two levels, the political and the military. Such meetings will take place hopefully between our representatives soon. We made a solemn pledge at our joint press conference in Jerusalem that there will be no more wars between us. This is a great moral victory. And we agreed that there be no future mobilizations or troop movements on either side, so that our mutual commitment of 'no more war' may be given a practical expression on the ground."

And then, shoulders back, head rising, forehead wrinkling, "No, no, Mr. President, I assure you – yes, yes – we still want to go to Geneva if you think it useful. It is all a matter of proper timing. President Sadat and I discussed this, but did not talk about an actual date. We exchanged ideas on the most substantial issues, and knowing we have differences of opinion we promised each other to discuss them further in the future. What is important is that the atmosphere throughout all our talks was friendly, frank and cordial."

Then, face all a-grin, voice bubbling, "Mr. President, without you it could never have happened. So allow me to express my deepest gratitude for your magnificent contribution. Peace-loving people the world over, and the Jewish people for generations to come, will be forever in your debt for the role you played in helping to bring this historic visit about. We shall need your understanding and help in the future. God bless you, Mr. President. Goodbye," and he hung up.

Privy to every word, his guests in the lounge fervently congratulated him on what was, assuredly, an affable conversation – all of them that is, but Gordie Zacks. Dumbfounded, he asked, "Why Mr. Prime Minister? *Why?* Why give Carter so much credit? Sadat came here because of what you did, and *despite* what Carter did, with his idea of Geneva with the Soviets."

"What does it cost?" answered Begin with an impish expression. "I'm still going to need him, aren't I? So giving him a bit of credit now might help us a little in the future. The important thing is that Sadat and I are agreed on making peace with or without Geneva."

A week later, on 28 November, in an address to the Knesset, the prime minister summarized the historic visit, and the initiatives which had brought it about. He reiterated his gratitude to the United States, and explained why eight o'clock had been deliberately chosen as the hour for the Egyptian President's arrival at Ben-Gurion Airport. He said:

> President Sadat indicated he wished to come to us on Saturday evening. I decided that an appropriate hour would be eight o'clock, well after the termination of the Shabbat. I decided on this hour in order that there would be no Shabbat desecration. Also, I wanted the whole world to know that ours is a Jewish State which honors the Sabbath day. I read again those eternal biblical verses: *"Honor the Sabbath day to keep it holy,"* and was again deeply moved by their meaning. These words echo one of the most sanctified ideas in the history of mankind, and they remind us that once upon a time we were all slaves in Egypt. Mr. Speaker: We respect the Muslim day of rest – Friday. We respect the Christian day of rest – Sunday. We ask all nations to respect our day of rest – Shabbat. They will do so only if we respect it ourselves.[71]

Author's corrections on initial draft of joint Egypt-Israel communiqué issued at the end of Sadat's visit to Jerusalem, 20 November 1977

The author with President Sadat, Ismailia, Egypt, 25 December 1977

Chapter twelve

Deadlock

Within a matter of weeks, all the protocols for the Egyptian-Israeli talks were in place, and meetings between the two sides began. An air of expectancy gripped the nation, as if some miracle was in the offing; the creation of a redemptive, instant peace treaty. But it was not to be. Like Sisyphus, whenever Menachem Begin pushed his boulder up the steep hill of negotiation, it always came rolling down again over his toes, with painful and prolonged consequences.

Anwar Sadat assumed that his grand reconciliatory gesture of coming to Jerusalem would be rewarded by a grand reconciliatory gesture on the part of Menachem Begin, in the form of a withdrawal on all fronts back to the pre–Six-Day War 1967 lines, and acquiescence in the establishment of a Palestinian state. Small wonder, then, that whenever the Egyptian and Israeli representatives met, they faced an unbridgeable abyss of misunderstanding and deadlock. Their joint committees broke up in angry dispute, indignant letters were exchanged, the Carter administration told American Jewish leaders that the Begin government was being unnecessarily obdurate, and the heavily censored Egyptian press treated Israel with disdain and its prime minister with malice. Begin was depicted as a Shylock.

This affront upset him deeply. His hurt was reflected in the withering sarcasm of the occasional working notes he would send me, addressing them, "From Shylock to Shakespeare," and signing them, "Menachem Mendel Shylock."

By the spring of 1978, the talks were in the doldrums and Jimmy Carter had to intervene urgently in an effort to rescue the waning hopes. He pressed Begin to come to Washington to thrash things out. The prime minister, knowing what lay in store, asked Foreign Minister Moshe Dayan to accompany him.

The acrimony of those talks, held in the White House Cabinet Room on 21 and 22 March, is vividly illustrated in the following exchange, which I recorded verbatim. What follows is the full version:

> *Begin:* ...We decided, in our July talks last year, to talk frankly. When I saw you [privately] at that time I read to you a three-point document. You sent me a five-point response and, in it, you used language that said we would have to withdraw 'on all fronts.' I said we would not agree to such language. I later said we had a claim and a right to sovereignty in Judea, Samaria, and Gaza, but that we would leave that claim open. So we did two things in an effort to make an agreement [with Egypt] possible: First, we did not apply Israeli law to Judea, Samaria, and Gaza, proposing that the question of their future sovereignty be left open. Secondly, we offered administrative self-rule for the Palestinian Arabs in these areas, and suggested that their autonomy would be reviewed after five years. After five years all questions would be open for renegotiation. These, I submit, Mr. President, are far-reaching proposals.
>
> *Carter:* They nevertheless represent a change compared to the position of previous [Labor] governments [i.e., a readiness for a withdrawal on all fronts, including the West Bank].
>
> *Begin:* Yes, but not a drastic change. Under previous governments, the River Jordan was to be designated as Israel's security boundary. There was to be no Israeli withdrawal from the river. The Labor governments planned to evacuate only a part of the West Bank. The Israeli Army was to remain along the Jordan River.
>
> *Carter:* In an effort to break the present deadlock, could you envisage that your security needs could be met by having Israeli military forces deployed for a period of five years in military positions along the river, or in the hills around Jerusalem? In other words, would you agree to withdraw into cantonments

Note attached to letter from author to Begin, with Begin's reply.
Translation: "Your letter to [Canadian premier] Trudeau."
Begin's reply: "From Shylock to Shakespeare – With thanks. No payment," 6 February 1978

in a manner that would satisfy Arab demands and yet preserve your security? Is that a possibility?

Begin: I don't know about the word cantonments. We could consider withdrawal into emplacements. In all circumstances, our forces must stay in Judea, Samaria, and Gaza.

Dayan: I would like to refer to the question of whether there has been a change in the policy of the present government compared to the [Labor] governments of the past. I was in previous Labor governments, and I can tell you that for several months after the Six-Day War, the Israeli position was that we would return the whole of Sinai and the Golan Heights in return for assurances, but we totally excluded the West Bank...the plan of the present government to offer the Palestinian Arabs a regime of self-rule grants them a far greater measure of genuine self-expression than any plan of previous Israeli governments. Our current plan begins with the proposition that we don't want our forces to rule over the Arabs. We don't want to impose ourselves on them. We don't want to tell them how to run their lives. But we must be in a position to check the movement of those who cross into our territory. Among the Palestinians are refugees, laborers, and, yes, terrorists. Speaking as an ex-soldier, I want to know who will be in charge of the border checkpoints from Jordan and Syria into the Palestinian and Israeli areas. If our own soldiers are not going to do the checking we shall have to fence off our whole country with barbed wire. I don't want Israel to become an isolated fortress. We will, therefore, have to deploy our soldiers in the West Bank and Gaza wherever they are needed for our security, without imposing ourselves on the daily lives of the Arabs who will, under this government's plan, enjoy self-rule.

Carter: Let me repeat one thing. I have no doubt that Sadat really wants a peace agreement with Israel. I have had hours of private talks with him, and he is flexible on the issues. He has obligations to the other Arabs, and he acts as spokesmen for their interests. He is the best Arab leader with whom you can negotiate. But because of the pressure of the terrorists, and the pressures on Sadat himself, I am afraid that the

chance for an agreement will slip away and the prospects for peace be lost.
[...]

Brzezinski: As we try to advance toward a solution, it is important to note that your self-rule proposal can be seen in different ways. To put it bluntly, it can be seen as a continuation of your military and political control over the West Bank and Gaza. This would make it clearly unacceptable. It would render Security Council Resolution 242 ambiguous, displaying unwillingness on your part to apply the term 'withdrawal' to the West Bank and Gaza. If Israel were to speak of its forces being withdrawn from *control* of the West Bank and Gaza to agreed emplacements, then your plan could be the basis for a solution, and open the way to peace. But if not, there could be strong suspicions that you intend to perpetuate your control over these occupied territories. Need I say that the Middle East is an essential area of interest to us? It is vital that the region be engaged with the West, and be set on a course of moderation and stability. This is in your interest as well as ours.

Begin: We all understand the need for an agreement with the Arabs. We have, therefore, elaborated a peace plan which will enable the Palestinian Arabs to elect their own Administrative Council – self-rule – and run their daily lives themselves without our interference. We only reserve for ourselves the maintenance of security and public order.

Carter: You envisage the autonomy agreement for the West Bank and Gaza to last for five years, am I not right?

Begin: Correct.

Carter: What will happen after that?

Begin: After that, we shall see. We have carefully considered the possibility of conducting a plebiscite in which the Palestinian Arabs would be given the choice of continuing the status quo, or opting for a tie with Jordan, or for a tie with Israel. However, with the pistols of the PLO pointing at their heads, and with the almost daily assassinations and the threats which the population constantly endures, a plebiscite will be futile and dangerous. The PLO will either force the people to boycott it or force them to vote for a Palestinian state. This we will not allow. Therefore, we suggest, let's wait and see how the [five-year] self-rule experiment works out – how the reality will unfold.

Carter: This practically gives Israel a veto – a de facto veto – even over Arab administrative affairs. And it keeps Israel in indefinite control of the West Bank. Without Israeli willingness to give the Palestinian Arabs a voice in determining their own future, there is no chance for a peace settlement. I know that Sadat won't agree to the perpetuation of Israeli control over the West Bank, if the Palestinians are not given a guaranteed chance to choose their future. If Israel insists they have no voice, there will be no prospect of a peace settlement. You are getting more and more demanding. You are slamming the door shut.

Brzezinski: We have to have an agreement that is satisfactory to you on security grounds, but which is politically realistic. If you want genuine security while giving the Palestinians genuine self-rule and an identity, that can work. Security – yes, political control – no.

Begin: In our self-rule plan, we give the Palestinian Arabs the option of [Israeli] citizenship after five years. They can even choose to vote for our Knesset.

Brzezinski: But it works both ways: Israelis are allowed to buy land in the West Bank, but there is no reciprocity for the Arabs in Israel proper. This is an unequal status.

Begin: This is a right of our citizens.

Brzezinski: But Israelis are not citizens of the West Bank.

Begin: But we are giving them the option of becoming our citizens.

Dayan: According to our plan, Palestinian Arabs after five years can opt for either Jordanian or Israeli citizenship, or they can retain the status quo, and keep their present local identity cards. We will make no obstacles to their choice. The main point about any referendum in the future is to allow individuals to decide their citizenship, but not to decide the sovereign status of Judea, Samaria, and Gaza. The kind of plebiscite you are suggesting will determine territorial sovereignty, not just the status of the people. If we allow what you call 'deciding their own future' in terms of territory, they will be deciding

Proposed

Proposed Principles

1. The Palestinian Arabs, inhabitants of Judea, Samaria and the Gaza District, will enjoy full autonomy.

2. For this purpose a self-governing authority (Administrative Council) shall be elected by the Arab inhabitants of Judea, Samaria and the Gaza District.

3. The Administrative Council will be composed of eleven members; it will operate in accordance with the principles laid down in this paper.

4. Details concerning the right to vote, or to be elected to the Administrative Council, e.g. age, personal status etc. will be determined in the negotiations.

5. The Administrative Council will operate a number of departments; their number and competence will be determined in the negotiations.

6. Arab inhabitants of Judea, Samaria and the Gaza District will be given free choice (option) of either Israeli or Jordanian citizenship.

7) Arab inhabitants in the aforementioned areas who will choose, and be granted, Israeli citizenship, will be entitled to vote and be elected to the Knesset in accordance with the Israeli election law;

The inhabitants, who are citizens of Jordan, or who will acquire such citizenship, will elect and be eligible to the

Begin's initial draft of "Proposed Principles" for Palestinian autonomy in Judea, Samaria and Gaza, December 1977, to which reference is made in this discussion. (Paragraph 7 offers Palestinians the future option of voting and election to the Knesset)

not only their own future, but ours, too. If they have a right to decide whether Israel gets out of the territories, they are, ipso facto, deciding our future.

Begin: Nothing is excluded. There will be a review after five years. But we are not ready to commit now to a referendum that will inevitably lead to a Palestinian state under the existing conditions of PLO intimidation and threat. Hence, we suggest that matters be left open for review. To agree now to a plebiscite could have incalculable consequences for our future.

Carter: Mr. Prime Minister, in my view the obstacle to a peace treaty with Egypt is your insistence on keeping political control over the West Bank and Gaza, not just now, but to perpetuate it even after five years. I had hoped we could reach a point of possible success of the peace process, but now we are on the verge of seeing it all lost.*

It was on this sour note that the first round of the White House talks ended. They continued the following day, again in the Cabinet Room, when President Carter, reading from a typed page, addressed the prime minister with disdain in his voice and fury in his eyes, saying:

"Mr. Prime Minister, the Israeli position, as I understand it, is that even if there were a clear statement by us *against* a total Israeli withdrawal from the West Bank and *against* a Palestinian state, and even if this were to be accepted by Egypt, Israel would still not stop building new settlements or the expansion of settlements; Israel would not give up the settlements in Sinai; Israel would not permit an Egyptian or UN protection over the Israeli settlements in Sinai; Israel will not withdraw its political authority from the West Bank and Gaza; Israel will not recognize that Resolution 242 applies on all fronts, including the principle of withdrawal from the West Bank; Israel will not give the Palestinian Arabs, at the end of the [five-year] interim period, the right to choose whether they want to be affiliated with Israel, with Jordan, or live under the interim arrangement. This is my understanding of the present situation. If I am correct, the likelihood that

---

* On a subsequent research visit to the Jimmy Carter Presidential Library, Atlanta, in November, 1999, I was handed a 'sanitized' transcript of this same meeting to which a note had been attached. It was addressed to Secretary of State Cyrus Vance and signed by National Security Adviser Zbigniew Brzezinski, and it said, "The subject memoranda of conversation are very sensitive and should be held close. They are forwarded for your records only."

the peace talks can be resumed with Egypt is very remote. There are no immediate prospects of a substantial movement toward a peace agreement. I would like to have your comment."

Carter's words were met with an oppressive silence. Dayan's face remained impassive; Begin's was ashen. But after a few moments of silence, this political combat brought out the defiance in him, and in a spitfire tongue, he declared:

"Mr. President, you have seen fit to couch all your definitions in negative terms. I shall state them positively. Israel has made a two-part peace proposal which is positive and constructive. Part one: we are resolved to negotiate peace treaties with a view to reaching a comprehensive settlement with all our neighbors. We have accepted Resolution 242 as the basis for negotiations with all our neighbors. We are determined that the negotiations be direct. We want secure and recognized boundaries, as called for in 242, but that same Resolution does not call for a total withdrawal on all fronts. The possibility of less than a total withdrawal applies not only to Judea and Samaria, but also to Sinai and the Golan. Nevertheless, Israel has stated its willingness for a total withdrawal to the international border in Sinai. We have asked for the demilitarization of the Sinai beyond the Gidi and the Mitla Passes. We have also suggested that after our total withdrawal from Sinai – which, I repeat, is not called for by 242 – two United Nations zones be established embracing our settlements there, which will be under the protection of Israeli contingents. We could have demanded border changes with Egypt, but again, I say, we have not done so, for the sake of peace.

"And now to part two of our positive peace proposals, dealing with Judea, Samaria and Gaza. We have proposed self-rule – or administrative autonomy – for the Palestinian Arabs in these areas. They will be enabled to elect their own administrative council which will deal with all issues of daily life, with no interference from Israel. Israel will reserve for itself control of security and public order only. This means that our forces will be in designated camps in Judea, Samaria and Gaza. The question of the future sovereignty of these areas shall remain open. We are dealing here with human beings, not with the status of the territory. The Palestinian Arabs shall have full self-rule and the Palestinian Jews security. We agree that there should be a review of the situation after five years. We suggest that people on both sides, Jew and Arab alike, be given the opportunity to work and live side by side together, and we shall see how this reality unfolds. After five years everything will be open to review. This, Mr. President, is part two of our positive peace proposal."

Begin's words made no impression. The stalemate was absolute. The White House encounter was simply nasty. Arriving back at Ben-Gurion Airport two days later, Menachem Begin made no bones about the seriousness of the situation. He told the waiting press,

"Our talks in Washington were difficult. Certain demands were made of us which we could not accept. Our lives would have been made much simpler had we been able to say 'yes' to the demands of the greatest power on earth, but we could not. We represent a small yet courageous nation, and we, its spokesmen, are concerned only with safeguarding our people's future. Always remember that what is, admittedly, a matter of important policy for the mighty United States of America, is for us a matter of life and death. On the table were issues which I cannot yet reveal. We shall, of course, continue to maintain contact with the president and his advisers. I have no doubt that the U.S. government desires peace in the Middle East. We, certainly, aspire to it with all our hearts. And so we hope the peacemaking process will continue, despite all the present difficulties."

Next, Begin answered some of the pointed questions the journalists had.

"It has been publicized that a senior U.S. representative has asserted that in order to make peace Israel will have to replace its prime minister. What is your reaction to that?"

"I do not know to whom you are referring, but the prime minister was chosen by the people of Israel, and not by a representative of the United States of America."

"While you were en route back to Israel, your Minister of Defense [Ezer Weizman] called for the establishment of an emergency national peace government. How do you view this proposal?"

"I have not read my colleague's remarks. If a peace government is required – it already exists. The government in which the Defense Minister is Defense Minister is a peace government."

"You said in your opening remarks that you hope the peace process will continue. In what way will it continue? What form will it take?"

"In every form available to us."[72]

In the tense and frustrating months that followed, the best way available turned out to be an enormous gamble on the part of President Carter. In September 1978, he invited Prime Minister Begin and President Sadat, together with their senior aides, to Camp David, the presidential retreat in Maryland. Here, confined behind locked gates, far from the maddening

The White House talks – Begin and his team face President Carter and his team across the table in the cabinet room, 1 May 1978

pressures of Washington and the ever-prying eyes of the press – in what Menachem Begin dubbed a "concentration camp deluxe" – the two parties went at it hammer and tongs for thirteen days and nights, with Carter serving as an indefatigable go-between. Finally, a two-part accord was reached, the first calling for the implementation of an autonomy plan for the Palestinian Arabs of Judea, Samaria and the Gaza Strip, to be followed after five years by a negotiated permanent settlement. The second was a framework for the conclusion of a peace treaty between Israel and Egypt, with full normalization and diplomatic relations, in return for Israel's complete withdrawal from Sinai within three years, and the dismantling of all of its settlements there. In recognition of these accords, Menachem Begin and Anwar Sadat were jointly awarded the Nobel Prize for Peace.

The Egyptian and Israeli teams went home, and continued their work of intensive negotiations to translate the general principles agreed upon at Camp David into the binding language of concrete contracts. This proved to be easier said than done, and necessitated a last-minute, whirlwind visit by President Carter to both Jerusalem and Cairo to dot the *i*'s and cross the *t*'s of the treaty with Egypt, and to put into place the machinery for a Palestinian autonomy negotiation. Although this latter ultimately came to naught, and despite the fact that the Arab world was in uproar, Sadat nevertheless decided to go ahead and sign his peace treaty with Israel.

Axiomatically, Washington, on the White House lawn, in the presence of Jimmy Carter, was where the ceremony would take place.

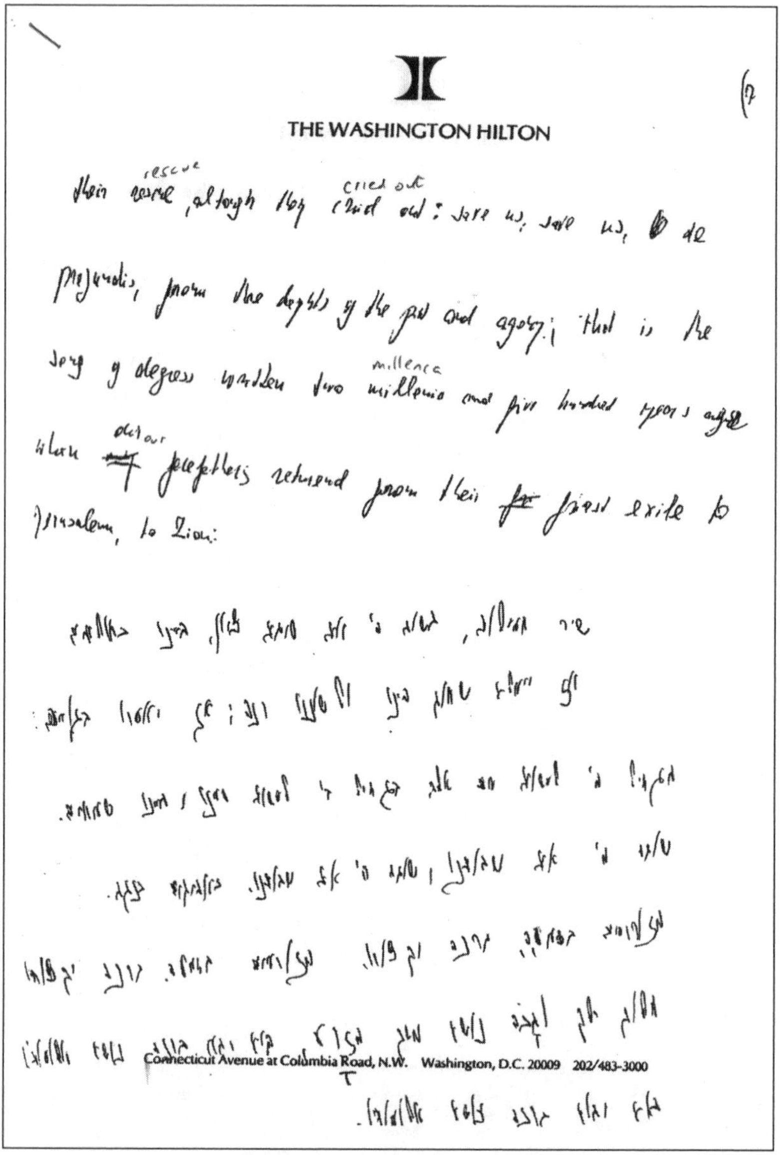

(7)

THE WASHINGTON HILTON

their rescue, altough they cried out: save us, save us, de profundis, from the depths of the pit and agony; that is the song of degrees written two millenia and five hundred years ago when our forefathers returned from their first exile to Jerusalem, to Zion:

שיר המעלות, בשוב ה' את שיבת ציון, היינו כחולמים

אז ימלא שחוק פינו ולשוננו רנה; אז יאמרו בגוים:

הגדיל ה' לעשות עם אלה. הגדיל ה' לעשות עמנו, היינו שמחים.

שובה ה' את שביתנו, כאפיקים בנגב.

הזורעים בדמעה, ברנה יקצרו. הלוך ילך ובכה

נשא משך הזרע, בא יבא ברנה נשא אלמתיו

Connecticut Avenue at Columbia Road, N.W. Washington, D.C. 20009 202/483-3000

Last page of Begin's draft of speech at Egypt-Israel peace-signing ceremony, written in his Washington Hilton suite on the morning of the ceremony, 26 March 1979

Chapter thirteen

Abie Finegold Saves the Peace Treaty

Tapping his temple and radiating an inscrutable smile, the prime minister quipped, "Yehuda, it's in here. You'll have it as soon as it's finished in here."

It was 25 March 1979, the ceremonial signing of the peace treaty was but a day away, and Menachem Begin's speech, scheduled for worldwide broadcast, was still incubating in his mind. His original intention had been to draft it during the long and tedious flight from Tel Aviv to Washington, but the journey turned out to be too distracting. We were traveling in an antiquated Israel Air Force Boeing 707, refurbished with discarded El Al seats, many of which were occupied by cabinet ministers, and, as a demonstration of national unity, a sizable contingent of opposition members, led by Yitzhak Rabin and Shimon Peres. His fellow travelers kept the prime minister engaged for much of the time, and the turbulence over the Atlantic was so severe it made me feel like a piece of salad in a colander tossed by a particularly energetic chef. So, by the time we'd unpacked at the Washington Hilton on Connecticut Avenue, where we were lodging, I was longing for bed.

"Go to bed," said the prime minister, when I walked into his suite to check on the status of his speech. "You look done in. I'll ring you first thing in the morning, when it's ready."

And so he did – at five A.M.

Still bedraggled and bleary-eyed, I dragged myself to his suite and found him in a dressing gown, full of beans. "Kindly shakespearize this," he said, passing me eight pages of his tight, vertical scrawl.

I immediately set to work, handing page after polished page to my secretary, Norma, who checked and rechecked it with particular attention to the English translation of Psalm 126, which the prime minister wrote down in its original Hebrew, and which I copied into English from a Gideon Bible I found in a bedside drawer. After going over the typed version one last time, I placed it in a luxurious black leather folder which I had brought with me from Jerusalem for the occasion, and carried it to the prime minister's suite, where I found him breakfasting with Foreign Minister Moshe Dayan and Defense Minister Ezer Weizman.

"Please place it on the desk by the window," he said. "If there are changes, I'll let you know."

Hearing nothing from him all morning, I pocketed his hand-written draft, and having shaved, showered and generally spruced myself up, boarded the minibus marked '*ISRAELI DELEGATION – Prime Minister's Staff*,' to be driven to Blair House, where Secretary of State Cyrus Vance was hosting a noon luncheon for the Egyptian, American, and Israeli delegations. The Begins and the Sadats were to lunch an hour later with the Carters at the White House, after which they were to step out onto the North Lawn for the signing ceremony before a crowd of dignitaries, at two o'clock sharp.

Traveling to Blair House down Connecticut Avenue, our American driver drew up at a traffic light, but General Poran suddenly began pounding the dashboard and ordered him not to stop. "Jump the light!" he commanded. But the man stared back at him bewildered, as did we all, not having seen what Freuka had seen in the rearview mirror – a band of thirty or so Arab demonstrators exiting a side street and rushing toward us, yelling slogans.

The driver inched forward, hooting, through the snarled traffic, but it was too late. The demonstrators swarmed around us, some carrying anti-peace placards, and all of them ranting wild curses and threats against Sadat and Begin and their peace treaty. Cowering, I peered out of the window at faces full of hate and venom, while my traveling companions seemed to be maintaining a remarkable sangfroid. But then a man with a kaffiyeh started to pound the roof with a stick; others whacked with their fists, booing, hissing, and spitting, and then they all began heaving the minibus from side to side. The driver, numb with dread, was incapable of running the tormentors down, even if he had wanted to. And as the vehicle pitched and tossed, we all stared fixedly ahead gripping our seats as best we might, until we were rescued by mounted police who, truncheons flying, cleared a path to let us through. The driver revved up the engine, gunned the vehicle forward, and pulled away with a tire-wrenching jerk, his knuckles white. When he brought us safely to our destination he acknowledged our thanks with a scowl, and hissed, "That's the last frigging time I'll ever drive Israelis again."

Checking ourselves in the large mirror of the Blair House entrance hall, we decided none of us looked the worse for wear, so we joined the crowd at the buffet table. Hardly had I picked up a salad plate when Ovad, a member of the prime minister's security detail, accosted me, telling me that Begin was searching for me urgently. He dialed a classified number and put me through.

"Mr. Begin, you're looking for me?" I panted.

"Yes, where's my speech?"

"On the desk by the window in your suite, where you told me to put it."

"No, not that one – my original."

"It's in my pocket. You need it?"

"Yes – immediately!"

"When are you leaving for the White House?"

"At twelve forty."

I looked at my watch. The dial said twelve twenty. A shiver ran down my spine. "I'll bring it over right away," I said, not having the slightest idea how. But then I spied Secretary of State Cyrus Vance casually chatting with an Egyptian, and in desperation, brandished the speech in his face and said with deadly seriousness, "Mr. Secretary, unless I get this document to Mr. Begin at the Hilton Hotel within ten minutes there will be no signing ceremony today."

He stared at me in disbelief.

"Come with me," he snapped, and he strode to the front door, where he collared a senior police officer who ran down the steps to a waiting police car, and ordered the cop inside, "Get this man to the Hilton in ten minutes or I'll have your head. Step on it."

Siren blaring, we hit eighty kilometers an hour within a block, whereupon the policeman extended a massive paw, and said, "*Sholom aleichem!* My name's Abie Finegold. I'm one of four Jewish cops on the Washington police force. Pleased to meet you."

"*Aleichem shalom*," I said, flabbergasted. "Are we going to make it?"

"Sure, you bet. When Abie Finegold presses on the gas, people know to keep out of my way. Hey, lady!" He was yelling at an aging driver in an aging car, at a signal light. "That light's green, and it isn't going to get any greener. Go! Go! Go!" He peeled off around her, and she made an obscene gesture as we passed by. Another car made the near fatal mistake of slowing at an intersection that had no stop sign or traffic light. Abie flashed his headlights, blasted his horn, raised the siren to an even higher hysterical pitch, did a sharp swerve, swore, and clucked, "Jeez, I almost hit the bastard." He swore again as he bore down on a forty-kilometer-an-hour sluggard, then tailgated a guy who, in despair, mounted the sidewalk to let him pass.

I was beginning to like this: High Noon on Connecticut Avenue, and I was Gary Cooper.

"*Mazal tov!* We made it!" chirped Abie, screeching to a halt in front of the Hilton.

The clock on the dashboard read 2:39.

I ran into the lobby just as Mr. and Mrs. Begin were exiting an elevator surrounded by a bevy of bodyguards.

"*Baruch Hashem!*" cried Begin when I handed him the pages. "Thank God you caught me!"

"The speech that I left on your desk – it's not what you wanted?" I asked, somewhat peeved. "You weren't happy with my changes?"

"Oh, no, they're fine," he assured me. "It's just that as I was going over the typed text I suddenly had the feeling that today of all days I want to read my own speech exactly as I wrote in my own hand." And to make the implicit explicit, he added, "I wrote it from the heart and I want to read it from the heart."

President Carter was the first to speak, then President Sadat, and then Prime Minister Begin. All three promised the sixteen hundred invited guests on the White House lawn, along with a worldwide television audience in the millions, that warfare between Egypt and Israel was banished forever. All three quoted, coincidentally, Isaiah's famous phrase about swords being beaten into plowshares. Yet even as they pronounced these stirring words, the shouts of thousands of Arab protestors from nearby Lafayette Park drifted across Pennsylvania Avenue toward the White House, a reminder that the whole of the Arab world was implacably opposed to the document to which the leaders had just put their signatures – the first treaty of peace between an Arab nation and the Jewish State.

Begin's address was by far the most highly charged with personal emotion. "Peace is the beauty of life," he sentimentalized. "It is sunshine. It is the smile of a child, the love of a mother, the joy of a father, the togetherness of a family. It is the advancement of man, the victory of a just cause, the triumph of truth."

To Sadat, he said, "It is a great day in your life, Mr. President of the Arab Republic of Egypt. In the face of adversity and hostility you have demonstrated the human value that can change history – civil courage. A great field commander once said, civil courage is sometimes more difficult to show than military courage. You showed both, Mr. President. But now it is time for all of us to show civil courage, in order to proclaim to our peoples and to others: no more war, no more bloodshed, no more bereavement – peace unto you; shalom, salaam, forever." And then, husky with emotion, "This is the proper place, and the appropriate time, to bring back to memory the song and the prayer of thanksgiving I learned as a child in the home of my father and mother, that doesn't exist anymore because they were among the six million people – men, women and children – who sanctified the Lord's name with their sacred blood which reddened the rivers of Europe from the Rhine to the Danube, from the Bug to the Volga, because – only because – they were born Jews; and because they didn't have a country of their own, nor a valiant Jewish army to defend them; and because nobody – *nobody* – came to their rescue, although they cried out 'Save us! Save us!' *de profundis*, from the depths of the pit and agony: that is the Song of Degrees written two millennia and five hundred years ago when our forefathers returned from their first exile to Jerusalem, to Zion."

Here Begin felt into his pocket and took out a black silk yarmulke, which he placed on his head, and in a gesture pregnant with symbolism, recited in the original Hebrew the whole of the Psalm of David – "*Shir hama'alot b'shuv Hashem et shivat Ziyon hayinu k'cholmim*" – without rendering it into English.

"I will not translate it," he said. "Every person, whether Jew, Christian or Moslem, can read it in his or her own language in the Book of Books. It is simply psalm one hundred and twenty-six."

A general applause greeted his remarks, and one could tell from the areas of louder applause where the Jewish groups were sitting. Everybody

Photograph credit: Ya'acov Sa'ar & Israel Government Press Office

The triple handshake: Sadat, Carter & Begin after signing the Israel-Egypt peace treaty, The White House, Washington, 26 March 1979

rose to their feet and clapped ecstatically when the three men wholeheartedly grasped each other in a three-way hand clasp, a picture of reconciliation so memorable that the cheers lingered on long after the three had departed the platform to reenter the White House.

That night, under a great orange and yellow marquee on the South Lawn – the marquee longer than the presidential mansion itself – more than thirteen hundred invitees gathered for a state banquet to celebrate the peace. The fifteen-page guest list offered the novel sight of Arab and Jewish names succeeding each other alphabetically. Practiced observers of Washington politics and politesse commented that it was the first time so many of the Washington social establishment had entered the Carter White House, making it the largest presidential dinner in memory.

Everybody seemed to know everybody else, and the guests mingled and table-hopped with all the informality of a high school reunion. I was chatting with Yitzhak Rabin when Henry Kissinger came threading his way through the crush, his arms open wide as though to embrace his old antagonist and friend.

"Yitzhak! What a day," he exclaimed, with a broad grin. "You and I can take pride in having helped to make this happen."

The former prime minister gave his half smile. "How many people here know that, Henry?" he said mildly. "How many people know that my nineteen seventy-five Sinai interim agreement with Sadat was the first step toward this peace?"

"And how many people know that I had to drive you crazy to make it happen?" quipped Kissinger, tease and truth in delicate balance.

"Forgive me, Henry," said Rabin in all seriousness. "We differed on details, but not substance. We both sought the same thing – disengagement and diffusion on the Egyptian front."

"And it sure worked," said Kissinger with a sparkle.

"Yes, it worked," concurred Rabin. "Imagine Sadat ever coming to Jerusalem if we'd still been shooting at each other in the Sinai, instead of building up mutual trust. Mind you" – this with undisguised admiration – "for all of Begin's opposition to my agreement at the time, once he assumed the premiership he handled matters brilliantly."

A flourish of trumpets and a standing ovation heralded the entry of the Egyptian president and the Israeli prime minister, along with their wives, accompanied by the American president and the first lady. All three men wore dark suits, while their wives displayed long dresses – Mrs. Carter in coral, Mrs. Sadat in beige, and Mrs. Begin in green. A protocol officer guided them to one of the scores of tables decorated with forsythia and yellow tulips, all illuminated by candles encased in miniature hurricane lamps.

"Excuse me, sir, are you Mr. Avner?" interrupted a middle-aged gentleman in a yarmulke, marking my own. "I'm general manager of Schleider's kosher caterers in Baltimore. I just want to make sure everything is satisfactory."

He had to pitch his voice high above the hubbub. His eyebrows rose in pleasure when I complimented him on the elegance of his catering.

"We had to prepare everything in such a rush," he said with professional pride. "It was only on Saturday night [this was Monday evening] that we got the call from the White House to supply one hundred and ten kosher meals for this banquet. They also asked us to prepare meals for Prime Minister and Mrs. Begin for the lunch with President Carter and President Sadat before the signing ceremony. I hope they enjoyed it."

"I'm sure they did," I answered, assuming they had.

He arched his neck and stood on his tiptoes, the better to see what was going on around him. "I have to keep an eye on my waiters to make sure they're serving the right people," he explained.

A discreetly colored place card marked the settings of the kosher farers, and his waiters wore a slightly different garb amid the small army of other waiters who were serving a menu of Columbia River salmon in aspic with cheese straws, followed by roast beef and spring vegetables, and a hazelnut and chocolate mousse for desert.

"As you see," he said, stretching out a hand toward a tray borne by one of his waiters, who was squeezing by us, "our kosher menu is similar to theirs – salmon mousse followed by boneless beef prime rib and the same variety of vegetables. For dessert we're serving chocolate mousse with non-dairy creamer."

Again, I expressed my admiration and he, now buoyant, elaborated, "We wanted to break out our finest gold flatware and our best service pieces for the occasion, but the White House told us to tone it down. Ours, they said, shouldn't be too different from theirs. And, as you see" – he was pointing to my own place setting – "they're not."

We were interrupted by the announcement of the toasts as waiters, squeezing between the densely packed tables, began passing out coffee, brandy, and cigars. Then came the entertainment, by artists representing the three signatory nations – the United States choosing soprano Leontyne Price, Egypt a trio playing guitar, drum, and electric organ, and Israel, the violinists Yitzhak Pearlman and Pinchas Zuckerman.

In the boisterous mingling that followed, I happened upon Ambassador Samuel Lewis, who had apparently just shared a joke with Secretary of State Cyrus Vance, a staid man as a rule, who was now bent over in a guffaw of laughter – until he saw me. With sudden earnestness he asked, "That document at Blair House you said you had to get to Mr. Begin without delay, otherwise there'd be no peace-signing – you weren't serious, were you?"

I described to him the stressful circumstances of that moment, and he took my explanation in the best of spirits. As we were talking someone squeezed up from behind, and Secretary Vance turned to greet a tall, pleasant-looking fellow in his sixties, whose keen, regular features and piercing blue eyes were wreathed in smiles. "Congratulations, Mr. Secretary," said the man. "I guess it's been a busy time for you these last few months, knocking this historic peace treaty together."

"And a few heads, too," said the Secretary, in jest.

He was speaking to Senator Henry "Scoop" Jackson, a cherished advocate of Israeli causes and a relentless champion on behalf of Jews locked behind the communist Iron Curtain.

"I don't pretend to know much about Sadat," said the senator, "but I know Mr. Begin to be a man of strong principle – tough to negotiate with, but his word is his bond."

"I'd certainly grant that," said Ambassador Lewis.

"Indeed so," said Vance, benevolently. "But one of the problems in this negotiation was that, unlike Sadat, Mr. Begin is a man of many words. It can be terribly irritating at times, but he relishes a good argument, sometimes just for the sheer sake of it. That's what makes him a good parliamentarian, I suppose. But in these peace negotiations we sometimes wasted a lot of time arguing about the meaning of words and, in the process, he occasionally got lost in the trees. That was one of the problems Sadat had with Begin. Sadat sees things broadly, his eye always on the horizon. He has no desire or willingness to get down to the nitty-gritty of arguing out the finer points of a document. He leaves that to his subordinates. Mr. Begin, on the other hand, can get lost in the small print; he's pedantic about semantics."

"But those semantics can be vital," said the senator, whose reputation as a tough negotiator was legendary, not least as a leading proponent of increased American aid to Israel, and blocking Soviet trade advantages with the U.S. so long as Russia's Jews were prohibited from leaving at will.

"Vital, yes, but you also have to take into account that Mr. Begin is a very good poker player," said Ambassador Lewis irreverently.

"Oh, that he is – a poker player, first class!" confirmed Vance. "He's as sharp as they come – one of the best interlocutors I've ever negotiated with."

"In what sense?" Jackson asked.

"In the sense that as I quickly learned when negotiating with him, he could sometimes display a wounded heart, as if to say in disbelief, 'How can you possibly ask me to make such a sacrifice?' And then he won't budge an inch, sitting his opponent out until *he* does the yielding. He can outsit the man on the other side of the table time and time again. That's what I call a good poker player."

"You make him sound devious," said Jackson. "I don't believe he is. The man genuinely believes what he says. He's haunted by the Holocaust. He's a patriot. He fears for his country's future. His whole life has been a struggle for Israel. There's no other side to him."

"I never suggested otherwise," said Vance defensively. "He certainly is a patriot, with the interests of his country at heart. Indeed, I've always found him very clear in his objectives, very precise in his thinking when it comes to Israel's defense. What I'm saying is, he sometimes will make a demand that he is later willing to sacrifice, as a bargaining chip. That's why he's such a skilful negotiator."

"I have to add, he has a masterly sense of timing," affirmed Lewis. "He can stonewall a situation, sending everybody nearly crazy, and then, at the very last minute, when everything seems about to collapse, he'll make a tiny concession that will, by then, look huge to everybody else. His instincts identify the very last moment to offer a compromise, by which time it looks like he's made a tremendous sacrifice. It's a brilliant negotiating technique."

"So, what comes next after this peace treaty?" Jackson asked.

"The West Bank and Gaza," replied Vance, solemnly. "Israel is committed to continuing ongoing talks with the Egyptians for self-rule for the Palestinians. Five years after the self-rule has been established it will be open to review."

"I hardly think Mr. Begin will be in a mood for West Bank concessions after those five years," said the senator, soberly.

"The Lord works in wondrous ways," said Vance, raising his eyes skyward as if in search of a miracle. "The Begin I know today won't budge from what he calls Judea and Samaria. He's made no bones about that. He said to me, 'I will never preside over the transfer of one inch of the Land of Israel to anyone else's sovereignty, because the country belongs to us. Others may come after me who might feel differently, but not me.' That's what he said."

"But he has agreed, has he not, to make no claims of Israeli sovereignty over the West Bank and Gaza during that five-year autonomy period, if and when it ever starts?" asked the senator.

"Indeed, he has. And when I've asked him what the sovereign disposition of the West Bank after those five years would be, the answer he gave me was, 'By that time I may not be around.'"

"That's what he said?"

"In those very words – 'I may not be around.'"[73]

The Washington ceremonies done, the prime minister flew to New York for a hero's welcome that included an extended weekend of public rallies, receptions, interviews, meetings with lay and religious leaders, and the mandatory fund-raising banquets for Israeli causes. It was a hectic, emotional, euphoric outpouring of Jewish wining, dining, and celebration, and Begin reveled in it. As was his wont, he spent the Sabbath day resting in his suite on the thirty-eighth floor of the Waldorf Astoria Hotel, but came Saturday eve and off he was, making a grand entrance into the hotel's grand ballroom where two thousand people, black-tied and evening-gowned, rose and roared their acclaim, and wrote out their checks for Israel with glittering abandon.

Then came the serious business of Sunday, whose morning program began with a visit to a modest Lower East Side apartment, there to pay respect to the world-renowned rabbinic luminary and leading halachic authority of the day, Rabbi Moshe Feinstein. This was followed by a CBS interview on *Face the Nation*, while in the prime minister's Waldorf Astoria suite on the thirty-eighth floor, another camera crew was setting up equipment for an interview of a different kind. It was to be a documentary for posterity – a relaxed soliloquy in which Mr. Begin would be given all the time he needed to talk candidly in depth about his life and times. The brainchild of Rabbi Alexander Schindler, head of the Conference of American Rabbis, the footage was intended for archival purposes, to be released at some unspecified future date. He and Begin were old friends, having worked closely together during Schindler's chairmanship of the Conference of Presidents of Major American Jewish Organizations.

As I sat with Schindler going over his notes, awaiting the prime minister's arrival, a demonstration was beginning to form on Park Avenue below. We knew that the police had granted a permit to an ultra-Orthodox group who were protesting an archeological dig in Jerusalem at a location called "Area G." Human bones had allegedly been uncovered at the site, thereby rendering the ground hallow. The group protesting were zealous disciples of the fanatically anti-Zionist, New York-based Satmar Rebbe, Rabbi Yoel Teitelbaum, many of whose followers were associated with a fanatical sect called *Neturei Karta* – Aramaic for Guardians of the City. To these Jews the State of Israel was, by its very existence, a secular blasphemy, a man-made obscenity, a sinful obstacle along the road to divine redemption.

The NYPD had assured us that while microphones would be used for speeches, the volume would not reach the prime minister's suite, thirty-eight floors above. Looking down, I could discern the cordoned-off area where the demonstration was beginning to assemble, between 49th and 50th Streets, right in front of the hotel. From where I stood, everything was in miniature. A mobile speaker's platform was positioned in the center of the block, on the south-bound lane. Hundreds of tiny beings, all garbed in black, were gradually filling the cordoned-off block in what seemed to be absolute silence. No street noise penetrated the multi-paned windows of the hotel suite; it all looked so neat, so symmetrical, so choreographed. The black was sprinkled with spots of dark blue, these being the policemen posted in no particular pattern. They wore no crash helmets, nor did they carry shields or batons. Jewish demonstrations were never violent, it was said. There was nothing sinister about the feel of it all. Indeed, I could not but marvel at the innocent civility of the occasion, how this great metropolis was taking in its stride an anti-Zionist, ultra-Orthodox Jewish demonstration on a Sunday afternoon in the very heart of Manhattan, and shrugging it off as just one more community of New Yorkers doing their own thing in their own way, as the law allows.

Unaware of the protestors below, the prime minister entered the lounge and greeted Schindler warmly. Then, observing me looking out of the window, he asked what was attracting my attention. When I told him he strode over to look down. "*Nu, nu,*" he said, "thank God America is a free country, where Jews can demonstrate without fear." He then clapped his hands, placed himself in the armchair facing the camera, and said with alacrity, "Shall we begin?" And the cameras rolled.

Schindler asked him about his home life as a youngster, his early years as a Zionist, his trials as commander of the Irgun underground, his frustrations as a politician, and his aspirations as a statesman. The most personal and difficult questions he left to the end – those about the fate of the Begin family during the Holocaust; what their slaughter had done to him as a man, and as a Jew. And, yes, where was God?

As Begin began to explain the meaning of *kiddush Hashem* – the sanctification of the Almighty's name, even in the hell of the Holocaust – something diabolical occurred. The sound system below was turned up full blast, and a speaker was heard damning Begin as a Nazi, and calling upon the United Nations to dismantle the Jewish State. Begin, seemingly unaware of the intrusion, continued to dwell at length on what he called his *ani ma'amin* – his credo – on why, even after the Holocaust, he remained a believing Jew.

But now the single voice grew to a chorus, which gradually swelled into a roar, as hundreds of distant voices from the street below welled up, yelling in unison a chilling curse in a rhythmic beat, "*Begin, yemach shimcha! Begin, yemach shimcha!*"

As the protestors were calling down the wrath of God upon the prime minister, to obliterate his name from the face of the earth, he did not stop talking about his undiminished belief in *Elokei Yisrael* – the God of Israel. In an almost whisper, staring straight into the camera, he said, "After the Holocaust, there is no command more supreme than that a Jew should never abuse another Jew, should never lift a finger against another Jew, and should endeavor to love his neighbor as himself." And as he said these words, his eyes reddened, and he left the room.

Chapter fourteen

The Child in El Arish

A couple of months later, in the early hours of Sunday morning 27 May, four tourist buses, two Egyptian and two Israeli, came from opposite directions along the coastal road of northern Sinai, bound for El Arish. In those days, El Arish was a sand swept, lazy oasis of some forty-five thousand souls, anchored in desert dunes and lapped by a velvet sea. It was also the administrative capital of the Sinai, which was why Prime Minister Menachem Begin and President Anwar Sadat had chosen to meet there on that May morning for its ceremonial transfer back to Egyptian rule. The implementation of the peace treaty had begun and, with it, the gradual withdrawal of the Israel Defense Forces from Sinai.

The passengers in the tourist buses were not tourists. They were disabled veterans of the two armies, who had charged at each other across the sands of Sinai, in tanks, in half-tracks, in gun carriers, in command cars, in helicopters, and in aircraft, attacking each other in combat in many wars, over many decades. Now, at Begin's instigation and with Sadat's concurrence, the wounded veterans had agreed to rendezvous at El Arish in a gesture of chivalrous reconciliation.

Prior to their arrival, honor guards and military bands of both armies had marched in unison across the parade ground in files of five, as the prime minister and the president took the salute. It was a thrilling spectacle to view at first, but then the bugles sounded, signaling the lowering of the Israeli flag and the raising of the Egyptian one. Watching it, many a

Jewish face turned momentarily melancholy, showing an indefinable disquiet. Who knew how long this peace would last?

In rigid homage, the two leaders listened to the playing of their national anthems, after which they retired for a private talk, while a number of us, members of the entourage, strolled to the nearby flag-bedecked recreation hall where the wounded veterans were to rendezvous.

The Egyptian buses arrived first. They churned up much desert dust as they came into view, and drew to a halt at the entrance to the hall. There must have been about seventy men in all, resplendent in fresh uniforms of different rank and insignia, and all lavishly decorated in campaign medals. Their descent from the buses was painfully slow. Some were missing a foot, others a leg. At least four had had both legs amputated. Some wore hook-like contraptions where their hands had been, and the sleeves of those without arms were neatly folded back and pinned at the shoulder. A number were grotesquely disfigured; others blind. They walked, wheeled and limped their way into the hall's cool interior, on crutches, with canes, and in wheelchairs. Medical orderlies guided them to the far end of the hall, where they were handed refreshments.

Five minutes later the two Israeli buses, red and cream-colored, pulled up, and the scene repeated itself. One by one, the Israeli war invalids emerged, some lame, some disfigured, some with artificial limbs, some paralyzed, some blind. Unlike the Egyptians, however, none wore uniforms or decorations of any sort. In wheelchairs, or leaning on crutches and canes, they were assisted by medical orderlies as they hobbled and rolled their way into the hall, lining up opposite the Egyptians.

Silence!

Eyes locked in a palpable maelstrom of conflicting emotions. The wounded appraised each other, as if striving to pick out the one who had pressed the trigger, pulled the pin, pushed the button. Gallant though this encounter was, no one had thought it through to the end. Nobody knew what to do or to say as the two groups of smashed men confronted one another across a distance of ten or twelve yards, that was an impassable no-man's land. A restless stirring gripped the hall. Some asked orderlies to get them out. The wounds were too fresh.

Close to where I was standing, an Israeli in his thirties, blind, bent low to embrace a whimpering child. The child was eight or nine, with big eyes as black as his curly hair. Their resemblance was striking.

"*Kach oti eleihem*" [Take me to them], whispered the father, but the child looked up at his father pleadingly. "*Ani m'fached mihem*," [I'm scared of them], he sniveled. Gently, the father nudged the child forward and, timidly, the boy led the father into the no-man's land. At his very first step, an Egyptian officer in a wheelchair, legless, began rolling himself toward them. They met in the middle and the officer placed the blind man's palm into his own, and shook it. Instantly, the tension eased. A Jew began to clap; he was joined by an Arab. The sprinkling of claps quickly swelled into a burst of boisterous applause as the two groups moved toward each other, melting into a huddle of embraces, handshakes, and backslapping. With laughter and tears, the maimed soldiers of the 1948 war, the 1956 Sinai War, the 1967 Six-Day War, the 1970 Attrition War, and the 1973 Yom Kippur War fell on one another, calling out "Shalom!" "Salaam!" "Peace!"

It was in the midst of this embrace that Prime Minister Begin and President Sadat entered, and the applause rose to an even higher pitch. The two leaders circulated among the men, asking about their wounds and where they had fought. And when the two leaders mounted the rostrum to laud their brave armies and their wounded veterans, many in the crowd wept and called out to each other in Hebrew, in Arabic, and in English: "L'chayim!" "Lihayot!" "To life!"

Enveloped in the midst of this raucous camaraderie, the child clung tightly to his blind father. He looked bewildered, his eyes darting back and forth at the animated faces of Arab and Jew. As long as he could remember, he had played escort to a father who would never see because he had been made blind by these Arabs. To him, they would always be the enemy and, by definition, bad. Sensing his son's apprehension, the blind man lifted his child into his arms, kissed him gently, and said, "*Al t'fached b'ni. Ha'Aravim ha'eyle tovim*" [Don't be afraid my son. These Arabs are good].

British Prime Minister Margaret Thatcher receiving Prime
Minister Begin at 10 Downing Street, 25 May 1979

Chapter fifteen

Begin's Bag and Baggage

A few months later, Mr. Begin was invited to London, as a guest of the Anglo-Jewish community. It was not all that long ago that many of its elders had cold-shouldered the man as a nationalist lunatic, but now they were opening their doors wide to him, as a world statesman. It was in this spirit that Prime Minister Margaret Thatcher hosted him for lunch at 10 Downing Street.

Few things tickled Mr. Begin's fancy more than walking across the threshold of Number 10, for it was there, in the mid-1940s, that the order had been given to promise ten thousand pounds – what was then a huge sum – as a reward for information leading to his capture, dead or alive. Amazingly, now, British reporters were still pillorying him, and one, a bald man with the shape of a beer barrel, bellowed from the other side of the street as the prime minister emerged from his limousine, "Mr. Begin, people in Britain still call you a wanted terrorist. Any comment?"

Begin crossed over to the scrum of newsmen, and in an eminently reasonable tone said to the man, "You really want my comment?"

"Yes, I do."

"Then you shall have it. Kenyan Mau Mau leaders visit Britain and they are called freedom fighters. Cypriot insurgents, Irish revolutionaries, and Malaysian militias visit Britain, and they are all called freedom fighters. Only I am called a terrorist. Is that because I was a *Jewish* freedom fighter?"

"Are you going to ask Mrs. Thatcher for her support of the recognition of Jerusalem as Israel's capital?" fired another, in a la-di-da accent. He was tall, smartly dressed in a blue serge suit, with a silk handkerchief neatly tucked into his breast pocket.

Frigidly, the prime minister answered. "No, sir – under no circumstances."

"Why not?"

"Because, sir, Jerusalem was a Jewish capital long before London was a British capital. When King David moved the capital of his kingdom from Hebron, where he had reigned for seven years, to Jerusalem, where he reigned for thirty-three years, the civilized world had never heard of London. In fact, they had never heard of Great Britain," and he turned on his heels toward the door, where Mrs. Thatcher was waiting to greet him.

Over pre-lunch drinks, the talk was largely about the British leader's support for the worldwide Jewish campaign on behalf of Jews in the Soviet Union who wished to emigrate to Israel.

"Those who manage to get out, are they readily absorbed in your country?" asked Thatcher. "Do they set down roots easily?"

Begin, who loved telling a story to illustrate a point, and who could be a flatterer if not a flirt in dealing with women, answered in a velvety tone, "Oh, they set down roots all right – excellent roots. Their contribution to our society is enormous. And I can well imagine your predecessor, Mr. Churchill, asking the very same question in this very same room."

"How so?" asked the lady, intrigued.

"Because," said Begin jovially, "when Churchill first visited us in nineteen twenty-one, Tel Aviv was little more than a few houses on sandy streets. So the then mayor, Meir Dizengoff, anxious to make a good impression, had several large trees transplanted to the entrance of his little town hall to give it color. However, the pressure of the crowd was so great that one of the trees toppled over, almost hitting Mr. Churchill. And he, dusting himself down, was heard to say, "My dear mayor, if you want to make an impression you must set down deeper roots. Without roots, it won't work.""

The general laughter was followed by the British prime minister regaling her guest with stories expressive of her fervent admiration of Jews. "It has to do with my Methodist upbringing," she exclaimed. "Methodism, you see, means method. It means" – her fingers bunched into a fist – "sticking to your guns, dedication, determination, triumph over adversity, reverence for education – the very qualities you Jews have always cherished."

Begin responded with a small, modest smile. "I cannot deny," he said, "that millennia ago, when monarchs did not even know how to sign their own names, our forefathers had already developed a system of compulsory education."

Thatcher's eyes were ablaze with enthusiasm: "Your marvelous chief rabbi here, Sir Immanuel [later Lord] Jakobovits, recently made exactly the same point. He said to me that the term, 'an illiterate Jew,' is an oxymoron. How right he is! He has ..." – she paused as if to replenish her stock of awe and respect – "such a high moral stature, such an inspiring commitment to the old-fashioned virtues, like community self-help, individual responsibility, and personal accountability – all the things I deeply believe in." And then, in a voice that was surprisingly acrid, "Oh, how I wish our own church leaders would take a leaf out of your chief rabbi's book."

Begin nodded, but said nothing. Perhaps this was because he thought it would be indiscreet to concur, or perhaps it was because he and the British chief rabbi did not always see eye-to-eye on the Jewish State's vision of itself.

The two prime ministers were standing chatting in the Blue Room. A butler appeared at the door and, emitting a discreet may-I-have-your-attention-please cough, announced, "Prime Ministers, Gentlemen, lunch is served."

"Do you know," continued Mrs. Thatcher doughtily, as she led the way into the oak-paneled dining room, "in all the many years I have represented Finchley, my parliamentary constituency, which as you know has a high proportion of Jewish residents, I have never once had a Jew come to me in poverty and desperation. They are always so well looked after by their own. And that is absolutely splendid!"

Pundits would postulate that it was this cast of mind that accounted for the remarkably high number of Jews in the various Thatcher governments – six at one time or another, not to speak of close advisers. And in a class-conscious society like Britain where the aristocracy was almost solidly Anglican, her Methodist roots made her an ambitious outsider. So it was perhaps natural for her, the daughter of a grocer, to see Jews as kindred spirits.

"Now, let's talk about your country," said Thatcher. They had reached the dining room table, accompanied by half a dozen cabinet colleagues and aides. Through the window one could catch a glimpse of the prime minister's lanky husband, Dennis, practicing putting on the back lawn, while from their gilded frames, Viscount Horatio Nelson and the Duke of

Wellington stared down haughtily at the oblong table that seated four on each side. As Begin took his place alongside Thatcher, he gestured toward me with his chin, and muttered, "Yehuda, *mach hamotzi.*"*

He was indicating a low corner table bedecked with a white silk Sabbath cloth draped over a plaited loaf of Sabbath bread – a challah – on a silver platter, together with an ornamental Sabbath bread knife, a jug of water, a glass bowl, and a hand towel embroidered with a Sabbath blessing, in Hebrew. A card placed discreetly by the bread, read, "Under the Supervision of the Sephardic Kashrut Commission."

In her eagerness to please, this ever-vigilant, tough woman known as the "Iron Lady" had gone overboard in ensuring our kosher fare by turning a regular Tuesday lunch into a traditional Sabbath-style feast, with all its attendant ritual regalia. This left me wondering what best to do. The room went as mute as a tomb and I could feel Mrs. Thatcher's sharp-edged gaze playing on my back, waiting for the ritual to begin. So, with nowhere to hide, I canonically performed the hand-washing libations, recited the blessing, cut the challah, which was so fresh it crumbled to pieces in my hands, chewed on a piece and, stomach tight, danced around the table, bowed, and proffered our hostess the crumbled bread on the silver platter, intoning, "Madame Prime Minister, wilt thou break bread with me?"

Thatcher was charmed. "Oh, what a delightful custom," she cooed. "I must tell protocol about this. We should do it more often."

Lord Peter Carrington, the foreign secretary, who was full of the self-confident repartee common to graduates of Eton and Sandhurst, ho-hummed in the authoritative, patronizing warble of the British upper class: "I bet you a wager, Mr. Begin, that I know what passed through your mind when I was introduced to you before."

"Do you, Lord Carrington? I'm not a betting man, but please tell me: what did pass through my mind?" An impudent smile hovered over Begin's features. All at the table were grinning at the banter.

The foreign secretary chuckled devilishly. "You were thinking to yourself: By George, those Camel Corps chaps at the British Foreign Office are a bunch of Arabists besotted with an irredeemable proclivity toward Arab interests. Am I not right? Come on – own up." He gave an audacious smile and wagged a finger to add to the tease.

Begin raised his arms in a don't-shoot pose, his eyes bright with

---

* Yiddish for "make the blessing over bread."

mirth. "How did you guess, Lord Carrington? You are totally correct! And you put it so succinctly."

Everybody let out peals of laughter, and Thatcher, laying on all her charm, said sportingly, "Oh, come, come, Prime Minister, you know Peter's just joking. Israel has good friends here in Whitehall, even if we don't always see eye-to-eye on everything." And then, solicitously, "How do you find the salmon? It's specially catered – kosher."

"Delicious. Your thoughtfulness is appreciated." And then, back to the foreign secretary, who was sitting opposite him: "What, pray, do we not see eye-to-eye about these days?" He was desirous of moving on to the crux of things.

Lord Carrington's gung-ho manner vanished. Flatly, he answered, "Your bag and baggage approach toward settlements, mostly."

A fiery light appeared in the Israeli prime minister's eyes. "Bag and baggage?"

"That's what I said," replied Carrington, and he stepped into the ring and began punching hard, one-two, one-two, one-two: "Your settlement policy is expansionist. It is intemperate. It is a barrier to peace. The settlements are built on occupied Arab soil. They rob Palestinians of their land. They unnecessarily arouse the animosity of the moderate Arabs. They are contrary to international law – the Geneva Convention. They are inconsistent with British interests."

In a voice like steel wrapped in velvet, Margaret Thatcher affirmed, "The foreign secretary is speaking on behalf of Her Majesty's government in this matter."

Begin chose to fight Carrington, not Thatcher. He leaned forward to focus his fullest attention on him, and the looks traded were malevolent. Then he let fly.

"The settlements, sir, are not an obstacle to peace. The Arabs refused to make peace before there was a single settlement anywhere. No Palestinian Arab sovereignty has ever existed in the biblical provinces of Judea and Samaria, where most of the new settlements are located, hence the Geneva Convention does not apply. Besides, we are building the settlements on state-owned, not Arab-owned land. Their construction is an assertion of our basic historic rights, not to speak of their critical importance to our national security."

Lord Carrington's face went blotchy. He would have none of it. Tempers were at flash point.

Abruptly, Begin turned to face Margaret Thatcher. "Madame Prime

Minister," he said, in a voice pitched to hit hard, "your foreign secretary dismisses my country's historic rights and pooh-poohs our vital security needs. So, I shall tell *you* why the settlements are vital: because I speak of the Land of Israel, a land redeemed, not occupied; because without those settlements Israel could be at the mercy of a Palestinian state astride the commanding heights of Judea and Samaria. We would be living on borrowed time. And," – his face went granite, like his eyes – "whenever we Jews are threatened or attacked we are always alone. Remember in nineteen forty-four, how we came begging for our lives – begging at this very door?"

The British premier's brow creased in concentration, and she muttered pensively, "Nineteen forty-four? Is that when you wanted us to bomb Auschwitz?"

"No, Madame, not Auschwitz. We asked you to bomb the railway lines *leading* to Auschwitz. In the summer of nineteen forty-four, Eichmann was transporting to their deaths a hundred thousand Hungarian Jews a week along those lines to Auschwitz."

Thatcher cupped her chin in profound contemplation, "You know, Prime Minister," she said bluntly, after a momentary pause, "I have at times wondered what I would have done had I been here at Number Ten in those days. And I have to tell you in all candor, the policy of the Allies in those years was to destroy the Hitlerite war machine as speedily as possible. I would have agreed to nothing that would have detracted one iota from that goal."

Menachem Begin went white. Clearly, the woman had not been briefed who this man was – a survivor of the Holocaust, orphaned of virtually his whole family.

"But Madame, this was nineteen forty-four," he said, in a low voice reserved for dreaded things. "The Allies had all but won the war. You were sending a thousand bombers a night over Germany. What would it have taken to divert fifty, sixty, seventy aircraft to bomb those lines?"

"And what does this have to do with the settlements?" Thus, Carrington, barging in with malign consistency.

Begin, livid, turned on him and snapped: "Lord Carrington, please have the goodness not to interrupt me when I am in the middle of a conversation with your prime minister. Do I have your permission to proceed?"

Carrington went puce.

The shocked silence was interrupted only when Mrs. Thatcher, in a gesture of uncommon informality, placed a calming hand on Begin's arm, and said, "Please do not allow yourself to get upset. You are truly among friends here. In my constituency, I go to synagogue more often than I go

to church. And whenever there is crisis in your country half of my con-
stituents disappear, and I know exactly where they are. They have gone to
you. They have gone to Israel, to help."

"Precisely, Madame Prime Minister," said Begin. "As I said, whenever
we are threatened or attacked, we have only our own fellow Jews to rely on."

"Peter," said Mrs. Thatcher softly, "I think an admission of regret is
called for."

The foreign secretary took off his spectacles, breathed on them, and
polished each lens in turn with a handkerchief from the top pocket of his
Saville Row suit. He seemed to be about to speak, but hesitated, and then
he made up his mind. "Quite right, Prime Minister," he said apologetically.
"Somehow, your little country, Mr. Begin, evokes all sorts of high emotional
fevers. Stirs up the blood, so to speak."

Begin, his composure regained, smiled at him, the smile not reaching
his eyes. "The story of our people is very much a tale of having to defend
ourselves against bouts of irrationality and hysteria," he said. "It happens
in every generation."

"Quite, quite," said Prime Minister Thatcher, seemingly mystified
at this reflection. And then, desirous of steering into calmer waters, she
said in a conciliatory tone, "Let's talk about our bilateral trade relations.
I believe they are excellent." And for the next ten minutes all concurred
that indeed they were, after which the talk began to peter out, and then it
was time to go.[74]

This conversation remained etched in my mind when, a few years later, still
during the Thatcher years, I served as Israel's ambassador in London, and
often encountered passionate expressions of disapproval of Israel's policies –
from journalists mainly – couched in a language that seemed to me to be
more offensive than necessary. When that happened, Lord Carrington's
words would invariably come to mind: "Somehow, your little country
evokes all sorts of high emotional fevers. Stirs up the blood, so to speak."

Why was this so? I wondered. Where did genuine criticism end
and bigotry begin?

It did not take long for me to realize that an anti-Semitic bigotry of
sorts still lingered in segments of the British landed class, which constituted the true aristocracy of Britain. I encountered it firsthand more than
once, sometimes subtly, sometimes brazenly, including one memorable
incident in 1985, during a banquet celebrating Queen Elizabeth's official
birthday, at Hampton Court Palace.

The tabloids were reaping an abundant harvest that year from the goings-on in the royal family, and Henry VIII's Great Hall at the palace, with its sixteenth-century Flemish tapestries and soaring ceiling, was abuzz with salacious gossip about Britain's future king, Charles Prince of Wales, husband of the widely adored Princess Diana, who, it appeared, had taken for himself a mistress. Her name was Camilla Parker Bowles, and she was a married woman. To my right sat a baroness whose name I do not recall, but whose appearance was unforgettable. She had the face of a haughty Pekingese, a long neck noosed in yards of pearls, a prominent Adam's apple, and she was dressed in a fussy fire-engine red.

"Charles has taken a feather out of Henry the Eighth's cap, I wager," she remarked in a tone ringing with reproach. "Did you know that after Henry married Anne Boleyn in fifteen thirty-three he still played hanky-panky with her sister, Mary – and their mother, too, right here in Hampton Court. Did you know that?"

I confessed that I hadn't.

"And at the very same time, he was also conducting an affair with a wench called Elizabeth Blount, also right here in Hampton Court. Did you know that?"

Again, I admitted that I hadn't.

"And did you know that not only was she his mistress, she gave birth to his only son?"

Once more, I acknowledged my ignorance.

The woman stared sharply at me through her pince-nez as if to say 'You are a nincompoop,' and then cast a jaundiced eye at the white-gloved butler, who was obsequiously placing a gold plate of kosher cuisine before me.

"Where are you from?" she snapped.

"Israel," I said.

"Oh, there. Bah!" and she tucked into her own dish, brimming with contempt.

Whether this was meant as a slur against my beliefs, a slight at my ignorance, or a sweep at my country I did not have time to fathom, for now the woman on my left – a Lady Carpenter, wife of the Dean of Westminster Abbey – marked my meal and began pontificating about the virtues of religious traditions. She was a trim, middle-aged dowager of pious appearance – no make-up, no jewelry, her silvery hair simply done, her dress unadorned. The fellow next to her, a husky, soldierly type in his early seventies, with an aristocratic nose, glossy bald head, and piercing blue eyes, joined in, declaring jovially, "By sheer chance, I partook of a kosher meal myself in New York last week."

"How interesting," gasped Lady Carpenter. She sounded quite spellbound.

"I was out with a Moslem chap, a Pakistani," he elaborated. "And since we couldn't find a hallal restaurant we ended up in a kosher one. Good chicken soup, I can tell you. Ha, ha!"

He spoke in a refined accent, and a crimson sash crossed his chest, decorated with royal insignia and military honors. Proffering his hand, he said, "My name is Howard, but people call me Norfolk."

I blushed at my gaucherie, for I had failed to recognize the Duke of Norfolk, Premier Earl of the English peerage and chief layman of the English Catholic church.

"Dr. Inamullah Kahn, that was the Pakistani's name – secretary-general of the World Moslem Congress," he explained. "And we'd just awarded him the Templeton Prize."

The Templeton Prize is one of the most munificent prizes in the world – a tidy $1,500,000 – and is awarded for innovative contributions to the harmonious coexistence of religion and science. I deduced that the Duke was a member of its panel of judges.

"And do you know," he piped on, "an influential New York lobby had the effrontery to try and pressure us at the last minute to withdraw the prize."

"Really, Your Grace?" sighed Lady Carpenter. "How dreadful! But why would they want to do such a thing?" Her voice trailed off into whispery woe.

"Because, Madame," answered the Duke with alacrity, "Dr. Inamullah Kahn is a friend and supporter of Yasser Arafat and his cause, that's why."

"And who is this lobby?" I asked, antlers rising.

"Oh, come, come, Ambassador, you know as well as I do who the lobby is." His expression was prim, his lips a tight smile.

"No. Who?"

"The Jew press of New York, of course."

"The what?"

"The Jew press of New York," he gamely repeated.

I could not believe my ears. "You're an anti-Semite, sir," I stuttered.

"Am I? It never occurred to me." He seemed genuinely taken aback.

Apparently alarmed at my breathlessness, Lady Carpenter began rubbing my back, cooing, "Ambassador, please do not let the wounds of two thousand years be reopened. Let me mollify them with the balm of Jerusalem."

And as she rubbed, the Duke of Norfolk said over and over again, "Nothing personal, old boy – nothing personal."

These theatrics were halted by former Prime Minister Harold Wilson, who stepped over and said to me, "What are *you* doing here?"

"I was invited," I said.

"But didn't the president ask you to accompany him to Moscow?"

"No," I said.

"Oh my God, don't tell me. I'm getting old. I've done it again. You're not Henry Kissinger. You're the Jordanian ambassador. Forgive me," and off he strode, genuinely aghast at himself.

Meanwhile, the red-liveried toastmaster began barking for silence, and commanded everybody to rise for the Loyal Toast. Everybody did, and then we all settled down for the speeches.

Orations done, the guests moved into an adjacent grand parlor, where brandy, liqueurs, coffee, and cigars were proffered, and a string quintet was playing Bach. Amid the hubbub I came face to face with the baroness, who was enjoying a tipple. She was standing under a Gainsborough, not far from the secretary of state for Scotland, Malcolm Rifkind, who was engaged in a vehement conversation with the head of the Liberal Party, David Steel. By now a trifle inebriated, the baroness, sneered "Look at them – politicians! Talk! Talk! Talk!"

"Scotsmen do seem to have much to talk about," I bantered, for want of anything better to say.

A derisive expression spread across the baroness's face, and with a jerk of her chin in Rifkind's direction, scoffed, "He's not a Scotsman, he's one of yours."

That was enough! Earlier, this insufferable woman had addressed me with a mixture of paternalism and hauteur. Now, it was pure hauteur – anti-Semitic hauteur. Irate, I retorted: "How can you say that a man born in Edinburgh, raised in Edinburgh, educated in Edinburgh, represents a constituency in Edinburgh, and is the secretary of state for Scotland, is not a Scotsman?"

The baroness's lips twisted into a disdainful smile as she pointed in the direction of yet another Jew who was a member of Prime Minister Thatcher's cabinet – the secretary of state for trade and industry, Lord David Young. Scornfully, she hissed, "Young's an Englishman as much as Rifkind's a Scotsman."

Aghast, I began scanning the big room in search of other Jewish members of Margaret Thatcher's cabinet. "Look," I said challengingly, "There's Keith Joseph, secretary of state for education. And over there is Leon Britain, the home secretary. And by the window is Nigel Lawson, the chancellor of the exchequer. And there's Michael Howard, minister of state for local government – in addition to Malcolm Rifkind and David Young. So what do you make of that? How come Mrs. Thatcher has so many Jews in her cabinet?"

Her eyes held a vicious glint, as smoothly, snottily, the baroness answered, "Because Margaret Thatcher is most comfortable among the lower middle class," and off she went.

Still, while I would come across many a haughty and hidebound aristocrat of the baroness's breed, there were also numerous high-ranking types who thought Jews admirable and the Jewish State remarkable. I had known one such for years, and had arranged to meet him during my trip to London with Prime Minister Begin shortly after the rather crabby luncheon at 10 Downing Street. The appointment was at yet another refined address, this one at the corner of Pall Mall and Waterloo Place – The Athenaeum. The Athenaeum is one of London's celebrated gentlemen's clubs, built at a time when Britain ruled the waves and when its masters concentrated their phenomenal power in the drawing rooms of gentlemen's clubs all along London's Pall Mall, once the epicenter of the world's largest empire.

When one enters the Athenaeum, a sign beneath a nude statue catches the eye: *TIES MUST BE WORN AT ALL TIMES.* A porter in the doorway, with a gaunt face made grand by white muttonchop whiskers, asked me my business. I told him I was looking for Sir Herbert Hardwick.

"Sir Erbert Ardwick is 'ere, upstairs, 'aving a drink," he advised me.

I found the gentleman at the entrance to an expansive chandeliered parlor. It was a mausoleum of a place, hung with portraits of the Victorian upper crust haughtily gazing upon an array of dozing, reclining and or conversing men: cabinet ministers, senior civil servants, church dignitaries, and other assorted celebrities, all of them over sixty. Sir Herbert had not changed a bit over the years I had known him. He wore a pinstripe suit, held a bowler hat in one hand and a tightly rolled umbrella in the other, and his face was staid and melancholy.

"I'll just pop these in the cloak room," he said, indicating his hat and umbrella, and off he strode, with the ramrod posture of a British grenadier.

We had initially met in early 1967, when I was at a gathering in

London to mark the anniversary of the Balfour Declaration, at which Sir Herbert spoke. It was hosted by a group of parliamentarians – friends of Israel – in a Westminster reception hall. When the proceedings were done, Sir Herbert asked me if I would care to join him for tea on the parliamentary terrace, and there, munching scones with Devonshire cream, he revealed that his father, whom he referred to as Pater, a former Colonial Office man, had been of the same old Scottish lineage as the famed Lord Arthur James Balfour, and a devout Presbyterian, as was he. It was due to this pedigree that he had been prevailed upon to speak at this annual commemoration of Lord Balfour's historic 1917 declaration proclaiming in the name of His Majesty's Government that Britain "views with favor" the establishment in Palestine of "a national home for the Jewish people," thereby giving the Zionist enterprise its first vote of approval from a significant power. I was to learn, further, that his father had been closely acquainted with Blanche (Baffy) Dugdale, Lord Balfour's niece, and one of Chaim Weizmann's closest confidantes.

"Baffy used to conduct a Zionist salon luncheon in the private room of a Soho restaurant, to which my Pater was often bid," he revealed. "They would dine in the company of such Christian Zionists as Orde Wingate, Wyndham Deeds, and C.P. Scott." And then, with some fervor, "Indeed, under Pater's influence, I have been strongly infused in the Hebraism of the Old Testament and the People of the Book. And I can tell you that the Christian religion and civilization owe to Judaism an immeasurable debt, shamefully ill-repaid. Hence, Israel's future welfare seems to me of immense moral importance."

He went on to recount with a self-deprecating chuckle how, back in the 1950s, he had pulled family strings to get himself appointed as a junior diplomat to the British Embassy in Tel Aviv. "But I didn't last very long," he said wistfully. "I was so pro-Zionist my ambassador cabled London to say I'd been stricken by what one nowadays calls the Jerusalem syndrome, and was promptly sent packing. All my subsequent postings were to Eastern Europe, where I became something of an expert on the Soviet bloc."

Upon retirement, given his expertise in Soviet affairs, Sir Herbert became a firm and useful advocate of the "Let My People Go" movement, which lobbied aggressively worldwide for the right of Jews to leave the Soviet Union. This, together with his passion for Israel, brought him periodically to Jerusalem, invariably accompanied by a colleague or two from the Institute of Strategic Affairs, of which he was a senior fellow. It was in the lobby of the King David Hotel that I had next bumped into him, in June 1967, during the excruciatingly tense days leading up to the Six-Day War. Not recognizing one another at first, we both hesitantly searched our memories for the right identification, and his penny dropped first.

"By George," he warbled, "you're the chap I had tea with at the Balfour affair a few months ago," and he pumped my hand, spilling over with goodwill. I responded in kind, and invited him to join the clusters of war correspondents sipping drinks on the hotel's terrace, in full view of the spectacular Old City walls. Incongruously, Sir Herbert was still wearing his pinstripe suit and bowler hat. His face was more staid and melancholy than ever as he confided the chilling thought that Israel's days were surely numbered.

"How can it be otherwise?" he had said gloomily, in his top-drawer accent. "How can you save yourselves now? How can your small army withstand the combined might of all the Arab armies that are ganging up against you even as we speak?"

He cast an eye at the Old City's walls, on whose ramparts Arab Legionnaires stood watch.

"And, besides, they have the Soviet Union behind them, in addition to the tens of millions of Muslims the world over, with their oil and other fabulous riches, while you have been abandoned even by your so-called friends." His depressing assessment was getting to me. He continued, lamenting, "And even if you do somehow stave them off now, in ten or twenty years time the Palestinians will catch up with you numerically. Egypt's population will have burgeoned to seventy-five million, and Saudi Arabia's to twenty-five. Multiply that by the Arab birthrate overall and what do you get? You get a raging horde of Arabs, most of whom will be younger than thirty-five. There is no way Israel will be able to withstand that kind of hostile demographic pressure."

He stared darkly into his empty glass, lips pursed in a frown of despondency, and ordered yet another drink. This last induced him to talk elliptically about "Nasser's rabble" and "America's perfidy," and "Europe's duplicity" and "plucky Israelis," and "IDF grit," and "we shall never surrender" and "silver linings."

When we rose to part, he did something very uncharacteristic for his class. He put a hand on my shoulder and let it linger for a while, as he said, in a voice cracked with anxiety, "It's simply bad luck, old boy. Bad luck has always stomped through the lives of you Jews. The balance is tipped against you. I'm flying home tonight. It will take a paradigm shift for you to survive this thing," and off he went, his torso rigid, as though he couldn't find the courage to turn around and bid a final farewell.

Now, twelve years later, in the stolid Victorian ambience of the Athenaeum Club, he was as tall and straight as ever, possessed of the rigor and energy which often went with Presbyterianism, and manifestly full of beans.

"Well, well, how things have improved," he enthused, and he began to tick off our changes of fortune one by one with the tips of his fingers, "One, you've beaten off all the Arab armies every time. Two, your Mr. Begin has signed a peace agreement with the biggest, the strongest, and the most influential of all the Arab states – Egypt. Three, the Arab states are helpless without Egypt, so the war option is all but dead. Four, your other neighbors will have to make peace with you sooner or later. Five, your victories have clipped the Soviet Union's wings good and proper. Six, the struggle for Soviet Jewry is bearing fruit and you'll soon be bringing in tens of thousands of Russian immigrants, boosting your population by God knows how many. And to think" – this with an abashed, self-deprecating smile – "I was stupid enough to predict your tribe would go under. I was talking rubbish, utter bollocks! Mind you" – his jolliness momentarily lagged – "there's still Iran and Iraq to reckon with. But, chins up, old chap! The tide is turning, nevertheless. The wind is at your back. Stand fast. Be strong and of good courage. Fear not – time is on your side!" And with this evangelistic flourish, he took a swig of his Black Label.

"Banjo, you old windbag, who's this you're yapping at?" I looked up to see a tall, balding fellow, with a sharp crooked nose and eagle eyes framed in square rimless spectacles. Banjo, I deduced, must be Sir Herbert's nickname.

Sir Herbert introduced him as a Sir Charles somebody, and when Sir Charles heard where I was from, he grabbed a chair, sat himself down, stared hard at me, and said, "I used to come across your Mossad chaps. A crafty lot. Sneaky, too."

I wasn't sure whether the man was speaking professionally or prejudicially, but whatever it was, Sir Herbert jumped in to explain that his colleague was a retired MI6 big shot, adding with the familiarity of an old pal, "Charlie's reputation in the British Intelligence Service was so awesome his underlings would leave his presence by walking backwards. Isn't that right, Charlie?"

The retired British spy saw nothing amusing in this. Combing a few strands of gray hair over the top of his balding head, he retorted ominously, "Tell your Mr. Begin to watch what's going on in his backyard."

"Which backyard is that?" I asked.

The retired MI6 man leaned toward me, and in a conspiratorial manner whispered, "Iraq to begin with. And then there's those bloody fanatics in Iran – those ayatollahs. They've deposed the Shah and they'll go on a rampage one day throughout the whole of the Middle East if we don't stop 'em."

A white-coated butler glided between the armchairs and potted palms toward us, affably holding up two liquor bottles, pausing to top up a glass of whisky here and bestow a drop of brandy there. His whisky refilled, the old spy rambled on.

"Western civilization has been locked in a historic war with Islam for a thousand years. We thought we'd settled it once and for all, thanks to our technological superiority. But see what's happening now.

"The fundamentalists are on the rise, besotted with a holy jihad mission to export their brand of Islamism from Afghanistan to Sudan, and then beyond. Your Mr. Begin must watch out. As far as Banjo and I are concerned, Israel constitutes our front line."

"Precisely," avowed Sir Herbert, brooding over his Scotch. "The Mohammedans' fanatical frenzy is as dangerous to a man as rabies is to a dog."

"Mohammedanism was always a militant and proselytizing faith," proffered Sir Charles, "and now that the Shiite zealots have taken over a whole country – Iran – they're capable of setting the whole Middle East ablaze."

To which Sir Herbert grunted, "There's a lot of combustible stuff lying out there. Charlie and I visited a number of Arab countries a few months back, and wherever we went, people were blaming you Israelis for all the blemishes of their own societies. To them, the peace treaty with Egypt is a disaster – "

"Begin should have no illusions – it's not peace between peoples, just between governments," butted in the MI6 fellow.

" – and nowhere did we encounter any form of introspection, self-criticism, or moral inquiry – nothing but a culture of victimhood," said Sir Herbert, rounding out his thought. "And Arab governments are deliberately promoting this scapegoat nonsense because they need an external enemy so they can retain their power."

It was at this point that I mentioned the prickly exchange between Foreign Secretary Lord Carrington and Prime Minister Begin over lunch at Downing Street, to which Sir Herbert replied, "I can read the minds of those foreign office blokes like an open book. Not a one of them, least of all Peter Carrington, is capable of grasping what we're talking about. We're talking about the future of our civilization and all they can think about is trade and oil."

"The problem is," said Sir Charles, "we don't have enough intelligence on what's bubbling beneath the surface even in our own country. It's not like Northern Ireland, where we can do our undercover work like fish in water. Even the most diehard Irish Republican nationalists crack under a little bit of coercion, or the promise of some cash. But your average Muslim fanatic, even if he's born here – he'd kill himself first, and take you with him. And as for what's happening where the fanatics gather in Muslim countries, all our state-of-the-art technology isn't worth a damn farthing. Deploy as much high falutin' satellite surveillance and computer decryption as you like, it won't track them down in a month of Sundays. The only way to go after him and his sort is by going back to the most elementary methods of intelligence: human intelligence collection; personal counter-espionage."

Added Sir Herbert, enigmatically, "Allah will not be mocked. He toys around with our clever gadgets and laughs in our faces. Islamists wage their holy war by simply outflanking our technology."

"So what we need," said the MI6 man, "are first-class operatives – people who look like Arabs, talk like Arabs, and think like Arabs. Your blokes are champions at that sort of thing."

"What do you mean, my blokes?" I asked.

"You Israelis – you're past masters at duplicity."

"What on earth are you talking about?"

Sir Herbert stepped in, placatory, "Your Mossad and Shin Bet chaps have any number of agents who can pass convincingly as Muslims – patriotic Jews from families born in Arab countries, who speak native Arabic and can adopt Islamic disguises at the drop of a hat."

"Dead right, Banjo," interjected the other fellow. Then to me, "Your intelligence is superb. You get your man into Arab lairs almost every time – through infiltration, dissimulation, and deception."

I was beginning to feel that this Athenaeum encounter with Sir Charles Thingamajig was no mere coincidence.

"But you've got lots of Arabic-speaking communities right here in Britain," I averred. "Why not recruit your agents from them?"

"Don't trust 'em," said Sir Charles dismissively.

Sir Herbert concurred. "Islam has such a powerful hold over its believers that the difficulty of recruiting Muslim undercover agents is acute."

"So what does all this have to do with me?" I asked.

"You're close to Begin. Tell him we could do with some of his intelligence assets," answered Sir Charles, knocking his liquor back and wiping his chin with the back of his hand. "Tell him from us we need people like yours – types who can pass muster as Arabs, win the trust of fundamentalists, understand their mindsets, gather for us hard intelligence. Will you tell that to him?"

"I shall do no such thing," said I, rising to leave.

"Why not?" asked Banjo, seeming peeved.

"Because you both know there are channels to pass such sensitive messages along, and I'm not one of them. Besides, you're both retired, with no authority to make any such proposal."

Their faces fell. I found myself gazing upon two well-meaning, withered old fogies, at home in an antiquated setting.

Grimly, with almost existential angst, Sir Charles brooded, "England has never had a security problem like this before." His words were slurred by the whisky, and he began to nod off even as he spoke. So I gathered up my belongings and, escorted by Sir Herbert, descended the stairs to the Athenaeum's exit, and stepped out into the street.

"Good Lord, look at that!" barked Sir Herbert, halting in his tracks.

Propped up against a nearby wall, an *Evening Standard* billboard bellowed: IRANIANS STORM U.S. TEHERAN EMBASSY – TAKE 52 AMERICAN DIPLOMATS HOSTAGE.

Sir Herbert, his face white with anger, blew out his cheeks and exclaimed, "God knows where this is going to lead," and off he marched at a defiant pace.

Flying home, I shared with the prime minister the essence of my Athenaeum encounter. He listened attentively, and remarked, "At least it reflects well on our intelligence community." A mere mention of Lord Carrington, however, ignited a deeply-felt fiery anger. "The insolence of the man," he growled. "He talks as if he were still a colonial governor, and we his natives." Of Margaret Thatcher, he said, "She is a strong woman of strong convictions, and is basically well-disposed toward us. True, her ignorance of the Holocaust particulars is appalling, but that is true of many other world leaders." And then, morosely, "I don't think I shall visit England again. It places too much of a burden on their security people."

It was true that wherever Begin went, the cordon of protection around him was unprecedentedly large. But whether this was the real cause for his decision, or merely a pretext – not wanting to have dealings with Carrington and his ilk – was something he never disclosed. The fact remains, he did not travel to England again.

Begin with General Ephraim (Freuka) Poran, 28 December 1980

Chapter sixteen

Purity of Arms

In May 1980, Defense Minister Ezer Weizman resigned from office over policy differences, and the prime minister took over the defense portfolio. Weizman thought Begin far too intransigent and Begin thought Weizman far too conciliatory in the ongoing negotiations with Egypt on the Palestinian autonomy idea. Ultimately, both were content to see the backs of each other.

The prime minister relied heavily on General Poran to guide him through the labyrinth of his new ministry, and it was Poran who brought him to an armored corps base in the foothills of the Judean Mountains one evening in June, to see firsthand how a brigade of tank reservists readied themselves to be deployed for a thirty-two-day stint in the Nablus sector of the West Bank to counter the terrorist incursions.

In addition to Freuka Poran, Begin was accompanied by the chief of staff, Lieutenant General Raphael Eitan, aka Raful, a stocky, phlegmatic, and highly decorated soldier. Yechiel and I tagged along to get an idea of the premier's new responsibilities.

He was received by the base commander, Assaf, a friendly, bulky fellow in his forties, dressed in drab olive green fatigues, with a shock of curly hair that was partially covered by a knitted yarmulke. A successful entrepreneur in civilian life, the officer's epaulettes ranked him as colonel.

The visit began in a hut which looked as if it had not seen a cleaning implement in a month. The place reeked of Lysol. A few flowers brightened the brown Formica tables and the sun-faded curtains. The only other decoration in the room was a floor-to-ceiling wall map which Assaf used to point out the tricky, rocky terrain his brigade was readying to patrol, and where suspected PLO terrorists were thought to be hiding. He then led us out to a gravel compound, where ammunition trucks were parked alongside a dozen tanks. In the glare of headlights, squads of reservists were loading shells under the watchful eye of the second-in-command. An unsmiling sort, he sharply ordered his sergeants to gather their crews so that the exercise could commence. Next he inundated Begin with a stream of technical data about top speeds, fire power, range, armaments, maneuverability, and other details.

"Crews, prepare to mount the tanks!" he barked. And then, "Crews, mount!"

We all watched while the engines of the Patton M-60s ignited, coughed and roared. Then, as the clanking armored column began to move off, snorting through a curtain of diesel fumes and whirling dust, Assaf slid into his command jeep with Freuka at his side, and Yechiel and me at the back. Mr. Begin and Raful followed in the Chief of Staff's 4WD.

The tanks clawed at the grey stones, moving down a rugged slope that terminated in a long, rock-strewn valley, stretching into a narrowing v, and dominated by steep, partially wooded hills. At the valley's tapered end was the rubble of broken concrete blocks, earthen bricks, and pulverized plaster. And rising out of the debris, like the effigies of some bizarre shrine, were the practice targets – a semicircle of blown-out tanks and half-destroyed armored personnel carriers.

Creaking and shuddering on their tracks, the steel beasts fired their practice salvos with savage precision, creating a cacophony of thunderclaps and flashes reminiscent of the thumping finale of Tchaikovsky's *1812 Overture*. Then, on some unseen signal, one of the behemoths began crawling along the valley floor, and Assaf plugged into the command network and held an open earphone toward us so that we could listen in.

"Driver, sharp right! Stop! Obstacle on left flank. Now, forward! Full speed! Reverse! Now, sharp right again! Go! Gunner, combat range! Two thousand meters! Fire! Loader, reload! Driver, faster! Watch out, another obstacle on your left! Gunner, combat range, fifteen hundred meters! Fire! Good! Direct hit!"

After a couple of hours of this, the crews eased themselves out of their protective gear and helmets, slipped off their rifles, and bivouacked around bonfires at an encampment on the valley's edge, where Begin peppered them with questions while they munched on hefty sandwiches. He asked why it was necessary for the tank commander to give such precise instructions to his driver. Couldn't the driver see where he was going?

"Yes and no," the brigade commander answered. "When a driver's hatch is closed, he can see virtually nothing on his flanks beyond a seventeen degree radius, which is about the range of his periscopes. He has to rely largely on his commander in the open turret to guide him."

A picture flashed through my mind of a CNN news report I had seen the week before. The reporter had stated that the Israeli tank we were watching on our screens, crawling along an alleyway in a West Bank town with its turrets closed, was maliciously grating its flanks against the shuttered storefronts to vandalize them.

When I mentioned this to Assaf he laughed in a cynical sort of way and said, "I can promise you that that driver was doing his level best to avoid hitting those storefronts. In such narrow confines, the slightest fraction of a turn can cause a scrape without the driver ever knowing it." To which the prime minister, in a mixture of challenge and mischief, turned to me and said, "Yehuda, why don't you check that out?"

"Check what out?"

"Climb in and see what a tank driver sees when his hatch is closed."

Dismayed at the prospect but too embarrassed to admit it, I submitted to big meaty hands bundling me onto a tank turret, giving me a helmet,

The author – an unhappy warrior

then seizing me by the waist and armpits and lowering me through a narrow hatch, shoulders crammed, torso twisted, legs dangling, and suspending me thus until my feet rested on the driver's seat below. I squiggled down further to squeeze my backside into the seat, and found myself entombed inside a cramped steel belly encrusted with instrument panels, packed shell racks, and other fearsome paraphernalia. The stench of cordite, diesel, oil, and sweat was overwhelming. So was the claustrophobia.

Assaf's tinny voice scratched through the helmet's earphones: "I'm sealing you in now – closing the hatch."

Everything went black. I was not a happy warrior.

By the eerie beam of a searchlight mounted on the turret I could make out three periscope slits, one directed forward and the other two angled off at either side. I was seeing what a tank driver sees – a constricted vision that gives no view either of the flanks or the rear.

I was ready to climb out, but Assaf's voice scraped through again, "On the floor there's the accelerator pedal. You're in neutral, so just press on it. Get the feel of the engine." I did, and had the sense of being inside a percussion instrument.

After what seemed an eternity, Assaf opened up the beast and hauled me out, whereupon the prime minister calmed my fevered senses by leading the soldiers in a round of benevolent applause. He then bid farewell to the men, saying he would meet up with them again later in the night, and drove off with Raful, Freuka, and Assaf for what Freuka was later to describe as Mr. Begin's induction into the challenges which reserve soldiers face during tough economic times. For in that season of 1980, Israel had slid into an economic trough.

Assaf, I was later told, had made a name for himself among the top brass for his groundbreaking initiatives to sustain the *esprit de corps* of his men, many of whom had hit upon hard times but nevertheless reported for duty when summoned. Senior military officials everywhere called upon him for advice on how to set up mutual aid programs, employment schemes, and morale-boosting family get-togethers, just as he had succeeded in doing for his troops.

It was not hard to figure out why such men were so willing to lend each other a helping hand: it was the infectious camaraderie of an army composed overwhelmingly of reservists aged anywhere between twenty-two and forty-five, who, year after year, tore themselves away from hearth and home to team up for hazardous front-line duties that joined them in a bond impossible to describe and just as impossible to break. This was why Freuka had deliberately chosen this particular base. He wanted Begin to meet Assaf and assess the results of his initiatives.

The high morale of his men was evident as Yechiel and I, awaiting the return of the prime minister and his party, sat chatting and munching with them around the bonfire. The second-in-command, whom I'd taken to be a hard-nosed sort earlier, tossed me a smart-ass grin, and said, "How did you enjoy the feel of sitting inside a tank?"

"Great," I lied.

"Then let's go for a spin; you'll see what it feels like on the move."

"Brilliant idea," cried Yechiel roguishly. "Put him in. He'll enjoy it."

Before I had a chance to protest, a bunch of grinning soldiers pounced on me with all the wisecracking banter of boy scouts at a summer camp, strapped a helmet and body gear onto me, and squeezed me into the loader's seat. When I looked up, I gazed upon the second-in-command grinning down at me from the commander's turret. Instantly, he switched on the searchlight, and speaking into his headset ordered, "Driver, take us across the valley, up the hill, and back."

The man in the tank's belly sent the monster jolting, rumbling, lurching, and crunching over the valley's rocky floor toward the target area, and then up a terraced slope, causing my head to bounce on my shoulders like a jack-in-the-box. I could not begin to imagine what the real thing was like, jammed into this creaky metal box in actual battle, in a world of screaming shells, fire, and explosions, deafened, befuddled, exhausted, and scared. By the time we clattered back to the bivouac I was utterly drained, my face assuredly as gray as my hair, and all I could do in response to the guffaws and backslaps that greeted me on every side was to muster a sheepish grin.

It was by now close to midnight, and Begin and his party returned. He stood on a rise, flanked by the chief of staff and the brigade commander, the reservists arrayed in front of them, some sitting, some lying down. A tank spotlight picked out the prime minister's heavy spectacles, high forehead, and powerful chin, and standing there against the blackness of the sky he looked ten years younger than his sixty-seven years, crisp in a chalk white, open-necked shirt.

"I'm speaking to you now as minister of defense," he began, "and I salute you all for your devotion and courage, and the assistance which you are rendering to each other."

The reservists' sun-beaten faces were all turned to him, smiling their approval. They liked that.

"As you know," continued Begin, "the IDF lives by a code of ethics in battle – a *Jewish* code of ethics – even when operating against the PLO's savage terror which you are about to counter in the Nablus sector. Ours is an army in which human rights transgressions are brought to light. Penalties are paid for the abuse of innocent civilians, and justice is done." Then, turning to Assaf, he said lightly, "But I don't suppose, Colonel, you have problems of that sort with men like these."

"Well," answered Assaf, looking Begin straight in the eye, as if wanting deliberately to take up the point, "occasionally problems of that sort do arise."

There was a faint stirring among the ranks.

"Like what?" asked Begin.

"Well, we quite often have to make difficult choices when operating in civilian areas where suspected terrorists are lurking."

"Can anybody here give me a concrete example of a difficult choice any one of you have had to make, personally?" called Begin to the men.

A hand shot up. "I have," answered a tall, gawky fellow, with deep-set eyes and yellow teeth.

"What do you do in civilian life?" asked Begin.

"I'm a truck driver, but I'm out of a job."

Begin nodded in empathy, and he said, "Tell me whatever is on your mind."

The man shrugged his shoulders and in a flat, inflectionless voice told how, on the outskirts of the West Bank town of Jenin, the tank he commanded had come face-to-face with a parked Mercedes partially blocking his way. It was standing outside an isolated Arab house. So he ordered his driver to crush the car, shove it aside, and move on.

"Why didn't you knock on the door and tell the car's owner to move it aside?" asked Begin sharply.

"And what – leave the safety of my tank?"

The chief of staff quickly intervened. "Standing orders, Mr. Prime Minister, are that a soldier may not leave his tank under any circumstances in an environment that is possibly hostile."

"I see," said the defense rookie.

"And, besides," added a sleek-looking fellow, who said he was the tank driver and a history lecturer in civilian life, "we were dead beat. We were sleep deprived. We hadn't closed our eyes in thirty-six hours. It was hot. We were fed up. And we were still hurting from the loss of two of our men who had exited their tank in that exact area."

Assaf explained somberly that on a previous tour of duty a small explosive device had slammed into the side of one of his brigade's tanks in a Jenin alleyway, causing minor damage. Contrary to orders, two of the crew got out to inspect the damage, and were gunned down.

"I see," said Begin morosely. *"Lo pashut"* [not simple]. And then, after a long pause, he squared his shoulders and began addressing the men in a precise and ministerial tone. "Let me explain to you what we – all of us – are up against. Classic warfare is fundamentally a contest of wills fought to impose so much stress on the enemy that he loses the will to fight. A war of terror has the same intent, but with a singularly insidious twist: the enemy can be anybody, anywhere. He is without uniform or identification. His targets are random. His weapon is fear. He knows no constraints. He comes in all guises, often in the dress of his victims. He seeks to shatter nerves and break morale by flaunting the impotence of the authorities to protect their people. He uses his own women and children as his shield. He seeks to goad the defender into ever-harsher counter measures so as to stoke the general hate. He goes all-out to sow despair and to brutalize the agitated hearts of the other side. And in so doing, he strives to corrupt the defender's military professionalism and discipline through combat stress, demoralization, fatigue, boredom and overkill, the very things we've been talking about. Well" – this in a final arpeggio – "no enemy is going to brutalize our hearts, nor corrupt our military professionalism and discipline. The IDF has a tradition of humanity, fighting a foe that knows no humanity. Ours is a Jewish army defending a cause that is moral and just. This is why we shall, with the help of the Almighty, vanquish those who seek our destruction."

With that, he half-bowed to the troops, as if in homage, and they applauded him with great admiration.

Israel Bonds dinner, Jerusalem Hilton, June 1980

Chapter seventeen

O Jerusalem

Amonth or so later, Menachem Begin could be found at the Hilton Hotel in Jerusalem, standing on a flag-bedecked platform adorned with a banner as big as a billboard, that read: "BONDS FOR ISRAEL – THE JERUSALEM SOLIDARITY MISSION – JUNE 1980." Cheers welled up from the crowded banqueting hall, where approximately two hundred American property moguls and entrepreneurs were boisterously demonstrating their fellowship with Jerusalem. They were listening to the Israeli prime minister with fierce approval, as he savaged the UN's recent resolution condemning Israel. A Knesset initiative had proposed legislation to enshrine Jerusalem as Israel's eternally united capital; the UN had issued a sharply-worded resolution condemning the initiative. The audience adored the prime minister's audacious declaration that, in response, he intended to transfer his own office from West Jerusalem to East Jerusalem – which the UN insisted was conquered territory, and not legally part of Israel.

Ablaze with defiance, he shook a finger in righteous ire at the battery of television cameramen who were recording his every word and gesture, and he thundered: "CHUTZPAH! INSOLENCE! By what right does the United Nations dare tell us where the capital of Israel should be? Who arrogated to them the right to tell us where the office of the prime minister of Israel should be? Did the founders of the proud American nation ever ask anybody's permission before they designated Washington as their capital? Did they?"

The speaker stared down at his approving visitors with glowing eyes and they responded with smiles and loud applause. When this died down, Begin's face creased into a roguish smile, and he snickered, "By the by, may I ask you a question? If Jerusalem is *not* the capital of Israel, where *is* our capital? Petach Tikva, perhaps?"

Laughs ricocheted around the hall.

"Just as the builders of Washington endowed their capital city with the letters DC, so did the builders of Jerusalem endow our capital with the letters DC – David's City."

More guffaws and claps.

"And what exactly is our crime, ladies and gentlemen? What wrong have we done that so irritates the United Nations?"

He stepped out in front of the podium, and in a stage whisper, said, "I'll tell you, confidentially, what our crime is. Our sovereign Knesset has the temerity to unilaterally declare Jerusalem our capital city. *Oy vey!* UNI-LATERALLY! Without the UN's permission! What a felony!"

Then, springing back to the podium, he threw up his arms, fists balled, and in a voice that was vibrant and trembling, he cried, "We Jews did not choose Jerusalem unilaterally as our capital city. HISTORY chose Jerusalem unilaterally as our capital city. KING DAVID chose Jerusalem unilaterally as our capital city. That is why reunited and indivisible Jerusalem shall remain the eternal capital of the Jewish people forever."

As the applause exploded, Begin's voice soared higher, above it, and he repeated "YES, FOREVER AND EVER!" And then he shared how, at the very end of his Camp David talks with Jimmy Carter and Anwar Sadat, in 1978, literally minutes before the signing ceremony was due to begin, the American president approached him with "Just one final formal item." Sadat, Carter said, was asking Begin to put his signature to a simple letter that committed him to placing Jerusalem on the negotiating table of the final peace accord.

"I refused to accept the letter, let alone sign it," rumbled Begin. "I said to the president of the United States of America, 'If I forgot thee, O Jerusalem, let my right hand forget its cunning, and may my tongue cleave to my mouth.'"

This ancient admonition was borne aloft as the premier concluded amid more cheers: "My fellow Jews: Jerusalem is an epic. It is the well-spring of a civilization. Without Jerusalem's civilization, the spiritual history of the world would be stagnant. Has anyone ever heard of a daughter or a son of a Saladin fasting each year in memory of ancient Jerusalem's

Photograph credit: Chanania Herman & Israel Government Press Office

Begin votes for the Jerusalem Bill, 29 July 1980

anguish? Not a one! Has anybody ever heard of a son of a Crusader who breaks a glass at his wedding ceremony in memory of ancient Jerusalem's torment? Not a one! Throughout all its three-thousand-year-long history Jerusalem has been capital to no one but the Jews. So it was. So it is. And so it shall forever be."

The entire audience leapt to their feet in a standing ovation, led by the chairman of the evening, Sam Rothberg, a sharp-chinned, plain-talking philanthropist, hewed from much the same flinty rock as the prime minister himself. A native of Peoria, Illinois, Sam Rothberg was an initiator of, and voluntarily led, the State of Israel Bonds campaign for years, often against the wishes of other prominent Jewish community leaders, who preferred tried and tested Israeli charities like the United Jewish Appeal. Menachem Begin respected Sam Rothberg enormously, at times treating him as a sort of ex-officio cabinet minister, charging him with helping top up the country's development budget while also raising funds for the expanding needs of the country's prestigious Hebrew University, whose governing board he chaired.

When the prime minister sat down, Rothberg shook his hand enthusiastically and bellowed above the hullabaloo, "Menachem, that was magnificent! Where on earth do you find the energy to cope with the two most grueling jobs in government – the premiership and the defense ministry, and yet still be as fresh as a daisy at this hour of the night?"

"I try to do what Napoleon did," responded Begin, smiling, rising again to bow and wave at the still-applauding crowd. "Napoleon said of himself that he compartmentalized an array of subjects in his head, and when he wished to focus on one he simply locked the doors on all the others. Tonight, I locked everything away but Jerusalem, and on that subject, the good Lord gives me great strength. Remember the ancient words of the Almighty, '*Hanoten l'ayef koach*'" [He who gives strength to the weary].

"So how much sleep do you manage on?" asked Rothberg, amid the din.

"Though I only managed a couple of hours last night, *Hanoten l'ayef koach* saw me through the day. So now I shall go home, have a quiet nocturnal chat with my wife, study the latest dispatches, get a few hours rest, and, *im yirtze Hashem* [God willing], be ready to start tomorrow afresh."

The next day, the prime minister was rushed to Hadassah Hospital with a heart attack. It turned out to be a relatively mild one, and the doctors indulged his doggedness by allowing him to work minimally behind a curtained-off corner in the coronary ward, which he shared in semi-privacy with eight other patients. Summoned to his bedside, I found him propped up reading cables. His pajama-clad shoulders were bowed and his cheeks sallow, but his eyes were as sharp as ever.

"*Hosht du gehert aza meisa?*" [Did you ever hear of such a thing?] he asked me impishly, in colloquial Yiddish. "Lord Carrington has the chutzpah to tell me what I should be doing here in my own capital. I read it in a press report from London this morning."

The British foreign secretary and the Israeli prime minister had, by this time, arrived at a no-exit stalemate of chronic dislike for one another.

"I shall write him a letter!" said Begin, and on the spot he began dictating to me a furious reprimand, essentially telling Lord Carrington to mind his own business, and repeating much the same thing as he had said to one of the journalists outside Number 10, when he had called on Mrs. Thatcher.

"Open your bible, Lord Carrington," he dictated, "and read the First Book of Kings, chapter two, verse eleven, where you will find that King

David moved his capital from Hebron, where he had reigned for seven years, to Jerusalem, where he ruled for another thirty-three years, and this at a time when the civilized world had never heard of London."

Released from hospital ten days later to recuperate at home, Begin seemed unfazed that eleven of the thirteen foreign embassies in Jerusalem – including the Dutch, which had been the first to open an embassy in Jerusalem – had withdrawn to Tel Aviv, in protest against the Knesset bill. Begin also received a fourteen-page letter from President Sadat which included a sharp protest against the Jerusalem bill. Annoyed though the Egyptian leader was, he nevertheless graciously opened with a solicitous inquiry about Mr. Begin's health after his heart attack. These were not empty words; as unlikely as the pairing of these two men was, they had, by now, taken a genuine liking to each other.

In his reply, which Begin drafted that night, he began on an equally personal note, marveling with intense lyricism at the fragility of the human heart. He wrote:

> May I tell you something of my thoughts during the illness which suddenly befell me? My good doctors put me under a big machine, made in Israel, unique in its sophistication. They made a photo of my heart and decided to show it to me. So, what is the human heart? It is, simply, a pump! God Almighty, I thought to myself, as long as this pump is working, a human being feels, thinks, speaks, writes, loves his family, smiles, weeps, enjoys life, gets angry, gives friendship, gets friendship, prays, dreams, remembers, forgets, forgives, influences others, is being influenced by other people – lives! But when this pump stops, one is no more. What a wonder is the cosmos and the frailty of the human body, without which the mind, too, becomes still, helpless and hapless. Therefore, it is the duty of every man who is called, to serve his people, his country, humanity, a just cause, to do his best – as long as the pump pumps.

Having delivered himself of these musings, he delved into the substance of the Egyptian president's letter, gently rebuking him for insinuating that he had misled him on the matter of Jerusalem:

> You will, I hope, forgive me for this quasi-philosophic introduction, but it is relevant. Both our nations yearn for peace. It is in this spirit, and for the sake of clarity, that I must make several corrections

in your detailed letter...You will agree with me that none of our meetings consisted of a monologue, either by you or by me. We conducted a mutual dialogue. You spoke, and I responded. I spoke, you responded. Let us therefore refresh our memory of the things we spoke about.

In your letter to me, you write, "You will recall that I agreed [in El Arish] to provide you with water that could reach Jerusalem, passing through the Negev. You, however, misunderstood the idea by saying that the national aspirations of your people are not for sale."

Mr. President: I believe that were you to recreate in your mind our short dialogue at El Arish you will agree that: (a) you suggested to me bringing water from the Nile to the Negev Desert. You never once mentioned bringing water to Jerusalem; (b) I never said that the national aspirations of my people are not for sale. I would never use such language in our exchanges. You took the initiative by making a double proposal. You said: "We must act with vision. I am prepared to let you have water from the Nile to irrigate the Negev," and you also said, "let us resolve the problem of Jerusalem, because if we solve this problem we solve everything." To which I responded: "Mr. President, water from the Nile to the Negev Desert – a great idea, indeed a great vision. But we must always distinguish between moral and historical values, which is the matter of Jerusalem, and material advances, which is the matter of watering the Negev. So let us separate the two – Jerusalem on the one hand, and water from the Nile to the Negev on the other."

He then went on to catalogue in immense detail the number of times he had emphasized his principled and consistent refusal to put Jerusalem on the negotiation table, and objected to the intimation that under Jewish sovereignty the religious rights of Muslims and Christians could not be guaranteed. Warming to that topic, he sermonized:

We know that from the point of view of religious faith, Jerusalem is holy to Christians and Muslims, but to the Jewish people Jerusalem is their history for three millennia, their heart, their dream, the visible symbol of their national redemption.

Anwar Sadat was not at all receptive to this lecture. Two weeks later he wrote a thirty-five page retort, much of it a recapitulation of his loves his family, smiles, weeps, & enjoys life gets angry, gives friendship, gets friendship, prays, dreams, remembers, forgets, forgives, influences other people, is being influenced by other people, — lives; but when this pump stops — no more. What a wonder is the *whole* Cosmos; and the frailty of the human body, without which the mind too becomes still, helpless, or hopless.

Therefore, it is the clear duty of every man, who is called upon to serve his people, his country, humanity, a just cause, *he* is in duty-bound to do his best — as long as the "pump" pumps.

I agree with you wholeheartedly that there is no nobler task than to work for the peace, yes indeed, a comprehensive peace between all nations, and notably between the nations which originate from and live in our region, *the* known as the Middle East,

Page from Begin's letter to Sadat in which he lyrically reflects on the heart attack he had recently suffered, 3 August 1980

previous epistle, but introduced now by a lengthy discourse on the religious imperative which had inspired all his negotiations. His inspiration, he wrote, was stirred while on a visit to Mount Sinai. Begin was so intrigued by this that he invited Deputy Prime Minister Yigael Yadin, Foreign Minister Yitzhak Shamir, and Interior Minister Yosef Burg to his home, to hear their impressions of the opening paragraph of the Sadat letter, which he read out to them:

> The thoughts which I am sharing with you now occurred to me as I was on the peak of Mount Moses, reciting the Koran and worshipping God in this sacred part of the land of Egypt which witnessed the birth of the great mission. As I was reciting the Koran on this unparalleled spot, I became more certain of a fact that I have stated before, that my peace initiative was a sacred mission. The story of the Israelites began in the Land of Egypt. It is apparent that it is the will of God that the story would find its completion in Egypt also.

Yosef Burg, himself a religious man of sharp wit and tranquil optimism, was genuinely mystified. "He really believes he talks directly with the Almighty," he said, drolly. "He is summoning us from the heights of Sinai."

Yitzhak Shamir, a hardheaded, hard-line realist, couldn't believe his ears. He asked the prime minister to show him the pertinent paragraph again, and as he read it, he translated it slowly into Hebrew, word for word, while the urbane Yadin evaluated the more ambiguous phrases to make sure of the right rendering. Knowing Begin's penchant for legalities, and his sometimes florid style, the three ministers suggested judicious points of reply. Thus it was that in the silence of his study that night, the prime minister reviewed the letter with patience, and answered it with ardor. "On Jerusalem," he wrote, "I have told you everything I can, both orally and in writing. Jerusalem is our capital, one city, indivisible, with guaranteed free access to all the Holy Places for all religions."

And then, totally fed up of platitudes and clichés, he cut through the claptrap.

> Prince Fahd of oil-rich Saudi Arabia calls on his Arab brothers to march on Israel in a holy war – jihad. We are not impressed. You know me by now, Mr. President. I hate war with every fiber of my soul. I love peace. My colleagues and I made great sacrifices for the sake of peace. If there are, anywhere, ungrateful men who prefer to

forget what we did, and the sacrifices we made for the sacred cause of peace – let them buy oil, let them sell arms, let them be friends of tyrants, like the ruler of Iraq, to mention just one. Let them sell principles and dignity. They will not change the irrefutable facts.

And then, soaring high on the winds of history:

Yes, we hate war and yearn for peace. But let me say this: should anybody at any time raise against us a modern sword in the attempt to rob us of Jerusalem, of our capital, the object of our love and prayers, we Jews will fight for Jerusalem as we have never done since the days of the Maccabees. And how Judah the Maccabee and his brothers fought and won the day, every student of history and strategy knows. The threats of Prince Fahd are of no concern to us. He does not know – how can he? – what this generation of Jews, who suffered the indescribable fall and the unprecedented triumph, is capable of sacrificing and doing in order to defend the people, the country, Jerusalem. He may have the billions of petro-dollars; we have the will and the unconditional readiness for self-sacrifice.

This was evidently enough for the Egyptian president. A week later he wrote a brief letter of acknowledgement, suggesting they meet sometime somewhere at a summit. No such summit ever took place and Menachem Begin held by his vow to never discuss the matter again in any forum. The United Nations remained equally obdurate, refusing to recognize Jerusalem as Israel's capital, even its pre-1967 Western half. As a matter of policy, all embassies remain located in Tel Aviv, including that of the United States, electoral promises to the contrary notwithstanding.

Chapter eighteen

Germany – the Eternal and Infernal Reverie

O n an afternoon in early May, 1981, a group of about thirty young Americans greeted the prime minister with spirited applause, as he entered his conference room. They were budding Jewish community activists affiliated with the United Jewish Appeal. With old-world charm, Begin made his way around the table, kissing the hands of the young ladies, shaking the hands of the young men, and asking everybody their first names and where they came from. His opening remarks were punctuated by coughs, and as he cleared his throat of rumbling phlegm he apologized, and explained that he had caught a slight chest cold at the opening ceremonies of the recently held Holocaust Memorial Day – the annual commemoration of the six million Jews who perished at the hands of the Nazis.

Irving Bernstein, the indomitable executive vice president of the uja, who was in charge of the group, asked in his typical straight-to-the-point manner, "Tell us, Mr. Begin, in which way does the memory of the Holocaust impact on your attitude toward Germany today?"

Everybody straightened up, attentive, as the prime minister buried his face in his hands. Looking through his fingers, he told them that the subject was deeply emotional for him. Softly, in sorrowful spirit, he added, "You see, I know how my mother, my father, my brother, and my two cousins – one four years old, one five years old – went to their deaths. My father was the secretary of the Brisk Jewish community. He walked to his death at the head of five hundred fellow Jews, leading them in the singing of "*Hatikva*," and "*Ani ma'amin*," the declaration of faith in the coming of the Redemption. The Germans drove them into the River Bug, which flows through Brisk. They opened fire with machine guns, and the river turned to blood. Their bodies were left to float down the river. That is how they died. And my mother – she was elderly and sick in hospital – they drove her and all the other patients out of the building, and slaughtered them on the spot. So yes, I live with this trauma. It colors everything I do. I shall live with it until my dying day."

Begin stared unseeingly at the faces of his young guests. After a few moments, he snapped out of his reverie, his composure restored, smiled a faint smile, and said, "Now, *baruch Hashem*, we Jews have the means to defend ourselves. We have our courageous Israel Defense Forces."

"But can there be no pardon, ever?" asked a young man named Bob, from Denver. He was short, intense, with piercing eyes, and spoke with a southern drawl. "Doesn't there ever come a time when we have to put the past behind us?"

"No, Bob, I can't do that," said Begin. "I cannot forget or forgive what the Germans did to our people. Every German I see of that generation, I think to myself, perhaps he's the one. Years ago, my wife and I visited the Vatican library in Rome. We had both studied Latin as students and were examining a Latin translation of a biblical text, comparing it with the original Hebrew, when a couple approached and asked us in English what language we were speaking. 'Hebrew,' we said. 'So you must be from Israel,' they said. And when they learned that we were, they shook our hands with tremendous enthusiasm, 'Oh, you have no idea how much we admire and respect your country,' they said. 'And where are you from?' I asked. 'Germany,' they said. 'How old are you?' I asked the man. 'Forty-five,' he said. So I said, 'In World War Two, you would you have been twenty or so.' He said, 'That's right.' Instantly and instinctively, my wife and I started to back away, and we did not say another word to them. I thought to myself, perhaps this man took part in the slaughter of my father and my mother, and our Jewish children. And when I speak of my father, I speak of all the slaughtered fathers, and when I speak of my mother, I speak of all the slaughtered mothers, and when I speak of my little brother and my little cousins, I speak of all the slaughtered little Jewish children – of all the Moysheles and the Surales and the Yankeles and the Rivkales and the

Dovidels. How much of the Jewish genius was choked and charred in the pit? How much was buried alive? Who can measure? To us the cost of the Holocaust will forever be paid."

A melancholy silence fell upon the room, and when Begin next spoke it was from behind clenched teeth. "The Germans bear collective responsibility for a horror the like of which has not been known since God created man and man created Satan. So long as that embodiment of all evil – Adolf Hitler – brought them their victories, the German people hailed him. Only when his fortunes declined did they begin to turn their backs on him, and even then, only a small minority. So, no, I shall never shake the hand of a German – NEVER!"

"But what do you do when you have to officially receive Germans as prime minister?" asked a young lady in a flowery frock. She had large, intelligent eyes, and her name was Hilary. She was from Cleveland. "Don't you shake their hands even then?"

"Oh, then it's quite a different matter," Begin reassured her. "As prime minister, I have my official duties to fulfill. When German representatives come to see me, I receive them with formal courtesy. That is my civic duty. We have important issues to discuss."

"Do you ever speak to them in German?" asked Hilary.

"No. I know German but I won't speak their language. We communicate in English."

"Rumor has it, though," said a husky, muscular type who introduced himself as Tony from Detroit, "that these days, you refuse to speak to the German Chancellor Helmut Schmidt, that you insulted him, causing something of a crisis with Germany. Is that correct?" He was looking at the prime minister with avid curiosity.

Silence.

Begin sat back in his chair, his eyes fixed on the ceiling, and slowly began repeating back word for word everything the young man had just said, mulling it over. A muscle quivered in his cheek when he answered with a cordiality he clearly did not feel, "You evidently are unaware, Tony, of what the German Chancellor recently said – how he trampled on our people's dignity, honor, and historic justice."

Tony shrugged. "Yes, I guess I am unaware."

"So I shall tell you," said Begin grimly. "During a recent visit to Saudi Arabia, Chancellor Helmut Schmidt made a public statement declaring that Germany owed particular obligations to a number of peoples, among them the Palestinian Arabs. But he made no mention of Germany's obligation toward the Jews. His nation destroyed more Jews than the population of Switzerland, of Norway, and almost as many as Sweden, yet he made no mention of his responsibility to the Jewish people. Oh yes" – this with acrid sarcasm – "he had the nicest things to say about his hosts, Saudi Arabia, to whom he intends to sell arms. He described Saudi Arabia as Germany's most important ally after America and the European Union – this about a society that is corrupt from top to bottom."

The prime minister's eyes were burrowing into Tony's, and his voice was raised when he added, "Is that not scandalous? Should not every German be ashamed? I was beside myself in astonishment when I heard about it. Could it be, I asked myself, that he, of all people, had consciously omitted to make mention of Germany's obligation to the Jews – and in Saudi Arabia of all places? So, yes, I delivered a speech and I told him what I thought of him."

"What did you say?"

"I publicly reprimanded him. I said his statement showed callous disregard for the Jews exterminated by his people in World War Two. I reminded him that he had been a soldier in the German Army – an officer, no less – and that he had remained steadfast to his personal oath of loyalty to Hitler to the very end. He served both on the Russian front and the Western front, until he was captured by the British in forty-four."

"And how did he react to that?"

"He demanded an apology."

"And did you offer one?"

"Certainly not! I said that I was speaking as a free man who had fought for the survival and liberation of my own people, and I counseled him. I said to him, Mr. Schmidt, take an example from your predecessor, Chancellor Willie Brandt. Go to Warsaw, as he did. Go to the site where the Jewish ghetto once stood, and go down on your knees as he did, and ask for the forgiveness of the Jewish people for the crimes perpetrated against us by the Nazi regime, which you so loyally served as an officer in the Wehrmacht."

Some slight unease came into Mr. Begin's voice as he added, a little shamefacedly, "But, Tony, I have to confess I made one mistake."

"What was that?"

"I was told that Lieutenant Schmidt had been among the select audience of viewers of a film that showed the hanging of the German officers who rebelled against Hitler in the July Plot of nineteen forty-four. I later learned, however, that Mr. Schmidt had been invited to the screening, but did not attend. Nevertheless, he did take part" – again, his voice picked up its earlier contempt – "in a shameful trial against Nazi oppositionists that was presided over by the infamous Judge Freisler, the 'hanging judge' of the Nazi People's Court of Berlin. Freisler had been a participant in the nineteen forty-two Wannsee Conference, which decided on the extermination of the Jews of Europe – the Final Solution."

"And did you apologize to the chancellor for that mistake – about the screening?" asked Tony.

"No, I chose not to. Rather, I informed a certain member of the Bundestag who wrote me on the matter, that while I have no hesitation in admitting my error concerning the film, Mr. Schmidt remains culpable for participating in an infamous trial that was held in the most dreaded tribunal of the Third Reich and presided over by the most dreaded of judges of the Third Reich – Herr Freisler. That, in itself, is an indelible stain on the record of any German officer of the Third Reich."[75]

Then, surprisingly, Begin beamed a sudden smile, the smile one flashes when sharing a juicy piece of gossip. "The irony of it all," he shared, "is that Chancellor Helmut Schmidt's father was the illegitimate son of a self-confessed Jew, or so I have been told."

"Whaddya know!" marveled Tony.

At this point, Yechiel Kadishai walked in to remind the prime minister of his next meeting.

"Before you leave, Mr. Prime Minister," said Irving Bernstein, anxious that his wards take away some parting wisdom, "would you share with us what you think is the relevant message of the Holocaust for the people here, who are the coming leaders of the American Jewish community?"

Menachem Begin scanned the circle of young men and women surrounding him, stroked his chin in prolonged contemplation, leaned across the table from the edge of his chair, and said, "I pray with all my heart that you shall forever enjoy lives of tranquility and security. However, you must always remember that we Jews have a certain collective national experience that goes back many centuries. And in light of that experience, I believe the lessons of the Holocaust are these. First, if an enemy of our people says he seeks to destroy us, believe him. Don't doubt him for a moment. Don't make light of it. Do all in your power to deny him the means of carrying out his satanic intent. Second, when a Jew anywhere is threatened, or under attack, do all in your power to come to his aid. Never pause to wonder what the world will think or say. The world will never pity slaughtered Jews. The world may not necessarily like the fighting Jew, but the world will have to take account of him. Third, a Jew must learn to defend himself. He must forever be prepared for whenever threat looms. Fourth, Jewish dignity and honor must be protected in all circumstances. The seeds of Jewish destruction lie in passively enabling the enemy to humiliate us. Only when the enemy succeeds in turning the spirit of the Jew into dust and ashes in life, can he turn the Jew into dust and ashes in death. During the Holocaust it was after the enemy had humiliated the Jews, trampled them underfoot, divided them, deceived them, afflicted them, drove brother against brother, only then could he lead them, almost without resistance, to the gates of Auschwitz. Therefore, at all times and whatever the cost, safeguard the dignity and honor of the Jewish people. Fifth, stand united in face of the enemy. We Jews love life, for life is holy. But there are things in life more precious than life itself. There are times when one must risk life for the sake of rescuing the lives of others. And when the few risk their own lives for the sake of the many, then they, too, stand the chance of saving themselves. Sixth, there is a pattern to Jewish history. In our long annals as a nation, we rise, we fall, we return, we are exiled, we are enslaved, we rebel, we liberate ourselves, we are oppressed once more, we rebuild, and again we suffer destruction, climaxing in our own lifetime in the calamity of calamities, the Holocaust, followed by the rebirth of the Jewish State. So, yes, we have come full circle, and with God's help, with the rebirth of sovereign Israel we have finally broken the historic cycle: no more destruction and no more defeats, and no more oppression – only Jewish liberty, with dignity and honor. These, I believe, are the underlying lessons to be learned from the unspeakable tragedy of the Holocaust."

The pall of the Holocaust clung to Menachem Begin like a shroud, unremittingly. This greatly influenced my own perceptions of Germany and the Germans. Indeed, were it not for those intense years I worked for Menachem Begin, I doubt whether I would have had the temerity to defy protocol and create the stir I did in Buckingham Palace, when the president of Germany made a state visit to London during my tenure as Israeli ambassador there.

It all began when the royal summons reached me on a July day in 1986, in the form of an envelope as soft and as thick as summer cream. It contained a gold-embossed card sealed with the Queen's seal, informing me in Florentine script that:

> The Lord Steward has received Her Majesty's command to invite His Excellency the Ambassador and Mrs. Avner to a State Banquet

to be given by the Queen and the Prince Philip, Duke of Edinburgh, at Buckingham Palace in Honor of the President of the Federal Republic of Germany and Freifrau von Weizsacker.

Came the day, and to the standing ovation of peers, government notables, civic dignitaries, and foreign envoys – many wearing dazzling insignia of high rank and ancient office – heralds trumpeted a ceremonial flourish as Queen Elizabeth II and her consort escorted the German president and his lady into the palace's spectacular banqueting chamber. Women in evening gowns curtsied and men in black ties bowed as the majestic procession glided across the crimson carpet under a chandelier-laden ceiling whose radiance cast a pleasing light on the Gainsboroughs, Reynolds, Holbeins, Hogarths, and Constables which Queen Victoria hung in 1856 to celebrate the end of the Crimean War.

Silver-buttoned butlers fussed over the sumptuous kosher fare that had been reserved for my wife and me, and which resembled in every detail the menu served to the rest of the guests: consommé, halibut dressed with herbs, chicken flavored with basil and served with Savoy cabbage, roast potatoes and salad, followed by vanilla praline and coffee ice cream. The only distinction of our kosher fare was that our plates were piled twice as high as everybody else's.

Heralded by a drum roll, a squad of royal bagpipers of the kilted Gordon Highlanders, complete with dashing tartan sashes, played traditional Scottish skirls, their melancholy ululations mingling with the peals of laughter that rose from along the table. Then, upon the fierce command of a red-liveried toastmaster who barked, "Pray silence…," the sounds in the glittering hall muted and the sovereign rose to toast her guest of honor. Glasses were raised, and all stood in honor of the strains of the German national anthem, rendered by the brass band of the Grenadier Guards.

My wife, Mimi, who was sitting next to the leader of the opposition, Neil Kinnock, stood up hesitatingly, her reluctance to rise all too obvious. I, too, made as if to stand, but faltered. My legs would not carry me. They had gone numb. A hard fist of indecision knotted my stomach as chamberlains, ladies-in-waiting, and other notables cast scandalized glances in my direction. But the image of Menachem Begin appeared before me and I could not stand for that anthem. Its stanzas had been sanitized, true, but not its notes. Its melody still echoed the *Sieg heils* of Hitler's Third Reich.

After dinner in the Throne Room, where brandy, liqueurs, coffee and cigars were proffered, a string quintet and harp vainly pitted Johann

Sebastian Bach against the high-pitched chatter of the elegant crowd. Amid the hubbub, a towering equerry wearing a black frockcoat, buckling at the breast with military ribbons, bore down upon my wife and me and informed us that His Excellency, the president of Germany, wanted a private word in my ear. He was standing at the far end of the room talking to Prime Minister Margaret Thatcher, next to the proscenium arch under which the opulent, regal "Chairs of State" stood.

President Von Weizsacker was a silver-haired, slender figure, with a distinguished presence made all the more imposing by the sash across his chest. When the equerry announced our names he half-bowed to my wife, took my hand, and said, "I noted you did not stand for my country's anthem."

There was nothing I could say but the truth: "I could not – "

He interrupted me mid-sentence. "I just want you to know, I take no offense."

"I meant no personal offense, sir."

"One cannot reverse history," he said. "Nothing of the Holocaust may ever be forgotten. Memory is everything."

His accented English rang with sincerity. The German president was well known for challenging those Germans who claimed they had known nothing of the Holocaust. On a state visit to Israel the previous October, he had openly confessed Germany's guilt.

"Excuse my butting in, but I could not but overhear what you were saying," said Prime Minister Thatcher. And in a robust voice, as if proposing a toast, declared, "We should be mighty proud, all of us, that after Dunkirk and after Auschwitz, here we all are, standing together in friendship – you, the president of Germany, and you, the ambassador of Israel, and me, the prime minister of Britain, all of us guests of Her Majesty the Queen in Buckingham Palace, right here in Churchill's London. Now, isn't that a splendid thing! It is proof, if any was needed, that while one should never forget the past, we should never let it determine the future."

"Good Lord, if we were always living in the past, I'd still be fighting Scotland, Spain, and America." Thus Queen Elizabeth, with an easy smile. She had been standing close by, with Freifrau von Weizsacker, and as she approached in her finery of royal blue, and her glittering regalia, she somehow managed to be regal yet relaxed at the same time.

"Ma'am," said Prime Minister Thatcher, picking up the jocular cue, "and we women would still not have the vote." And then, to me, "I have yet to thank you, Ambassador, for the wonderful hospitality I enjoyed in your country."

Margaret Thatcher, accompanied by her husband, Denis, had paid an official visit to Israel the week before, the first British prime minister ever to do so.

"What's Jerusalem like?" asked Princess Diana, who had sidled up to join the circle, exquisite in a simple creation of red. "I hear it's fascinating."

"Indeed it is," trumpeted Mrs. Thatcher with enormous gusto, "but it's going to be a tough nut to crack if there is ever going to be peace. And then there's the issue of settlements which Mr. Begin started, and we certainly don't see eye-to-eye about that. But one cannot but admire their good old-fashioned patriotism. And they are doing more for the interests and protection of the free world in that unstable part of the globe than any number of NATO divisions."

The German president said something about Israel's tiny geography being a complicating factor in advancing a peace process because the risks were so high. Meanwhile, his wife was asking Princess Diana how her little princes, William and Harry, were faring. Laughing, Princess Diana answered with an infectious candor that William, at four years old, and Harry, at two, were "a pair of daredevils up to all kinds of mischief."

The Queen's husband, Philip, Duke of Edinburgh, came rambling over. He was chatting with the German ambassador, a tall, silver-haired aristocrat named Baron Rüdiger von Wechmar. He was a highly professional and gregarious diplomat who, at our very first meeting, had insisted I call him Rudi. He wanted us to be friends.

"Are you two friends?" asked the Duke, in his typically gauche fashion.

The Queen's husband had a provocative way about him, presumably born out of years of boredom. After all, what exactly was his job other than to trail behind his wife at official functions, hands behind his back, making meaningless small talk? Whenever he encountered a diplomatic line-up where protocol prescribed that I stand between the ambassadors of Iraq and Iran, this being the order in which we had presented our credentials, he would invariably toss out some wisecrack, like, "You three having fun together, are you?" or "Going at each other, are you?" All three of us would return him a forced smile, while continuing to ignore one another with the well-drilled habitual silence of hereditary enemies.

On this occasion, the Duke of Edinburgh facetiously said to me, "Did you know Baron von Wechmar fought with Rommel's Afrika Corps in the Western Desert during the war? He's just been telling me about it."

Again, the image of Begin entered my mind. The very thought of this German envoy, such a nice man, attired in a Wehrmacht uniform, was so repellent it must have shown on my face, for he instantly sought to reassure me, saying self-deprecatingly, "Don't worry, Yehuda, I spent most of my time running away from General Montgomery, until I was captured by the Americans. And then I spent the rest of the war in a prisoner of war camp studying for my degree to join the diplomatic corps of the new Germany."

"How interesting," yawned the Duke, and he turned to his wife. "My dear, time to retire, don't you think? President and Mrs. von Weizsacker have had a long day."

"Yes, indeed," said the Queen. "And all these good people won't leave until we do. So, time for bed everybody."

Instantly, the equerry, accompanied by chamberlains and ladies-in-waiting, emerged out of nowhere, ready to escort their charges to their chambers. Whereupon, the red-coated toastmaster once more emitted a stentorian "Pray silence...," causing all of us to bow and curtsy as Her Majesty, her consort, and her royal guests, bedecked in sashes, stars and crosses, glided through the gilded doors, nodding regally, and bidding everybody a good night.

Chapter nineteen

When Yet Another Holocaust Loomed

Not a week had passed since the prime minister had shared with the UJA young leadership mission his credo on the lessons of the Holocaust, when he and his fellow cabinet ministers spent a long morning listening in solemn and tense silence as the chief of army intelligence and the head of the Mossad reviewed the incontrovertible evidence that Osirak, the French-built installation outside Baghdad, was not a power plant, as the Iraqis had been claiming, but an almost completed nuclear facility, capable of being speedily converted to the manufacture of atomic weapons.

Three weeks later, on the eve of Shavuot, while busy with my pre-festival chores at home, the phone rang. It was General Poran. "We have an emergency," he said in a supercharged voice. "Drop whatever you're doing and come directly to the prime minister's residence. He's waiting for you."

"What's it about?" I asked, my stomach tightening.

"Not on the phone. Just come!"

When I panted through the doorway of Begin's book-lined study, I found him sitting in shirt sleeves at his desk, immersed in a document. He threw me a perfunctory glance, and in a tone that was cold and hard-pinched, said, "Freuka will tell you what it's about."

I could tell by his tone, his sunken shoulders, and the ashen circles around his eyes, that whatever was afoot was taking its toll.

The red emergency telephone startled us with its shrill, piercing ring. Begin sat up sharply and locked eyes with Freuka, who had grabbed the receiver. The military secretary listened, nodded, said, "Repeat that," nodded again, returned the receiver, and in a stony voice said to Begin, "The aircraft have just taken off. The chief of staff briefed the pilots personally. He told them that the alternative to success might be our destruction."

"*Hashem yishmor aleihem*" [May God protect them], said the prime minister, with an air of consecration. I could see the veins throbbing in his neck.

Freuka took me aside to tell me what was happening. The world's first air strike against a nuclear plant was underway. Our aircraft had taken off for Baghdad to destroy Osirak, which was estimated by our intelligence to be on the brink of going live, with the capacity to produce one or more bombs. The operation, code-named Opera, was highly hazardous. It required our pilots to fly 680 miles (1,100 kilometers) over enemy territory, skimming low across the desert floor in close formation, beneath Jordanian, Saudi Arabian, and Iraqi radar defenses. Within the hour – five o'clock – they would be over their target. My job, Freuka told me, was to assist the prime minister in composing the English text of the official communiqué, for cabinet approval.

"What does the cabinet know about this?" I asked.

"Most know nothing," said Freuka. "It's so secret, Begin instructed me to phone each member individually, to be here at five sharp. Each one thinks he's coming for a private meeting. Some of the religious members grumbled that five o'clock was too close to the onset of sundown and Shavuot."

"I advise you to take a look at this," interrupted Begin, handing me the document he had been studying. "See what a brutal tyrant we're up against – the Butcher of Baghdad."

It was a psychological portrait of Saddam Hussein created by the Mossad, and when I read the opening paragraph my heart thumped against my rib cage. It read, "Saddam Hussein is a hard-headed megalomaniac, cunning, sophisticated, and cruel. He is willing to take high risks and drastic action to realize his ambition for self-aggrandizement. His possession and use of a nuclear weapon will enable him to threaten and strike Israel and, thereby, win supremacy over the Arab world. He is prepared to act at an early opportunity, even in the awareness that retaliation might follow."

Rising stiffly to his feet, Begin began prowling the room, head down, face grim, arms behind his back, his lips moving almost imperceptibly in the manner of one muttering prayers to himself. Mid-stride, painfully, he growled, "Here we are awaiting news that could mean life or death for Israel, and Shimon Peres [still leader of the Labor opposition] has the temerity to ask me to desist from taking action. Have you heard of such a thing?"

He took a letter from his pocket, shook it open, and passed it to us. "See for yourselves."

Dated 10 May, it was classified "Personal" and "Top Secret," and it read:

At the end of December 1980, you called me into your office in Jerusalem and told me about a certain extremely serious matter. You did not solicit my response and I myself (despite my instinctive feeling) did not respond under the given circumstances. I feel this morning, however, that it is my supreme civic duty to advise you, after serious consideration, and in weighing the national interest, to desist from this thing. I speak as a man of experience. The deadlines reported by us (and I well understand our people's anxiety), are not realistic. Materials can be changed for other materials. And what is meant to prevent [disaster] can become a catalyst [for disaster]. Israel would then be like a thistle in the desert. I am not alone in saying this, and certainly not at the present time under the given circumstances.

Repocketing the letter, Begin said, "We'll have elections soon, and I'm convinced Peres will claim I launched this attack for my own electoral purposes [this did indeed prove to be the case]. Would I risk the life of a single one of our pilots for electoral purposes, I ask you? I'm convinced that if we lose the election, Peres will be incapable of deciding on such a raid, and then I would never forgive myself for not having acted when I could. The future of our people is at stake. All the responsibility is on our shoulders." He glanced at his watch and asked dourly, "How much longer?"

"They'll be over the target within ten minutes," said Freuka softly.

"Time to inform the cabinet," and out he strode to the adjacent lounge, which was filled with puzzled ministers surprised at seeing one another. When he broke the staggering news there was a stunned silence, followed by a cacophony of questions. Some wanted to immediately consider what options to take in the event the attack should fail, but Begin insisted that such discussion was premature.

"I am awaiting a call from the chief of staff, and then we shall debate how best to proceed under the circumstances, whatever they are," he said.

Back in the seclusion of his study, he walked over to the window, pulled aside the curtain which was perpetually drawn for security reasons, and said, "The sun is beginning to go down. It will be Shavuot within the hour. I don't want to keep the cabinet here after the festival begins, and yet I can't allow them to disperse before the mission is over – one way or another. There must be no leaks." Again, he retreated to the privacy of his thoughts, his lips moving mutely.

An excruciating silence descended on the room. There was no movement, and not even a whisper of sound. The man's expression was undecipherable; it revealed nothing of what he was feeling. This was a moment much more given to private prayer than to conversation.

And then, RING! RING! RING!

With glacial slowness Menachem Begin turned from the window as Freuka dived for the phone.

"Yes? When? How long? Are you sure? Can you totally confirm that?" Thus Freuka, his voice sharp. Then, arms rigid, Brigadier-General Ephraim Poran turned to face Prime Minister Menachem Begin, stood to attention, and stated, "Sir, I am able to report on behalf of the chief of staff that our aircraft have just destroyed Saddam Hussein's nuclear reactor, Osirak, by direct hits. Our planes are now on their way home. The raid took fewer than ninety seconds."

"To what extent destroyed?" interrogated the premier.

"Totally," answered the general.

"*Baruch Hashem!*" cried Begin, clapping his hands in jubilation. "Oh, thank God! Oh, thanks to the Almighty for having blessed us with such fine sons as pilots." Then, to me, "Please connect me with the American ambassador."

When Ambassador Samuel Lewis came on the line, I automatically picked up the extension to record the exchange.

"Sam, I would like you to convey an urgent message from me to the president," said Begin, desperately trying to restrain the exhilaration in his voice. "Our air force has just destroyed Osirak. Please transmit this news as quickly as possible to the Oval Office."

"Completely destroyed?" Lewis sounded shocked at the audacity of the deed and its stupefying success.

"Yes, direct hits."

"Well, I hear what you say, Mr. Prime Minister, and I'll get in touch with Washington right away." And then, following the briefest of pauses, "Is there anything else you'd like to tell me about this?"

"Not now, Sam. Our military people will give a full briefing to your military people."

"I understand. I shall faithfully convey your message to the president. Thank you, Mr. Prime Minister."

Then Begin began to stride around the room again, but this time at a much slower pace than before. He asked Freuka what dangers the aircraft still had to confront on their return flight home.

"Anti-aircraft fire, SAM ground-to-air missiles, interception by Saudi, Iraqi, or Jordanian fighters, some technical hitch perhaps." Freuka spelled this out with the dispassion of a housewife going over her grocery list.

As he paced unhurriedly to and fro, the prime minister grew progressively more pensive until, by degrees, his features became firmly set, and I could tell he had begun to mentally organize what he wanted to report to the world about the raid. Eventually, his voice tranquil, he began to dictate to me the language of the communiqué, for the approval of the cabinet.

"On Sunday, 7 June," he began, "the Israeli air force launched a raid on the atomic reactor near Baghdad, Osirak. Our pilots carried out their mission fully. The reactor was destroyed. The atomic bombs which the reactor was capable of producing, whether from enriched uranium or from plutonium, would have been of the Hiroshima size. Thus, a mortal danger to the people of Israel progressively arose – "

The red telephone shrieked again.

"Wonderful!" said Freuka into the receiver, after listening for a few seconds. He turned to the prime minister. "All our aircraft have just landed without a scratch."

"Add that to the last paragraph," Begin said to me spiritedly. "Write 'All our aircraft returned safely to base.'" Then he continued, delving into the military, moral, and judicial justifications for the raid, ending with a warning that was to become a doctrine. "Let the world know that under no circumstances will Israel ever allow an enemy to develop weapons of mass destruction against our people. If ever such a threat reoccurs we shall take whatever preemptive measures are necessary to defend the citizens of Israel with all the means at our disposal."

When the news got out, there was uproar worldwide. Ronald Reagan, president of the United States, was said to be "thunderstruck" on receiving Begin's message through Ambassador Lewis. This is confirmed by the entry in his diary:

> June 7 – Got word of Israeli bombing of Iraqi nuclear reactor. I swear Armageddon is near. PM Begin informed me after the fact. Begin insists the plant was preparing to produce nuclear weapons for use on Israel. If he waited til the French shipment of 'hot' uranium arrived he couldn't order the bombing because the radiation would be loosed over Baghdad. I can understand his fear but I feel he took the wrong option. He should have told us and the French; we could have done something to remove the threat.[76]

Begin *had* told the Americans how perilous the situation was becoming, but the outgoing Carter administration had failed to inform the incoming Reagan administration of what was afoot. No one in the upper echelons of the new U.S. government had been aware that Begin had more than once warned the American ambassador, "Either the U.S. does something to stop this reactor or we shall have to!"

As Lewis himself put it, "I contacted Washington informally to make sure that a full paper on this subject was prepared by the transition team. The paper was prepared, I was later told, but with such a high classification and such extreme restrictions on its distribution that neither Secretary of State–designate Alexander Haig nor any of the key incoming White House officials ever saw it. That real bureaucratic 'glitch' during the change of administration meant that President Reagan apparently had never been properly briefed on the history, and was both astounded and 'blind-sided' by the Israeli action."[77]

The UN Security Council condemned Israel, and the United States suspended its delivery of military aircraft to Israel on the grounds that they were supposed to have been procured for self-defense purposes only. U.S. lawyers and senior officials questioned whether Israel's attack fell into this category. If not, the U.S. was required by law to suspend *all* military deliveries to Israel.

Menachem Begin parried this salvo of international condemnation with defiance. He fumed over what he described as "Western do-gooders who never once raised a voice against Saddam Hussein's murderous intent." Scrutinizing a file of press reports one morning, he told us, his personal staff: "Listen to the thrashing Margaret Thatcher is giving me. She says, 'Armed attack in such circumstances cannot be justified; it represents a grave breach of international law.' Tut tut – what a naughty boy I am." His voice was scathing. "And here's a *New York Times* editorial which says, 'Israel's sneak attack' – note: *sneak* attack – 'was an act of inexcusable and shortsighted aggression.' And *Time* magazine is informing its readers that I have 'vastly compounded the difficulties of procuring a peaceful settlement of the confrontations in the Middle East.' *Oy vey!* It's all my fault! But best of all is French Foreign Minister Claude Cheysson. He says: 'France doesn't think Israel's action serves the cause of peace in the area.' Well, well. *Really! Our* action does not serve the cause of peace! And what about" – a corner of his mouth twisted upwards – "the action of French president Giscard d'Estaing, who equipped the Iraqis with the nuclear reactor in the first place – did *that* serve the cause of peace in the area?"

Snapping the file shut he leaned toward us, dropped his voice to a mock conspiratorial whisper, and murmured, with a rascally glint in his eyes, "I'll share a personal secret with you. Whenever I have to choose between saving the lives of our children or getting the approval of the Security Council and all those other fair-weather friends, I much prefer the former. But keep that to yourselves. Now I want to write a letter to U.S. Defense Secretary Caper Weinberger, who I'm told has been particularly keen on punishing us. Yehuda, take this down:

> "Dear Mr. Secretary, I feel I have the moral obligation to ask you that in any of your actions and judgments you consider the following: At a time when your children and grandchildren live and continue to live in the big country of America, my children and grandchildren will keep on living in small Israel which has many enemies that would like to see her be totally destroyed and disappear. Does Israel have to be punished by a weapons embargo because of this? … After you read this letter, when looking at pictures of your children and grandchildren, you might think that a million like them are living in Israel. It is about them that I write."

A secretary stuck her head around the door to tell us that Max Fisher had arrived.

Begin rose to greet a powerful-looking, heavy-set man of advanced age who was a head taller than any of us in the room. He had made his millions from oil and real estate, and in recognition of his philanthropic largesse was chairman of the Jewish Agency board of governors. But more importantly for Mr. Begin on that July afternoon, Mr. Fisher was known to have clout in Washington's Republican circles, most notably in the White House, being a longtime contributor and a trusted adviser on Israel and Jewish affairs to every Republican president since Eisenhower.

"Take a seat, Max," said the prime minister affably, gesturing toward an armchair in his cozy lounge corner.

"I'd like a word with you alone, if I may," said his guest, lowering his well-tailored bulk into the chair.

There were three other people in the room: Yechiel, the new press secretary Shlomo Nakdimon, and myself.

"We *are* alone," said Begin. "My friends here enjoy my absolute trust. Speak as freely as you wish."

"In that case," said Fisher in his characteristically unflappable fashion, "I personally think that what you pulled off the other week in Baghdad was something mighty, but I need hardly tell you what a hornet's nest you've stirred up in Washington. As you know, they think you overdid it." Begin was not offended. "Oh, I'm fully aware of that," said the prime minister. "Our American friends differed with our experts as to the exact timing the Iraqi reactor would go 'hot.' But in all honesty, that was irrelevant to me. We had incontrovertible evidence that the reactor was going to go lethal sooner than later, and with an enemy as savage as a nuclear Iraq, tens of thousands of our children could have been annihilated or mutilated in one go. And what about the Iraqi children? They would have been incinerated or contaminated for generations by the pall of radioactive dust that would have shrouded Baghdad. It doesn't bear thinking about." Begin paused, and when he next spoke the anger within him found expression in an emotional eruption. It was hard to tell whether this was spontaneous, or a bit of theater designed to impress his guest, and through him President Reagan.

"No nation can live on borrowed time, Max," he snapped. "For months I had sleepless nights. Day after day I asked myself: to do or not to do? What would become of our children if I did nothing? And what would become of our pilots if I did something? I couldn't share my anxiety with anyone. My wife would ask me why I was so disturbed, and I couldn't tell her. Nor could I tell my son, whom I trust implicitly. I had to carry the responsibility and the burden alone."

His voice trailed off, and for a fraction of a second he seemed lost in his own reveries, but he quickly reimposed his iron control on himself, and stated caustically:

"I hear Defense Secretary Caspar Weinberger was the one to press hardest for the aircraft suspension. Does his name suggest Jewish blood flows through his veins?"

A glimmer of amusement lurked in Max Fisher's eyes: "I understand his paternal grandfather left Judaism because of a dispute with a Czech synagogue, and he became an active Episcopalian. But that's just hearsay. The story goes that in his younger days, Caspar Weinberger lost a bid to become state attorney general for California, and when asked why, he answered, 'Because the Jews knew I wasn't Jewish and the Gentiles thought I was.'"

This triggered a chortle from Begin, although it faded fast, and he asked "But by what moral standards does a man like that live? Who is he trying to punish – Israel, which acted in self-defense, or the tyrannical Iraqi slaughterer who seeks to wipe us off the map?" And then, even more furiously, "Hasn't Mr. Weinberger heard of the one-and-a-half million Jewish children who were thrown into the gas chambers and choked to death with Zyklon-B gas? What greater act of self-defense could there be than to destroy Saddam Hussein's nuclear potential, that was intended to bring Israel to its knees, slaughter our people, vaporize our infrastructure, destroy our nation, our country, our very existence?"

Max Fisher simply sat, eyes veiled, a picture of solidity and strength. Gently, he probed, "You're a man of belief, are you not?"

The question so surprised Begin it doused his fury. He answered, "If by that you mean, am I a mystic, then the answer is no. But am I a believer – do I believe in *Elokei Yisrael*, the God of Israel? The answer is a categorical yes. How else to account for our success in accomplishing the virtually impossible? Every conceivable type of enemy weaponry was arraigned against our pilots when they flew in and out of Baghdad. They had to face anti-aircraft guns, ground-to-air missiles, fighter planes – all there to defend Osirak – yet not a one touched us. Only by the grace of God could we have succeeded in that mission."

"The reason I ask," said Fisher, in his slow manner, "is because the president is also a devout man, and because of his innate commitment to Israel, I think you and he will eventually get along just fine once you get to know each other."

"What do you mean, his innate commitment to Israel?"

Mr. Fisher indulged in a satisfied smile. "Well, I myself once heard him say that for all the differences between Christianity and Judaism, we both worship the same God, and the Holy Land is the Holy Land to us both. All of us in America, he said, have our ancestry in some other part of the world, and there is no nation like us except Israel. Both are melting pots, he said, everyone coming from somewhere else, to live in freedom. Those were his words, and I believe he meant every one of them. Also, the horrors of the Holocaust seem to have left such a mark on him that I believe he feels a certain sense of moral guilt and a degree of protectiveness toward Israel."

Begin said nothing, and Fisher elaborated. "Reagan served in an army film unit during the war. On one occasion he processed classified films of the Nazi death camp atrocities, and these evidently shocked him so deeply that he created a film of the most graphic footage in color, which he called *Lest We Forget*. He kept one copy for himself, which was probably against regulations. Nevertheless, he still has it, and I'm told he occasionally takes it out to screen privately. Word has it that when each of his two sons, Ron and Michael, turned fourteen he had them sit through it. That's how deeply he feels."

Begin still said nothing.

"And you know, of course, that the Reagan administration views the Middle East quite differently from the Carter administration."

The mere mention of Jimmy Carter's name caused an expression of exasperation to spread across the prime minister's features. Tartly, he said, "Mr. Carter certainly played a historic role in helping to achieve our peace treaty with Egypt. However, he showed an increasing ambiguousness toward us, a prejudice even, when I deemed it necessary on occasion to reject his demands for excessive unilateral concessions that could put our security in jeopardy. After Camp David he even accused me, unjustifiably, of going back on my word with regard to freezing settlement activity. It was a pure misunderstanding, but to him it became a perpetual grudge."

"Well, I think that once we get this present Iraqi mess sorted out, you'll be pleasantly surprised as to how our new president views the Middle East."

"You say he will pleasantly surprise me?" said Begin.

"To begin with, he admires your anticommunism and tough stance. He sees the region almost exclusively through Cold War lenses; it's black and white. We stand by Israel because Israel is on our side, while many of the Arab countries are allies of the Soviet Union. It's as simple as that. That's how he views the Lebanon situation, for instance."

Half-jokingly, the prime minister remarked, "Given his Hollywood background I've been told he sometimes confuses movies with real life."

Fisher laughed. "Some do say that in his mind, history is the saga of the brave, good-hearted men and women battling daunting odds, forever trying to do the right thing. It's said his favorite TV show is the *Little House on the Prairie*."

Once more there was silence – a long silence. Begin sat there musing. He had heard similar reports from others of President Reagan's favorable predisposition toward Israel. And if these reports were correct, if, for example, Reagan viewed the worsening situation in Lebanon in much the same way as Begin did – a Syrian occupation army backed by the Soviet Union bearing down on the downtrodden Maronite Christian community while bolstering the PLO's takeover of southern Lebanon, creating there an armed enclave, a state within a state, to relentlessly harass and bleed Israel – if, indeed, President Reagan shared this read, the ramifications for a future formal alliance with Israel would be momentous. It would mean Washington no longer regarded Israel merely as a small, worthy ward or client state, to be helped by dint of common democratic values, but as a genuine ally standing side by side with America against Soviet expansionism. Here lay the makings of a fully fledged treaty of strategic cooperation between the two nations, so Begin thought.

His musings were interrupted by Max Fisher, who asked, "How are things progressing with Bud McFarlane?"

Bud McFarlane, counselor at the state department, had been dispatched by President Reagan to try and hammer out some kind of a joint U.S.-Israel statement which would put an end, or at least paper over, the dispute arising out of the attack on the Iraqi nuclear reactor, thus permitting the resumption of American aircraft deliveries to Israel.

Bleakly, Begin answered, "I had a three-hour session with him this morning, but we've not yet reached an understanding on language. We are due to meet again this evening."[78]

"How do you find the man?" asked Fisher.

"He seems a decent sort of a fellow, but I get the impression he's not entirely comfortable with his mission."

"In what sense?"

"Either he lacks experience, or deep down he knows justice is on our side and he feels awkward trying to foist on me language I cannot accept, insinuating that in some way we are culpable."

"I think his job is to smooth your ruffled feathers and move on with outstanding business," said Fisher optimistically.

"I hope you're right."

He was. That evening, in the course of the onerous effort to find language that would exonerate Israel while accommodating Washington, Bud McFarlane left the room to phone the White House with a revised proposal penned personally by Mr. Begin. He soon returned, with a grin on his face and his thumbs up. "Message from the president: Well done!" he trumpeted.

The date was 13 July 1981, and the agreed U.S.-Israel joint statement read:

> The governments of the United States and Israel have had intensive discussions concerning the Israeli operation against the nuclear reactor near Baghdad which gave the Iraqi government the option of developing nuclear explosives. These discussions have been conducted with the candor and friendship customary between friends and allies. The governments of the two countries declare that any misunderstandings which might have arisen in the wake of the aforementioned operation have been clarified to the satisfaction of both sides.[79]

Congressmen of both Houses joined in proclaiming their gratitude, and foreign media, which had been particularly abusive toward Begin, apologized. Most moving of all for Begin was the letter of tribute he received, signed by one hundred of the hundred and twenty members of the Knesset – Yitzhak Rabin among them – saluting him for his courage and leadership in ordering the attack.

The final postscript to Operation Opera came ten years later, in June 1991, when U.S. Defense Secretary Richard Cheney presented to Major General David Ivri, commander of the Israeli Air Force at the time of the raid, a satellite photograph of the destroyed Iraqi reactor. His inscription

Begin's draft of proposed joint U.S.-Israel statement designed to end the dispute with Washington following Israel's destruction of Iraq's nuclear reactor, 13 July 1981

read: "With thanks and appreciation for the outstanding job on the Iraqi nuclear program in 1981, which made our job much easier in Desert Storm."

Still, when Menachem Begin and Max Fisher were having their tête-à-tête, the issue uppermost in the prime minister's mind, besides resolving his differences with the U.S. over the Baghdad raid, was how to substantially upgrade Israel's relationship with the new administration. Learning that the new president viewed Israel as a partner in the struggle against communist expansionism, an idea grew in his mind: to seek a formal agreement of strategic cooperation with the United States, and it was with this in mind that he readied himself to fly to Washington for his first meeting with President Ronald Reagan.

Begin and Reagan in the Oval Office, 9 September 1981

Chapter twenty

Asset or Ally?

It was common knowledge that President Reagan had a craving for jelly beans. He started chewing them in the early 1960s when he gave up smoking, and on entering the White House he had crystal jars of jelly beans placed on his desk in the Oval Office, on the table in the Cabinet Room, in the suites of his guest house, and on Air Force One, where a special container was fashioned to prevent spillage during take-off, landing, and turbulence. The tabloids reported that guests at Ronald Reagan's inaugural balls consumed forty million jelly beans, almost equaling the number of votes he received in the election.

"I can hardly start a meeting or make a decision without first passing around a jar of jelly beans," quipped Reagan to Begin when they met for the first time in early September 1981. "You can tell a lot about a fella's character by whether he picks out all of one color, or just grabs a fistful. Here, take a few."

Begin grinned and obliged, scooping up a small handful. "In my early Knesset days, during a particularly boring debate," the prime minister told Reagan jovially, "I would sometimes slip out to a local movie house, where I was far more entertained by you than by my parliamentary colleagues. I owe you a debt for having once chosen an acting career." Reagan laughed. "You know," he said, "someone asked me how an actor could become a president, and I answered, how can a president *not* be an actor?"

The jest had them both laughing. Without a doubt, his host's genial tone and infectious bonhomie were giving Menachem Begin a sense of ease, and when the president beseeched, "Please, call me Ron. And may I call you Menachem?" – he pronounced it Menakem – Begin responded with the widest of smiles. With false modesty, he protested, "Oh, no, Mr. President," he said, "I'm a mere prime minister and you are the president of the mightiest power on earth. So by all means call me by my first name, but I cannot call you by yours."

"You sure can, Menakem. I insist," said the president.

"In that case, Ron, I shall," said the prime minister, elated.

They were sitting across from one another on floral-patterned settees in the Oval Office, two note-taking aides in attendance – I being one of them. The sunny rose garden was in view through the tall windows, the presidential colors were draped next to a prominent portrait of Thomas Jefferson, and dotted around the room were mementos, plaques and signed photographs – all the bric-a-brac of a public man who had been a middling film star and a popular state governor. Begin had arrived in Washington after a summer of political success at home – beating Shimon Peres to win his second general election – yet internationally, in this, Israel's most important relationship, the situation had been more tense. Reagan and Begin had first clashed over the bombing of the Iraqi nuclear reactor, and then, not long after, over a U.S. sale of sophisticated military equipment to Saudi Arabia. Begin could not be certain how much of Reagan's affability was Hollywood, and how much was sincere, but having learned that the man had a genuine admiration for Israel, and already highly buoyed by his electoral triumph, he allowed himself to relax into Reagan's big-hearted fellowship.

The first-class reception had begun an hour earlier, when the president pulled out all the stops in a ceremony of spectacular pomp and circumstance on the White House lawn: red carpet, honor guards, flags waving and bands playing. Immaculately groomed, dashingly handsome, and looking a decade younger than his seventy years, President Reagan addressed an invited crowd of hundreds, declaring, "I welcome this chance to further strengthen the unbreakable ties between the United States and Israel, and to assure you, Mr. Prime Minister, of our commitment to Israel's security and well-being. Your strong leadership, great imagination, and skilled statesmanship have been indispensable in reaching the milestone of the past few years on the road toward a just and durable peace in the Middle East."

Reagan then turned to address Begin directly, and the rich timbre of his voice almost cracked when he said, "I know your entire life has been dedicated to the security and the well-being of your people. It wasn't always easy. From your earliest days you were acquainted with hunger and sorrow, but as you have written, you rarely wept. On one occasion you did – the night your beloved State of Israel was proclaimed. You cried that night, you said, because 'truly, there are tears of salvation as well as tears of grief.' Well, with the help of God, and us working together, perhaps one day for all the people of the Middle East there will be no more tears of grief, only tears of salvation. Shalom, shalom, to him that is far off and to him that is near."[80]

Stirred to the core by these sentiments, so publicly expressed, the prime minister responded in kind: "Our generation, Mr. President, lived through two world wars, with all the sacrifices, the casualties, and the miseries involved. Ultimately, mankind crushed the darkest tyranny that ever arose to enslave the human soul." This reference to Nazism was a precursor to an assault on totalitarianism, phrased in language calculated to appeal to this anticommunist crusader. Begin wanted to reassure Reagan that America could rely wholeheartedly on Israel as a faithful ally in the incessant battle against the Soviet evil: "After World War Two, people believed we had reached the end of tyranny of man over man. It was not to be. Country after country is being taken over by totalitarianism. So liberty is still endangered and all free women and men must stand together to defend it and to ensure its future for all generations to come." And then, softly, with deep gratitude: "Mr. President, thank you for your heartwarming remarks about my people and my country, and for your touching words about my life. I am only one of the uncountable thousands and millions who suffered and fought and persisted, until after a long night, we saw the rising of the sun."[81]

All stood to attention as the national anthems were played. Had Mr. Begin used the moment to wonder how such a lavish and splendid welcoming ceremony had come about, he would probably have guessed – correctly – that Ambassador Samuel Lewis, in whom he placed much trust, had persuaded those around the president to receive Begin with full ceremonial honors, treating him as the head of an allied government, not an obdurate dependant – which some of the president's men considered him to be.

The subsequent one-on-one in the intimacy of the Oval Office was in and of itself a singular gesture. It seemed to Begin that the president was deliberately seeking to break the ice in a public display of camaraderie, in order to give him the rare opportunity to open his heart and say what was on his mind in an intimate tête-à-tête. Imagine, then, his astonishment, even bewilderment, when hardly had he opened his mouth to talk about the

Israel-U.S. relationship, his hopes for peace, PLO terrorism, the Lebanon escalation, and the stalled Palestinian autonomy negotiations, when Reagan interrupted him to say: "You must forgive me, Menakem, but we have only a quarter of an hour before we have to join the others in the Cabinet Room. So I would just like to make" – he slipped his hand into his pocket and extracted a pack of three-by-five-inch cards – "a few points. The first is…."

The prime minister stared in disbelief as the American president began reciting in a mechanical tone a series of "talking points" consisting largely of standard reaffirmations of America's known positions on Israel and the Middle East.

This was the fifth president I had met, after Johnson, Nixon, Ford, and Carter, but Reagan was the only one who resorted to this bizarre practice of using cue cards. When he paused, which he did twice, Begin assumed it was to allow him to engage, but it was not. It was simply Reagan making sure of his lines.

Could it be that he was so uninformed that he needed to read elementary issues from cards, like a third-rate actor? All the other presidents had been in total command of their material; they needed no coaching, no cue cards. Evidently, Reagan's advisers did not want their man plunging extemporaneously into exchanges on complex issues, for fear he would get lost in their intricacies. So Begin sat and listened. It was not an easy thing for him to do. Coming from a centuries-old culture of polemicists, analysts, conversationalists, and nonconformists, he was, by nature, a passionate debater. Ronald Reagan was destined to enter history as a brilliant public communicator, the man who reinvigorated the American people after the lackluster years of Jimmy Carter, who restored his country's self-confidence, and who initiated policies which ultimately brought the communist empire to its knees. But little of this was evident at that first meeting, which ended with the president re-pocketing his cards and saying, "And that, Menakem, is how America sees things." Begin responded with a gracious, "I thank you, Ron, for that comprehensive overview."

"And now let's join the people in the Cabinet Room," said the president, and he led the way into the adjacent chamber. The room had colonial-style, off-white paneled walls, a brass chandelier, golden drapes, and a grand oak conference table with high-backed leather chairs, behind which senior aides were standing in respectful attendance. Mr. Begin made a beeline for the secretary of defense, Caspar Weinberger, shaking him by the hand with an affected, "Ah, Mr. Weinberger, at last! How delighted I am to make your acquaintance."

Cap Weinberger, a diminutive man with sleek black hair, reciprocated with frigid civility, his expression a blank. Secretary of State Alexander Haig, by contrast, was an admirer of Begin, and he welcomed him with the robust muscle of the soldier that he was. The principals worked their ways around the table, Reagan extending a particular welcome to the recently appointed Defense Minister Ariel Sharon, as well as to Foreign Minister Yitzhak Shamir and Interior Minister Yosef Burg, who was now in charge of the negotiating team dealing with the long-stalled Palestinian autonomy talks.

Seating himself at the table's center, facing Begin, Reagan extracted another pack of cards, and in the practiced style of a late-night talk-show host, suavely welcomed Begin and his entourage with the briefest but most cordial of introductions, describing Israel as "a strategic asset," and inviting the prime minister to make any comments he wished.

Begin obliged, presenting a comprehensive review of all the relevant issues, and making reference to Israel's role as "America's most reliable and stable ally of freedom against Soviet expansionism in the Middle East." Then, choosing his words most cautiously, he added, "You, Mr. President, kindly referred to my country just now as a strategic asset. While that certainly has a positive ring to it, I find it, nevertheless, a little patronizing. Given the bipolar world in which we live – democracy versus communism – the cherished values we share, and our confluence of interests on so many fundamental issues, might I suggest the time has come to publicly acknowledge that Israel is not just a strategic asset, but a fully fledged strategic ally."

Had Begin floated this thought in Jimmy Carter's Cabinet Room, he would have been met with a steely gaze and an icy rejection. Carter had issued explicit instructions to all his aides never to use the terms "ally" or "alliance" when characterizing the U.S.-Israel relationship. And, indeed, there were some around President Reagan's table now who were looking faintly disconcerted. Weinberger was actually frowning. But the president continued to give Begin his fullest attention, and he chuckled when his guest continued with, "You know, Mr. President, I sometimes get the impression that our relationship is a little like Heinrich Heine's famous couplet about the bourgeois gentleman from Berlin who implores his mistress not to acknowledge him while walking in that city's most fashionable boulevard, begging her, 'Greet me not Unter den Linden.' I fear there are some who would say much the same to Israel today."

On all sides, the American faces seemed either bemused or irritated, but not the president's. He looked at the prime minister with respect, and he affirmed, "I'd be proud to acknowledge you in public anywhere, any time."

The way he said it gave Begin the distinct feeling that this was a decent man who was both a good listener and open to persuasion. If only he would be permitted to talk with Reagan alone whenever policy differences arose – as arise they must – surely they would find a common language with which to iron things out. But scanning the faces on the other side of the table he knew that some of those flanking the president would never allow that to happen.

Encouraged, Begin continued. "Certainly, in this alliance, Israel is very much the junior partner, but a partner we are. And I dare say" – a faint smile curled his lips and his voice sank into understatement – "over the decades Israel has done a thing or two which might have contributed to the American strategic interest in our region. And much as we deeply appreciate the military and economic aid we have received over the years, I venture to suggest it has not been an entirely one-way street – not a charity, so to speak."

There, he had said it: He had spelt it out. No other Israeli prime minister had quite put it that way before – that Israel was not merely a receiver, but also a giver. As Begin spoke he noted that Reagan was nodding in agreement. The president looked around to invite discussion, but since everyone seemed rather taciturn, Begin seized the moment to continue: "Might I suggest, Mr. President, that consideration be given to an agreed document on this matter – on the strategic relationship between our two countries. And in employing that expression 'strategic relationship' I do not mean for our own defense. We've defended ourselves in five wars, and we've never asked any nation to endanger their lives for our sake. We shall continue to defend ourselves if war is again thrust upon us, God forbid. What I do speak about is strategic cooperation in defense of our common interests, in a region which is the target of Soviet expansionism, more aggressive than at any time since the end of the Second World War."

Caspar Weinberger's gray eyes were cold as they glared at Begin. He grunted some sort of a reservation. Alexander Haig, in contrast, seemed far more amenable.

President Reagan said, "What the prime minister proposes sounds like a good idea to me. Let's look into it."

This caused Menachem Begin to sit up abruptly, energy coursing through him. He had been waiting for this moment for a long time, the moment when the United States of America would grant the State of Israel the status of a fully fledged strategic ally. So he said, "With your permission, Mr. President, may I call on Defense Minister Sharon to share with you and your colleagues a number of ideas which might give expression to this concept?"

"By all means," said Reagan. "Go ahead."

Sharon, frequently called "the Bulldozer" because of his girth, his autocratic style and his military daring, stood up, and referring to a set of maps, proceeded to give an elaborate presentation of the ways in which Israel and America might cooperate strategically. Weinberger, always extremely sensitive about America's relationships with major Arab countries – most notably Saudi Arabia, with which he had done much business before joining the administration – reddened at Sharon's swashbuckling style. Others on the American side exchanged uneasy glances, but Sharon plowed on imperviously, proposing what was essentially a wide-ranging mutual defense treaty. For his part, Begin, sensing the growing uneasiness around the table, suggested that the president authorize the two defense ministers to confer about finding a mutually acceptable formula.

"Good idea," said Haig.

"So why don't you two fellas get together and see if you can work something out in this area?" Reagan said to Weinberger and Sharon.

Weinberger seemed dumbfounded. It was clear that he was seething, stuck with a presidential request to deliberate with a man he could not abide, about an agreement he totally opposed.[82]

The next day, the prime minister was interviewed by Israel Radio:

> *Question:* You've described your meeting with the president as highly successful, telling us you've reached an agreement in principle for a far-reaching memorandum of understanding on strategic cooperation. How far-reaching does it go?

> *Answer:* I hear some people back home are saying that the whole strategic security cooperation memorandum will boil down to a bit of stockpiling and the construction of a few hospitals. That's not so. We are talking about genuine cooperation. We haven't signed anything yet, but we have come to an agreement in principle on the matter. The details are many and very serious. We are talking about true cooperation on land, at sea, and in the air.

At the very same hour that the Prime Minister was saying this on Israeli Radio, Secretary of Defense Caspar Weinberger was telling his senior aides, "I want no publicity on this matter. I want as little said as possible. The Israelis, of course, are going to do just the opposite. They'll want a binding document with lots of detail and publicity. We're not going to subscribe to anything like that at all. Whatever we'll sign will be so general and so empty of content that we'll be able to defend it in the Arab world. And I want the negotiations to be held right here in Washington. Is that clear? I intend to control the whole process personally myself."[83]

And control it he did.

Shortly after the preliminary talks, and within a matter of weeks, the Israeli defense ministry presented the Pentagon negotiators with a twenty-nine page booklet containing a sweeping list of military cooperation proposals. This spawned further back-and-forth negotiations which, in the words of one American participant, "was like being in a washing machine where sometimes things went very smoothly and the water was warm. Then suddenly cold water would come out of nowhere and you'd be turned the other way and get hit across the head with some unexpected action or development. It was a funny time: On the one hand, things were done at the president's direction that were unprecedented, but then they would be undone by his secretary of defense."[84]

Soon enough, Sharon became so disenchanted he wanted to wash his hands of the whole concept, but Begin insisted he persist. He sought a symbol of the alliance, if nothing more. What he got in the end was a brief, seven-hundred-word memorandum of understanding, that contained little that was new or substantive. It was signed in November, 1981, by Sharon and Weinberger without fanfare, at an informal dinner at the National Geographic Society in Washington. In what was a calculated resolve to play down the whole exercise, no press was invited, and the Pentagon did not even give its customary briefing to the media afterward. Nowhere are there photographs of Weinberger signing the agreement with Sharon.

Chapter twenty-one

Death of a President

Whatever misgivings Begin might have had regarding the watered-down version of the strategic cooperation agreement were swept aside by the devastating news which reached him at his home on the afternoon of 6 October. His peace partner, President Anwar Sadat, was dead, mowed down at a Cairo military parade by Muslim fanatics.

"Are you sure he's dead?" asked a shocked Begin, with a quick intake of breath. "Is it absolutely confirmed?" He was talking to General Poran, who had conveyed the news to him on the phone. I was sitting there rigid, my pen frozen mid-air, primed to continue the dictation for which the prime minister had summoned me to his residence.

Freuka's answer was evidently not unequivocal, for Begin said, "I need full and final confirmation." Then, to me, "Switch on the radio. See what the foreign stations are reporting."

I began fiddling with the receiver on his desk, seeking a shortwave band. The Voice of America was saying that Sadat had been wounded, but was not in danger. Radio Monte Carlo was saying that two of Sadat's bodyguards had been killed, but that he had been led away untouched. The BBC World Service, however, announced unambiguously that the president of Egypt had been assassinated.

Begin's expression was as pained as though he himself had taken a bullet. "If the BBC announces it so categorically, it has to be true," he said. And then, "Please connect me back to Freuka."

"Freuka," he said, in a commanding tone, "contact the chief of staff at once. We must be on full alert for any contingency. Who knows what's going on in Cairo. It may be a coup."

His military secretary evidently assured him that all precautions were well in hand, because Begin began to nod his head up and down, saying, "Good. Good. Good."

And then, back to me, "I need to speak to Yechiel."

Yechiel informed him that our ambassador to Cairo, Moshe Sasson, had finally been able to get through on the clogged Egyptian telephone lines, to report that he had witnessed the shooting, and that yes, Sadat was indeed dead.

"Tell him," instructed Begin, "that he should tell the Egyptians that I wish to attend the funeral at the head of an official Israeli delegation."

This thought seemed to have touched a nerve, as if the consequences of the catastrophe had only just now truly sunk in, for his features went suddenly taut and his face grayer as he heaved a tormented sigh, leaned heavily back in his chair, and murmured, "God knows what this will do to the peace treaty. In a few months we're supposed to complete our final withdrawal in Sinai, and dismantle our settlements there."

"Do you want to issue a statement of condolence?" I asked warily, for fear of upsetting him further.

"Yes, yes, of course," he answered, and he dictated:

President Sadat was murdered by the enemies of peace. His decision to come to Jerusalem and the reception accorded him by the people, the Knesset and the government of Israel will be remembered as one of the great events of our time.... Unforgettable is the hour in which he, the President of Egypt and I, the Prime Minister of Israel, signed a treaty of peace between our two countries. During our many meetings a personal friendship was established between us. I have therefore lost not only a partner to peace, but also a friend.... We hope the peace process will continue, as we know Sadat would have wished.[85]

But the question on everybody's lips was, would the peace process indeed hold?

Menachem Begin found out when, the following Friday, he flew to Cairo with three of his senior ministers to attend the state funeral, much

Photograph credit: Chanania Herman & Israel Government Press Office

The Israeli delegation to Sadat's Cairo funeral, led by Begin, and including Ministers Burg, Sharon & Shamir, walk a hefty distance to join the funeral cortege, Shabbat, 10 October 1981

to the discomfort of the Egyptian authorities, who were saddled with a twofold predicament: the unprecedented security the visit necessitated, and the unprecedented protocol headache it posed because of the attendance of numerous Arab enemies of the Jewish State. Since the funeral took place on Saturday – Shabbat – the security headache was further compounded when the Israelis refused to ride in the armored vehicle meant to carry them from their accommodation to the funeral procession, insisting instead on walking. This was staggeringly courageous, and a significant physical effort on their part, and an unmitigated nightmare for the Egyptians.

Nevertheless, all passed off without mishap. Upon returning home on the Saturday night, a fatigued prime minister spoke to the waiting press. He told them that he and his colleagues had felt it vital to attend the funeral as a gesture of respect and tribute to his peace partner, and to personally express condolences to Mrs. Jehan Sadat and her family. "Those who came to console her," he said, "were themselves consoled by her. To me and my colleagues she said, 'I was always afraid that I would lose him. But God is stronger than those who killed him, and he gave his life for peace, and the peace shall continue.'"

"Mr. Prime Minister," asked a journalist, "will the peace process indeed continue?"

Unhesitatingly, the prime minister answered, "I am convinced it will. I had a long private talk with President-designate Mubarak, and that is what we mainly talked about. There is no doubt in the minds of both of us that this is going to be a fact."

"Mr. Prime Minister, there is a lot of concern in Israel about the stability of the regime in Egypt. You've just come back from there. Can you say anything about it?"

"There is no reason to believe in the instability of the regime. We found a bereaved government who had lost a great and respected leader. But we also found a strong government. In a couple of days' time, the new president, Hosni Mubarak, will be sworn in."

"Can you tell us something about your relationship with President-designate Mubarak?"

"Yes, I can. I can tell you of a very simple human and dramatic moment when we met. As we were walking toward each other we extended our hands to one another, and we both said simultaneously, and with absolute spontaneity, 'Peace forever.' Of course, one cannot guarantee anything forever. But what we meant was that we shall both endeavor to establish a peace that our children and grandchildren can inherit."[86]

On a November evening just weeks after the Sadat assassination, while moving between the basin and the towel rail in his bathroom, Menachem Begin slipped and fell. Excruciating pain shot through his body when he attempted to pick himself up. Wincing, he called to his wife for help, but she didn't hear him because his bathroom radio was blaring so loud it drowned out his cries.

Fortuitously, soon afterward, Mrs. Begin had cause to go to the bathroom herself. Upon opening the door, she discovered her husband prostrate on the floor.

"Menachem, what happened?" she asked in alarm.

"I fell."

"So get up."

"I can't."

Their daughter, Leah, heard them talking and ran to the scene. "Daddy, what's wrong?"

"I fell. I can't get up. Just leave me to lie here a while and then I'll try and raise myself again."

After a brief consultation, wife and daughter decided they would gently ease him up as best they could, and carry him to his bed.

"Don't," grimaced the prime minister. "You don't have the strength, and you'll only make the pain worse. I might have broken something. Call the security guards. I'll tell them how to carry me."

Within minutes, two strapping young men hovered over the prime minister, awaiting his instructions.

"Place your hands under my back and lift me up in one go, and carry me to my bed," he told them. "But try not to jerk any limbs, please."

An ambulance took the prime minister to the Hadassah Hospital, where he was examined by three senior doctors, among them his personal physician, Dr. Mervyn Gotsman. X-rays confirmed he had a fractured left femur, and he was swiftly operated upon. Later, when it was over, firmly convinced that the public had a right to know every detail of their leader's state of health, Begin penned an article describing in vivid detail the circumstances of his accident and what had gone through his mind while on the operating table, when the local anesthetic had already taken effect and a screen had been placed to hide his gaze from what was being done to his thigh:

The operation began. I did not feel it begin. I felt nothing. I spoke with Professor Gotsman who was by my side, and he talked to me.

Suddenly, I heard the pounding of a hammer on a nail. The pounding increased. I felt nothing. I did not count, but I think I distinguished nine or ten intermittent hammer-blows. After a while they told me the operation would soon be over and that everything had gone well. A little while later they said it was done.[87]

When the Prime Minister was discharged from hospital eighteen days later, a long convalescence began. Overnight, he seemed to have aged a decade. Sometimes the pain was so excruciating he could hardly function, and the medications he had to take tired him out. The only way he could get about was in a wheelchair. His desk was too uncomfortable for him to work at, so he ran the government from the couch in the corner of his office. Far worse than his own discomfort, though, was his anxiety about the country, and his family: The economy was in the dumps with no signs of an early improvement, some of his cabinet colleagues were getting him down because of petty squabbles over petty grievances, and most disquieting of all, his beloved wife Aliza, who had a long history of asthma attacks, had become very sick indeed.

So there he sat, alone in his apartment on a mid-December evening, steeped in a deep melancholy, brooding. But for the purr of the radio broadcasting the evening news, to which he was hardly listening, the room was as quiet as a crypt. Suddenly, however, his ears pricked up, when the announcer began quoting a report in a Kuwaiti newspaper on a statement by Syrian President Hafez al-Assad:

> He will not recognize Israel even if the Palestinians deign to do so. There can be no question of making peace between Israel and the Arabs so long as the strategic balance plays into Israel's hands. He called upon the Arab states to persist in their rejectionist stand until they attain the power necessary to impose peace conditions on Israel in the spirit of Arab demands.

Begin, dabbing at the sudden film of sweat on his forehead, meditated over this statement. The situation with Syria had already deteriorated greatly. The Syrians had all but taken over Lebanon, and had deployed their advanced ground-to-air missiles on its territory, hampering Israel's freedom of the skies. Worse still, Yasser Arafat's PLO had taken control of Lebanon's south, from which it was mounting ever more deadly salvoes on northern Israel. This in turn was harming the Israel-U.S. relationship, because President Reagan had made plain his opposition to an Israeli incursion into Lebanon to clear the PLO out.

The prime minister picked up the phone to Yechiel Kadishai. "Yechiel, please find out the current population of the Golan Heights and call me straight back."

A half hour later, Yechiel called back. "There are some ten to twelve thousand Druze living on the Golan, and a few thousand Israeli settlers, no more," he reported.

Begin closed his eyes and forced himself to think through his pain. The Golan Heights rose a thousand feet over the farm-rich Huleh Valley. Were it governed by a friendly neighbor, the Heights would be unimportant, but in enemy hands it was a strategic nightmare. Its capture in the Six-Day War had put an end to years of Syrian bombardment of the villages and towns below. When the Syrians almost recaptured the Heights during the Yom Kippur War, their forces had advanced within reach of the road to Haifa. Now, Hafez al-Assad, the most intractable and intransigent of all the Arab leaders, was saying for the umpteenth time that Syria would never recognize the Jewish State. So why wait? Why leave this sparsely populated, critically strategic plateau in a state of legal limbo under military administration when, by a simple act of legislation it could be incorporated under Israel's sovereign law? And what better time to do it than now, when international attention was distracted by a crisis in Poland, where the communists were suppressing the anticommunist *Solidarity* movement, and by turmoil in Argentina, presaging the Falklands war with Britain.

Crisply, Begin set things in motion. "Yechiel," he said, "arrange a special cabinet session first thing tomorrow morning here at the residence, and alert the Knesset Speaker to a possible legislative session later in the afternoon. Also, tell the attorney general to call me."

Yechiel Kadishai, forever the perfect factotum, did not ask why.

"Gentlemen, I am pleased to propose to you the Law of the Golan Heights," the prime minister told his astonished ministers the following morning. He was sitting propped up in his wheelchair, his ministers fanned out in a semicircle around him.

"The law of what?" asked one, thinking to himself the medication was beginning to affect Begin's mind, so the minister was to later to tell me. Others were so perplexed by the grandness of this sudden ambition that they just sat there wondering what had gotten into their leader.

"After consultation with the attorney general, I wish to go over the language of what I term the Golan Law," answered the prime minister. After citing the law's proposed clauses, he proceeded to make his case:

"Following the renewal of our independence, the Syrians dominated the Golan Heights and demonstrated what they were capable of doing to our civilian population in the towns and villages below. The Syrians turned the lives of tens of thousands of our people into hell. Driven by their deep and abiding hatred, they would open fire from the Heights, instituting a reign of blood and terror throughout the area. Their targets were men, women, and children, and the attacks took their toll in killed and wounded. It was said in those days that the children born in that valley were 'children of the shelters.' Why? Because at every alert – and there were so many – they ran for their lives to the shelters. No wonder that in this matter of the Golan Heights the nation is virtually in consensus that Israel cannot come down from the Golan Heights and hand them back to the Syrians, ever."

"So what are you proposing?" asked one.

"I am proposing that we apply the law of Israel to the Golan Heights."

"Isn't that tantamount to annexation?" asked another.

Either the prime minister did not catch the question, or he chose not to hear it. "The question I have to ask myself is whether we should wait indefinitely, in the hope that one day a Syrian ruler will display willingness to conduct peace negotiations. I, personally, have no illusions. Time and again I have called upon the Syrian president from the rostrum of the Knesset to come to Jerusalem or, alternatively, to invite me to Damascus, to negotiate peace. For almost fifteen years he has consistently refused the approaches of every Israeli government. But most significant is his most recent refusal which I heard last night. Unlike the previous ones, this time he actually specifies why."

"In what sense?" asked the same minister, skeptically.

"The cabinet should know that we have all the information from an impeccably reliable source as to exactly what happened at the recent Fez conference.* There, the Syrian foreign minister declared," – Begin picked up a paper stamped "Top Secret," and adjusted his spectacles – "he declared, and I quote, 'We Arabs must not put forth any peace proposal. We must be willing to wait a hundred years and more until Israel's military prowess wanes, and then we shall act.'" He replaced the document on the small table beside his wheelchair, and picked up another. "Just yesterday, President Assad himself said much the same thing, publicly. I heard it with my

---

* A summit of Arab leaders held on 25 November, 1981.

own ears over the radio, and it appears here in today's review of the Arab press." His voice was firm as he quoted the Kuwaiti newspaper.

"So I ask you, after such words, should Israel wait in vain for the Syrians to talk peace, knowing that when they deign to do so, it will only be at a time when they feel they can dictate their terms either because they have grown so strong or we, God forbid, have grown so weak? Meanwhile, Syria is extending its domination over Lebanon, and the murderous PLO have taken over the south of the country. What do we have to wait for?"

One worrier, "How do you suppose the United Nations will react to your proposed Golan Law?"

"A fair question. Clearly, what I'm suggesting is a bold move, and I do not dismiss for one minute that the international repercussions will be harsh. For one, I anticipate a Security Council resolution roundly condemning us."

"And the United States?" asked another. "How do you suppose Reagan will react?"

"In all likelihood, the U.S. will support such a UN resolution and will lodge its own direct protest. Our American friends will argue that the Golan Law is a unilateral step which they will not recognize. I would expect a letter in such a vein from Secretary of State Haig, or from President Reagan himself. We will answer them with what we genuinely believe – that justice is on our side, and that we deem our action fully valid under the circumstances we face."

A number of faces in the chairs around him continued to display uneasiness, prompting Begin to say with some vehemence, "With all due respect to our great friend the United States of America, with whom we recently signed an agreement on strategic cooperation, Israel is a sovereign state and ours is an elected government. We are not talking here about some whim, some caprice; we are talking about our lives and our future as a nation. No one on earth has a moral right to dictate to us what to do after we have waited this long, fully fifteen years since the end of the Six-Day War, to negotiate peace with Syria, only to be rebuffed time and again by their rejectionism." And then, with even greater conviction. "I am convinced that our people will back the government to the hilt on this matter. Therefore, I propose to submit the Golan Law to the Knesset for legislative approval this afternoon, subject to cabinet approval."[88]

The subsequent ministerial debate was not as straightforward as the prime minister would have wished, but by the end all were in agreement. That afternoon, they took their seats at the cabinet table in the well of the Knesset chamber, as the prime minister, immobile in his wheelchair, opened by beseeching the Speaker to allow him to remain seated where he was, and not mount the podium.

"Permit me, Mr. Speaker, for reasons beyond my control, to address the House today from my place at the government table," he said, in grand parliamentary style. "And permit me, not withstanding custom, to deliver my remarks while seated." He then launched into much the same rhetoric as he had used at the cabinet session, and before the day was done, the Golan Law was passed by a majority of sixty-three to twenty-one, creating an instant firestorm in Washington.

Begin in his wheelchair at the Knesset, 14 December 1981

Photograph credit: Chanania Herman & Israel Government Press Office

"You know, Al," said President Reagan to his secretary of state, Alexander Haig, who for once was in agreement with Caspar Weinberger, "I'm madder about this Golan Law thing than I was about the Iraqi reactor business. I would think Israel's unilateral action has complicated Middle East peacemaking tremendously."

"Frankly, I feel quite double-crossed," agreed an angry Haig. "I didn't expect this. I favored the memorandum of understanding which you tasked Weinberger to negotiate, because I assumed a formal strategic relationship, however vague, would put paid to their penchant for taking us by surprise, like they did with the bombing of Osirak. I simply took it for granted the Israelis would, from now on, consult with us fully before taking such drastic unilateral action."

"Does the memorandum oblige them to consult with us?" asked the president.

Haig shrugged, and his sharp eyes narrowed when he answered, "Well, nowhere does it say so specifically. The Israelis never actually promised to consult us, but we had every reason to understand that as strategic allies we could expect not to be taken by surprise again by an act as far-reaching as this, which clearly affects our interest as well as theirs."

"So what do you propose?" The president popped a few jelly beans into his mouth.

Haig took his time answering, and when he did, his voice was pensive and measured. "Well, Mr. President, I don't think we should risk weakening Israel's defensive capabilities by suspending aircraft deliveries like we did the last time, in the case of the Iraqi affair. But we have to convey a message to Mr. Begin that is sharp enough that he'll sit up and take note, and not surprise us again."

"Such as what?"

"I think the first thing we've got to do is to straighten out the ground rules between us, so that we'll know in future how to deal with one another. No more surprises! I therefore recommend that we suspend the strategic cooperation agreement which Begin wanted so much, until we have conducted a joint review of our interpretations of the agreement and the implications of Israel's action."

The president mulled this over and said, "You're right, Al. That's the way to go. Let's do it."

"I'll instruct our ambassador, Mr. President," said the secretary of state.[89]

The next day, Ambassador Sam Lewis phoned Yechiel Kadishai. "Yechiel, I need an appointment with the prime minister. It's quite pressing."

"What's so urgent, Sam? Has somebody in Jerusalem given somebody in Washington a headache?"

The ever-irreverent Yechiel enjoyed ribbing the American ambassador, and the ambassador, knowing him well enough, took it in the best of spirits.

"Something like that," he answered. "I have a message from my boss."

"Well, I think the prime minister has a message for your boss, too," said Yechiel, as if relishing what Mr. Begin had in mind for Mr. Lewis.

The prime minister received the ambassador the following morning in his residence. He was sitting in a chair, with one foot propped on a stool and, by him, a table covered with papers.

The men had come to like each other a great deal. Begin respected Lewis's urbane and well-honed diplomatic skills, which made him and his charming wife, Sallie, regulars in the social calendars of Israel's elite. In fact, during Lewis's eight years in Israel, which spanned the Carter and the Reagan administrations, he became so well connected, and was so well trusted, that frustrated politicians of whatever political hue would occasionally unburden their souls to him.

"Come on in, Sam," called Begin, when Lewis appeared at the door, accompanied by a note-taker.

"How are you feeling, Mr. Prime Minister?" asked the ambassador solicitously, shaking him by the hand. He noted that the premier's cheekbones and chin were more pronounced than ever, and there was pain in his eyes.

"Much better, thank you," answered the prime minister, vainly trying to pump a bit of cheer into his voice. "The trouble is, I can't bend my leg. But you know me by now, Sam – a Jew bends his knee to no one but to God."

Whether this was a bit of banter or a declaration of defiance was hard to tell.

Lewis shook the hands of two of the other men in the room, Defense Minister Ariel Sharon and Foreign Minister Yitzhak Shamir, each of whom grunted a gruff 'Shalom,' and gave him only glares. The prime minister invited him to take a seat, reached for the stack of papers by his side, and with a stony face and a steely voice, began a speech that would last for almost an hour. He never once paused to look at his notes. He gave a thunderous recitation of the perfidies perpetrated by Syria over the decades; its endless attacks on the residents of the Huleh Valley from the Golan Heights, the almost-successful Syrian seizure of the Heights during the Yom Kippur War, the Israeli sacrifices in pushing them back, and, finally, "Mr. Ambassador, I therefore have a very personal and urgent message for President Reagan, which I want you to transmit immediately."

"Of course," said Lewis, having been through this sort of ritual before. Everybody knew their roles and recited their lines.

"Mr. Ambassador, during the last six months, the U.S. Government punished Israel thrice. On June seventh we destroyed the atomic reactor near Baghdad. We did not have any doubt whatsoever about when that reactor would go 'hot.' Therefore, our act was one of salvation in the highest sense of the term. Nevertheless, you announced you were punishing us by breaching a written and signed contract for the delivery of F-16 aircraft."

"Not punishing you, Mr. Prime Minister, merely suspending – "

Begin galloped on, in a tone that told Lewis this was no fleeting squall. "Not long after, we bombed the headquarters of the PLO in Beirut – in self-defense, after a PLO massacre of our people, one of them an Auschwitz survivor. Regretfully, there were civilian casualties, and again you punished us. You suspended delivery of F-15 aircraft."

"Excuse me, Mr. Prime Minister, it was not – "

"By what right do you lecture us on civilian casualties, Mr. Ambassador? We wrack our brains to avoid civilian casualties. We sometimes risk the lives of our soldiers to avoid civilian casualties. We've read the history of the Second World War, Mr. Ambassador. We know what happened to civilians when you carried out your military operations against the enemy. We've also read the history of the Vietnam War, and we know all about what you called the 'body counts.'"

"Mr. Prime Minister, I must correct you – "

"A week ago, on the recommendation of the government, the Knesset adopted the Golan Law by a two-thirds overwhelming majority, and again you declare you are punishing us. What kind of language is this – punishing Israel? Are we a vassal state? Are we a banana republic? Are we fourteen-year-old boys that have to have our knuckles slapped if we misbehave?"

"This is not a punishment, Mr. Prime Minister; it's merely a suspension until – "

"Let me tell you, Mr. Ambassador, what kind of people this government is composed of. It is composed of men who fought, who risked their lives, and who suffered. You cannot and will not frighten us with punishments. Threats will fall on deaf ears. We are always willing to listen to reasoning. But you have no right to punish Israel, and I protest the very use of the term."

"But we've not used the term. The intention is to – "

"Excuse me, Mr. Ambassador, you announced that you are suspending the memorandum of understanding on strategic cooperation, and that its resumption is now contingent on progress in the autonomy talks concerning the Palestinian Arabs, and on the situation in Lebanon."

"That's not correct at all – "

"In other words you are making Israel a hostage to the memorandum of understanding. I regard your announcement as a renunciation of the agreement on the part of the American government of the memorandum of understanding. We shall not allow a sword of Damocles to hang over our heads. The people of Israel have lived for three thousand seven hundred years without a memorandum of understanding with America, and it will continue to live without it for another three thousand seven hundred years!"

"Please allow me to explain – "

"Moreover, in imposing upon us pecuniary sanctions, you have broken the word of the president. When Secretary of State Haig was here, he read to us the words of the president of the United States, that the United States would purchase from Israel military and other hardware to an amount of two hundred thousand dollars. Now you are saying this commitment will not be honored. That is breaking the word of the president. Is this proper, Mr. Ambassador? Is it done? What are you trying to do, hit us in our pockets?"

"If only you'd allow me to – "

"In nineteen forty-six, in this house where we are sitting today, there lived a British general whose name was Barker. Today, I live in this house. When we fought against him he called us terrorists, and yet we continued our struggle. After we blew up his headquarters in the King David Hotel, Barker said, 'You can punish this race only by hitting them in their pockets,' and he issued an order to his British troops that all Jewish coffee shops were to be out of bounds. 'Hit them in their pockets,' he said. That was the Barker philosophy. Well, I now understand why the whole great effort in the Senate to win a majority for the arms deal with Saudi Arabia was accompanied by such an ugly, anti-Semitic campaign."

"Not so – "

"Yes so. First came the slogan, *'Begin or Reagan!'* – the inference being that to oppose the deal with Saudi Arabia was tantamount to supporting a foreign prime minister while being disloyal to the president of the United States. Are such eminent senators as Kennedy, Jackson, Moynihan, Packwood, and of course Boschwitz, who expressed opposition to the deal, disloyal citizens? Are they? Then came another slogan: *'We will not allow the Jews to determine the foreign policy of the United States.'* Well, let me tell you something, Mr. Ambassador: no one will frighten the great and free Jewish community of the United States. No one will succeed in intimidating them with anti-Semitic propaganda. They will stand by us. This is the land of their forefathers, and they have a right and a duty to support it."

"Mr. Prime Minister, you surely don't believe that – "

"There are those who say the Golan Law adopted by the Knesset has to be rescinded. The word 'rescind,' Mr. Ambassador, is a concept from the time of the Inquisition. Our forefathers went to the stake rather than rescind their faith. We are not going to the stake, Mr. Ambassador. Thank God, we have enough strength to defend our independence and defend our rights. Rescinding the Golan Law – "

"We are merely suggesting a review – "

"Rescinding the Golan Law, which is what you would have us do, does not depend on me. It depends on the Knesset. And it is my firm belief that there is not a man alive who can convince the Knesset to annul this law. So please tell the secretary of state that the Golan Law shall remain in force. Nothing and nobody can bring about its abrogation."

Lewis had clearly had enough. Dispensing with even the pretense of nicety, he shot back, "Mr. Prime Minister, you have not allowed me to explain what I have to say. I shall certainly deliver your urgent and private message to the president. But in the meantime, I have a message for you: between friends and allies there should be no surprises. There should be consultations by either party on issues which affect the other's interests."

"Correct, but the surprise on this occasion was because we did not want to embarrass you, by putting you in a predicament vis-à-vis the Arab capitals with which you have ties. Had we told you beforehand what we intended to do, you would have said no. We did not want you to have to say no, and then proceed with the legislation, which is what we would have done under all circumstances."

Faced with this unending barrage, which to the ambassador seemed somewhat hyperbolic and, in part, even paranoid, he saw no point in carrying on, so he took his leave and set out on the drive back to his Tel Aviv Embassy, to cable off his report. On the way out of Jerusalem, he switched on the radio, and what he heard flummoxed him totally.

"I don't believe this is happening," he said morosely to his note-taker. "Is this Begin's idea of a private and urgent message to the president of the United States? Boy, is Washington going to have something to say about this."

What he was hearing was the voice of the cabinet secretary, repeating almost word for word, in English, for the benefit of the foreign correspondents assembled outside Begin's residence, the fieriest of all the passages of Begin's harangue.

The White House was livid. It deemed the language of the prime minister's message intemperate, it deemed its tone improper, and it deemed the treatment of its envoy an affront to America itself. That same day, President Reagan was seen heaving a huge sigh of bewilderment upon reading the report, scratching his head, and wheezing, "Boy, that guy Begin sure does make it hard to be his friend."

Shortly thereafter, Ambassador Lewis escorted a senior senator to meet Mr. Begin and assess the frozen situation. When the meeting was done, the ambassador said, "Mr. Prime Minister, there is something I wish to talk to you about. It concerns me personally."

Begin gave him an amiable look, and said, "Go ahead, Sam. What's on your mind?" There was not the slightest hint of guile in his voice.

"It has to do with the handling of the urgent and private message you asked me to deliver to the President," said Lewis. "The fact that you authorized the release of that message to the media almost immediately after I had left you, was, to put it mildly, a violation of every diplomatic norm and practice. And the way you did it made me feel I was being treated like an idiot."

"But surely, you realize there was nothing personal in what I said or did," said the prime minister, surprised at Lewis's rancor. "I considered your government's act of such grave national consequence that I felt compelled to fully inform our people of our stand, there and then, to make it plain that we, too, have red lines."

"Yes, but hardly had I left Jerusalem when I heard your spokesman on the radio quoting what you'd said to me almost word for word, in what was supposed to have been a personal message to the president."

Begin pursed his lips in thought, and said, "I simply never thought of it in that light, Sam. My one consideration was that, given the sharpest difference of views we had – and still have – on a matter so vital to our future as the Golan Heights, I felt our public had a right to know exactly what was said and where we stood. I apologize if I embarrassed you personally. Forgive me, please."

The tone of contrition in the prime minister's voice filled Sam Lewis with a sense of uncommon bemusement. Never had he thought this proudest of men capable of such humble apology.[90]

Chapter twenty-two

Pacta Sunt Servanda

There were those who would describe what occurred subsequently in the Reagan-Begin relationship as a deep freeze, others as a temporary lapse. The first spoke of rupture and schism, the others of a mere wobble. But the relationship recovered somewhat when, within Israel itself, a violent convulsion occurred: in preparation for a final withdrawal of Israeli troops from Egyptian territory, the Jewish settlements in Sinai were dismantled. Some in Washington had feared that, as a consequence of Sadat's assassination, the uncertainty surrounding the appointment of his successor, Hosni Mubarak, and the prospect of a surge in Islamism, Begin might well have second thoughts and seek a last-minute pretext not to withdraw. But when the day came for the final phase of the peace treaty to be enacted – April 25 1982 – withdraw he did.

"*Pacta sunt servanda* – agreements must be kept, treaties must be carried out," said Begin, with severe conviction. "It is the golden rule of international law. The observance of an international agreement is an absolute duty. If one side carries out their part, it obligates the other side to do the same. If one side commits a breach, it entitles the other side to do the same."

We were in his apartment, where he was now managing to hobble about with the help of a cane, which was what he was doing now, after having perused letters and other documents which I had brought to him for approval. But his mind was elsewhere. I could see it in his eyes, which were clouded with sadness as he picked up a week-old newspaper and stared at the photograph which dominated its front page. It portrayed the wrenching spectacle of Israeli soldiers scaling barricaded buildings on ladders, forcefully evicting protesting inhabitants and other anti-withdrawal diehards from Yamit, a brand-new town of pristine beauty that had been built out of the sand dunes of Sinai's Mediterranean coastline. But Yamit had to go, if the peace treaty was to stand.

Begin put the paper down, but I could sense that he was still seeing that photo. "What a tragedy," he mumbled. "What a trauma." And then, affirming the validity of forcefully evacuating and destroying Yamit, he said with utter finality, "We have to honor our signature. We must remain true to our commitment. *Pacta sunt servanda!*"

Fifteen years of Israeli presence in Sinai would end at noon the following day – fifteen years that had involved incessant toil, infrastructural investment, oil exploration, desert reclamation, and widespread settlement construction. At noon, the last Israeli flag would be lowered in a low-key military ceremony at the resort which Israel had begun building, Ophira, on a spit of land abutting the Straits of Tiran. As of tomorrow it would revert to its original Arabic name: Sharm el-Sheikh.

The operative paragraph of the IDF order of the day read:

"We are leaving Sinai primarily for our own sake – for the sake of our children and future generations, to try and find a way other than warfare – a way of the outstretched hand of peace."

Beneath these words a military intelligence officer had scribbled:

"The Egyptians have distributed national flags to the locals, and it is expected that as our contingent pulls back to the Israeli frontier they will be followed by cheering, jeering and waving Bedouin, who will slaughter sheep along the roadside in celebration."

"So be it," sighed the prime minister, reading the note. "Let them slaughter sheep to their heart's content. Were Sadat alive things might have been a little different. Time alone will tell." And then, almost fatalistically, "Mubarak is certainly no Sadat. With Anwar, whatever our differences, we developed a very close relationship, based, in the first instance, on mutual trust. We used to open our hearts to one another. Often we would speak about our beliefs and our ancient traditions, and our experiences, and how they impacted on our lives and made us what we are. And he used to tell me things which he told nobody else, including the fact that he did not hold his Mubarak, his vice president, in the highest esteem."

Leaning on his cane, he limped back to where he'd been sitting, and in a voice permeated with nostalgia, said, "Our families became very close. We were drawn to one another – our wives, our children. His family became like my own. And when Anwar was assassinated we grieved, oh how we grieved. I said to Jehan, and to Anwar's son and daughters, I said, and I meant every word of what I said, that his death was a loss to the world, to the Middle East, to Egypt, to Israel, and to my wife and to myself personally. We invited all the family to Israel. The invitation still stands. They will be our personal guests."

"And how will Mubarak take to that, you maintaining such a close personal relationship with Mrs. Sadat?" I asked.

Begin gave me an impatient shrug, as if not wishing to even contemplate the implications of my question and, instead, rambled on in a husky, distant voice, "I trusted Anwar. By the time it came to implementing the clauses of the peace treaty, I sensed that despite all the ups and downs he genuinely wanted this to be a reconciliation between our peoples, not simply a contract between our governments. We once said to each other that our lives are short, but the peace must surely outlive us. One day we were sitting together on his terrace in Alexandria, just the two of us, he puffing on his pipe and looking out to sea, and he said, 'You know, Menachem, there will come a time when I will no longer be president of Egypt.' And I said to him, 'You know, Anwar, there will come a time when I will no longer be prime minister of Israel.' And then we laughed, and embraced, and said to one another with true affection that while we will inevitably go the way of all flesh, our nations will never pass away, and neither, with the grace of God, will the peace."

Eyes glittering, fixed on images from an unforgettable time and place, he continued his reminiscences. "Ah, remember El Arish? Remember how the war invalids, ours and theirs, casualties of five wars, met and embraced? One had to see it to believe it – to see with one's own eyes that such reconciliation was possible: soldiers, some without hands, some without legs, some blinded, maimed for life, hugged and kissed, and cried out to each other over and over, 'Never again war! No more war ever again.' I doubt if such a thing has ever happened anywhere, at any time, in any other country."

And then, beseechingly, like a prayer, "May the Almighty induce in Hosni Mubarak's heart the belief in this sort of peace – the peace which Anwar and I believed in."[91]

With that, he leaned across the table, took pen and paper in hand and began to write a note to Jehan Sadat with intense concentration:

Our hearts, Madame, go out on this day to you and your children and grandchildren. Anwar Sadat, of blessed memory, should have been with us to see the glory of his efforts to make peace and achieve reconciliation between the good peoples of Egypt and Israel. To prove that his memory did not die, that it will live on forever in the hearts of women and men of goodwill, we have to work for the sacred cause: "No more war, no more bloodshed, peace, salaam, shalom, between our nations."

We embrace you, our dear friend,
Aliza and Menachem Begin

He laid down his pen, handed me the page, and said, "Try and make sure our ambassador in Cairo delivers this personally to Mrs. Sadat as soon as possible."

Our hearts, Madam, go out on this day to you and the children and grandchildren.

Anwar Sadat of blessed memory should have been with us to see a the

Glory of his efforts to make peace and achieve reconciliation between the good

peoples of Egypt and Israel. To prove that his memory did

not die, that it the will live forever in the hearts of women and men

of goodwill will, we all to to work for the sacred cause :, no more war,

no more bloodshed, peace, salam, shalom between our nations."

We embrace you, our dear friend

Aliza Menachem Begin

Personal message from the Begins to Mrs. Jehan Sadat on the day
of Israel's final withdrawal from Sinai, 25 April 1982

Chapter twenty-three

The Sabbath Queen

Once the last phase of the peace treaty was completed, the prime minister began devoting himself with renewed vigor to domestic affairs. For a long time he had been itching to take on one of the most powerful labor unions in the country – the El Al workforce. He wanted to put a stop to the operations of Israel's national airline from sundown Friday to sundown Saturday (the hours of the Jewish Sabbath), as well as on the major Jewish festivals. It was on this topic that Mr. Begin addressed the Knesset in May 1982, from the rostrum rather than from a wheelchair – the first time he had done so since breaking his hip almost six months before. However, since he was still in pain, it was with heavy steps that he mounted the platform, leaning on the arm of an usher and supported by his cane.

For days, the Knesset had been permeated with a rising tension as muscular, stocky men roamed its corridors and canteens, and approached its committees, their numbers rising daily. These were the El Al union bosses, accompanied by their whispering lawyers, intent on scotching Prime Minister Begin's plan to halt the carrier's flights on holy days. Without letup, they pressured, pestered, and petitioned the parliamentarians. Even the strictly observant interior minister, Dr. Yosef Burg, was collared. He was waylaid by a union man who placed an amicable arm around his shoulder and then jabbed a forefinger into his chest and barked into his face so sharply that Dr Burg's head was jerked backward, as though the arguments were being shoved physically down his throat.

"Mr. Speaker, ladies and gentlemen, members of the Knesset," Begin began, "the government has decided that following a time lapse of three months, the aircraft of our national airline, El Al, will no longer fly on the Jewish Sabbath and festivals."

This announcement resulted in looks of sheer hatred appearing on the faces of the union men, who sat watching the proceedings in the public gallery. The opposition benches erupted into paroxysms of heckling: "So why don't you shut down the television on Shabbat, too?" screamed one.

"Are you going to stop Israel merchant ships at sea, too?" yelled another.

The derision fazed the premier not one bit. On the contrary, it supplied him with new inspiration. "Shout as much as you want," he taunted, scanning the opposition faces with scorn, his gaze finally settling on the young radical leftist, Yossi Sarid. "I have nothing to say to you and your kind. In fact, I have nothing to say to anyone who supports a Palestinian state, which is a mortal danger to our people." And then, changing his tone, altering his voice to a muted, sonorous pitch, this man who believed in oratory as the supreme weapon, an artful combination of style, cadence, and the application of formidable intellectual energy, argued, "Forty years ago I returned from exile to Eretz Yisrael. Engraved in my memory still are the lives of millions of Jews, simple, ordinary folk, eking out a livelihood in that forlorn Diaspora, where the storms of anti-Semitism raged. They were not permitted to work on the Christian day of rest, Sunday, and they refused to work on *their* day of rest, Saturday, for they lived by the commandment, 'Remember the Sabbath day to keep it holy.' So each week they foreswore two whole days of hard-won earnings. This meant destitution for many. But they would not desecrate the Sabbath day."

"So, stop football on Shabbat, too?" heckled Sarid, triggering off yet another squall of jeers, hissing and name-calling.

Adroitly, cutting through the pandemonium, Begin told the tale of Salonika, and as he did so the House listened. "In Greece there is a port city called Salonika, which had an extensive Jewish population before the war. Most of the port workers there were Jewish, and on Shabbat they did not work. Those stevedores would forego their pay rather than desecrate the Shabbat. The goyim accepted this as a fact of life, and the port was closed on the Sabbath day. Imagine that!"

"And you want to close down the whole country, turn us back to the Dark Ages," yelled somebody.

Photograph credit: Chanania Herman & Israel Government Press Office

Prime Minister Begin with Minister of the Interior Dr. Yosef Burg

Photograph credit: Chanania Herman & Israel Government Press Office

*An enthused and dynamic Prime Minister Begin using his powers of
persuasion on colleagues MKs Yosef Rom and Chaim Kaufman*

"Ah, the Dark Ages," echoed the prime minister sarcastically, and to the delight of his supporters, he calmly raised his right hand as if to catch a ball, tossed it back toward the heckler, and resumed his rhetorical flow. "The Dark Ages, you say. Well let me tell you something, my dear socialist friend: Shabbat enshrines a social-ethical principle without peer. Shabbat is one of the loftiest values in all of humanity. It originated with us, the Jews. It is all ours. No other civilization in history knew a day of rest. Ancient Egypt had a great culture whose treasures are on view to this day, yet the Egypt of antiquity did not know a day of rest. The Greeks of old excelled in philosophy and the arts, yet they did not know a day of rest. Rome established mighty empires and instituted a system of law which is relevant to this day, yet they did not know a day of rest. Neither did the civilizations of Assyria, Babylon, Persia, India, China – not one of them knew a day of rest."

"So, put on a yarmulke," sneered somebody.

"Chutzpah!" boomed Begin, bristling. "I speak of our people's most hallowed values and you dare stoop to mockery. Shame on you!" With arms held high, he thundered, "One nation alone sanctified the Shabbat, a small nation, the nation that heard the voice at Sinai, 'so that your man-servant and your maidservant may rest as well as you.' Ours is the nation that bequeathed to humanity the imperative of a day of rest to apply to the most humble of beings. Ours is the nation that gave the laborers the dignity equal to that of their employers, that both are equal in the eyes of God. Ours is the nation that bequeathed this gift to other faiths: Christianity – Sunday; Islam – Friday. Ours is the nation that enthroned Shabbat as sovereign Queen."

A chorus of approval from the government benches went up, muffling every last vestige of dissent. Begin, idol of the common folk, caught up in his enthusiasm and sense of mission, rose to a crescendo. "So are we, in our own reborn Jewish State, to allow our blue and white El Al planes to fly to and fro, as if to broadcast to the world that there is no Shabbat in Israel? Should we, who by faith and tradition heard the commandment at Sinai, now deliver a message to all and sundry through our El Al planes – 'No, do not remember the Sabbath day. Forget the Sabbath day! Desecrate the Sabbath day.' I shudder at the thought that the aircraft of our national carrier have been taking off the world over on the seventh day over these many years, in full view of Jews and Gentiles alike."

The ensuing rumpus was terrific. The Speaker sat, vainly banging his gavel, which thudded as soundlessly as a velvet mallet. So Begin himself raised his palms and then lowered them gently, once, twice, thrice, until the furor quieted. Once it had, he fixed his eyes on the public gallery and cast a solemn stare at its occupants. "Let me say this to you, the good workers of El Al. The government has been the object of threats from some of you if we go ahead with our decision. We disregard these threats. In a democracy, government decisions are not made under threat. We cannot engage in profit-and-loss calculations when it comes to the eternal heritage of the Jewish people. There is no way of assessing the religious, national, social, historical, and ethical values of the Sabbath day by the yardstick of financial loss or gain. In our revived Jewish State we simply cannot engage in such calculations. If it were not for the Shabbat that restored the souls and revived the spiritual lives, week by week, of our long-suffering nation, our trials and vicissitudes would have pulled us down to the lowest levels of materialism and moral and intellectual decay." And to hammer his point home, he ended his speech with the celebrated saying, "More than the Jews have kept the Sabbath day, the Sabbath day has kept the Jews."

With that he turned to limp back to his seat, amid cheers and jeers, but hardly had he taken a step when, struck by a sudden additional thought, he hobbled back to the microphone, and declared, "Mr. Speaker, allow me just one further point. This House should know, it is not necessary to be an observant Jew to appreciate the full historic and sacred aura that enshrines this 'perfect gift' called Shabbat. Its prohibitions are not arbitrary. They provide insulation against corrosive everydayness, they build fences against invasions by the profane, and they enrich the soul by creating a space for sacred time. In a word, one need not be pious to accept the cherished principle of Shabbat. One merely needs to be a proud Jew."

The Speaker bellowed that he was putting the prime minister's statement to a vote, and instructed the tellers to start counting. The tally was 58 in favor and 54 against, and Menachem Begin exhaled a long sigh of relief as he limped his way out of the hall.[92]

His sense of satisfaction at this moral victory was short-lived when, back in his office he met at length with Minister of Defense Ariel Sharon who painted him a stark picture of the situation along Israel's border with Lebanon.

This mountainous frontier had long been a tinderbox, ever since Yasser Arafat had established his PLO headquarters in west Beirut in the late nineteen seventies, and then sent his men to occupy southern Lebanon, which they quickly transformed into a Palestinian ministate, dubbed Fatahland. The townships and villages of the northern Galilee were bombarded from its strongholds, sporadically but consistently, often bringing normal life to a standstill. Many fled southward, and those who remained spent many long and anxious days and nights huddled in shelters. As the escalation intensified, an apprehensive President Reagan dispatched a special emissary, Philip Habib, to try and broker a truce. This he had done, in July 1981. It lasted for eleven months, but it was honored mainly in the breach. Thus it was that when Sharon met Begin, on the day of his El Al speech, the first thing he did was to hand him a dossier registering two hundred and forty ceasefire violations – shellings, incursions, and outright terrorist attacks, some horrendous.

"Unless they stop and calm is restored," the defense minister warned, "the situation could well deteriorate into full-scale war."

Photograph credit: Ya'acov Sa'ar & Israel Government Press Office

Prime Minister Begin with Ariel Sharon

Chapter twenty-four

Waging War, Preaching Peace

If the amber light for the war in Lebanon flashed on when the PLO persisted in its terrorist attacks in direct violation of an American-sponsored ceasefire, it turned red on 3 June 1982, when an assassination attempt was made against one of Israel's most senior and gifted diplomats – Israel's ambassador to Great Britain, Shlomo Argov, who was shot in the head as he left a banquet at the Dorchester Hotel in London. In the words of one pundit, not since the shooting of Archduke Ferdinand in Sarajevo in 1914 had a hit squad – this one Palestinian – made war such a likely outcome.

The morning after the shooting, the prime minister sought out Dr. Yosef Burg, head of the National Religious Party, and invited him to his office for an urgent consultation. He wanted to persuade him to support the plan drawn up by Defense Minister Sharon for a massive IDF incursion into south Lebanon to drive the PLO terrorists out. Begin wanted unanimous cabinet consent, and he knew that Burg, an influential minister, had sharp reservations.

"Strike them by all means," said Burg, "but not a full-blown ground invasion."

Dr. Yosef Burg was a witty man, with chubby cheeks and a permanent twinkle in his sharp eyes. He was also an ordained rabbi, a doctor of philosophy, a master of eight languages and a Knesset member since the founding of the state. He had headed multiple governmental ministries under six prime ministers. With credentials like those, he knew enough to know that once the Lebanon curse struck it would be hard to get rid of it.

Beautiful Lebanon, once a tranquil country, had years before become bitterly factionalized, smitten with ethnic and religious insanity. Havoc, slaughter and treachery were by then a way of life: Shiite against Sunni; Sunni and Shiite against Druze; Christians against Sunni and Shiite; Druze and Christians against Syrians; in short, Lebanon had become a cursed land where the PLO had found it easy to carve out a formidably armed fiefdom – literally, a state within a state.

"We've already carried out air strikes against their bases in Beirut, and yet they are still bombarding our towns and villages along the border relentlessly. It's intolerable!" Begin replied in response to Burg's cautionary advice.

"But full-scale war will be even more intolerable," said Burg with determination.

"Yosef, we simply cannot allow an attack on our ambassador to go unanswered," countered Begin with impatience. "Ambassador Argov was chosen as a target because he is a Jew, because he is an Israeli, and because he is a symbol of the state. An attack on an ambassador is tantamount to an attack on the state itself."

"That's as may be, but we are not dealing here with international protocol," said Burg, in a tone of biting irony.

Begin gave him a solemn look: "And I tell you, we would have to bury our heads in shame were we not to respond in force and clear the killers out."

A thought drifted across Burg's face and his eyes darkened. "Supposing I support the plan," he said, "what are the casualty estimates?"

Begin stared back at him sadly. "My feelings of trepidation are no less than yours, believe me. We will suffer casualties. Only a fool would say this is a cut-and-dried affair. The PLO thugs have modern Soviet-supplied armaments, and they will put up a fight. But our IDF will put up a stronger fight, and we'll vanquish them."

"Yes, we shall. But again I ask, at what cost?"

In slow, solemn tones, Begin answered. "Everything will be done to prevent casualties. Given the limited nature of the operation, which is to remove our towns and villages from beyond the range of the terrorists' fire – that is to say, to push the enemy back forty kilometers from our border – I am assured the casualty rate will be relatively small. But nobody can deny that military action means losses, and losses mean bereavement and orphans. If Operation Peace for Galilee – that is the code name of the intended operation – succeeds in freeing northern Galilee from perpetual threat, that in itself will be a worthwhile accomplishment, even if the quiet doesn't last indefinitely."

"But how can you call it an accomplishment when, once we've withdrawn, the terrorists will regroup and come back to harass us?"

Begin's eyes went hard. "I tell you that even though I cannot promise anything conclusively, by launching this operation now we will make sure to destroy and uproot the bulk of the terrorist infrastructure. If thousands of terrorists are killed in the process that, too, will be an accomplishment."

"And what of the Syrians?" argued Burg. "They have thirty thousand troops in northern and eastern Lebanon, as well as ground-to-air missiles."

"Our intention," said Begin cautiously, "is to make every effort to avoid confrontation with the Syrians, unless the Syrians decide to confront us."

"Fine! And what about the day after Operation Peace for Galilee? Where do we go from there?"

"None of us can answer that question now. I am not going to play charlatan. I certainly cannot give a guarantee of what will come after. Perhaps our intervention will enable the Lebanese Christians to gain the upper hand. Perhaps it will break the back of the Nazi-PLO organization altogether. All I can say now is that once we've completed Operation Peace for Galilee we can then review how best to consolidate it. One thing for sure, we're not in Lebanon to stay. Israel certainly does not seek a single centimeter of Lebanese territory."

Burg threw him a melancholy smile, and said, "And have you put our American friends on notice so that they won't complain we're taking them by surprise again?"

The prime minister breathed an exasperated sigh, and said, "Yes and no. Sharon was in Washington last month and he all but forewarned Secretary of State Haig and others that they shouldn't feel we've taken them by surprise if we respond massively to the incessant violations of the ceasefire which they themselves brokered."

"And what was their response?"

"Haig is certainly sympathetic to our problems. He doesn't doubt our inherent right to self-defense. But he gave us no green light. Perhaps he gave us an amber one, but I wouldn't count on that either."

Burg mulled this over in silence, his face studying the framed map on the wall by the prime minister's desk. Its uppermost sector, marking the Galilean mountains, was colored a deep brown, which merged into the even deeper brown of southern Lebanon, with its craggy slopes, deep ravines, and dry stream beds. Perhaps Burg was thinking of his son, Avrum, a parachutist officer in the reserves, who would almost assuredly be conscripted to fight in that forbidding and fractured terrain.

Begin, as if reading his colleague's mind, fixed his eyes unblinkingly on him, and in a voice full of the irrepressible drama always present in his rhetoric, said, "Yosef, the question is, who is going to prevail – the brutes over us or we over the brutes? The decision is ours to make. I don't believe we have a choice. We will be nobody's cowering Jew. We won't wait for the Americans or the United Nations to save us. Those days are over. We have to defend ourselves. Without our readiness for self-sacrifice, there will be another Auschwitz. And if we have to pay a price for the sake of our self-defense, then we will have to pay it. Yes, war means bloodshed, bereavement, orphans – and that is a terrible thing to contemplate. But when an imperative arises to protect our people from being bled, as they are being bled now in Galilee, how can any one of us doubt what we have to do?"[93]

On Saturday night, 5 June, the prime minister convened the cabinet for a final vote on Operation Peace for Galilee, set to begin the following morning. There were three abstentions, one of them Dr. Burg's. The next day, Ambassador Samuel Lewis rushed to Jerusalem to hand the prime minister an urgent letter from President Reagan:

> Dear Menachem,
>
> Following the abominable shooting of Ambassador Argov and the subsequent escalation of violence, I am sure you are aware of our efforts with the interested parties in Europe and the Middle East to urge that no actions be taken against Israel that could worsen the situation. As we continue our efforts, I hope you will ... do what you can to avoid military steps that could lead to a widening of the conflict and even greater Israeli casualties.
>
> [...]
>
> I hope you will agree on the need to work together to bring about those conditions, which, over time, will recreate a stable and secure Lebanon, and ultimately lead to security on Israel's northern border. I pray our efforts will succeed to ensure the situation does not go beyond the violence of recent hours. As you know,

the security of Israel remains of the utmost concern to me. With warm regards,

Ronald Reagan

To which the prime minister replied:

Dear Mr. President, Dear Friend,

I thank you for your letter. Your words of sympathy, friendship and understanding touched me deeply. I am in permanent contact with the surgeon – a wonderful man – who operated on Ambassador Argov. His last call from London came yesterday evening; the good doctor informed me that he still could not make a definite prognosis. It seems already clear, however, that if the ambassador survives the assassination attempt, he will be left paralyzed. Nothing can be determined as yet about how his intellectual faculties will function.

For the last seventy-two hours, twenty-three of our towns, townships, and villages in Galilee have been under the constant shelling of Soviet-supplied heavy artillery and Katyusha rockets by the PLO terrorists. Tens of thousands of men, women, and children remain day and night in shelters. We have suffered casualties…. The purpose of the enemy is to kill – to kill Jews. Is there a nation in the world that would tolerate such a situation? Does not Article 51 of the UN Charter [the inherent right of self-defense] apply to us? Is the Jewish State an exception to all the rules applying to all other nations? The answer to these questions is enshrined in the questions themselves….

The army has been instructed to push back the terrorists to a distance of forty kilometers to the north, so that our citizens and their families can live peacefully and carry on their daily lives without the lurking permanent threat of sudden death.

I do hope, Mr. President, you will take into consideration the unique situation in which we find ourselves as a result of the repeated aggression against us perpetrated by a Soviet-promoted terrorist organization bent on shedding the blood of our people in our Land and abroad.

We shall do our sacred duty, so help us God.

Yours respectfully and sincerely,

Menachem

Just over a week later, while the war was raging as the IDF was advancing and occupying large swaths of Lebanese territory, the prime minister readied himself to travel to the United States. His purpose was to deliver an address at a special session of the United Nations General Assembly on international disarmament, and, more importantly, to meet with President Reagan in the hope of settling their sharp differences over the Lebanon war.

As I busied myself polishing the prime minister's disarmament speech, he was becoming ever more embroiled in meetings with Defense Minister Ariel Sharon over the war in Lebanon. Clearly, it was not going according to plan. The Syrians had entered the fray, and the fighting was broadening into fierce encounters resulting in an ever-mounting number of casualties. Understandably, he was not happy when he was waylaid by a clutch of Israeli journalists waiting for him outside the airport VIP lounge as he was about to board his flight to the United States:

"Mr. Begin, in view of the fighting in Lebanon and the criticism in the world press about the alleged thousands of Lebanese casualties inflicted by the IDF, shouldn't your U.S. visit be postponed?"

"No, it didn't even occur to me to postpone it. I received an invitation to address the UN General Assembly on the disarmament issue, and I think this an excellent time for the prime minister of Israel to deliver such an address to such a forum. Moreover, the president of the United States, Mr. Ronald Reagan, has invited me to the White House. We have much to talk about and to clarify, not least the grossly exaggerated claims concerning Lebanese casualties. So, yes, this is a visit of high national importance."

A second journalist stepped up. "Mr. Prime Minister, our forces are now in Beirut, and – "

"Correction, our forces are not in Beirut, they are at the approaches to Beirut."

"Sorry, at the approaches. This is far beyond the forty-kilometer security line which was the officially declared goal of Operation Peace for Galilee – to push the PLO weaponry beyond the range of our towns and villages along our northern border."

"Correct. But this was a necessary maneuver to out-flank the enemy. It is not a strategic goal."

"But now that the enemy has been pushed northward, what do you intend to do with their bases and command centers in Beirut itself?"

Menachem Begin pondered for a moment, stared hard at his shoes, and not without self-consciousness, answered, "I would like to answer your question, since I don't like evasion, but there is a matter of field security involved, and in a few days' time you will find out."

"How do you intend to respond to President Reagan's general criticism of this war?" asked a third man.

"Well, it's true, we have some differences in nuance, but there is also a basic agreement that the situation that existed in the past in Lebanon should not be restored. And now you will please excuse me, I have to address a UN disarmament conference on the eighteenth of June, and that is tomorrow, and I don't want to keep the good passengers of El Al waiting. Thank you. Shalom."

Menachem Begin's decision to personally attend a conference in Washington during wartime was not because of his esteem for the stature and integrity of the United Nations, dominated as it was by countries which could not tell right from wrong and which spent an inordinate amount of time castigating the Jewish State. As a student of history and an aficionado of Winston Churchill, he was familiar with the legendary war leader's admonishment on the eve of the UN's founding in 1946: "We must make sure that the UN's work is a reality and not a sham, that it is a force for action and not merely a frothing of words, that it is a true temple of peace in which the shields of many nations can some day be hung up, and not merely a cockpit in a Tower of Babel."

Over the years, no nation had been more pecked in that cockpit than Israel, which was precisely why Begin relished this opportunity to preach to that body about how the prophets of Israel had been the first to envision a world where nations would hang up their shields. What he had prepared for delivery was not oratory, but a homily based on the Book of Isaiah.

As he approached the dais, the representatives of the Arab and communist countries predictably walked out. However, the array of prime ministers, foreign ministers, ambassadors and other dignitaries who remained seated in the vast hall of the General Assembly numbered more than the count of those who often stayed to hear him in the Knesset, so he felt satisfied with that.

Holding his text close to his face, the prime minister read:

"Two ancient universal prophets in Israel, Yeshayahu ben Amotz and Micha Hamorashti, brought forth similar, although not identical, visions of complete disarmament and eternal peace. The vision of Isaiah is older. I shall, therefore, quote from chapter two of the book of his prophecies, which reads: 'And it shall come to pass in the last days, that the mountain of the Lord's House shall be established on the top of the mountains and shall be exalted over the hills…. And many people shall go and say, Come ye, and let us go to the mountain of the Lord…. For out of Zion shall go forth the Law, and the word of the Lord from Jerusalem…. And they shall beat their swords into plowshares and their spears into pruning-hooks; nation shall not lift up sword against nation, neither shall they learn war anymore."

Staring fixedly at the United Nations secretary-general, Javier Pérez de Cuéllar of Peru, Begin mused, "Mr. Secretary-General, is not Isaiah here predicting a remarkable vision of world disarmament and universal peace, millennia before disarmament conferences were ever thought of?"

Javier Pérez de Cuéllar drew his lips in thoughtfully, and nodded a vague assent.

"Moreover, this universal peace – when shall it come into being?"

The prime minister scanned the representatives of the nations, adjusted his spectacles, and again peered closely at his prepared text, as though studying a museum manuscript. "Honorable delegates, please note that in the original Hebrew it is written, *'vehaya b'acharit hayamim,'* which in classic English translation is generally rendered as 'in the last days,' or 'in the end of days.'"

His audience strained to follow his interpretation, which he proceeded to amplify. "Would this phrase not imply that we will have to wait until the last days – or the end of days – in order to merit universal peace and the tranquility of disarmament? Yet it is widely preached that with the coming of the last days – or the end of days – ice shall cover the earth and volcanic lava the continents. Well, then" – there was a sudden wryness in his tone – "where is the blessed peace? Where is the solace? Where is the succor? What consolation does Isaiah's vision bring to suffering mankind if in the last days – or the end of days – ice and lava shall cover the earth? Where is the cure for humanity's afflictions?"

A buzz of bafflement droned around the great hall, but it faded when the speaker declared with a sudden vibrancy, "Fellow delegates, Hebrew synonyms are rich and its homonyms are resonant. But they often suffer in translation. However, to those familiar with the original language of the Bible they are poetry."

Smiling faintly with the satisfaction of knowing that he alone in that mammoth chamber commanded the knowledge of the original language, the language of the Bible, he postulated, "In Hebrew, we would translate, 'in the last days,' or 'in the end of days' as, *B'ACHARON hayamim,'* However, Isaiah does not use those words, but an entirely different phrase:

'B'ACHARIT *hayamim*.' And though *'b'acharon'* and *'b'acharit'* are phonetically similar, their meanings are entirely different. *'Acharit hayamim'* does not mean 'the last days' or 'the end of days.' On the contrary! The key word, *'acharit,'* is a synonym for a bright future. It means *'tikva,'* – hope, as we find in Jeremiah chapter twenty-nine, verse eleven: *'latet lachem acharit v'tikva'* – 'to give to you a future and a hope,' or, 'to give you a hopeful future.' *'Acharit'* can also mean progeny, as we find in Ezekiel chapter twenty-three, verse twenty-five – and in progeny, too, there is future. Hence, *'b'acharit hayamim'* really means the days of hope, of future, of redemption, when mankind shall enjoy the full blessings of eternal peace for all generations to come. Such is the true vision of the prophet Isaiah."

Rising to his full height, in a tone that evoked high purpose, pride, conviction, and a Jewish sense of mission, Menachem Begin declared, "Nearly three millennia have passed since Isaiah's immortal words were uttered – *'vehaya b'acharit hayamim.'* Thousands of wars have devastated lands and destroyed countless millions of people. Whole nations have been on the brink of extermination, as manifested in the Holocaust of my people. Plowshares have been beaten into swords, pruning-hooks into spears. What then of the prophet's vision? Shall we, mankind, despair?"

Sitting there among the delegates, I looked around to gauge how they were taking this lesson on disarmament. The Chinese ambassador seemed sphinx-like in his inscrutability, while the Japanese representative simply looked like a tired bureaucrat. There were the bourgeois features of the Frenchman, and the unsure look of the Indian. The English delegate looked aloof; the Italian perplexed; the Austrian indifferent. I couldn't read the expression of the Egyptian – the only Arab to remain in the chamber – but I was heartened by the firm and encouraging gaze of the American delegate.

"Certainly not," thundered Begin, in answer to his own question, his voice sonorous and trembling. "To us, the Jews, so often the victims of man's inhumanity to man, Isaiah's words resonate as if they were spoken but yesterday. They declare: Never despair! His vision is like a lode star. It is distant yet bright. It shows us the way. And, indeed, one day in the bright future, *'b'acharit hayamim,'* universal peace shall surely come to pass. So, yes, let us strive on. Let us have faith."

With that, the prime minister moved on to his political remarks, expanding with concrete proposals for a global nuclear non-aggression pact, the establishment of nuclear-free zones, and the extension of strategic arms limitation treaties. These proposals he wound up with the words, "Fellow delegates: There is one question we have to ask ourselves:

whatever our animosities, our recriminations, and our states of war, can we nations still talk to one another? Israel's answer is a resounding, 'YES! WE MUST! WE CAN!'"

Thumping the lectern, he plunged into the story of how he and President Sadat of Egypt, enemies for decades, had finally made peace. "So, yes, we can do it. And yes, there shall surely come a time in the bright future – *vehaya b'acharit hayamim* – when our children and our children's children will beat their swords into plowshares and their spears into pruning-hooks. Nation shall not lift up sword against nation, neither shall they learn war anymore."

When he descended the rostrum, the delegate of some obscure Pacific archipelago rushed over to shake him by the hand, while in the public gallery one could tell by the pockets of applause where, exactly, Jews were sitting.

And then he flew on to Washington.

Chapter twenty-five

"I Did Not Mislead You"

M r. Prime Minister, I have a speech that I feel I must make to you, and since I want to be quite sure not to leave anything out I have made some notes for myself."

It was 21 June 1982, and the speaker was President Ronald Reagan. He held in his hand a pack of cue cards which instructed him to begin by saying, "Welcome, Mr. Prime Minister."

None of us on the Begin team scoffed any longer at this strange cue card practice of Reagan's. Between this meeting and the last, the prime minister had come to realize that this president's forte lay in knowing how to delegate authority, and in trusting his intuition over his brain power. Hence, when it came to the one-on-ones of the sort now taking place in the Oval Office, he preferred to go strictly by a preprepared script, which on that day he read in the same laconic tone one might use to discuss balmy weather, although there were definite signs of dark gray storm clouds approaching. So Begin leaned forward, fingers clenched, waiting for the storm clouds to burst.

"While I am delighted to see you again," said the president, "I wish very much the circumstances could be different. Events have occurred such that we are now forced to focus our attention on the grave risks and opportunities that your operation in Lebanon has created. When I learned, on the morning of June the sixth, that Israel's forces had launched a massive invasion into a country whose territorial integrity we are pledged to respect, I was genuinely shocked. In the past I tried to make clear that I shared your concern for the implications of the situation in Lebanon for your security, but repeatedly I have expressed the view that diplomatic solutions were the best way to proceed."

Begin gazed at Reagan earnestly, intent on absorbing his every word, while the latter paused to switch a card:

"I wrote to you immediately upon hearing of the hideous attack on Ambassador Argov in London. There can be no rational excuse for such terrorism, and I've been praying with you for his recovery. But Israel has lost ground to a great extent among our people as a result of your action. They cannot believe that this vile terrorist attack, nor even the accumulation of losses that Israel has suffered from the PLO terrorist activity since last summer, justified the death and destruction that the IDF has brought to so many people over the past two weeks."

"Death and destruction?" interrupted the prime minister, his expression pained. "You make it sound – "

"Obviously, what is done is done," continued Reagan, unyielding. "But I am determined to salvage from this tragedy a new Lebanon, one which will no longer constitute a threat to Israel and which can become a partner in the peace process. I know that these are also primary objectives of yours. This crisis is an opportunity to rid Lebanon of foreign military forces for the first time in many years, particularly the Syrian forces and the armed Palestinian elements. Palestinian fighting units must certainly be disarmed and/or evacuated. Those Palestinians remaining in Lebanon will have to live as peaceful residents, responsive to the authority of the central government."

Begin pinched his lower lip with his teeth and gently nodded his head, as if to say, *'Halaveye!'* (Yiddish for 'If only that was possible!')

The President again switched cards, and droned on, "In keeping with the objective you stated to me in your letter of June the sixth, you must move your forces back to a distance of forty kilometers from your northern border. We can then discuss a realistic time table for the phased withdrawal of Israeli forces and the introduction of a peacekeeping force to maintain the situation until Lebanon is stable. There will also have to be a realistic timetable for the withdrawal of Syrian forces. And as I have stated many times," – he again paused to swap a card – "you must have enough confidence in us that we can pursue our broader objectives in the Middle East."

And then, resolutely, "Mr. Prime Minister, your actions in Lebanon have seriously undermined our relationship with those Arab governments whose cooperation is essential to protect the Middle East from external threats, and to counter the forces of Soviet-sponsored radicalism and Islamic fundamentalism now growing within the region. These governments want to see Israel punished. U.S. influence in the Arab world, and our ability to achieve our strategic objectives, have been seriously damaged. I am determined to maintain our relationships with our Arab friends."

He flipped over the last card. "Our success in enhancing the U.S. strategic posture in the region and making strides in the peace process are also certainly in Israel's interests. From time to time, I may take actions with which you do not agree. I don't expect you to come out and approve them, but for heaven sakes" – this with uncommon intensity – "please don't oppose us. I want again to stress my commitment to maintain Israel's qualitative edge. Our ultimate purpose is to create more Egypts ready to make peace with Israel. And that's about all what I wanted to say." He pocketed his cards. "And now I would appreciate your comments."

For a moment Menachem Begin seemed to hesitate between civility and anger, but then he opted for the former, and answered, "Mr. President, I have listened carefully and have remembered everything you have said, including all your criticisms. Of those you've made many, and I shall answer each one candidly, as befits good friends. But first I want to tell you about the weapons we found in Lebanon. We found ten times more Soviet weaponry than even we anticipated. Three days ago our forces discovered a PLO arms depot in Sidon which will require five hundred truckloads to remove. Imagine that: five hundred truckloads."

His voice had dropped to an ominous rumble, but judging by Reagan's expression, his words were having no effect. So he continued in an even deeper, darker pitch. "Mr. President, we now estimate that it will take ten huge Mack trucks running day and night for six weeks to transport all the Soviet arms and ammunition we've captured, to Israel. In fact, we now realize that Lebanon had been turned into a major Soviet base. It had become the principal center of Soviet activities in the Middle East. It was a formidable international terrorist center. We have the documents to prove it, and we shall be happy to share them with you. Furthermore, among the documents were specific orders to shell and bombard our civilian centers. That's the kind of people we're dealing with."

"I will be glad to see the documents," said Reagan, his voice neutral.

The prime minister knew that anything to do with the Soviets grabbed this president's attention, so he pressed that angle further. "Mr. President, by our action we have not only set free our northern population from the constant threat of death, but have also rendered a great service to the United States and to the free world. We uprooted a Soviet base and the headquarters of an international terrorist organization in the heart of the Middle East."

The president carefully studied his manicured nails, still seemingly unimpressed. When he finally looked up, he asked, "But what about Syria? Why did you have to engage Syria?"

"We did our level best, Mr. President, to keep our distance from the Syrian forces, but they insisted on joining the enemy. In air battles the like of which have not been seen since World War Two, our Air Force downed one hundred Soviet-Syrian MIGs, without a single loss to ourselves. We also took out their Soviet-made SAM-6 missile batteries, employing a new technology which we ourselves developed and which we will be happy to share with you for the good of the free world." And then, triumphantly, "Mr. President, in every single engagement, the quality of U.S. weaponry far exceeded that of the Soviets, adding greatly to the free world's prestige."

Still, no positive response. A crease of grief furrowed Mr. Begin's brow when he softly and balefully said, "Of course, there were casualties. And you must believe me when I tell you that my heart aches for each casualty, and most of all for my own fellow countrymen. We've had two hundred and sixteen killed and one thousand wounded. For us, the Jewish people, who lost six million in the Holocaust, this is a heavy price."

Begin searched Reagan's eyes, as if pleading for understanding, but saw only an unfathomable remoteness. So he raised his voice a notch, and in a tone that was adamant yet still gentle, said, "Mr. President, there is something else on my mind that is deeply troubling me. I have been given to understand that you believe I misled you?"

The president looked the prime minister directly in the eye, and said, "Well, you did assure me in your letter of June sixth that your forces would not advance beyond a forty-kilometer line from your border. Yet in certain sectors they've gone far beyond that. They've almost reached Beirut."

"The forty-kilometer limit of our advance was and remains our goal," answered Begin intrepidly. "But we've had to go beyond it in a number of sectors in order to secure our objective. These are purely tactical measures, which any army would have to do to assure the security of the forty-kilometer zone which we have designated." And then, with unrestrained earnestness: "Mr. President, I did not mislead you. I am an old man, and in all my life I have never knowingly misled anyone. I would surely not mislead the president of the most powerful nation on earth."

Reagan nodded his understanding, encouraging Begin to spell out what hurt him the most in the inventory of complaints which had just been read out to him. "You asserted at the outset, Mr. President, that we massively invaded Lebanon. Now, for God's sake" – Reagan cocked an eyebrow at the intensity of the other man's umbrage – "we did not *invade* Lebanon. We were being attacked by bands operating across our border and we decided we had to defend ourselves. What would you have done if Russia was still occupying Alaska and was permitting armed bands to operate across your border? Did not the United States do exactly the same on at least two occasions, to defend itself across the Mexican border? Abraham Lincoln made a famous speech prior to the Mexican war, explaining why it was impossible to tolerate such incursions. And didn't Woodrow Wilson do the same when armed Mexican bands crossed into Texas and General Pershing was sent after them? We behaved no differently. We defended ourselves from aggression that had been going on for months. When the murderers tried to assassinate our ambassador in London we could remain passive no longer. Ambassador Argov is dying, and if by any chance he survives, he will be paralyzed for life. So, how could we not have reacted?"

"Yes, but in the process you've inflicted enormous civilian casualties."

The prime minister's face blanched, and a tremulous timbre entered his voice. "Not so, sir. When Ambassador Argov was shot we very carefully selected two purely military targets in Beirut – a sports stadium which the terrorists had turned into an arms depot, and a terrorist training base. Our forces exercised extreme caution not to hit civilians, and not one was hurt."

"But the perception here among our public is that you bombed Beirut after the shooting of the ambassador, and that the PLO shelled you in retaliation. These are the public perceptions we have to deal with."

"Those allegations are completely outrageous lies and exaggerations. We did not bomb Beirut. We very carefully struck two military targets in retaliation to the shelling of our civilian centers and to the shooting of our ambassador."

"That's as may be, but unfortunately this is not the perception among our public. Our people and the world saw the television news of damaged buildings in Beirut, and interpreted your action differently."

"Mr. President" – Begin was truly irate now – "after we struck those military targets, the PLO bombed our towns for three days without interruption. We had to act. Our people in the north have been hostages to the PLO for far too long. Whenever the murderers carried out terrorist attacks we could not retaliate without them bombarding our civilian centers in

*Begin with Reagan and their respective advisers during a working
session in the White House Cabinet Room, 21 June 1982*

*Begin and Reagan in animated discussion
in White House garden, 21 June 1982*

return. So our army just had to go in, clear them out, and resolve the problem once and for all."

"Well, I have to say again, the perception of your actions in Lebanon accent the human tragedy for innocent people."

"That perception is unfair. The media is biased against us, and the casualty figures have been grossly exaggerated. The PLO has widely circulated a figure that six hundred thousand people have been rendered homeless by our action in southern Lebanon. That is impossible. There are not six hundred thousand people in southern Lebanon. The actual figure is about twenty thousand. That, surely, is bad enough without multiplying it thirty times over. There were about four hundred killed in Sidon, not four thousand as was widely publicized. Even four hundred deaths are surely awful, but the stories circulated are ten times higher. Why accept as fact these false allegations against us?"

For anyone who has ever questioned the veracity of media reporting on matters to do with the Israel-Arab conflict in wartime, this contentious exchange between Reagan and Begin is, surely, instructive. Here was an American president shaping policy on the basis of perception, and not upon facts on the ground as the prime minister knew them to be. The president's perception was fed, first and foremost, by the voracious impatience – indeed tyranny – of a twenty-four-hour media cycle that is ravenous for news but is often out of sync with the incessantly changing military reality on the ground. Here was proof, if any was needed, that in a transparent real-time wartime information environment, rebuttal is persuasive only if done with instant and accurate information – an exercise in which Israel has been out-foxed time and time again.

On this occasion, at least, Begin did seemingly succeed in persuading the president that the truth did not tally with the news reports, for as Reagan rose to his feet, he said, "It's time we join our colleagues in the Cabinet Room, and I would like them to hear what you've just told me, so I suggest we start with that."[94]

As they walked into the Cabinet Room where their senior advisers were waiting, Menachem Begin had the sense that he had reestablished a measure of rapport with the president which, surely, would help foster their dialogue in the months ahead. It certainly helped when, after the usual pleasantries and photo-op, the president asked Begin, using his first name for the first time on the trip, "Menakem, please repeat for my colleagues what you just told me concerning the bombing of the sports stadium and PLO training base in Beirut."

The prime minister readily responded.

After he made his point, Secretary of State Alexander Haig remarked, "The latest wire service reports from Beirut say that shelling is continuing, and that the Soviet Embassy has reportedly been hit by artillery fire, inflicting casualties."

"That report is only from one source," said the head of Israel's military intelligence, General Sagui, who was a member of the premier's entourage. "It has not been corroborated, so I suggest we refrain from commenting on it until it is confirmed one way or another."

Begin added, "There has been firing on both sides, and perhaps a Palestinian shell hit the Soviet Embassy. We certainly have no interest in interfering with Soviet diplomats in Beirut." (Later reports would support his claim.)

"Would not the bulk of the Palestinians prefer to stay in Lebanon as part of Lebanese society and under Lebanese authority?" asked the president, of no one in particular.

"According to our information," answered Haig, "the Lebanese President, Elias Sarkis, has said the Palestinians could remain, but only as non-voting residents."

"And what's your view, Menakem?" asked Reagan.

"I think that for the sake of the future of Lebanon, a portion of the Palestinians should leave. After all, Libya and Iraq are almost empty countries, and perhaps they could take them in. One thing is for sure, if the PLO is disarmed and allowed to stay in Lebanon, they will re-arm in no time. It is impossible to stop Soviet gun-running. No central Lebanese authority is strong enough to do that. They have to go."

"That might well be true," conceded Reagan, "but surely you will agree that there can be no full answer to the Middle East problem until this Palestinian refugee situation is resolved."

"I agree, and it is doable," said Begin. "It is a humanitarian problem, and if only the Arabs had the will they could resolve it in short order. After all, that is how the refugee problems in Europe were resolved after World War Two. That's how the refugee issue was handled between Pakistan and India. That's how the refugee problem between Greece and Turkey was tackled. And that's how we tackled our own refugee problem. Israel took in and resettled some eight hundred thousand Jewish refugees expelled from Arab countries. But the Arabs keep *their* refugees in permanent camps and reject any suggestion of resettlement because, for them, their refugees are a weapon against us."

The President, wanting to move on, glanced at a cue card and read, "Cap, will you say a few words about our military strategy for the Middle East generally."

"Certainly, Mr. President," said Defense Secretary Caspar Weinberger, and he proceeded to explain to the prime minister and to the rest of us seated around the burnished oak conference table how America was trying to woo strategic Arab countries, some fabulously oil-rich, away from the Soviet influence.

"The U.S. is determined to pursue, as a strategic goal, an ability to protect Middle East oil countries," he said in his clipped, rapid speech. "This is a matter of acute national interest, because were these oil fields to fall to the East, the West would have a hard time surviving."

Smelling a rat, Begin looked hard at the defense secretary and the defense secretary looked back hard at him.

"The Soviets will soon need to import energy from the Arabs, and they may not choose to do so by conventional means," Weinberger went on. "So we have to be ready for any contingency. To secure these areas we have talked to Saudi Arabia, Jordan, and Oman, primarily. Thus far we have naval rights in Oman and bases in Egypt. We are striving to promote relations with other Arab countries, but they are reluctant to associate with us. For example, we have talked to Jordan and urged them to buy U.S. weapons, but instead King Hussein has turned to the Soviets for weaponry. This means no control by us over the supply, the number, or the use of such weaponry. I can't overstate how important it is for us to win over the Arabs, but it is terribly hard to carry out our policy of military supply, because the Arabs do not perceive us as a reliable supplier."

Weinberger sounded like he was making a diagnosis, but to Begin it came across as an existential threat. A low buzz of disaffection started in our ranks. Begin was twisting his lips in a way that as much as said, "How callous and voracious and shortsighted can a man be?" This sentiment entered his voice when he said contemptuously, "Mr. President, I absolutely differ with this presentation. Don't arm Jordan! Jordan is linked militarily with Iraq, and Iraq with the Soviet Union. Even as I speak, Soviet ships are docked in Akaba port unloading weapons for Iraq."

Sympathetically, yet firmly, Reagan responded, "But how long can Israel exist as an armed camp in a hostile world, Menakem? As I've said before, we have to create more Egypts. So yes, we are seeking to encourage Jordan to follow Sadat's path. But to influence King Hussein in that direction we must raise his confidence in us by agreeing to sell him arms. We would never sell arms to Jordan and then simply stand back when they use them. In this matter Israel must trust us. I've had a very good meeting with King Hussein, and I have the confidence to say to you, Menakem, that the U.S. will proceed in asking Jordan to express its willingness to deal with Israel, just as Egypt did. We believe that Jordan is prepared to be brought into the picture. Jordan bought Soviet weapons because the weapons we sold them in the past were so restricted in how they could use them as to be almost useless to them. On the other hand, we know that the king is very unhappy with the purchases he made from the Soviet Union. He wants ours. We would never try selling arms to Syria, for example, but only to those regimes which show signs of responsibility. And, believe me, we would not deal on trust alone, but would insist on assurances. We are using good judgment, Menakem."

As he was talking, Begin was shaking his head.

"I see you disagree," said the president. "So tell me, what are the alternatives? How can you live everlastingly surrounded by hostile neighbors, with your economy forever stretched to the limit, and your standard of living constantly drained? This is no future! So yes, we have made overtures to Jordan, Saudi Arabia, and Oman."

Begin was about to answer, but the president pre-empted him. "Just let me finish this thought. We intend to provide military equipment to those Arab nations who have come to rely on us, such as Jordan and Saudi Arabia, for the means to defend themselves. I believe that in so doing, Arab confidence in us is strengthened, our strategic position in the region is improved, and thereby we encourage these Arab nations to take risks for peace. And now let me hear your response."

Begin took aim and fired his salvo. "Mr. President, it is my responsibility to tell you that arming Jordan will pose a mortal threat to our survival. Yours is a mighty country, ours is Lilliputian. Does Jordan's goodwill really depend on airplanes? Of course, we trust the United States, but Jordan has never kept its promises. Supply Jordan with weaponry, and in minutes it could hit Israel's centers of population. Of course it's important to try to influence King Hussein to join the peace process. I am ready to receive him in Jerusalem at any time, or let him invite me to Amman. But for the United States to arm him, in addition to Saudi Arabia, and the others – they, with their unprecedented wealth – could bankrupt us merely by our trying to keep up."

"So, if that's the case, what's your future, Menakem? What's your solution?" Reagan sounded genuinely empathetic.

"My solution is to say to you that five years ago, no one would have believed there would be a peace treaty with Egypt. It was achieved through great Israeli sacrifice and by maintaining Israel's deterrent strength. That is what brought Egypt to the peace table. That is what will bring the others to the peace table. If the Lebanon problem is solved, and I pray Operation Peace for Galilee will help solve it, Israel will have peace with Lebanon. If present policies are maintained by guaranteeing Israel's deterrent strength, Jordan, too, will have good reason to join the peace process. And as for Saudi Arabia, well, the only thing I can say about that so-called country – if it is a country at all – is that it is the most fanatical of all the Arab states in their striving to destroy Israel. I go further: the U.S. money which goes to pay for Saudi oil often ends up enabling the Soviets to buy weapons for the PLO."

"That's not so!" barked an angry defense secretary, a muscle jumping in his jaw. "The U.S. relationship with Saudi Arabia enabled us to get the PLO to accept the ceasefire in Lebanon which we'd sponsored, and which lasted for almost a year until you invaded that country. This was solely because Saudi Arabia was able to use its influence with Syria which, in turn, used its influence with the PLO."

"Is that how it came about?" asked Reagan, searchingly.

"No, Mr. President, that is not how it came about," answered Begin. "Secretary Weinberger is wrong. Saudi Arabia did not persuade Syria – "

"Excuse me, they did – "

"Mr. Weinberger, please have the goodness not to interrupt me. The president has given me the floor."

The defense secretary went red and turned away, and Begin, turning his back on him, faced the president squarely and declared, "Anwar Sadat told me, personally and directly, that the so-called ceasefire, which the PLO honored only in the breach, came about solely because the Saudis paid twenty million dollars – TWENTY MILLION DOLLARS – directly into Yasser Arafat's bank account. It's as simple as that! And as for Saudi Arabia, I say again, they are the most extreme haters of my country."

"You could have said as much about Egypt at one time," said the president, a trifle sardonically. "Saudi Arabia is deeply anxious about its own future. It is fearful of domestic turmoil as well as of Soviet designs on its oil. And as Cap has pointed out, our strategic interest in that country is paramount. So you have to trust us, Menakem, that we won't pursue that interest at Israel's expense."

"Oh, we trust the United States absolutely," said the prime minister, "but even the best of intentions are sometimes hard to fulfill."

He might as well have said the road to hell is paved with good intentions, because that is how it came across.

Reagan, catching the nuance, countered, "I accept that over the last few years [meaning the Carter administration] the United States showed little muscle in world affairs. But now, things are different. Now, we are again growing muscular, and nations are beginning to take note. That's why the Soviets are ready to talk to us about arms reductions. And that is why, if only Israel had more confidence in what we are doing, we could proceed to a wider peace in the Middle East."

At some unseen signal, presumably from the president, Secretary of State Haig, who had remained largely reticent throughout the proceedings, took the floor, and said, "Time is running out and we need to sum up. While all of us are paying a price over Lebanon, something good might yet come out of it. We must get out of the Lebanese tragedy as soon as we can and get back to the work of peacemaking. After Egypt, Jordan is the next obvious choice and so, yes, we want to bring Jordan in, and we want Saudi Arabia in too, to endorse the outcome. Yet, as the president has pointed out, the United States cannot be oblivious to these countries' security concerns and expect at the same time to win them over to the peace process. So, Mr. Prime Minister, we ask you to join us in understanding why we have to conduct the policy the president has outlined with respect to those two countries. If we don't, the United States and Israel will be left isolated in the Middle East, and that is untenable for us. So this has to be our first order of business – the renewal of the peace process, beginning with Jordan and backed by Saudi Arabia, and I know that to make this happen all parties concerned will have to shed some attitude."

"I agree," said Begin surprisingly. "There are no eternal enemies. Today we even have a German ambassador in Tel Aviv."

Whether he said this for tactical or for other reasons was hard to tell. What mattered was that the president threw him a nod of satisfaction, and together they walked out to the South Lawn to meet the waiting press. As they stepped through the door, Reagan laughed out loud when Begin quipped: "I need hardly say, Ron, how grateful we are for your assistance. American aircraft with Israeli pilots are an unbeatable combination."

Speaking to the news people, Ronald Reagan exuded confidence and natural charm, making the session sound as if it had been a warm and casual chat: "It has been worthwhile to have Prime Minister Begin at the White House again. All of us share a common understanding of the need to bring peace and security to the Middle East. Today, we've had an opportunity to exchange views on how this cause can be advanced. On Lebanon, it is clear that we and Israel both seek an end to the violence there, and a sovereign, independent Lebanon under the authority of a strong, central government. We agree that Israel must not be subjected to violence from the north, and that the United States will continue to work to achieve these goals and to secure withdrawal of all foreign forces from Lebanon. And now, I invite our guest, Prime Minister Begin, to say a few words."

A far less sanguine Begin was more forthright. "Everybody knows that we now face a situation in the Middle East which calls for activity, great attention and understanding. I have read in some newspapers in this great country that Israel invaded Lebanon. This is a misnomer. Israel did not invade any country. You invade a land you want to conquer or annex. We don't covet even one inch of Lebanese territory, and we shall willingly withdraw our troops and bring them back home as soon as possible – as soon as arrangements are made that never again will our citizens – men, women and children – be attacked, maimed and killed by armed bands operating from Lebanon, and armed and supported by the Soviet Union and its satellites. There is hope that such arrangements will be made, and that all foreign forces, without exception, will be withdrawn from Lebanon, based on its territorial integrity. And we pray the day is near that such a Lebanon will sign a peace treaty with Israel, and live in peace forever. Thank you."

Chapter twenty-six

An Inept Attempt at
a Flawed Peace

I n his memoirs, *An American Life*, Ronald Reagan writes about the depth of his feelings for Israel, coupled with his exasperation in his dealings with its leadership – presumably a reference to Menachem Begin, though he does not mention him by name. He writes:

> I've believed many things in my life, but no conviction I ever held has been stronger than my belief that the United States must ensure the survival of Israel. The Holocaust, I believe, left America with a moral responsibility to ensure that what happened to the Jews under Hitler never happens again. We must not let it happen again. The civilized world owes a debt to the people who were the greatest victims of Hitler's madness. My dedication to the preservation of Israel was as strong when I left the White House as when I arrived there, even though this tiny ally, with whom we share democracy and many other values, was a source of great concern to me when I was President.[95]

One reason for this "great concern" was what happened after he had sent a top secret cable to Ambassador Samuel Lewis on 31 August 1982, containing a letter which he was to deliver without delay to Prime Minister Begin, who was vacationing in Nahariya, a small seaside town a few miles south of the Lebanese border.

By the time this letter was written, the IDF had not only cleared the PLO out of the south of Lebanon, but had also put such a squeeze on the last surviving PLO enclave in West Beirut that Yasser Arafat and his minions were driven out of that savagely fragmented land altogether, and dispersed to other Arab destinations, mainly Tunis. It took vicious fighting and tortuous negotiations brokered by the president's special emissary, Philip Habib, to make this happen, and once accomplished, the curtain rose again on another blow-up between Washington and Jerusalem. As before, the will of the prime minister was pitted against that of the president, who, believing the Peace for Galilee campaign had achieved its goal, concluded it was time for him to achieve his by launching a far-reaching Middle East peace initiative, just as he had indicated to Begin at their last meeting. It came to be called the Reagan Plan.

Ambassador Lewis knew that by delivering the president's letter he would be intruding on Begin's well-earned rest after the strains and the stresses of the war. He picked up the phone with enormous reluctance to ask for an appointment, feeling all the more uncomfortable because he was not entirely happy with the instructions he had received, but who was he to question a presidential order?

"Hello, this is the American ambassador speaking," said Lewis into the phone. "Please forgive me but – "

"Ah, Mr. Lewis, how are you?" answered Mrs. Aliza Begin, in her tobacco-roughened voice.

Mrs. Begin, though still an ailing woman, had recovered sufficiently to resume her normal routines.

"I'm well, thank you. I do apologize for intruding – " Lewis began.

"I presume it's not me you want to talk to, but my husband. Hold on, I'll call him."

He felt a little hot under the collar as he listened to the background talk of Mrs. Begin telling Mr. Begin that the American ambassador wanted to talk to him on the phone.

"Sam, good afternoon. How can I help you?"

The prime minister sounded like he was in fine fettle. He had good reason to be buoyant, for though the cost of the war had turned out to be bloodier than he had hoped and prayed for, its outcome was, by his lights, a resounding victory: not only had the IDF expelled the PLO from Lebanon, it had also taught Syria a lesson it would not readily forget, and the new Lebanese president-elect, Bashir Gemayel, a pro-western Christian, seemed amenable to negotiating a peace treaty with Israel.

"Forgive me, Mr. Prime Minister," said Lewis, "I wouldn't be bothering you, but I've just received instructions – "

"Speak up, Sam, the line is not very good."

"I said I've just received instructions to deliver to you personally a most urgent message from the president."

The prime minister sighed. "I hear what you say, Sam, but please understand, these have been rather stressful weeks, and I'm taking a few days' rest. So I hope whatever the message is can wait a few days."

"I'm afraid not, sir."

Begin sounded put out. "Sam, the last holiday I took was four years ago. I simply need a vacation, and I'm sure the president will appreciate that."

"I understand, but – "

"And I chose to come here to Nahariya, so that everybody should know that things are quiet again on our northern border. So, I suggest you speak to Yechiel to set up an appointment for when I return to my desk in a few days' time."

Lewis's hands went clammy. "In normal circumstances I'd do that, Mr. Prime Minister, but this really can't wait. My instructions are from the president himself."

Begin capitulated with a grunt: "In that case I suppose you'll have to do what you've been told to do."

"Thank you, Mr. Prime Minister. I'll leave Tel Aviv right away and be with you in a couple of hours."

"I shall be expecting you," said an irked Begin.

Sam Lewis was about to perform one of the more distasteful duties of his career. He was to go through the motions of consulting with the prime minister about a blueprint for a Middle East peace which carried the imprimatur of the president himself. He was to tell Begin that President Reagan intended to make his peace plan public in a nationwide address within the next seventy-two hours, hence the hurry. And while he was to assure the prime minister that he would report back everything he said concerning the presidential plan, he was to leave no impression that the plan itself was open to modification.

The letter in effect said that while the U.S. had hitherto functioned as mediator, it was now publicly expressing its own view. And that view was that for peace to endure, it must involve all those who have been most deeply affected by the conflict. Only through broader participation in the peace process – most immediately by Jordan and the Palestinians – would Israel be able to rest confident in the knowledge that its security and integrity would be respected by its neighbors. Hence, it was essential, wrote the president, to find a way, "to reconcile Israel's legitimate security concerns with the legitimate rights of the Palestinians." The preferred American solution was not a Palestinian state in the West Bank and the Gaza Strip, since that would not be viable, but rather a transitional five-year period of Palestinian self-government in the occupied territories as envisioned in the Camp David Accords, evolving into a political association with the Kingdom of Jordan. Moreover, "The United States will not support the use of any additional land for the purposes of settlements during the transition period. Indeed, the immediate adoption of a settlement freeze by Israel, more than any other action, could create the confidence needed for wider participation in these talks."

Identical démarches were made at exactly the same time by the American ambassadors in Riyadh, Cairo, and Amman which, unlike Jerusalem, were essentially in the picture, since Washington had already consulted with them.

As he was being driven along the coastal highway to Nahariya, Lewis read and reread the presidential letter and its attendant talking points, and the more he studied them, the more irritated he became. For one, he was uncomfortable with the style and contents of the talking points which he was instructed to deliver orally to Begin, together with the letter. They appeared to him to be ineptly and inappropriately phrased, couched (as he would later learn) in the identical language as that being employed by his ambassadorial colleagues in Jordan, Egypt, and Saudi Arabia when delivering their letters – as if Menachem Begin could possibly be persuaded to enter into negotiations swayed by the same arguments as those tailored to appeal to the Arab mind and interest.

Lewis could only assume that George Shultz, the new secretary of state in place of Alexander Haig, was a man of such high purpose and hidebound integrity that he mistakenly believed it was imperative that all his ambassadors follow the exact same script in all the Middle Eastern capitals, so that no one could later accuse him of double-dealing.

The ambassador was also chagrined at not having been consulted more than perfunctorily about this peace plan, which elaborated in far greater detail than any previous American initiative a solution to the most complicated political and territorial issues, and this without even attempting to solicit the thinking of the one party whose stakes were arguably the highest: Israel.

As his car sped northward to what he knew would be a thorny rendezvous, Samuel Lewis could not rid himself of these frustrations: why had he been left largely in the dark during the preparation of such a far-reaching plan? He did not disagree with its essence, but he bridled at having been excluded from the tightly knit coterie which the new secretary of state had gathered around him – and whom he'd sworn to absolute secrecy. He was the most qualified to offer significant input on the Israeli aspect of things, and the most competent to advise the president and the secretary how and when to present the plan to a man like Menachem Begin. The whole thing seemed to him to be so tactically flawed that it was bound to fail. As in life, so in diplomacy, timing can be as important as substance, and in this instance, the timing was abysmal. Had he been asked, Lewis would have urged prudence and patience: this was the worst of times to expect Israel to entertain an initiative in which it, alone, was being asked to make enormous sacrifices and take tremendous risks in surrendering up the West Bank and the Gaza Strip when the dust of the war in Lebanon had hardly settled; when the IDF was still deployed there and things were still messy; when the nation was still mourning its dead; and when the Israeli Right and Left were locked in a furious tug-of-war over the human cost of the war, the excessive length of the war, and the political gains of the war. Acceptance of the plan now, in whatever modified form, would be regarded by Begin as both a capitulation and an outright betrayal of everything his government stood for.

Such were his troubled thoughts as his car drew up to a small boarding house on a partially paved Nahariya street with a view of the sea. Its façade was the color of diluted mustard. His usual cheery smile, which he bestowed on the posse of security guards in attendance on the premier, was artificial. As he walked toward the door, Mrs. Begin, comfortably dressed in a housecoat and slippers, came padding out to usher him in with a gush of hospitality. Cheerfully, she explained that the advantage of not staying in a large seaside hotel was that her husband could avoid boisterous holidaymakers with rowdy children.

"Ah, here you are, Sam," said the prime minister, rising from an armchair to shake his hand, as the ambassador walked into a marvelously comfortable-looking room filled with overstuffed chairs strewn with needlepoint pillows.

"I really am sorry, Mr. Prime Minister, to disturb you – "

"Say no more about it, Sam. You have your duty to perform, and if your duty can't wait, you must perform it."

Lewis had never seen the prime minister looking so relaxed. Instead of his usual suit and tie he was wearing a sports shirt and slacks, and the spontaneity of his reception – warmed all the more by Mrs. Begin's freshly brewed tea and biscuits – made him feel all the more discomfited because of the unpleasant duty he was about to perform.

"Well, Sam," said the prime minister, after a pleasant preliminary chitchat, "what's on President Reagan's mind that can't wait?"

"I am instructed by the president to deliver this to you, Mr. Prime Minister," said Lewis gravely, handing over the letter.

"With your permission I shall read it in your presence. May I?" asked Mr. Begin, with his old-world courtesy – a set ritual the ambassador knew well.

"Please do."

Begin adjusted his spectacles, drew the page closer to his face, and began studying it with intense concentration, taking in the meaning of the words. The further he read, the more his brow puckered and his face dropped, so that by the time he reached the president's signature his features were a scowl and his mouth thin with displeasure.

"Sam," he said, "this is the saddest day of my life since becoming prime minister. Could you not have allowed us to enjoy our victory for just a day or two longer? Did you have to bring this to me now?" And then, eyes as steely as his face, he flared, "Mr. Ambassador, is this it, or do you have anything orally to add?"

"Yes, Mr. Prime Minister, I do," answered Lewis, hiding a thick swallow, and he proceeded to read out his talking points, which caused the expression on the prime minister's face to mutate from anger to angst and back again. When the ambassador related that Washington was consulting simultaneously with Jordan, Egypt and Saudi Arabia on the presidential plan, Begin became so angry that he bit his lip, and said from between clenched teeth, "Did I hear you say you were consulting with Saudi Arabia? What on earth does Saudi Arabia have to do with peace with Israel?

Are you telling me that your superiors in Washington are involving those anti-Israel, Islamic fanatics in determining our future, our very fate?"

"My instructions state – "

"I hear exactly what your instructions state, Mr. Ambassador. You have told me. They state that Washington has been consulting with everybody but with the government of Israel. And they state that the king of Jordan already seems favorably disposed to the presidential initiative which concerns Israel most of all, but about which my government knows least of all."

The premier stared at the letter in silence, his face grim. The ambassador held his tongue. The room went as quiet as a catacomb. Finally, Begin threw the ambassador a livid look, and with bitterness said, "Please inform the president that I have read his letter and am most unhappy both with its contents and its implications. I have also listened very carefully to your oral message and am extremely upset by its contents. You may tell the president and the secretary of state that I am astonished that your government did not see fit to indicate that such an initiative was in the making, or to consult with the government of Israel at any stage of its elaboration. This is entirely unacceptable. The whole initiative is utterly contrary to all our understandings with your country. It is not in accordance with the Camp David agreements; in fact it is a violation of those agreements. Of course, I will consult with my cabinet, and then give you a response. We being a democracy – unlike those others with whom your government has seen fit to consult – necessitates my being given time before giving a formal response."

"I understand," said Lewis – he really did – "but I am required to tell you that the president intends to make his plan public within the next seventy-two hours."

"In that case I ask you to please ask the president, on my behalf, to defer his speech for five or six days so as to enable me to return to Jerusalem to convene the cabinet for a full debate."

"I will certainly report your request, Mr. Prime Minister, but I have no way of knowing if the president can wait that long. He is very sensitive to premature leaks."

With weary dignity and a voice full of entreaty, Begin said, "Sam, this plan has been thrust upon us. It bears upon our very existence. I think President Reagan owes me at least that much; to give my government time to render a considered response."

"I promise I will do my very best," said the ambassador, rising and slipping his notebook into his briefcase. "I've made a record of everything you've said, and I shall now dash back to Tel Aviv and cable off your reaction and your request. And again, forgive me. I regret I had to interrupt your holiday for this purpose."

"So do I, Sam. So do I," muttered an unhappy prime minister.

The next evening, while the ambassador was attending a cocktail reception, one of his staff members nudged his way through the cluster of guests to deliver an urgent and highly classified cable which had just reached the embassy. When Lewis read it in the privacy of an out-of-the-way hallway, his left eyebrow rose a fraction, his heart missed a beat, and he muttered a sigh of dismay. His instruction was to deliver this message to the prime minister without delay, before the cabinet had time to formulate its response, which was set for the following morning. He pondered what best to do – drive straight to Nahariya and deliver the message personally, or take the inevitable flack over the telephone? He looked at his watch. It was late – too late to drive to Nahariya, so he sought out his chauffeur and told him to take him back to his embassy. "I have a call to make," he said, and on his way over, he pondered how best to make it.

"Good evening, Mrs. Begin. Forgive me for disturbing you again. It's Sam Lewis. May I – "

"Hold on. My husband is right here. Menachem, pick up the extension. It's Mr. Lewis."

"Hello, Sam. You have news?"

"I do, Mr. Prime Minister, and I'm afraid it's not as good as I would have wished."

Silence.

"Mr. Prime Minister, are you there?"

"Oh, yes, Mr. Ambassador, I am here, waiting to hear what you have to tell me." There was a spike of reproach in his voice.

Lewis spoke in as reasonable a tone as he could manage. "My instructions are to tell you that the president is unable to postpone his public address as you requested."

"Unable to postpone? Why not?" Begin's bitterness spilled through the receiver.

"Because some of its substance has already been leaked and, therefore, the president has decided to deliver his speech this evening, Washington time."

"This evening?! The president is making his initiative public this evening – even before my cabinet has the opportunity to deliberate upon it tomorrow morning?"

"I'm, afraid so, Mr. Prime Minister. I'm sorry."

"As well you might be, Mr. Ambassador."

The outrage in Begin's voice was peppered with a bitter cynicism. "Is this the way to treat a friend? Is this the way to treat an ally? Your government consorts with our despotic enemies and yet you choose to ignore us on a matter of vital import to our future? What kind of a discourse is this between democratic peoples who purport to cherish common values? Is this the way to make peace? We do not deserve this kind of treatment." And then, in a voice that had hardened ruthlessly: "Mr. Ambassador, please convey to the president exactly what I've just said. Tell him I am hurt to the core. And tell him that our cabinet will convene tomorrow as planned, and then we shall provide your government with our official response. Good night!"[96]

The response came in the form of a meticulously detailed and comprehensive refutation of every single point of the president's plan. The penultimate paragraph read, "Since the positions of the government of the United States seriously deviate from the Camp David agreements, contradict it, and could create a serious danger to Israel, its security and future, the government of Israel has resolved that on the basis of these positions it will not enter into any negotiations with any party."[97]

That done, the prime minister called me in to request I go over the draft of his accompanying letter to the president, which he had composed on paper from the boarding house before leaving Nahariya. After some minor 'shakespearizations' this is how it read:

Dear Ron,

Thank you for your letter of 31 August, 1982, which Ambassador Lewis was kind enough, upon instructions from his government, to bring to me to Nahariya, now free of rockets and shells.

I enclose, herewith, the resolution of the cabinet, September 2, 1982, adopted unanimously. As each of the paragraphs is elaborated, I have little to add except to state – taking if I may a leaf from your book – that the government of Israel will stand by the decision with total dedication.

I have also read your speech, which preceded by twenty-four hours the cabinet consultation with my colleagues. It serves as additional testimony to your opinion or resolve. Indeed, my friend, great events did take place since we last met in Washington in June. May I, however, give you a somewhat different version of those events? On 6 June, the Israeli Defense Forces entered Lebanon in order not to conquer territory, but to fight and smash the armed bands operating from that country against our land and its citizens. This, the IDF did. You will recall that we could not, regrettably, accept your suggestion that we proclaim a ceasefire on Thursday, 10 June, at 06:00 hours, because at that time the enemy was still eighteen kilometers from Metula, on our northern border. However, twenty-four hours later we pushed the enemy further northwards and we proclaimed a unilateral ceasefire on Friday 11 June at 12 noon. This was rejected by the terrorists. So the fighting continued, and it went on until 21 June when we suggested that all the terrorists leave Beirut and Lebanon, which they did with the help of the important good offices of Ambassador Philip Habib many weeks later. In the ensuing battles Israel lost 340 men killed and 2,200 wounded, 100 of them severely.

When the Syrian Army entered the fray – against all our appeals – we destroyed 405 Soviet-Syrian tanks, downed 102 Soviet-Syrian MIGs (including one MIG-25) and smashed 21 batteries of SAM-6, SAM-8, and SAM-9 air-to-ground missiles – all deadly weapons. Yet, in your letter to me, as in your speech to the American people, you didn't, Mr. President, see fit to mention even once the bravery of the Israeli fighter, and the great sacrifices of the Israeli army and our people. The impression one could have gotten was that Ambassador Philip Habib, with the help of expeditionary units, achieved this result. It is my duty to tell you, Mr. President, that I was struck by this omission. I state a fact. I do not complain.

What I do protest against is the omission to consult with us prior to sending out your proposals to Jordan and Saudi Arabia, the former an outspoken opponent of the Camp David Accords, the latter a complete stranger to, and an adversary of, those accords.

In face of the fact that there was no prior consultation, the U.S. government adopted the position that the 'West Bank' be re-associated with Jordan. What some call the 'West Bank,' Mr. President, is Judea and Samaria, and this simple historic truth will never change. There are cynics who mock history. They may deride history as much as they wish. I stand by the truth – the truth that millennia ago there was a Jewish kingdom of Judea and Samaria, where our kings knelt to God, where our prophets brought forth the vision of eternal peace, where we developed our rich civilization which we took with us in our hearts and minds on our long global trek for over eighteen centuries and, with it, we came back home.

By aggressive war and by invasion, King Abdullah [of Jordan] conquered parts of Samaria and Judea in 1948. Subsequently, in a war of most legitimate self-defense in 1967, after having been attacked by King Hussein [of Jordan], we liberated, with the Almighty's help, that same region of our homeland.

Judea and Samaria will never again be the 'West Bank' of the Hashemite Kingdom of Jordan, created by British colonialism after the French Army expelled King Faisel from Damascus [at the end of World War One].

At Camp David we suggested – yes, it was our initiative – full autonomy for the Arabs of Palestine, inhabitants of Judea and Samaria and the Gaza district, with a transitional period of five years. It is a generous suggestion of the widest scope of autonomy existing on earth in our time....

Geography and history have determined that the matter of security remains paramount, for Judea and Samaria are mountainous country; two-thirds of our population lives in the coastal plain below. From those mountains you can hit every city, every town, each township and village, and last but not least, our principal airport [Ben-Gurion] in the plain below. We used to live penned up in eight miles from the seashore and now, Mr. President, you suggest to us in your proposals that we return to almost that same situation.

True, you declare you will not support the creation of a Palestinian state in Judea, Samaria, and the Gaza district. But such a state will arise of itself the day Judea and Samaria are given to Jordanian jurisdiction. Then, in no time, we and you will have a Soviet base in the heart of the Middle East. Under no circumstances shall we accept such a possibility ever arising, which would endanger our very existence.

Mr. President, you and I chose for the last two years to call our countries 'friends and allies.' Such being the case, a friend does not weaken his friend, and an ally does not put his ally in jeopardy. This would be the inevitable consequence were the 'positions' transmitted to me on August 31, 1982, to become reality.

I believe they won't.

'*L'ma'an Zion lo echeshe, u'l'ma'an Yerushalayim lo eshkot*' – For Zion's sake I will not hold my peace, and for Jerusalem's sake I will not rest. (Isaiah, chapter 62).

Yours respectfully and sincerely,
Menachem[98]

מלון קרלטון בע"מ
נהריה
CARLTON HOTEL LTD.
NAHARIYA

Dear Ron,

Thank you for your letter of 31 August which Ambassador Lewis was kind enough, upon instruction from his Government, to bring to me *It* ⟨struck⟩ to Nahariya, *Il* now free of rockets and shells.

I enclose the ⟨decision⟩ *resolution* of the Cabinet, adopted ⟨struck⟩ *unanimously*

As every paragraph is elaborated, I have little *but* to add except to state, if I may take a leaf from your book, that the Government of Israel will stand by this decision with total dedication. I ⟨may⟩ ⟨struck⟩ ⟨say⟩, ⟨struck⟩ and with ⟨struck⟩ ⟨struck⟩.

I have also read your speech which preceded by 24 hours the consultation with my ⟨colleagues⟩ colleagues. It *was* ⟨struck⟩ an additional testimony to ⟨struck⟩ your opinion, or ⟨struck⟩ well.

Indeed, ⟨struck⟩ my friend, grad events took place since we met in June. May I, however, give you a somewhat different description of these events.

On the sixth of June, the Israeli Defence Forces entered

22101 NAHARIYA —ISRAEL— TELEPHONE : 922211— P. O. B. 124 — ת.ד. — 922211 : סלפון — 22101 — נהריה
CABLES : CARLTON NAHARIYA — מברקים : קרלטון נהריה TELEX 46299 סלקס

Chapter twenty-seven

The Rosh Hashanah of Sabra and Shatila

T he ambitious Reagan initiative was so flawed it was, as we have seen, doomed to failure before it even got off the ground. Moreover, it was swiftly overtaken by events, when yet another ghastly calamity rocked Lebanon. On 4 September that country's president-elect, Bashir Gemayel, on whom Begin had pinned his hopes for peace, was assassinated. In revenge, Christian militias slaughtered hundreds of Muslim civilians in two Palestinian refugee camps in West Beirut, known as Sabra and Shatila. This horrendous massacre occurred on the eve of Rosh Hashanah, 16 September. On the following morning, Mr. Begin stood waiting for me in the hallway of his residence, where I was meeting him to escort him to synagogue. His face was like stone. Contemptuously he snapped, "*Host du gehert aza meisa?* [Have you heard of such a thing?] Christians massacre Muslims and the goyim blame the Jews."

Dumbfounded, I said, "I don't understand."

"Precisely what I'm telling you. I first heard it on the BBC. I checked with our commanders on the spot. They told me it was true. Christian militias entered two Palestinian refugee camps in West Beirut to flush out residual PLO terrorist nests, and then set upon civilians, massacring hundreds. Our own men put a stop to it, yet predictably, the foreign media are blaming us." He looked at his watch. "Come, let us go. I'll tell you about it on the way."

Still not totally recovered from his broken hip, the prime minister grasped his cane, handed me the velvet pouch containing his prayer shawl, gripped my arm for support and, surrounded by bodyguards, began limping the few blocks toward Jerusalem's Great Synagogue, pausing periodically to acknowledge the New Year greetings of respectful passersby. While he walked, he leaned heavily on my arm and recounted what he knew of the hideous events that had occurred in Beirut over the past several days.

According to reports, buildings filled with people had been dynamited to the ground. The alleyways in the two refugee camps were filled with entangled corpses, hastily dug mass graves, and bodies bulldozed to the sides of lanes. Lebanon was slowly bleeding to death in the abattoir of its civil war, which had been ravaging its people since 1975. And even though everyone knew that in years past, Lebanese Arab Muslims and Lebanese Arab Christians had inflicted far more terrible slaughters on each other, and even though everyone knew that no Israelis were directly involved in these latest massacres, the Jewish State had been put in the dock of public opinion for allegedly having allowed the slaughter to happen.

"There's no one more respectful of world opinion than me," said Begin, with a hint of sarcasm, as we approached the synagogue. "But when papers in Washington, London and Paris brand us as aggressors and don't have a single accusatory word to say about those trying to kill our innocents, then we have to conclude that we face a blatant media bias."

"In other words, anti-Semitism," I said.

He paused, looked at me morosely, and said what he really meant: "There are many bleeding hearts among the goyim who say, 'God forbid – us, anti-Semites? Never! We're just anti-Israel.' Believe me, there comes a point where it's impossible to distinguish one from the other. This is why we have to stand up to these people and never be apologetic. We have to constantly remind them how their papers didn't say a single word while six million of our brethren were being slaughtered. Never once did they make an effort to pressure their governments to come to the rescue of even a single Jewish child. So I'm not at all surprised at this innate bias. It's always been the same" – this with a snarl – "goyim kill goyim and they hang the Jews."

This was not the only source of grief for the prime minister on that Rosh Hashanah. He deeply lamented the demise of the prospect of another treaty of peace with a neighbor. President-elect Bashir Gemayel had been so well disposed toward Israel that he had begun to deliberate seriously about being the next signatory to a treaty. Indeed, the prime minister, along with his defense minister Ariel Sharon, had been intensely engaged with Gemayel, negotiating its details. But just as the young president-elect was about to be officially inaugurated and assume formal control of his fractious domain, he was murdered, and the fragments of the peace treaty draft were left scattered among his remains.

And there was something else besides that distressed the prime minister as we walked to the Jerusalem Great Synagogue that day. Although the Peace for Galilee campaign had ended to his satisfaction, the fact that Israeli troops were still engaged deep inside Lebanon, with mounting casualties, had caused ever-increasing numbers of the public to regard the war without conviction. Angry and frustrated by the souring of events – what was originally conceived as a brief campaign had stretched from June into July, August, and now September – Israel was enduring protests and demonstrations almost daily. One group of antiwar protestors had mounted an around-the-clock vigil directly in front of the prime minister's residence, with a huge placard displaying the rising toll of the fallen, which, by that Rosh Hashanah, totaled more than six hundred. Whenever the newest casualty figures were brought to Begin's attention we, his staff, had marked his deep sorrow. His heart broke silently and a dull throb of grief possessed his spirit. "It's as though I do not have a home anymore," he told Dr. Burg wearily, speaking of the demonstrators outside his house. "It's as though I'm living on the street."

"I shall have them removed," declared Burg, who possessed the ministerial authority to do so.

"Under no circumstances," said Begin.

"But they are such a disturbance to you. In no other country are demonstrators allowed to demonstrate right in front of a prime minister's house."

"It is their democratic right," Begin had insisted. "Let them stay. I only pray they don't disturb the neighbors too much."

It was perhaps natural that Begin should accuse the leader of the Labor opposition, Shimon Peres, for the deepening civic rift. He had charged him with being more interested in pulling down national pillars than pondering the rights and wrongs of the war, the first in which partisan political divisions were ripping the country apart.

The man Peres wanted to bring down most, as, indeed, did some of Mr. Begin's own cabinet, was Defense Minister Sharon. To his antagonists, Sharon's purposes were as clear as that of a fox in a hen coop. The warrior who had long earned a reputation for boldness, decisiveness, and tactical skill was now being depicted as a satanic militarist. The Labor opposition had fingered him for every foul-up, and now they were demanding he be dismissed or be made to resign for mishandling the war and for allowing the Christian militia to enter Sabra and Shatila, even though he could not have possibly foreseen the terrible consequences.

"There will be no resignations and no dismissals," said the prime minister as we mounted the steps to the sanctuary. Once inside, he immediately calmed down, as if surrendering to the embrace of its sanctity. Wrapped in his prayer shawl, he worshipped with quiet passion, reading from a tattered prayer book that had been given to him as a bar mitzvah gift, pronouncing the words in the soft Ashkenazi intonations of his Warsaw youth. And when the cantor and the choir reached the pinnacle of the service in chanting the mournful prayer, *"U'Netaneh Tokef Kedushat Hayom"* [Let us tell how utterly holy is this day for it is awesome and terrible], his eyes glistened, and he swayed back and forth in profound piety.

Slowly and sorrowfully, the cantor came to the wrenching and brokenhearted incantation, "On Rosh Hashanah it is inscribed, and on Yom Kippur it is sealed: How many shall pass away, and how many shall be born. Who shall live and who shall die." Sighs and sobs swelled from the throats of the Jews in those pews where Menachem Begin stood, as the cantor's voice swelled in an agony of reverence, his eyes closed, his body swaying, his hands stretched out and up: "Who shall perish by the sword and who by wild beast, who by famine and who by thirst...who shall be at peace and who shall be pursued. Who shall be at rest and who tormented. Who shall be exalted and who shall be brought low. Who shall prosper and who shall be impoverished."

In answer to the suspended verdict of this dirge, the cantor rose on his toes in a finale of trembling and exulted conviction, and cried out at the top of his voice, in thunderous unison with the entire congregation, many of whom had endured the torment of the Holocaust and the bereavement of Israel's wars, *"U'teshuvah u'tefillah u'tzedakah ma'avirin et ro'a ha'gzeirah"* [But repentance, prayer and charity shall avert the severe decree].

Whereupon, I felt a gentle tap on my shoulder as if from on High, but it was only Zabush, chief of the prime minister's security detail that day.

"There's an ugly demonstration building up outside," he whispered into my ear. "You will have to take the prime minister out through the rear exit. We'll cut through the back alleyway and across the street to his home."

I transmitted this discreetly to Mr. Begin, behind whom I was sitting, but he gave no sign of acknowledgement. He was bent over his prayer book, steeped in the cantorial renditions and the congregational recitations, mouthing each supplication with the fervor of a believer. Upon the service's culmination, in buoyant optimism that prayers will indeed be answered, multitudes of congregants swarmed around him to wish him a *Shanah Tovah* – a happy new year.

Beaming, he shook every hand, and when he finally took my arm to go, Zabush hissed, "Follow me." I did, leading the prime minister through the last remaining clusters of well-wishing congregants, and toward the synagogue's rear exit.

"Where are you taking me?" demanded Begin, halting mid-stride.

Zabush explained.

"Under no circumstances will I go out this way," he retorted angrily. "I will not slink out of the synagogue. I will leave the way I came, through the front door, demonstration or no demonstration."

Zabush spoke into his walkie-talkie urgently, alerting his squad outside. As the prime minister emerged into the synagogue's forecourt, a horde of demonstrators tried to crush in upon him. Spittle, clenched fists, and cries of "Murderer!" assaulted the sanctity of the day as anxious policemen and guards pushed, kicked, and elbowed the baying crowd, cutting a channel through the crush to form a close cordon around us, while swarms of reporters recorded the pandemonium.

The prime minister's bespectacled, bony features showed nothing but boldness, but rage was swelling within him. I could feel it in the sharp nip of his fingers pinching into my arm as he leaned on me. He was deliberately limping at an artificially slow pace in a show of defiance that made my every nerve shudder.

All the frustrations over the long Lebanese war seemed to explode on that Rosh Hashanah outside the Great Synagogue, as protestors yelled over and over again, "Begin is a murderer!" Some surged ahead to join the pickets encamped across the street from the prime minister's home, and as Begin advanced toward it at a snail's pace, encircled by ring upon ring of policemen and bodyguards, he leaned so hard against me that my arm went numb. Once safely inside, the protesters yelled at him to come outside again. "Come outside, man of blood," they roared. "Come outside, killer of Sabra and Shatila!"

I left Menachem Begin to limp upstairs alone to his private quarters and his ailing wife, whereupon I beat a quick retreat through a side door to join my family, who had all the while been witness to this Rosh Hashanah horror.

Predictably, the demonstrators clamored for an official commission of inquiry to pass judgment as to what had truly happened at Sabra and Shatila. Thus was the Kahan Commission born, named after its chairman, the president of the Supreme Court, Yitzhak Kahan. It was composed of persons of high repute who subjected those appearing before them, the prime minister included, to a most exhaustive, though always polite, cross examination.

The commission issued its report in February, 1983, and concluded that Ariel Sharon, as minister of defense, carried an "indirect responsibility" for the atrocity at Sabra and Shatila by allowing the Christian Phalangists to enter the camps. At that point, it was up to the government to decide what to do – to reject the Commission's findings in whole or in part, or to accept them. The cabinet sat for three consecutive sessions to determine its position, while Ariel Sharon waited impatiently through a parade of interminable monologues, as each minister was invited to speak his piece. When the vote finally came, it was sixteen to one in favor of adopting the commission's findings in their entirety.

Begin testifying before the Kahan Commission on the Sabra and Shatila massacre, 8 November 1982

With his marvelous incapacity to admit error, Sharon utterly rejected this stigmatization. Controversy raged for years after, between critics and partisans alike, over the Kahan Commission findings, and Sharon's guilt or innocence, and over the true nature of Menachem Begin's feelings toward him. What is undisputable is that Begin accepted Sharon's resignation as defense minister, although he did retain him in the cabinet, as a minister without portfolio.

However harsh the self-examination to which Israel subjected itself in probing the facts of Sabra and Shatila, nothing seemed to help in stemming the tide of overseas criticism and condemnation, even from some of the Jewish State's staunchest supporters. One such was Senator Alan Cranston who, days after the massacre, issued a public letter addressed to Prime Minister Begin in which he wrote, inter alia:

> I did not condemn Israel's initial move into Lebanon for the avowed purpose of protecting Israel's citizens against repeated PLO attacks launched from that country. And I refrained, despite deep misgivings, from commenting publicly on your siege of Beirut and your entry into its western section. I am reluctant to criticize a treasured friend and ally in the midst of a military struggle. But the massacre of hundreds of men, women and children is another matter. It will be some time before we know who was to blame for the massacre. We may never know. […] Perhaps the most somber consequence of the current strife in Lebanon is the dimming of the inspiring moral beacon which shone so brightly from beleaguered Israel.[99]

Cold anger drove Menachem Begin's pen across a sheet of paper in response to the Senator's letter. In sentences that were unmarked by the slightest erasure and second thought, he wrote:

> The whole campaign of blaming Israel for the massacre, of placing moral responsibility on Israel seems to me, an old man who has seen so much in his lifetime, to be almost unbelievable, fantastic and utterly despicable. After the September 14 assassination of president-elect Bashir Gemayel we decided to move the IDF into West Beirut to prevent a Christian revenge of the Muslim population. It never occurred to anyone dealing with the Lebanese military units which subsequently entered the Shatila and Sabra camps that they would perpetrate a massacre. The first horrific truth is that Arabs murdered

Arabs. The second truth is that Israeli soldiers stopped the carnage. And the third truth is that if the current libelous campaign against Israel should go on without a reaction of outrage by decent men – yes, outrage – then within a matter of weeks or months everyone everywhere will have gotten the impression that it was an Israeli military unit which perpetrated the horrible killings.[100]

How right he was. Surf the Internet and see.

Begin in talks with Sec. of State Schultz and Ambassador Lewis, with author

Chapter twenty-eight

"To Everything There Is a Season"

I t's time I met President Reagan again," said the prime minister, in a resigned voice. "There are misunderstandings that only I can clear up. If I could just sit down with him face to face I'm sure I could convince him that we were in no way blameworthy for Sabra and Shatila, and that the Lebanon war was a well considered and justifiable action. What we did was as much in the American interest as our own – to set Lebanon free of the PLO thugs, and clip Syria's wings. Surely Reagan can be made to see that?"

"According to what I hear from Sam Lewis," I answered, in a futile attempt to cheer him up, "there are people in the administration who are angry, but not – "

"I'm well aware of that," interjected Begin in a sapped voice.

" – but not the president. He's unhappy about the war and upset about your having turned down his peace initiative, but he still looks upon us as a barrier to Soviet expansionism, and remains an admirer of Israel. What's more, he retains his high regard for you personally."

"That's nice to hear," said Begin sullenly, and he stared ahead of him, as if some troubling spectacle was taking place in his mind.

"I have to rebuild the personal relationship and confidence not only with the president but also with those around him," he murmured. "And I must speak to the Jews as well."

This exchange took place in mid-October, 1982. The Kahan Commission's findings would not be announced for several months, and the Sabra and Shatila massacre was still a fresh wound. It was triggered by a report I had prepared on Diaspora Jewish attitudes toward Israel following the massacre. In certain important quarters they had soured alarmingly. Begin studied the three-page report for several minutes and emitted a long sigh. Finally, he looked up and in a weary voice repeated, "Yes, I have to speak to the Jews."

There was no self-pity in his voice, but the manner of his speech indicated that his troubles and infirmities were growing upon him. He had lost weight. His face was worn, devoid of its usual commanding expression. His public speeches had become perfunctory. He was hurting from the condemnation of antagonists over his Lebanon war policy, frustrated that the Lebanese turn of events had deprived him of another peace treaty, and physically drained by the cumulative attrition of his past frailties – heart trouble, a minor stroke, the broken hip, and perhaps most of all, his constant anxiety over the health of his beloved wife and lifelong companion, Aliza. By this time she was hooked up to a respirator at Jerusalem's Hadassah Hospital, having suffered an acute attack of her chronic asthma. Once, twice a day sometimes, he would repair to the hospital to sit by her bedside. His detractors were beginning to make the claim that the prime minister of Israel was becoming immobilized due to a serious depression.

Pondering his misfortunes, he did seem to be sinking into a cocoon of melancholy. Yechiel tried to bolster his spirits by suggesting he arrange some visits to the development towns, where he was very much loved – a suggestion he had been making repeatedly. But Begin shut down on the topic and said he didn't want to hear any more about it. "The important thing for me now is to see Reagan," he reiterated.

Grasping at this intent as if it was proof positive that the prime minister of Israel was functioning perfectly well, Yechiel Kadishai said he'd get onto the matter right away with Ambassador Lewis.

"But don't fix a definite date yet," cautioned Begin. "I won't leave the country while Alla is in hospital." Then, to me, with a restored air of professional poise, "Start thinking about what Jewish forums in America I should be addressing. We have to get our message across to them, our own people, first and foremost. And when you bring my greetings tonight to the Bonds leadership at the King David Hotel, tell them what that message is. And tell Sam Rothberg I really am sorry I can't do it myself."

That night was a big night at the King David. The elated greetings and excited laughter of the cocktail throng in the lobby made it seem as if nothing could be more euphoric than being together in that place, which was still the most important networking axis in the Jewish world. Anybody who was anybody passed through the portals of the King David at one time or another. On this particular night, Israel Bonds big shots from all over the world were straining their voices as they greeted each other under the lobby's high ceiling, rich with ancient Semitic motifs that evoked the glorious period of the legendary King David.

I had known many of these big Bonds buyers for years, so it took me a while to squeeze my way through the boisterous groups, returning "hellos" and hearty handshakes as I inched my way forward in search of Sam Rothberg, world chairman of the Bonds organization, and a dear personal friend. Eventually I found him amid the crush, good-naturedly teasing an overdressed, aging lady who was attired in a sparkling evening gown as well as winged sunglasses. "Gloria," he was saying to her, eyes twinkling mischievously, "you look stunning! And it's a good thing you remembered your sunglasses, because sometimes late at night here in Jerusalem the sun gets really, *really* bright, and then it snows."

In spite of herself, the woman laughed richly along with Sam, but his face turned sober when he saw me. We retreated to the privacy of the adjacent reading room.

"How is he?" he asked.

"He sends his personal apologies. I'm afraid you'll have to make do with me tonight as his understudy."

"That's fine, but why won't he see me privately as he always does?"

"He's hardly seeing anyone. He's not in the best of spirits. It's happened before. His doctors say he'll snap out of it. He always has in the past."

"Peres tells me he's dysfunctional."

"Nonsense! He's low, but he has all his wits about him. I've just come from a meeting where he decided it's time for him to visit America again – to see the president and speak to the Jews. That's not the talk of a dysfunctional prime minister. He's concerned about Jewish support after Sabra and Shatila, and that's what I'm going to be talking to the audience about tonight."

"Good! When does he plan to come to America?"

"As soon as possible, I guess – once Mrs. Begin is out of hospital and the appointment with the president is set."

"Tell him to come to Los Angeles."

"Why Los Angeles?"

"Because he's forever meeting the Jewish *macher*s in New York, but Los Angeles is the fastest-growing Jewish community in America, and it's been a long time since he's been there. In mid-November we're planning the biggest international banquet ever – two thousand people: Hollywood stars, political big shots, the lot. And if he comes as guest of honor I can guarantee him massive exposure and top notch meetings. It'll be worth the effort. Tell him I said so."

"I will."

"Tell him I want him there."

"I shall quote your every word."

This was vintage Sam Rothberg – obstinate and determined. Once he'd gotten an idea into his head he wouldn't let go.

When I put the proposal to the prime minister the following morning, his spontaneous response was, "How can I say no to Sam? If he thinks Los Angeles is important, include it in my itinerary." And then, softly, to himself, "Assuming of course Alla is well enough to enable me to go."

I put LA into the itinerary, and told Sam that, everything else being equal, the prime minister would be happy to be guest of honor at the Bonds black-tie gala at the Los Angeles Century Plaza Hotel, on Saturday night, 13 November. The schedule had him flying from there to Dallas the following morning, to address a mass rally of Christian supporters, and then on to Washington for his meeting with the president. Given the tightness of the scheduling and the complex logistics involved we decided to make use of an antiquated Boeing 707 belonging to the Israel Air Force, and to cover the costs by billing the sizeable press contingent accompanying the premier. Departure date was set for Friday morning, 12 November, and the plan was to fly directly to California, landing en route only to refuel, and arrive in Los Angeles well in time for Shabbat, thanks to the ten-hour time difference.

Everything was falling nicely into place when a few days before the departure date, Yechiel Kadishai stuck his head around my door and groused, "We have a problem."

"How big a problem?"

"Massive! Begin doesn't want to go. The doctors have performed a tracheotomy on Aliza to relieve her breathing, and he refuses to leave her. We have to cancel everything. I'll speak to Sam Lewis and to the Dallas people. You handle Rothberg."

He turned and left, and I felt frantic. How was I to break this news to Sam Rothberg, after he had promoted his whole Bonds razzmatazz around Begin's presence? I asked Norma, my secretary, to get him for me on the phone, but then changed my mind, and told her not to. It was still the middle of the night in America. I had a reprieve for a few hours, at least.

Came the afternoon and Yechiel was back, beaming.

"Why the smile?" I asked.

"Have you spoken to Rothberg yet?"

"No, I was just about to."

"Well don't. We're going."

"How come? What's happened?"

"Alla insists. They've stuck tubes down her throat, so she can't talk. She communicates with notes. When Menachem told her he'd decided not to go she scribbled to him. 'You've got to go. It's a meeting with the president. It's important for the country. I'll be all right.' He was truly tormented, not knowing what best to do. Finally, he consulted the doctors and they assured him that though Alla was still frail, her condition was reasonably stabilized, and they saw no reason for him to change his plans. So we're going."

Being in charge of the programming I flew on ahead, to make sure that every final detail of the prime minister's schedule was in place. Upon my arrival in Los Angeles, Sam Rothberg asked me to join him at a pre-banquet cocktail party for the biggest Bonds buyers. It would get the ball rolling for the big night. The gathering turned out to be a diamond-studied affair in a Beverly Hills mansion, with about fifty guests. My task was to say something inspirational, and when I had finished, our hostess rose to ask what on earth had induced me, way back in 1947, a mere boy of eighteen, to leave the comforts and safety of my Manchester home for what was already then war-torn Palestine. In response, I described the atmosphere of those tortured post-Holocaust days, and the thrill that had come over me on catching my first sight of Haifa from the deck of a ship called the *Aegean Star*.

"*Aegean Star?* Did you say *Aegean Star?*" interrupted a fellow in the audience. He spoke with a thick European accent, and he sounded thunderstruck.

"Does that name mean anything to you, Jay?" asked our hostess, who introduced him to the room as Jay Cole.

"Are you kidding?" retorted Jay Cole, brimming with incredulity. "I was on that ship, goddamnit!"

He looked to be in his mid-fifties, short and plump, with a tan that spoke of golf courses, cruises, and beach clubs. His thin hair was tinted blond, and he wore a sky-blue, short-sleeved silk shirt with a heavy gold necklace hung around the points of its collar, like a decoration. But despite the swanky outfit and bleached hair, I could still see scars cutting through his eyebrows. Those, and the death camp tattoo on his arm were the unmistakable signature of another name I recalled from my youth, more than thirty years before.

"Yossel Kolowitz," I called out with unrestrained excitement.

He waded through the fan of chairs with a smart-ass grin, seized me by the hand, and said, "Damn right I am. And you're the kid from Manchester."

"You two have met before?" asked our hostess, bemused.

The quickening interest flowing through the room was palpable as, for the next half hour, Jay Cole told the story of Yossel Kolowitz – his survival in Auschwitz, his failed attempt to jump ship, his internment by the British, his enlistment into Begin's Irgun, his heroic adventures during the War of Independence and, finally, his life on Kibbutz Mishmar HaEmek.

Later, over drinks by the pool, Yossel told me the rest of his story. He had ultimately chosen to live with the uncle on a non-religious kibbutz rather than with the uncle in a Jerusalem yeshiva. The kibbutz had been good for him. He had learned the trade of plumbing, married a local girl, and had two sons. An IDF reservist, he was called up to serve during the Six-Day War, and was wounded. He went to America to recuperate. He decided to stay, and chose Los Angeles because of the climate, where he made a decent living as a plumber. In due course, his two sons joined him and, together, they prospered in the plumbing accessories business.

When I asked him how his boys had taken to America, a blush of pleasure rose to his cheeks. "They've made me a *zaydie*, a grandfather," he beamed. "I've got six *eineklich*" (grandchildren). "My older boy is married to a girl from Utah, and my younger one to a girl from Wyoming."

He must have seen my smile falter because he quickly moved his face very close to mine, almost threateningly, and in a mulish whisper that was shot through with his old swagger and bluster, he hissed, "Sure, I would have wanted my boys not to have married *shikses*. So what am I supposed to do, hotshot – disown them? This is America, right? These things happen all the time in America, right?"

I nodded, wanting to distance myself from his pain, but he drove on relentlessly.

"Don't think I'm not heartbroken. Of course I'm heartbroken. People here call me Jay Cole. It's a masquerade. I'm back to my old Auschwitz cabaret tricks. I put on fancy clothes and fancy airs, and at my country club I make people laugh. They think I'm one of them, but underneath I'm crying; I'm forever a survivor. So just keep your opinions to yourself, hotshot, and don't start telling me what's right and what wrong. Menachem Begin is a survivor. He'll understand. Goodbye!" And with that, off he went.

The weather in Los Angeles the following Shabbat afternoon, 13 November, the day after Begin's arrival, was a glorious mix of sun, breeze, and shade. The plaza in front of the hotel where we were staying boasted fountains and foliage; winter flowers bloomed in circular beds and cascaded from pedestals. As I approached the hotel I spied Yechiel Kadishai striding back and forth, eyes darting hither and thither. It looked like he was desperately in search of someone.

"What's up?" I asked.

"Where have you been?"

"With friends over Shabbat. Why? Anything wrong?"

"I'm waiting for Dr. Gotsman. I need him urgently."

Dr. Mervyn Gotsman habitually accompanied Begin on his travels overseas.

"What's wrong? I asked.

"Aliza's dead!"

An icicle of horror and sadness trickled down my spine. Distraught though Yechiel was, he remained admirably contained as he explained how the prime minister's son, Benny, had phoned him from Jerusalem with the heartbreaking news. Yechiel's first act was to try and track down Dr. Gotsman on his beeper, but he didn't answer. He needed him by his side when conveying the bitter news to Begin, and to his daughter, Leah, who had accompanied him on this trip.

"Presumably we'll be turning around and flying straight home tonight," I ventured.

"Yes. I've already instructed the crew to ready the plane for departure at nine. Meanwhile, don't tell a soul."

By the time Dr. Gotsman turned up, it was twilight. He'd gone to synagogue for the afternoon service and had been in the process of reciting the blessing over the Torah when his beeper went off. He promptly phoned the Israeli duty officer on the hotel's nineteenth floor, where the prime minister's suite was located, but she had no idea what it was about. So he hurried back, and, given the news, grabbed his medical bag and went off with Yechiel and Hart and Simona Hasten, old friends of the Begins, to the prime minister's suite. Filing silently inside they found Begin sitting on a sofa reading a book, splendidly attired in his tuxedo, in readiness for the evening's banquet.

"What's happened?" he asked, looking up, his face suddenly waxen.

"Alla has gone," said Yechiel in a hushed and sorrowful tone.

Anguish overcame him and tears began welling up in his eyes. "*Lama azavti otta?*" [Why did I leave her], he wailed, shaking back and forth in grief. Over and over again he cried this lament, refusing all consolation.

Yechiel went in search of the prime minister's daughter, Leah. When he escorted her back into the room she took one look at her father, and cried, "Ima! It's Ima! What's happened to my mother?" Told of her passing, she slumped into the embrace of Simona Hasten, who gently lowered her onto the couch where she leaned against her father, sobbing.

Yechiel described this to me when he left the room, and told me to inform Sam Rothberg of our imminent departure. I found Sam at the end of the corridor, looking drained of all color. He already knew; Hart Hasten had told him. They had bumped into one another as Sam was on his way to the prime minister's suite for a relaxed chat prior to escorting him to the grand ballroom for the gala affair.

An hour or so later, with an ashen face and haunted eyes, Menachem Begin shambled onto the plane and allowed Yechiel to settle him in the aircraft's tiny sleeping cabin, from which he hardly emerged throughout the tedious sixteen-hour flight back to Tel Aviv. When we landed briefly in New York for refueling, the traveling journalists rushed to the telephone booths to phone in their pieces. Taking advantage of the stopover to stretch my legs, I caught snippets of what they were dictating into the receivers; all seemed to be saying much the same thing:

"It was a simple, old-fashioned, lifelong love affair…"

"The prime minister relied on her totally…"

"She was the only person he really confided in…"

"She managed all his personal affairs…"

"Only with her was he absolutely candid and open…"

"Begin needed three things above all – devotion, tranquility, and companionship, and she gave him all three…"

Over the Atlantic, I asked Yechiel where Mrs. Begin was to be buried, and he answered that he had broached the matter gingerly with the prime minister, prior to leaving Los Angeles.

"I didn't want to use the word bury," he said. "I thought it too awful. So I said funeral. 'Menachem,' I said, 'where do you want Alla's funeral to be?' He said, 'The same place as for me.' So I said, 'But I don't know where that is.' He said, 'You have it in my will. I gave it to you a long time ago in a sealed envelope.' I said I had the envelope, but I'd never opened it because it was my understanding I was to open it only after he'd gone. He seemed to assume he'd go first. He understood the predicament and said, 'I want the funeral to be on the Mount of Olives, as near as possible to Moshe Barazani and Meir Feinstein. That's what's written in the envelope.'"

Moshe Barazani and Meir Feinstein had been two heroes of Menachem Begin's underground days. Condemned to death, they resolved that rather than swing on a rope tied by a British executioner, they would take their own lives, and this they did by embracing each other and blowing themselves up with an improvised hand grenade lodged between them.

Aliza Begin, sixty-two, was laid to rest on the Mount of Olives alongside these martyrs, and Yechiel made sure that the adjacent plot was reserved for Menachem Begin.

At Aliza's graveside, November 1982

During the *shiva* week, the seven days of ritual mourning following the funeral, when the bereaved sit on low chairs, wear ripped garments and male mourners go unshaven, the prime minister received all comers in what was an extraordinary display of shared grief. People lined up in droves to convey their condolences, people from every walk of life: shopkeepers, professors, politicians, yeshiva students, entrepreneurs, soldiers, rabbis, diplomats, housewives; even men and women who had served jail sentences, and former drug addicts and prostitutes whom Aliza Begin had discreetly helped rehabilitate. Her husband knew absolutely nothing about this until they told him.

As we have seen, Begin revered religious Jews who spent their time immersed in rabbinical texts, and he had a particular admiration for the scholarship of his colleague Dr. Yosef Burg, who was a prewar graduate of the famed Berlin Hildesheimer Rabbinical Seminary and of the Berlin University. His erudition was amply displayed when he was gave the eulogy for the deceased during the *shiva*.

"The Kabbalah tells us," Dr. Burg began, "that there is a Torah that cannot be memorized or written down. It is a Torah not of study or of learning, not of intellect or of scholarship, not of innovation or of disputation. It is a Torah without words. It is a Torah of the *nefesh*, of the soul, and it is the sweetest Torah of all.

"Nothing we say or write, could ever do justice to, or truly fathom, the *nefesh* of Aliza Begin – the warmth and love that flowed from her inner being, the demands she made of herself day by day, her sacrifices in the underground for the sake of Eretz Yisrael, her work for the needy and for the sick, for those ailing in body and in spirit; her courage, her vigor, her faith, her fortitude; her love and laughter, her readiness to spare nothing of herself for the sake of her children and her husband. Only when we come together, as we do now at this *shiva*, and talk of her virtues, can we share a little something of the nobility and stature of the *nefesh* of Aliza Begin.

"In Judaism, memory is everything. No less than one hundred and sixty-nine times does the Torah command us to remember the past. The significance of memory is that, by it, the past is made part of the present. If you erase the power of memory you shatter the sense of time. Time is past, present and future. And the existence of a future in Judaism is *netzach* – eternity. To the bereaved the future is also a *ma'aseh chesed* – a divine act of loving kindness. It is a *ma'aseh chesed* because even as one remembers the passing of a loved one, the future is a promise that the agony of grief will, in time, mellow.

"In Judaism there are two kinds of memory: *zikaron* and *yizkor*. *Zikaron* is ephemeral; it fades. *Yizkor* is eternal. If one loses a distant friend, one has pangs of memory and a sense of a place that he or she once filled. The most dismaying thing about such a death is not the gap that it leaves, but how the memory of it becomes a mere echo of the past. That is *zikaron*.

"However, there is that other quality of memory that never dims. It never dims because the person we recollect is a part of oneself: *'basar m'basarcha, nefesh m'nafshecha'* [flesh of your flesh, soul of your soul].The deceased remains a living being within one's soul forever. And that is *yizkor*.

"And in *yizkor* we acknowledge that the finality of death is part of life. Or, in the words of Ecclesiastes, 'To everything there is a season: A time to be born, and a time to die.' Often, we see the Almighty plucking a beautiful life just when, to us, he or she appears in full blossom. And then we ask, *lama*? Why? The prophet Isaiah gives the answer. His answer is that the thoughts of the Almighty are beyond the capacity of mortal minds. And so we are confused and frightened, and ask questions to which there are no answers, except for the one in Deuteronomy, chapter thirty-two, verse four: *'Hatzur tamim po'alo, ki kol devarav mishpat'* [The Rock, the Almighty, His work is perfect, for all His ways are justice].

"This means that in Judaism there is no such thing as an irrational, meaningless fate. In the words of the eminent rabbinic scholar, Rabbi Yosef Ber Soloveitchik, Judaism rejects the notion of random events in life. Judaism rejects any belief in a determinate luck or in a blind fate. We do not believe in fate as did the Greeks, who saw everything affected by absurd, unalterable, and ruthless decrees which emanated from some remote unknown. Such a belief crushes a man's dreams, irrespective of what he does or does not do. This, to the Greeks, was the source of human tragedy. Man becomes a helpless pawn in the hands of inexorable forces which cannot be thwarted, even by the gods.'"

Here, Dr. Burg paused, and looking directly at the prime minister, his son Benny, and his daughters, Hassya and Leah, who were sitting low by their father's side, he ended, "Even as Judaism tries to comprehend catastrophic events which cruelly destroy man's dreams, Judaism cannot accept the existence of the ultimately irrational in human life. Events which we label as tragic belong to a higher divine order into which man has not been initiated. The world is governed not by decrees of fate but by reasons beyond our comprehension. We have been granted insights into the physical nature of life through the accumulation of scientific knowledge, but we are excluded from the realm of divine understanding. The relationship between the individual and what becomes of him or her eludes our grasp. Thus it is that even as we mourn the passing of your beloved wife and mother, Aliza, we acknowledge that to God there are no arbitrary happenings. This is why upon hearing of her passing we declared, '*Baruch Dayan ha'emet!*' [Blessed be the Judge of the truth]. And this is why we affirmed at her graveside, '*Hashem natan, Hashem lakach, yehi shem Hashem l'olam va'ed,*' [The Lord has given, the Lord has taken away, blessed be the name of the Lord forever]. And blessed shall be the remembrance of Aliza Begin forever."

The prime minister, his face worn, his skin as gray as the leaden November sky outside, rose to shake Yosef Burg's hand, but Burg restrained him, saying, "It is not customary in a house of mourning for the bereaved to express thanks."

"Nevertheless, you have my gratitude," said Begin. "Your words are a great comfort."

"Time for *ma'ariv,*" somebody cried out, and as befitted the son of the deceased, Benny Begin led the prayers of the evening service. To the uninitiated, of which there were many that night, the words of the congregants must have sounded like a Babel of mutterings and chantings, punctuated every now and again by a loud "*Oomeyn*" [Amen]. At one point, the chattering of the non-congregants grew so loud it elicited a reproachful "Sh-sh-sh!" from the congregants. However, all stood in solemn silence as Benny Begin rounded off the service by reciting the mourner's Kaddish, which opens with a vision of God becoming great in the eyes of all nations, and ends with a supplication for peace, to which all chorused "Amen!"

When she heard that Aliza Begin had died, Mrs. Jehan Sadat, widow of the slain President Anwar Sadat, picked up the phone in her Cairo home, with its spectacular view of the Nile, and placed a call to Israel's ambassador to Egypt, Moshe Sasson. She invited him for coffee, and Sasson, a man with vast experience in Arab affairs assumed, correctly, that the former first lady of Egypt wished to speak to him privately.

Though more than a year had passed since her husband's assassination, Jehan Sadat remained a highly popular figure among influential circles in Egyptian society, thanks to her sharp mind, her stunning beauty, and her continuing outspoken and courageous activism on behalf of Egyptian women. Given the autocratic nature of Arab society, and the fact that Jehan Sadat's image far outshone that of Mrs. Mubarak, it was certainly possible that President Hosni Mubarak was keeping a watchful eye on her comings and goings.

"I have a letter of condolence for your prime minister," said Jehan, upon receiving Ambassador Sasson. "I would appreciate it if you could communicate it as soon as possible." She handed him an envelope.

"Of course," said Sasson, pocketing it.

"Coffee?" asked Mrs. Sadat, as a maid walked in.

"Please."

Jehan Sadat felt at ease with Moshe Sasson, not only because his Arabic was refined and absolutely fluent, but more so because she knew her husband had established a close relationship with him.

"I imagine Mr. Begin must be taking his loss very hard," she said compassionately. "They were very close, I know."

"I'm told his grief is all the greater because he feels guilt at having been out of the country when she passed away," said Sasson.

"You know," said Jehan, in a confessional tone, "I knew instinctively that my husband was going to die. I remember sitting here in Cairo, with my grandson perched on my knee, watching the live television broadcast of Anwar's plane landing at Ben-Gurion Airport, and I felt terrified. I just knew he would be killed for what he was doing. I did not know when or where it would happen, or who would pull the trigger. All I knew was that my days on earth with my husband were numbered."

The ambassador put down his cup, and in a voice that was both soothing and respectful, said, "Since you raise the matter, allow me to share an episode. About two months before your husband's assassination, we were sitting together alone and he suddenly turned to me and said, 'Moshe, I feel my meeting with my Maker is very close.' 'Why are you saying that?' I asked him. But he merely continued puffing on his pipe and gave no answer."

Jehan Sadat offered him a small and sad smile, and said: "I had an absurd argument with him. I knew he'd originally stipulated in his will that he wanted to be buried on Mount Sinai. He'd told Mr. Begin that he planned to build there a mosque, a church, and a synagogue. A beautiful idea! But when he told me in all seriousness that that was where he wanted to be buried, I said to him, Anwar, who of your children – meaning the Egyptian people – will want to climb up to the top of Mount Sinai to visit you? He gave me no answer, but he understood what I was saying. The trouble was that he had not yet altered his will when he was assassinated, and it was I who insisted he be buried here in Cairo, by the Tomb of the Unknown Soldier."[101]

Returning to his embassy, Ambassador Sasson summoned his chief security officer and requested that the courier designated to carry the diplomatic pouch to Jerusalem that evening take pains to ensure that Mrs. Sadat's letter reach the prime minister as speedily as possible. Thus it was that early the following morning, as Menachem Begin was wrapping away his *tefillin* [phylacteries] at the end of the morning service in his *shiva* house, Yechiel Kadishai handed him the letter. It was written in Jehan Sadat's own bold hand, and it said:

> Dear Menachem,
>
> I imagine your shock and feelings of helplessness when the news was broken to you of Aliza's cruel death. A lifetime of shared hopes and disappointments, of joy and sadness, suddenly smashed in a moment. Surely, only those who have suffered in the same way can understand fully what you are feeling now. Let me add my own heartfelt tribute to a grief which nothing will ever truly brush away from your heart. These are times when sympathy is not enough, but please accept the spontaneous overflow of my feelings for a great lady who I grew to love and respect. And please accept the hand of friendship and solidarity in this moment of utter loneliness which you will find difficult to live with.
>
> Remember, I too have had to travel through the bitter valley of shock and loneliness and I well remember your kindness and genuine sympathy towards me little more than a year ago. I too have felt what you are feeling now, and I too have had to find reasons to overcome despair. We share a belief in Divine Providence and that is one of the great consolations of all the bereaved. But you and my late husband shared as well a deep commitment to the cause of peace and I am certain that we owe it to the memory of our dearest to continue to serve the ideal which inspired them. Let us live, warmed by the memory of past happiness and sustained by the hope that we in our own turn may leave the world a better and a kinder place for generations to come.
>
> Take comfort, dear friend. I know that Anwar El Sadat had great confidence in your own faith in peace and human concord, and he may have differed with you on the means towards a noble end, but I am certain you were both dedicated to the same ideal of peace.
>
> Jehan Sadat, 15 November 1982.

Shortly thereafter, on 8 December, after a restless night, the prime minister pulled on his dressing gown, and with the half-light of dawn he composed his reply in a meticulous hand. He wrote:

Dear Jehan,

Thank you from the heart for your personal message. I will remember it all my life. In your words I have found real friendship, humanity and profound compassion. Since we met in other days for all of us you won our respect and admiration. Aliza and I often talked about you. Always remembering the courage and vision of my unforgettable friend Anwar, Aliza and I used to say to each other: but Jehan is a personality in her own right. You proved it, dear friend, to everybody for years. And all those who saw you in pain and suffering bowed their head before your dignity.

Now bereavement struck my dear ones and myself. I met Aliza when she was a young girl. Except for a period of separation, as a result of my arrest in Russia, we were together for more than forty years – a lifetime. Her devotion to the cause for which we fought and suffered was limitless. She was prepared for every sacrifice, and in adversity was fearless. In fact, she suffered more than her husband: worry was her inseparable companion for many years. But she never complained. And in such circumstances she took care of the children and raised a happy family.

Aliza helped many people who needed help. During the last years we didn't even know the scope of her humanitarian work. Now, more and more details are revealed to us, from what people wrote to us or came to tell us during the days of mourning and expressions of sympathy. I know that in this humanitarian work you had much in common. I know that this good human work deepened the friendship between you and her. She herself told me about your common visits to the suffering, and the consolation you brought to them.

Great is our loss. I have to accept in humility and even be grateful for the years of happiness we spent together.

Thank you for your wonderful letter. We shall continue to share the memory of our dear ones who left us. You and I shall always believe in the good, just cause of peace for which we all made so great endeavors. God bless you dear friend.

Yours wholeheartedly,
Menachem[102]

our dearest to continue to serve the ideal which inspired them. Let us live, warmed by the memory of past happiness and sustained by the hope that we in our turn may leave this world a better and a kinder place for generations to come.

Take comfort, dear friend. I know that Anwar El Sadat had great confidence in your own faith in peace and human concord, and I may have differed with you on the means towards a noble end, but I am certain that you were both dedicated to the same ideal of peace.

Jehan Sadat

15 November 1982

Last page of condolence letter from Jehan Sadat to Menachem Begin after Aliza's death

Jerusalem, December 8th 1982.

ראש הממשלה

Dear Jehan,

Thank you from the heart for your personal message. I will remember it all my life. In your words I have found real friendship, humanity and profound compassion. Since we met - in other days for all of us - you won our respect and admiration. Anwar and I often talked about you. Always remembering the courage and vision of my unforgettable friend Anwar, Anwar and I used to say to each other: ... but Jehan is a personality in her own right. *it has been a toughby of years* You passed it, dear friend, to everybody for years. And all ~~those~~ *who* who saw you in pain and suffering bowed their head before your dignity.

~~Now because~~ *Your bereavement struck my dear ones and myself.* I met Anwar when she was a young girl. Except for a period of separation, as a result of my *recent* arrest in Russia, we were together for more than forty years - a life-time. Her devotion to the *cause,* for whole we fought and suffered was limitless. She was prepared for every sacrifice, and in adversity was fearless. In fact she suffered more than her husband: worry was her inseparable companion for so many years. But she never complained and in such circumstances she took care of the children and raised a happy family.

Anwar helped many people, who needed help. During the last years we didn't even know the scope of her humanitarian work. Now, more and more details are revealed to us from what people write to us or come to tell us during the days of mourning and expression of sympathy. I know that in the humanitarian work you had much in common. I know that the good human work deepened the friendship between you and her. She briefly told me about your common visits to the suffering and the *consolation* you brought to them.

~~Great loss~~ *Great is our loss.* I have to accept in humility and *even* be grateful for the years of happiness we spent together.

Thank you again for your wonderful letter. We shall continue to serve the memory of our dear ones who left us. You and I will always labour in the good good cause of peace, for which we all made so great endeavours. God bless you, dear friend.

Yours wholeheartedly,
Menachem

A bearded Begin sits solitary at the government table in the Knesset during the shloshim – the ritual month-long mourning period for his wife – November, 1982

Chapter twenty-nine

"I Cannot Go On"

The months that followed Aliza's death were a period of intense trial for Menachem Begin. Even after the *shiva* ended, he chose to remain at home for the further three weeks of intense mourning which Jewish tradition prescribes even though, by custom, he could have resumed his normal duties. He could not bring himself to leave the house. Still unshaven, he then got a rash on his face that prevented him shaving, so he continued to stay at home in a deep funk, saying he did not want to be seen at the office or in public in such a state. When he did return to the office at the beginning of January 1983, he gave fewer interviews, met fewer people, attended fewer cabinet meetings, engaged in fewer negotiations, and when he did participate, he tended to deal with matters more in the macro than in the micro, passively. Indeed, as time went by, he became less and less accessible to all but his closest advisers; I would bring him drafts of letters for approval a few times a week, but he hardly glanced at them. He appended his signature in a listless sort of way, and I would leave without saying a word. Yechiel urged us to push him into activity by setting him appointments in the hope of getting him focused, and some of us quietly sounded out Lewis about rescheduling a Washington trip. But, clearly, the vitality of his premiership was hemorrhaging.

This was manifestly and embarrassingly apparent when, on 15 June 1983, he decided to answer in person a provocative opposition motion to establish yet another commission of inquiry on the Lebanon war, this time to investigate the effectiveness of the government's decision-making throughout the hostilities.

Mr. Begin had difficulty climbing the steps to the podium, so he allowed a steward to cup his elbow to help him up. Once there, leaning against the long-familiar pedestal, he became something of his old self again, as if energized by the magic of the spot where, for years, he had been clever, quick and intrepid.

Finding his words easily, he began, "Mr. Speaker, the cabinet resolved on Operation Peace for Galilee with but one aim: to ensure that the inhabitants of the Galilee wouldn't have to run to their shelters any longer, and deadly terror would cease raining down upon them day and night. I am truly amazed at opposition members who, by their statements, seek to make people forget that this was the goal. At issue" – he thumped the lectern – "was an operation of legitimate national self-defense. We were facing the destruction of Kiryat Shmona, God forbid, or the ruin of Nahariya, heaven forefend. The danger was real. The inhabitants of Galilee were hostage to enemy rockets. Not any longer!"

He paused to take a deep breath, but when he resumed, his tone grew progressively weaker, his voice huskier, and his delivery less forthright.

"Is this the first war in which we encountered problems?" he asked the House. "Even in the most justified and best planned military operations, complications and hitches arise. So why do my opposition colleagues always try to create the impression that at some point in the Lebanon campaign Israel suddenly became the aggressor? What will yet another commission of inquiry accomplish?"

His voice faded away as he continued, and losing track, he fumbled with his notes, repeated phrases, and mumbled, "So yes...so yes...what will another inquiry...what will yet another inquiry commission accomplish? We already carried out all the recommendations of one commission that inquired, and it was not a simple thing to do. And now the opposition wants another? What for?...For what? To undermine national morale? To give our enemies aid and comfort? Surely...surely...this is a time...surely this is a time to stand together, not to establish more inquiry commissions."

Those listening to him were struck at how tired he looked as he rambled on. The fire in his belly was doused, his once incisive oratory stale, his eloquence washed out. Increasingly, he was resorting to vague rhetoric and tired gibes, stripped of the ardor that had once thrilled supporters and angered opponents.

He exuded deep melancholy as he descended from the podium to return to his seat at the head of the government bench. And though the opposition motion was defeated, it took fortitude for this infirm, prematurely old man to preserve his dignity as he shuffled out of the Knesset chamber to his customary table in the dining room, there to pick at a meager plate of vegetables instead of the usual bowl of steaming chicken soup his wife had prescribed as mandatory midday fare.

Without Aliza to take care of him, Menachem Begin was in physical decline, and his appetite was gone. The despair he felt at her death had been awful enough to endure, but it was cruelly compounded by a sense of lost opportunity and the disintegration of his political dreams about peace with Lebanon. His unmarried daughter, Leah, now living with him, took care of him devotedly, but could be no substitute for her mother. These were days when the prime minister's deeply wrinkled face sometimes looked emaciated. His neck was just skin and bones. His shirt was too big on him, and his suit hung on him pathetically. He looked so thin and frail that his head seemed excessively large. At seventy, he looked eighty.

Five days after the Knesset debate, on 20 June, Yechiel Kadishai strode buoyantly into the prime minister's room to say that Ambassador Samuel Lewis had called for an appointment to renew the presidential invitation to Washington. Begin responded to this with a sudden and unexpected spurt of energy. "Yes, by all means, I shall see him. Make the appointment."

On the following day Lewis entered with a hearty "How good it is to see you again, Mr. Prime Minister." Begin rose unsteadily from behind his desk to return the warm handshake, and if the ambassador was taken aback at what he saw – the sunken face, the suit that hung loosely on Begin's skeletal frame – he succeeded in camouflaging it remarkably well. Equally, Mr. Begin pulled himself together sufficiently to invite his guest to take a seat, and gave him a warm smile that belied the misfortunes which had come crashing down on him like an avalanche over the past months. For an instant Menachem Begin's commanding magnetism returned, and the ambassador sweetened the moment by telling him, "Mr. Prime Minister, President Reagan has asked me to tell you that it is his desire to bring the relationship back to what it was before the Lebanon war. This is why he is eager to meet you."

Genuinely moved, the premier said, "Please thank the president for his invitation and for the goodwill behind it, which I heartily reciprocate."

"I shall certainly do that. It really has been unfortunate that because of Lebanon the relationship between the two of you has become a little distant."

The tension in Begin's jaw betrayed his deep feeling when he replied,

"You will recall, Sam, that this was why I flew to the States last November. My purpose was to patch things up. But then, as you know, while I was in Los Angeles my wife – "

Pain flickered in his eyes, and Lewis returned his look with a compassionate nod, and then stared at his shoes.

" – I honestly believed then, as I do now," continued Begin, "that if the president and I could sit down together we would be able to iron out all misunderstandings."

"Which is why he really is looking forward to seeing you after so long," said Lewis spiritedly. "He would like to know what dates might be possible. We were thinking, perhaps, sometime in mid-July, in about three weeks."

The prime minister offered the ambassador a distracted nod and said, "I shall examine my schedule and let you know."

"That's fine!"

There followed a morose pause, the prime minister retreating back into his grief-stricken reminiscences. It was only broken when Lewis made reference to the impending changes of senior White House officials designated to deal with the affairs of the region – Bud McFarlane was to replace Philip Habib as the president's special envoy to the Middle East.

"I see," said Begin distantly, without amplification of any sort.

This struck Lewis as odd. The prime minister had spent countless hours in assiduous deliberation, intense negotiation and, yes, occasional spats, with Philip Habib, a professional, tireless, frequently harassed, and by now totally exhausted presidential envoy. He had been in the thick of things throughout the Lebanon war, valiantly putting himself and his health at risk in the effort to reach truces and ceasefires while conducting the tricky negotiations which led to the expulsion of Arafat's PLO forces from Beirut. Phil Habib had followed this up by helping mediate the attempted long-term Israel-Lebanon peace arrangement which at one point had seemed so tantalizing close. Surely, thought Lewis, after such a rigorous engagement, the prime minister would have a little more to say about Philip Habib's departure than a mere "I see." Where, he wondered, was Begin's characteristic cross examination, his probing for the finer points that always fascinated him? His perfunctory "I see" made him sound like a passive and unengaged observer in what, surely, had been one of the most hectic and intensive and challenging chapters of his entire stewardship.

Lewis all but said as much to me when I escorted him to his car at the end of the meeting. He said, "He's not his old self, is he? He doesn't look good at all."

Loyally, I replied, "Need I tell you, Sam, he's been through a pretty rough time? He's still mourning. He's been inconsolable, but he's coming out of it. He's keeping more regular hours at the office now, and the American visit will do him the world of good."

Lewis gave me a questioning look and asked point blank, "Do you think he's up to a Washington trip?"

"Of course he is," I said dismissively. "You know the importance he attaches to his relationship with the president, and you saw for yourself how pleased he was with the invitation."

"Yes, but as you know, a Washington visit is a demanding act at the best of times, and I'm wondering whether he'll be up to the heightened public exposure and pressure he'll have to withstand this time round."

"What do you mean, this time round? You know he's an old pro at the game. He relishes the cut and thrust of it all."

"Yes, when he is his old self, but he's not now. He'll be encountering a lot of skeptical audiences. He'll have to defend his conduct of the Lebanon war that was supposed to end forty kilometers from your border, not in Beirut. He'll have to meet with a dubious Congress, some of whose members are on important committees. He'll have to face a critical press. He'll still have some explaining to do about Sabra and Shatila. And he'll have a lot of questions from certain Jewish quarters, too."

"Sam," I answered, my guard up, "I think you're making it sound worse than it is. Every one of those assertions has been answered time and again. We still have lots of friends and much goodwill in America. Letters of support keep pouring in every day by the sack-load."

"Nonetheless, it's going to be a tough trip."

He bent to enter his car and, with one leg in and one leg out, said, his mouth curving into a smile, "The most important thing is that Reagan is genuinely looking forward to his coming. But for Pete's sake" – this with a wag of the finger – "you fellows go easy on his programming. Keep it as light as you can. Make sure he doesn't overdo it."

"Can I quote you on that?" I asked lightly.

"You sure can. You know I care for the man."[103]

On the following Sunday afternoon, 24 June, the prime minister summoned me to his room, and with almost ceremonial formality, said, "Yehuda, upon my recommendation, and with the approval of Foreign Minister Yitzhak Shamir, the cabinet this morning approved your appointment as ambassador to Great Britain in place of Shlomo Argov. And since the position has remained vacant for almost a year," – Shlomo Argov lay paralyzed in a Hadassah Hospital bed – "it would be helpful if you could commence your duties as soon as feasible, once arrangements have been made for Harry to take your place here."

Harry Hurwitz was a longtime political associate of the prime minister who, at the time, headed the information division at our Washington Embassy (in years to come he would be founder and president of the famed Menachem Begin Heritage Center, Jerusalem).

Begin's announcement came to me as no surprise, since I had known for weeks that my London candidacy was in the offing. The appointment passed without fuss, since throughout all the years during which I had worked part- or full-time in the prime minister's bureau, I had remained officially seconded from the foreign office and hence was a career diplomat.

It was while I was conversing with the prime minister about the technicalities of the changeover, that an obviously bothered Yechiel Kadishai walked in to say that Sam Lewis was on the phone – for the third time in as many days – asking for the official letter of confirmation of the Washington visit. I knew that Lewis had been having a hard time pinning Begin down, because he had told me so, just as I knew that Begin was still hesitating over the very prospect of making the journey. Nevertheless, a date – 15 July – had finally been agreed upon, and President Reagan had accordingly dispatched a formal letter of invitation. I was charged with drafting the prime minister's official response confirming his acceptance, and the letter was lying on his desk, untouched, when Yechiel came barging in. Dolefully, Begin stared at the page, picked it up, read it, put it down again, and resting his wrinkled hands on it like a pair of worn-out gloves, lamented, "How can I represent the State of Israel as I presently am? How can I possibly travel to meet the president of the United States in the condition I'm in?"

The sight of him was so pitiful that my heart sank, and I stole out of the room, leaving him and Yechiel to mull over the terrible knowledge that the prime minister of Israel was too feeble to carry out a mission of high importance to the president of the United States.

Back at my desk, the telephone rang. It was Ambassador Lewis.

"Yehuda, what's going on?" he asked.

"About what?"

"You know about what – Mr. Begin's Washington visit."

"Why do you ask?" I asked.

"Because I'm hearing whispers he's not going to make it."

"From what sort of people?"

"People in the know."

"Speak to Yechiel," I said. "He's dealing with it."

"Is this a tip-off that he's going to resign?"

"What are you talking about? Speak to Yechiel." I did not know what else to say.

The next day, Begin spent tortuous hours agonizing over exactly how to communicate to the president that he was unfit to travel in a manner that would not diminish the dignity of his office nor his self-respect. Yechiel asked me to try and draft some appropriate language, but I could find none. Eventually, Begin was prevailed upon to speak directly to Reagan over the phone, and put the matter to him man to man.

"Mr. President," said Begin, "I deeply regret to inform you that for personal reasons – not official ones – for personal reasons, I am unable to travel to Washington at this time. If it is acceptable to you, I would like to take up your invitation at some future date."

The prime minister listened attentively to whatever the president was saying in response, and repeated softly, "Yes, that is correct, Ron, the reasons are purely personal."

Again, he paused to listen, and then said, "I appreciate what you have just told me, and I reciprocate your kind words of goodwill. As for the idea of the two ministers traveling instead of me, I shall await your letter of invitation. And again, I thank you for your understanding and friendship. God bless you, my friend."

When he replaced the receiver, he emitted an audible sigh of relief, and muttered, "*Baruch Hashem!* Thank God that's over and done with."

As my office colleagues, all smiles and teases, raised their glasses to me at my farewell shindig, I felt self-conscious, but enormously flattered. Begin had waxed overly lyrical about my contributions as an aide, toasting me as "a cherished friend, an indispensable colleague, a veritable Shakespeare who will make a proud ambassador of our nation."

Pleased though I was at my appointment to London, I was sorry to say goodbye to some of the people around me, most particularly Prime Minister Begin and, of course, Yechiel. Equally poignant was the thought of taking leave of this room, whose occupants had changed more often than the furnishings. These remained much the same as they were on the day in 1963 when I had first nervously entered, to be greeted by Prime Minister Levi Eshkol, who had put me at ease with his Yiddish witticisms and repartee.

I had witnessed so much here. I had seen how that most affable of men would, four years later, on the eve of the Six-Day War, display nerves of steel while facing a frightened nation that accused him of indecisiveness. Restraining his generals from precipitate action, he had not only won a war in six days, but sown the seeds of a virtual future alliance with the United States. I had seen Golda Meir sitting there in that same prime minister's seat, confiding her personal intimacies to Oriana Fallaci. And in 1973, I had seen her steer the nation unflinchingly through the horrors of the Yom Kippur War, despite her advanced age and her ignorance of all things military. Then had come the no-nonsense, analytical-minded Yitzhak Rabin, with whom I had already formed a relationship in Washington. My promotion to the senior rank of adviser had allowed me the vantage point to observe him close-up as he oversaw the most daring rescue mission in living memory – the raid on Entebbe. And now here was Prime Minister Menachem Begin, bidding me farewell as I prepared to return to the country of my birth, carrying the credentials of the country of my birthright.

Packing!

Packing is one aspect of relocation which should never be done under stress. The more organized you are prior to packing, the less tiring and strenuous it is going to be, and fewer are the items likely to be misplaced or forgotten. It was the night before my family and I were scheduled to depart for London, 5 July. We had already shipped off the bulky furniture by container, but we still had to pack our personal belongings. In leaving the packing until the last minute, I had failed to take into consideration the incessant interruptions: telephone calls from well-wishers, and the comings and goings of relatives and friends – terrific handshakes, heavy hugs, thumpings on the back, kisses – so it was close to midnight before I got round to bagging my own belongings, and the situation had certainly become stressful. And yet again, the phone rang, and Mimi answered.

"The prime minister wants to speak to you," she called impatiently.

"My passport's missing," wailed Yael, our youngest daughter, who was joining us in London for a while, having recently completed her army service.

"Hello, Mr. Begin?"

"Yehuda, excuse my calling so late. I've just received a most important cable from the president of the United States and I would appreciate it if you would draft a reply. One of my *bachurim metzuyanim* (that's what he called his bodyguards – "outstanding young men") will deliver the letter to you immediately, along with my suggested points of reply."

"Anybody seen my passport?" called Yael.

"Mr. Begin, if you want me to call off London, I'll do so," I said, almost at the end of my tether. "I won't leave tomorrow."

"No, no. It's important you go...."

"Abba, I can't find my passport. Will somebody help me, please?" groaned Yael.

"Excuse me, one moment, Mr. Begin." I cupped the receiver. "Yael, look in my briefcase. Maybe it's there." And then, "You were saying, Mr. Begin..."

"Harry Hurwitz will be starting in a couple of days, so you should go. It's just that it's urgent I send President Reagan my cabled reply tonight. And again, I'm deeply sorry for troubling you. My warmest best wishes to your wife. Travel well. And thank you once more for everything."

The president's cabled letter turned out to be a page and a half long, while the prime minister's points of reply were a few paltry, almost illegible lines. They read:

> Yehuda – Attached is the letter from President Reagan to me. With regard to the response, these are my suggestions:
> a) Thanks.
> b) Expressions of good wishes to Philip Habib and satisfaction at the appointment of McFarlane.
> c) With regard to the visit of the two ministers – affirmative.
> M.B.

My instant reaction was one of acute exasperation. Well did I recall Begin's first day in office, when he had told me he never put his signature to anything he had not written or dictated himself. Yet here I was, under the stress of imminent departure on a major ambassadorial posting that was not without risk, and instead of packing and helping Yael find her passport, I was desperately trying to decipher the prime minister's cramped and cryptic scribble. Still, soon enough my vexation gave way to a second and far more distressing thought: the realization that the man I had come to love and admire over these past six years was so weakened as to be virtually incapable of composing his own reply, in his own inimitable style. This wrenched at my heart.

So I plunked myself down, and frantically began to flesh out the note into a full-blown epistle. In it, the prime minister thanked the president for his generous remarks and expressions of friendship, praised Philip Habib

Begin's urgent note to author on eve of his ambassadorial posting to London, 24 July 1983 (Translation, page 677)

expansively for his dedicated professionalism and invaluable contributions as the president's Middle East envoy and noted with satisfaction the appointment of Bud McFarlane in his stead. He expressed gratification at the president's invitation to Foreign Minister Yitzhak Shamir and Defense Minister Moshe Arens – both of whom had picked up much of the slack during Begin's moments of relative inertia – for talks on all the issues of common interest, in place of himself who, regrettably, could not presently travel for personal reasons, and signed off with a fanfare to the everlasting friendship between the two peoples and countries.

With no secretary at hand to type the letter out, I speedily rewrote the whole thing in clear block letters, telephoned the foreign ministry's communications center and gave instructions for someone to pick it up and send it off, and finished packing as best I could. On the morrow, I set out with my wife and daughter for London.

We were met at Heathrow Airport by a grand welcoming party, consisting of a bevy of embassy staff members, leaders of the Anglo-Jewish community, a squad of Scotland Yard bodyguards who instantly took me under their protection, and a Colonel from the British protocol office who addressed me grandly as "Your Excellency."

The day soon came when I was to present my credentials to Queen Elizabeth II, a ceremony that required my being trussed up in a tightly noosed and inflexible winged collar and white bow tie. Collar and tie were mounted by studs to a dress shirt, its starched-pleated front as unyielding as a breastplate. A white waistcoat held my middle in like a corset, and all was framed by a black, long-tailed morning coat.

I must have looked grand seated in an eighteenth-century gold- and black-lacquered ceremonial coach, with wheels as high as my head, attended by liveried, top-hatted royal horsemen who handled the team of four white horses as they clip-clopped through Hyde Park toward the gates of Buckingham Palace. There, crimson-uniformed ceremonial guards marching their sentry paths snapped to attention in salute at my entry, while tourists, delighted by the pageantry, applauded and clicked their cameras. I waved back feeling ridiculous, sweating profusely.

Escorted into the Queen's chamber by an equerry dressed like the Duke of Wellington, I executed the choreographed dance of obeisance in which I had been thoroughly rehearsed by the chief of protocol: one bow of the head at the door, two steps forward, another bow, two further steps forward, one more bow, and then, within reach of the sovereign lady, I duly handed her an embossed document and proclaimed, "Your Majesty, I have the honor to present to you my credentials from President Chaim Herzog as the ambassador of Israel to the Court of St. James's."

The credentials read:

> To her Majesty Elizabeth the Second…My Great and Good Friend,
>   Holding in esteem the relations of friendship and mutual understanding existing between your realm and the State of Israel, and being desirous to develop these friendly relations, I, in accordance with the powers vested in me by law, have decided to appoint Mr. Yehuda Avner to reside near Your Majesty as our Ambassador Extraordinary and Plenipotentiary. The character and abilities of Mr. Avner lead me to believe that he will fulfill the mission with which he is charged in such a manner as to merit Your Majesty's trust and approbation, and prove himself worthy of the confidence I place in him. I, therefore, request Your Majesty to receive our Ambassador favourably and to give credence to all that he shall have the honour to communicate to Your Majesty on the part of the Government of

*Author mounting carriage to Buckingham Palace for presentation
of his credentials to the Queen, 8 August 1983*

Israel. May I express to Your Majesty my sentiments of high esteem and send you my best wishes for your well-being and the well-being and prosperity of your realm.

      Your good friend,

      Chaim Herzog

The Queen nodded an acknowledgement, took the document into her white-gloved hand, passed it on to her chamberlain, and in a slightly mystified voice, said, "I do believe this is the first time I have ever received credentials from a foreign ambassador actually born in this country. How did you manage that?"

Anticipating the question, I had prepared a rather high-minded response. "Your Majesty," said I, "though physically born in this country, I was given birth spiritually in Jerusalem, from whence my ancestors were exiled by Roman legions two thousand years ago."

"Were they really?" said the Queen. "How unfortunate!" And she began to talk about the weather.

This was something to behold. There I was, alluding to the mysteries of Jewish history's conundrums and there she was, talking about the weather.

Upon presenting my wife, the Queen was intrigued to learn that she, too, was of English origin. Somehow, they began talking about their mothers. My mother-in-law was of a similar age to that of Elizabeth, the Queen Mother.

"My mother," Queen Elizabeth was saying to Mimi, "makes me feel quite inept sometimes, as if I am a little girl. Unlike me, my mother, who is now eighty-three, does not need spectacles. And there's nothing wrong with her legs at all. She can stand about for ages. And she walks very well, too. So if I ever dare say to her that I'm a little tired she snaps back, 'Utter nonsense,' and carries on without the slightest sign of weariness. I presume people born in the horse-and-carriage age have more stamina than our generation." And then, with a sigh, hands folded in a pose of acceptance, "They seem to function at a much more measured pace than we do, don't you think? They know how to conserve their energies."

The royal chamberlain interrupted with a judicious signal that it was time I introduce the senior staff members of the embassy, after which he sounded a discreet cough to indicate the audience was over. We all bowed or curtsied in perfect configuration, took two steps back, bowed or curtsied again, took two more steps back, bowed or curtsied one last time, and made our way out of the chamber in faultless formation.

It was while the ancient carriage clattered and clanked its way back through Hyde Park to my embassy in Palace Green that my mind wandered back to Jerusalem and to Begin, and it suddenly dawned on me that under the stress and the mess of packing, I had composed and authorized the dispatch of a full-fledged communication from the prime minister of Israel to the president of the United States without the prime minister having approved its language. I took comfort in the thought, however, that having heard nothing to the contrary, the communication must have said what the prime minister wanted it to say.

A few weeks later, on 20 August, while at my desk at the embassy, Harry Hurwitz called.

"Harry, good to hear from you," I said. "How's the job going?"

"I'm not sure I still have one," he answered. "Begin's just resigned."

"You're joking! When?"

"An hour ago, at the cabinet meeting. He arrived at the office this morning looking even paler than usual. He called in Yechiel. When Yechiel came out, he looked as white as a sheet. I asked him what was going on, and he told me that Begin had just told him he was going into the cabinet to submit his resignation there and then. And that's exactly what he did. He simply told the ministers, 'I cannot go on.'"

"Just like that?"

"They were stunned. They appealed to him to reconsider. But he told them that if he'd had any doubts he might have been open to persuasion, but since he had none, nothing would make him change his mind."

"And what did he do then?"

"Then he went back to his room, called me in, took me by the hand, and said, 'Harry, I'm sorry for what I'm doing to you and to my other friends, but I hope you understand. I simply cannot go on.'"

"But why today? Why not last week? Why not next week?"

"I have a theory, but you won't believe it."

"Try me."

"After he said what he said to me, he walked over to the window, and he stood there staring at something."

"At what?"

"German flags."

"German flags?"

Begin leaving hospital after second hip operation during his period of seclusion, March 1991

"That's what I said. And as he was standing there a strange smile came over his face, and I distinctly heard him whisper to himself, 'So that problem has been resolved, too.'"

"What problem?"

"The German chancellor, Helmut Kohl, is arriving tomorrow on an official visit. Normally, Begin would have had to receive him at the airport. But can you imagine him standing to attention while the German national anthem was being played? I can't. And can you imagine him making a toast to Germany at the official banquet? I can't. This must have been preying on his mind for God knows how long. That's my theory as to why he chose today to resign. But if I know anything about Menachem Begin, he'll never admit it to a soul."

To the best of my knowledge, Menachem Begin never did tell anyone what last straw broke his inner drive, causing him to resign and go into seclusion for nine years, distant and withdrawn till the end of his days. He made no public statement when he stepped down, no speech to the nation. He became a man of silence. Speculation abounds as to what made him do it – his failing health, the death of his wife, the heavy toll of the Lebanon war, the Inquiry Commission that followed, the furor over Sharon, the deteriorating economic situation. But nobody knows for sure.

During all those years of his public silence, I saw him only once, in 1984, while I was on home leave from London. Yechiel Kadishai astonished me by returning my call to say that yes, Mr. Begin was agreeable to my calling on him. I was astonished because I had been told he was seeing no one but his immediate family, a very few old associates and, of course, Yechiel, his ever faithful factotum.

"You'll find his mind as sharp as ever," Yechiel told me when he ushered me in to Mr. Begin's modest, simply furnished apartment located in the leafy Jerusalem suburb of Yefe Nof, close to his son, Benny. When I walked into the lounge I found him sitting on a couch strewn with newspapers, clothed in a dressing gown. His complexion was bloodless, and he gave me a joyless smile.

"I was saddened to hear of the murder of Police Officer Yvonne Fletcher outside the Libyan Embassy. When you return to London please convey my condolences to her family, and to her commander."

Those were his first words to me, and I heard them with incredulity.

Yvonne Fletcher was a British police officer who, a few days earlier, had been shot and killed by a gun fired from inside the Libyan Embassy in the heart of London, during an anti-Libyan demonstration which she was policing. This enfeebled man was asking me to convey his commiserations over a human tragedy in a far-off foreign capital, the details of which he was fully conversant with. Our chat was in equal measure wistful and wry. During the course of it, he asked me about the probability of a member of the British royal family accepting an invitation to visit Israel officially. None ever had. I told him that from the feelers I had put out, the prospects were slim.

"When President and Mrs. Herzog recently made an unofficial visit to London," I told him, "Lord Rothschild used his good offices to elicit a royal invitation for a private lunch at Windsor Castle. The press asked me if President Herzog intended to use the occasion to invite the Queen and the Duke of Edinburgh to visit Israel. I said I had no doubt that he would. Within the hour, I received a phone call from the Queen's secretary, a Sir Humphrey somebody, who said President Herzog must do no such thing. 'It's simply not protocol to issue such an invitation at a private luncheon,' he said. When I reported this to President Herzog he laughed and extended an invitation just the same. The reply he got was a polite 'Thank you. One day.'"

Menachem Begin smiled at this, and he actually laughed when I went on to tell him about a lunch at Kensington Palace held in honor of a visit by Shimon Peres, who by then was prime minister of Israel. Kensington Palace was home of the Prince and Princess of Wales, Charles and Diana. Peres had attended without his wife, Sonya, but my wife Mimi had accompanied me, and there had been a handful of other guests.

The whole occasion was an informal and cozy affair, Prince Charles elegant in a navy blazer, buttoned-down collar and regimental tie, Diana lovely in a simple high-necked, long-sleeved summer dress. They welcomed their guests in a comfy, happy-looking parlor, papered in a bold floral design and draped with pinkish curtains. Following a prelude of pleasantries and drinks, the suave and urbane Shimon Peres said with a semi-bow, "Your Royal Highnesses, I come carrying gifts from Jerusalem," and he presented to Diana, a Roman coin bearing the likeness of Diana the goddess of the hunt, and to the passionate equestrian Charles, a statuette of a terracotta horse of ancient Greek provenance, both unearthed in Jerusalem.

Princess Diana inspected her coin with huge delight, while Charles handled his horse a tad awkwardly, saying, "Wonderful piece! Most appreciated! But I'm afraid my gift to you is far less grand." He picked up two volumes from a piano top and said, "You have a reputation, Prime Minister, of being a man of letters, so I pray you will find these of interest. They are the latest biographies of our poet, T.S. Eliot, and of my late great-uncle, Lord Mountbatten of Burma."

"They come highly recommended," added a jovial Antonia Fraser, a prolific writer of historical biographies, and wife of playwright Harold Pinter.

"And they will make a fine addition to your library, I promise you," guffawed the famed academic Lord Annan, a vaguely soldierly type in his seventies, with a glossy pate as bald as a billiard ball.

Shimon Peres expressed his gratitude and then said, formally, "It is my privilege, Your Royal Highnesses, to extend to you an official invitation to visit Israel at a time of your convenience, where you will be received with all honor as most welcome guests."

Diana's eyes sparkled, and her husband responded, "How kind! We'd love to come," adding quickly the usual reservation, "at the appropriate time."

"Lunch is about ready," Princess Diana said with an easy smile, and she led us into a cozy dining room, its windows framing a view of a splendid walled garden. We were eleven, amicably seated at a single round table under a chandelier, surrounded by canvases of priceless masterpieces.

"Is Mr. Peres married?" whispered Princess Diana hurriedly in my ear as I sat down next to her.

"Very much so," I whispered. "But his wife, Sonya, prefers not to get involved in his public activities."

"I totally empathize with her," murmured the princess.

Princess Diana had a reputation for common sense and practicality, and it was said that her outward softness masked an inner shrewdness and candidness. This she amply displayed when she said, "If one is not careful one can shrivel up in this fishbowl. I love getting out and about and meeting real people. You Israelis are said to be an informal lot, not ones to stand on ceremony."

"I suppose that's true," said I meaninglessly.

"I remember at school," continued Diana, rather mischievously, "how us girls would confide nothing to our parents except things we couldn't hide, like end-of-term results and weather reports. We were too scared to be thought ninnies by our mummies and daddies, so the last thing we would do was to bare our souls, show our emotions. Not done! But I won't let that happen to my children."

"Come to think of it," said Prince Charles to the whole table, apropos of nothing, "I almost did visit Israel once. It was last year – illegally."

The high-pitched chatter ceased as we all beamed at the prospect of a tale.

"Oh yes, indeed," the prince continued in his top-drawer fashion. "I was in Jordan, you see, guest of King Hussein, and I was water skiing in Akaba Bay. Suddenly" – his voice took on a roguish tone – "I found my speedboat being chased by Jordanian coastguards. They began blaring at me through a klaxon to turn around immediately; otherwise I'd be accosted by the Israeli navy as I was almost in Eilat waters – something like that."

"Pity you turned around," said Peres wittily. "Our coastguard would have cast a red carpet upon the waters in your honor."

We all chuckled politely, while a butler refilled our glasses.

"Mr. Peres, I always think of Israel as a plucky little country," said Diana, resting her chin on her hand, a bemused smile on her lips.

"That is kind of you to say so," said Peres.

"Well, as for me, Prime Minister," brooded Charles, "I always find the Middle East so full of impenetrable intricacies. Do you think a day will ever come when you and your neighbors will get along together?"

"One day," said Peres wistfully. And then, poetically, as was his wont, "One must remember, just as a bird cannot fly with one wing and a man cannot applaud with one hand, so a country cannot make peace just with one side, with itself."

"Of course," said Charles, and he went on to express high praise for the kosher menu, engendering a discourse of veneration for the virtues of tradition. This was followed over dessert by gossip and funny stories concerning world leaders whom the royals and their guests had met, and it was during this chitchat that Princess Diana, her big, dazzling eyes focusing beseechingly on my wife, leaned over to her, and quietly said, "Do me a favor. Please tell people I'm not anorexic. Look, I've just taken a second helping of pudding." She chuckled at herself, and then joined in the general conversation about the London arts scene. Mr. Peres was saying he had enjoyed a fine production of *Les Miserables* the previous evening.

"Oh, I saw that when it first played at the Barbican, before it moved to the Palace Theater," said Diana gamely. The trouble with the Palace is it's so hard to find parking there."

"You, a royal princess, have parking problems?" asked Peres astonished.

"Not now," replied Diana demurely. "I'm talking about before I became a princess."

"Are you going to allow us to see the little princes?" ventured Antonia Fraser. "How are they?"

"True little devils!" laughed Diana infectiously, somehow managing to be regal and jolly at the same time. "They're up to all kinds of tricks! William is four and Harry is two, and yesterday, at Buckingham Palace, I let William loose in the throne room. That child is an absolute bull in a china shop. He went running around the thrones going 'Bang! Bang! Bang!'"

She said this aiming two fingers at her husband, like a pistol.

Stiffly, Prince Charles rose, and said, "Prime Minister, friends, shall we retire?" and he led us back to the parlor for coffee and liqueur, where a nanny soon appeared with the little princes. Diana reached out to cradle Harry adoringly in her arms, while William, bouncing across every barrier of protocol, ran to the center of the room, and pointing a finger at the towering figure of the bald-headed Lord Annan, cried, "Mummy, why does that big man have no hair?"

"William, you must not say that," admonished Diana, stifling a giggle that was drowned out by Lord Annan's great roar of laughter. Even Prince Charles could not contain a smile.

My wife, seemingly overwhelmed by her motherly instincts, gave William a warm hug, planted him on her knee, and softly instructed him in how to say 'Hello' and 'Goodbye' in Hebrew. Thus it was that when the time came to bid farewell, the boy born to be king stretched out his hand to Prime Minister Shimon Peres and, at his mother's urging, said to him, "Shalom."

As I was relating all this to Mr. Begin, I caught a hint of the old impish look in his eyes. Being a formidable history buff, he responded by regaling me with a saga of his own, about the origins of the name of the British royal family. They were originally of German stock, he recalled, and he cited a number of close relatives of the royal family who had served the Nazis as *gauleiters*, and had fought with crack Wehrmacht units, including the SS. Then he went on to catalogue the royal pedigree in immense detail, explaining that the House of Windsor sprang from the marriage of Queen Victoria to Prince Albert, who was the son of the German Duke of Saxe-Coburg-Gotha.

"Saxe-Coburg-Gotha, not Windsor, is therefore the true surname of the royal family," he said, with the faintest hint of a sassy smile. "However, in nineteen seventeen, when World War One was raging and anti-German sentiment was at its height, King George the Fifth ordered the royal family to scrap Saxe-Coburg-Gotha in favor of the English-sounding Windsor. Likewise, Prince Phillip, the Duke of Edinburgh, though of Greek extraction, was also of German stock, from the house of Schleswig-Holstein-Sonderburg-Glücksburg. This, arguably, should be the surname of his heirs, not Mountbatten-Windsor, which he adopted."

At that point, Mr. Begin screwed up his gaunt features into a scowl, and said, "But the one who should be put in the dock was King Edward the Eighth. His admiration of Hitler was a national scandal. He had an affair with an American divorcee named Wallis Simpson and abdicated the throne in nineteen thirty-six to marry her. In nineteen thirty-seven they visited Germany and paid their respects to Hitler. When they parted, Edward described him as a decent sort of a chap, and Hitler was heard to say of Wallis Simpson that she would have made a good queen. But instead of the throne, Edward was reduced to the rank of a mere duke, and was shipped off to Bermuda as its governor, there to live out World War Two, and he quickly faded into obscurity."

As he was rattling this off I got the distinct impression he was doing so not to engage me in discourse, but to exercise his own mind and put his memory to the test. Once he was finished with his recitation, he held out a lean hand in a limp farewell, and asked me to remember him to Prime Minister Margaret Thatcher.

That was the last I ever saw of Menachem Begin. There was one final bit of correspondence on the occasion of his seventy-eighth birthday, in 1991, when I sent him greetings, to which he replied:

> My Dear Friend,
>
> I thank you from the heart for your greetings on the occasion of my birthday. We both share good memories of the days when I called you 'my Shakespeare' and until the day when you welcomed immigrants from Ethiopia to Eilat [a reference to my peripheral involvement in the secret mission of smuggling Jews out of Ethiopia during that country's most turbulent days]. Our working together was always a deep source of satisfaction to me. My best wishes to your wife and family.
>
> Most sincerely, and warmest greetings,
> Menachem Begin

מנחם בגין
תל-אביב

תל-אביב, כ"א   באב   תשנ"א
1   באוגוסט 1991

לכבוד
השגריר יהודה אבנר
רח' דיסקין 13
ירושלים

ידידי היקר,

קבל נא את תודתי מקרב לב על ברכתך לרגל יום הולדתי.

לשנינו זכרונות טובים מן הימים בהם קראתי לך: "השקספיר שלי", ועד ליום בו
קיבלת את פניהם של עולי אתיופיה באילת.

עבודתנו המשותפת תמיד הביאה לי סיפוק עמוק.

דרישת שלום לרעייתך ולכל בני ביתך.

בכבוד רב ובברכה לבבית,

מנחם בגין

Begin's last letter to author, 1 August 1991 (Translation, page 689)

Begin's 'will' deposited with Yechiel Kadishai (Translation, page 693)

Chapter thirty

Journey's End

The curtain descended and the lights went out on 9 March 1992. Menachem Begin, Israel's sixth prime minister, died of a heart attack, and Yechiel Kadishai opened the envelope which Begin had entrusted to him. The handwritten note it contained read:

> My Dear Yechiel,
>   When the day comes, I request that you read to my dear ones, to my friends and comrades, this request: I ask to be buried on the Mount of Olives next to Meir Feinstein and Moshe Barazani. I thank you and all those who will carry out my request.
>   With love,
>   Menachem Begin.

World leaders readied to fly to Jerusalem to attend the funeral, but Israeli embassies were swiftly instructed to inform governments that, at the request of the deceased, the funeral was to be a traditionally Jewish one: no lying in state, no military guard of honor, no official delegations, not even eulogies.

Despite the previous nine years of silence which Menachem Begin had mysteriously imposed on himself, a dense throng of hundreds of thousands spontaneously spilled into the streets in a mass display of grief and honor for the man whose voice had spoken for them, to a sometimes hostile or indifferent world, about Jewish faith, Jewish honor, Jewish patriotism and Jewish pride.

The arteries of Jerusalem were clogged in total gridlock as friends and foes, those who had loved him and those who had opposed him, the exalted and the humble, stood vigil while the body was prepared for burial at the Sanhedria funeral home. Under a pewter sky, the 1978 Nobel Prize laureate was carried by his pallbearers – all former Irgun commanders – to the cinnamon slopes of the Mount of Olives, the oldest Jewish cemetery in the world, there to be laid to rest alongside his beloved Aliza and his two comrades-in-arms. Countless lips trembled and countless eyes brimmed, and many openly sobbed as the procession of mourners, which extended over four kilometers, accompanied the bier that bore Menachem Begin's body, wrapped in a simple shroud and a prayer shawl. Never before had Jerusalem seen such a funeral, that did such unique homage to the man and to the country's unity.

I was one of literally thousands stumbling among the Mount of Olives tombstones and wandering the terraces of the ancient cemetery in search of a vantage point. It was only when one of Menachem Begin's old bodyguards recognized me that I was able to squeeze through the barrier that enclosed the burial site where the family stood. There, Benny Begin recited *Kaddish* and Yechiel Kadishai read *"Eil malei rachamim"* – the prayer for the tranquility of the soul. And as many took turns to shovel earth into the grave, the aged Irgun veterans stood to attention and sang their old Irgun anthem in a final salute to their commander-in-chief who, for much of his life, had been a figure of controversy but who, on this day, was buried with a nation's veneration.

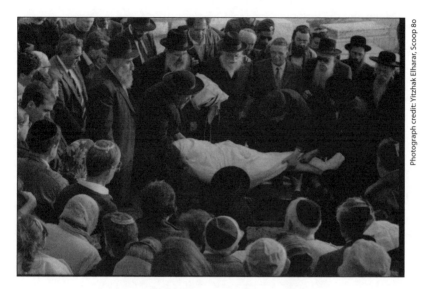

*Menachem Begin's body being lowered into his grave on
the Mount of Olives, Jerusalem, 9 March 1992*

Afterword

Eaton Square is a leafy London enclave, surrounded by pristine period properties where the wealthy and the celebrated, the great and the good, make their homes. Arguably London's premier quadrangle, the roster of its former residents reads like a *Who's Who* of English political and cultural lore. It is the sort of place where tour buses stop.

Ninety-three Eaton Square comes with a particular cachet. Two ex–prime ministers once lived there: Sir Stanley Baldwin in the mid–nineteen thirties, and Margaret – later Baroness – Thatcher, for a brief period in the early nineteen nineties.

The Thatcher occupancy was fortuitous. Henry Ford Jr. offered Baroness Thatcher and her husband, Denis, the use of his London residence at 93 Eaton Square while their own home was being renovated. And it was to this mansion that I repaired on a sunny, crystal clear April morning in 1992, to keep an appointment with the ex-prime minister, who had been ousted by her Conservative Party two years before. My acquaintanceship with Mrs. Thatcher went back, of course, to my London days, when I had served as Israeli ambassador, and she was still very much the prime minister. I was now the inspector general of the foreign service, and was in London on government business. Hearing that Mrs. Thatcher had invited me to tea, friends of mine at the Bar Ilan University in Ramat Gan had asked me to use the opportunity to enquire whether she would be willing to accept an honorary doctorate at the next conferment.

"Come in, come in," piped Denis in a rush of companionability, as he opened the door. "Margaret is in the lounge. I'm just dashing out. Be back in a jiffy." And off he strode, a groomed, gray-haired, bespectacled English gentleman in his late seventies, wearing a brown trilby hat, a well tailored suit, polished black brogues, and carrying a tightly rolled umbrella.

The author on visit with Margaret Thatcher

Baroness Thatcher, ten years his junior, received me genially in the hallway, dressed in an apple-green outfit, with a formidable string of pearls around her neck. She led me into an elegant and spacious room, with a grand piano, superb furnishings, Modiglianis on the walls, and french doors giving on to a manicured terrace decorated with a medley of spring flowers. Admiring the setting, I asked her about the honorary doctorate and she agreed on the spot, with gusto. She then patted a comfortable-looking couch and said, "Now, why don't you and I sit down and have a bit of a natter. Here, have a peppermint!"

She pushed a brass tray of wrapped green sweets in my direction, and tinkled a little bell that was handily placed by her side. "I'm sure you'll join me in a nice cup of tea, won't you?"

A maid appeared, bearing a china service, a silver teapot and all the other necessary accoutrements, which she placed on a coffee table whose surface was largely obscured by old copies of the *Illustrated London News* and *Country Life*.

"Now tell me about Mr. Begin," said Mrs. Thatcher stoutly, pouring the tea. And then, in a leap of sympathy, voice dropping into tenderness, "I read in the newspapers that there was much mourning in Israel at his passing. A massive funeral, I hear."

Hardly a month had passed since his burial, and it was with deep-felt solemnity that I said, "Mr. Begin's death did occasion profound national mourning."

"Well, I have to tell you," she returned, her voice sharpening, "I, for one, made no bones about my opposition to his settlement policies, but I greatly admired his convictions and principles." Whereupon, between sips of tea, she began reminiscing about her Israeli associations, beginning with the large Jewish presence in her old North-West London parliamentary constituency of Finchley, moving on to highlights of the few occasions she had visited Israel, and concluding with the one major encounter she had had with Menachem Begin.

"I remember it was a lunch at Number Ten, shortly after I'd entered office in seventy-nine," she said. "And, as I recall, there was some sort of a spat between him and Peter Carrington."

I reminded her that I had been present, and that Begin had expressed strong feelings about how European Jewry had been abandoned to their fate in World War II.

Thatcher clamped her jaw, stared hard in recollection, and pensively said, "Yes, I remember. He spoke bitterly about how the Allies had not bombed the railway lines to Auschwitz. And I have to tell you" – this almost in sorrow – "at the time of that luncheon I was hardly aware of what Auschwitz truly was. I knew it was a concentration camp, but it was only later, when I visited Yad Vashem in Jerusalem, that I fully realized it was a hideous death camp. It brought tears to my eyes."

This winded me. "You really didn't know?"

"Back then there were a number of things of which we were not as fully cognizant as we ought to have been about the Holocaust," she said broodingly.

"One cannot begin to understand Menachem Begin without understanding the Holocaust," I ventured. "Virtually his whole family was exterminated. The Jewish helplessness and homelessness of those times dominated his whole being. They were at the core of many of his policies."

"Here, let me refill your cup," she said, as if wanting to move off the subject, and she raised the teapot and poured. "So, remind me – when exactly was it that Mr. Begin first entered office?" she asked.

"In nineteen seventy-seven," I said.

"Oh yes. I have a vague recollection of our foreign office know-it-alls putting it about that you Israelis had elected a warmonger and a demagogue. But then he surprised us all, being such a world-class statesman, negotiating that historic peace treaty with Egypt. It was a masterstroke. He won the Noble Peace Prize for that, did he not – he and Sadat together?"

I confirmed that they had, and added, "In my opinion Mr. Begin was worthy of a second Nobel Prize, too."

"For what, pray?"

"For securing Israel's parliamentary democracy."

Thatcher's voice acquired a serrated edge. "Surely, you exaggerate. Israel is universally famous for its democracy. It's one of the most robust in the world."

"But not at the outset," I said. "On two occasions, just before and just after our independence, he saved us from civil war."

"Civil war?" She sounded aghast.

Briefly, I related the tale of the 'Hunting Season' in 1944, and of the *Altalena* in 1948, and added, "I once asked Mr. Begin what was the single most important thing he'd ever done in his life, and his unreserved answer was, 'Twice I prevented civil war.'"

"I had no idea," said Thatcher, sounding genuinely amazed.

I drove on. "In fact, he can be credited for bringing the whole nation together into the democratic parliamentary system. Most of our people come from countries with no democratic tradition whatsoever, and had no idea how to work the levers of power in a democracy."

"What countries are you talking about?"

"The Arab countries mainly, in the Middle East and North Africa; also immigrants from Asia. They hardly had a voice. It was Begin who championed their cause, and they were the ones who initially put him in office."

A maid entered to hand Baroness Thatcher a note. Thatcher shot her a sharp glance and, rising, said, "You'll have to excuse me a moment. I have to take a call from President Bush [Senior]."

She exited briskly and I took the opportunity to gaze about me, noting the fantasies of power which still clung to her in that room that was a feast of opulence: the large oil painting above the fireplace displayed her statuesque image in the full grandeur of her peerage regalia, the silver sculpture on the table was engraved with the names of her cabinet, the huge plain silver bowl next to it was inscribed as a parting gift of her parliamentary constituency, and a needleworked cushion on an armchair depicted the front door of 10 Downing Street.

"Am I interrupting?" It was Denis Thatcher, peering through the doorway, back from whatever errand he'd been on. "Where's Margaret?"

I told him, and he explained that he was searching for an atlas, which was probably in the bookcase by the french window. He stood before the mahogany antique and surveyed its shelves with his hands behind his back, in the manner of an officer inspecting a guard of honor, until he found what he was after. He lowered himself into an armchair, leafing through the atlas, and said, "We've been invited to Bahrain, and I'm doing a bit of homework. Aha, here it is – another one of those sunny little oases, I see."

A smile entered his voice and then spread across his features, until, in a burst of conviviality, he shared, "Gosh! I hope they've got decent showers there. Your country's got all the mod cons, I know, but you can never tell in these other places. A few years back we were invited to Abu Dhabi. Got there late at night, and as we were being piled into our cars our chief security chap whispered into my ear, 'When you get to the palace, sir, you should know there's no water.' I said, 'You're joking.' And he said, 'I'm not, sir, there's no water.' When I got there I found I had a bathroom half the size of the Albert Hall – marble walls and a line of basins – there must have been four or five – but no water. I turned the taps full on, but each tap gave only a dribble. And I thought to myself, ah well, I'm going to have to let these run all night. In the morning, I went along to Margaret's bedroom, which was twice the size of the Queen's in Buckingham Palace, and I said, 'You know, there's no water.' She said, 'I know there's no water.' 'Well,' I said, 'come to my bathroom and I'll give you a shower.' She said, 'You've got a shower?' 'No,' I said, 'I've got a few basinfuls of water and I'll scoop them over you with my hat. Come along.' She came along. 'Strip off,' I said, and she stripped off. I then threw the water in the air with my hat. But I'm afraid it wasn't a success. Ah, here comes Margaret."

He pecked his wife on the cheek and exited, explaining that he had to shove off to his club. She resumed her seat and said, "that was George on the phone – I should say President Bush. He stays in touch, which is gracious of him considering I'm no longer in office, and that I still have a bone to pick with him about Desert Storm."

"And what bone is that?"

Her whole demeanor grew severe as she moralized with cast-iron confidence: "When the Gulf War began, I was still prime minister. I was attending a conference at Aspen, Colorado, and Bush was there. When we heard about the invasion of Kuwait by that monster Saddam Hussein he asked me my view of things. I told him I'd experienced aggression in the Falklands, and I had no doubt there was only one way to deal with aggressors. 'Look George,' I said, 'this is no time to be wobbly. Liberate Kuwait, then go into Iraq and destroy Saddam Hussein and his National Guard. We, Britain, will stand by you. We'll be at your side all the way.'"

Glowering at the teapot, she raised her chin for added conviction and confided, "the trouble with George is that he was badly advised. James Baker [his secretary of state] is no Henry Kissinger. He is a lawyer from Texas, and he operates like a lawyer from Texas. He doesn't make policy, he makes deals. I suspect he thinks Sinai is the plural of sinuses."

She rose to stare out of the french windows, arms folded, her features fixed in a pose of melodramatic self-righteousness, saying nothing – a nothing that said everything, a nothing that said, 'If only I was still prime minister everything would be different.'

When she finally spoke her face showed contempt, and she lamented, "I was unseated from the premiership at the critical moment, just when George Bush needed all my backing to keep his nerve. But he faltered. He became obsessed with casualties. He tried to win the war from high altitudes, where everything is clean and sterile. So instead of going into Baghdad and finishing off the job by destroying the National Guard, capturing Saddam Hussein and putting him on trial as a war criminal, George declared a premature victory."

"At least he and the Allies didn't have to face a nuclear bomb," I hazarded.

I say 'hazarded,' because one had to tread carefully with this 'Iron Lady' who, by reputation, allowed no interruptions, heard no excuses, and permitted no questioning.

"Why do you say that?" she glared.

"Because of Saddam Hussein's nuclear reactor in Baghdad, which Mr. Begin ordered our Air Force to destroy in eighty-one, just as it was about to go hot. Hussein was on the point of manufacturing the atomic bomb, remember?"

She cupped her chin and nodded slowly, as the recollection began to seep in. Then she strode back to the couch, sat down, turned to face me with a cold hard stare, but still didn't say a word.

So I marched on. "You will recall that the Americans protested Begin's action, as you did. But in the end, the Americans thanked him wholeheartedly for destroying that reactor. The nineteen ninety war against Iraq, they said, could have ended in utter disaster had that Baghdad reactor not been knocked out in time."

If Baroness Thatcher had any opinion on the matter she chose to keep it to herself.

It was time to go. As she accompanied me into the hallway, she asked, "Did Mr. Begin write his memoirs? Has he left us anything of what you've been telling me about? I'd love to read it."

"I'm afraid not," I answered. "He'd intended to, but he never got round to it."

"Not even in all his years of retirement from public life?"

I shook my head, not knowing how to explain the mystery of his silence to myself, let alone to her. "All I can tell you," I said, "is that I remember him once giving an interview to *Time* magazine, in which he said he was planning a memoir in his head. It would consist of a number of volumes, and he was going to call it *From Destruction to Redemption*. It would tell the story of his generation of Jews, which he described as being almost unique in the whole of Jewish history for the depth of its suffering and the crowning heights of its deliverance. When the interview was over, and the *Time* man rose to go to the door, I recall him turning and asking, 'Just one last question, Mr. Begin. How would you like to be remembered in history?'"

"And what answer did he give to that?"

"As a decent human being, and a proud Jew."

Endnotes

1. From a stenciled propaganda sheet distributed by local Begin supporters.
2. Menachem Begin, *The Revolt* (Jerusalem: Steimatzky's, 1951), 43.
3. Ibid., 87. NOTE: Unless otherwise stated, the section on Begin's life in the underground is largely based on the author's recollections of conversations with Begin; his memoir, *The Revolt*; J. Bowyer Bell's *Terror Out of Zion* (Dublin: Academy Press, 1977); and Harry Hurvitz's *Begin: His Life, Words, and Deeds* (Jerusalem: Gefen, 2004).
4. Begin, *Revolt*, 221.
5. Bell, *Terror Out of Zion*, 184.
6. Menachem Begin Heritage Center Archives, Jerusalem.
7. Reconstructed from Begin's *Revolt*, chapters X and XI, and the author's notes.
8. Golda Meir, *My Life* (London: Futura, 1975), 266.
9. Israel State Archives.
10. Reconstructed from the author's notes.
11. Reconstructed from Begin's tribute to Eshkol on resigning from the national unity government, 4 August 1970.
12. Israel State Archives.
13. Based largely on interviews with Yechiel Kadishai.
14. Begin Center Archives.
15. In the possession of the author.
16. Reconstructed from Memorandum of Conversation, RG 59, U.S. National Archives and Records Administration; and the author's personal notes.
17. Based on Yitzhak Rabin's *The Rabin Memoirs* (Jerusalem: Steimatzky's, 1994), 95.
18. Ibid., 111.
19. Robert Dallek, *Nixon and Kissinger* (New York: HarperCollins, 2007), 222.
20. Rabin, *Memoirs*, 127.
21. Golda Meir, *My Life*, 316.
22. Abba Eban, *Personal Witness* (New York: Putnam's, 1992), 336.
23. Oriana Fallaci, *Interview with History* (Boston: Houghton Mifflin, 1977), 88.
24. Reconstructed from Golda Meir's *My Life*, 351, and the author's notes.
25. Rabin, *Memoirs*, 137.

26. Henry Kissinger, *Years of Upheaval* (London: Weidenfeld & Nicolson, 1982), 483.

27. Based on Golda Meir's *My Life*, 205.

28. Reconstructed from *My Life*, 361.

29. Henry Kissinger, *Crisis* (New York: Simon and Schuster, 2003), 483.

30. Golda Meir, *My Life*, 371.

31. Ibid., 375.

32. Rabin, *Memoirs*, 189.

33. Dallek, *Nixon and Kissinger*, 588.

34. Author's notes; "Excerpts from Secretary of State Kissinger's Press Conference," Jerusalem, 17 June 1974, document 11, in Meron Medzini, ed., *Israel's Foreign Relations: Selected Documents*, vol. 3, 1974–1977 (Jerusalem: Israel Ministry of Foreign Affairs). www.mfa.gov.il.

35. "Press Conference with Prime Minister Rabin," Jerusalem, 17 June 1974, document 12, in Meron Medzini, ed., *Israel's Foreign Relations: Selected Documents*, vol. 3, 1974–1977 (Jerusalem: Israel Ministry of Foreign Affairs). www.mfa.gov.il.

36. *Letter from President Nixon to President Sadat*, June 25, 1974, Anwar Sadat Archives. www.sadat.umd.edu/archives/correspondence.htm.

37. Dan Caldwell, ed., *Henry Kissinger: His Personality and Policies* (Durham, NC: Duke University Press, 1983), XI.

38. Rabin, *Memoirs*, 200.

39. Ibid., 201; plus author's notes.

40. Based on Begin's Knesset speech, March 24, 1975.

41. Israel State Archives.

42. *Meeting between President Sadat, President Gerald Ford, Secretary Kissinger, and Egyptian Foreign Minister Ismail Fahmi*, June 2, 1975, Memorandum of Conversation, Anwar Sadat Archives, www.sadat.umd.edu/archives/negotiations.htm.

43. Gerald Ford, *Telephone Conversations with Secretary of State Kissinger, Prime Minister Yitzhak Rabin of Israel, and President Anwar el-Sadat of Egypt on the Egyptian-Israeli Agreement*, September 1, 1975, document 516, Public Papers of the Presidents, American Presidency Project. www.presidency.ucsb.edu.

44. Reconstructed from Begin's Knesset speech, March 24, 1975; article by Begin, *Maariv*, August 29, 1975; Rabin, *Memoirs*, 215.

45. Rabin, *Memoirs*, 212.

46. Ibid., 215.

47. Based on the memoir of the former commander of the Israel Air Force: Benjamin Peled, *Days of Reckoning* [in Hebrew], ed. Moshe Shurin (Ben Shemen: Modan, 2004); and Rabin, *Memoirs*, 226.

48. Rabin, *Memoirs*, 221.

49. Ibid., 208.

50. Uri Dan, "My Scoop with Idi Amin," *Jerusalem Post*, July 6, 2006, 13.

51. Knesset speech, July 4, 1976.

52. Jimmy Carter, *Keeping Faith* (Fayetteville, AR: University of Arkansas Press, 1995), 287.

53. Rabin, *Memoirs*, 234.

54. In 1992, Yitzhak Rabin was again elected prime minister. By now an experienced and mature politician, he reached a full reconciliation with Shimon Peres, who served as his foreign minister, and was applauded for his economic and educational initiatives. Most significantly, he was hailed worldwide for his statesmanship in negotiat-

ing the Oslo accords with the Palestinians, (for which he received the Nobel Prize), followed by his peace treaty with Jordan.

Nothing, however, proved more contentious at home than the Oslo accords, signed at the White House on 13 September 1993. At the ceremony, Rabin famously shook the hand of Yasser Arafat, acknowledging that henceforth he would be his partner for peace in negotiating a final settlement with the Palestinians. That was the essence of Oslo.

At that time I was the Israeli ambassador to Australia. In late 1995, on the eve of my return home and retirement, Rabin called to say he wanted me back on his team. I met him at his Jerusalem office on Wednesday, 1 November. My first question was, "Why did you shake Yasser Arafat's hand?"

Typically, he rose and walked over to the window, and after a moment's thought, articulated his considerations one by one:

"Number one: Israel is surrounded by two concentric circles. The inner circle is comprised of our immediate neighbors – Egypt, Jordan, Syria, and Lebanon and, by extension, Saudi Arabia. The outer circle comprises their neighbors – Afghanistan, Iran, Iraq, Sudan, Somalia, Yemen and Libya. Virtually all of them are rogue states, and some are going nuclear.

"Number two, Iranian-inspired Islamic fundamentalism constitutes a threat to the inner circle no less than it does to Israel. Islamic fundamentalism is striving to destabilize the Gulf Emirates, has already created havoc in Syria, leaving twenty thousand dead, in Algeria, leaving one hundred thousand dead, in Egypt, leaving twenty-two thousand dead, in Jordan, leaving eight thousand dead, in the Horn of Africa – the Sudan and Somalia – leaving fourteen thousand dead, and in Yemen, leaving twelve thousand dead. And now it is gaining influence in the West Bank and the Gaza Strip.

"Iran is the banker, pouring millions into the West Bank and Gaza in the form of social welfare and health and education programs, so that it can win the hearts of the population and feed religious fanaticism.

"Thus, a confluence of interest has arisen between Israel and the inner circle, whose long-term strategic interest is the same as ours: to lessen the destabilizing consequences from the outer circle. At the end of the day, the inner circle recognizes they have less to fear from Israel than from their Muslim neighbors, not least from radicalized Islamic powers going nuclear.

"Number three: The Israel-Arab conflict was always considered to be a political one: a conflict between Arabs and Israelis. The fundamentalists are doing their level best to turn it into a religious conflict – Muslim against Jew, Islam against Judaism. And while a political conflict is possible to solve through negotiation and compromise, there are no solutions to a theological conflict. Then it is jihad – religious war: their God against our God. Were they to win, our conflict would go from war to war, and from stalemate to stalemate.

"And that, essentially, is why I agreed to Oslo and shook hands, albeit reluctantly, with Yasser Arafat. He and his PLO represent the last vestige of secular Palestinian nationalism. We have nobody else to deal with. It is either the PLO or nothing. It is a long shot for a possible settlement, or the certainty of no settlement at all at a time when the radicals are going nuclear."

I made full notes of these words, and I had a lot to chew over. Rabin instructed his chief aide, Eitan Haber, to arrange for a second meeting the following Sunday 5

November – but it never took place. The evening before, as Yitzhak Rabin was leaving a Tel Aviv peace rally, he was murdered by a Jewish nationalist zealot.

55. Based on Eric Silver's *Begin: A Biography* (London: Weidenfeld and Nicolson, 1984), 156, and the author's notes.

56. Carter, *Keeping Faith*, 295.

57. Had he lived to hear the BBC in more recent times, Begin would have been shocked to the point of righteous anger at the manner of its coverage of the Jewish State. He would have summoned me to dictate letters to its chairman, railing against the opinionated, slanted and emotional advocacy which has replaced the accurate, honest, and straightforward journalism of yesteryear. He would express indignation at interviewers who hold forth without a drop of sympathy or empathy for Israel's predicaments; who utter words like 'Zionism' and 'settler' through curled lips, while in the same breath describing Arab terrorists as mere 'radicals' or 'militants,' or 'gunmen,' not the killers of innocents they know them truly to be.

58. Yaakov Herzog, *A People That Dwells Alone* (London: Weidenfeld and Nicolson, 1975), 52.

59. *Israel Government Press Office Bulletin*, July 15, 1977.

60. *Visit of Prime Minister Menahem Begin of Israel: Remarks of the President and the Prime Minister at the Welcoming Ceremony*, July 19, 1977, Jimmy Carter, Public Papers of the Presidents, American Presidency Project. www.presidency.ucsb.edu.

61. Mark Twain, *The Innocents Abroad*, part 5, chapter 47.

62. Reconstructed from the official transcript; the author's personal notes; and Carter, *Keeping Faith*, 297.

63. Author's notes; Moshe Dayan, *Breakthrough* (New York: Knopf, 1981), 19.

64. Ibid., p. 20.

65. Reconstructed from the author's notes; Zbigniew Brzezinski, *Power and Principle* (New York: Farrar, Straus and Giroux, 1983); Samuel Lewis (Ambassador), interview by Peter Jessup, 1998, Foreign Affairs Oral History Collection of the Association for Diplomatic Studies and Training (ADST). http://memory.loc.gov.

66. Menachem Begin Heritage Center, Jerusalem, Newsletter, August 2, 2006.

67. Based on *Israel Government Press Office Bulletin*, September 2, 1977.

68. *Israel Government Press Office Bulletin*, November 11, 1977.

69. Carter, *Keeping Faith*, 300.

70. Dayan, *Breakthrough*.

71. *Israel Government Press Office Bulletin*, November 28, 1977.

72. *Israel Government Press Office Bulletin*, March 24, 1978.

73. Reconstructed from Vance and Lewis interviews and the author's notes.

74. Reconstructed from the author's transcript of the meeting, and from Sir John Mason (former British ambassador to Israel), *Diplomatic Despatches*, (Canberra: National Library of Australia, 1998), 172.

75. Author's notes; "Statement Made by Prime Minister Begin on Remarks Made by Chancellor Shmidt," Jerusalem, 25 February 1982, document 108, in Meron Medzini, ed. *Israel's Foreign Relations: Selected Documents*, vol. 7, 1981–1982 (Jerusalem: Israel Ministry of Foreign Affairs). www.mfa.gov.il.

76. Ronald Reagan Presidential Library.

77. Lewis, interview, ADST.

78. *Israel Government Press Office Bulletin*, July 13, 1981.

79. Israel Government Press Office.

80. *Remarks at the Welcoming Ceremony for Prime Minister Menahem Begin of Israel*, September 9, 1981, The Public Papers of President Ronald W. Reagan, Ronald Reagan Presidential Library. www.reagan.utexas.edu.

81. Israel Government Press Office.

82. Author's notes.

83. Reconstructed from Lewis, interview, ADST.

84. Dan Raviv and Yossi Melman, *Friends in Deed* (New York: Hyperion, 1994), 200.

85. Begin Center Archives.

86. *Israel Government Press Office Bulletin*, October 11, 1981.

87. *Haaretz*, December 4, 1981.

88. Based on cabinet minutes, December 12, 1981.

89. Extrapolated from Lewis, interview, ADST.

90. Reconstructed from the author's notes; *Israel Government Press Office Bulletin*, December 20, 1981; interview with Ambassador Samuel Lewis; and Lewis, interview, ADST.

91. Reconstructed from the author's notes, and *Israel Government Press Office Bulletin*, January 26, 1982.

92. Reconstructed from the Knesset minutes, May 3, 1982.

93. Based on the author's conversations with Dr. Yosef Burg, and Begin's remarks to the cabinet, June 5, 1982.

94. *Remarks of the President and Prime Minister Menachem Begin of Israel Following Their Meeting*, June 21, 1982, The Public Papers of President Ronald W. Reagan, Ronald Reagan Presidential Library. Reconstructed from the official transcript. www.reagan. utexas.edu.

95. Ronald Reagan, *An American Life: The Autobiography* (New York: Simon and Schuster, 1990).

96. Reconstructed from the author's notes based upon conversations with Menachem Begin; Lewis, interview, ADST.

97. "Cabinet Resolution on the Reagan Plan," Jerusalem, 2 September 1982, document 68, in Meron Medzini, ed., *Israel's Foreign Relations: Selected Documents*, vol. 8, 1982–1984 (Jerusalem: Israel Ministry of Foreign Affairs). www.mfa.gov.il.

98. *Israel Government Press Office Bulletin*, September 5, 1982.

99. "Senator Cranston Speaks Out," *The Link* (Americans for Middle East Understanding) 15 (December 1982): 8–9.

100. Israel State Archives.

101. Based on an interview with Ambassador Moshe Sasson, September 5, 2001; and Jehan Sadat, *A Woman of Egypt* (London: Bloomsbury, 1987).

102. Copies of the letters are in the author's possession; reconstructed from the author's notes; interview with Yechiel Kadishai; referenced from Hart N. Hasten, *I Shall Not Die!* (Jerusalem: Gefen, 2003).

103. Reconstructed from the author's notes; Lewis, interview, ADST.

Bibliography

A s indicated in the acknowledgements to this work, much of the author's material is sourced from his personal diary, recollections of events to which he was witness, the testimony of others present at happenings when he was not, official and unofficial transcripts, and minutes. Additional sources to which the author had recourse in one degree or another are:

Agress, Eliyahu. *Golda*. [In Hebrew, with photographs.] Tel Aviv: Levin-Epstein, 1969.

Begin, Menachem. *The Revolt*. Jerusalem: Steimatzky's, 1951.

Bell, J. Bowyer. *Terror Out of Zion*. Dublin: Academy Press, 1977.

Bradford, Sarah. *Elizabeth*. New York: Farrar, Straus and Giroux, 1996.

Brzezinski, Zbigniew. *Power and Principle*. New York: Farrar, Straus and Giroux, 1983.

Caldwell, Dan, ed. *Henry Kissinger: His Personality and Policies*. Durham, NC: Duke University Press, 1983.

Carter, Jimmy. *Keeping Faith*. Fayetteville: University of Arkansas Press, 1995.

Clarke, Thurston. *By Blood and By Fire*. London: Hutchinson, 1981.

Dallek, Robert. *Nixon and Kissinger*. New York: HarperCollins, 2007.

Dayan, Moshe. *Breakthrough*. New York: Knopf, 1981.

Dellheim, Charles. *The Disenchanted Isle: Mrs. Thatcher's Capitalist Revolution*. New York: Norton, 1995.

Eban, Abba. *Personal Witness*. New York: Putnam's, 1992.

Eshkol. [In Hebrew, with photographs.] Tel Aviv.

Friedman, Thomas L. *From Beirut to Jerusalem.* New York: Anchor, 1990.

Gilbert, Martin. *Exile and Return.* London: Weidenfeld and Nicolson, 1978.

———. *Jerusalem in the Twentieth Century.* London: Chatto and Windus, 1996.

———. *Israel: A History.* London: Doubleday, 1998.

Golan, Aviezer, and Shlomo Nakdimon. *Begin.* [In Hebrew.] Jerusalem, 1978.

Grosbard, Ofer. *Menachem Begin: A Portrait of a Leader.* [In Hebrew.] Tel Aviv: Resling, 2006.

Hasten, Hart N. *I Shall Not Die!* Jerusalem: Gefen, 2003.

Herzog, Chaim. *The Arab-Israeli Wars.* New York: Vintage, 1984.

Herzog, Yaakov. *A People That Dwells Alone.* London: Weidenfeld and Nicolson, 1975.

Horovitz, David, ed. *Yitzhak Rabin: Soldier of Peace,* London: Halban, 1996.

Hurwitz, Harry. *Begin: His Life, Works, and Deeds.* Jerusalem: Gefen, 2004.

Isaacson, Meron. *Begin.* [In Hebrew, with photographs.] Tel Aviv, 2003.

Katz, Samuel. *Battleground: Fact and Fantasy in Palestine.* Rev. ed. New York: Taylor, 2002.

Keegan, John. *Intelligence in War.* New York: Knopf, 2003.

Kissinger, Henry. *Years of Upheaval.* London: Weidenfeld and Nicolson, 1982.

———. *Years of Renewal.* New York: Simon and Schuster, 1999.

———. *Diplomacy.* New York: Simon and Schuster, 1995.

———. *Crisis.* New York: Simon and Schuster, 2003.

Kurzman, Dan. *The Life of Yitzhak Rabin.* New York: HarperCollins, 1998.

Laqueur, Walter. *A History of Zionism.* London: Weidenfeld and Nicolson, 1972.

Lewis, Samuel (Ambassador). Interview by Peter Jessup. *Foreign Affairs Oral History Collection of the Association for Diplomatic Studies and Training* (ADST), 1998. http://memory.loc.gov.

Mason, John. *Diplomatic Despatches.* Canberra: National Library of Australia, 1998.

Meir, Golda. *My Life.* London: Futura, 1975.

Medzini, Meron, ed. *Israel's Foreign Relations: Selected Documents.* 17 vols. Jerusalem: Israel Ministry of Foreign Affairs, 1947–1981.

Morris, Edmund. *Dutch: A Memoir of Ronald Reagan.* New York: Random House, 1999.

Nakdimon, Shlomo. *Altalena.* [In Hebrew.] Tel Aviv, 1978.

Nixon, Richard. *Memoirs.* New York: Grosset & Dunlap, 1978.

O'Brien, Conor Cruise. *The Siege: The Saga of Israel and Zionism*. London: Weidenfeld and Nicolson, 1986.

Oren, Michael B. *Six Days of War*. U.S.A.: Oxford University Press, 2002.

Peled, Benjamin. *Days of Reckoning*. [In Hebrew.] Ben Shemen, Israel: Modan, 2004.

Perlmutter, Amos. *The Life and Times of Menachem Begin*. New York: Doubleday, 1987.

Prittie, Terence. *Eshkol of Israel*. London: Museum Press, 1969.

Rabin, Yitzhak. *The Rabin Memoirs*. Boston: Little, Brown, 1979.

Raviv, Dan, and Yossi Melman. *Friends in Deed: Inside the U.S.-Israel Alliance*. New York: Hyperion, 1994.

Reagan, Ronald. *An American Life: The Autobiography*. New York: Simon and Schuster, 1990.

Reeves, Richard. *President Reagan: The Triumph of Imagination*. New York: Simon and Schuster, 2005.

Sadat, Jehan. *A Woman of Egypt*. London: Bloomsbury, 1987.

Schechtman, Joseph B. *The Vladimir Jabotinsky Story*. New York: Yoseloff, c. 1956–1961.

Silver, Eric. *Begin: A Biography*. London: Weidenfeld and Nicolson, 1984.

Slater, Robert. *Rabin of Israel*. London: Robson, 1993.

Stein, Kenneth W. *Heroic Diplomacy: Sadat, Kissinger, Carter, Begin, and the Quest for Arab-Israeli Peace*. New York: Routledge, 1999.

Summers, Anthony, with Robbyn Swan. *The Arrogance of Power: The Secret World of Richard Nixon*. New York: Viking, 2000.

Sykes, Christopher. *Crossroads to Israel*. London: Collins, 1965.

Syrkin, Marie, ed. *Golda Meir Speaks Out*. London: Weidenfeld and Nicolson, 1973.

Thatcher, Carol. *Below the Parapet: The Biography of Dennis Thatcher*. London: HarperCollins, 1996.

Tuchman, Barbara. *Bible and Sword: England and Palestine from the Bronze Age to Balfour*. New York: Ballantine, 1956.

Vance, Cyrus. *Hard Choices: Critical Years in America's Foreign Policy*. New York: Simon and Schuster, 1983.

Weizmann, Chaim. *Trial and Error*. New York: Harper, 1949.

About the Author

Ambassador Yehuda Avner was born in Manchester, England, in 1928, and first reached Israel shortly before independence, in 1947. He is a founding member of Kibbutz Lavi in Galilee, and entered the Israel Foreign Service in the late 1950s. During a lengthy diplomatic career he served as consul in New York, counselor at the Washington Embassy, ambassador to Great Britain, non-resident ambassador to Ireland, and ambassador to Australia. Between overseas postings he served as speech writer and secretary to Prime Ministers Levi Eshkol and Golda Meir, and adviser to Prime Ministers Yitzhak Rabin, Menachem Begin, and Shimon Peres. He is the author of *The Young Inheritors: A Portrait of Israel's Children*, and a frequent guest columnist with the *Jerusalem Post*.

The fonts used in this book are from the Arno family